KING ARTHUR IN
LEGEND AND HISTORY

KING ARTHUR IN
LEGEND AND HISTORY

Edited by
RICHARD WHITE

With a Foreword by
ALLAN MASSIE

J. M. Dent   London

First published in Great Britain in 1997
by J. M. Dent, a division of Orion Books Ltd,
Orion House, 5 Upper St Martin's Lane,
London WC2H 9EA

Introduction and selection © J. M. Dent 1997

Foreword © Allan Massie 1997

Cover illustration: *Livre de Messire Lancelot du Lac*, Ms.Fr. 112 f.5, *The Round Table and the Holy Grail*, Gaultier Map, 1470, Italy. Courtesy of the Bridgeman Art Library, London/Bibliothèque National, Paris.

A CIP catalogue record for this book is
available from the British Library.

Typeset by Selwood Systems, Midsomer Norton
Printed and bound in Great Britain by Butler & Tanner Ltd, Frome and London

CONTENTS

NOTE ON THE EDITOR

RICHARD WHITE has a BA in Ancient and Medieval History and an MA in Medieval Studies from London University, where he also undertook postgraduate research on Arthurian Literature. He is currently visiting lecturer at Tamagawa University, Tokyo. While primarily interested in Arthurian literature and medieval history, he is also interested in a wide range of other literary, historical and cultural issues.

CHRONOLOGY OF KEY ARTHURIAN TEXTS

Pre-12th Century

c. 548	GILDAS, The Ruin of Britain
early 9th century	NENNIUS, History of the Britons
by 10th century	The Annals of Wales
c. 950?	The Mabinogion: 'Culhwch and Olwen'
c. 1019?	The Life of St Goeznovius
c. 1075	LIFRIC OF LLANCARFAN, The Life of St Cadoc
c. 1100?	The Life of St Carannog
c. 1100?	The Life of St Iltud

12th Century

12th century	The Life of St Padarn
c. 1125	WILLIAM OF MALMESBURY, The Deeds of the English Kings
c. 1136	GEOFFREY OF MONMOUTH, History of the Kings of Britain
c. 1150?	BÉROUL, The Romance of Tristan
before 1155?	CARADOC OF LLANCARFAN, The Life of Gildas
1155	WACE, Brut
c. 1170	CHRÉTIEN DE TROYES, Erec and Enide
c. 1175–1200	ROBERT BIKET, The Lay of the Horn
c. 1176	CHRÉTIEN DE TROYES, Cligés
c. 1177	CHRÉTIEN DE TROYES, Lancelot, or the Knight of the Cart; Yvain, or the Knight of the Lion
c. 1182	CHRÉTIEN DE TROYES, Perceval, or the Story of the Grail
c. 1190	The First Perceval Continuation; The Bridleless Mule
c. 1190–1200	The Second Perceval Continuation

13th Century

c. 1200–10	LAWMAN (LAYAMON), Brut
c. 1200–12	Didot Perceval; Perlesvaus
c. 1200–20	RAOUL DE HOUDENC, Meraugis de Portlesguez; My Lord Gawain, or the Avenging of Raguidel
c. 1210–25	HEINRICH VON DEM TÜRLIN, The Crown

c. 1210–25	MANESSIER, Perceval Continuation; GERBERT DE MONTREUIL, Perceval Continuation; GUILLAUME LE CLERC, Fergus of Galloway; Yder; Gliglois; *Non-cyclic* Prose Lancelot; The Grail Quest; Huth Merlin; The Story of Merlin
c. 1225	The Death of Arthur (Mort Artu)
c. 1235	The Knight With Two Swords
c. 1250	The Perilous Cemetery
c. 1250–75	The Romance of Hunbaut; The Rise of Gawain; The Romance of Laurin; The Book of Arthur; ROBERT DE BLOIS, Biausdous
1268	Claris and Laris
c. 1266–1300	JEHAN, The Marvels of Rigomer; GIRART D'AMIENS, Escanor
c. 1270	ROBERT OF GLOUCESTER, Metrical Chronicle
c. 1300	The Knight of the Parrot

14th Century

c. 1300?	Of Arthour and of Merlin
c. 1330–40	Sir Percyvell of Gales
1338	ROBERT MANNYNG OF BRUNNE, Chronicle
c. 1350	Ywain and Gawain; *The Stanzaic* Morte Arthur
c. 1365–1400	*The Alliterative* Morte Arthure; The Anturs of Arther
c. 1385–90	Sir Gawain and the Green Knight; The Parlement of the Thre Ages; JOHN DE FORDUN, Chronicle of the Scottish People
c. 1400	Syre Gawene and the Carle of Carelyle; THOMAS OF CHESTRE, Syr Launfal

15th/16th Century

c. 1425	The Avowing of King Arthur; ANDREW OF WYNTOUN, Chronicle
c. 1450	HENRY LOVELICH, The Romance of Merlin; The Weddynge of Sir Gawen and Dame Ragnell
c. 1460–70	SIR THOMAS MALORY, The Works (Le Morte d'Arthur)
c. 1471	JEHAN DE WAURIN, Chronicles and Ancient Histories of Great Britain
1535	WILLIAM STEWART, The Buik of the Chronicles of Scotland

FOREWORD
by Allan Massie

Milton pondered the Arthurian cycle – the Matter of Britain – as the subject for his epic before turning to the Fall and the loss of Paradise. Tennyson devoted the middle years of his life to the elaboration of the Idylls of the King. His *Morte d'Arthur* is one of the most magnificently sounding of his poems. In our century the Arthurian legends have engaged the attention and occupied the imagination of writers as diverse as David Jones, Charles Williams, T. H. White and Rosemary Sutcliff; though the last-named is best known as a children's novelist, her Arthurian novel *The Sword at Sunset* is the most convincing imaginative version of what may be called the possibility of Arthur.

Arthur, it seems, will not die. This is appropriate since he is, in legend, the Once and Future King – *rex quondam rexque futurus*. Arthurian legends recur in different parts of our island, and numerous resting-places have been proposed for the king and his knights who await the call that will restore them to life. In the last war Francis Brett Young wrote a long poem, *The Island*, which is not very good on the whole but takes on a moving and mysterious vitality when he turns to Arthur:

> They were so few ... We know not in what manner
> Or where or when they fell – whether they went
> Riding into the dark under Christ's banner
> Or died beneath the blood-red dragon of Gwent ...

Field-Marshal Lord Wavell included it – '*Hic Jacet Arthurus*' – in his anthology *Other Men's Flowers*, and observed in a note that

> I carried a pocket edition of Malory with me in the early days of the late war. Malory is excellent reading, but only a court or fancy dress version of the real story which no man knows. Arthur was probably a grim figure in a grim unromantic struggle in a dark period of history.

No doubt this is true, and trying to reconstruct that struggle is for some the challenge of Arthur. For others, however, Malory remains the fountain from which we drink.

Though Malory offers a tangle of stories, some of which – like that of Tristram and Iseult – are well-nigh separate novels and have spawned other works barely concerned with the Arthurian cycle, nevertheless two great themes may be discerned.

The first is the story of the Grail. What the Grail was and how memories of folk-magic and old religions were woven into the tapestry of Christian legend furnish matter for scholarly debate, but for the poet or novelist the Grail stories are the pattern of the Quest: by way of danger and great hardship the hero is tested till he proves himself fit to attain his goal.

The second and still more dramatic theme is the story of Arthur's betrayal and failure. The great enterprise of the Round Table – that 'goodliest fellowship of noble knights' – is destroyed by the all too human passions of lust, jealousy and the desire for revenge. The theme is betrayal. Lancelot's guilty, yet beautiful, love for Guenevere, Arthur's Queen, is a betrayal of the ideals for which the Round Table stands, just as surely as Mordred's rebellion against Arthur – who in some versions is his uncle and in others his father, Mordred then being the fruit of the incestuous coupling of Arthur with his sister Morgan le Fay – is at the same time the revolt of disorder against order and the expression of mean resentment against high ideals. It may be that Arthur, like the Christian God, demands more of human nature than men can bear.

It is because the stories told with such easy certainty by Malory are all found in later ages to be capable of carrying a variety of interpretation, while still working simply as narratives, that the Matter of Britain has offered such a rich store to be drawn on over the centuries. T. H. White for instance, working on the last volume of his tetralogy, suddenly observed that the great theme of the cycle was how to avoid war.

It is because they can yield such diverse meanings, such a variety of significance, without losing their essential nobility and pathos, that the Arthurian stories retain a perpetual freshness, so that writers in every century have turned to them for inspiration and as a means of exploring matter of enduring value.

ALLAN MASSIE

INTRODUCTION

Today, many people are familiar with the figure of Arthur as portrayed in films and novels; these will have fixed a number of ideas in the minds of audiences and readers: such as Arthur being a powerful king who holds his court at Camelot and sits at the Round Table with his knights. In this way the modern depiction of Arthur has become narrow in focus. Thus, while a number of Arthurian knights reappear in modern films, it is Lancelot with his adulterous love for Queen Guenevere, rather than Gawain, the loyal supporter of his uncle Arthur's rule, who almost invariably tends to be emphasized. It is hoped that the reader of this anthology will acquire a greater awareness of the richness and diversity of the representation of the figure of King Arthur which existed in medieval literature and history, and which deserves to be better known today.

Did Arthur really exist? Was he a powerful king or just a warrior? What sort of a role did he perform in the defence of Britain against the ravages of invading Saxons, Picts and Irish? Historians remain undecided about whether Arthur was a real person or not. Since his name is Roman, Arthur would presumably have belonged to the surviving Romano–British aristocracy who remained in Britain after the traditional departure of the Romans in AD 410. In some works he is the nephew of Aurelius Ambrosius, an earlier Romano–British leader against the Saxon invaders. Whatever the facts, for over a thousand years Arthur has symbolized British resistance to invasion. Although he may have been merely a regional warlord in late Romano–Celtic Britain, Arthur was such a fascinating figure that stories about him were told and retold in many different languages during the medieval period alone.

In some works, Arthur is portrayed simply as a warlord whose activities are restricted to only a small region of Britain, such as the South West. But in many other stories he is a famous king of considerable wealth and reputation, who rules the whole of Britain and frequently possesses sufficient military resources to invade Continental Europe in pursuit of glory and territorial expansion. In many works, Arthur is fond of hunting and other royal amusements such as tournaments and lavish banquets. The reader will be able to perceive in the various extracts in *King Arthur in Legend and History* that Arthur's interest in these activities is not just for personal pleasure. Rather, they enable him to recruit new followers and ensure the loyalty of his knights.

Bringing together an extensive range of diverse material which reveals the development of the legendary figure of Arthur, this anthology enables the reader to understand how the Arthurian legend developed over a period of over five hundred years. The extracts are arranged in approximate chronological order to give the reader an idea of the various directions in which the Arthurian legend was simultaneously developing.

The Earliest Evidence about Arthur

First of all, the reader is presented with glimpses of what the real figure of Arthur might have been like through tantalizingly fragmentary early references to Arthur in Latin chronicles and saints' lives, together with early Welsh legendary material which provides obscure allusions to Arthur's reputed exploits.

According to some of the earliest chroniclers, Arthur won a number of battles against the Saxon invaders and was responsible for the major British victory at Badon, while a single source provides the brief and ambiguous statement that both Arthur and Mordred were slain at the battle of Camlann, the exact date of which is uncertain.

Arthur in the Saints' Lives

The recorded lives of several Celtic saints, where material about Arthur is often employed in order to enhance the reputation of the holy men, are generally of too late a date and spurious a character to be of much use as historical evidence. Some of these works are of interest because they introduce material which is employed by later writers of Arthurian romance. The attitude towards Arthur varies considerably in the different saints' lives, but in many cases he is depicted as a tyrant and oppressor of holy men. Yet Arthur was clearly a Christian, since early works describe him carrying the image of the Virgin Mary into battle, either on his shoulders or on his shield.

The Arthur of Welsh Legend

While some of the extant Welsh Arthurian material may be of early date, it survives only in relatively late manuscripts and is extremely difficult to date. The mid-thirteenth-century *Black Book of Carmarthen*, the early fourteenth-century *Book of Taliesin* and the *Red Book of Hergest* (c. 1375–1425) contain the most important surviving early Welsh Arthurian material. Unfortunately, much of it is too obscure or fragmentary to be of much interest to the general reader. The *Goddoddin*, a Welsh elegy which may have been composed as early as *c.* AD 600, compares a contemporary hero's exploits unfavourably with those of Arthur, who is clearly regarded by the poet as an outstanding warlord, but Arthur is not described in any detail. *The Spoils of Annwn*, an obscure early Welsh poem composed around AD 900 or even earlier, contains another early reference to the figure of Arthur, although the text is corrupt and makes numerous unidentifiable allusions.

In *The Mabinogion*, a collection of eleven early Welsh tales, Arthur appears in the early 'Culhwch and Olwen' and the three short Arthurian romances, which are of considerably later date, since they show clear signs of substantial French cultural influence. The Arthurian romances – *The Lady of the Fountain*, *Peredur* and *Gereint* – tell the same basic stories as Chrétien de Troyes's *Yvain*, *Perceval* and *Erec and Enide* respectively. While it is hard to determine the relationship of these works with their French counterparts, critics now generally believe that they derive from a common Celtic source which has now been lost.[1]

Geoffrey of Monmouth and the 'Brut' Chronicle Tradition

Geoffrey of Monmouth's *History of the Kings of Britain* (*c.* 1136), which he claimed to have translated from an ancient Welsh chronicle, is the first major contribution to the Arthurian legend, providing a complete account of Arthur's life in Latin prose for an erudite audience. Geoffrey's Arthur is a warrior–king who defeats the Saxon invaders and establishes peace throughout Britain; he then embarks on a series of territorial expansions until he is betrayed by his nephew Mordred. The popularity of Geoffrey's work made the Arthurian legend famous; its direct impact was a range of summaries, translations and adaptations. Although most people during the medieval period accepted Geoffrey's *History* as a truthful account of Arthur's reign, William of Newburgh was an exception, criticizing the work as a piece of ludicrous fantasy without any historical value.

Wace's *Brut* (1155) is the first French translation of Geoffrey of Monmouth's *History*. While Wace preserves the basic story and much of the original material, he augments courtly elements already present in Geoffrey's work. One of Wace's most significant contributions to the Arthurian legend is Arthur's famous Round Table, which is mentioned in numerous subsequent works.

Lawman's (or Layamon's) *Brut*, the first of a number of different English versions of Geoffrey's work, is translated from Wace's French version rather than directly from Geoffrey's original Latin. Despite this, Lawman's Arthur, unlike Wace's more courtly figure, is depicted in terms of early English war-leaders, ironically the kind of people whom Arthur struggled to drive out of Britain. Among the various other versions of the Arthurian legend closely derived from Geoffrey's *History* are French works by Pierre de Langtoft and Jehan de Waurin, and English poems by Robert Mannyng of Brunne and Robert of Gloucester.

In addition to material from Geoffrey's *History* and related works, this anthology contains substantial extracts from later works, which expand and develop Geoffrey's basic story of Arthur in a variety of different ways. Many of the later Arthurian stories of romance and chivalry are set during the twelve years when Geoffrey's Arthur rules Britain in peace, inviting brave men from remote countries to join his magnificent court.

Chrétien de Troyes and the Arthur of French Romance

In French works written during the twelfth century, apparently in order to entertain a more sophisticated courtly audience which included a significant proportion of women, Arthur was converted into the figure familiar to readers of romance. In this period, the status of women was improving so that noble ladies like Eleanor of Aquitaine and her daughter, Marie de Champagne, were in a position to patronize the arts and commission romances.

It is Chrétien de Troyes, the twelfth-century French poet, who first converts Geoffrey's warrior hero of outstanding prowess into a less bellicose and more sedentary figure of chivalric romance. Since Chrétien and subsequent French writers visualized Arthur as an English king, they were naturally more derogatory about him than writers of Welsh or English origin.

In each of his five Arthurian romances Chrétien focuses on the exploits of a young Arthurian knight, rather than on King Arthur himself, who now appears in only a few scenes in each story. Arthur is no longer the central figure, since Chrétien's stories are concerned with the themes of love and chivalry, whether within marriage, as in *Erec and Enide* and *Yvain*, or outside it, as in *Cligés* and *Lancelot*. From the opening of the first Arthurian romance, *Erec and Enide*, Arthur is depicted as a weak and possibly incompetent ruler who ignores his nephew Gawain's warning that his decision to revive the custom of hunting the white stag will cause disorder at court.

After Chrétien de Troyes had introduced the genre, numerous French Arthurian romances were composed in celebration of chivalric adventure, most of which concentrate on the exploits of a single, often unknown, hero and generally devote a very limited but frequently highly critical amount of attention to King Arthur.

While Chrétien sometimes appears disapproving of Arthur, Raoul de Houdenc, who wrote two Arthurian poems in the early thirteenth century, represents Arthur in a particularly derisive manner. In *My Lord Gawain, or the Avenging of Raguidel*, which like many works opens at King Arthur's court, since it is his custom to refrain from eating on important occasions until he has met with an adventure, Arthur becomes depressed and neglects his royal duties when no unusual event has occurred. This episode typifies Arthur's passive role in French romance since, although he initially discovers Raguidel's corpse, Arthur himself takes no further active role in avenging his death. This poem also includes another common Arthurian theme: the don constraint, or 'obligatory gift', where Arthur rashly promises to grant unspecified wishes to strangers arriving at his court, and then is honour-bound to fulfil them, despite his reluctance. This motif, which particularly occurs in French romances, suggests that Arthur rather gullibly maintains impractical customs which cause him to become an inadequate and irresponsible ruler. Perhaps it was originally intended by Chrétien to associate Arthur with Henry II of England, whose desire to preserve the customs of his grandfather, Henry I, was renowned.

Writers of Arthurian romance usually employ Arthur's court as the centre of civilization, a starting-point for chivalric adventures, to which a hero eventually will return to truthfully relate his exploits to Arthur and his followers. Today it is popularly believed that Arthur held his court at Camelot, the location of which has been much disputed, but remains uncertain. In the medieval period a number of other places were also associated with Arthur's court, especially Carlisle in the north of England, and Caerleon and Caerwent in south Wales. Chrétien's *Lancelot* contains the first known reference to Camelot, although Arthur was obviously seen as a peripatetic ruler, since he also holds court elsewhere in this poet's other works.

In most romances, Gawain frequently acts as his uncle's chief adviser and champion; in some works, he is given the role of Arthur's viceroy, presiding over the court in Arthur's absence, depicted fighting with Arthur's famous sword, Excalibur, and even acknowledged as Arthur's heir-apparent by his uncle's barons when they believe the king to be dead. Gawain's prominent position at Arthur's court and in Arthurian society is reflected in the large number of romances in which he figures as a major hero. He is, in fact, the hero of more stories than any other Arthurian knight. Owing to his particular concern for the safety and happiness of women, Gawain is often described as 'the Ladies' Knight' and it is Gawain, rather than Arthur himself, who is the model of chivalry which young heroes endeavour to emulate and amorous damsels seek to encounter. For all these reasons it is difficult to obtain an adequate knowledge of either Arthur's character or Arthurian society without becoming familiar with the fascinating figure of his nephew Gawain.

In many romances Arthur is particularly concerned to persuade valiant young heroes to join his retinue and become members of his Round Table fellowship, since this is an important means of increasing his military power. A good example of this occurs in the lengthy French romance *Claris and Laris* (1268), where Arthur is eager to secure the two young heroes as his followers.

In many works Arthur is concerned about the safety of his followers, but in a number of French romances he fails in his duty to reward his knights' loyal service and protect his vassals. In the early thirteenth-century *Yder*, Arthur neglects to reward the hero for saving him from two knights who attacked him while out hunting. Arthur then increases the young hero's disgust when he refuses to offer assistance to one of his vassals, the Lady of the Maidens' castle, whose safety it is the king's duty to ensure. Arthur displays a similar lack of concern for his knights' well-being in *The Romance of Hunbaut*. In this poem, the king is depicted as a strong and prosperous ruler, although his character is rather more aggressive than in most other romances. While eager to use threats of military force to extend his kingdom, Arthur appears unprepared to provide his followers with the requirements essential to execute his commands. When Gawain requests an assistant to accompany him on his mission to subdue a foreign king refusing Arthur homage, his uncle commands that the hero shall take his sister!

The only French romance in which King Arthur himself is the hero is *The Knight of the Parrot*, which opens with Arthur's coronation. The king vows to undertake the first adventure to arrive at his court. As a knight-errant Arthur assumes the titular pseudonym after winning a parrot in a contest, and he follows the common practice of sending defeated opponents back to court to surrender to Gawain's father Lot, whom he has appointed as regent during his absence. This is an interesting variant of Lot's usual role, since in several works he is Arthur's enemy.

The Vulgate Prose Cycle

Chrétien's *Lancelot*, which introduces the figure of Lancelot and his love for Queen Guenevere into the Arthurian story, was written at the request of his patroness, Marie de Champagne. While Chrétien's poem opens with the hero already at Arthur's court and in love with Queen Guenevere, the early thirteenth-century *Prose Lancelot* provides a much more detailed account of the Lancelot story, beginning with the hero's childhood education from the Lady of the Lake, and relating how he falls in love with Guenevere. While Chrétien's story deals with a single theme, this bulky French romance contains substantial episodes describing the adventures of other heroes, including Gawain and Hector, which are incorporated into the main story. *The Prose Lancelot* is later expanded and incorporated into a collection of French Arthurian prose works, usually called 'The Vulgate Cycle', which comprises *The Story of Merlin*, *The Prose Lancelot*, *The Grail Quest*, *The Death of Arthur* and *The Book of Arthur*.

The Story of Merlin (*Lestoire de Merlin*), preceding *The Prose Lancelot* in the cycle, was composed in the early thirteenth century, and despite its title is not merely concerned with Merlin. The early part is derived, through the prose version, from Robert de Boron's lost poem, *Merlin*, and includes various elements familiar to readers of Malory, such as the Sword in the Stone and the Lady of the Lake. A substantial proportion of the story relates the civil war which erupts after Arthur's accession due to opposition from the five kings, who are defeated with the help of a group of young squires led by Arthur's nephew, Gawain. This story was frequently transformed into English during the medieval period, appearing in poetic form as *Of Arthour and of Merlin* and the mid-fifteenth-century version by Lovelich, while Malory's prose version is preceded by that of Wheatley, Lovelich's contemporary.

The massive mid-thirteenth-century *Book of Arthur* (*Livre d'Artus*), which survives only in a single manuscript, is the least well known part of 'The Vulgate Cycle'. The principal hero of the romance is Gawain, although the exploits of various other Arthurian heroes are celebrated and a section of the work relates Arthur's adventures as a knight-errant.

The Death of Arthur (*Mort Artu*), a French prose text written about 1225, became the final part of 'The Vulgate Cycle', thus incorporating the character of Lancelot into Geoffrey of Monmouth's original narrative of Arthur's death. In fact, whereas Geoffrey's version is relatively brief, this long romance encompasses much more than just the final battle against Mordred. This particular work provides the basis for various English accounts of Arthur's final wars, notably the stanzaic *Morte Arthur*, while admirers of Malory should recognize his debt to these works for his account of Arthur's downfall. In this story, Arthur learns of Lancelot's adultery with Guenevere from his sister, Morgan, and pretends to go hunting in order to catch Lancelot with the queen. Gawain, who had formerly been one of

Lancelot's closest friends, vows to avenge his brothers killed during Lancelot's rescue of the queen, and Arthur declares war on Lancelot and his kinsmen. After the final duel between Lancelot and Gawain, Arthur fights a war against the Romans, the details of which differ from those given by Geoffrey. Finally, learning of Mordred's treachery, Arthur decides to settle their quarrel without seeking Lancelot's assistance.

The Grail Quest (*La Queste del Saint Graal*) appears as the penultimate part of 'The Vulgate Cycle'. Opening at Arthur's Pentecostal feast at Camelot, it relates the adventures encountered by all the leading Round Table knights when they leave court in search of the Holy Grail. In this version of the story the usual role of Perceval as the occupant of the Perilous Seat is replaced by Lancelot's son, Galahad, who finally achieves the Grail since, unlike his father, he is untainted by mortal sins of the flesh.

Perceval and the Grail

Chrétien de Troyes's *Perceval* (also known as the *Story of the Grail*) introduces the enigmatic Holy Grail to Arthurian legend, together with the Grail Castle and the mysterious lance. While the Grail and lance are evidently mystical objects, Chrétien does not provide them with the Christian associations which they are later to acquire. In fact, they probably derive originally from Celtic mythology. Despite the existence of a number of versions of the Grail legend, King Arthur himself rarely has much directly to do with the Grail. However, in *Perlesvaus*, also called *The High Book of the Grail* (a Perceval romance in which various Arthurian figures undertake chivalric adventures), King Arthur himself sets off on adventure with Gawain in quest of the Fisher King, taking part *en route* in a three-day tournament on behalf of a pair of damsels. Unusually, in this work Arthur and Guenevere have a son called Loholt, who is murdered by Kay.

Chrétien de Troyes's uncompleted *Perceval*, which deals with adventures undertaken by both the worldly hero Gawain and his more spiritual counterpart, Perceval, inspired a number of continuations and adaptations of the story of their different quests for the Grail. During all of these the action rarely returns to Arthur, save when news of the two heroes arrives at court. *The First Perceval Continuation*, written about 1190, deals more with Gawain's subsequent adventures than those of Perceval, and also contains a long episode relating the adventures of Caradoc, another Welsh hero inserted into the Arthurian story. *The Second Perceval Continuation* is devoted to the exploits of Perceval rather than Gawain, but this work also leaves the story incomplete at the point where Perceval fails to mend the broken sword at the Grail Castle. Gawain's son, Giglain, the hero of a contemporary French poem, Renaut de Beaujeu's (*Li Biaus Descouneus*), also appears in this poem.

In the early thirteenth-century two French poets, Gerbert and Manessier, almost simultaneously wrote Perceval Continuations which attempted to complete the story from the point where the anonymous *Second Continuation* had ended. In Gerbert's version, Perceval returns to Arthur's court after failing at the Grail Castle, and sits in the Perilous Seat at Arthur's Round Table, which has hitherto swallowed up every knight who attempted to sit there. Manessier's *Third Continuation* finally successfully concludes the lengthy story of Perceval and the Grail, in which Arthur attends Perceval's coronation as the Fisher King.

Other French versions of the Perceval story include the *Didot Perceval*, which provides an alternative version of Perceval's assumption of the Perilous Seat. Merlin also appears in this text and Arthur's wars against both the Romans and Mordred complete the story.

The German View of Arthur

The various medieval German translations and adaptations of French Arthurian romances provide a different viewpoint of King Arthur, reflecting the unique political situation in Germany.

Although a number of episodes in Heinrich von dem Türlin's *Diu Krône* (*The Crown*) are derived from material and ideas found in earlier French writers, in other sections he offers a more original portrayal of King Arthur's character. Arthur is a mere child when his father, Uterpandragon, dies, but he regrets that he acquired his kingdom by inheritance, rather than through his own endeavours. Later, when he is an adult, Arthur listens to Lady Fortune's advice, which always turns to his advantage in this work.

Arthur in Middle English Romance

Although many of the surviving Middle English Arthurian romances are translations or adaptations of more sophisticated French originals, owing to nationalistic considerations, English writers tend to display Arthur in a more positive light than do their French counterparts. In a number of original English works, such as *The Anturs of Arther, The Avowing of King Arthur* and *The Weddynge of Sir Gawen and Dame Ragnell*, Arthur is depicted hunting, often in the vicinity of Carlisle, and frequently encounters adventure while enjoying this favourite pastime of medieval rulers.

The alliterative *Morte Arthure*, a late fourteenth-century poem from the north of England, is an imaginative reworking of the concluding section of Geoffrey of Monmouth's basic Arthurian story. One of the poet's most important additions to the basic story is Arthur's Dream of Fortune's Wheel, which indicates that the king's period of good fortune has come to an end. Fortune's Wheel was a popular medieval theme and also appears in the late fourteenth-century *Anturs of Arther*, where Arthur's greed for territorial expansion is the cause of his change in fortune.

Sir Gawain and the Green Knight, a late fourteenth-century poem composed in the dialect of the north-east Midlands, displays a familiarity with earlier Arthurian literature. Arthur's custom of refusing to eat at a great feast until he has observed an adventure, which first appears in Chrétien de Troyes's *Perceval* and becomes a traditional feature of French Arthurian romance, is here refashioned to produce an original representation of the king's character, which differs substantially from that found in any other known work.

Thomas Malory's *Works* (more often known by the title *Le Morte d'Arthur* [*The Death of Arthur*]), cover Arthur's entire life. Malory, unlike a number of his French sources, prefers to eulogize Arthur, although he allows Lancelot and Tristan to be the main heroes of much of his romance. While Malory's works, following his sources, are largely concerned with relating various Arthurian knights' adventures rather than Arthur's own exploits, the Accolon episode is an exception. Here, Arthur is the main hero, who manages to overcome a very serious danger to his life posed by his hostile half-sister, Morgan.

The Scottish View of Arthur

The medieval Arthur is generally depicted as an English king with territorial claims to both Scotland and France. Scottish writers are therefore inclined to treat Arthur less sympathetically than their English counterparts. The Scottish historians John de Fordun and John Major use Arthur's illegitimacy in order to discredit him as a usurper who supplants the true heirs, his nephews Gawain and Mordred, who are only boys at the time. Subsequent Scottish chronicles develop Fordun's criticism of Arthur into outright hostility. Arthur becomes not merely a bastard and usurper, but also a glutton and a breaker of oaths, who breaks his promise to accept Loth's son Mordred as his heir.

The British belief that Arthur did not die was clearly not invented by Geoffrey of Monmouth, since it was apparently widespread in the Celtic regions during the medieval period. It is even possible that the legend may have originated as early as just after Arthur's death, in order to inspire courage in the demoralized Britons so that they would continue their resistance against the Saxon invaders. Writing about a decade before Geoffrey of Monmouth's *History*, William of Malmesbury declared that 'Arthur's tomb is nowhere to be found, for which reason ancient fables declare that he will return again.'

The Welsh continued for centuries to believe in Arthur's return, and frequently rose in revolt against English overlordship in the hope that Arthur would come back to lead them to victory. The apparent discovery of Arthur's tomb at Glastonbury in 1191 was therefore a significant political benefit for the English Crown. Several different accounts of this discovery are extant, including contemporary ones by Ralph of Coggeshall and Gerald of Wales. There are also two later accounts relating to the Glastonbury discovery, written nearly a century later when Edward I and his wife Eleanor visited Glastonbury and opened the tomb.

Considered the highest paragon of chivalry and kingship, Arthur was a model for emulation by medieval English kings, particularly Edward I and Edward III, but also for great nobles and foreign magnates such as the German Emperor Maximilian I.[2] Writing in the early fourteenth century, Pierre de Langtoft's *Chronicle* relates how Edward I made use of Geoffrey of Monmouth's 'Prophecies of Merlin', and Arthur's legendary conquest of numerous kingdoms, to assert his right to the Scottish Crown and to Continental possessions. Edward III's short-lived foundation of a Round Table fellowship at Windsor Castle in the 1340s is mentioned by Adam of Murimuth.

King Arthur in Legend and History will enable the reader to become aware of how a kernel of truth about the quasi-historical figure of Arthur has been surrounded by layers of legendary material and developed over centuries into the famous figure of chivalric romance.

RICHARD WHITE

References
1. For a brief discussion of this problem see D. D. R. Owen's introduction to the Everyman translation of Chrétien de Troyes's *Arthurian Romances* (London: Everyman, 1987; rev. 1993), p. xvi.
2. See Gerhild S. Williams, 'The Arthurian Model in Emperor Maximilian's Autobiographic Writings *Weisskunig* and *Theuerdank*' in *The Sixteenth Century Journal* XI, 4 (1980), pp. 3–22.

NOTE ON THE TEXT

Apart from Lawman, whose early and deliberately archaic language is difficult for the modern reader to decipher, the Middle English extracts are given in the original. In most cases the original spelling is retained although, in accordance with Everyman house style, the letters i and j, u and v have been altered to conform with modern usage. The Middle English letters þ (thorn) and ȝ (yog) have been replaced by their modern equivalents: th and y, g or gh.

Arthurian Great Britain

Arthurian Wales

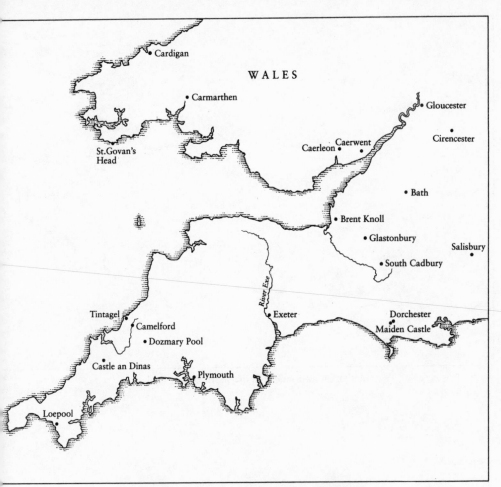

Arthurian associations in the South West of England

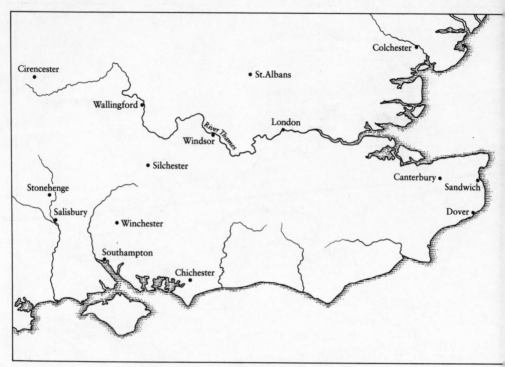

Arthurian associations in the South East of England

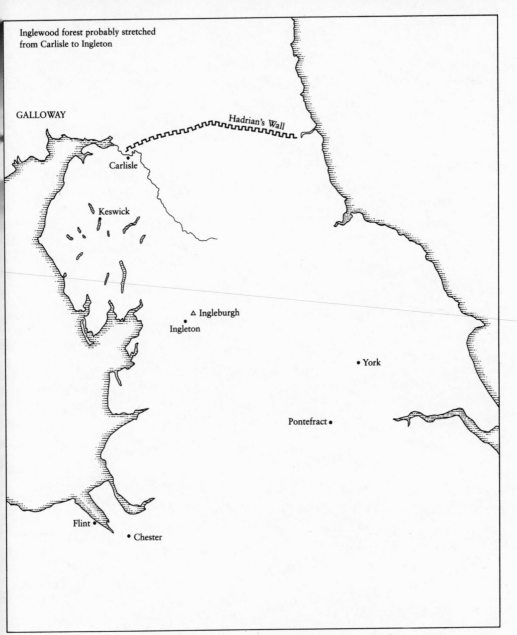

Inglewood forest probably stretched
from Carlisle to Ingleton

GALLOWAY

Hadrian's Wall

Carlisle

Keswick

△ Ingleburgh
Ingleton

York

Pontefract •

Flint •
• Chester

Arthurian associations in the north of England and Scotland

KING ARTHUR IN
LEGEND AND HISTORY

PART I
EARLY WORKS

GILDAS, The Ruin of Britain (c. 548)*

Born in Strathclyde, Gildas was a Romano–British historian and monk. In The Ruin of Britain *he relates how, after the departure of the Romans (which traditionally occurred in AD 410) Britain was subject to devastating plundering raids by Saxons, Picts and Scots, until God gave strength to the surviving Britons in the person of Ambrosius Aurelianus. Gildas refers to the siege of Badon (probably modern Bath), but it is interesting that he makes no mention of Arthur. Perhaps this is explained by Gildas's assertion in the concluding sentence of this extract that the British rulers do not deserve to hand their names down to posterity. Passages in the eleventh-century* Life of St Gildas, *substantiated by Gerald of Wales, suggest a personal reason for the saint's specific antipathy towards Arthur.*

Their leader was Ambrosius Aurelianus, a gentleman who, perhaps alone of the Romans, had survived the shock of this notable storm: certainly his parents, who had worn the purple, were slain in it. His descendants in our day have become greatly inferior to their grandfather's excellence. Under him our people regained their strength, and challenged the victors to battle. The Lord assented, and the battle went their way.

From then on victory went now to our countrymen, now to their enemies: so that in this people the Lord could make trial (as he tends to) of his latter-day Israel to see whether it loves him or not. This lasted right up till the year of the siege of Badon Hill, pretty well the last defeat of the villains, and certainly not the least. That was the year of my birth; as I know, one month of the forty-fourth year since then has already passed.

But the cities of our land are not populated even now as they once

* For a List of Sources to the extracts see pp. 555–61.

were; right to the present they are deserted, in ruins and unkempt. External wars may have stopped, but not civil ones. For the remembrance of so desperate a blow to the island and of such unlooked for recovery stuck in the minds of those who witnessed both wonders. That was why kings, public and private persons, priests and clergymen kept to their own stations. But they died; and an age succeeded them that is ignorant of that storm and has experience only of the calm of the present. All the controls of truth and justice have been shaken and overthrown, leaving no trace, not even a memory, among the orders I have mentioned: with the exception of a few, a very few.

The Complaint: Kings

Britain has kings, but they are tyrants; she has judges, but they are wicked. They often plunder and terrorize – the innocent; they defend and protect – the guilty and thieving; they have many wives – whores and adulteresses; they constantly swear – false oaths; they make vows – but almost at once tell lies; they wage wars – civil and unjust; they chase thieves energetically all over the country – but love and even reward the thieves who sit with them at table; they distribute alms profusely – but pile up an immense mountain of crime for all to see; they take their seats as judges – but rarely seek out the rules of right judgement; they despise the harmless and humble, but exalt to the stars, so far as they can, their military companions, bloody, proud and murderous men, adulterers and enemies of God – if chance, as they say, so allows: men who should have been rooted out vigorously, name and all.

NENNIUS, History of the Britons (Historia Britonum) (early ninth century)

Although a Welshman, Nennius wrote in Latin. His History of the Britons *contains one of the first references to Arthur, not as one of the various kings discussed by Nennius, but merely as the war-leader against the invading Saxons. Nennius briefly relates the location of twelve battles fought by Arthur against the invading Saxons. The last battle, which takes place at Mount Badon, is also mentioned by Gildas, Bede and* The Annals of Wales (Annales Cambriae). *Although intimating that Arthur is a Christian whose victory is attributed to the intervention of Christ and Mary since he carries the image of the Virgin on his shoulders, in another passage Nennius endows the hero with mystical qualities.*

At that time the Saxons became powerful, increasing their numbers in Britain. Upon the death of Hengist, his son Octa crossed into the kingdom of Kent in the eastern part of Britain; the kings of Kent are descended from him. It was during this period that the war-leader Arthur, together with the kings of Britain, was fighting against the Saxons.

The first battle took place on the bank of the River Glein, while the second, third, fourth and fifth battles occurred beside another river, called the Dubglas, which is in the Linnuis region. The sixth battle was sited on the River Bassus, and the seventh in the Celidon Wood, which is called 'Cat Coit Celidon'.

The eighth battle was at Castle Guinnion, where Arthur bore the image of the Holy Virgin Mary on his shoulders; on that day the pagans turned in flight and were slaughtered in great numbers, through the grace of Our Lord Jesus Christ and of his Holy Mother, the Virgin Mary.

The ninth battle was fought in the city of the Legions (Caerlion), the tenth on the bank of a river called Tribruit, and the eleventh on a mountain called Agned. The twelfth was the battle of Mount Badon, in which nine hundred and sixty men were slain in a single charge by Arthur: all these were slain by Arthur himself, and he was victorious in every conflict.

Since they were defeated on each encounter, the Saxons sought help from Germany; they greatly increased their forces without interruption, bringing kings from Germany who ruled over them in Britain until the reign of Ida, the son of Eobba, who was the first king of Beornica.

The mythical associations relating to King Arthur are already present in Nennius's work, appearing in two miraculous incidents, one concerned with Arthur's dog, Cabal, and the other with his son, Anir.

There is another marvel in the region which is called Buel. There is a pile of stones there, and the stone placed on the top has the mark of a dog on it. When hunting the boar Troynt, Cabal, who was the soldier Arthur's dog, left his pawprint on the stone, and afterwards Arthur piled up stones beneath the stone on which the dog's pawprint was, and called it Carn Cabal. And men came and raised up stones in their hands for the space of a day and a night, and on the following morning the stone with the pawprint was found at the top of the pile.

There was another wonder in the place which was called Ercing. There was a tomb beside a fountain there which was known as Licat Anir and the name of the man who was buried in the tomb was Anir. He was the soldier Arthur's son, and Arthur himself killed him and buried him there. And men came to measure the length of the tomb and one found it six feet, another nine feet, someone twelve feet, and somebody else fifteen feet. By whatever means you measure it you will not find it the same again, and I myself have proved this.

The Annals of Wales *(Annales Cambriae)*
(by tenth century)

The Annals of Wales *gives a brief glimpse of two of Arthur's battles, Badon and Camlann, in which both Arthur and Mordred fall. This first reference to Mordred is ambiguous, since it is unclear whether Mordred is fighting against Arthur (as in later Arthurian works) or on the same side. Unfortunately, this tantalizingly brief reference to* Gueith Camlann *(the battle of Camlann) is not clarified elsewhere, being overlooked by Gildas, Bede and Nennius.*

AD 516 LXXII. The year of the battle of Badon, in which Arthur [*Variant reading*: King Arthur] carried the cross of our Lord Jesus Christ for three days and three nights on his shoulders,[2] and the Britons were victorious.

AD 537 XCIII. The year of the battle of Camlann, in which Arthur and Medraut [i.e. Mordred] fell; and there was a plague in Britain and Ireland.
(A late manuscript has: The battle of Camlam, in which the famous Arthur king of the British and Mordred his betrayer, fell by wounds inflicted by each other.)[3]

The Mabinogion: *'Culhwch and Olwen'*

(*The Mabinogion* is of uncertain date. Perhaps some stories are tenth-century or even earlier, although it is possible that the collection did not reach its present form until *c.* 1200–50.)

The Mabinogion is a collection of eleven early Welsh tales which can be divided into three distinct groups. Arthur appears in the early 'Culhwch and Olwen' and the three short Arthurian romances, which are of considerably later date and show clear signs of substantial French cultural influence. The Arthurian romances – The Lady of the Fountain, Peredur *and* Gereint – *tell the same basic stories as Chrétien's* Yvain, Perceval *and* Erec and Enide *respectively. The stories are preserved in two later manuscripts: the* White Book of Rhydderch *(c. 1300–25) and the* Red Book of Hergest *(c. 1375–1425).*[4] *It is difficult to determine their exact relationship with their French counterparts; most critics now believe that the parallel Welsh and French works derive from a common Celtic source which has now been lost.*[5]

'Culhwch and Olwen': (c. 950?)

In this story, Culhwch requests assistance from Arthur and his warriors to help him woo Olwen, daughter of Ysbaddaden the Chief Giant. The figures of Cei, Bedwyr and Gwalchmei correspond to the later Arthurian characters Kay, Bedevere and Gawain, although here Cei possesses a number of marvellous qualities and is Arthur's principal warrior.

Arthur said, 'Ah, chieftain, I have never heard tell of the maiden thou tellest of, nor of her parents. I will gladly send messengers to seek her.' From that night till the same night at the end of a year the messengers were a-wandering. At the end of the year, when Arthur's messengers had found nothing, said the chieftain, 'Every one has obtained his boon, yet am I still lacking. I will away and take thine honour with me.' Said Cei, 'Ah, chieftain, overmuch dost thou asperse Arthur. Come thou with us. Till thou shalt say she exists not in the world, or till we find her, we will not be parted from thee.'

Then Cei arose. Cei had this peculiarity, nine nights and nine days his breath lasted under water, nine nights and nine days would he be without sleep. A wound from Cei's sword no physician might heal. A wondrous gift had Cei: when it pleased him he would be as tall as the tallest tree in the forest. Another peculiarity had he: when the rain was heaviest, a handbreadth before his hand and another behind his hand what would be in his hand would be dry, by reason of the greatness of his heat; and when the cold was hardest on his comrades, that would be to them kindling to light a fire.

Arthur called on Bedwyr, who never shrank from an enterprise upon which Cei was bound. It was thus with Bedwyr, that none was so handsome as he in this Island, save Arthur and Drych son of Cibddar, and this too, that though he was one-handed no three warriors drew blood in the same field faster than he. Another strange quality was his; one thrust would there be of his spear, and nine counter-thrusts.

Arthur called on Cynddylig the Guide. 'Go thou for me upon this enterprise along with the chieftain.' He was no worse a guide in the land he had never seen than in his own land.

He called Gwrhyr Interpreter of Tongues: he knew all tongues.

He called Gwalchmei son of Gwyar, because he never came home without the quest he had gone to seek. He was the best of walkers and the best of riders. He was Arthur's nephew, his sister's son, and his first cousin.

Arthur called on Menw son of Teirgwaedd, for should they come to a heathen land he might cast a spell over them, so that none might see them and they see every one.

Away they went till they came to a wide open plain and saw a fort, the greatest of forts in the world. That day they journeyed. When they thought they were near to the fort they were no nearer than at first. And the second and the third day they journeyed, and with difficulty did they get thereto. However, as they were coming to the same plain as it, they could see a great flock of sheep without limit or end to it, and a shepherd tending the sheep on top of a mound, and a jerkin of skins upon him, and at his side a shaggy mastiff which was bigger than a nine year old stallion. It was the way of him that never a lamb had he lost, much less a grown beast. No company had ever fared past him that he did not do it harm or deadly hurt; every dead tree and bush that was on the plain, his breath would burn them to the very ground.

Quoth Cei: 'Gwrhyr Interpreter of Tongues, go and have word with yonder man.' 'Cei, I made no promise to go save as far as thou thyself wouldst go.' 'Then let us go there together.' Quoth Menw son of Teirgwaedd: 'Have no qualms to go thither. I will cast a spell over the dog, so that he shall do harm to none.'

They came to where the shepherd was. Quoth they, 'Things are well with thee, shepherd.' 'May things never be better with you than with me.' 'Yea, by God, for thou art chief.' 'There is no affliction to do me harm save my wife.' 'Whose are the sheep thou tendest, or whose is the fort?' 'Fools of men that you are! Throughout the world it is known that this is the fort of Ysbaddaden Chief Giant.' 'And thou, who art thou?' 'Custennin son of Mynwyedig am I, and because of my wife Ysbaddaden Chief Giant has wrought my ruin. You too, who are you?' 'Messengers of Arthur are here, to seek Olwen.' 'Whew, men! God protect you! For all the world, do not that. Never a one has come to make that request that went away with his life.'

The shepherd arose. As he arose Culhwch gave him a ring of gold. He sought to put on the ring, but it would not go on him, and he placed it on the finger of his glove and went home and gave the glove to his wife. And she took the ring from the glove. 'Whence came this ring to thee, husband? 'Twas not often that thou hast had treasure-trove.' 'I went to the sea, to find seafood. Lo! I saw a body coming in on the tide. Never saw I body so beautiful as that, and on its finger I found this ring.' 'Alas, husband, since sea does not tolerate a dead man's jewels therein, show me that body.' 'Wife, the one whose body that is, thou shalt see him here presently.' 'Who is that?' the woman asked. 'Culhwch son of Cilydd son of Cyleddon Wledig, by Goleud-dydd daughter of Anlawdd Wledig, his mother, who is come to seek Olwen.' Two feelings possessed her: she was glad that her nephew, her sister's son, was coming to see her; and she was sad because she had never seen any depart with his life that had come to make that request.

They came forward to the gate of the shepherd Custennin's court. She heard the noise of their coming. She ran with joy to meet them. Cei snatched a log out of the wood-pile, and she came to meet them, to try and throw her arms about their necks. Cei thrust a stake between her two hands. She squeezed the stake so that it became a twisted withe. Quoth Cei, 'Woman, had it been I thou didst squeeze in this wise, there were no need for another to love me ever. An ill love, that!'

They came into the house and their needs were supplied. After a while, when all were letting themselves be busied, the woman opened a coffer alongside the hearth, and out of it arose a lad with curly yellow hair. Quoth Gwrhyr, ''Twere pity to hide a lad like this. I know that it is no fault of his own that is visited upon him.' Quoth the woman, 'He is all that is left. Three-and-twenty sons of mine has Ysbaddaden Chief Giant slain, and I have no more hope of this one than of the others.' Quoth Cei, 'Let him keep company with me, and we shall not be slain save together.'

They ate. Quoth the woman, 'On what errand are you come

hither?' 'We are come to seek Olwen.' 'For God's sake, since none from the fort has yet seen you, get you back!' 'God knows we will not get us back till we have seen the maiden. Will she come to where she may be seen?' 'She comes hither every Saturday to wash her head; and in the bowl where she washes she leaves all her rings. Neither she nor her messenger ever comes for them.' 'Will she come hither if she is sent for?' 'God knows I will not slay my soul. I will not betray the one who trusts in me. But if you pledge your word you will do her no harm, I will send for her.' 'We pledge it,' said they.

She was sent for. And she came, with a robe of flame-red silk about her, and around the maiden's neck a torque of red gold, and precious pearls thereon and rubies. Yellower was her head than the flower of the broom, whiter was her flesh than the foam of the wave; whiter were her palms and her fingers than the shoots of the marsh trefoil from amidst the fine gravel of a welling spring. Neither the eye of the mewed hawk, nor the eye of the thrice-mewed falcon, not an eye was there fairer than hers. Whiter were her breasts than the breast of the white swan, redder were her cheeks than the reddest foxgloves. Whoso beheld her would be filled with love of her. Four white trefoils sprang up behind her wherever she went; and for that reason was she called Olwen.

She entered the house and sat between Culhwch and the high seat, and even as he saw her he knew her. Said Culhwch to her, 'Ah maiden, 'tis thou I have loved. And come thou with me.' 'Lest sin be charged to thee and me, that I may not do at all. My father has sought a pledge of me that I go not without his counsel, for he shall live only until I go with a husband. There is, however, counsel I will give thee, if thou wilt take it. Go ask me of my father. And however much he demand of thee, do thou promise to get it, and me too shalt thou get. But if he have cause to doubt at all, get me thou shalt not, and 'tis well for thee if thou escape with thy life.' 'I promise all that, and will obtain it,' said he.

She went to her chamber. They then arose to go after her to the fort, and slew nine gatemen who were at nine gates without a man crying out, and nine mastiffs without one squealing. And they went forward to the hall.

Quoth they, 'In the name of God and man, greeting unto thee, Ysbaddaden Chief Giant.' 'And you, where are you going?' 'We are going to seek Olwen thy daughter for Culhwch son of Cilydd.' 'Where are those rascal servants and those ruffians of mine?' said he. 'Raise up the forks under my two eyelids that I may see my future son-in-law.' That was done. 'Come hither tomorrow. I will give you some answer.'

They rose, and Ysbaddaden Chief Giant snatched at one of the three poisoned stone-spears which were by his hand and hurled it after them. And Bedwyr caught it and hurled it back at him, and pierced Ysbaddaden Chief Giant right through the ball of his knee. Quoth he, 'Thou cursed savage son-in-law! I shall walk the worse up a slope. Like the sting of a gadfly the poisoned iron has pained me. Cursed be the smith who fashioned it, and the anvil on which it was wrought, so painful it is!'

That night they lodged in the house of Custennin. And on the morrow with pomp and with brave combs set in their hair they came into the hall. They said, 'Ysbaddaden Chief Giant, give us thy daughter in return for her portion and her maiden fee to thee and her two kinswomen. And unless thou give her, thou shalt meet thy death because of her.' 'She and her four great-grandmothers and her four great-grandfathers are yet alive. I must needs take counsel with them.' 'So be it with thee,' said they. 'Let us go to our meat.' As they arose he took hold of the second stone-spear which was by his hand and hurled it after them. And Menw son of Teirgwaedd caught it and hurled it back at him, and pierced him in the middle of his breast, so that it came out in the small of his back. 'Thou cursed savage son-in-law! Like the bite of a big-headed leech the hard iron has pained me. Cursed be the forge wherein it was heated. When I go uphill, I shall have tightness of chest, and belly-ache, and a frequent loathing of meat.' They went to their meat.

And the third day they came to court. Quoth they, 'Ysbaddaden Chief Giant, shoot at us no more. Seek not thy harm and deadly hurt and death.' 'Where are my servants? Raise up the forks – my eyelids have fallen over the balls of my eyes – so that I may take a look at my future son-in-law.' They arose, and as they arose he took the third poisoned stone-spear and hurled it after them. And Culhwch caught it and hurled it back, even as he wished, and pierced him through the ball of the eye, so that it came out through the nape of the neck. 'Thou cursed savage son-in-law! So long as I am left alive, the sight of my eyes will be the worse. When I go against the wind they will water, a headache I shall have, and a giddiness each new moon. Cursed be the forge wherein it was heated. Like the bite of a mad dog to me the way the poisoned iron has pierced me.' They went to their meat.

On the morrow they came to court. Quoth they, 'Shoot not at us. Seek not the harm and deadly hurt and martyrdom that are upon thee, or what may be worse, if such be thy wish. Give us thy daughter.' 'Where is he who is told to seek my daughter?' ''Tis I who seek her,

Culhwch son of Cilydd.' 'Come hither where I may see thee.' A chair was placed under him, face to face with him.

Said Ysbaddaden Chief Giant, 'Is it thou that seekest my daughter?' ''Tis I who seek her.' 'Thy pledge would I have that thou wilt not do worse by me than is just.' 'Thou shalt have it.' 'When I have myself gotten that which I shall name to thee, then thou shalt get my daughter.'

The Life of St Goeznovius (Legenda Sancti Goeznovii) (c. 1019?)

The Life of St Goeznovius provides a short account of British legendary history before Arthur's reign. Since it contains material also found in Geoffrey of Monmouth's History of the Kings of Britain, *it is probable that both writers possessed lost British/Welsh chronicles containing this material. According to this work, Arthur drove the invading Saxons out of most of Britain and subdued them. However, after he had won many victories in both Britain and France, Arthur was 'recalled at length from worldly actions', and the Saxons again prevailed. This is probably the first text to insinuate that Arthur does not actually die. The original Latin phrase 'Ab humanis tandem actibus evocato' is ambiguous; it may be a Christian euphemism for 'died', but the literal meaning might imply knowledge of Arthur's legendary survival.*

We may read in British history that the British, under Brutus and Corineus, by their strength subdued the place Albidia (Albion), with the surrounding islands, which they then called Britain. With their growing multitude of followers and the kingdom prospering under their control, Conanus Meriadoc, an upright and warlike man, who had risen in power because he had captured one of the lesser kingdoms, crossed the sea to Armoric Gaul with a great number of people. The first place where he settled was beside the River Guilidona at the edge of Plebis Columbae (Plougoulm) in an area which is still called Meriadoc's Castle.

Conanus, with his British followers, won all that land from both shores of the sea to the city of Andegavora by his praiseworthy valour, together with all the land of Nannetensus and Redonicus. Having killed all the native pagan inhabitants, they renamed it Pengouet. The women, whose tongues were cut out lest they should corrupt the language of the Britons, were employed as wives and for other services, as the occasion demanded. Churches were built to the glory of God, and by the grace of God the whole land was named Lesser Britain. Thus the Britons of Armorica and of the island, using the same laws and bound by fraternal treaties, were ruled as one people in a single empiric region.

After a passage of time, Vortigern became king by usurpation; and, to preserve himself while ruling most of Britain, which he had subdued unjustly, he summoned warlike men from parts of Saxony and made them companions in his kingdom. Since these men were pagans and of a diabolical nature, they covered themselves with spilt human blood and brought much evil to the Britons.

The pride of these Saxons was later suppressed by the great Arthur, king of the Britons, and they were driven from the greater part of the island and forced into servitude. However, when that same Arthur, after many splendid victories which he won in parts of Britain and Gaul, was recalled at length from worldly actions, the way was again clear for those Saxons who had remained in the island. Great oppression befell the British, and the Holy Church was persecuted.

This persecution lasted for the reigns of many kings, both Saxons and Britons. The Saxons, remembering Anglia, an ancient Saxon city, imposed its name on both themselves and the island, and called themselves either 'Angles' or 'Anglici', although to this day they are called 'Saxons' by the Britons. During this stormy period, many holy men willingly offered themselves to martyrdom; others, following evangelical advice, left Great Britain, which now was the land of Saxons, crossing into lesser Britain [Brittany], where they evaded the tyranny of pagans; many in truth left everything for a secret life of devotion, thankfully and happily serving the Lord in solitary places.

LIFRIC OF LLANCARFAN, The Life of St Cadoc (Vita Cadoci) (c. 1075)

The Prologue of Chapter 18 of Lifric's Life of St Cadoc *portrays Arthur as a selfish warlord who wastes his time gambling with his followers. Seeing a beautiful girl approaching, Arthur desires to rape her rather than offer her protection. The concept of a knight possessing the right of conquest over a damsel whose escort he has defeated is a prominent theme in the later* Prose Tristan, *which attributes the downfall of Arthurian chivalry, especially that of heroes such as Gawain, to its practice. Malory follows this text closely in the* Book of Sir Tristram de Lyones. *The reprimand of Arthur's evil remark by Kay and Bedevere is probably the first recorded mention of the chivalric practice of assisting the weak and helpless.*

When, after great slaughter, Gundleius, king of Demetia, physically uninjured but dejected by fighting his adversaries, together with the aforementioned virgin Gladusa, daughter of Brachan, reached the boundaries of his lands, behold, they encountered three powerful heroes: Arthur, with two of his knights, Cei and Bedguir, were sitting together on the summit of the aforesaid hill, playing dice.

Perceiving the king approaching with this girl, Arthur was immediately inflamed with illicit passion for the adolescent girl and, full of wicked thoughts, addressed his companions, 'You should know that I burn with violent desire for that girl whom the horseman is conducting.' But they spoke forbiddingly to him, 'Remove such wicked thoughts from your mind, for we are accustomed to aid those who are weak and defenceless: for which reason we have come in haste to assist in this critical battle.' Then Arthur said, 'Since you both prefer to assist Gundleius rather than violently snatch the girl from him on my behalf, go and intercept them, and diligently enquire of them who is the heir of this land.'

When they had quickly departed and enquired on behalf of their king, Gundleius replied: 'I call on God and all my deceased British ancestors to witness that I am the heir of this land.' Returning to their lord, the messengers repeated what they had heard from Gundleius. Arthur and his companions then armed and attacked Gundleius' enemies, who, turning their backs in great confusion, fled to their native land. Then Gundleius, triumphing through the protection of Arthur, returned to his palace with the aforesaid virgin Gladusa.

In Chapter 18 of The Life of St Cadoc, *there is a dispute between St Cadoc, the son of Gundliac, and King Arthur.*

A most powerful leader of the Britons, called Ligessauc, son of Eliman, who also had the nickname Lauhiir, meaning 'long hand', killed three knights of Arthur, the most famous king of the Britons. Then he was pursued by Arthur wherever he turned, and he found nowhere that was safe, and nobody would protect him for fear of the aforesaid king. Finally, after a very swift flight, he came, exhausted, before a man of God. Having compassion for his suffering, the holy man received him kindly, trusting in God, and not fearing Arthur at all, according to the Lord's precept: 'Do not fear those who kill the body, for they cannot slay the spirit, but rather fear him who can send both spirit and body into Hell.' He remained in this manner with the holy man in the territory of Guunliauc for seven years in security, without Arthur's knowledge.

After this period of time, a message was sent to the aforesaid King Arthur asking for a peaceful settlement, since nobody would have dared to use force against a man of God, but Arthur came to the River Usk with a large body of soldiers. Sending messengers to the king, the holy man asked him if the dispute could be settled by a wise judgement. However, Arthur remained silent since, before his arrival, St Cadoc had gathered on the bank of the great River Usk three main leaders: namely, David, Teliauno and Dochu, summoned by Keneder and Maidoc, from the various regions of his land, together with many other clerics and senior judges from the whole of Britain.

There, in the manner of enemies, on opposite banks of the river, they argued the matter with bitter words on both sides for a long time. After this dispute, the more learned of the judges decreed that Arthur should receive in recompense for each of his slain men three of the finest cows.[6] Others considered that Arthur should receive a hundred cattle as recompense for the three men, since from former times it was an established custom among the British for a king or duke to receive such recompense. Accepting this judgement, Arthur insolently refused to accept cattle of a single colour; indeed he wished to receive mixed-coloured cows, with the front part red and the rear part white, for he was most eager to use the difference in colour as an excuse for refusal.

Since they did not know where they could find cattle of such a colour, they hesitated, deliberating how they might come by them; concerning this, the holy man called upon God the Father, the Son and the Holy Spirit to determine whether nine or a hundred cattle of this colour should be given to Arthur. As the aforesaid animals were brought before his eyes and those of the other servants of God, by divine intervention, because of the depravity of Arthur's greed, the cows were immediately changed into the aforementioned colours through the prayers of the just. All the assembled clergy, together with all those who believed in God, attributed the miracle to this holy man and, rejoicing greatly, praised God enthusiastically.

The holy man consulted with his supporters about whether the aforesaid cows should be given to Arthur by right. They all replied: 'It is just that you drive them out into the middle of the ford.' So he drove them towards the place where Arthur, Kay and Bedevere were sitting on the river bank; but when Kay and Bedevere were boasting that they would drag them by the horns to the other bank, as soon as they had laid hands on them, in the sight of all, the cows were transformed by divine intervention into fern bundles.

When Arthur saw this spectacle, since that which he had demanded had been snatched away unjustly, he whipped the holy man humiliatingly. However, forgiveness is freely bestowed on the wrongdoer: according to the Gospel: 'Give, and it shall be given unto you.' Therefore, the aforesaid King Arthur took counsel with his followers, and condemned the saint to exile for seven full years and an equal number of months and days.[7]

Arthur and all his leaders, with the agreement of all the elders of the whole of Britain, proclaimed: 'We, in the hearing of all, give our word of sanction to this dispute, and whoever contests it, may God bestow on him all the plagues written in the Old and New Testaments, and may his name be removed from the Book of Life. May those who maintain this agreement be filled with all the blessings of the Old and New Testaments, and may their spirit rest in eternal peace.' After this judgement was made, all the cows which had been transformed into sticks were discovered unharmed in their cattle-sheds by their owners. From that day onwards, the place was called in Welsh 'Trefredinauc', meaning 'the town of sticks'. The ford at which this incident took place was called Rithguutebou.

The Life of St Carannog (Vita Carantoci) (c. 1100?)

The Life of St Carannog *contains a short episode involving Arthur and Cato (who is probably one of Arthur's earliest followers, Kay). In this story, Arthur requests the saint's assistance against an enormous dragon,[8] which has been terrorizing the local people. Perhaps this reference to feeding the dragon suggests that Kay is already holding the office of Arthur's steward.*

St Carannog returned to his own homeland of Cardigan, to his cell with many clergy, and there he performed many virtuous deeds which it is impossible for anyone to enumerate. Christ gave him a magnificent altar from Heaven, the colour of which nobody could discern. Afterwards, he came to the River Severn, intending to cross, and he placed the altar in the sea, since it went before him wherever God wished him to go.

At that time Cato and Arthur were ruling in this region, living in Dindraithov; and as Arthur was travelling around he came across an enormous, terrible and most powerful dragon, which had devastated a twelfth of the fields of Carrum. Then Carannog came and greeted Arthur, who was glad to receive benediction from him. Then Carannog asked Arthur if he knew where his altar had landed, and Arthur replied, 'If I received a boon I would inform you.' And he replied, 'What favour do you request?' He replied, 'You should subdue the dragon which is near here so that we may perceive that you are a servant of God.'

Then the blessed Carannog proceeded and prayed to the Lord, and behold the dragon came with a great noise, just as a calf hastens to its mother, and bowed its head before God's servant, as a servant obedient to his master, with a humble heart and downcast eyes. The saint placed his robe around its neck and led it like a lamb; it did not raise up its wings or its claws, and its neck was like the neck of a seven-year-old bull, so it was hardly possible for the robe to go around it.

Then they went on together to the citadel, and they greeted Cato, and they were well received by him. He led this dragon into the middle of the hall and fed it before the people, but they attempted to kill it. However, the saint would not permit them to slay it, but declared that it had come from the Word of God to destroy the sinners who were in Carrum and to display the virtue of God through him.

Afterwards, Carannog led it through the fortress gate and dismissed it, ordering it to injure nobody and to return no more, and it departed, although hesitating, as the Law of God had anticipated. Then Carannog took back his altar, which Arthur had intended to use as a table, but whatever was placed on it was thrown off a long way. Then the king asked Carannog in a written document to receive Carrum, and afterwards he built a church there.

Later on a voice came from Heaven ordering the altar to be placed on the sea. Then Carannog sent to Cato and Arthur to find out about the altar, and he was informed by them that it had landed in the harbour of Guellit. Then King Arthur said, 'Carannog should be given a twelfth part of the fields where the altar was found.' Afterwards Carannog returned and built a church there, and called the city Carrov.

The Life of St Iltud (Vita Illuti) (c. 1100?)

In his youth Iltud, son of Bican and of Rieingulid, daughter of Anblaud, king of Brittany, is drawn to King Arthur's court by news of his renown, as many young knights were later to be.

The splendid knight, Illytud, having heard about all the victories of his cousin King Arthur, was eager to visit the king's magnificent court. He left the place called Further Britain [Brittany], and came sailing to where he saw an enormous force of soldiers. There he was received honourably, and given gifts according to his warlike taste; having fulfilled his desire of receiving gifts, he returned most satisfied from the royal court.

The Life of St Padarn (Vita Paterni) (twelfth century)

In this saint's life the representation of Arthur is positively hostile, making Arthur a local tyrant rather than a great king, and presenting him as an enemy of the Church rather than as its defender.

When St Padarn was recuperating in the church after a lengthy sea-journey, a certain tyrant of that region, called Arthur, came one day to the cell of St Padarn the bishop. Whilst he was speaking to Padarn, he caught sight of his tunic and, filled with jealousy, he asked if it could be his. The saint replied, 'This tunic is too worthy a garment for anyone wicked, since it is a clerical habit.'

Arthur left the monastery swearing, and he returned once more in indignation, in order to snatch away the tunic, against the advice of the holy brethren. One of the disciples of Padarn, seeing Arthur returning in anger, hastened to St Padarn and said, 'The tyrant who came here before has returned insolently, kicking to the ground everything that he feels like.' Padarn replied, 'Well, then, let the earth swallow him up.' As soon as he said this, the earth opened and swallowed up Arthur as far as his chin. Arthur, who immediately realized his offence, began to beseech both God and Padarn until he obtained mercy, and the earth threw him back up. From this place, he sought forgiveness from the saint on bended knees, which Padarn granted. Arthur asked Padarn to become his permanent mentor, but he refused.

CARADOC OF LLANCARFAN, The Life of St Gildas (Vitae Gildae) (before 1155?)

Caradoc of Llancarfan's assertion that Gildas was Arthur's con-
temporary is probably correct, since Gildas himself states that he
was born in the year of the battle of Badon.[9] The silence sur-
rounding Arthur in Gildas's own work has sometimes been explai-
ned as his revenge for the death of his beloved brother, Hueil, at
Arthur's hands.

In this work, it appears that the area of Britain controlled by
Arthur may have been only Devon and Cornwall.[9] In Chapter 10,
there is a brief account of Guenevere's abduction by Melvas, king
of Somerset, and the intervention by Gildas the Wise and the
abbot of Glastonbury to restore her to Arthur peacefully. The
abduction of Guenevere is depicted on the archivolt of Modena
Cathedral in Italy, which can be satisfactorily dated to c. AD 1116,
and is later recounted in Chrétien de Troyes's Lancelot. *According*
to Rachel Bromwich, another written reference to such an incident
is found in two Triads in the Red Book of Hergest, *where Medraut's*
raid on Arthur's court at Kelliwic and subsequent violation of
Gwenhwyfar is said to have been responsible for the battle of
Camlann.

From Chapter 5

Gildas, a most holy man, was a contemporary of Arthur, king of the
whole of Great Britain, and, since he held Arthur in great esteem, he
wished always to obey him. However, twenty-three of Gildas' brothers resisted the aforesaid king in rebellion, being unwilling to put
up with his domination, but they were repeatedly put to flight and
driven off in assaults and by war.

The eldest brother, Hueil, a habitual warrior and a most famous
soldier, refused to obey any king, even Arthur. He used to harass
Arthur, and they provoked each other with the greatest fury. Hueil
invaded from Scotland on many occasions, setting fire to the land
and bearing off booty with victory and praise.

For this reason, Arthur, king of all Britain, hearing about the
achievements of this brave, excellent and most victorious youth, felt
oppressed, since the native people said and hoped that he would be
their future king. So, by fierce persecution and in open warfare,
Arthur killed the young pillager on the Isle of Minau.[10] After slaying

him, Arthur returned victorious, rejoicing greatly that he had overcome his strongest enemy.

Gildas, a historian of the British, was staying in Ireland at that
time, studying about kings and preaching in the city of Armagh, when
he heard that his brother had been killed by Arthur. He grieved at the
news, weeping and groaning, as a brother might for his dearest
brother; he prayed for his brother's spirit every day; moreover, he
prayed on behalf of Arthur, his brother's persecutor and killer...

...Meanwhile Gildas came to Britain...That night he was honourably received by Cadoc, the venerable abbot, in the valley of Carbana
... Hearing of Gildas the Wise's reception by King Arthur and the
principal bishops and abbots of all Britain, numerous clergy and
people gathered to make peace with Arthur regarding the aforesaid
homicide. However, Gildas, as he would have done at first, although
aware of the report of his brother's death, forgave his enemy, gave a
kiss of peace when asked for forgiveness, and, with a benevolent
spirit, gave his blessing. After Gildas had performed this, King Arthur,
grieving and in tears, received penance from the surrounding bishops,
making amends in whatever way he could for as long as his life lasted.

From Chapter 10

Gildas ... climbed into a little ship and went to Glastonbury ...
Melvas was the king ruling in Somerset (the summer region). Given
a warm welcome by the abbot of Glastonbury, Gildas taught his
fellow-brethren and various common people, sowing the seed of
heavenly faith. Here he wrote the history of the kings of Britain.
Glastonbury (that is, 'Glass City'), which took its name from glass,[11]
is a city originally called Ynisgutrin in the British [i.e. Welsh] language.

Glastonbury was besieged by the tyrant Arthur with an enormous
army, on account of Guenevere his wife, who had been snatched
away and raped by the aforementioned wicked King Melvas and
taken to Glastonbury since it was an impregnable refuge on account
of the reed defences, the river and the boggy ground.[12] The rebel king
[i.e. Arthur] had been searching everywhere for the queen for an
entire year, and had at last discovered her whereabouts. Then he
assembled the military forces of all Cornwall and Devon, and the two
enemies prepared for battle.

Perceiving this, the abbot of Glastonbury, together with his clerical
followers and Gildas the Wise, entered the battlefield and advised
Melvas to make peace with his king and restore the captive queen.
So she was returned, as she should have been, peacefully and in good
faith. Having done this, the two kings bestowed extensive lands on

the abbot and, coming to the church of St Mary, at the abbot's instigation they prayed in brotherly affection for a stable peace and for the benefits which it brought and would bring in addition. Then the pacified kings respectfully promised to obey the most reverend abbot of Glastonbury and never to violate the most sacred place nor the surrounding area.

From Chapter 14

Ynisgutrin was the ancient name for Glastonbury, and it is still called this by the native British; *ynis* in the British language means 'island', and *gutrin* means 'glass'. However, after the arrival of the English and the expulsion of the British (or Welsh), it was renamed 'Glastigberi', from the English word *glas* ('glass') and *beri* ('city'), meaning 'City of Glass'.

Gerald of Wales, The Description of Wales

In this interesting extract, Gerald relates a British belief that Gildas' failure to mention King Arthur was due to his anguish at his brother's death at Arthur's hands.[13]

The Britons maintain that, when Gildas criticized his own people so bitterly, he wrote as he did because he was so infuriated by the fact that King Arthur had killed his own brother, who was a Scottish chieftain. When he heard of his brother's death, or so the Britons say, he threw into the sea a number of outstanding books which he had written in their praise and about Arthur's achievements. As a result you will find no book which gives an authentic account of that great prince.

WILLIAM OF MALMESBURY, The Deeds of the English Kings (De Regum Gestis Anglorum) (c. 1125)

Nennius's account of the battle of Mount Badon was accepted without question by later historians. William of Malmesbury discusses the successful repulsion of the invading Saxons during the reign of Ambrosius, the last Roman ruler. Whereas Geoffrey of Monmouth states that Arthur was born after the death of Ambrosius (his uncle), in William's account Arthur is his valorous general.

On the death of Vortimer, the strength of the Britons dwindled, their diminished hopes receded; they would have been totally destroyed had not Ambrosius, the last remaining Roman leader, who was sole ruler of the realm after Vortigern, repressed the swelling hordes of barbarians through the distinguished achievements of the warlike Arthur.

It is about this Arthur that the Britons tell such trifling stories even today. Clearly, he is a man more worthy to be extolled in true histories, as the leader who long preserved his tottering homeland and kindled an appetite for war in the shattered minds of his countrymen, than to be dreamed of in fallacious fables. Finally, at the siege of Mount Badon, trusting in the Mother of our Lord, whose image he had sewn upon his armour, he attacked single-handedly nine hundred of the enemy and overthrew them with incredible slaughter.

William of Malmesbury makes only one other reference to Arthur, when he recounts the discovery in Wales, in the reign of William the Conqueror, of the tomb of Gawain, Arthur's nephew, whose deeds were celebrated by later English writers. It is possible that his statement on Arthur's lack of a burial-place and fabled return may indicate an awareness of the 'Graves' Triad, and testifies to the existence of legends concerning Arthur's promised return.

At this time was found, in the province of the 'Welsh' called Ros, the tomb of the noble Walwen (Gawain), who was the nephew of Arthur by his sister. He reigned in that part of Britain which is still called *Walweitha* [Galloway]. Although a warrior most renowned for his valour, he was expelled from his kingdom by Hengist's brother and nephew (about whom I have written in the first book), but not before he had been compensated for his exile by causing them considerable damage. He deserves to share the praise justly given to his uncle, since together they delayed for many years the destruction of their collapsing country.

The tomb of Arthur is nowhere to be found, for which reason ancient fables claim that he will return again. However, as I have said, the tomb of his nephew, which is fourteen feet in length, was found in the time of King William upon the seashore. Some maintain that he was wounded by his foes and cast out in a shipwreck, but according to others he was killed by his fellow-citizens at a public banquet. Therefore, the truth remains in doubt, although neither story could tarnish his fame.

PART 2

GEOFFREY OF MONMOUTH AND THE 'BRUT' CHRONICLE TRADITION

GEOFFREY OF MONMOUTH, History of the Kings of Britain (Historia Regum Britanniae) (c. 1136)

Geoffrey of Monmouth was a Welsh chronicler and ecclesiastic, thought to be the son of Breton parents. He studied at Oxford and was archdeacon of Llandarff or Monmouth (c. 1140) and was appointed bishop of St Asaph in 1152.

His famous History of the Kings of Britain *provides us with the first full-length account of Arthur's life from his dramatic conception at Tintagel Castle in Cornwall, to his death at the hands of Mordred. Geoffrey asserts that he has translated his work from an ancient Welsh chronicle presented to him by Walter Archdeacon of Oxford. While Welsh versions of Geoffrey's story are still extant today, they are all in manuscripts later than Geoffrey's* History, *so some critics believe that they are derived from Geoffrey's work.[14]*

Although knowledge of Arthur had already spread beyond the Celtic world before Geoffrey's History *was written, it was this influential work that made the Arthurian legend famous. A number of summaries, translations and adaptations of Geoffrey's work subsequently appeared, including French versions by Wace, Pierre de Langtoft and Jehan de Waurin, and English translations by Lawman, Robert of Gloucester and Robert Mannyng.*

The Arthurian section of Geoffrey's History *is about fifty pages long; about a third of which is included here. The rest of the story is told through the various other works derived from Geoffrey's original version. Since Geoffrey's work is an important text, it is useful to give the reader a summary of its contents.*

Geoffrey's story of Arthur begins with Uther Pendragon's lust for Ygerna, wife of Duke Gorlois of Cornwall, and Merlin's use of magic to transform Uther into the likeness of Gorlois so that he can visit Ygerna in Tintagel Castle, where he begets Arthur (see first extract, pp. 27–30).[15]

When the Saxon invaders poison Uther at St Albans, the young Arthur becomes king and fights first the Saxons and then the Picts and Scots, using his famous sword Caliburn (in other works also known as Excalibur). After Arthur has defeated all these invaders and restored peace to Britain, he marries Guenevere (see second extract, pp. 30–37).[16]

Arthur then embarks on a series of overseas conquests. First, he defeats the Irish King Gilmaurius and subdues Ireland, then he takes possession of Iceland, Gotland and the Orkneys. He then returns to Britain, which he rules in peace for twelve years, inviting men of valour from distant lands to join his splendid court.[17]

Arthur then undertakes a second period of conquest, invading first Norway and then Gaul (France), where he kills the Roman tribune Frollo in single combat. He divides up Gaul to reward his followers, giving Neustria (Normandy) to his cup-bearer, Bedevere, and Anjou to Kay the seneschal (see Wace, pp. 45–52).

On his triumphal return to Britain, Arthur holds a splendid Pentecostal court at Caerleon upon Usk, attended by all the king's vassals and involving much ceremonial pomp and an ostentatious display of wealth. There is also a lavish feast, where the women dine separately from the men in accordance with an ancient 'Trojan' custom,[18] *as well as various competitions and games. The festivities are interrupted by the arrival of messengers from the Roman Emperor Lucius with a demand that Arthur appear in Rome to stand trial for his invasion of Gaul and for his failure to pay tribute to Rome.*[19]

After holding a council of war, Arthur entrusts Britain to the safe-keeping of his nephew, Mordred, and Queen Guenevere. While at sea he has a dream in which a dragon fights a bear; he is disturbed by this dream until he is informed that the interpretation is favourable. Arriving at Barfleur, Arthur learns of the abduction of Helena, niece of Hoel, duke of Brittany, by a savage giant. Arthur goes to Mont-Saint-Michel to fight the giant, whom he overcomes in fierce single combat (see Mannyng).[20]

Arthur and his followers now have to fight a large Roman army under Lucius. After an unsuccessful attempt at a parley, Arthur's nephew, Gawain, skirmishes with the Romans before returning to Arthur's camp with prisoners and booty. Then, after the Romans have attempted to destroy the Britons in an ambush, the two armies draw up at Saussy for a pitched battle. In the battle, Gawain and

Hoel display their prowess in arms, and Arthur eventually routs the Roman army.[21]

Finally, Arthur learns that his treacherous nephew Mordred has crowned himself and is living adulterously with Guenevere. He hastens back to Britain, where he engages in a fight to the death with Mordred. Arthur is seriously wounded, and is taken to the Isle of Avalon so that his wounds can be healed. Arthur entrusts the Crown of Britain to his cousin, Constantine, son of Cador, duke of Cornwall (see third extract, pp. 37–40).[22]

Arthur's Conception at Tintagel Castle

The next Eastertide Uther told the nobles of his kingdom to assemble in that same town of London, so that he could wear his crown and celebrate so important a feast-day with proper ceremony. They all obeyed, travelling in from their various cities and assembling on the eve of the feast. The King was thus able to celebrate the feast as he had intended and to enjoy himself in the company of his leaders. They, too, were all happy, seeing that he had received them with such affability. A great many nobles had gathered there, men worthy of taking part in such a gay festivity, together with their wives and daughters.

Among the others there was present Gorlois, Duke of Cornwall, with his wife Ygerna, who was the most beautiful woman in Britain. When the King saw her there among the other women, he was immediately filled with desire for her, with the result that he took no notice of anything else, but devoted all his attention to her. To her and to no one else he kept ordering plates of food to be passed and to her, too, he kept sending his own personal attendants with golden goblets of wine. He kept smiling at her and engaging her in sprightly conversation. When Ygerna's husband saw what was happening, he was so annoyed that he withdrew from the court without taking leave. No one present could persuade him to return, for he was afraid of losing the one object that he loved better than anything else. Uther lost his temper and ordered Gorlois to come back to court, so that he, the King, could seek satisfaction for the way in which he had been insulted. Gorlois refused to obey. The King was furious and swore an oath that he would ravage Gorlois' lands, unless the latter gave him immediate satisfaction.

Without more ado, while the bad blood remained between the two of them, the King collected a huge army together and hurried off to the Duchy of Cornwall, where he set fire to towns and castles. Gorlois' army was the smaller of the two and he did not dare to meet the King in battle. He preferred instead to garrison his castles and to bide his time until he could receive help from Ireland. As he was more worried about his wife than he was about himself, he left her in the castle of Tintagel, on the sea-coast, which he thought was the safest place under his control. He himself took refuge in a fortified camp called Dimilioc, so that, if disaster overtook them, they should not both be endangered together. When the King heard of this, he went to the encampment where Gorlois was, besieged it and cut off every line of approach.

Finally, after a week had gone by, the King's passion for Ygerna became more than he could bear. He called to him Ulfin of Rid-caradoch, one of his soldiers and a familiar friend, and told him what was on his mind. 'I am desperately in love with Ygerna,' said Uther, 'and if I cannot have her I am convinced that I shall suffer a physical breakdown. You must tell me how I can satisfy my desire for her, for otherwise I shall die of the passion which is consuming me.' 'Who can possibly give you useful advice,' answered Ulfin, 'when no power on earth can enable us to come to her where she is inside the fortress of Tintagel? The castle is built high above the sea, which surrounds it on all sides, and there is no other way in except that offered by a narrow isthmus of rock. Three armed soldiers could hold it against you, even if you stood there with the whole kingdom of Britain at your side. If only the prophet Merlin would give his mind to the problem, then with his help I think you might be able to obtain what you want.' The King believed Ulfin and ordered Merlin to be sent for, for he, too, had come to the siege.

Merlin was summoned immediately. When he appeared in the King's presence, he was ordered to suggest how the King could have his way with Ygerna. When Merlin saw the torment which the King was suffering because of this woman, he was amazed at the strength of his passion. 'If you are to have your wish,' he said, 'you must make use of methods which are quite new and until now unheard-of in your day. By my drugs I know how to give you the precise appearance of Gorlois, so that you will resemble him in every respect. If you do what I say, I will make you exactly like him, and Ulfin exactly like Gorlois' companion, Jordan of Tintagel. I will change my own appearance, too, and come with you. In this way you will be able to go safely to Ygerna in her castle and be admitted.'

The King agreed and listened carefully to what he had to do. In the end he handed the siege over to his subordinates, took Merlin's drugs, and was changed into the likeness of Gorlois. Ulfin was changed into Jordan and Merlin into a man called Britaelis, so that no one could tell what they had previously looked like. They then set off for

Tintagel and came to the castle in the twilight. The moment the guard
was told that his leader was approaching, he opened the gates and
the men were let in. Who, indeed, could possibly have suspected
anything, once it was thought that Gorlois himself had come? The
King spent that night with Ygerna and satisfied his desire by making
love with her. He had deceived her by the disguise which he had
taken. He had deceived her, too, by the lying things that he said to
her, things which he planned with great skill. He said that he had
come out secretly from his besieged encampment so that he might
make sure that all was well with her, whom he loved so dearly, and
with his castle, too. She naturally believed all that he said and refused
him nothing that he asked. That night she conceived Arthur, the
most famous of men, who subsequently won great renown by his
outstanding bravery.

Meanwhile, when it was discovered at the siege of Dimilioc that
the King was no longer present, his army, acting without his instructions, tried to breach the walls and challenge the beleaguered Duke
to battle. The Duke, equally ill-advisedly, sallied forth with his men,
imagining apparently that he could resist such a host of armed men
with his own tiny band. As the struggle between them swayed this
way and that, Gorlois was among the first to be killed. His men were
scattered and the besieged camp was captured. The treasure which
had been deposited there was shared out in the most inequitable way,
for each man seized in his greedy fist whatever good luck and his own
brute strength threw in his way.

Not until the outrages which followed this daring act had finally
subsided did messengers come to Ygerna to announce the death of
the Duke and the end of the siege. When they saw the King sitting
beside Ygerna in the likeness of their leader, they blushed red with
astonishment to see that the man whom they had left behind dead in
the siege had in effect arrived there safely before them. Of course,
they did not know of the drugs prepared by Merlin. The King put his
arms round the Duchess and laughed aloud to hear these reports. 'I
am not dead,' he said. 'Indeed, as you see, I am very much alive!
However, the destruction of my camp saddens me very much and so
does the slaughter of my comrades. What is more, there is great
danger that the King may come this way and capture us in this castle.
I will go out to meet him and make peace with him, lest even worse
should befall us.'

The King set out and made his way towards his own army, abandoning his disguise as Gorlois and becoming Utherpendragon once
more. When he learned all that had happened, he mourned for the
death of Gorlois; but he was happy, all the same, that Ygerna was

freed from her marital obligations. He returned to Tintagel Castle, captured it and seized Ygerna at the same time, she being what he really wanted. From that day on they lived together as equals, united by their great love for each other; and they had a son and a daughter. The boy was called Arthur and the girl Anna.

Arthur's Early Reign

After the death of Utherpendragon, the leaders of the Britons assembled from their various provinces in the town of Silchester and there suggested to Dubricius, the Archbishop of the City of the Legions, that as their King he should crown Arthur, the son of Uther. Necessity urged them on, for as soon as the Saxons heard of the death of King Uther, they invited their own countrymen over from Germany, appointed Colgrin as their leader and began to do their utmost to exterminate the Britons. They had already over-run all that section of the island which stretches from the River Humber to the sea named Caithness.

Dubricius lamented the sad state of his country. He called the other bishops to him and bestowed the crown of the kingdom upon Arthur. Arthur was a young man only fifteen years old; but he was of outstanding courage and generosity, and his inborn goodness gave him such grace that he was loved by almost all the people. Once he had been invested with the royal insignia, he observed the normal custom of giving gifts freely to everyone. Such a great crowd of soldiers flocked to him that he came to an end of what he had to distribute. However, the man to whom open-handedness and bravery both come naturally may indeed find himself momentarily in need, but poverty will never harass him for long. In Arthur courage was closely linked with generosity, and he made up his mind to harry the Saxons, so that with their wealth he might reward the retainers who served his own household. The justness of his cause encouraged him, for he had a claim by rightful inheritance to the kingship of the whole island. He therefore called together all the young men whom I have just mentioned and marched on York.

As soon as this was announced to Colgrin, he assembled the Saxons, Scots and Picts, and came to meet Arthur with a vast multitude. Once contact was made between the two armies, beside the River Douglas, both sides stood in grave danger for their lives. Arthur, however, was victorious. Colgrin fled, and Arthur pursued him; then Colgrin entered York and Arthur besieged him there.

As soon as Baldulf, the brother of Colgrin, heard of the latter's flight, he came to the siege with six thousand troops, in the hope of freeing the beleaguered man. At the time when his brother had gone into battle, Baldulf himself had been on the sea-coast, where he was awaiting the arrival of Duke Cheldric, who was on his way from Germany to bring them support. When he was some ten miles distant from the city of York, Baldulf decided to take the advantage of a night march, so that he could launch an unexpected attack. Arthur heard of this and ordered Cador, Duke of Cornwall, to march to meet Baldulf that same night, with six hundred cavalry and three thousand foot. Cador surrounded the road along which the enemy was marching and attacked the Saxons unexpectedly, so that they were cut to pieces and killed, and those who remained alive were forced to flee. As a result Baldulf became extremely worried at the fact that he could not bring help to his brother. He debated with himself how he could manage to talk with Colgrin; for he was convinced that by consulting together it would be possible for them to hit upon a safe solution – that is, if only he could make his way into his brother's presence.

Once Baldulf had come to the conclusion that no other means of access was open to him, he cut short his hair and his beard and dressed himself up as a minstrel with a harp. He strode up and down in the camp, pretending to be a harpist by playing melodies on his instrument. No one suspected him and he moved nearer and nearer to the city walls, keeping up the same pretence all the time. In the end he was observed by the besieged, dragged up over the top of the walls on ropes and taken to his brother. When Colgrin set eyes on Baldulf he had the solace of embracing him and kissing him to his heart's desire, as though Baldulf had been restored to him from the dead. Finally, when, after exhaustive discussions, they had abandoned all hope of ever escaping, messengers returned from Germany to say that they had brought with them to Albany six hundred ships which were commanded by Cheldric and loaded with brave soldiery. When Arthur's advisers learned this, they dissuaded him from continuing the siege any longer, for if so large an enemy force were to come upon them they would all be committed to a most dangerous engagement.

Arthur accepted the advice of his retainers and withdrew into the town of London. There he convened the bishops and the clergy of the entire realm and asked their suggestion as to what it would be best and safest for him to do, in the face of this invasion by the pagans. Eventually a common policy was agreed on and messengers were dispatched to King Hoel in Brittany to explain to him the disaster which had befallen Great Britain. This Hoel was the son of Arthur's sister; and his father was Budicius, the King of the Armorican Britons. As a result, as soon as he heard of the terrifying way in which his uncle was being treated, Hoel ordered his fleet to be made ready.

Fifteen thousand armed warriors were assembled and at the next fair wind Hoel landed at Southampton. Arthur received him with all the honour due to him, and each man embraced the other repeatedly.

They let a few days pass and then they marched to the town of Kaerluideoit, which was besieged by the pagans about whom I have already told you. This town is situated upon a hill between two rivers, in the province of Lindsey: it is also called by another name, Lincoln. As soon as they had arrived there with their entire force, keen as they were to fight with the Saxons, they inflicted unheard-of slaughter upon them; for on one day six thousand of the Saxons were killed, some being drowned in the rivers and the others being hit by weapons. As a result, the remainder were demoralized. The Saxons abandoned the siege and took to flight.

Arthur pursued the Saxons relentlessly until they reached Caledon Wood. There they re-formed after their flight and made an effort to resist Arthur. The Saxons joined battle once more and killed a number of the Britons, for the former defended themselves manfully. They used the shelter of the trees to protect themselves from the Britons' weapons. As soon as Arthur saw this, he ordered the trees round that part of the wood to be cut down and their trunks to be placed in a circle, so that every way out was barred to the enemy. Arthur's plan was to hem them in and then besiege them, so that in the end they should die of hunger. When this had been done, he ordered his squadrons to surround the wood and there he remained for three days. The Saxons had nothing at all to eat. To prevent themselves dying of sheer hunger, they asked permission to come out, on the understanding that, if they left behind all their gold and silver, they might be permitted to return to Germany with nothing but their boats. What is more, they promised that they would send Arthur tribute from Germany and that hostages should be handed over. Arthur took counsel and then agreed to their petition. He retained all their treasure, and took hostages to ensure that the tribute should be paid. All that he conceded to the Saxons was permission to leave.

As the Saxons sailed away across the sea on their way home, they repented of the bargain which they had made. They reversed their sails, turned back to Britain and landed on the coast near Totnes. They took possession of the land, and depopulated the countryside as far as the Severn Sea, killing off a great number of the peasantry. Then they proceeded by a forced march to the neighbourhood of Bath and besieged the town. When this was announced to King Arthur, he was greatly astonished at their extraordinary duplicity. He ordered summary justice to be inflicted upon their hostages, who were all hanged without more ado. He put off the foray with which he had begun to harass the Scots and the Picts, and he hastened to break up the siege. Arthur was labouring under very considerable difficulties, for he had left behind in the city of Alclud his cousin Hoel, who was seriously ill. He finally reached the county of Somerset and approached the siege. 'Although the Saxons, whose very name is an insult to heaven and detested by all men, have not kept faith with me,' he said, 'I myself will keep faith with my God. This very day I will do my utmost to take vengeance on them for the blood of my fellow-countrymen. Arm yourselves, men, and attack these traitors with all your strength! With Christ's help we shall conquer them, without any possible doubt!'

As Arthur said this, the saintly Dubricius, Archbishop of the City of the Legions, climbed to the top of a hill and cried out in a loud voice: 'You who have been marked with the cross of the Christian faith, be mindful of the loyalty you owe to your fatherland and to your fellow-countrymen! If they are slaughtered as a result of this treacherous behaviour by the pagans, they will be an everlasting reproach to you, unless in the meanwhile you do your utmost to defend them! Fight for your fatherland, and if you are killed suffer death willingly for your country's sake. That in itself is victory and a cleansing of the soul. Whoever suffers death for the sake of his brothers offers himself as a living sacrifice to God and follows with firm footsteps behind Christ Himself, who did not disdain to lay down His life for His brothers. It follows that if any one of you shall suffer death in this war, that death shall be to him as a penance and an absolution for all his sins, given always that he goes to meet it unflinchingly.'

Without a moment's delay each man present, inspired by the benediction given by this holy man, rushed off to put on his armour and to obey Dubricius' orders. Arthur himself put on a leather jerkin worthy of so great a king. On his head he placed a golden helmet, with a crest carved in the shape of a dragon; and across his shoulders a circular shield called Pridwen, on which there was painted a likeness of the Blessed Mary, Mother of God, which forced him to be thinking perpetually of her. He girded on his peerless sword, called Caliburn, which was forged in the Isle of Avalon. A spear called Ron graced his right hand: long, broad in the blade and thirsty for slaughter. Arthur drew up his men in companies and then bravely attacked the Saxons, who as usual were arrayed in wedges. All that day they resisted the Britons bravely, although the latter launched attack upon attack. Finally, towards sunset, the Saxons occupied a neighbouring hill, on which they proposed to camp. Relying on their vast numbers, they considered that the hill in itself offered sufficient protection. However, when the next day dawned, Arthur climbed to the top of the peak with his army, losing many of his men on the way. Naturally enough, the Saxons, rushing down from their high position, could inflict wounds more easily, for the impetus of their descent gave them more speed than the others, who were toiling up. For all that, the Britons reached the summit by a superlative effort and immediately engaged the enemy in hand-to-hand conflict. The Saxons stood shoulder to shoulder and strove their utmost to resist.

When the greater part of the day had passed in this way, Arthur went berserk, for he realized that things were still going well for the enemy and that victory for his own side was not yet in sight. He drew his sword Caliburn, called upon the name of the Blessed Virgin, and rushed forward at full speed into the thickest ranks of the enemy. Every man whom he struck, calling upon God as he did so, he killed at a single blow. He did not slacken his onslaught until he had dispatched four hundred and seventy men with his sword Caliburn. When the Britons saw this, they poured after him in close formation, dealing death on every side. In this battle fell Colgrin, with his brother Baldulf and many thousands of others with them. Cheldric, on the contrary, when he saw the danger threatening his men, immediately turned away in flight with what troops were left to him.

As soon as King Arthur had gained the upper hand, he ordered Cador, the Duke of Cornwall, to pursue the Saxons, while he himself hurried off in the direction of Albany. It had reached his ears that the Scots and the Picts had besieged his nephew Hoel in the town of Alclud, where, as I have explained already, Arthur had left him because of his poor health. Arthur therefore hastened to his nephew's assistance, for he was afraid that Hoel might be captured by the barbarians.

Meanwhile the Duke of Cornwall, accompanied by ten thousand men, instead of pursuing the fleeing Saxons, rushed off to their boats, with the intention of preventing them from going on board. Once he had seized their boats, he manned them with the best of his own soldiers and gave those men orders that they were to prevent the pagans from going aboard, if these last came running to the boats. Then he hurried off to pursue the enemy and to cut them to pieces without pity once he had found them: this in obedience to Arthur's command.

The Saxons, who only a short time before used to attack like lightning in the most ferocious way imaginable, now ran away with fear in their hearts. Some of them fled to secret hiding-places in the woods, others sought the mountains, and caves in the hills, in an attempt to add some little breathing-space to their lives. In the end they discovered safety nowhere; and so they came to the Isle of Thanet, with their line of battle cut to pieces. The Duke of Cornwall pursued them thither and renewed the slaughter. Cador drew back in the end, but only after he had killed Cheldric, taken hostages, and forced what remained of the Saxons to surrender.

Once peace was restored in this way, Cador set out for Alclud. Arthur had already freed the town from the harassing attentions of the barbarians. He now led his army to Moray, where the Scots and the Picts were under siege. They had fought three times against the King and his nephew, suffering defeat at Arthur's hands and then seeking refuge in this particular district. When they reached Loch Lomond, they took possession of the islands in the lake, hoping to find a safe refuge on them. This lake contains sixty islands and has sixty streams to feed it, yet only one of these streams flows down to the sea. On these islands one can make out sixty crags, which between them support exactly the same number of eagles' nests. The eagles used to flock together each year and foretell any prodigious event which was about to occur in the kingdom: this by a shrill-pitched scream which they emitted in concert. It was to these islands, then, that the enemies of whom I have told you fled, hoping to be protected by the lake, although in effect they gained little help from it. Arthur collected together a fleet of boats and sailed round the rivers. By besieging his enemies for fifteen days he reduced them to such a state of famine that they died in their thousands.

While Arthur was killing off the Scots and the Picts in this way, Gilmaurius, the King of Ireland, arrived with a fleet and a huge horde of pagans, in an effort to bring help to those who were besieged. Arthur raised the siege and began to turn his armed strength against the Irish. He cut them to pieces mercilessly and forced them to return home. Once he had conquered the Irish, he was at liberty once more to wipe out the Scots and the Picts. He treated them with unparalleled severity, sparing no one who fell into his hands. As a result all the bishops of this pitiful country, with all the clergy under their command, their feet bare and in their hands the relics of their saints and the treasures of their churches, assembled to beg pity of the King for the relief of their people. The moment they came into the King's presence, they fell on their knees and besought him to have mercy on their sorrowing people. He had inflicted sufficient suffering on them, said the bishops, and there was no need for him to wipe out to the last man those few who had survived so far. He should allow them to have some small tract of land of their own, seeing that they were in any case going to bear the yoke of servitude. When they had petitioned the King in this way, their patriotism moved him to tears.

Arthur gave in to the prayers presented by these men of religion and granted a pardon to their people.

When all this had been accomplished, Hoel took a good look round the side of the loch which I have described to you. He was surprised to see so many rivers, islands, rocks and eagles' nests, and, what is more, to find exactly the same number of each. While he was meditating upon this remarkable circumstance, Arthur came up to him and told him that in the same neighbourhood there was another pool which was even more extraordinary. It was not very far away from where they were standing. It was twenty feet wide and the same distance long, and its depth was just five feet. Whether it had been shaped into a square by the artistry of man, or by nature, it remained true that, while it produced four different kinds of fish in its four corners, the fish of any one corner were never found in any of the others.

Arthur also told Hoel that there was a third pool in the parts of Wales which are near the Severn. The local people call it Lin Ligua. When the sea flows into this pool, it is swallowed up as though in a bottomless pit; and, as the pool swallows the waters, it is never filled in such a way as to overflow the edges of its banks. When the tide ebbs away, however, the pool belches forth the waters which it has swallowed, as high in the air as a mountain, and with them it then splashes and floods its banks. Meanwhile, if the people of all that region should come near, with their faces turned towards it, thus letting the spray of the waters fall upon their clothing, it is only with difficulty, if, indeed, at all, that they have the strength to avoid being swallowed up by the pool. If, however, they turn their backs, their being sprinkled has no danger for them, even if they stand on the very brink.

Once he had pardoned the Scottish people, the King moved to York, where he proposed to celebrate the coming feast of the Nativity of our Lord. As he rode into the city, Arthur grieved to see the desolate state of the holy churches. Samson, the saintly Archbishop, had been driven out, and with him all men of the Christian faith. The half-burnt churches no longer celebrated God's holy office. The fury of the pagans had been so great that it had brought everything to an end. Arthur therefore summoned the clergy and the people, and appointed his own chaplain, Piramus, as Metropolitan of that see. He re-built the churches, which had been razed to the ground, and he graced them with religious communities of men and women. He restored to their family honours the nobles who had been driven out by the Saxon invasions.

There were in York three brothers sprung from the royal line, Loth,

Urian and Auguselus, who had been Princes in those parts before the Saxon victories. Arthur was determined to do for them what he had done for the others: that is, to grant them back their hereditary rights. He returned the kingship of the Scots to Auguselus; to Urian, the brother of Auguselus, he gave back the honour of ruling over the men of Moray; and Loth, who in the days of Aurelius Ambrosius had married that King's own sister and had had two sons by her, Gawain and Mordred, he restored to the dukedom of Lothian and other near-by territories which formed part of it.

Finally, when he had restored the whole country to its earlier dignity, he himself married a woman called Guinevere. She was descended from a noble Roman family and had been brought up in the household of Duke Cador. She was the most beautiful woman in the entire island.

Arthur's Last Battle

Arthur spent the following winter in this same locality and found time to subdue the cities of the Allobroges. When summer came, he made ready to set out for Rome, and was already beginning to make his way through the mountains when the news was brought to him that his nephew Mordred, in whose care he had left Britain, had placed the crown upon his own head. What is more, this treacherous tyrant was living adulterously and out of wedlock with Queen Guinevere, who had broken the vows of her earlier marriage.

About this particular matter, most noble Duke, Geoffrey of Monmouth prefers to say nothing. He will, however, in his own poor style and without wasting words, describe the battle which our most famous King fought against his nephew, once he had returned to Britain after his victory; for that he found in the British treatise already referred to. He heard it, too, from Walter of Oxford, a man most learned in all branches of history.

As soon as the bad news of this flagrant crime had reached his ears, Arthur immediately cancelled the attack which he had planned to make on Leo, the Emperor of the Romans. He sent Hoel, the leader of the Bretons, with an army of Gauls, to restore peace in those parts; and then without more ado he himself set off for Britain, accompanied only by the island kings and their troops. That most infamous traitor Mordred, about whom I have told you, had sent Chelric, the leader of the Saxons, to Germany, to conscript as many troops as possible there, and to return as quickly as he could with those whom he was to persuade to join him. Mordred had made an agreement with Chelric that he would give him that part of the island which stretched from the River Humber to Scotland and all that Hengist and Horsa had held in Kent in Vortigern's day. In obedience to Mordred's command, Chelric landed with eight hundred ships filled with armed pagans. A treaty was agreed to and Chelric pledged his obedience to the traitor Mordred as if to the King. Mordred had brought the Scots, Picts and Irish into his alliance, with anyone else whom he knew to be filled with hatred for his uncle. In all, the insurgents were about eighty thousand in number, some of them pagans and some Christians.

Surrounded by this enormous army, in which he placed his hope, Mordred marched to meet Arthur as soon as the latter landed at Richborough. In the battle which ensued Mordred inflicted great slaughter on those who were trying to land. Auguselus, the King of Albany, and Gawain, the King's nephew, died that day, together with many others too numerous to describe. Ywain, the son of Auguselus' brother Urian, succeeded him in the kingship; and in the wars which followed he became famous because of the many brave deeds which he accomplished. In the end, but only with enormous difficulty, Arthur's men occupied the sea-shore. They drove Mordred and his army before them in flight and inflicted great slaughter on them in their turn. Profiting from their long experience in warfare, they drew up their troops most skilfully. They mixed their infantry with the cavalry and fought in such a way that when the line of foot-soldiers moved up to the attack, or was merely holding its position, the horse charged at an angle and did all that they could to break through the enemy lines and to force them to run away.

However, the Perjurer re-formed his army and so marched into Winchester on the following night. When this was announced to Queen Guinevere, she gave way to despair. She fled from York to the City of the Legions and there, in the church of Julius the Martyr, she took her vows among the nuns, promising to lead a chaste life.

Now that he had lost so many hundreds of his fellow-soldiers, Arthur was more angry than ever. He buried his dead and then marched on the third day to the city of Winchester and laid siege to his nephew who had taken refuge there. Mordred showed no sign of abandoning his plans. He gave his adherents every encouragement he could think of, and then marched out with his troops and drew them up ready for a pitched battle with his uncle. The fight began and immense slaughter was done on both sides. The losses were greater in Mordred's army and they forced him to fly once more in shame from the battlefield. He made no arrangements whatsoever for the burial of his dead, but fled as fast as ship could carry him, and made his way towards Cornwall.

Arthur was filled with great mental anguish by the fact that

Mordred had escaped him so often. Without losing a moment, he followed him to that same locality, reaching the River Camblam, where Mordred was awaiting his arrival. Mordred was indeed the boldest of men and always the first to launch an attack. He immediately drew his troops up in battle order, determined as he was either to win or to die, rather than run away again as he had done in the past. From his total force of troops, about which I have told you, there still remained sixty thousand men under his command. From these he mustered six divisions, in each of which he placed six thousand, six hundred and sixty-six armed men. From those who were left over he formed one single division, and, when he had assigned leaders to each of the others, he placed this last division under his own command. As soon as they were all drawn up, he went round to encourage each of them in turn, promising them the possessions of their enemies if only they stood firm and were successful in battle.

On the other side, Arthur, too, was marshalling his army. He divided his men into nine divisions of infantry, each drawn up in a square, with a right and left wing. To each he appointed a commander. Then he exhorted them to kill these perjured villains and robbers who, at the request of one who had committed treason against him, the King, had been brought into the island from foreign parts to steal their lands from them. He told them, too, that this miscellaneous collection of barbarians, come from a variety of countries – raw recruits who were totally inexperienced in war – would be quite incapable of resisting valiant men like themselves, who were the veterans of many battles, provided always that they made up their minds to attack boldly and to fight like men.

While the two commanders were encouraging their men in this way in both the armies, the lines of battle suddenly met, combat was joined, and they all strove with might and main to deal each other as many blows as possible. It is heartrending to describe what slaughter was inflicted on both sides, how the dying groaned, and how great was the fury of those attacking. Everywhere men were receiving wounds themselves or inflicting them, dying or dealing out death. In the end, when they had passed much of the day in this way, Arthur, with a single division in which he had posted six thousand, six hundred and sixty-six men, charged at the squadron where he knew Mordred was. They hacked a way through with their swords and Arthur continued to advance, inflicting terrible slaughter as he went. It was at this point that the accursed traitor was killed and many thousands of his men with him.

However, the others did not take to flight simply because Mordred was dead. They massed together from all over the battlefield and did their utmost to stand their ground with all the courage at their command. The battle which was now joined between them was fiercer than ever, for almost all the leaders on both sides were present and rushed into the fight at the head of their troops. On Mordred's side there fell Chelric, Elaf, Egbrict and Bruning, all of them Saxons; the Irishmen Gillapatric, Gillasel and Gillarvus; and the Scots and Picts, with nearly everyone in command of them. On Arthur's side there died Odbrict, King of Norway; Aschil, King of Denmark; Cador Limenich; and Cassivelaunus, with many thousands of the King's troops, some of them Britons, others from the various peoples he had brought with him. Arthur himself, our renowned King, was mortally wounded and was carried off to the Isle of Avalon, so that his wounds might be attended to. He handed the crown of Britain over to his cousin Constantine, the son of Cador Duke of Cornwall: this in the year 542 after our Lord's Incarnation.

WILLIAM OF NEWBURGH, History of English Affairs (Historia Rerum Anglicarum) (1196–8)

In the prologue to his History of the recent past, *William of Newburgh ridicules Geoffrey of Monmouth's* History of the Kings of Britain *as a fiction of no historical value, declaring much of his work to be lies. He concentrates his attack on the figure of Arthur, whom he asserts must have been invented either by Geoffrey or someone else, since Bede does not mention him. William fails to consider that Bede's sources for the fifth century would probably have been exclusively Anglo-Saxon, and so unlikely to mention a successful British leader.*[23]

Prologue to the History that follows

The venerable priest and monk Bede has composed a history of our race the English. In fact in his preface he went further back so as to approach the special subject of his researches more appropriately, and with elegant brevity he touched also on the more famous achievements of the Britons, who are known to have been the first inhabitants of our island.

The race of Britons had their own historian before our Bede in the person of Gildas, as Bede attests when he includes some of his words in his writings. I proved this to my satisfaction when some years ago I came across this same Gildas' book for reading purposes. Since his language is unpolished and lacks flavour, few people have bothered to transcribe or possess it, and so it is rarely found. But it is no slight proof of integrity that he does not spare his own nation in revealing the truth; though quite sparing of compliments to his fellow-Britons, he condemns many evil traits in them. So that the truth may not remain unstated, he does not hesitate to write as a Briton about Britons that they were neither brave in war nor trustworthy in peace.

But in our own day a writer of the opposite tendency has emerged. To atone for these faults of the Britons he weaves a laughable web of fiction about them, with shameless vainglory extolling them far above the virtue of the Macedonians and the Romans. This man is called Geoffrey and bears the soubriquet Arthur, because he has taken up the stories about Arthur from the old fictitious accounts of the Britons, has added to them himself, and by embellishing them in the Latin tongue he has cloaked them with the honourable title of history. More audaciously still he has taken the most deceitful predictions of a certain Merlin which he has very greatly augmented on his own account, and in translating them into Latin he has published them as though they were authentic prophecies resting on unshakeable truth.

His story is that this Merlin was born of a woman and sired by a demonic incubus; accordingly he ascribes to him a most outstanding and extensive foreknowledge of the future, on the grounds that he took after his father. In fact we are instructed by both true reasoning and the sacred writings that demons are shut out from God's light, and are wholly unable to have prior knowledge of the future by mentally observing it, though they apprehend certain future events by guesswork rather than knowledge, through signs better known to them than to us. In short, they are often deceived and deceive by their guesses, though these are quite sophisticated, but by means of trickery in their predictions they lay claim amongst naive people to a fore-knowledge of the future which they do not at all possess.

Certainly the predictions of Merlin are clearly false in the events known to have occurred in the kingdom of the English after the death of this Geoffrey, who translated the infantile stories of these prophecies from the British tongue, and according to well-founded belief added considerably to them from his own imagination. More-over he doctored the events which took place before or during his own time with his own readily-added inventions in such a way that they could bear a concordant interpretation. Then too none except those ignorant of ancient histories can possibly doubt the extent of his wanton and shameless lying virtually throughout his book, which he calls *A History of the Britons*, when they come across it. He has not learnt the truth about events, and so without discrimination he gives space to fables without substance. I do not mention all his fictions about the achievements of the Britons before Julius Caesar held sway, or his adoption of the false statements of others as authentic. I do not mention all his lunacies uttered in praise of the Britons against the evidence of historical truth from the days of Julius Caesar, under whom the Britons began to come under Roman control, up to the time of the emperor Honorius, under whom the Romans voluntarily withdrew from Britain because of more pressing business affecting the state.

When the Romans retired and the Britons gained independence – or rather were left to their own destruction and exposed as plunder to the Picts and the Scots – the accounts certainly say that Vortigern was their king. He invited the Saxons or Angles to defend the kingdom, and they came to Britain under the leadership of Hengist. They repelled the invasions of the barbarians for the moment; but when they had ascertained the fertility of the island and the sluggishness of its inhabitants, they broke the treaty and turned their arms on those who had invited them. The Britons were gradually crushed by them, and the invaders penned the wretched remnants, now called the Welsh, in trackless mountains and forests.

They had in unbroken succession very brave kings with extensive sway. Amongst them were Ethelbert, great-grandson of Hengist, who after extending his dominion from the English Channel to the Humber embraced Christ's gentle yoke in response to Augustine's preaching: Aethelfrith, who controlled Northumbria and subdued both Britons and Scots with boundless slaughter: Edwin, Aethelfrith's successor who governed both Angles and Britons: Oswald, who succeeded him, and ruled over all the peoples of Britain.

Since these events accord with the historical truth as expounded by the Venerable Bede, it is clear that Geoffrey's entire narration about Arthur, his successors, and his predecessors after Vortigern, was invented partly by himself and partly by others. The motive was either an uncontrolled passion for lying, or secondly a desire to please the Britons, most of whom are considered to be so barbaric that they are said to be still awaiting the future coming of Arthur, being unwilling to entertain the fact of his death.

In brief, he claims that Vortigern was succeeded by Aurelius Ambrosius, who after conquering and expelling the Saxons, whom Vortigern had summoned, held impressive sway throughout Britain. As his successor he names Utherpendragon his brother, who reigned with equal power and glory; and with his gushing and untrammelled lying he interlards several incidents concerning this Merlin of his. After Utherpendragon too had died, Geoffrey makes his son Arthur succeed to the kingdom of Britain as fourth in succession from Vortigern, just as our Bede names Ethelbert, who welcomed Augustine, as fourth in line from Hengist in the kingdom of the English. Thus Arthur's reign and Augustine's arrival in Britain ought to have coincided.

But even a person of dim mental vision can observe how much the unadulterated historical truth preempts the falsehood which has been compiled at this point. Geoffrey makes Arthur himself outstanding and remarkable above all others; he seeks to present him in his achievements according to the free reign of his fancy. In brief, first and foremost he makes him triumph at will over the English, Picts and Scots. Then he depicts him as bringing under his sway Ireland, the Orkneys, Sweden, Norway and Denmark, partly by war and partly by the mere awe inspired by his name. To these he adds as well Iceland, which some call furthest Thule, so that the flattering words addressed to the Roman Augustus by the celebrated poet seem in truth to refer to that Briton: 'Furthest Thule will be your slave.'

Next he makes Arthur strike the provinces of Gaul in war, speedily subduing and most happily triumphing over them, whereas Julius Caesar could barely master them after ten years of the utmost hazards and toils; this is doubtless to make this Briton's little finger appear thicker than the mighty Caesar's loins. Next he brings him back to Britain in manifold triumph, and has him celebrate a most notable feast in the company of conquered kings and princes. Three British archbishops, of London, Caerleon and York, are present, and this at a time when the Britons never had even a single archbishop, for Augustine was the first to receive the pallium from the Roman pontiff and to become archbishop in Britain. In fact the barbarian nations of Europe, even if they had been converted to belief in Christ long before, were content with bishops, and did not trouble about the prerogative of the pallium; in short the Irish, Norwegians, Danes and Swedes, though known to have been Christians long before and to have had bishops, have only now in our own day begun to have archbishops.

Subsequently our story-teller, in seeking to exalt Arthur to the heights, makes him declare war on the Romans. Before this war commences he has him felling a giant of monstrous size in single combat, though we read of no giants after David's day. After that his undisciplined lying pours forth in greater flood. He makes the great kings of the world ally themselves with the Romans against Arthur; these are the kings of Greece, Africa, Spain, the Parthians, the Medes, the Ituraeans, Libya, Egypt, Babylonia, Bithynia, Phrygia, Syria, Boeotia, Crete. He recounts that they were all conquered by Arthur in a single battle, whereas the celebrated Alexander the Great, renowned in every age, sweated for twelve years in overcoming certain princes of these great kingdoms. He certainly makes his Arthur's little finger broader than the back of Alexander the Great, especially as before this victory over so many great kings he has him at an assembly remind his troops of the subjugation of thirty kingdoms already achieved by himself and them. Yet our story-teller will not find that number of kingdoms in the world we live in, over and above the ones listed which Arthur clearly had not yet conquered.

Is he dreaming of another world containing kingdoms without number, in which the events took place which are mentioned by him earlier? Certainly in our world nothing of this kind took place; for how could the historians of old, who took immense pains to omit from their writings nothing worthy of mention, and who are known to have recorded even modest events, have passed over in silence this man beyond compare and his achievements so notable beyond measure? How, I ask, have they suppressed in silence one more notable than Alexander the Great – this Arthur, monarch of the Britons, and his deeds – or Merlin, prophet of the Britons, one equal to our Isaiah, and his utterances? In what sense does he attribute to his Merlin lesser foreknowledge of the future at any rate than we attribute to our Isaiah, except that he does not presume to insert in his prophecies 'Thus saith the Lord', and he was ashamed to insert 'Thus saith the devil' as should have been appropriate to a prophet who was the son of a demonic incubus? So since the historians of old have made not even the slightest mention of these persons, clearly all that Geoffrey has published in his writing about Arthur and Merlin has been invented by liars to feed the curiosity of those less wise.

We should further note that he subsequently reports that this same Arthur was mortally wounded in war, and that once he had set his kingdom in order he departed to nurse his wounds to the island of Avalon, famed in the invented tales of the Britons; and because of fear of the Britons, Geoffrey does not dare to pronounce him dead, for the brutish Britons believe that he really will still come. Then too he lies with equal shamelessness about Arthur's successors, assigning to them the monarchy of Britain until about the seventh generation. Those who the Venerable Bede says are most brave kings of the English, ruling with renown over the whole of Britain, Geoffrey makes subordinate princelings of these men. So to ensure that confidence in all matters is reposed in Bede, whose wisdom and integrity it is

sacrilegious to doubt, that story-teller and all his tales must be unhesi-
tatingly spurned by all.

Writers were certainly not lacking after Bede to continue from his
day the sequence of periods and events in our island up to the days
which we ourselves can recall. They are in no sense comparable to
him, yet they are praiseworthy because their work is scrupulous and
faithful, though their presentation is less eloquent. But in our own
day such great and notable events have occurred that the indifference
of moderns would be rightly adjudged worthy of censure if these
events were not consigned to the literary record to make them remembered for ever. Perhaps this work has already been begun or completed
by some individual or individuals. But revered persons to whom we
must defer deign to impose this task on my puny person, so that I
too at least in the company of the poor widow (for I cannot associate
with the rich) can put something from my slender store into the
treasure-chest of the Lord.

Since we are aware that the sequence of English history has been
taken by certain writers as far as the death of king Henry I, I shall
begin with the arrival of the Normans in England and run briefly
through the intermediate period, so that God willing I can begin
to extend a fuller narrative from the time of Henry's successor
Stephen. In the first year of his reign, I, the least of Christ's servants,
was born in the first Adam to death, and was reborn in the second
Adam to life.

WACE, Brut *(1155)*

*Robert Wace (c. 1115–83) was an Anglo-Norman, born in Jersey,
who studied in Paris. His* Brut *is the first French translation of
Geoffrey of Monmouth's* History *and, like most medieval trans-
lators, Wace felt free to alter and transform his source to suit the
interests of his audience. While Wace's version retains much of the
original material, he tends to increase the elements of courtly
society already present in Geoffrey of Monmouth's* History.

*The extract selected deals with the period from the twelve-year
peace to Arthur's magnificent Pentecostal court at Caerleon, which
is described in detail. The passage is particularly significant for its
introduction of Arthur's famous Round Table (absent in Geoffrey
of Monmouth) at which all the knights sit as equals.*

Twelve years he abode in his realm in peace and content, since none was so bold as to do him a mischief, and he did mischief to none. Arthur held high state in a very splendid fashion. He ordained the courtesies of courts, and bore himself with so rich and noble a bearing, that neither the emperor's court at Rome, nor any other bragged of by man, was accounted as aught besides that of the king. Arthur never heard speak of a knight in praise, but he caused him to be numbered of his household. So that he might he took him to himself, for help in time of need. Because of these noble lords about his hall, of whom each knight pained himself to be the hardiest champion, and none would count him the least praiseworthy, Arthur made the Round Table, so reputed of the Britons. This Round Table was ordained of Arthur that when his fair fellowship sat to meat their chairs should be high alike, their service equal, and none before or after his comrade. Thus no man could boast that he was exalted above his fellow, for all alike were gathered round the board, and none was alien at the breaking of Arthur's bread. At this table sat Britons, Frenchmen, Normans, Angevins, Flemings, Burgundians, and Loherins. Knights had their place who held land of the king, from the furthest marches of the west even unto the Hill of St Bernard. A most discourteous lord would he be deemed who sojourned not awhile in the king's hall; who came not with the countenance, the harness, and the vesture that were the garb and usage of those who served Arthur about his court. From all the lands there voyaged to this court such knights as were in quest either of gain or worship. Of these lords some drew near to hear tell of Arthur's courtesies; others to marvel at the pride of his state; these to have speech with the knights of his chivalry; and some to receive of his largeness costly gifts. For this Arthur in his day was loved right well of the poor, and honoured meetly by the rich. Only the kings of the world bore him malice and envy, since they doubted and feared exceedingly lest he should set his foot upon them every one, and spoil them of their heritage.

I know not if you have heard tell the marvellous gestes and errant deeds related so often of King Arthur. They have been noised about this mighty realm for so great a space that the truth has turned to fable and an idle song. Such rhymes are neither sheer bare lies, nor gospel truths. They should not be considered either an idiot's tale, or given by inspiration. The minstrel has sung his ballad, the storyteller told over his story so frequently, little by little he has decked and painted, till by reason of his embellishment the truth stands hid in the trappings of a tale. Thus to make a delectable tune to your ear, history goes masking as fable. Hear then how, because of his valour, the counsel of his barons, and in the strength of that mighty chivalry he had cherished and made splendid, Arthur purposed to cross the sea and conquer the land of France. But first he deemed to sail to Norway, since he would make Lot, his sister's lord, its king. Sichelin, the King of Norway, was newly dead, leaving neither son nor daughter of his body. In the days of his health, as alike when he fell on death, Sichelin had appointed Lot to succeed him in his realm and fief. The crown was Lot's by right, even as Sichelin proclaimed, since Lot was the king's nephew, and there was no other heir. When the folk of Norway learned that Sichelin had bequeathed his realm to Lot, they held his command and ordinance in derision. They would have no alien for their lord, nor suffer a stranger to meddle in their business, lest he should deem them an ancient and feeble people, and give to outland folk what was due to the dwellers in the realm. The Norwegians resolved to make king one of their own house, that he might cherish them and their children; and for this reason they chose from amongst them a certain lord named Ridulph to be their king.

When Lot perceived that his right was despised, save that he took his heritage by force, he sought help of Arthur, his lord. Arthur agreed to aid him in his quarrel, promising to render him his own, and to avenge him bitterly on Ridulph. Arthur gathered together many ships and a mighty host. He entered into Norway with this great company, wasting the land, seizing on the manors, and spoiling the towns. Ridulph was no trembler, and had no thought to leave the country to its fate. He assembled his people, and prepared to give battle to the king. Since however his carles were not many, and his friends but few, Ridulph was defeated in the fight and slain. The greater part of his fellowship perished with him, so that no large number remained. In this manner Lot the King of Lyones destroyed the Norwegians from the land. Having delivered Norway from itself Arthur granted the kingdom to Lot, so only that he did Arthur homage as his lord. Amongst the barons who rode in this adventure was Gawain, the hardy and famous knight, who had freshly come from St Sulpicius the Apostle, whose soul may God give rest and glory. The knight wore harness bestowed on him by the Apostle, and wondrously was he praised. This Gawain was a courteous champion, circumspect in word and deed, having no pride nor blemish in him. He did more than his boast, and gave more largely than he promised. His father had sent him to Rome, that he might be schooled the more meetly. Gawain was dubbed knight in the same day as Wavain, and counted himself of Arthur's household. Mightily he strove to do his devoir in the field, for the fairer service and honour of his lord.

After Arthur had conquered Norway, and firmly established his justice in the land, he chose of his host those men who were the most valiant and ready in battle, and assembled them by the sea. He brought to the same haven many ships and barges, together with such mariners as were needful for his purpose. When a quiet time was come, with a fortunate wind, Arthur crossed the sea into Denmark; for the realm was very greatly to his desire. Acil, the Danish king, considered the Britons and the folk from Norway. He considered Arthur, who had prevailed against so many kings. Acil knew and was persuaded that Arthur was mightier than he. He had no mind to suffer hurt himself, or to see his goodly heritage spoiled in a useless quarrel. What did it profit to waste wealth and honour alike, to behold slain friends and ruined towers? Acil wrought well and speedily. He sought peace, and ensued it. He gave costly gifts, and made promises which were larger still; till by reason of his words, his prayers, and supplications, concord was established between Arthur and the king. Acil paid fealty and homage; he became Arthur's man, and owned that of Arthur's grace he held his fief. King Arthur rejoiced greatly at this adventure, and of the conquest he had made. He desired honour the more greedily because of the worship he had gained. From out of Denmark he chose, by hundreds and by thousands, the stoutest knights and archers he could find. These he joined to his host, purposing to lead this fair company into France. Without any long tarrying the king acted on his purpose. Towns, cities, and castles fell before him, so that Flanders and the country about Boulogne were speedily in his power. Arthur was a prudent captain. He perceived no profit in wasting his own realm, burning his towns, and stealing from his very purse. His eyes were in every place, and much was forbidden by his commandment. No soldier might rob nor pill. If there was need of raiment, meat, or provand, then must he buy with good minted coin in the market. Nothing he dared to destroy or steal.

Now in Arthur's day the land of France was known as Gaul. The realm had neither king nor master, for the Romans held it strongly as a province. This province was committed to the charge of Frollo, and the tribune had governed the country for a great space. He took rent and tribute of the people, and in due season caused the treasure to be delivered to the emperor at Rome. Thus had it been since the time of Caesar, that mighty emperor, who brought into subjection France and Germany, and all the land of Britain. Frollo was a very worthy lord, come of a noble Roman race, fearful of none, however hardy. He knew well, by divers letters, the loss and the mischief done by Arthur and his host. Frollo had no mind tamely to watch the Romans lose their heritage. The tribune summoned to his aid all the men abiding in the province who carried arms and owned fealty to Rome. He assembled these together, ordaining a great company, clad in harness and plenteously supplied with stores. With these he went out to battle against Arthur, but he prospered less than his merit deserved. The Roman tribune was discomfited so grievously that he sought safety in flight. Of his fellowship he had lost a great number. Many were slain outright in battle, others were sorely wounded, or made captive, or returned sorrowing to their own homes. Out of the meinie Frollo had gathered from so many cities, more than two thousand were destroyed. This was no great marvel, since the count of Arthur's host was more than Frollo might endure. From every land he had subdued to himself, from every city that was taken, Arthur saw to it that not a spearman nor knight of fitting years and strength of body, but was numbered in the host, and commanded to serve Arthur as his lord. Of these outland folk, Arthur chose a fair company of the hardiest knights and most proven champions to be of his private household. The very French began to regard him as their king, so only that they had the courage of their minds. This man loved him for his wise and comely speech: this by reason of his liberal hand: this because of his noble and upright spirit. Whether men were driven to his presence by fear, or considered him a refuge in the storm, all found cause enough to seek his court, to make their peace, and to acknowledge him as their suzerain. Now Frollo, after his discomfiture by the king, fled to Paris with all the speed he might, making no stop upon the road. The tribune feared Arthur and his power very sorely, and since he sought a fortress to defend his person, he would not trust his fortune to any other city. He resolved, therefore, to await Arthur within Paris, and to fight the king beneath the walls. Frollo called to himself such legions as were yet in towns near by. Because of the number of the fugitives who were come to that place, together with the burgesses abiding therein, a great concourse of people filled the city. All these folk toiled diligently to furnish the city with corn and meat, and to make sure the walls and gates against their foes.

Arthur learned that Frollo was making strong his towers, and filling the barns with victuals. He drew to Paris, and sat down without the city. He lodged his men in the suburbs beyond the walls, holding the town so close that food might not enter whether by the river or the gates. Arthur shut the city fast for more than a month, since the French defended them well and manfully. A mighty multitude was crowded within the walls, and there was a plentiful lack of meat. All the provand bought and gathered together in so short a space was quickly eaten and consumed, and the folk were afterwards anhungered. There was little flesh, but many bellies; so that the women and children made much sorrow. Had the counsel of the poor been taken, right soon would the keys of the city have been rendered. 'Diva,' clamoured the famished citizens, 'what doest thou, Frollo? Why requirest thou not peace at Arthur's hand?' Frollo regarded the common people who failed for famine. He looked upon the folk dying by reason of their hunger, and knew that they would have him yield the city. Frollo perceived that of a surety the end of all was come. The tribune chose to put his own body in peril – yea, rather to taste of death, than to abandon Paris to her leaguers. Frollo had full assurance of Arthur's rectitude. In the simplicity of his heart he sent urgent messages to the king, praying him to enter in the Island, that body to body they might bring their quarrel to an end. He who prevailed over his fellow, and came living from the battle, should take the whole realm as his own and receive all France for his guerdon. Thus the land would not perish, nor the folk be utterly destroyed. Arthur hearkened willingly to the heralds, for very greatly was their message to his mind. He accorded that the battle should be between the two captains, even as Frollo desired. Gauntlets were taken from one and the other, and hostages given on behalf of Paris and on the part of the besiegers for better assurance of the covenant that was made.

On the morrow the two champions arrayed them in harness, and coming to the Island, entered boldly in the lists. The banks were filled with a mighty concourse of people, making great tumult. Not a man or woman remained that day in his chamber. They climbed upon the walls, and thronged the roofs of the houses, crying upon God, and adjuring Him by His holy Name to give victory to him who would guard the realm in peace, and preserve the poor from war. Arthur's meinie, for their part, awaited the judgement of God, in praying the King of Glory to bestow the prize and honour on their lord. The two champions were set over against the other, laced each in his mail, and seated on his warhorse. The strong destriers were held with bit and bridle, so eager were they for the battle. The riders bestrode the steeds with lifted shields, brandishing great lances in their hands. It was no easy matter to perceive – however curiously men looked – which was the stouter knight, or to judge who would be victor in the joust. Certainly each was a very worthy lord and a right courageous champion. When all was made ready the knights struck spurs to their steeds, and loosing the rein upon the horses' necks, hurtled together with raised buckler and lance in rest. They smote together with marvellous fierceness. Whether by reason of the swerving of his destrier, I cannot tell, but Frollo failed of his stroke. Arthur, on his side, smote the boss of his adversary's shield so fairly, that he bore him over his horse's buttock, as long as the ash staff held. Arthur drew forth his sword, and hastened to Frollo to bring the battle to an end. Frollo climbed stoutly on his feet. He held his lance before him like a rod, and the king's steed ran upon the spear, so that it pierced deeply in his body. Of this thrust the destrier and his rider alike came tumbling to the ground. When the Britons saw this thing, they might not contain themselves for grief. They cried aloud, and seizing their weapons, for a little would have violated the love-day. They made ready to cross the river to the Island, and to avenge their lord upon the Gauls. Arthur cried loudly to his Britons to observe their covenant, commanding that not a man should move to his help that day. He gripped Excalibur sternly in his hand, resolving that Frollo should pay dearly for his triumph. Arthur dressed his shield above his head, and handselling his sword, rushed upon Frollo. Frollo was a passing good knight, hardy and strong, in no whit dismayed by the anger of his adversary. He raised his own glaive on high, striking fiercely at Arthur's brow. Frollo was strong beyond the strength of man. His brand was great and sharp, and the buffet was struck with all his power. The blade sheared through helm and coif alike, so that King Arthur was wounded in his forehead, and the blood ran down his face.

When Arthur felt the dolour of his hurt, and looked upon his blood, he desired nothing, save to wreak evil on the man who had wrought this mischief. He pressed the more closely upon Frollo. Lifting Excalibur, his good sword, in both hands, he smote so lustily that Frollo's head was cloven down to his very shoulders. No helmet nor hauberk, whatever the armourer's craft, could have given surety from so mighty a blow. Blood and brains gushed from the wound. Frollo fell upon the ground, and beating the earth a little with his chausses of steel, presently died, and was still.

When men saw this bitter stroke the burgesses and sergeants raised a loud cry. Arthur's household rejoiced beyond measure; but those of the city wept, making great sorrow for Frollo, their champion. Nevertheless, the citizens of Paris ran to their gates. They set the doors wide, and welcomed Arthur, his meinie, and company within their walls. When Arthur perceived the French were desirous to offer him their fealty, he suffered them so to do, taking hostages that they would abide in peace. He lodged within the city certain days, and appointed governors, for the assurance of his power. After quiet was established, Arthur divided the host into two parts. The one of these companies he delivered into the charge of Hoel, the king's nephew. With the other half he devised to conquer Anjou, Auvergne, Gascony, and Poitou; yea, to overrun Lorraine and Burgundy, if the task did not prove beyond his power. Hoel did his lord's commandment, even as Arthur purposed. He conquered Berri, and afterwards Touraine,

Auvergne, Poitou, and Gascony. Guitard, the King of Poitiers, was a valiant captain, having good knights in his service. To uphold his realm and his rights Guitard fought many a hard battle. The luck went this way and that. Sometimes he was the hunter, sometimes the quarry: often he prevailed, and often, again, he lost. At the end Guitard was persuaded Arthur was the stronger lord, and that only by submission could he keep his own. The land was utterly wasted and ravaged. Beyond the walls of town and castle there was nothing left to destroy; and of all the fair vineyards not a vine but was rooted from the ground. Guitard made overtures of peace, and accorded himself with Hoel. He swore Arthur fealty and homage, so that the king came to love him very dearly. The other parcels of France Arthur conquered them every one by his own power. When there was peace over all the country, so that none dared lift a spear against the king, Arthur sought such men as were grown old in his quarrels, and desired greatly to return to their homes. To these feeble sergeants Arthur rendered their wages and gifts, and sent them rejoicing from whence they had come. The knights of his household, and such lusty youths as were desirous of honour, having neither dame nor children to their hearths, Arthur held in his service for yet nine years. During these nine years that Arthur abode in France, he wrought divers great wonders, reproving many haughty men and their tyrannies, and chastising many sinners after their deservings. Now it befell that when Easter was come, Arthur held high feast at Paris with his friends. On that day the king recompensed his servants for their losses, and gave to each after his deserts. He bestowed guerdon meetly on all, according to his zeal and the labour he had done. To Kay, the master seneschal of his house, a loyal and chivalrous knight, the king granted all Anjou and Angers. Bedevere, the king's cup-bearer and very privy counsellor, received that fief of Normandy, which aforetime was called Neustria. These lords, Kay and Bedevere, were Arthur's faithful friends, knowing the inmost counsel of his mind. Boulogne was given to Holden: Le Mans to Borel, his cousin. On each and all, according to his gentleness of heart and diligence in his lord's service, Arthur bestowed honours and fees, and granted largely of his lands.

After Arthur thus had feoffed his lords, and given riches to his friends, in April, when winter was gone, he passed the sea to England, his own realm. Marvellous joy was shown of all good folk at the return of the king. Dames held those husbands close from whom they had been parted so long. Mothers kissed their sons, with happy tears upon their cheeks. Sons and daughters embraced their fathers. Cousin clipped cousin, and neighbour that friend who once was his companion. The aunt made much of her sister's son. Ladies kissed long that lover who had returned from France; yea, when the place was meet, clasped him yet more sweetly in their arms. Wondrous was the joy shown of all. In the lanes and crossways, in the high-ways and by-ways, you might see friends a many staying friend, to know how it fared with him, how the land was settled when it was won, what adventures chanced to the seeker, what profit clave to him thereof, and why he remained so great a while beyond the sea. Then the soldier fought his battles once again. He told over his adventures, he spoke of his hard and weary combats, of the toils he had endured, and the perils from which he was delivered.

Arthur cherished tenderly his servants, granting largely, and promising richly, to the worthy. He took counsel with his barons, and devised that for the louder proclamation of his fame and wealth, he would hold a solemn feast at Pentecost, when summer was come, and that then in the presence of his earls and baronage he would be crowned king. Arthur commanded all his lords on their allegiance to meet him at Caerleon in Glamorgan. He desired to be crowned king in Caerleon, because it was rich beyond other cities, and marvellously pleasant and fair. Pilgrims told in those days that the mansions of Caerleon were more desirable than the palaces of Rome. This rich city, Caerleon, was builded on the Usk, a river which falls within the Severn. He who came to the city from a strange land, might seek his haven by this fair water. On one side of the town flowed this clear river; whilst on the other spread a thick forest. Fish were very plentiful in the river, and of venison the burgesses had no lack. Passing fair and deep were the meadows about the city, so that the barns and granges were very rich. Within the walls rose two mighty churches, greatly praised. One of these famed churches was called in remembrance of Saint Julius the Martyr, and held a convent of holy nuns for the fairer service of God. The second church was dedicated to Saint Aaron, his companion. The bishop had his seat therein. Moreover, this church was furnished with many wealthy clergy and canons of seemly life. These clerks were students of astronomy, concerning themselves diligently with the courses of the stars. Often enough they prophesied to Arthur what the future would bring forth, and of the deeds that he would do. So goodly was the city, there was none more delectable in all the earth. Now by reason of the lofty palaces, the fair woods and pastures, the ease and content, and all the delights of which you have heard, Arthur desired to hold his court at Caerleon, and to bid his barons to attend him every one. He commanded, therefore, to the feast, kings and earls, dukes and viscounts, knights and barons, bishops and abbots. Nor did Arthur bid Englishmen alone, but Frenchman and Burgundian, Auvergnat and Gascon,

Norman and Poitivin, Angevin and Fleming, together with him of Brabant, Hainault, and Lorraine, the king bade to his dinner. Frisian and Teuton, Dane and Norwegian, Scot, Irish, and Icelander, him of Cathness and of Gothland, the lords of Galway and of the furthest islands of the Hebrides, Arthur summoned them all. When these received the king's messages commanding them to his crowning, they hastened to observe the feast as they were bidden, every one. From Scotland came Aguisel the king, richly vested in his royal robes; there, too, was Urian, King of Murief, together with his son Yvain the courteous; Lot of Lyones also, to take a brave part in the revels, and with him that very frank and gentle knight Gawain, his son. There besides were Stater and Cadual, kings of South Wales and of North; Cador of Cornwall, right near to Arthur's heart; Morud, Earl of Gloucester; and Guerdon, Earl of Winchester. Anavalt came from Salisbury, and Rimarec from Canterbury. Earl Baldulph drew from Silchester, and Vigenin from Leicester. There, too, was Algal of Guivic, a baron much held in honour by the court. Other lords were there a many, in no wise of less reputation than their fellows. The son of Po that was hight Donander; Regian, son of Abauder; Ceilus the son of Coil; that son of Chater named Chatellus; Griffin, the heir of Nagroil; Ron, the son of Neco; Margoil, Clefaut, Ringar, Angan, Rimar and Gorbonian, Kinlint, Neco and that Peredur, whom men deemed to be gotten by Eladur. Besides these princes there drew to Caerleon such knights as were of the king's house, and served him about his court. These were his chosen friends, who had their seats at the King's Round Table, but more of them I cannot tell. Many other lords were there of only less wealth and worship than those I have named. So numerous was this fair company that I have lost count of their numbers. A noble array of prelates came also to Arthur's solemn feast. Abbots and mitred bishops walked in their order and degree. The three archbishops of the realm came in his honour, namely, the Archbishop of London, his brother of York, and holy Dubricius, whose chair was in that self same city. Very holy of life was this fair prelate. Very abundantly he laboured, being Archbishop of Caerleon and Legate of Rome. Many wonderful works were wrought by his hands. The sick were brought to him gladly, and by reason of his love and his prayers, oftentimes they were healed of their hurt. In olden days this Dubricius abode in London, but now was Bishop in Wales, by reason of the evil times when kings regarded not God, and the people forsook the churches of their fathers. These clergy assembled at Arthur's court, for the king's feast, together with so great a fellowship of barons that I know not even to rehearse you their names.

Yet these must be remembered, whomsoever I forget. Villamus,

King of Ireland, and Malinus, King of Iceland, and Doldamer, lord of that lean and meagre country, known as the land of Goths. Acil, the King of the Danes; Lot, who was King of Norway, and Gonfal, jarl of the lawless Orkneys, from whence sail the pirates in their ships. From the parts beyond the seas came Ligier, holding the dukedom and honour of Burgundy; Holden, Earl of Flanders; and Guerin, Earl of Chartres, having the twelve peers of France in his company, for the richer dignity and splendour of his state. Guitard was there, the Earl of Poitiers; Kay, whom the king had created Earl of Angers; and Bedevere of Neustria, that province which men now call Normandy. From Le Mans drew Earl Borel, and from Brittany Earl Hoel. Passing noble of visage was Hoel, and all those lords who came forth from France. They voyaged to Arthur's court in chased harness and silken raiment, riding on lusty horses with rich trappings, and wearing jewels, with many golden ornaments. There was not a prince from here even unto Spain, yea, to the very Rhine in the land of Germany, but hastened to Arthur's solemn feast, so only that he was bidden to that crowning. Of these some came to look on the face of the king; some to receive of his largeness costly gifts; some to have speech with the lords of his council. Some desired to marvel over the abundance of Arthur's wealth, and others to hear tell of the great king's courtesies. This lord was drawn by the cords of love; this by compulsion of his suzerain's ban; this to learn by the witness of his eyes whether Arthur's power and prosperity exceeded that fame of which the whole world bragged.

When this proud company of kings, bishops, and princes was gathered together to observe Arthur's feast, the whole city was moved. The king's servants toiled diligently making ready for so great a concourse of guests. Soldiers ran to and fro, busily seeking hostels for this fair assemblage. Houses were swept and garnished, spread with reeds, and furnished with hangings of rich arras. Halls and chambers were granted to their needs, together with stables for the horses and their provand. Those for whom hostelries might not be found abode in seemly lodgings, decently appointed to their degree. The city was full of stir and tumult. In every place you beheld squires leading horses and destriers by the bridle, setting saddles on hackneys and taking them off, buckling the harness and making the metal work shining and bright. Grooms went about their business. Never was such a cleansing of stables, such taking of horses to the meadows, such a currying and combing, shoeing and loosing of girths, washing and watering, such a bearing of straw and of grass for the litter, and oats for the manger. Nor these alone, but in the courtyards and chambers of the hostels you might see the pages and chamberlains go swiftly about their tasks, in divers fashions. The varlets brushed and folded the habiliments and mantles of their lords. They looked to the stuff and the fastenings of their garments. You saw them hurry through the halls carrying furs and furred raiment, both vair and the grey. Caerleon seemed rather a fair than a city, at Arthur's feast.

Now telleth the chronicle of this geste, that when the morning was come of the day of the high feast, a fair procession of archbishops, bishops, and abbots wended to the king's palace, to place the crown upon Arthur's head, and lead him within the church. Two of these archbishops brought him through the streets of the city, one walking on either side of his person. Each bishop sustained the king by his arm, and thus he was carried to his throne. Four kings went before Arthur and the clerks, bearing swords in their hands. Pommel, scabbard, and hilt of these four swords were of wrought gold. This was the office of these kings when Arthur held state at his court. The first of the princes was from Scotland, the second from South Wales, the third was of North Wales, and as to the last it was Cador of Cornwall who carried the fourth sword. All these fair princes were at one in their purpose, being altogether at unity, when Arthur was crowned king. To holy Dubricius it fell, as prelate of Caerleon and Roman legate, to celebrate the office and perform such rites as were seemly to be rendered in the church.

That the queen might not be overshadowed by her husband's state, the crown was set on her head in another fashion. For her part she had bidden to her court the great ladies of the country, and such dames as were the wives of her friends. Together with these had assembled the ladies of her kindred, such ladies as were most to her mind, and many fair and gentle maidens whom she desired to be about her person at the feast. The presence of this gay company of ladies made the feast yet more rich, when the queen was crowned in her chamber, and brought to that convent of holy nuns for the conclusion of the rite. The press was so great that the queen might hardly make her way through the streets of the city. Four dames preceded their lady, bearing four white doves in their hands. These dames were the wives of those lords who carried the golden swords before the king. A fair company of damsels followed after the queen, making marvellous joy and delight. This fair fellowship of ladies came from the noblest of the realm. Passing dainty were they to see, wearing rich mantles above their silken raiment. All men gazed gladly upon them, for their beauty was such that none was sweeter than her fellows. These dames and maidens went clothed in their softest garments. Their heads were tired in their fairest hennins, and they walked in their most holiday vesture. Never were seen so many rich kirtles of divers colours, such costly mantles, such precious jewels and rings. Never were seen such furs and such ornaments, both the vair and the grey. Never was known so gay and noble a procession of ladies, as this which hastened to the church, lest it should be hindered from the rite.

Now within the church Mass was commenced with due pomp and observance. The noise of the organ filled the church, and the clerks sang tunably in the choir. Their voices swelled or failed, according as the chant mounted to the roof, or died away in supplication. The knights passed from one church to the other. Now they would be at the convent of St Julius, and again at the cathedral church of St Aaron. This they did to compare the singing of the clerks, and to delight their eyes with the loveliness of the damsels. Although the knights passed frequently between the churches, yet no man could answer for certain at which they remained the longer. They could not surfeit the heart by reason of the sweetness of the melody. Yea, had the song endured the whole day through, I doubt those knights would ever have grown weary or content.

When the office drew to its appointed end, and the last words were chanted, the king put off his crown that he had carried to the church. He took another crown which sat more lightly on his head; and in such fashion did the queen. They laid aside their heavy robes and ornaments of state, and vested them in less tiring raiment. The king parted from St Aaron's church, and returned to his palace for meat. The queen, for her part, came again to her own house, carrying with her that fair fellowship of ladies, yet making marvellous joy. For the Britons held still to the custom brought by their sires from Troy, that when the feast was spread, man ate with man alone, bringing no lady with him to the board. The ladies and damsels ate apart. No men were in their hall, save only the servitors, who served them with every observance, for the feast was passing rich, as became a monarch's court. When Arthur was seated in his chair upon the daïs, the lords and princes sat around the board, according to the usage of the country, each in his order and degree. The king's seneschal, hight Sir Kay, served Arthur's table, clad in a fair dalmatic of vermeil silk. With Sir Kay were a thousand damoiseaux, clothed in ermine, who bore the dishes from the buttery. These pages moved briskly about the tables, carrying the meats in platters to the guests. Together with these were yet another thousand damoiseaux, gentle and goodly to see, clothed likewise in coats of ermine. These fair varlets poured the wine from golden beakers into cups and hanaps of fine gold. Not one of these pages but served in a vesture of ermine. Bedevere, the king's cup-bearer, himself set Arthur's cup upon the board; and those called him master who saw that Arthur's servants lacked not drink.

The queen had so many servitors at her bidding, that I may not tell you the count. She and all her company of ladies were waited on, richly and reverently. Right worshipfully were they tended. These ladies had to their table many rich meats, and wines and spiced drink of divers curious fashions. The dishes and vessels from which they ate were very precious, and passing fair. I know not how to put before you the wealth and the splendour of Arthur's feast. Whether for goodly men or for chivalrous deeds, for wealth as for plenty, for courtesy as for honour, in Arthur's day England bore the flower from all the lands near by, yea, from every other realm whereof we know. The poorest peasant in his smock was a more courteous and valiant gentleman than was a belted knight beyond the sea. And as with the men, so, and no otherwise, was it with the women. There was never a knight whose praise was bruited abroad, but went in harness and raiment and plume of one and the self-same hue. The colour of surcoat and armour in the field was the colour of the gown he wore in hall. The dames and damsels would apparel them likewise in cloth of their own colour. No matter what the birth and riches of a knight might be, never, in all his days, could he gain fair lady to his friend, till he had proved his chivalry and worth. That knight was accounted the most nobly born who bore himself the foremost in the press. Such a knight was indeed cherished of the ladies; for his friend was the more chaste as he was brave.

After the king had risen from the feast, he and his fellowship went without the city to take their delight amongst the fields. The lords sought their pleasure in divers places. Some amongst them jousted together, that their horses might be proven. Others fenced with the sword, or cast the stone, or flung pebbles from a sling. There were those who shot with the bow, like cunning archers, or threw darts at a mark. Every man strove with his fellow, according to the game he loved. That knight who proved the victor in his sport, and bore the prize from his companions, was carried before the king in the sight of all the princes. Arthur gave him of his wealth so goodly a gift, that he departed from the king's presence in great mirth and content. The ladies of the court climbed upon the walls, looking down on the games very gladly. She, whose friend was beneath her in the field, gave him the glance of her eye and her face; so that he strove the more earnestly for her favour. Now to the court had gathered many tumblers, harpers, and makers of music, for Arthur's feast. He who would hear songs sung to the music of the rote, or would solace himself with the newest refrain of the minstrel, might win to his wish. Here stood the viol player, chanting ballads and lays to their appointed tunes. Everywhere might be heard the voice of viols and harp and flutes. In every place rose the sound of lyre and drum and shepherd's pipe, bagpipe, psaltery, cymbals, monochord, and all manner of music. Here the tumbler tumbled on his carpet. There the mime and the dancing girl put forth their feats. Of Arthur's guests some hearkened to the teller of tales and fables. Others called for dice and tables, and played games of chance for a wager. Evil befalls to winner and loser alike from such sport as this. For the most part men played at chess or draughts. You might see them, two by two, bending over the board. When one player was beaten by his fellow, he borrowed moneys to pay his wager, giving pledges for the repayment of his debt. Dearly enough he paid for his loan, getting but eleven to the dozen. But the pledge was offered and taken, the money rendered, and the game continued with much swearing and cheating, much drinking and quarrelling, with strife and with anger. Often enough the loser was discontented, and rose murmuring against his fellow. Two by two the dicers sat at table, casting the dice. They threw in turn, each throwing higher than his fellow. You might hear them count, six, five, three, four, two, and one. They staked their raiment on the cast, so there were those who threw half naked. Fair hope had he who held the dice, after his fellow had cried his number. Then the quarrel rose suddenly from the silence. One called across the table to his companion, 'You cheat, and throw not fairly. Grasp not the dice so tightly in your hand, but shake them forth upon the board. My count is yet before yours. If you still have pennies in your pouch bring them out, for I will meet you to your wish.' Thus the dicers wrangled, and to many of Arthur's guests it chanced that he who sat to the board in furs, departed from the tables clothed in his skin.

When the fourth day of the week was come, on a certain Wednesday, the king made knights of his bachelors, granting them rents to support their stations. He recompensed those lords of his household who held of him their lands at suit and service. Such clerks as were diligent in their Master's business he made abbots and bishops; and bestowed castles and towns on his counsellors and friends. To those stranger knights who for his love had crossed the sea in his quarrel, the king gave armour and destrier and golden ornaments, to their desire. Arthur divided amongst them freely of his wealth. He granted lordship and delights, greyhound and brachet, furred gown and raiment, beaker and hanap, sendal and signet, bliaut and mantle, lance and sword and quivers of sharp barbed arrows. He bestowed harness and buckler and weapons featly fashioned by the smith. He gave largesse of bears and of leopards, of palfreys and hackneys, of chargers with saddles thereon. He gave the helm as the hauberk, the gold as the silver, yea, he bestowed on his servants the very richest and most precious of his treasure. Never a man of these outland knights, so only he was worthy of Arthur's bounty, but the king granted him such gifts as he might brag of in his own realm. And as with the foreign lords, so to the kings and the princes, the knights and all his barons, Arthur gave largely many precious gifts.

LAWMAN (LAYAMON), Brut (c. 1200–10)

Little is known of Lawman, save that he was priest at Areley Kings near Stourport-on-Severn in Herefordshire. Lawman's Brut, *the first English version of Geoffrey of Monmouth's* History, *is written in an archaic poetic style using a long alliterative line. Although he translated mainly from Wace's version, French words and concepts which had already started to infiltrate the English language are deliberately avoided by Lawman, whose poem is intensely English in character. While Lawman's Arthur is reminiscent of early English warleaders such as Beowulf, his most significant contribution to the Arthurian section is perhaps his increased use of the 'supernatural'.*[24]

The Battle of Badon (Bath)

Arthur attacks Childric's army, routing the Saxons, who flee into Calidon Wood in Caledonia [Scotland], where Arthur besieges them. Colgrim suggests to Childric that they should make peace with Arthur, promising to leave Britain. Arthur laughs at the Saxon messengers, comparing Childric to a fox pursued by men and hounds, but he acts unwisely when he decides to show mercy on condition that the Saxons give hostages as a pledge of good faith, and hand over their horses and weapons.

After sailing out to sea, the Saxons return to Britain, devastating the South-West and slaughtering the inhabitants. They then besiege Bath, all without Arthur's knowledge, while he is securing control of Scotland. When Arthur discovers that the Saxons have broken their word not to return, he hastens to Bath and destroys their army, sending Cador to intercept the survivors before they can reach their ships. This passage contains some excellent imagery, particularly Arthur's comment about the 'steel fish' in the Avon, which resemble dead Saxons.

Arthur started riding, the army was stampeding
10300 As if the whole earth were eaten up with flames;
In among Childric's tents they swooped down in the fields,
And the man who was the first there to start the battle cry
Was Arthur the great warrior, the son of King Uther,
Who shouted loudly and with courage, as comes best from a
    king:
'Now may Mary aid us, the meek mother of our God,
And I am praying to her Son that he be our assistance!'
    At these very words they took aim with their spears,
Stabbing and striking all those they came close to,
And knights from the city strode out towards them.
10310 If they fled back to the city, there they would perish,
If they fled to the woodland they would be destroyed there:
Let them go where they could, they would still be attacked.
It's not recorded in a book that there was ever any fight
Within this realm of Britain where destruction was so rife,
For they were the most wretched of all races who have come
    here!
There was a deal of bloodshed: there was destruction among
    men;
Death there was rife and the earth was resounding.
Childric the emperor had a single castle there
On the plain of Lincoln – he was lying up inside it –
10320 Which was recently constructed and really well defended,
And in there also with him were Baldulf and Colgrim,
Who saw that their army was undergoing huge fatalities,
And right away at once it was on with the mail-coats
And they fled from the castle, bereft of all their courage,
And fled right away at once to the wood of Calidon.
They had as their companions seven thousand riders,
And behind them they left slain and deprived of their life's days
A full forty thousand who were felled to the ground:
Men who came from Germany all of them damned in misery,
10330 And all the Saxon men levelled to the ground.
    Then Arthur was aware, the most admirable of kings,
That Childric had fled, into Caledonia he'd sped,
And Colgrim and Baldulf, both had made off with him,
Into the high wood, into the high hurst.
And Arthur went on their track with sixty thousand knights:
The soldiers of Britain surrounded all the wood,
And on one side they felled it for a seven mile extent,

One tree on another, and 'truly' they worked fast!
On the other side he laid siege to it with his levied army
10340 For three days and three nights: it put them in tremendous
plight.
Then Colgrim realized as he was holed up in it
(Who was there without food, in sharp hunger and distress)
That not for them nor their horses was there any help at all.
And in this way Colgrim called to the emperor:
'Tell me, my lord Childric, in words which are truthful,
Can there be any reason why we are lurking here like this?
Why don't we sally forth and summon up our armies,
And start up the fighting against Arthur and his knights?
It's better for us to be laid out on the land but with our honour
10350 Than like this in here to perish with hunger.
It's tormenting us terribly and our men are held in contempt;
Or else let's send straight out to him, and seek a truce from
Arthur,
And plead for his mercy and pass hostages to him
And create an alliance with the noble king.'
Childric was listening as he sheltered in the fort,
And he gave his reply in a really sad voice:
'If Baldulf your own brother wants this and agrees,
And more of our confederates who are here with us inside,
That we should sue for peace from Arthur and set up a treaty
with him,
10360 Then just as you want, that's what I'll do,
Since in the realm this Arthur is reckoned a most noble man,
Beloved among his followers and a man of royal stock;
Entirely from kings he comes: he was King Uther's son,
And often it does come to pass in many kinds of peoples,
Where valiant knights embark on fierce fight,
That what they win at first they will lose again at last;
And for us right here and now it's turning out like that,
But if only we can live, then for us things will improve.'
There came an instant and forthright response from the
knights:
10370 'We all approve of this proposal, for you have put it well.'
They selected twelve knights and sent them off straight
To where he was in his pavilion by the edges of the wood.
One of them began to shout at once in a sturdy voice:
'Lord Arthur, your safe-conduct: with you we wish to speak!
Childric, styled the emperor, has sent us over here,
As did Colgrim and Baldulf, both of them together;

Now and for all eternity they request your clemency:
They will become your vassals and your renown they will
    advance,
And they will hand over to you hostages in plenty,
10380 And regard you as their lord, as you will like most of all,
If only they may leave and go from here alive
Into their own land and take there the loathed report;
For here we have experienced many kinds of evils:
At Lincoln we left behind our most beloved kinsmen,
Sixty thousand men who are lying there slain,
And if it might be the wish of your heart
That we across the sea may travel under sail,
Then never any more shall we come back here,
For here we have lost for good our own loved relations;
10390 As long as will be for ever here shall we come back never!'
    Then Arthur laughed, and with a loud voice:
'May thanks be given to God who governs all decisions
That Childric the strong has had sufficient of my land!
He divided up my land among all his doughty knights,
Me myself he had planned to drive from my native land,
To regard me as a wretch and to retain all my realm,
And to have destroyed all my family and condemned all my
    folk.
But things have turned out for him as they do with the fox:
When he is most brazen, up in the forest,
10400 And has his freedom for playing and has fowls a-plenty,
In his wild sport he climbs and he seeks out the crags;
Out in the wild places he excavates dens:
Let him roam wherever he wishes, he never has any distress,
And thinks he is in valour the finest of all creatures,
When towards him up the mountains here come men climbing,
With horns and with hounds, and with hallooing voices;
There hunters are yelling; there foxhounds are belling,
Driving the fox on across dales and over downland:
He dashes to the highwood and seeks out his den;
10410 At the nearest point he presses down into the hole.
Then the bold fox is quite bereft of bliss,
And men are digging down to him upon every side;
Then he there becomes the saddest who of all beasts was the
    proudest.
    'That's how it was with Childric, the powerful and mighty:
All my kingdom he intended to get into his clutches,
But now I have driven him to the very edge of death,

Which of the two I decide to do, to behead or hang him.
Now I decide to give him peace and allow him speech with me;
I shall neither behead nor hang him but will accede to his
    request:
10420 I wish to take hostages from his highest-ranking men,
Horses and their weapons, before they go from here,
And so they are to travel like wretches to their ships,
To sail across the sea to their splendid land,
And dwell there dutifully within their realm,
And announce the tidings of Arthur the king,
Of how I have set them free for my father's soul's sake,
And from my own generosity have dealt gently with the
    wretches.'
    In this affair King Arthur was short of all good judgement,
There was no man who was quite so rash as to dare to put him
    right;
10430 This he regretted bitterly a very short time after.
Childric came from under cover to Arthur who was king,
And he became his vassal there with each one of his knights.
Fully twenty-four hostages Childric handed over there:
They were all selected specially and born in the nobility.
They gave up their horses and their fine mail-coats,
Their spears and their shields and the long swords of theirs:
Everything they had there they then left behind;
They started their journey till they came to the sea
Where their fine ships were standing by the sea.
10440   They had the wind they wanted, and very pleasant weather:
They pushed out from the shore ships massive and long;
They all left behind the land and laid course along the waves
Until they could not see any sight of land at all.
The water was still, which suited their will;
They set their sails gliding right alongside,
Plank against plank; people spoke to one another,
Deciding that they wanted to come back to this land
And avenge with honour their own loved relations,
And lay waste King Arthur's land and kill those who lived here,
10450 And conquer the castles and do acts of wild delight.
So they travelled on the sea for such a long time
That they arrived midway between England and Normandy;
They went about on their luff and laid course towards land,
Till they came (no doubt of this) to Dartmouth reach at Totnes;
In the very greatest joy they jumped down ashore.
    As soon as they came to land they slaughtered the people:

They put to flight the peasants who were ploughing the soil;
They hanged all the knights who had command of the lands;
All the dutiful wives they stabbed to death with knives,
10460 All the young girls they gang-raped to death,
And the men of learning they laid out on hot coals;
All the serving-men at court they killed by clubbing them;
They demolished the castles, they laid waste the land,
They burned down the churches; there was distress in the land!
The babies at the breast they drowned in the waters;
The livestock which they seized they slaughtered completely,
To their quarters dragged it and stewed it up and roasted it;
Everything they grabbed which they could get close to.
All day long they were singing about Arthur the great king,
10470 Claiming they had won for themselves homes
Which were going to be their holdings in their own control,
And there they would be staying in winter and in summer,
And if Arthur had such courage that he wanted to come
To fight against Childric the powerful and mighty,
'[We]'ll make a bridge, really fine, from the bits of his spine
And pick out all the bones from the admirable king,
And join them together with links of gold chain,
And lay them in the hall doorway which each man has to go
     through
In tribute to Childric, the mighty and the rich!'
10480   All this was just how they played, to King Arthur's disgrace,
But all happened quite another way very shortly after:
Their boasts and their games turned into their own shame,
As it does almost everywhere when a man behaves like that.
The emperor Childric conquered everything he looked at:
He took Somerset, and he took Dorset,
And all Devonshire's people he entirely destroyed,
And he treated Wiltshire with the utmost wickedness;
He seized all the lands down to the sea sands;
Then ultimately he ordered men to start blowing
10490 Horns and brass trumpets, and his host to assemble,
And he wanted to be off and completely besiege Bath,
And also to blockade Bristol round about the coastline;
Such was their boasting before they came to Bath.
     To Bath came the emperor and besieged the castle there,
And the men inside it with valour proceeded
To mount upon the stone walls, well supplied with weapons,
And they defended the place against the mighty Childric.
There encamped the emperor and Colgrim his companion,

And Baldulf his brother and very many others.
10500   Arthur was in the north, and knew nothing of this;
He travelled all through Scotland and set it all into his own
        hand:
Orkney and Galloway, the Isle of Man and Moray,
And all of the territories which were their tributaries.
Arthur assumed that it was a certain thing
That Childric had laid course back to his own land,
And that never again would he ever come back here.
    Then to Arthur the king there came the tidings
That Childric the emperor had come to the country
And in the south region was wreaking great chaos.
10510 Then Arthur announced (most admired of kings):
'I am deeply sorry that I spared my enemy,
That in the hilltop wood I did not [kill him off] with hunger,
Or did not slice him right up with slashes from my sword!
Now this is how he pays me back for my good deed!
But so help me the Lord who made the light of day
For this he shall endure the most extreme of all agonies,
Harshest contests; I shall be his killer,
And both Colgrim and Baldulf I myself shall kill,
And all of their supporters shall suffer death.
10520 If the Ruler of heaven wishes to grant this,
I shall honourably avenge all his evil deeds;
If the life in my breast is able to last in me,
And if he who created moon and sun is willing to grant me
        this,
Then Childric will never cheat me again!'
    Now the call went from Arthur, the most admired of kings:
'Where are you, my knights, brave men and valiant?
To horse, to horse, worthy warriors,
And swiftly towards Bath we shall now be on our way.
Get men to erect really high gibbets
10530 And bring here the hostages in front of our knights,
And they shall be hanged there upon the high trees.'
    There he had executed all twenty-four children,
From the German race, of very noble families.
Then came the tidings to Arthur the king
That his cousin Howel was sick (and this news made him sad)
Lodged in Dumbarton by the Clyde; and there then he had to
        leave him.
With exceeding haste he started making off
Until beside Bath he moved on to a plain,

And there he dismounted, and all of his knights,
10540 And on with their mail-coats, those stern men of war,
And he divided his forces into five sections.
    When he had stationed them all and all were surveyed
Then he put on his mail-coat fashioned from steel mesh
Which an elvish smith had made with his excellent skill:
It was called Wygar, which Wiseman had smithied.
His thighs he covered up with cuisses of steel;
Caliburn his sword he strapped by his side –
It was made in Avalon and endowed with magic powers;
His helmet he set on his head, high and made of steel:
10550 On it was many a gem and it was all bound with gold –
It had once belonged to the noble King Uther –
It was known as Goosewhite, among all others quite unique.
He hung about his neck a shield which was precious:
Its name in British was entitled Pridwen;
Inside it was engraved with red gold stencilling
A most precious image of the mother of our Lord;
In his hand he took his spear which bore the name of Ron.
When he had donned all his armour, then he leaped on his
        charger;
Then the bystanders were able to behold
10560 The most handsome knight who ever led forth host:
Never did any man see a more splendid knight
Than was this Arthur who was most aristocratic.
    Then Arthur called out in a loud voice:
'Look here now, ahead of us, those heathen hounds
Who slaughtered our ancestors with their evil tricks,
And who for us in the land are the most loathsome of all things.
Now let us charge towards them and fiercely set upon them
And avenge with acclaim our race and our realm,
And avenge the great disgrace by which they have debased us
10570 When over the billows they came to Dartmouth sound.
And they are all utterly forsworn and they are all utterly cast
        down:
They are all doomed, with the Lord's divine aid.
Now let us hasten forward in combined formation
Every bit as gently as if we had no harsh intentions,
And when we come up to them, I myself will start:
Among the very foremost I shall begin the fighting.
Now we shall ride and across the land we'll glide
And no man for his very life must move at all loudly,
But travel with all speed. Now the Lord give us support!'

10580   Then Arthur the great man set off at a gallop,
          Headed over the plain and was making for Bath.
          The tidings came to Childric, the powerful and mighty,
          That Arthur with his forces was coming all prepared for fight.
          Childric and his bold men leaped upon their horses,
          Firmly grasped their weapons, knowing Arthur was their
              enemy.
          Arthur, most admired king, noticed this thing;
          He noticed one heathen earl making straight for him
          With seven hundred knights all prepared for fight,
          The earl himself advancing in front of his contingent;
10590   And Arthur himself was riding at the head of all his army.
          Arthur the resolute took Ron in his hand,
          He steadied the sturdy shaft, that stout-hearted king,
          He set his horse galloping so that the earth resounded,
          And raised his shield before his breast: the king was enraged!
          He struck the earl Borel straight through the chest
          So that his heart was split; and the king called out at once:
          'The first one is fated! Now may the Lord afford us aid,
          And the heavenly Queen who gave birth to the Lord.'
              Arthur, most admired of kings, called out again:
10600   'Now at them, now at them! the first deed was well done!'
          The British set upon them as must be done with scoundrels:
          They gave savage slashes with axes and with swords.
          From Childric's men there fell fully two thousand,
          While Arthur did not lose a single one of his!
          There the Saxon men were the most abject of people,
          And the men of Germany the most mournful of all nations.
          Arthur with his sword sent many to their doom:
          Everything he struck with it was instantly done for.
          The king was every bit as enraged as the wild boar is
10610   When among the oakmast he meets many [pigs].
              Childric was aware of this and began to turn away,
          And he set off across the Avon to find safety for himself,
          And Arthur leaped into pursuit just like a lion
          And flushed them into the water: many there were fated;
          To the depths sank there two thousand five hundred,
          And all the River Avon was spanned with a bridge of steel.
          Childric fled across the water with fifteen hundred knights,
          Intending to slip off and pass across the sea.
          Arthur spotted Colgrim climbing to the mountains,
10620   Making a break towards the hills which look down on Bath,
          And Baldulf made off after him, with seven thousand knights,

Supposing that up in the hills they could make a noble stand,
Defend themselves with weapons and wound Arthur's force.
　　Then Arthur noted, that most admired king,
Where Colgrim offered resistance and made his stand too;
Then the king called out, loudly and with courage:
'My bold-hearted warriors, march to the hills!
For yesterday Colgrim was of all men most courageous,
Now he's just like the goat holding guard on its hill:
10630 High on the hillside it fights with its horns;
Then the wild wolf comes, on its way up towards them;
Even though the wolf's alone, without any pack,
If there were in one pen a full five hundred goats,
The wolf would get to them and would bite them all.
In just that way today I shall quite destroy Colgrim:
I'm the wolf and he's the goat: that guy is going to be doomed!'
　　Once again Arthur called out, most admired of kings:
'Yesterday Baldulf was of all knights the boldest;
Now he's standing on the hill and staring at the Avon,
10640 Sees lying in the stream fishes made of steel,
They're girded with swords but their swimming is all spoiled;
Their scales are fluttering like shields adorned with gold;
Their spines are floating just as if they were spears.
These are remarkable sights to see in this land:
Such beasts on the hill, such fish in the spring;
Yesterday the emperor was the most audacious monarch,
Now he's become a hunter and horns are his accompaniment,
He's dashing over the broad plain and his dogs are barking;
There beside Bath he has abandoned his hunting:
10650 He's in flight from his own quarry, so we'll be the ones to
　　　　kill it
And so bring to nothing those brazen boasts of his,
And in this way we'll regain true rights of ownership.'
　　And with those very words which the king was speaking
He raised high his shield in front of his chest,
Grasped his long spear and set spurs to his horse;
Almost as fast as a bird in its flight
There went following the king twenty-five thousand,
Of valiant men in wild rage, armed with their weapons.
They made towards the mountains with very mighty force
10660 And into Colgrim they struck with most savage whacks.
And Colgrim took them on and felled the British to the ground,
Fully five hundred in the first onrush.
This Arthur noted, that most admired king,

And marvellously and mightily he became maddened,
And in this way started shouting Arthur the great man:
'Where are you, my British, my bold and brave soldiers?
Here ahead of us are standing all our noted enemies!
Good warriors of mine, let us grind them to the ground!'
   Arthur grasped his sword in his right and he struck a Saxon
      knight,
10670 And the sword (it was so splendid) sliced till at his teeth it
      ended!
And then he struck another who was the first knight's brother
So his helm and the head with it fell upon the ground;
At once he gave a third blow and he cut one knight in two.
Then the British men were strongly emboldened
And imposed upon the Saxons some most severe contusions
With their spears which were long and with their swords which
      were strong.
There the Saxons fell in their last fatal hour,
In hundreds upon hundreds they fell in heaps upon the ground,
In thousands upon thousands they went on falling on the
      ground.
10680   Then spotted Colgrim that Arthur was coming to him:
Because of all the corpses Colgrim couldn't slip aside;
Baldulf was fighting there right beside his brother.
Then Arthur called out in challenging tones:
'Here I come, Colgrim! we two are reaching for this country
And now we're going to share this land in a way you'll find
      least pleasing!'
After these words which the king was uttering
He lifted high his broad sword and heavily struck down
Striking Colgrim on the helmet and carving down the centre,
And through the coif on his mail-coat, till it stuck in the man's
      chest,
10690 And he reached out to Baldulf with his right hand
And swiped his head right off together with his helmet.
   Then noble King Arthur gave a great laugh,
And began to recite these words of rejoicing:
'Lie there now, Colgrim: you certainly climbed high,
And your brother Baldulf who is lying by your side,
Now's the time I invest all this realm in your possession,
The dales and the downland and all my doughty men!
You climbed up this hill marvellously high
As if you were on your way to heaven; now you've got to go
      to hell;

10700 There you will recognize a good many of your tribe.
Give my regards to Hengest who was the most handsome knight,
Ebissa and Octa and from your tribe lots more,
And ask them to stay there all winter and all summer;
Then in this land we shall live in joy,
And pray for your souls – that they will never have salvation! –
And your bones shall lie here, right beside Bath.'
Arthur the king called Cador the courageous
(He was the Earl of Cornwall and a most courageous knight):
'Listen to me, Cador, you come from my own family;
10710 Childric has now run off and has gone away from here;
He thinks that he'll be safe to come travelling back again.
But take from my forces five thousand men,
And travel directly, by day and by night,
Until you arrive at the sea in advance of Childric,
And everything you can conquer, enjoy that with pleasure,
And if you manage to kill the emperor with the greatest cruelty,
I'll give you as reward all of Dorsetshire.'
As soon as the noble king had spoken these words
Cador sprang to horse as a spark does from the fire;
10720 A full seven thousand accompanied the earl.
Cador the courageous and many of his kindred
Went across the wolds and over the wild places,
Over dales and over downlands over deep waters;
Cador knew the way which towards his own lands lay:
Westwards he went, this is the case, right on to Totnes,
By day and by night; he got there directly,
So that Childric never discovered the least detail of his coming.
Cador came to his country in advance of Childric
And had all folk in the area marshalled in front of him,
10730 Vigorous peasants with enormous clubs
With spears and great cudgels collected for that very purpose,
And he put every single one of them into the ships' bilges,
Ordered them to keep well hidden so that Childric wasn't aware of them,
And when his men arrived and were trying to climb in
They were to grab their cudgels and vigorously thump them,
And with their staves and with their spears to slaughter Childric's adherents.
The peasants did exactly as Cador had instructed:
Off to the ships went the peasants in grim fury;
In each of the ships there were a hundred and fifty,

10740 And Cador the courageous moved towards a high wood
Five miles from the spot where the ships were stationed,
And hid his men as he desired in the utmost silence.
Childric came soon after marching on the plain,
Intending to rush to the ships and run away from the land.
As soon as Earl Cador, a man of courage, could clearly see
That Childric was on the plain between him and the peasants
Then Cador called out in a clear voice:
'Where are you, my knights, my good, valiant fighters?
Remember what Arthur, our admirable king
10750 Commanded us at Bath before we left the company!
Now see Childric flying, trying to flee from the land
And making for Germany where his ancestors lie
Where he'll collect up an army and come back here again
And invade our interior, intending to avenge that Colgrim
And Baldulf his brother, who lie dead beside Bath.
But may he never survive to see that hour! He will not if we
     have the power!'
Upon concluding that speech the great earl had spoken
In a mood of harsh anger he rode at their head;
The valiant soldiers strode out of the wood-shaw
10760 And went after Childric, the powerful and mighty.
Childric's knights looked back behind them:
Saw battle standards proceeding across the plain,
And five thousand shields gliding across the fields.
Then Childric became most distressed in his emotions,
And the mighty emperor ventured these words:
'This is King Arthur and he wants to eliminate us all!
Let's run off now quickly and rush into the ships
And get away from here by water and not bother about where
     we go to!'
When the emperor Childric had uttered these remarks
10770 He set off in flight fearfully quickly
With Cador the courageous coming after him at once.
Childric and his knights came to their ships straightaway
Intending to shove off those sturdy ships from land.
The peasants were hiding, with their cudgels, inside them:
They raised up their cudgels and brought them down hard;
By their clubs many knights there were instantly slain,
And stabbed by their pitchforks and pinned to the ground.
Cador and his knights attacked them from behind.
Then Childric realized they were facing disaster
10780 When all his great force fell in heaps on the ground!

Now he spotted to one side a very lofty hill;
That river flows beneath it which is termed the Teign
And the hill is called Teignwick: that's the way Childric fled
As quickly as he could manage with twenty-four knight
    companions.
Cador was aware how things were going there,
That the emperor was in flight and heading for the heights
And Cador went after him with as much speed as he could,
And gained on him steadily and caught up with him.
Then announced Cador, the most courageous earl,
10790 'Wait, Childric, wait; I want to give you Teignwick!'
Cador raised his sword and struck and killed Childric.
Many who were fleeing made for the water:
In the waters of the Teign there they met their end:
Cador killed everyone whom he found alive,
And some crawled into the woodland and he destroyed all
    these there.
    When Cador had conquered all of them and had seized all
    that land as well
He imposed a very firm peace which remained a long time
    after:
Even were a man wearing gold rings upon his arms
10799 No man whatever would dare to treat another man with wrong.

The Foundation of the Round Table

*One Christmas Day, when Arthur is holding court in London,
attended by all his numerous vassals, a serious fight breaks out
during the meal over the respective rank of the diners. Arthur
restores order and pronounces a dire punishment for the man who
started the fight and for his kinsfolk. After the feast, Arthur goes
to Cornwall, where a skilled craftsman offers to make a round
table for him, so that all his knights will be equal and will have no
cause for dispute in the future. Lawman then goes on to describe
British fables about Arthur, notably the myth about Arthur's
journey to Avalon to be healed of his wounds by Argante the
Gracious.*[25]

It happened one Christmas day, when Arthur was lodged in
    London,
People had come to him from each of his dependencies:
From Britain's land, from Scotland, from Ireland and from
    Iceland

And from all the other lands which Arthur held in hand,
11350 All the greatest leaders with their horses and their squires:
There were seven sons of kings with seven hundred knights
          who'd come,
Not counting the courtiers paying service to Arthur.
Each of them was feeling proudly exultant,
Giving out that he himself was better than his fellows;
The folk came from many realms: there was much rivalry,
Since if one would count himself so high, the second would
          much higher.
   Then the brass trumpets were blown and the trestle-tables
          covered:
Fine golden bowls were carried out to the hall floor,
And with them soft towels, all made of white silk;
11360 Then Arthur sat down, and beside him Queen Guinevere,
Then all the earls were seated, and after them the barons,
Then next the knights, as they were assigned;
The nobly connected then brought in the food,
Exactly in decorum, first to the knights,
Then to the foot soldiers and then to the squires,
Then to the baggage-men, right down the tables.
   The company became aroused: blows were freely given;
First they started throwing loaves, as long as there were some
          left,
And then the silver goblets which were filled with wine,
11370 And after that, clutching palms quickly caught up throats!
   Then a young man jumped forward who'd come there from
          Wendland;
He'd been given to Arthur to be held as hostage;
He was the son of Rumareth who was king of the Wends;
In this way the knight spoke there to Arthur the king:
'Lord Arthur, be off quickly, into your bedroom,
And your queen with you, and your close relations,
And we'll decide this conflict between these foreign combatants!'
Having spoken these words he leaped up to the trestle-boards
Where carving knives were lying in front of the lord king:
11380 Three knives he caught up and with one quickly struck
Into the neck of the knight who first began that very fight
So that down to the hall floor his head went crashing;
Fast he slew another, this same fighter's brother:
Before the swords came out he had finished off seven.
There was a huge fight there: every man struck the other;
There was enormous blood-shed, consternation in the court!

Then the king emerged from out of his chamber;
With him a hundred courtiers, with helmets and with corslets,
Each carrying in his right hand a broadsword of bright steel.
11390 Then shouted Arthur, most admired of kings:
'Sit down, sit down at once, all of you, or you will lose your
    lives!
Anyone who refuses to will be condemned to death.
Seize and bring me the actual man who first started this fight,
Clap a noose around his neck and drag him to the marshes,
And fling him in a deep bog and there let him lie,
And seize all his closest relatives whom you can discover,
And strike off their heads with your broadswords;
From the women you can discover among his closest relations
Carve off the noses and let their beauty be destroyed;
11400 In that way I'll quite obliterate the tribe from which he came,
And if ever any more I subsequently hear
That any of my courtiers, whether great or humble,
From this same slaughter should [seek] revenge after,
Then no compensation from gold or treasure will atone,
Neither strong steed nor war gear, to buy him off from death
Or from being drawn apart by horses, which is the punishment
    for traitors.
Bring here the sacred relics and I shall swear upon them,
As shall all you knights who were present at this fight,
You earls and barons, that you will never break it.'
11410   The first to swear was Arthur, most admired of kings,
Then the earls took the oath, and then the barons took the
    oath,
Then the landholders took the oath, then the servitors took the
    oath,
That they would never again instigate a brawl.
The dead were all taken up and carried to their resting-place,
And then brass trumpets were blown with very rousing sound:
Whether they liked it or loathed it, each one took water and a
    cloth,
And then, reconciled, they sat down at the table,
All in awe of Arthur, most admired of kings.
Cup-bearers were jostling, minstrels were singing,
11420 Harps gave out joyful sounds: courtiers were jubilant.
For a whole week like this the court was employed.
   Next, it says in the story, the king went to Cornwall;
There a man came quickly to him who was a skilled craftsman,
And he encountered the king and gave courteous greeting:

'All health to you, Arthur, most admired of kings!
I am your own vassal; many a land I have traversed;
I know a marvellous number of the skills of woodworking.
I heard tell beyond the sea such novel tidings
About your own knights who at your table started fighting
11430 At the midwinter feast; many fell there.
In their mighty arrogance they were acting games of murder,
And because of their high connexions each must sit near
      top-table.
But I shall make for you a most suitable table
Where sixteen hundred and more can easily be seated,
Each in turn all round so that no one gets left out,
No inclusion and exclusion, just one man opposite another.
When you want to ride you can carry it alongside,
And set it up wherever you want, according to your fancy,
And you need never again be afraid in all the wide world
11440 That ever any proud knight would at your table start a fight,
Since the important there must be equal with the simple.'
     Timber was obtained and the table was begun:
In the space of four weeks the work was completed.
On a certain festival the court was assembled,
And Arthur himself turned quickly to the table,
And ordered all his knights to the table straightaway.
When all those knights were seated at their food
Then each was chatting to the other just as if he were his
      brother;
They were all seated around it and none was excluded;
11450 Every single kind of knight was very well placed there;
Each was seated equally, the important and the simple,
And no one there could boast about a different kind of toast
Than the drink of his companions who were sitting at the table.
     This was the very table which the Britons boast about,
And they tell many kinds of fiction about Arthur who was
      king,
But so does every man who has great love for another:
If he loves that man too much then he is bound to lie,
And in his fine praise he'll say more than he deserves;
However bad a man he is, his friend will back him up still;
11460 On the other hand if should arise in the community,
On any occasion between two individuals,
Lies will be invented about the one who isn't liked:
Even if he were the best man who ever ate bread at table
The man who found him hateful would invent some vices for

him:
It's not all true, it's not all false which poets are proclaiming,
But this is true fact about Arthur the king:
There has never been a king so valiant in everything;
It's found as fact in the annals just as it actually was,
From the start to the end, concerning Arthur the king,
11470 No more and no less, just as his deeds were recorded,
But the Britons loved him greatly and often lie about him
And recount many things about Arthur the king
Which never really happened in the whole of this world!
A man can say enough, if he just tells the truth,
Of outstanding things about Arthur the king.
    Arthur was then very great, his court very glorious,
So that no knight was valued nor his actions reckoned valiant,
– Not in Wales, nor in England, in Scotland nor in Ireland,
In Normandy nor in France, in Flanders nor in Denmark,
11480 Nor in any land whatever which lies on this side of the Alps –
No knight (as I said) would be thought good, nor his deeds
    reckoned bold
Unless, concerning Arthur and his outstanding court –
His weapons and his garments and also his war-mounts –
He was able to tell in song, about Arthur the young
And about his knightly courtiers and about their great prowess,
And about their magnificence and how well it suited them;
Then he would be welcome anywhere in this world's span,
Wherever he might come to, even if he were in Rome.
    All those who heard the stories told about Arthur
11490 Found accounts of the good king very extraordinary;
And so it had been prophesied before he was even born,
So the famous prophet Merlin had foretold about him,
Saying that a king would come from Uther Pendragon
Such that minstrels should make a board for food from the
    king's own breast
And at it would be seated really splendid poets,
Who would eat their fill before they fared away;
And they would draw draughts of wine from the king's tongue
And be drinking and delighting by day and by night;
This sport was to endure for them as long as this world lasts.
11500   In addition Merlin stated that more was to come:
That everything he looked at was to bow down at his feet;
In addition Merlin stated a marvel which was greater:
That there would be immoderate sorrow at this king's
    departure,

And as to this king's end – no Briton would believe it,
Unless one means the final death at the last great Judgment
When our Lord God is to judge all the nations;
Otherwise we can't determine as to Arthur's death
Because he himself said to his splendid Britons,
Down south in Cornwall where Gawain had been killed
11510 And he himself was badly wounded, grievously severely,
That he was to voyage into Avalon,
Into the island, to Argante the gracious,
Because with health-giving lotions she would heal his wounds,
And when he was entirely healed he would instantly come to
    them.
The Britons believ[e] this: that he will come like this,
And they are always looking for his coming to his land,
Just as he promised them before he went away.

ROBERT OF GLOUCESTER, Metrical Chronicle (c. 1270)

Robert of Gloucester's Chronicle, *written in the second half of the
thirteenth century, provides another English version of Geoffrey of
Monmouth's* History. *The following short extract gives a slightly
different account of Arthur's great Whitsun feast at Caerleon after
his conquest of France.*

3861 The king wan Normandye and also god Angeo.
And withinne a nye yer al this was ydo.   *done*
The king wende tho to Parys, tho he adde ydo al this.
And alle the heye men of the lond. Thuder come
        ywis.   *Thither, indeed*
Their omage of hom and hor servise he nom.   *took*
And lawes as he wolde in sulf sette in the kinedom.
He gef that lond of Normandye. Bedwer is boteler.   *his*
And that lond of Aungeo, Kaye is
        paneter.[26]   *pantler/master of the pantry*
And other king other heye men and syker it made   *true enough*
        ynou.
3870 And suththe aboute Leinte toward this londe drou.   *then*
Tho the King Arthure com here in to this londe.
And so moche lond adde ywonne, and adde al so an
        honde.   *hand*

In joye and blisse he was ynou, and all that with him were.
And agen Witesontyd. hit was in the yere.
He thoghte the heye feste of Wytesonetyd do.
With honour among is men, and that alle come therto.
Bothe kinges and dukes and erles echon. *everyone*
Barons and knightes and squiers monyon. *many a one*
Leuedies and maidens, and ech mon that
    aght were. *was of any rank*
3880 In eny lond that it was, that hii were alle there. *they*
Of this Rounde Table. is ban aboute he sende. *message*
That ech a Witesonetyd to Carleon wende.
A toun that is in Glammorgan. upe the water of Osk ydo.
A lute bisyde Severne in murye stude al so. *a pleasant location*
Vor me may there in the southhalf al bi the se lede.
Fram other londes god ynou, to endy such a dede. *relate*
In the other half beth grete wodes, lese and *were pastures,*
    mede al so. *meadows*
So that ther nas non defaute, such noble thing to do.
Ther come to this Rounde Table, as he sende is ban. *summons*
3890 Auncel King of Scotland, and also Uryan.
That was King of Murifens and King of Northwalis.
Cadwal and al so Scater, King of South Walis.
Cador King of Cornwayle, and erchbissopes also.
Of Londone and of Everwyk, and of Carleon ther to.
Erles ther come ek monion, as the erl of *also, many*
    Gloucestre.
Moroud and Ingemer, erl of Leicestre.
Mauron erl of Warewik and Cursal of Cicestre.
Gallut erl of Salesbury, Jonatal of Dercestre.
Kyninnar erl of Kanterburi, of Bathe Sir Urgen.
3900 Bose erl of Oxenford, that were alle noblemen.
The barons and knightes that of this londe a day,
At this Rounde Table were, noman telle ne may;
Kinges that were of yles, as King of Yrlonde,
Gillam and al so Malveys, King of Yslonde,
Lot King of Northwey, and Doldam of Godlonde,
And the King of Orcadas, and of Denemarch ich under stonde.
Kinges ek of by yonde se, as Kay of Aungeo.
Bedwer of Normandye. Gwider of Peyto.
Ligger of Coloyne and al so the dosse pers. *twelve companions*[27]
3910 Of France were ther echon. that so noble were and
    fers. *fierce*
His neveu King Howel. of the lasse Brutayne al so.

Mid so vair volc thuder com. and mid so gret charge ther
    to.   *folk*
Of mules and of cartes. and of hors mid alle gode.
That ther nas non so wyttimon that it al under stode.   *wise*
Ther nas bitwene this and Spayne no prince withoute al
    this.
That nas at this Rounde Table. and at is feste ywis.
And no wonder uor the kinges los. so wyde sprong
    ynou.   *for, renown*
Of godnesse and of cortesye, that hor herte to him drou.
Tho this hey men were alle ycome, and the heye tyme al so.
3920 Of the Wytesonetid. the feste uor to do.
The erchebissopes were ybroght to sette the kinges croune
On is heued; ac Sein Dubric of the sulve toune.   *head, but, same*
Was erchebissop him bivel the croune on him do.   *befell*
And the servise ek of holi chirche, that bivel ther to.
Tho the croune was on is heued, and ydo ech other thing.
Tueye erchebissopes ladde this noble king.   *two, led*
To the chirche of the heye munstre. and that yede bivore him
    there.   *went*
Four kinges and four suerdes of golde bivore him bere. *swords*
Verst the King of Scotland and the King of Northwalis.
3930 And the King of Cornwaile and the King of Southwalis.
Other bissopes and prelats bivore this King Arthure.
And clerkes songe as right was, that joye it was to hure.
In the other half the quene was of erchebissops al so.
Ylad and ycrouned ek. as right was vor to do.   *led*
And to another munstre ylad and vour quenes bivore hire
    wende.
The voure kinges wives. that we bivore nemde.   *mentioned*
And foure wite colfren. al so bivore hire bere.   *doves*
The compainye of leuedies. wel gret al so were.
Tho hii were to chirche ybroght. eyther in is side.
3940 So murye and so gret was that song that me song therinne
    wyde.
That thet folc stod that ther was. as hii were ynome.
Ne hii nuste to wether chirche. murgore it was to   *merrier*
    come.
The king was to is paleys. tho the servise was ydo.
Ylad with is meyne. and the quene to hire al so.   *retainers*
Vor hii hulde the olde usages. that men with men were.
Bi hom sulve and wymmen. bi hom sulve al so there.
Tho hii were echon yset. as it to hor stat bicom.

Kay King of Aungeo. a thousend knightes nom.   *took*
Of noble men. yclothed. in ermine echon.
3950 Of o sywte and servede. at this feste anon.
Bedwer the boteler. King of Normandye.
Nom al so in is alf. a uayr compaynie.   *fair*
Of o sywte vor to servi. of the botelerye.
Bivore the quene it was al so with a such corteisye.
Vor to telle al the nobleye. that ther was ydo.
They my tonge were of stel. me ssolde noght dure ther to.
Womman ne kepte. of no knight. as in druerye.   *love*
Bote he were in armes wel yproved. and atte leste thrie.
That made lo the wimmen. the chastore lif lede.
3960 And the knightes the stalwordore. and the betere in hor dede.
Sone after this noble mete. as right was in such tyde.
The knightes atyled hom aboute in eche syde.
In feldes and in medes to provy hor bachelerye.   *prowess*
Some with launce and some with suerd. withoute vileynie.
With pleyn de atte tables. other atte chekere.   *dice*
With castinge other with sssetinge, other in som manere.
And woch so of eny game. adde the maistrie.   *did best*
The king hom of is giftes dude large corteysie.
Upe the alvres of the castles. the leuedyes thanne   *battlements*
     stode.
3970 And bihulde this noble game. and wuche knightes were gode.
All the thre nexte dawes. laste this nobleye.   *days*
In halles and in veldes. of mete and eke of pleye.   *also*
This men come the verthe day. bivore the kinge there.   *fourth*
And he gif hom large giftes. evere as hii worthe were.

Robert of Gloucester provides an interesting reference to the dis-
covery of Arthur's tomb, which may shed light on other material
about the request of a monk for burial at Glastonbury being the
cause of the discovery.

Vorte the Yonge king Henri. deide attelaste.   *therefore*
A sein Barnabes day. & as it wolde be.   *on*
Endleue hundred yer of grace. & eighteti & thre.   *eleven*
In Normandye he deyde. & thulke yer also.   *the same*
Seint Egwine at Evesham. in ssrine was verst ido.   *buried*
Glastinguri was ther after. and to ther ibroght to grounde.
Vorbarnd & of king Arthure. the bonres verst ifounde.   *first*

ROBERT MANNYNG OF BRUNNE, Chronicle (1338)

Mannyng's Chronicle is a closer rendering of Wace's Brut into English than Lawman's version, although there is a certain element of originality in Mannyng's work. The first extract relates how Arthur becomes king after the death of his father, Uther, and Mannyng transfers the place of coronation to Cirencester. Mannyng's choice of language gives the passage a chivalric tone not present in Geoffrey's original version, and he describes Arthur's good qualities in some detail.

Arthur, son of Uther, is made king and crowned at Cirencester

9735	The Erchebishop his conseil held	
	Of erles, barons, and knyghtes of scheld;	
	Ilkon after other sent	*each one*
	To come to comune Parlement,	
	And after sire Uteres sone Arthorghe	*Arthur*
9740	To come to Circestre, the noble burghe;	*town*
	And there bitaught hym the coroun,	*he received*
	Thorow comun graunt of ilka baroun.	*every*
	Fful yonge then was he, lond to welde;	*very, to rule*
	Ffyftene yer than was his elde;	*age*
	At Circestre that tyme thar	
	Was first tyme that he croune bar;	*wore*
	Some of his thewes y wil descrye;	*manners*
	I trowe y schal nought mykel lye:	*much*
	Craftily dide he mannes dedes,	*skilfully*
9750	Doughtiest knyght at alle nedes;	
	Than of myrthe most was in halle,	
	Glad-chered, lovely, and lordlyest of alle;	
	Ageyn the proude, proud herted was he;	*towards*
	Ageyn the meke, debonere and ese;	*lenient*
	The hardiest man hym self to fende,	
	Blethely gaf, largely wold spende;	*gave cheerful*
	That nedful was, and him bysought,	
	That he myghte, he werned him nought;	*drove off*
	Mykel loved he joie and worthly thynge,	*much*
9760	Doughti dedes made of menyng;[28]	
	Nobliche his court he ledde,	
	Richely alle hyse he fedde;	*his followers*
	Ilka day come tydynges newe;	*every*

Gestes of joye, wyth knyghtes trewe;   *deeds*
Over alle prynces the pris he nam   *won*
Of curteseye and of wysdam;
Was no kyng so noble of thewes,
As men reden of hym, and schewes.   *read*

*In this second extract, Mannyng describes the magnificence of
Arthur's court, to which all men of honour flock, during Arthur's
twelve years of peace. He then goes on to talk about the various
stories which have been written about Arthur, which he considers
are of some value even if they are not entirely truthful. He laments
that Arthur is written about more in other countries, especially
France, than in England.*

The Splendour of Arthur's Court

10543 What knyght has ben in al the werld,
       Had his los be nevere so wel byherd,   *renown, known*
       Were he ffrenche, were he Bretoun,
       Normaund, fflemyng, or Burgoiloun,
       Spaynard, Gascoyn, or Angevyn,
       Scot, Irische, Pykard, or Peytevyn,
       Daneys, Norneys, or Selander,
10550 Henner, ffryson, or Katelaner,
       Arragoneys, Lombard, or Brabaunt,
       Provyncial, Naverner, or Alemaunt,
       Of wham he held his fe, or how,
       ffro the Weste or Est until Moungow,
       He was told of non honour   *considered*
       Bot he had ben wyth kyng Arthour,
       And hadde taken of his livere,
       Cloth or queyntise, that knowe myght be.   *finery*
       Of ferne landes many on nanem,   *distant, took*
10560 And til that court for worschyp camen,   *to*
       To lere honur and curtesy,   *learn*
       And here the prowesse of knyghtes hardy,
       And to here the faire gestes
       That knyghtes broughte and telde at festes.
       Somme come to se his faire wonyng,   *dwelling*
       And se and here there selcouth thynge;   *marvellous*
       Pouere men, they lovede hym alle,
       And rich honured hym in halle;

ffele kynges of ferne stede   *many, place*
10570 Sent hym gyftes for doute and drede;
They wyst hit wel, yf they wold ryde,
His werre durste no kyng abide;
Kynges aforced ther casteles aboute,   *fortified*
ffor alle landes of hym hadde doute,
That yf he come, he scholde them lese,   *lose*
Or gyve hym truwage as he wold chese;   *homage*
ther-fore ilkon at there myght   *each one*
Aforced ther cites, and well theym dight.   *prepared*
But in thyse twelf yeres tyme
10580 ffel auentures that men rede in ryme;
In that tyme were herd and sen
That somme seye, that nevere hath ben.
Of Arthur ys seid many selcouth   *marvels*
In diverse landes northe and south
That men holdeth now for fable,
Be they nevere so trew ne stable.
Al ys nought soth, ne nought al lye,   *true*
Ne al wysdam, ne al folye;
Ther nys no thyng of hym seyd   *is no*
10590 That hit ne may be to godnesse leyd.   *it, put*
More than othere were his dedes,
That men of him so mykel redes;   *much*
Ne were his dedes hadde be writen,
Of hym no thyng men scholde haue wyten.   *known*
Geffrey Arthur of Monemu,   *Monmouth*
He wrot his dedes that were of pru,   *prowess*
And blamed bothe Gyldas and Bede,
Why they wolde nought of him rede,   *write*
Syn he bar the pris of all Cristen kynges,
10600 And write so litel of his preysynges,
And more worschip of hym spoke ther was
That of any of tho that spekes Gildas,
Or of any that Bede wrot,
Save holy men that we wot.   *know*
In alle landes wrot men of Arthur,
Hys noble dedes of honur:
In ffraunce, men wrot, and yit men wryte,
But herd have we of hym but lyte;   *little*
There-fore of hym more men fynde
10610 In farre bokes, als ys kynde,   *natural*
Than we have in thys lond:

That we have, ther men hit fond;
Til Domesday men schalle spelle, *write stories*
And of Arthures dedes talke and telle.

The third passage from Mannyng's Chronicle *describes Arthur's dream and his single combat against the giant of St Michael's Mount. This material is also derived from Geoffrey of Monmouth's* History,[29] *although in Mannyng's version, Mordred already is having a secret affair with the queen before Arthur's departure.*

Concerning Gawain's Brother Mordred, the Traitor

12033 Sir Arthur hadde a cosyn,
  Moddred he highte, a traitur fyn; *was called, absolute*
  A noble knyght he was in stour *battle*
  But til his eme he was a traytour. *to, uncle*
  Arthur bitaughtym his lond to kepe; – *entrusted to him*
  Hym hadde ben bettere have leid to slepe;
  ffor he had loved the quene prively,
12040 Arthures wyf, and leyn hure by;
  Nought was perceyved bytwyxte hem to: *the two of them*
  Who schuld have trowed hit had be so? *believed*
  Who wold have went so synful lyf *imagined*
  That the cosyn had leyn by the emes wyf?
  And namely of swylk a man? *such*
  Thorow al the werld his los of ran. *reputation was known*
  Arthur bitaught hym Genevere the quen, *entrusted*
  (Alas that evere hit scholde so ben!)
  And al the lond save the coroune,
12050 And schop his host to Southaumptoune, *brought*
  Ther schipes y the haven ryden, *in*
  That Arthur and his folk abiden.
  Ther myghte men se the mariners,
  Many wyght man in schipes fers, *nimble, bold*
  Ropes to righte, lynes to leye,
  By banke and brymme to tache and teye,[30]
  Cables to knytte aboute the mast,
  The sail on yerde they feste ful fast, *fasten*
  Ancres, ores, redy to hande,
12060 Rotheres, helmes, right for to stande,
  Bowlyne on bouspret to sette and hale,[31]
  Cordes, kyuiles, atached the wale;[32] *keels*

When al was redy in god point,
Unto the lond the schipes joynt;   *together*
Somme stode in schipe, somme on sand,
Brygges and plankes they caste to land,
Wyth men and hors for to charge[33]
Cogges, barges, and schipes large;
Brought yn helmes, hauberks and scheldes,
12070 And al that men yn bataille weldes,   *uses*
Hors in to drawe, hors in to dryve;
Men hyed ther-after yn ful blyve.   *hurried, glad*
When alle were inne, and mad al yare,   *all made ready*
And they on ther weye schulde fare,
To theym on land they preieden eft   *bid again*
To grete ther frendes that they had lefte:
On bothe parties was hevy chere
[Whan frendes departed leve and dere.]   *cherished*
When alle were ynne, and were o flote,
12080 Mariners dighte them to note,   *prepared*
Ther takel for to righte and taille,   *tally*
By the wynd wel for to saylle;
Ancres o bord, sayl drowen heye,   *hoist*
The wynd blew wel, ther schipe gon fleye,
And the mariners that weren sleye,   *clever*
Ilkon dide ther maistrie: *each one, work*
Somme aforced the wyndas,   *windlass*
Somme the loof, somme the bytas;   *cords*
The mayster mariner was byhynde,
12090 The schip to stere by the wynde.
(Queynte he was, and right hardy,   *strange*
And engynous man and sley,   *ingenious, clever*
That first fond schip on se to fare,   *sail*
And turnde wyth the wynd ther he nyste whare,
Lond to seke that he saw nought,
Ne whiderward he schulde be brought.)   *whither*

Arthur's Dream

Sir Arthur hadde weder at wille,   *fair weather*
Saflyk he seyled, wythouten ylle;   *safely*
Hys folk was joiful and gladly let,
12100 ffor theire pathe fare to Bareflet.
Atte midnyght men gaf god kep,   *bid good night*
Arthur fel on slomber and slep;

In his slepying als he gan lye,   *as, lay*
Hym thoughte he sey a Bere flye   *saw*
An hugely gret, a lothly best,   *extremely huge*
And fley faste towardes the est.
O that other syde a Dragon up stey;   *start*
In to the west hym thoughte he fley;
Of his mouth a flaume cam out,
12110 The lond, the water, schon al about.
The bere assailled the dragoun,
And he defended hym as a lyoun;
Wonderly ilk other gan assaille,   *each*
And strong was thanne the bataille;
Scharply ther ilk other smot,
Bitterly bothe they blewe and bot.   *bit*
The dragon was swyft, and sleyly swypte,
The bere in his clawes he clypte,   *caught*
And thriste hym so that he to-barst,   *burst*
12120 And doun unto the erthe hym cast.
Arthur of his slepying wok,
Gret tent of his drem he tok;   *anxiety*
He askede clerkes sete hym aboute,
Whether hit mente drede or doute: *uncertainty/danger*
'Y wolde wyt what hit wolde mene,
And whether hit tokned joye or tene,   *signified, trouble*
And whether hit was help or dere,   *good or bad*
That the dragoun slow the bere.'

Interpretation of Arthur's Dream

Somme ther were thus hit descried,
12130 Hym self the dragon signefied,
And the bere som geaunt
That he schuld make recreaunt,   *admit defeat*
ffro fer schold come, and do gret wo,
And thorow force he schulde hym slo.
Somme other weys gan hit rede,   *interpret*
But alle they seyde he schulde wel spede;
Then seide hym self, 'y trowe hit menes
This werre, and manye other tenes   *difficulties*
Bytwyxt me and the Emperour.'
12140 Let God al worthe, my creatour!'
At that word the day gan sprynge,
The sonne ros faire y the mornynge,

And at the sonne rysyng in god tyme
They come to Bareflete er pryme.   *before 6 a.m.*
ffro schip to londe ful sone they yede,   *went*
And in the contre aboute gon sprede;
He seide he wolde his folk abyde
Tho that were nought come that tyde.
Longe while dwelled he nought,
12150 That tydynges men hym brought,
That thider was comen a geaunt,
And longe ther hadde ben his haunt;
Out of Spayne was he comen,
And had Sir Oheles nece y-nomen;   *seized*
Mayde Eleyne was hure name,
He had hure taken to do hure schame,
And had hure brought unto an hil,
That non ne myghte ne durste com til. –   *approach*
Micheles Mount men calles hit now,
12160 There the geaunt Eleyne slow;
Was ther non auter ne no chapel   *altar*
That ilke tyme that his chaunce fel;   *same*
Aboute that hil the water flowes,
Cometh ther non that he ne rowes. –   *rues/regrets*
Ther was non that hadde that myght
That wyth the geaunt durst ones fight;   *once*
Somme ther were umwhile wylde fonde,   *had tried before*
And hym assailled by water and londe,
But he gaf nought of their assaut,   *thought nothing*
12170 ffor they fulle evere in their defaut;   *always failed*
ffor grete roches at them he cast,
And ther schipes to-rof and brast.   *smashed, broke*
Many were drenkled, fele were slayn,   *drowned, many*
Tho that ascaped, hit was wyth payn;   *difficulty*
Ther-fore the contre was ner al fled,
Their wonyng fursoke, their godes led,   *dwellings, left*
And lefte that lond wast and wylde,
ffor man or best, wyf or childe.
The geauntes name was Dynabrok,
12180 A grysly man was on to loke.

The Giant Dynabrok

When Arthur hadde herd the pleynt,	*lament*
How wyth the geaunt the folk was teynt,	*by, beset*
He calde sire Caye and Bedver,	
And ilk of theym tok a squyer;	*each*
Armure dide they with them lede,	*bring*
And ilk of theym tok hym a stede.	
He nolde schewe hit to namo	*did not inform anyone else*
That he wolde to the geaunt go;	
If all had wyst he went so one,	*alone*
12190 The ost had ben abaischt ilkone;	*army, ashamed*
He tristed wel in Godes grace	
That he durste him schewe his face,	
And on his grete vaillauntise	*valour*
Ar he durst take that emprise.	*before, enterprise*
Al that ilke night they ryden,	
That they no whar stynte ne biden,	*stopped or delayed*
Til hit was y the morne tyde	*in*
That they seye wel there bysyde	*saw*
A bot standynge at a stage;	*boat, quay*
12200 Then hoped they there was the passage.	
Two hilles wythynne the water wore,	
That on was lasse, that other more;	
O the more hil ther was a fyr,	
ffo ferre they sey hit brenne schir;	*far, saw, bright*
The lasse hil was nought so drey	
ffro the more, but evene ney;	
An other fir was on that hil;	
Ther-fore Arthur was al wyl	*uncertain*
On whilk hil the geaunt was,	*which*
12210 Ne non couthe kenne hym the righte pas.	*know*
Then bad he sir Beduer 'go	*bade/told*
To serche the hilles to and fro;	
And when thou wost the certeyn	*knows*
Hye the thanne to me ageyn.'	*hasten*

Thenne Bedver dide hym in the bot,	*got in*
And on the nexte hil he smot.	*landed*
Bedver stod, and hym avysed	*he considered*
Whider-ward the weyes wysed;	*which way to go*
The nexte wey he tok vp hey,	*high*
12220 And als he wente he herde a cry;	

Gret pleynte he herde on make;   *someone*
A party gan his herte quake;   *a little*
He wende hit hadde the geaunt ben,
That his comyng had wist or sen;
He drow hys swerd al so smert,   *quickly*
And gadered hardinesse of hert,
And thought that if he wyth hym mette,
Wyth hym to fighte he wolde nought lette.
But al that thenkyng was in vayn,
12230 ffor on the hil above the playn
He fond a fir brennyng an hy,   *burning on high*
And a toumbe newe ther-by;
Als he bar his swerd in hande,
By the toumbe he sey on sittande,   *saw, someone*
A womman, ner al naked,
About hure hed hure her to-schaked;   *hair, tangled*
Biside the toumbe this womman lay,
And often cried 'wey la way!'   *alas*
And mente the vilenye and the peyne,
12240 And seide, 'alas for the, Eleyne!'

About Elaine's Tomb, and Her Nurse

Bedver sey the toumbe was newe,
And of hure deol his herte gan rewe.   *grief, take pity*
When scheo perceyved sire Bedver,
Scheo saide, 'cheytyf, what wiltow her?[34]   *wretched fellow*
Som synne hath the hyder y-brought,
That thy deth her hastow sought;   *here, you have*
This day ys the schape to deye,   *appointed*
If the geaunt the se wyth eye.
This ilke hil swythe thou weyve,   *quickly, leave*
12250 So that he the nought perceyve.'
'Wyf' he seide, 'for charite,   *woman*
Let thy gretyng, and spek wyth me,   *lamenting*
And sey me what thou art, and why   *tell, who*
Thou wepest here so delfully,   *dejectedly*
And ho ys leyd here on this grave;   *who*
And sey me soth, so God the save!'   *tell me truthfully*
'I am,' scheo seyde, 'a wo-bygon,   *wretched*
An helples thyng, a waryed on,   *cursed being*
And grete for a maydens myshap   *grieve*
12260 That whilom y norisched at my pap,   *once*

And souke y gaf hure of my brest;
And this ys hure toumbe that thou sest;
Eleyne scheo highte, Oheles nece,   *was called*
Of flesche was non so fair a pece.
To norische sche was me taught,
Alas the while y evere hure aught!³⁵
So cam this fend to thys contre,
And tok bothe Eleyne and me,
And broughte us here unto this hyl,
12270 So that no man dar come us tyl.   *approach us*
Eleyne he wolde have furlayn,   *ravished*
But sche ne myghte nought wyth that payn;
He was so huge, ouer mesure,
And scheo so yong, that myght nought dure.   *endure*
Thorow gret destresse hire herte brast,
In his armes scheo yald the gast,   *gave up the ghost*
And yn thys toumbe y have hure leyd;
And thus hit was als y have seid.'
Then seid he, 'wherto dwellest thou here,   *why*
12280 Sythen sche ys ded that was the dere?'   *since*
'Sire,' scheo seyde, 'y wil the telle
If thou durstest so longe dwelle.
Sire, for y the se of body avenaunt,   *graceful*
And gentil man by thi semblaunt,   *appearance*
When y sey Eleyne so schamely deye,   *saw*
My wit was lorn, and al aweye;   *lost*
Wyth force he dide me leve stille,   *remain*
His lecherie in me to fulfille,
Om God hym selve y take witnes,
12290 That al maugre myn hit es!³⁶
And ilka tyme that y him se,   *every*
Y wilde be sonken, for y ne may fle;³⁷
And y trowe he cometh right sone,   *believe*
His lecherie wyth me to done
Y telle the ded, if thou here bydes,   *you are dead*
No thyng ne saveth the, ne hides;
Swythe thou fle, y gyve the red,   *quickly, advise you*
Y wolde nought thou were so ded.
Yonder ys he, y schal the kenne,   *inform*
12300 On yone hil ther thou sest brenne;
Sone to come his tyme schal be,
Ther-fore, sir knyght, y rede thou fle,
And let me have my self my sorewe,

My will ys to be ded to morewe.'
Of hure wo sore hym over thought;
But he ne wiste what hure dought,   *did not know, do for her*
Ne to make long dwellyng.
He turned ageyn unto the kynge;
And als scheo seide, so he hym tolde,
12310 How Eleyne deyde, and scheo in holde,
And he scholde fynde the geaunt
Y the more hil, ther was his haunt;   *on, bigger*
'Out of that stede the smoke cam fro,   *place*
We may hym fynde if that we go.'
ffor Eleyne had Arthur sorewe ynow,
And abod til the flod wyth-drow.   *waited*
Until the ebbe a stounde they bod,   *while, waited*
With ther hors then over they rod,
And wenten bote a softe pas   *at a quiet pace*
12320 Tyl thei perceived wher he was.
Their stedes and ther palfreys
Their squiers helde, with other harneys;
But sir Bedver and sir Kay
Yede with Arthur up the way.   *went*
Arthur seide, 'y wil prove my might,
With the geaunt alone to fight;
Hold yow here byhynde a lyte;   *little*
Alone on hym wil y first smite;
While y may my selve save,
12330 Other help wil y non have;
Me thynketh hit were no vasselage,   *prowess*
Thre til on, hit were outrage!   *against one*
Nere the les, if that ye se nede,
Bettere ys help than over drede;
ffor men seye hit ys folye
In strengthe to mikel for to affye.'   *too much, trust*
They seide, 'for prowesse ne for yelp,   *boast*
Yf hit were ned, they wolde hym help.'

Arthur kills the Giant Dynabrok

Arthur alone the hil he tok
12340 Unto the geaunt Dynabrok.
By a mykel fir he sat,   *great*
Rostyng a swyn gret and fat,
And other flesche biside was sode;   *boiled*

His bryn, his berd, ther-with al lothen, *eyebrows, hideous*
And al to-soiled wyth the spyk: *fat*
I trowe that syght was ful lothlyk;
But Arthur thoughte to have the grace
To smyte er he tok his mace. *before*
When the geaunt of him was war, *aware*
12350 fferly he hadde how he cam thar, *he was amazed*
And stirte up thenne al o glyft, *in a hurry*
His grete mace for to lyft;
But Arthur avised hym wel ynow; *prepared himself*
Als he hys mace upward drow,
Arthur bar on hym wyth his launce
To combren hym, als of chaunce; *impede*
Longe they foughte, a wel god while,
But Arthur couthe mykel of gyle; *knew a lot of tricks*
Nere sleighte and queyntise hadde ben, and gile,[38]
12360 Somme had be combred ther in a whyle;
ffor kyng Arthur nevere er was
Bystad in so hard a cas. *beset*
Dynabrok ageyn hym stod
Wyth his mace, as geaunt wod, *mad*
ffor thre men, wythoute the forthe,
Schuld nought haue stired his mace from erthe;
He sey wel how he made his mynt, *mark*
And with his mace he teysed his dynt; *aimed, blow*
He wiste the strok schulde be gret; *believed*
12370 Under his scheld al he schet, *sheltered*
And ageyn his strok hit held.
Then smot the geaunt on his scheld,
And wyth that dynt so hevy and stronge
The hilles alle aboute ronge,
And al that was ther-inne, hit schok
When Arthur that dynt so huge tok.
Arthur was stoneyd, stakered, and stynt, *stunned, staggered*
But yut fel he nought for that dynt.
Another strok wold he nought byde,
12380 But peyned him to smyte a syde
With his swerd Caliborne;
Scharply he gan hym torne;
That swerd he lifte wel on hey, *high*
And valede his scheld a party; *lowered, a little*
Endlong his forehed he hym smot, *across*
The swerd bot wel, and he was hot *bit*

And entamed both his bryn *opened, brows*
That al the skyn heng over hys eyn.
Wyth that strok he hadde ben slayn:
12390 His mace he held wel ther agayn,
And his heued a party glent, *head, glancing blow*
That som of the strok hit hent; *took*
Netheles, wel was hit set;
The blod al over his eyen hit schet; *covered*
Then lost he ther al his sight,
Then wax he woder for to fyght, *grew, angrier*
Then was he woder then he was or, *before*
ffightyng als a wylde bor,
The same weys so dide he;
12400 When he sey that he myghte nought se,
He ne lefte for swerd ne other hirt
That he until Arthur stirt; *against, rushed*
Aboute his middel his armes he leyd,
And on Arthur so sore he breyd, *grasped*
On heighte he lifte hym four fet;
And als he there hym doun let,
Vpon his knees he hym kast. *threw*
Then Arthur proved his force fast,
Our lady hym halp, his wille was god,
12410 Wyth force he ros, and he up stod;
And Arthur was algate queynte, *always skilful*
And his wille was nevere feynte;
On that syde he bar his scheld,
And the geaunt nought ne held,
Wyth that he wroth, and turnde his syde,
And dide his armes opene wyde.
When he hym self was fro hym broken,
And that his body was nought loken, *held*
fful lyght hym thoughte that he was oute; *relieved*
12420 With Caliborne then ran he aboute,
And evere on the geaunt smot,
And Caliborne sore upon hym bot. *cut*
The geaunt glente hider and tyder, *glanced*
The blod so blent him, he nyst whider; *did not know where*
He groped aboute hym for to hent, *seize*
And Arthur aboute hym evere went,
And smot hym sore woundes fel, *many*
Nought of hym ne wold he spele; *spare*
And at a turn the geaunt stynt, *stopped*

12430 Arthur gaf hym so gret a dynt
    O the hed, that in to the nekke hit dref,   *cut*
    And in to the schuldres the panne he clef;   *head*
    Yyt he after Arthur raught, –
    Arthur wyth-drow his swerd a draught, –
    That he stombled, and gaf a cry,
    A dredful and a lothly;
    When he fel, he gaf a lasche
    As wyth a blast had falle an asche;   *ash tree*
    And for that fal Arthur low,   *laughed*
12440 He was venged hym thoughte y-now;
    ffro ferre he stod, and loked on hym,
    And seyde he was a geaunt grym;
    He bad Badver he schulde go   *bade*
    To smyte the heued the body fro,   *head*
    And bytake hit a squier   *give*
    To schewe hit al the host plener.   *to the whole host*

Here Arthur Told Bedver and Kay About the Giant Ryton

    Then telde Arthur to Bedver and Kay,
    That he nadde nevere such affray,   *fight*
    Of no geaunt but of on,
12450 And that geaunt highte Ryton;   *was called*
    fful manye kynges had he don slo,
    And flow the berdes of alle tho;
    Til a pane, as a furour, he did hem tewe;[39]
    Loke if Ryton were nought a schrewe!   *rascal*
    That geaunt Riton sende his sonde   *message*
    Til Arthur fro ferne londe,   *distant*
    And seide he scholde make hym a-ferd
    But he flowe of his owen berd   *cut off*
    And sent hit hym until his pane,   *for his cloak*
12460 To menske hit ther hit was wane;   *honour*
    And if he sent hit hym blethely,   *willingly*
    He schulde set hit most worschipfuly,
    ffor he wolde urle his pane wyth-al
    Aboute with a ffylet smal;
    And if Arthur wylde nought   *would not*
    Do als Ryton hym bisought,
    Greythe hym as sone as he myght,   *prepare*
    ffor Ryton wolde wyth hym fight;
    And whilk of them might other slo,   *which*

12470 His berd he scholde don of flo,   *flay*
       And have the pane ilka del,   *whole cloak*
       Ther-wyth aboute vrle hit wel.
       Arthur then til Ryton went,
       In bataille he slow hym and schent,   *overcome*
       And wan the pane and his berd;
       On the mount Derane he was conquerd.
       Sithen fond Arthur nevere non   *since*
       But Dynabrok, as was Ryton,
       That nevere dide til hym in dede,
12480 That he had of so mykel drede.   *great dread*
       Ther they hym slowe, ther they hym leued,
       And Bedver tok a squier the heved,   *head*
       To bere and schewe the host aboute,
       Wher that they were, and in what doute.   *concern*
       Sir Ohel ful sore byment   *lamented*
       That his nece was so schent;   *lost*
       A fair chapel for hure dide make,
       Of oure lady, for Eleynes sake.
       Sithen that tyme scheo was ther leyd,
12490 ffor Eleyne, Eleynes toumbe ys seid;
       And so men han cald hit ay   *always*
       Eleynes toumbe unto thys day.

The Alliterative Morte Arthure *(c. 1365–1400)*

This work is found only on the Thornton Manuscript, a miscellany of many poems, including The Parlement of the Thre Ages *and several Arthurian works:* The Anturs of Arther *and unique texts of both* Percyvell of Gales *and the alliterative* Morte Arthure.

The manuscript, which dates c. 1440, was compiled by Robert Thornton and once belonged to Lincoln cathedral. The date of the poem has been a matter of some dispute, with Benson's proposal of a date c. 1400 being accepted by Mary Hamel in her edition of the poem, but rejected by Juliet Vale who considers that the poem was written during 'the middle years of the fourteenth century'.[40]

Since Edward III endeavoured to emulate Arthur, some critics have associated the alliterative Morte Arthure *with Edward's French campaigns,*[41] *a viewpoint which is questioned by others.*[42] *Hamel's critical edition of the poem provides a detailed analysis of* the poet's selective use of his 'Chronicle' sources, which she considers to be Geoffrey of Monmouth, Wace, Lawman and Robert Mannyng.[43] While it might appear improbable that the poet knew Lawman's rather obscure work, there is, however, a single factor apparently unobserved by critics, which provides a possible association between the two poems: both works depict Arthur actually dining at the Round Table, a practice absent from other French and English Arthurian literature, although present in German works.

In subject matter, the alliterative Morte Arthure omits the early part of Arthur's career, covering only the latter part of his reign from the Carlisle feast. While retaining the basic structural framework of Arthur's fight with the giant, his war against the Roman emperor, and his death at the hands of his treacherous nephew Mordred, the poet's selectivity and his choice of additional material indicate more than poetic embroidery and are of vital importance for assessing the figure of Arthur in the poem as a whole.

Arthur is clearly the centre of attention in the poet's chronicle sources, but it is significant that, although he plays a prominent part in the alliterative Morte Arthure, it is the Round Table knights whose deeds of arms have won him glory. It is their prowess, and perhaps rashness (notably that of their most prominent members, Gawain and Cador), rather than Arthur's leadership, that contributes to military success. Arthur readily acknowledges this himself in the baronial council convened to debate the emperor's message (ll. 399–402).

Both Finlayson and Hamel see a deterioration in Arthur's character during the course of the poem, which they believe becomes evident at the point when he decides to invade Lorraine and Lombardy.[44] However, it is clear from Arthur's vow (ll. 349–54) and from his reply to the Romans (ll. 429–31) that right from the beginning he has every intention of subduing both regions entirely to his will. In fact, there is little evidence to support the view that Arthur's character is corrupted by power and success after his defeat of Lucius, particularly since the opening section of the poem reveals the unjust nature of his earlier victories.[45]

The first extract is taken from the opening scene of the poem, which provides a list of Arthur's conquests before introducing the New Year's challenge of the Roman senator and the reaction of Arthur and his followers. The vows made by Arthur's followers in the council meeting, not found elsewhere, are perhaps similar to those attributed to Edward III and his followers in a rather obscure poem called The Vows of the Heron,[46] said to refer to promises

*made to take part in Edward's invasion of France, which led to the
victories of Crecy and Poitiers.*

26 When that the King Arthur by conquest had wonnen   *won*
    Casteles and kingdomes and countrees many,   *countries*
    And he had covered the crown of that kith
        riche   *recovered, country*
    Of all that Uter in erthe ought in his time: *earth, owned*
30 Argayle and Orkney and all these oute-iles   *outer-isles*
    Ireland utterly, as Ocean runnes,   *entirely, where the*
    Scathel Scotland by skill he skiftes as him likes
    And Wales of war he won at his will,   *by, to*
    Bothe Flaunders and Fraunce free til himselven,   *to*
    Holland and Hainault they held of him bothen,   *both*
    Burgoigne and Brabaunt and Bretain the less,
    Guienne and Gothland and Greece the rich,
    Bayonne and Bourdeaux he belded full fair,   *dwelt in*
    Touraine and Toulouse with towres full high,   *towers*
40 Of Poitiers and Provence he was prince holden;
    Of Valence and Vienne, of value so noble,
    Of Overgne and Anjou, those erldoms rich,   *Auvergne, earldoms*
    By conquest full cruel they knew him for lord   *acknowledged*
    Of Navarre and Norway and Normandy eek   *also*
    Of Almaine, of Estriche, and other ynow;
    Denmark he dressed all by drede of himselven   *directed, dread*
    Fro Swynne unto Swetherwike, with his sword keen!

    When he these deedes had done, he dubbed his knightes,
    Devised ducheries and delt in diverse rewmes,
50 Made of his cosins kinges annointed   *relatives*
    In kithes there they covet crownes to bere.   *countries, where, bear*
    When he these rewmes had ridden and rewled the
        pople,   *realms, ruled, people*
    Then rested that real and held the Round Table;   *royal (one)*
    Sujourns that seson to solace himselven   *sojourns, season, please*

²⁹ [Uter: Uther Pendragon, Arthur's father.]
³² Harmful Scotland he skilfully rules as it pleases him. [Scotland and England were often
   at war in the fourteenth century; hence 'harmful' Scotland.]
³⁶ Burgundy, Brabant, and Little Britain (i.e. Brittainy). [All areas of what is now France.]
⁴⁵ Of Germany, of Austria, and many others.
⁴⁷ From Swynn (an arm of the North Sea near Zeeland) to Sweden (Swetherwike); i.e.
   the whole extent of Denmark.
⁴⁹ Created and gave out dukedoms in diverse realms.

In Bretain the brodder, as him best likes; *pleases*
Sithen went into Wales with his wyes all, *then, men*
Sways into Swaldie with his snell houndes *swift*
For to hunt at the hartes in those high landes,
In Glamorgan with glee there gladship was
    ever, *where, gladness*
60 And there a citee he set, by assent of his lordes *city*
That Caerlion was called, with curious walles, *skilfully made*
On the rich river that runnes so fair,
There he might semble his sorte to see when him liked.
Then after at Carlisle a Christenmass he holdes, *Christmas*
This ilk kidd conquerour and held him for lord *same, famous*
With dukes and douspeeres of diverse rewmes, *realms*
Erles and erchevesques and other ynow,
Bishoppes and bachelers and bannerettes noble
That bowes to his banner, busk when him
    likes *go, it pleases him*
70 But on the Christenmass-day when they were all *assembled*
    sembled,
That comlich conquerour commaundes himselven *comely*
That ilk a lord sholde lenge and no leve
    take *each, should, remain, leave*
To the tende day fully were taken to the end. *tenth*
Thus on real array he held his Round Table *royal*
With semblaunt and solace and selcouthe *splendour, rare foods*
    metes;
Was never such noblay in no mannes time *nobleness*
Made in mid-winter in tho West Marches! *those*

    But on the New-Yere day, at the noon
      even, *New Year's, exactly*
    As the bold at the borde was of bred served,
80 So come in sodenly a senatour of Rome, *suddenly*

---

55 In Britain the broader (i.e. Great Britain).
63 Where he might assemble his troop to see when it pleased him.
66 [*Douspeeres*: originally Charlemagne's twelve peers, but here simply 'high noblemen'.]
67 Earls and archbishops and many others.
68 Bishops and young knights (*bachelors*) and noble senior knights (*bannerets*). [A banneret was a knight entitled to bear his own banner; a bachelor ranked somewhat lower and was either a newly made knight or a young man about to be knighted.]
77 [West Marches: the countries bordering on Wales.]
79 As the bold men at the table were served with bread. The bread is the first course (since the other food was heaped upon it), and the first course is the traditional time for the arrival of a messenger.

With sixteen knightes in a suite, sewand him
    one;   *company, following, alone*
He salued the soveraign and the sale after   *saluted, hall*
Ilk a king after king, and made his inclines;   *each, bows*
Gaynor in her degree he grette as him
    liked   *greeted, it pleased him*
And sinn again to the gome he gave up his needes:
'Sir Lucius Iberius, the Emperour of Rome,
Salues thee as subjet, under his sele rich;   *salutes, subject, seal*
It is credans, Sir King, with cruel wordes;   *credentials*
Trow it for no troufles, his targe is to shew!
90   Now in this New-Yeres Day, with notaries sign,
I make thee summons in sale to sew for thy
    landes,   *hall, plead*
That on Lamass Day there be no let
    founden   *August 1, hindrance, found*
That thou be redy at Rome with all thy Round Table   *ready*
Appere in his presence with thy pris knightes   *appear, excellent*
At prime of the day, in pain of your lives,   *first hour, on*
In the kidd Capitoil before the king selven   *famous, himself*
When he and his senatours bes set as them
    likes,   *are, it pleases them*
To answer only why thou occupies the landes   *alone*
That owe homage of old til him and his elders,   *to*
100   Why thou has ridden and raimed and ransound the
    pople   *robbed, ransomed*
And killed down his cosins, kinges annointed;   *kinsmen*
There shall thou give reckoning for all thy Round Table,
Why thou art rebel to Rome and rentes them   *revenue*
    with-holdes!
Yif thou these summons withsit, he sendes thee these
    wordes: *if, resist*
He shall thee seek over the se, with sixteen kinges,   *sea*
Brin Bretain the brode and britten thy knightes
And bring thee buxomly as a beste with brethe where him likes,
That thou ne shall route ne rest under the heven rich
Though thou for reddour of Rome run to the erthe!

---

[85] And then (he bowed) again to the man (Arthur) and delivered his message.
[89] Think it not a trifle, his shield (armorial device) is to be seen (hereon).
[106-9] Burn Britain the broad (Great Britain) and beat down your knights; And with anger bring you compliantly as a beast where he pleases; And you shall not sleep nor rest under the rich heaven, though for fear of Rome you run to the earth (i.e. into a hole, like a hunted animal)!

110 For if thou flee into Fraunce or Frisland other,   *France, Frisia*
Thou shall be fetched with force and overset   *overthrown*
   forever!
Thy fader made fewtee we find in our
   rolles,   *father, fealty, records*
In the regestre of Rome, who-so right lookes;   *registry*
Withouten more troufling the tribute we ask   *trifling*
That Julius Cesar won with his gentle knightes!'   *noble*

The king blushed on the berne with his brode eyen,
That full bremly for brethe brent as the gledes,
Cast colours as the king with cruel lates   *features*
Looked as a lion and on his lip bites.
120 The Romanes for radness rusht to the erthe,   *fear, earth*
For ferdness of his face as they fey were;   *fear, fated to die*
Couched as kennetes before the king
   selven;   *crouched like hounds*
Because of his countenaunce confused them
   seemed!   *they seemed*
Then covered up a knight and cried full
   loud: *got up (on his knees)*
'King, crowned of kind, courtais and noble,   *by nature, courteous*
Misdo no messanger for mensk of thyselven,   *harm, honour*
Senn we are in thy manrede and mercy
   thee beseekes;   *since, power, beseech you*
We lenge with Sir Lucius, that lord is of Rome,   *belong*
That is the marveloustest man than on molde
   lenges;   *most marvellous, earth, lives*
130 It is lelful til us his liking til work;
We come at his commaundment; have us excused.'

Then carpes the conquerour cruel wordes:
'Ha! cravand knight, a coward thee seemes!   *craven, you seem*
There is some segge in this sale, and he were sore greved
Thou durst not for all Lumbardy look on him ones!'

'Sir,' says the senatour, 'So Crist mot me help,   *as, may*

---

115 [The Romans claim title to Britain on the basis of Caesar's conquest, as recorded in
chronicles based ultimately on Book V of Geoffrey of Monmouth's *History of the Kings
of Britain*.]
116-17 The king looked on the man with his large eyes, which burned very fiercely like
coals because of (his) anger.
130 It is loyal (our duty) for us to do his pleasure.
134-5 There is a certain man in this hall, and he was sorely grieved that you dared not look
on him once for all Lombardy (as a reward)!

The vout of thy visage has wounded us all!   *expression*
Thou art the lordliest lede that ever I on looked.   *man*
By looking, withouten lees, a lion thee seemes!'   *lies, you seem*

140   'Thou has me summoned,' quod the king, 'and said what
         thee likes.   *said*

For sake of thy soveraign I suffer thee the more;
Senn I crowned was in kith with crisom
         annointed,   *since, country, holy oil*
Was never creature to me that carped so large!   *talked so big*
But I shall take counsel at kinges annointed   *from*
Of dukes and douspeeres and doctours
         noble,   *high noblemen, theologians*
Of peeres of the parlement, prelates and other   *parliament*
Of the richest renkes of the Round Table;   *most powerful, men*
Thus shall I take avisement of valiant bernes,   *advice, men*
Work after the wit of my wise knightes.   *do, according to*
150   To warp wordes in waste no worship it were,   *utter, honour*
Ne wilfully in this wrath to wreken myselven.   *nor, avenge*
Forthy shall thou lenge here and lodge with these
         lordes   *therefore, remain*
This seven-night in solace to sujourn your horses,   *pleasure, rest*
To see what life that we lede in these low landes.'   *lead, humble*
For by the realtee of Rome, that richest was
         ever,   *royalty, most powerful*
He commaundes Sir Kayous, 'Take keep to those
         lordes   *care of*
To stightel tho stern men as their state
         askes,   *arrange, those, requires*
That they be herbered in haste in those high
         chambres,   *lodged, noble chambers*
Sithen sittandly in sale served thereafter,   *then, suitably, hall*
160   That they find no faute of food to their horses,   *lack*
Nother wine ne wax ne welth in this erthe;
Spare for no spicery, but spend what thee likes
That there be largess on loft and no lack founden;   *generosity*
If thou my worship wait, wye, by my trewth,
Thou shall have gersoms full grete that gain shall thee ever!'

---

[161] Neither wine nor wax (candles) nor wealth on this earth.
[162] Don't save money on spices, but spend what you please.
[164-5] If you guard my honour, man, by my pledged word, you shall have very great rewards
that will profit you for ever.

Now are they herbered in high and in host holden,
Hastily with hende men within these high
    walles.   *courteous, noble*
In chambers with chimpnees they changen their
    weedes,   *chimneys, change, clothes*
And sithen the chaunceller them fetched with chevalry
    noble;   *then*

170 Soon the senatour was set as him well seemed,   *befit*
At the kinges own borde; two knightes him served,
Singulere, soothly, as Arthur himselven,
Richly on the right hand at the Round Table.
By resoun that the Romans were so rich
    holden,   *reason, powerful*
As of the realest blood that regned in erthe.   *most royal, reigned*
There come in at the first course, before the king selven,
Borehevedes that were bright, burnisht with
    silver   *boar-heads, adorned*
All with taught men and towen in togges full rich,
Of sank real in suite, sixty at ones;

180 Flesh flourisht of fermison, with frumentee noble,
There-to wild to wale, and winlich briddes,
Pacockes and plovers in platters of gold   *peacocks*
Pigges of pork despine that pastured never;   *piglets, porcupine*
Sithen herons in hedoyne heled full fair,   *plumage, concealed*
Grete swannes full swithe in silveren chargeours,
Tartes of Turky, taste when them likes;   *pies, Turkey*
Gumbaldes graithly, full gracious to taste;   *beef pies, readily*
Senn bowes of wild bores with the brawn leched,
Bernakes and botoures in batterd dishes,

190 Thereby braunchers in bred, better was
    never,   *young hawks, bread*

[166] Now are they nobly lodged and regarded as guests.

[168] [Chambers with chimneys are heated rooms, a luxury at this time.]

[171-2] At the king's own table (a place of honour); two knights served him alone (singly), in truth, as (was done for) Arthur himself.

[176] [The elaborate feast that follows might actually have been served in a royal household of the late fourteenth century. Menus for royal feasts are printed in *Two Fifteenth-Century Cookery-Books*, ed. Austin, EETS, O.S., 91 (London: 1888; repr. 1964).]

[178-9] All with men trained and taught, in very rich clothes, all of royal blood in a troop, sixty together.

[180-81] Flesh fattened in season, with noble frumentee (a dish made of wheat), along with wild (game) to choose, and pleasant birds.

[185] Very many large swans on silver platters.

[188-9] Then shoulders of wild boars, with the lean meat sliced, barnacle geese and bitterns in pastry-covered dishes (i.e. baked in pies).

With brestes of barrowes that bright were to
    shew;   *breasts, pigs, be seen*
Senn come there sewes sere with solace
    thereafter,   *then, stews, various*
Ownde of azure all over and ardaunt them seemed,
Of ilk a leche the lowe launched full high,
That all ledes might like that looked them upon;   *men*
Then cranes and curlewes craftily rosted,   *roasted*
Connies in cretoyne coloured full fair,   *rabbits, milk and spices*
Fesauntes enflourished in flamand
    silver,   *pheasants, adorned, flaming*
With darielles endorded and dainties ynow;
200   Then Claret and Crete clergially rennen
With condethes full curious all of clene silver,
Osay and Algarde and other
    ynow   *Alastian and Spanish wines, many others*
Rhenish wine and Rochelle, richer was never,
Vernage of Venice, virtuous, and Crete,   *white wine*
In faucetes of fine gold, fonde who-so likes;   *to try*
The kinges cup-bord was closed in silver,
In grete gobletes overgilt, glorious of hew;
There was a chef butler, a chevaler noble   *chief, chevalier*
Sir Kayous the courtais, that of the cup served;   *courteous*
210   Sixty cuppes of suite for the king selven,   *cups, a set*
Crafty and curious, corven full fair,   *skilfully made, carved*
In ever-ilk a party pight with precious stones,   *each part adorned*
That none enpoison sholde go privily there-under
But the bright gold for brethe sholde brist all to peces,
Or else the venom sholde void through virtue of the stones;
And the conquerour himselven, so clenly arrayed,   *handsomely*
In colours of clene gold cledde, with his knightes,   *pure, clad*
Dressed with his diadem on his dese rich,

[193-4] Wavy with azure-coloured sauce all over, and they appeared to be flaming; from
each slice the flame leaped very high.

[199] With pastries glazed with egg yolks and many (other) dainties.

[200-201] Then Claret and Cretan wine were cunningly made to flow by conduits that were
skilfully made, all of pure silver.

[206-7] The king's cup-board was enclosed in silver and with great jewels gilded over, glorious
of hue [i.e. a cabinet for storing cups, which were often very valuable, as in this case].

[213-15] So that if any poison should go secretly under them (i.e. in the cup), the bright gold
would burst all to pieces with anger, or else the poison should empty (lose its power)
by means of the virtue of the precious stones. [The virtues (powers) of precious stones
were commonplace in the Middle Ages. See *English Medieval Lapidaries*, eds Evans
and Serjeantson, EETS, O.S., 190 (London: 1932; repr. 1960).]

For he was deemed the doughtiest that dwelled in erthe.

220   Then the conquerour kindly carped to those lordes,   *spoke*
Reheted the Romans with real speche: *cheered, royal, speech*
'Sirs, bes knightly of countenaunce and comfortes
            yourselven;   *be*
We know nought in this countree of curious metes;
In these barrain landes breedes none other;   *barren*
Forthy, withouten feining, enforce you the more
To feed you with such feeble as ye before find.'   *poor food*

'Sir,' says the senatour, 'So Crist mot me help,   *as, may*
There regned never such realtee within Rome
            walles!   *reigned, royalty, Rome's*
There ne is prelate ne pope ne prince in this erthe   *is no, nor*
230   That he ne might be well payed of these pris
            metes!'   *pleased, excellent, foods*

After their welth they wesh and went unto
            chamber,   *wealth, washed*
This ilk kidd conquerour with knightes
            ynow;   *same, famous, many knights*
Sir Gawain the worthy Dame Waynor he ledes,   *Gaynor, leads*
Sir Owghtreth on tother side, of Turry was lord.   *the other*
Then spices unsparely they spended
            thereafter,   *unsparingly, expended*
Malvesy and Muskadell, those marvelous
            drinkes,   *malmsey and muscatel*
Raiked full rathely in rosset cuppes
Til all the rich on row, Romans and other.
But the soveraign soothly, for solace of himselven,   *pleasure*
240   Assigned to the senatour certain lordes
To lede to his levere, when he his leve
            askes,   *lead, assigned place, leave*
With mirth and with melody of minstralsy noble.   *musicians*

Then the conquerour to counsel kaires thereafter   *goes*
With lordes of his legeaunce that to himself
            longes   *allegiance, belong*
To the Giauntes Towr jollily he wendes   *tower*

---

[223] In this country we know nothing of skilfully prepared foods.
[225] Therefore, without pretending (that you are enjoying it), force yourself all the more.
[237-8] Went round very quickly in russet-coloured (i.e. gold) cups, to all the powerful ones in turn, Romans and others.

With justices and judges and gentle knightes.   *noble*

Sir Cador of Cornwall to the king carpes,   *speaks*
Laugh on him lovely with likand lates: *at, pleasing, features*
'I thank God of that thro that thus us thretes!   *trouble, threatens*
250 You must be trailed, I trow, but yif ye tret
          better!   *dragged, believe, unless, treat*
The lettres of Sir Lucius lightes mine herte.   *lighten, heart*
We have as losels lived many long day   *wastrels*
With delites in this land with lordshippes many   *delights*
And forlitened the los that we are
          laited.   *lessened, praise, esteemed*
I was abashed, by our Lord, of our best bernes,   *by, men*
For grete dole of disuse of deedes of armes.
Now wakenes the war! Worshipped be Crist!
And we shall win it again by wightness and strength!'   *vigour*

'Sir Cador,' quod the king, 'thy counsel is noble;   *said*
260 But thou art a marvelous man with thy merry wordes!
For thou countes no case ne castes no further,
But hurles forth upon heved, as thy herte
          thinkes;   *head, heart*
I moste trete of a trews touchand these needes,
Talk of these tithandes that teenes mine herte.   *tidings, grieves*
Thou sees that the emperour is angerd a little;
It seemes by his sandesman that he is sore
          greved;   *messenger, grieved*
His senatour has summoned me and said what him liked,
Hethely in my hall, with heinous wordes,   *scornfully, hateful*
In speche despised me and spared me little;   *speech*
270 I might not speke for spite, so my herte trembled!   *could, speak*
He asked me tyrauntly tribute of Rome,
That teenfully tint was in time of mine elders,   *sorrowfully, lost*
There alienes, in absence of all men of armes,
Coverd it of commouns, as cronicles telles.   *obtained*
I have title to take tribute of Rome;
Mine auncestres were emperours and ought it
          themselven,   *owned*

²⁶¹ You take account of no circumstances, nor consider (the matter) any further.
²⁶³ I must bargain for a truce (with you, Cador) concerning this message.

Belin and Bremin and Bawdewyne the third;
They occupied the empire eight score winters,
Ilkon eier after other, as old men telles;   *each one, heir*
280   They covered the Capitol and cast down the walles,   *seized*
Hanged of their hedesmen by hundrethes at
    ones;   *head men, hundreds, once*
Senn Constantine, our kinsman, conquered it after,
That eier was of Yngland and emperour of
    Rome,   *heir, England*
He that conquered the cross by craftes of armes,
That Crist was on crucified, That King is of heven.   *heaven*
Thus have we evidence to ask the emperour the same,
That thus regnes at Rome, what right that he claimes.'   *reigns*

Then answerd King Aungers to Arthur himself:
'Thou ought to be overling over all other kinges,   *overlord*
290   For wisest and worthyest and wightest of handes,   *strongest*
The knightlyest of counsel that ever crown bore.
I dare say for Scotland that we them scathe
    limped;   *suffered harm from them*
When the Romans regned they ransound our
    elders   *reigned, ransomed*
And rode in their riot and ravished our wives,
Withouten resoun or right reft us our
    goodes;   *reason, bereft us of*
And I shall make my avow devotly to Crist   *devoutly*
And to the holy vernacle, virtuous and noble,
Of this grete vilany I shall be venged
    ones,   *villainy, avenged, once*

[277] [In Book III of Geoffrey's *History* we are told that, long before Caesar came to Britain, Belinus and Brennius conquered and ravaged Rome. In fact, Benson is mistaken: see Livy Book V, Chapters 38–9, where the Gallic chieftain, Brennus, captures Rome. RDW.]

[282] [According to Geoffrey (Bk V, Ch. 6), Constantine was the son of a Roman Senator and a British Princess, and he succeeded to the kingship of Britain. Then he overthrew the Emperor Maxentius and became Emperor. According to legend, his mother, Helen, discovered the True Cross. Arthur claims kinship with Constantine because of his supposed British mother. Constantine actually did proclaim himself Caesar while in York, but he was never king of Britain and was not of British descent.]

[297] [The vernacle (Veronica) is the handkerchief with which St Veronica wiped the face of Christ on His way to the Crucifixion. Miraculously, the image of His face was preserved on the handkerchief, which still survives. The cult of the Veronica was especially strong in the fourteenth century; Pope John XXII granted an indulgence of 10,000 days for a prayer to the Veronica, and its legend had an important part in the popular romances about Titus and Vespasian.]

On yon venomous men with valiant knightes!
300　I shall thee further of defence fostred ynow　　　　*well trained*
Twenty thousand men within two months
Of my wage to wend where-so thee likes,　　　　　*at my expense*
To fight with thy fomen that us unfair ledes!'

　　Then the burlich berne of Bretain the
　　　　little　　　　　　　　　　　*stately, man, Brittany*
　　Counsels Sir Arthur and of him congee
　　　　beseekes　　　　　　　　　　*leave, beseeches*
　　To answer the alienes with austeren wordes,　　　　*bold*
　　To entice the emperour to take over the mountes.
　　He said: 'I make mine avow verily to Crist,
　　And to the holy vernacle, that void shall I
　　　　never　　　　　　　　　　*Veronica, retreat*
310　For radness of no Roman that regnes in erthe,　　*fear, reigns*
　　But ay be redy in array and at erest founden;　*ready, the first*
　　No more dout the dintes of their derf
　　　　wepens　　　　　　　　*fear, strong, weapons*
　　Than the dew that is dank when that it down falles;
　　Ne no more shoun for the swap of their sharp
　　　　swordes　　　　　　　　　*shunt, sweep*
　　Than for the fairest flowr that on the folde　*flower, ground*
　　　　growes!
　　I shall to batail thee bring of brenyed knightes　*battle, armoured*
　　Thirty thousand by tale, thrifty in armes,　*count, prosperous*
　　Within a month-day, into what march　*whatever country*
　　That thou will soothly assign, when thyself likes.'

320　　'A! A!' says the Welsh king, 'Worshipped be Crist!
　　Now shall we wreke full well the wrath of our elders!　*avenge*
　　In West Wales, iwis, such wonders they wrought
　　That all for wandreth may weep that on that war　*sorrow*
　　　　thinkes.
　　I shall have the avauntward witterly
　　　　myselven,　　　　　　　*vanguard, certainly*
　　Til that I have vanquisht the Viscount of Rome,
　　That wrought me at Viterbo a vilany ones,　*villainy, once*
　　As I past in pilgrimage by the Pount Tremble.　*Pontremoli*
　　He was in Tuskane that time and took of our
　　　　knightes,　　　　　　　*Tuscany, some of*

³⁰³ To fight with your foes, who treat us unfairly.

Arrest them unrightwisly and ransound them after.
330 I shall him surely ensure that saghtel shall we
   never   *be reconciled*
Ere we sadly assemble by ourselven ones *ourselves alone*
And dele dintes of deth with our derf wepens!
And I shall wage to that war of worshipful
   knightes,   *bring at my expense*
Of wightest of Welshland and of the West Marches, *strongest*
Two thousand in tale, horsed on steedes,   *number*
Of the wightest wyes in all yon West Landes!' *strongest, men*

  Sir Ewain fitz Urien then egerly fraines, *eagerly, asks*
Was cosin to the conquerour, corageous
   himselven: *kinsman, courageous*
'Sir, and we wiste your will we wolde work
   thereafter;   *if we knew, would*
340 Yif this journee sholde hold or be ajourned
   further,   *journey, adjourned*
To ride on yon Romans and riot their landes, *ravage*
We wolde shape us therefore, to ship when you
   likes.'   *would prepare*

  'Cosin,' quod the conquerour, 'Kindly thou
   askes   *kinsman, said*
Yif my counsel accord to conquer yon landes.
By the kalendes of Juny we shall encounter ones *first day, June*
With full cruel knightes, so Crist mot me help! *as, may*
Thereto I make mine avow devotly to Crist *devoutly*
And to the holy vernacle, virtuous and noble; *Veronica*
I shall at Lamass take leve to lenge at my large
350 In Lorraine or Lumbardy, whether me leve thinkes;
Merk unto Meloine and mine down the walles *go, Milan*
Both of Petersand and of Pis and of the Pount
   Tremble;   *Pietrasanta, Pisa, Pontremoli*
In the Vale of Viterbo vitail my knights, *victual*
Sujourn there six weekes and solace myselven, *sojourn, refresh*
Send prikers to the pris town and plant there my
   sege   *riders, excellent, siege*
But if they proffer me the pees by process of
   time.'   *unless, peace*

329 Arrested them unjustly and afterwards held them for ransom.
332 And deal blows of death with our strong weapons.
349–50 At Lamastide (1 August) I shall take my leave, to remain freely in Lorraine (in
France) or Lombardy (in Italy), whichever seems preferable to me.

'Certes,' says Sir Ewain, 'And I avow after,   *certainly, vow*
And I that hathel may see ever with mine eyen   *if, man, eyes*
That occupies thine heritage, the empire of Rome,
360   I shall aunter me ones his egle to touch   *adventure, eagle-standard*
That borne is in his banner of bright gold rich,
And rase it from his rich men and rive it in
        sonder,   *snatch, cut, asunder*
Be he be redily rescued with riotous knightes.
I shall enforce you in the feld with fresh men of
        armes,   *reinforce, field*
Fifty thousand folk upon fair steedes,
On thy fomen to founde there thee fair
        thinkes,   *foemen, go, where*
In Fraunce or in Frisland, fight when thee likes!'   *Frisia*

'By our Lord,' quod Sir Launcelot, 'Now lightes mine
        herte!   *lightens*
I lowe God of this love these lordes has avowed!   *praise*
370   Now may less men have leve to say what them
        likes,   *lesser, leave*
And have no letting by law; but listenes these
        wordes: *hindrance*
I shall be at journee with gentle knightes   *the day's fight, noble*
On a jamby steed full jollily graithed,   *active, equipped*
Ere any journee begin to joust with himselven
Among all his giauntes, genivers and other,   *Genoese*
Strike him stiffly fro his steed with strenghe of mine
        handes,   *stoutly, from, strength*
For all the steren in stour that in his stale hoves!
Be my retinue arrayed, I reck it but a little   *reckon*
To make route into Rome with riotous knightes.
380   Within a seven-night day, with six score helmes,
I shall be seen on the se, sail when thee likes.'   *sea*

Then laughes Sir Lot and all on loud meles: *speaks*
'Me likes that Sir Lucius longes after sorrow;   *for*
Now he wilnes the war his wandreth beginnes;   *desires, sorrow*
It is our werdes to wreke the wrath of our elders!   *fates, avenge*
I make mine avow to God and to the holy vernacle: *Veronica*

363 Unless he (the eagle) is quickly rescued by vigorous knights.
374 Before any day's fight (the major battle) begins, to joust with himself (Lucius).
377 Despite the strong (ones) in battle that remain in his troop.
380 Within a week from today with 120 knights.

And I may see the Romans that are so rich holden,
Arrayed in their riotes on a round feld,
I shall at the reverence of the Round Table   *for*
390   Ride through all the rout, rereward and other,
Redy wayes to make and renkes full rowm,
Runnand on red blood, as my steed rushes!
He that followes my fare and first comes after   *route*
Shall find in my fare-way many fey leved!'   *dead, left*

Then the conquerour kindly comfortes these knightes,
Alowes them gretly their lordly avowes: *praises, vows*
   'Allweldand God worship you all!   *All-ruling, honour*
And let me never want you, whiles I in world regn;
My mensk and my manhed ye maintain in
    erthe,   *honour, manhood*
400   Mine honour all utterly in other kinges landes;
My wele and my worship of all this world rich,   *prosperity*
Ye have knightly conquered that to my crown longes.   *belongs*
Him thar be ferd for no foes that swilk a folk
    ledes,   *he need, afraid, such*
But ever fresh for to fight in feld when him likes.   *field*
I account no king that under Crist lives;   *take account of*
Whiles I see you all sound, I set by no more.'   *depend on*

When they trustily had treted they trumped up after,
Descended down with a daunce of dukes and
    erles.   *group (dance), earls*
Then they sembled to sale and souped als
    swithe,   *assembled, hall, dined, quickly*
410   All this seemly sorte, with semblaunt full
    noble.   *company, splendour*
Then the roy real rehetes these knightes   *king, royal, cheers*
With reverence and riot of all his Round   *riotous amusement*
    Table
Til seven dayes was gone. The senatour askes
Answer to the Emperour with austeren wordes.   *bold*
After the Epiphany, when the purpose was taken   *January 6*
Of peeres of the parlement, prelates and other,   *parliament*

387-8 If I can see the Romans, who are considered so powerful, arrayed in their riotous
    groups on a broad field.
390-91 Ride through all the company, rear guard and the rest, to make a ready way and
    plenty of room for men (who come after me).
407 When they had confidently discussed (this business), they blew on trumpets afterwards
    (as a signal that the council was concluded).

The king in his counsel, courtais and noble,   *courteous*
Uters the alienes and answers himselven: *brings out*
'Greet well Lucius, thy lord, and laine not these
    wordes;   *conceal*
420 If thou be legemen lele, let him wite soon   *liege-man, loyal, know*
I shall at Lamass take leve and lodge at my
    large   *August 1, freely*
In delite in his landes with lordes ynow,   *delight, many lords*
Regne in my realtee and rest when me likes;   *reign, royalty*
By the river of Rhone hold my Round Table,
Fang the fermes in faith of all tho fair rewmes
For all the menace of his might and maugree his
    eyen!   *despite, curses to*
And merk sithen over the mountes into his main
    landes,   *go, then, mountains, strong*
To Miloine the marvelous and mine down the walles;   *Milan*
In Lorraine ne in Lumbardy leve shall I
    nother   *Lombardy, leave, neither*
430 Nokine lede upon life that there his lawes
    yemes;   *No kind of man, keeps*
And turn into Tuskane when me time thinkes,   *Tuscany*
Ride all those rowm landes with riotous
    knightes.   *spacious, vigorous*
Bid him make rescues for mensk of himselven,   *honour*
And meet me for his manhed in those main
    landes!   *manhood, strong*
I shall be founden in Fraunce, fraist when him likes!   *to try*
The first day of Feveryer in those fair marches!   *February*
Ere I be fetched with force or forfeit my landes,
The flowr of his fair folk full fey shall be leved!   *dead, left*
I shall him sekerly ensure under my sele rich   *certainly, seal*
440 To sege the citee of Rome within seven winter   *besiege, city*
And that so sekerly ensege upon sere
    halves   *securely, besiege, all sides*
That many a senatour shall sigh for sake of me one!   *alone*
My summons are certified and thou art full served   *provided*
Of cundit and credens; kaire where thee likes.
I shall thy journee engist, enjoin them myselven,
Fro this place to the port there thou shall pass over: *from*

---

425 Seize the revenues, in faith, of all those fair realms.
444 With safe-conduct and credentials; go where you please.
445 I shall assign the resting-places for your journey, order them myself.

Seven days to Sandwich I set at the large;   *freely*
Sixty mile on a day, the sum is but little!
Thou moste speed at the spurs and spare not thy
    fole;   *must, foal*
450 Thou wendes by Watling Street and by no way elles;   *else*
There thou nightes on night needes moste thou lenge;
Be it forest or feld, found thou no further;   *field, go*
Bind thy blonk by a busk with thy bridle even,   *horse, bush*
Lodge thyselven under linde as thee lefe thinkes;
There owes none alienes to ayer upon nightes,   *ought, wander*
With such a ribawdous rout to riot thyselven.   *ribald, company*
Thy license is limit in presence of lordes,   *limited*
Be now loth or lefe, right as thee thinkes,
For both thy life and thy limm ligges thereupon,   *limb, lie*
460 Though Sir Lucius had laid thee the lordship of
    Rome,   *laid on you*
For be thou founden a foot withoute the flood
    marches   *edge of the sea*
After the aughtende day when undern is
    rungen,   *eighteenth, nine a.m.*
Thou shall be heveded in hie and with horse drawen,
And senn hiely be hanged, houndes to gnawen!
The rent ne red gold that unto Rome longes   *belongs*
Shall not redily, renk, ransoun thine
    one!'   *man, ransom, you alone*

    'Sir,' says the senatour, 'So Crist mot me help,   *as, may*
Might I with worship win away ones   *could, go*
I sholde never for Emperour that on erthe
    lenges   *should, remains*
470 Eft unto Arthur ayer on such needes;   *again, go, a message*
But I am singely here with sixteen knightes;   *singly*
I beseek you, sir, that we may sound pass.   *beseech, safely*
If any unlawful lede let us by the way,   *man, hinder*
Within thy license, lord, thy los is inpaired.'   *fame, impaired*

    'Care, not,' quod the king, 'Thy cundit is

450 [*Watling Street*: the old Roman road leading from the southern coast by way of
London to Cardigan in Wales.]
451 Wherever you are caught by night you must by necessity remain.
454 Lodge yourself under trees, wherever it seems good to you.
458 Whether (my order) is now hateful or pleasing (to you).
463-4 You shall be speedily beheaded and torn apart by horses, and then quickly hanged
for dogs to gnaw.

knowen   *said, safe conduct*
Fro Carlisle to the coste there thy cogge
    lenges;   *from, coast, ship*
Though thy coffers were full, crammed with silver,
Thou might be seker of my sele sixty mile further.'   *secure, seal*

    They enclined to the king and congee they
        asked,   *bowed, leave*
480 Kaires out of Carlisle, catches on their horses;   *go*
Sir Cador the courtais kend them the wayes,   *courteous, taught*
To Catrik them conveyed and to Crist them
    bekenned.   *entrusted*
So they sped at the spurres they sprangen their
    horses,   *exhausted*
Hires them hackenayes hastily thereafter.   *horses*
So for reddour they ridden and rested them never,   *fear, rode*
But yif they lodged under linde whiles them the light
    failed;   *Unless, tree, when*
But ever the senatour forsooth sought at the
    gainest.   *went, nearest (way)*
By the sevende day was gone the citee they reched.

In the second extract Arthur, who has just defeated the Romans, has reached the pinnacle of his power. He now experiences a dreadful dream in which he is wandering alone through a wood inhabited by wild beasts which have devoured his knights. He flees into a beautiful meadow, where he encounters the figure of Lady Fortune carrying her wheel, on which six kings sit. Each of the kings tells Arthur about himself, then Fortune addresses him honourably, sets him on a throne, but then crushes him under her wheel. When Arthur wakes up he consults a philosopher, who explains the identity of the kings, and informs Arthur that his time of good fortune is over. This is soon confirmed by the arrival of Sir Craddok with news of Mordred's treachery.

3218   Then this comlich king as cronicles telles,
        Bounes brothly to bed with a blithe herte;
3220 Off he slinges with sleght and slakes his girdle,
        And for slewth of slomour on a sleep falles.   *sloth, slumber*
        But by one after midnight all his mood changed;

---

[488] By the time the seventh day was gone they reached the city.
[3220] He throws himself quickly on the bed and loosens his belt.

He mette in the morn-while full marvelous
     dremes;   *dreamed, morning, dreams*
And when his dredful dreme was driven to the ende,
The king dares for doute, die as he sholde,   *cowers*
Sendes after philosophers, and his affray telles: *terror*
'Senn I was formed, in faith, so ferd was I never!
For-thy ransackes redily and rede me my
     swevenes,   *search, interpret, dreams*
And I shall redily and right rehersen the sooth.   *rehearse (tell)*

3230   'Me thought I was in a wood, willed mine
     one   *wandered by myself*
That I ne wiste no way whider that I
     sholde,   *knew, whither, should go*
For wolves and wild swine and wicked bestes
Walked in that wastern wathes to seek,   *waste place, prey*
There lions full lothly licked their tuskes   *loathly*
All for lapping of blood of my lele knightes!
Through that forest I fled there flowres were high,
For to fele me for ferd of tho foul thinges,   *hide*
Merked to a medow with mountaines enclosed   *meadow*
The merriest of middle-erthe that men might behold.

3240 The close was in compass casten all
     about   *enclosed place, extent, covered*
With clover and clevewort cledde even over;   *small grass, clad*
The vale was enveround with vines of silver,   *encircled*
All with grapes of gold, greter were never,
Enhorild with arbory and alkins
     trees,   *surrounded, groves, all kinds of gardens*
Erberes full honest, and herdes there-under;
All fruites foddemed was that flourished in erthe,   *produced*
Fair frithed in fraunk upon the free bowes;
Was there no danking of dew that ought dere sholde;
With the drought of the day all dry were the flowres.

3250   'Then descendes in the dale, down fro the cloudes,
A duchess dereworthily dight in diapered
     weedes,   *expensively, patterned*

3247-8 Beautifully enclosed (lit. protected in an enclosure) upon the noble boughs; There
was no moisture of dew that could harm anything.
3251 [Dame Fortune, with her Wheel of Fortune, is a familiar figure in late medieval poetry,
as are the Nine Worthies whom Arthur sees in his dream. The Nine Worthies first
appear in fourteenth-century works such as *The Parlement of the Three Ages* and
reappear as late as Shakespeare's *Midsummer Night's Dream*.]

In a surcote of silk full selcouthly hewed,   *surcoat, rarely*
All with loyotour overlaid low to the hemmes   *otter fur*
And with ladily lappes the lenghe of a yard,   *ladylike, lappets*
And all redily reversed with rebanes of gold,   *trimmed, ribbons*
With brouches and besauntes and other bright
    stones;   *brooches*
Her back and her breste was broched all over,   *adorned*
With kell and with coronal clenlich arrayed,   *hair net, diadem*
And that so comly of colour one knowen was never.

3260   'About sho whirled a wheel with her white handes,
Overwhelm all quaintly the wheel, as sho
        sholde;   *skilfully turned*
The rowel was red gold with real stones,   *wheel*
Railed with riches and rubies ynow;   *adorned*
The spekes was splented all with speltes of
        silver,   *spokes, plated, bars*
The space of a spere-lenghe springand full fair;   *spear length*
There-on was a chair of chalk-white silver
And checkered with charbocle changing of hewes   *carbuncle*
Upon the compass there cleved kinges on row,   *outer edge, clung*
With crowns of clere gold that cracked in sonder;
3270   Six was of that settle full sodenlich fallen,   *seat*
Ilk a segge by himself and said these wordes:
"That ever I regned on this roo me rewes it ever!   *wheel*
Was never roy so rich that regned in erthe!
When I rode in my rout rought I nought elles   *I thought of*
But rivaye and revel and raunson the pople!   *to hunt*
And thus I drive forth my dayes whiles I drie might, *endure*
And therefore derflich I am damned for ever!"   *direly*

    'The last was a little man that laid was beneth;   *beneath*
His leskes lay all lene and lothlich to shew,   *loins, lean*
3280   His lockes liard and long the lenghe of a yard,   *grey*
His lire and his ligham lamed full sore,   *face, body, crippled*
The tone eye of the berne was brighter than silver   *one*
The tother was yellower than the yolk of a nay.   *other, egg*

    ' "I was lord," quod the lede, "of landes ynow,
And all ledes me louted that lenged in erthe.   *bowed to me*
And now is left me no lap my ligham to hele   *rag, body*
But lightly now am I lost, leve eche man the

3256 [*Besauntes*: coins (originally from Byzantium), here coin-shaped golden discs.]
3259 And one so comely of complexion was never known.

sooth."   *quickly, believe*

'The second sir, forsooth, that sewed them after   *followed*
Was sekerer to my sight and sadder in
    armes;   *stronger, more determined*
3290 Oft he sighed unsound and said these wordes:
"On yon see have I sitten als soveraign and lord,   *throne*
And ladies me loved to lap in their armes,   *fold*
And now my lordshippes are lost and laid for ever!"

'The third thoroughly was thro and thick in the
    shoulders,   *stout*
A thro man to thret of there thirty were gadered;   *threat*
His diadem was dropped down, dubbed with stones,   *adorned*
Endented all with diamaundes and dight for the
    nones;   *adorned, diamonds, occasions*
"I was dredde in my dayes," he said, "in diverse
    rewmes,   *dreaded*
And now damned to the dede, and dole is the more!"

3300 'The fourt was a fair man and forcy in
    armes,   *fourth, forceful*
The fairest of figure that formed was ever.
"I was frek in my faith," he said, "whiles I on folde regned,
Famous in fer landes and flowr of all kinges;
Now is my face defaded and foul is me happened,
For I am fallen fro fer and frendles beleved."

'The fift was a fairer man than fele of these other,   *fifth*
A forcy man and a fers, with fomand lippes;   *forceful, foaming*
He fanged fast on the feleighes and folded his
    armes   *gripped, rim*
But yet he failed and fell a fifty foot large;
3310 But yet he sprang and sprent and spradden his
    armes,   *leaped, spread*
And on the spere-lenghe spekes he spekes these
    wordes: *spokes*
"I was in Surry a Sire and set by mine one
As soveraign and seinyour of sere kinges landes;   *lord*
Now of my solace I am full sodenly fallen
And for sake of my sin yon sete is me
    rewed."   *yon seat is denied me*

'The sixt had a sawter seemlich bounden   *sixth, psalter, bound*
With a surepel of silk sewed full fair,   *surplice (cover), sewn*

A harp and a hand-sling with hard flint-stones;
What harmes he has hent he hallowes full soon: *announces*
3320 "I was deemed in my dayes," he said, "of deedes of armes
One of the doughtiest that dwelled in erthe;
But I was marred on molde in my most strenghes   *injured*
With this maiden so mild that moves us all."

'Two kinges were climband and claverand on
           high,   *clambering*
The crest of the compass they covet full yerne.
"This chair of charbocle," they said, "we challenge
           hereafter,   *carbuncle*
As two of the chefest chosen in erthe."

'The childer were chalk-white, cheekes and other,
But the chair aboven cheved they never.   *achieved*
3330 The furthermost was freely with a front large   *noble, forehead*
The fairest of fisnamy that formed was ever,   *physiognomy*
And he was busked in a blee of a blew noble   *dressed, colour, blue*
With flourdelys of gold flourished all over;   *fleur-de-lis (lilies)*
The tother was cledde in a cote all of clene silver,   *other, clad*
With a comlich cross corven of gold;   *carved*
Four crosselettes crafty by the cross restes   *little crosses*
And thereby knew I the king, that cristened him seemed.

'Then I went to that wlonk and winly her
           greetes,   *bright (one), graciously*
And sho said: "Welcome, iwis, well art thou founden;   *come*
3340 Thou ought to worship my will, and thou well
           couthe,   *knew how*
Of all the valiant men that ever was in erthe,
For all thy worship in war by me has thou wonnen;
I have been frendly, freke, and fremmed til
           other.   *strange (hostile) to others*
That thou has founden, in faith, and fele of thy bernes,
For I felled down Sir Frolle with froward knightes;   *hostile*
For-thy the fruits of Fraunce are freely thine owen.

3325 The top of the wheel they eagerly covet.
3345 [Frollo was the ruler of France whom Arthur killed in single combat when he
conquered that country as part of the conquests that immediately precede the action of
this poem and that are summarized in the opening lines. The story is told in Geoffrey
of Monmouth's *History of the Kings of Britain*, Bk IX, Ch. 11, where Arthur's adversary
is called Flollo, and in Wace's *Brut* (which our poet may have known), where he is
called Frolle or Frollo.]

Thou shall the chair escheve, I chese thee myselven,   *achieve*
Before all the cheftaines chosen in this erthe."

   'Sho lift me up lightly with her lene handes   *lean*
3350 And set me softly in the see, the septer me
      reched;   *throne, sceptre, gave*
Craftily with a comb sho kembed mine heved,   *combed*
That the crispand krok to my crown
      raught;   *curling, lock, reached*
Dressed on me a diadem that dight was full fair,
And senn proffers me a pome pight full of fair stones,   *orb, set*
Enameld with azure, the erthe there-on depainted,
Circled with the salt se upon sere halves,
In sign that I soothly was soveraign in erthe.

   'Then brought sho me a brand with full bright hiltes
And bade me braundish the blade: "The brand is mine owen;
3360 Many swain with the swing has the swet leved,   *lifeblood*
For whiles thou swank with the sword it swiked thee
      never."   *laboured, failed*

   'Then raikes sho with roo and rest when her liked,   *quiet*
To the rindes of the wood, richer was never;   *trees*
Was no pomerie so pight of princes in erthe,   *orchard*
Ne none apparel so proud but paradise one.
Sho bade the bowes sholde bow down and bring to my
      handes   *boughs*
Of the best that they bore on braunches so high;
Then they helded to her hest, all holly at
      ones,   *bowed, command*
The highest of ech a hirst, I hete you forsooth.   *grove, promise*
3370 Sho bade me frith not the fruit, but fonde whiles
      me liked: *spare, try*
"Fonde of the finest, thou freelich berne,   *try, noble*
And reche to the ripest and riot thyselven.   *reach, enjoy*
Rest, thou real roy, for Rome is thine owen,
And I shall redily roll the roo at the gainest   *wheel*
And reche thee the rich wine in rinsed cuppes."

   'Then sho went to the well by the wood eves,
That all welled of wine and wonderlich runnes,
Caught up a cup-full and covered it fair;
Sho bade me derelich draw and drink to
      herselven;   *dearly, take a draught*

3380   And thus sho led me about the lenghe of an hour,
       With all liking and love that any lede sholde.   *should want*

       'But at the mid-day full even all her mood changed,
       And made much menace with marvelous wordes.
       When I cried upon her, she cast down her browes:
       "King, thou carpes for nought, by Crist that me made!
       For thou shall lose this laik and thy life after;   *pleasure*
       Thou has lived in delite and lordshippes ynow!"   *delight*

       'About sho whirles the wheel and whirles me under,
       Til all my quarters that while were quasht all to
           peces,   *time, crushed*
3390   And with that chair my chin was chopped in sonder;
       And I have shivered for chele senn me this chaunce
           happened.   *chill*
       Thus wakened I, iwis, all wery fordremed,   *wearied from dreaming*

       And now wot thou my wo; worde as thee likes.'   *speak*

       'Freke,' says the philosopher, 'thy fortune is passed,
       For thou shall find her thy fo; fraist when thee likes!
       Thou art at the highest, I hete thee forsooth;   *promise*
       Challenge now when thou will, thou cheves no more!
       Thou has shed much blood and shalkes destroyed,   *men*
       Sakeles, in surquidrie, in sere kinges landes;   *innocent, pride*
3400   Shrive thee of thy shame and shape for thine
           end.   *confess, prepare*
       Thou has a shewing, Sir King, take keep yif thee
           like,   *revelation*
       For thou shall fersly fall within five winters.
       Found abbeyes in Fraunce, the fruites are thine owen,
       For Frolle and for Feraunt and for thir fers knightes
       That thou fremedly in Fraunce has fey beleved.
       Take keep yet of other kinges, and cast in thine
           herte,   *consider*
       That were conquerours kidd and crowned in erthe.

       'The eldest was Alexander that all the world

3404 [For Frollo see note on line 3345; Feraunt is a Roman noble, one of Lucius' knights,
   first mentioned in line 2760.]
3405 Whom you unkindly (as a stranger) left dead in France.
3408-10 [Alexander the Great, Hector of Troy, and Julius Caesar are the three Pagan
   Worthies.]

	louted,	bowed to
	The tother Ector of Troy, the chevalrous gome;	other
3410	The third Julius Cesar, that giaunt was holden,	
	In eche journee gentle, ajudged with lordes.	
	The fourth was Sir Judas, a jouster full noble,	
	The masterful Macabee, the mightiest of strenghes;	
	The fift was Josue, that jolly man of armes,	fifth
	That in Jerusalem host full much joy limped;	befell
	The sixt was David the dere, deemed with kinges	sixth
	One of the doughtiest that dubbed was ever,	
	For he slew with a sling by sleight of his handes	skill
	Golias the grete gome, grimmest in erthe;	Goliath
3420	Senn endited in his dayes all the dere psalmes	composed
	That in the sawter are set with selcouthe wordes.	psalter

'The tone climband king, I know it forsooth,   *one*
Shall Karolus be called, the kinge son of Fraunce;   *king's*
He shall be cruel and keen and conquerour holden,
Cover by conquest countrees ynow;   *obtain*
He shall encroch the crown that Crist bore
  himselven,   *capture*
And that lovelich launce that lepe to His herte   *leaped*
When He was crucified on cross, and all the keen nailes
Knightly he shall conquer to Cristen men handes.   *i.e. for*

3430   'The tother shall be Godfray, that God shall revenge   *other*
On the Good Friday with galiard knightes;   *jolly*
He shall of Lorraine be lord by leve of his fader
And senn in Jerusalem much joy happen,
For he shall cover the cross by craftes of armes
And senn be crowned king with crisom annointed.   *holy oil*
Shall no dukes in his day such destainy happen,   *destiny*
Ne such mischief drie when trewth shall be tried.   *suffer, proved*

'For-thy Fortune thee fetches to fulfill the number,
Als ninde of the noblest named in
  erthe;   *ninth (of the Nine Worthies)*
3440   This shall in romaunce be redde with real knightes,
Reckoned and renownd with riotous kinges,

3412–16 [Judas Maccabeus, Joshua, and King David are the three Jewish Worthies.]
3423 [Carolus (Charlemagne) is the first of the three Christian Worthies. The second is
  Godfrey of Bouillon (3430), and the third is Arthur himself.]
3434 He shall recover the Cross (when he conquers Jerusalem). [Godfrey's deeds, like
  Charlemagne's, and prophesied, since historically Arthur comes before both.]

And deemed on Doomesday for deedes of armes,
For the doughtiest that ever was dwelland in erthe;
So many clerkes and kinges shall carp of your deedes   *thus*
And keep your conquestes in cronicle for ever.

'But the wolves in the wood and the wild bestes
Are some wicked men that werrayes thy rewmes,   *attack*
Is entered in thine absence to werray thy pople,
And alienes and hostes of uncouthe landes.   *foreign*
3450   Thou gettes tidandes, I trow, within ten dayes,   *i.e. will get*
That some torfer is tidde senn thou fro home
          turned.   *trouble, happened*
I rede thou reckon and reherse unresonable
          deedes   *tell (i.e. confess)*
Ere thee repentes full rathe all thy rewth workes.   *sad*
Man, amend thy mood, ere thou mishappen,   *have misfortune*
And meekly ask mercy for meed of thy soul.'   *reward*

Then rises the rich king and raght on his weedes,
A red acton of rose, the richest of flowres,   *quilted jacket*
A pesan and a paunson and a pris girdle;
And on he hentes a hood of scarlet full rich,   *draws*
3460   A pavis pillion-hat that pight was full fair   *large cloth hat*
With perry of the Orient and precious stones;   *pearls*
His gloves gaylich gilt and graven by the hemmes   *decorated*
With graines of rubies full gracious to shew.   *small stones*
His bede greyhound and his brand and no berne
          else   *(He takes), saucy*
And bounes over a brode mede with brethe at his
          herte.   *meadow*
Forth he stalkes a sty by tho still eves,   *path*
Stotays at a high street, studyand him one.

At the sours of the sun he sees there comand,   *rising*
Raikand to Rome-ward the rediest wayes,   *going, quickest*
3470   A renk in a round clok with right rowme clothes
With hat and with high shoon homely and
          round;   *shoes, comfortable*
With flat farthinges the freke was flourished all
          over   *coins, adorned*

3458 An armour neckpiece, a stomach guard, and an excellent belt.
3467 Pauses at a main road, thinking by himself.
3470 A man in a round (full cut) cloak, with right roomy (full cut) clothes. [Fully cut
clothes were very fashionable in the late fourteenth century.]

Many shreddes and shragges at his skirtes hanges
With scrip and with sclavin and scallopes ynow
Both pike and palm, als pilgrim him sholde;
The gome graithly him grette and bade good
      morwen;   *greeted, morning*
The king, lordly himself, of langage of
      Rome,   *language, i.e. Italian*
Of Latin corrumped all, full lovely him
      menes: *corrupted, speaks*
'Wheder wilnes thou, wye, walkand thine one?   *whither, seek*
3480 Whiles this world is o war, a wathe I it hold;   *at war, danger*
Here is an enmy with host, under yon vines;   *enemy*
And they see thee, forsooth, sorrow thee betides;
But if thou have condeth of the king selven,   *safe-conduct*
Knaves will kill thee and keep at thou haves,   *what*
And if thou hold the high way, they hent thee also,   *take*
But if thou hastily have help of his hende knightes.'

    Then carpes Sir Craddok to the king selven:
'I shall forgive him my dede, so me God help,
Any gome under God that on this ground walkes!
3490 Let the keenest come that to the king longes,
I shall encounter him as knight, so Crist have my soul!
For thou may not reche me ne arrest thyselven,   *seize, stop (me)*
Though thou be richly arrayed in full rich weedes;
I will not wonde for no war to wend where me likes   *hesitate*
Ne for no wye of this world that wrought is on erthe!
But I will pass in pilgrimage this pas to Rome   *way*
To purchase me pardon of the Pope selven,
And of the paines of Purgatory be plenerly
      assoilled;   *fully, forgiven*
Then shall I seek sekerly my soveraign lord,
3500 Sir Arthur of England, that avenaunt berne!   *seemly*
For he is in this empire, as hathel men me telles,   *noble*
Hostayand in this Orient with awful knightes.'

    'Fro whethen come thou, keen man,' quod the king
      then,   *whence*
    'That knowes King Arthur and his knightes also?

[3473] [The 'shreds' and 'shragges' are scalloped edges, a fashionable touch.]
[3474-5] With wallet and with pilgrim's mantle and many scallop shells, both staff and palm
branch, as if he were a pilgrim. [The scallop shells were the mark of a pilgrimage to St
James of Compostela in Spain, the palm branch of a pilgrimage to the Holy Land.]
[3502] Warring in this eastern land, with awesome knights.

Was thou ever in his court whiles he in kith lenged?
Thou carpes so kindly it comfortes mine herte!
Well wele has thou went and wisely thou seekes,   *nobly*
For thou art Breton berne, as by thy brode speche.'   *British*

'Me ought to know the king; he is my kidd lord,
3510   And I was called in his court a knight of his chamber;
Sir Craddok was I called in his court rich,
Keeper of Caerlion, under the king selven;
Now I am chased out of kith, with care at my herte,
And that castel is caught with uncouthe ledes.'   *foreign*

Then the comlich king caught him in armes,
Cast off his kettle-hat and kissed him full soon,
Said: 'Welcome, Sir Craddok, so Crist mot me help!
Dere cosin of kind, thou coldes mine herte!   *blood relative*
How fares it in Bretain with all my bold bernes?
3520   Are they brittened or brint or brought out of life?   *burned*
Ken thou me kindly what case is befallen;   *tell*
I keep no credens to crave; I know thee for trew.'

'Sir, thy warden is wicked and wild of his deedes,
For he wandreth has wrought senn thou away passed.
He has castels encroched and crownd himselven,   *captured*
Caught in all the rentes of the Round Table;
He devised the rewm and delt as him likes;   *divided*
Dubbed of the Denmarkes dukes and erles,   *i.e. Danes*
Dissevered them sonderwise, and citees destroyed;
3530   Of Sarazenes and Sessoines upon sere halves   *Saxons*
He has sembled a sorte of selcouthe bernes,   *foreign*
Soveraignes of Surgenale and soudeours many   *mercenaries*
Of Peghtes and paynims and proved knightes   *Picts, pagans*
Of Ireland and Argyle, outlawed bernes;
All tho laddes are knightes that long to the mountes,
And leding and lordship has all, als themselve likes;   *command*
And there is Sir Childrik a cheftain holden,
That ilke chevalrous man, he charges thy pople;   *burdens*
They rob thy religious and ravish thy nunnes   *nuns*
3540   And redy rides with his rout to raunson the poor;   *rob*
Fro Humber to Hawyk he holdes his owen,

3522 I need ask for no credentials; I know you are true.
3529 Scattered them in every direction (throughout the realm).
3541 From the Humber river (at the southern border of Yorkshire) to the town of Hawick
(in southern Scotland; i.e. the whole North Country).

And all the countree of Kent by covenant
     entailled,   *in his possession*
The comlich castles that to the crown longed,
The holtes and the hore wood and the hard
     bankes,   *hoar (grey)*
All that Hengest and Hors hent in their time;
At Southampton on the se is seven score shippes,
Fraught full of fers folk, out of fer landes,   *filled*
For to fight with thy frap when thou them assailes. *company*
But yet a word, witterly, thou wot not the worst! *certainly*
3550 He has wedded Waynor and her his wife holdes,
And wonnes in the wild boundes of the west marches, *dwells*
And has wrought her with child, as witness telles!
Of all the wyes of this world, wo mot him
     worthe,   *woe be to him*
Als warden unworthy women to yeme!
Thus has Sir Mordred marred us all!   *injured*
For-thy I merked over these mountes to mene thee the
     sooth.'   *came, tell*

   Then the burlich king, for brethe at his herte
And for this booteless bale all his blee
     changed;   *without remedy, colour*
'By the Rood,' says the roy, 'I shall it revenge!
3560 Him shall repent full rathe all his rewth workes!'

The Parlement of the Thre Ages *(c. 1390)*

This fourteenth-century poem, generally believed to have been written c. 1390, survives in two manuscripts, of which the most important is the Thornton copy made c. 1440. The other extant, but incomplete, copy of this short poem is in the Ware manuscript (BM Additional Ms. 33994).

In an account of the Nine Worthies, ll. 462–512 of the poem relate a version of the story of Arthur, containing material probably derived from the French Grail Quest and The Death of Arthur. The poem mentions Carlisle as the usual place where Arthur held his

---

3545 [Hengest and Horsa were traditionally the first Germanic (that is, Anglo-Saxon) invaders of Britain; Geoffrey of Monmouth (*History of the Kings of Britain*, Bk VI, Ch. 11) gives the traditional account.)

court, Merlin's construction of the Round Table and the Siege
Perilous, and the episode of King Rion's (here Roystone's) 'beard
mantle'. The poet has a confused (or variant) version of the St
Michael's Mount story, in which Arthur fights a dragon and inserts
the return of Excalibur to the lake, a task here undertaken by
Gawain (or in another manuscript Ywain), rather than Bedevere.

462	Of the thre Cristen to carpe couthely there-aftir	speak highly
	That were conquerours full kene and kyngdomes wonnen:	
	Areste was Sir Arthure, and eldeste of tyme,	first
	For alle Inglande he aughte at his awnn will,	owned
	And was kynge of this kythe and the crowne hade.	land
	His courte was at Carlele comonly holden,	
	With renkes full ryalle of his rownnde table,	knights
	That Merlyn with his maystries made in his tyme,	mysteries
470	And sett the sege perilous so semely one highte;	seat
	There no segge scholde sitt bot hym scholde schame tyde,	man, happen
	Owthir dethe with-inn the thirde daye demed to hym-selven,	doomed
	Bot Sir Galade the gude that the gree wanne.	prize
	There was Sir Launcelot de Lake full lusty in armes,	
	And Sir Gawayne the gude, that never gome harmede,	man
	Sir Askanore, Sir Ewayne, Sir Errake fytz Lake,	son of
	And Sir Kay the kene and kyd of his dedis,	noble
	Sir Percevalle de Galeys that preved had bene ofte,	proved
	Mordrede and Bedwere, men of mekyll myghte,	great
480	And othere fele of that ferde, folke of the beste.	many, company
	Then Roystone the riche kyng, full rakill of his werkes,	rash
	He made a blyot to his bride of the berdes of kynges,	gown[47]
	And aughtilde Sir Arthures berde one scholde be;	considered
	Bot Arthure oure athell kynge another he thynkes,	noble, otherwise
	And faughte with hym in the felde till he was fey worthen.	dead
	And than Sir Arthure oure kyng ames hym to ryde;	turns
	Uppon Sayn Michaells Mounte mervaylles he wroghte,	performed
	There a dragone he dreped, that drede was full sore.	slew[48]
	And than he sayled over the see in-to sere londes,	many
490	Whils alle the beryns of Bretayne bewede hym to fote.[49]	
	Gascoyne and Gyane gatt he there-aftir,	Guinnes
	And conquered kyngdomes and contrees full fele.	many

Than ames he in-to Inglonde in-to his awnn kythe: *returns*
The gates to-wardes Glassthenbery full graythely he
    rydes;   *road, promptly*
And ther Sir Mordrede hym mett by a more syde,   *moor*
And faughte with hym in the felde to alle were fey
    worthen,   *'til*
Bot Arthur oure athell kyng, and Wawayne his
    knyghte.   *except*
And when the felde was flowen & fey bot
    thaym-selven,   *dead*
Than Arthure Sir Wawayne athes by his trouthe   *orders*
That he swiftely his swerde scholde swynge in the mere,   *lake*
And whatt selcouthes he see the sothe scholde he
    telle.   *marvels, truth*
And Sir Wawayne [start] swith to the sworde and swange it in
    the mere,   *swiftly, threw*
And ane hande by the hiltys hastely it grippes,
And brawndeschet that brighte swerde and bere it
    a-waye;   *brandished*
And Wawayne wondres of this werke, and wendes
    by-lyve   *hastens*
To his lorde, there he hym lefte, and lokes abowte,
And he ne wiste in alle this werlde where he was
    by-comen.   *knew*
And then he hyghes hym in haste, and hedis to the
    mere,   *goes*
And seghe a bote from the banke and beryns there-inn.   *saw*
There-inn was Sir Arthure and othire of his ferys,   *companions*
And also Morgin la Faye that myche couthe of sleghte.
And there ayther segge seghe othir laste, for sawe he hym no
    more.   *each man saw the other*

500 (line marker)
510 (line marker)

JEHAN DE WAURIN, Chronicles and Ancient Histories
of Great Britain (Croniques et anchiennes istories
de la Grant Bretaigne, a present nomme Engleterre)
(c. *1471*)

(The author, a French knight who fought at Agincourt, subsequently joined the English, becoming a retainer of Sir John Fastolf. He continued his history to 1471).

This late French 'Brut Chronicle', unlike Geoffrey of Monmouth's History and other versions of the 'Brut', begins with an account of the destruction of Troy and Jason's voyage to Colchis in search of the Golden Fleece. The Arthurian section of Waurin's chronicle displays the influence of French romance, and is especially enthusiastic about Gawain. The following extract describes what happens to King Arthur after the death of Mordred.

After the traitor Mordred was dead and King Arthur had been mortally wounded, the two armies collided with such great force and hostility that most of the criminal traitors fell dead; but those who saw that Mordred was dead, losing all hope of refuge or mercy from Arthur and his barons, hurled themselves against King Arthur's forces with such a great fury that everybody on both sides was killed in that place except ten men on the side of King Arthur: that is to say, nine knights and he was the tenth.

When the battle was over, the nine knights came to the place where King Arthur was lying as if half-dead; but when he saw Giflet and his nephew Constantine, he suddenly raised himself to his feet as if he felt neither injury nor grief. Finally, since it was already night, the king and his nine companions went to a nearby hermitage; not long after they had arrived at that place, six of the nine knights, who were all grievously wounded, died. Then Arthur, perceiving the gravity of this situation, confessed his sins to the hermit and made his will, leaving his kingdom to Constantine, the son of Cador king of Cornwall. Then, having put his affairs in order, he embraced one of the three knights so affectionately that he died in his arms. The two others who remained, since they were wounded and exhausted, fell asleep, and the noble King Arthur disappeared, so that no one knew what had become of him; but others said that he had been carried off to the Isle of Avalon for his wounds to be healed, just as Merlin had prophesied, where he lived in joy and repose, and would remain there until the Day of Judgement.

The History of the Holy Grail gives a different account, which I shall refrain from discussing, but I tell you truly that it was a great pity to lose such a great and noble, powerful, generous, honourable, virtuous, renowned figure as the valiant King Arthur was, and still is, through the damned treason of the disloyal Mordred.

Other writers maintain that when King Arthur realized that all his companions except Gifflet were dead, he called him, and the two of them went on to the seashore; then Arthur kissed Gifflet and gave him his good sword Caliburne. He entered a boat which he found nearby, which put to sea as soon as King Arthur had entered, so suddenly that in a short time Gifflet was unable to tell what had become of it. Alas! Through the accursed treason of that disloyal Mordred, the Round Table was deprived of its knights-errant; thus ended the quests, the exploits of noble knights, and the honour and prowess of arms which had been so honoured and exalted by this noble King Arthur.

JOHN DE FORDUN, Chronicle of the Scottish People (Chronica Gentis Scotorum) (c. 1385)

While Geoffrey of Monmouth's Arthur is a British king, and the Saxons (or English) are his enemies, by the time Fordun writes his Chronicle of the Scottish People, *the figure of King Arthur has been adopted as a model by English monarchs and transformed by English writers into an English king. For this reason, Scottish writers are inclined to treat Arthur less sympathetically than their English counterparts.*

In his account of Arthur, Fordun utilizes the issue of illegitimacy in order to discredit Arthur as a usurper who displaces the rightful heirs, Gawain and Mordred. Fordun explains that, since Arthur's nephews are mere boys, Arthur is accepted as king because of his military prowess – Britain is facing serious danger from Saxon invasion.

When Uther, king of the Britons, like his brother, Aurelius of good memory, had died from poison through the treachery of the Saxons, his son Arthur succeeded to part of the kingdom. This he should not lawfully have done, since the kingdom should have been given to his sister Anna or her children, since she had legitimate offspring by Loth, consul of Scotland and lord of Laudon, who was of the household of Duke Fulgens. From this marriage were born two sons, the noble Gawain and Mordred, whom some maintain was of illegitimate birth, but this was not the case.

It is certain that Arthur's rule followed that of Gonranus, although this was seven years after his death. For Arthur died in the year of

Our Lord 542, according to various writers, but I am not aware of the year in which his rule began. However, why Arthur was chosen to rule, ignoring the legal heirs, is revealed by Geoffrey [of Monmouth], who declares that, on the death of Uther Pendragon, the leaders of the Britons were gathered from all parts into the city of Silchester, where, following the lead of Dubricius, archbishop of the City of the Legions,[50] they consecrated Uther's son Arthur as king; for Dubricius argued the necessity of this because, on hearing of Uther's death, the Saxons had invited their fellows from Germany and, with Colgerin as their leader, were planning to destroy the Britons.

Chapter 25

Therefore Dubricius, lamenting the country's calamity, gathered the bishops together and crowned Arthur king. Although Arthur was only a youth of fifteen years, he possessed unheard-of virtue and generosity; he had such kindness and inherent goodness that he was loved by almost all the people. Having received the regalia, he maintained the prevalent custom of bestowing largesse; however, such a multitude of soldiers gathered around him that even what he handed out was insufficient. Thus it is possible for a man who has both inherent generosity and honesty to be in want on occasion, but he will not be afflicted by continual poverty. This is what he [Geoffrey of Monmouth] says.[51]

Returning to the previous subject, it was maintained that necessity rendered lawful that which was not the law, for otherwise it would not have been acceptable. How and why this was necessary should be explained. However, it is clearly possible to conclude that Arthur's accession was due to the fact that Gawain, who was also called Walwain, and his brother Mordred were young boys, while as we have said already, Arthur was fifteen years old when he became king,[52] in a period of various uprisings and, in the meanwhile, wars already under way against the Saxons. According to Geoffrey, a short while after these wars were concluded, Walwain, the son of the aforesaid Loth, a youth of twelve years, was sent by his uncle [Arthur] to serve Pope Sulpicius, from whom he received arms.[53]

For this reason, encountering such necessity, an adolescent approaching manhood deservedly was chosen, rather than a baby in his cradle, and, as it happened, for this cause Mordred raised war against Arthur in which one or the other would be cut off by Fate. However Geoffrey writes that Mordred and Gawain were sons of Anna, sister of Aurelius, Arthur's paternal uncle, saying as follows:

'However, Loth married Aurelius Ambrosius' sister, on whom he begot Gawain and Mordred.' However, he later calls Arthur his uncle, saying this: 'Then Gawain was the son of the aforesaid Loth, a youth of twelve years, who was sent by his uncle to serve Pope Sulpicius, from whom he received arms.' That is what Geoffrey has; but it is clear that neither Aurelius nor Uther was still alive, so it must be Arthur who is meant by the word 'uncle'. I leave it to the more sagacious reader to reconsider these words. I do not see how to reconcile these statements easily; however, I do believe I have in fact read elsewhere that Mordred was Arthur's sister's son, and that was my intention in writing this chapter.

ANDREW OF WYNTOUN, Chronicle (c. 1420)

This Scottish chronicler gives a brief account of Arthur's career, listing his early conquests and war against Lucius, Mordred's treachery, and Arthur's journey to an island to be healed of his wounds. Unlike Fordun and some other Scottish writers, Wyntoun is not critical of Arthur. However, he does not seem particularly interested in Arthur, but is more concerned about whether Lucius was the Roman emperor or just a procurator. Wyntoun's lack of enthusiasm in writing about Arthur may be due to his belief that he has nothing original to contribute. He feels that Huchon of the Aule Realle has already treated the subject satisfactorily. He relates that Huchon wrote various works, including 'a gret Gest of Arthure and the Awntyre of Gawane'.[54]

4257 And qwhen this Leo was emperoure	
Kynge of Brettan was Arthoure,	
That wan al Frawnsse and Lumbardy,	
4260 Gyan, Gaskoyn and Normandy,	
(Burgon), Flanderis and Brabande,	
Henaude, Holande and Goutlande,	
Sweys, Swetheryk and Norway,	
Denmark, Irland and Orknaye;	
And al the Ilis in the se	
Subjet war til his pouste;	*to, power*
And al thir landis evir ilkan	*each one*
To the crowne of Brettane	
He ekyt hail, and made thaim fre,	*released wholly*

4270   Bot subdit til his realte,
       Withe out serwis or homage,
       Or ony payment of (trewage)
       Mad to Rome, as before thai
       Lange tyme oyssit for to pay.   *obliged*
       (Qwarfor) the state of the impyre,   *empire*
       Hely mowit in to gret ire,
       The hawtane (message) til hym sende
       That wryttyn in the Brute is kende;   *known*
       And Huchon of the Aule Reale   *old*
4280   In til his Gest Historyalle
       Has tretyt that mater cunnandly   *skilfully*
       Mar sufficiande than to pronowns can I.
            As in our mater we procede,
       Sum (man) may fal this buk to rede
       Sal cal the auttoure to rekles,
       And argw perchans his connandnes,   *perhaps, knowledge*
       Syn Hucheon of the Aule Realle   *since*
       In til his Gest Historyalle,
       Owhen kynge of Brettan was Arthoure,   *when*
4290   Callyt Lucyus Hyberyus emperoure.
       Hucheon baythe and the auttour   *both*
       Gyltles ar of gret erroure.
       For the auttour is fyrst to say,
       The storis qwha that wil assay   *whoever*
       Off Iber, Frere Martyn and Wyncens,
       Wrat storis to cun diligens,
       And Orosyus, all foure,
       That mony storis had seyn oure,
       Callit noucht this Lucyus emperoure
4300   Qwhen kynge of Bretan was Arthoure;
       Bot of the Brute the story sayis
       That Lucyus Hyberyus in his dayis
       Was of the hee state procuratoure,   *high*
       Nouthir callit hym kynge, na emperoure.
       Fra blame than was the auttour qwyte,
       As befor hym he fande to wryte;
       And men of gud discrecion
       Sulde excusse and loyff Hucheon,   *love/admire*
       That cunnande was in littratur.
4310   He made a gret Gest of Arthure,
       And the Awntyre of Gawane,
       The Pistil als of Suet Susane.

He was curyousse in his stille,
Fayr of facunde and subtile,   *eloquence*
And ay to pleyssance hade delyte,
Mad in metyre meit his dyte,
Litil or noucht nevir the lesse
Waverande fra the suythtfastnes.   *truth*
    Hade he callyt Lucyus procuratoure,
4320 Qwhar that he callit hym emperoure,
He had ma grewit the cadence   *rhythm*
Than had relewit the sentence.
Ane emperoure, in propyrte,
A commawndour sulde callit be;
Lucyus swylk micht haf beyn kende   *such, known*
Be the (message) that he sende.   *by*
Heyr sufficiande excusacyonys
For wilful defamacionys;
He mon bewar in mony thynge   *must*
4330 That wil hym kep fra mysdoynge.
    Off Arthouris gret douchtynes,   *generosity*
His worschep and his prysse prowes,   *worthy*
His conquest and his ryale state,
As in this buk befor I wrate,
How he helde in his yheris   *time*
His Tabil Rounde withe his Ducheperis,   *twelve companions*
How that he tuk syne his [wayage],   *since*
Fra Lucyus had sende hym the [message],
Til Italy withe hie mychtis
4340 Off kyngis, lordis, and of knychitis,
And discomfit the emperoure,
And wan gret worschepe and honoure
Off Frawnsse nere the bordowris set,   *borders*
In were as thai to gedur met,
And of tresson til hym don
Be Modrede, his systyr son,
Qwaharfor in hast he coym agan,
And withe hym faucht in to Brettan,
Qwhar he and his Rounde Tabil qwyte
4350 Was wndon and discomfyte,
Hucheon has tretyt curyously
In Gest of Brutis aulde story.
Bot of his ded and his last ende   *death*
I fande na wryt couythe mak me kende;   *learn*
Sen I fande nane that thar of wrate,   *since*

I will say na mar than I wate.
Bot qwhen that he had fouchtyn fast,
Eftyr in til ane Ile he past,
Sare wondit, to be lechit thar,   *healed*
4360 And eftyr he was seyn na mare.

WILLIAM STEWART, The Buik of the Chronicles of Scotland *(1535)*

William Stewart's Chronicles *is a translation of Hector Boece's Latin chronicle (1527) into Scottish verse. These nationalistic works expand Fordun's criticism of Arthur's illegitimacy into utter hatred. Arthur now also becomes a glutton and a vow-breaker, who reneges on his agreement to accept Loth's son Mordred as his heir. After he has restored Britain to peace with Scottish assistance, Arthur appoints Constantine as his heir, thus contravening his earlier pledge to Mordred, who subsequently declares war on Arthur. The Picts and Scots are victorious in a battle beside the River Humber and Guenevere is taken off to Scotland as a captive. Her grave can still be seen near Dundee.*

Uther begets Arthur on the Wife of Gothlous, Lord of Cornewall

26225 That samin tyme he tuke his wyfe him fro,
       He gat with hir, my author sais so,
       Ane sone wes callit Arthour to his name;
       In all Britane wes none of grittar fame.
       Thocht he wes gottin in adulterie,   *although*
26230 Yit efterwart he wan grit victorie,
       As I sall schaw within ane litill space,
       Sone efterwart quhen I haif tyme and place.   *when*
       And of his getting Uther sum men sais,
       Be meane of Merling in tha samin dais;
       The quhilk Uther transformit mervelus   *same*
       Into the figour of this Gothlous,
       Syne in his liknes with his wyfe he la.   *since, lay*
       Gif this be suith I can nocht to yow sa.   *true, say*
       Becaus sic thing is nocht kyndlie to be,   *such, natural*

26240 Thairfoir my self will hald it for ane lie.
    This ilk Arthure, fra tyme he grew to eild,   *same, old age*
    In all Britane wes nocht ane farar cheild,
    And all prattik he preissit ay to prewe;
    In him Uther had so gude beleif,
    That he sould be baith worthie, wyse and wycht;
    And so he wes quha reidis of him richt.   *reads*
    Gif it be suith heir as my author sais,
    No lauchfull sone Uter had in his dais;   *lawful*
    That wes the caus, alss far as I haif feill,   *as, found*
26250 This yound Arthour be lovit than so weill.
    For love of him richt far he brak the law,
    As I sall tell, and tak tent to my saw.   *listen to my story*

How Uter For Inordinat Affectioun That He Had To This Arthure, Gart All The Lordis Of Britane Sueir [swear] In Plane Parliament, That Efter Him Tha Sould Mak This Arthour Thair King

    Upoun ane tyme, the lordis him beforne
    In Parliament he gart thame all be sworne,
    Efter his tyme tha suld mak Arthure king.
    And no uther in Britane for to ring.   *other, rule*
    The king of Pechtis, hecht Loth, into tha dais,   *called*
    Had to his wyffe, as that my author sais,
    Uteris sister, baith plesand and fair,   *Uther's*
26260 Quhilk wes to him narrest and lauchfull air;   *lawful*
    And of Uter he wes richt evill content,
    And sindrie syis his servandis to him sent,   *many times*
    Beseikand him with plesand wordis fair,
    That he wald nocht defraud the rychtuous air,   *would*
    Cristane his wyfe, that wes ane ladie brycht,
    Wittand so weill that scho had all the richt.
    For no requeist that he culd send him till,   *to*
    This ilk Uter wald nocht brek of his will
    Nocht worth ane hair,[55] bot at his purpois baid,
26270 And wald nocht heir requeistis that war maid.   *hear*
    The king of Pechtis that tyme quhen he knew,
    That justlie than he micht nocht weill persew,
    Als lang as Uter levand war on lyfe,   *as, living*
    No kynd of richt pertenand to his wyffe,
    All Uteris tyme this ilk schir Loth thairfoir,
    He held him cloiss and spak thairof no moir. [...]   *close*

26947 This same king Arthure, as my author sais,
  In Eborac into tha samin dais,   *York*
  He wes the first with glutony and guill
26950 That evir begouth to mak sic feist in Yule;   *such*
  Continuand unto the threttene da.   *thirteenth day*
  Quhilk wes the caus thairfoir that all the Britis
  Fell in sic folie, as my author writis,
  That tha forget thair greit honour and gloir,
  And victorie that tha had win befoir;
  Quhilk maid thame all unabill for the feild,
  To walk and fast, and waponis for to weild.
  All that wynter, quhen tha usit sic glew, *made such glee*
  This king Occa his power did renew
26960 With nobill men out of Saxonia,
  Him to supplie brocht in Norththrumbia,
  That worthie war thair waponis for to weild.
  In symmer syne, quhen Arthure take the feild,
  The Britis all, war wond so bald to be,
  War sopit so with sensualitie,   *drenched*
  With gluttony and lichorus appetyte,
  Quhair in that tyme tha put thair haill delyte *whole*
  Of weir that tyme tha had no moir desyre,
  Nor for to put thair feit into the fyre.
26970 For that same caus, as my author judgis rycht,
  This king Arthure thocht he wes wyss and
    wycht,   *wise and valiant*
  Quhilk in his time sic fortoun had and chance, *who, good luck*
  Quhairfoir richt mony dois him now advance, *does*
  Agane his fa richt semdill culd prevaill, *foe, very little*
  And of his purpois oft wes maid to faill.

How Arthure maid ane Band to Loth, That efter Arthuris Time Loth and his Airis suld Succeid to the Kinrik of Britane For Ay

26976 And for that caus, quha richt can understand,
  With king Lothus King Arthure maid ane band, *pact*
  Agane Occa than for to tak his part;
  Syne all malice and rancour in his hart
26980 Glaidlie forgif, without ony invye,
  Stryfe and injure in tymes passit by.
  Of that conditioun I sall to yow schaw,
  Concord was maid be cours of commoun law;

That is to say, foroutin ony stryfe,
That king Arthure for terme of all his lyfe
Evin so him list, and at his awin lyking,   *while he wished*
Sould bruke the croun of Britane and be king   *wear*
Efter his deid the croun suld than retour
To schir Modred, quhik wes of hie honour,
26990 King Lothus sone and als his lauchtfull air,
The quhilk his wyfe Cristina to him bair,
That sister wes to king Uter also,
And lauchfull air withoutin ony mo.
Schir Gawin als, that wes young Modredis bruther
Bot he alone that tyme tha had na uther,   *other*
With king Arthure he sould remane ay still,
And for to have, at his plesour and will,
Lordschip and land of Arthour in his fie,
And in the court richt greit auctoritie.
27000 Decretit wes also amang the lawe,
That Modredus in mariage sould have
The fairrest ladie that wes in Britane,
That dochtor wes than of ane nobill man,
Quhilk callit wes Gualanus to his name.
The fair ladie of all bewtie but blame,
Into Britane that tyme scho buir the bell,   *she was most lovely*
Gif all be trew that I hard of hir tell.
Hir father als, of honour and renoun,
27010 Grittest he wes in Britane nixt the croun.
The caus it wes, gif I richt understude,
Modred suld wed into the Britis blude,
His barnis borne and fosterit be also,   *children*
Into Britane quill tha culd speik and go;
And all thair tyme sould haldin be for Britis,
And no Pechtis, as that my author writis;
And first Brit langage for to speik and use,
So that the Britis culd nocht weill refuse,
Quhen that tyme come, Modred to be thair king,
And his barnis to succeid to his ring.   *rule*

*When, with the help of the Picts and Scots, the Saxons are finally
subdued and the country enjoys peace, Arthur conveniently forgets
his bond with Loth and names Constantine as heir to his throne.
When Mordred, now king of the Picts, hears the news, he sends a
messenger to Arthur, requesting that he should honour his promise.*

How Arthure Gafe Ansuer to the Herald

27683 'Gude freind,' he said, 'ye be in wrang for-thy,
       'That blamis us withoutin caus or quhy,
       'Sayand to yow we haif brokin promit;
       'That is nocht trew, as thow sall rhycht weill wit.
       'And for this causs, oure band and oblissing   *obligation*
       'Wes to schir Loth and to na uther king.
       'Quhilk all his tyme we keipit richt perfite.   *which*
27690 'Thairfoir,' he said, 'we ar nocht for to wyte,
       'Efter his tyme thow ma weill understand,
       'Suppois to yow we keip nocht that same band.'
       This was the ansuer that king Arthure gaif,
       With loud lauchter and scornying of the laif;   *rest*
27700 Syne but reward, with mekill bost and blame,   *much*
       To king Modred the herald passit hame,
       And schew to him ilk word, boith les and moir,   *informed*
       At greit lasar, as I haif said befoir.   *length*
       The king Modred quhen he thair ansuer knew,
       And his lordis all, in sic anger grew,
       Into the tyme ilkane baith said and swoir,   *each one*
       Other to die or of that grit injure
       Revengit be, micht tha haif tyme and space,
       Richt suddantlie with help of Goddis grace.

*Despite an attempt by the Bishops to make peace, the British refuse
to keep their bond, and in the ensuing battle beside the River
Humber, the Picts and Scots are victorious.*

27857 Gude schir Gawane that da, with Arthure king,
       The second wing he had at his gyding,
       Tytest that tyme he wes of ony uther   *most determined*
27860 Agane Modred, suppois he wes his bruther.
       Ewgenius and schir Modred also,
       Into the feild agane Arthure did go
       With sic ane counter, like ane thunder crak,
       Quhill scheildis rawe and mony speiris brak;
       Birny and basnet brist wer all in schunder,
       Heidis war hewin in pecis that war under.
       The rappit on with mony rout full rude,   *struggle*
       Quhill breistis brist and bockit out of blude;   *while*
       Full mony freik war fellit thair on force,   *knight*
27870 And mony stout man stickit on his horss;

Full mony berne lay bulrand in his blude;   *man, wallowing*
And mony stalwart stickit quhair he stude.
Into that stour that stalwart wes and strang,   *battle*
With dyntis dour ilkane on uther dang,   *hard blows struck*
Quhill all the water into Humber flude,
Als reid as roissis ran all ovir with blude,
And all the coist full of deid corsis la.   *field, corpses*
Continuallie fra morne airlie that da,   *early*
Tha faucht ay still quhill nune wes passit by,   *noon*
27880 And no man wist quha had the victorye;   *knew*
Quhill at the last ane stalwart Scot and stout,
In Brit langage full loud he gaif ane schout
That all the Britis understude richt plane;
'Allace!' he said, 'oure nobill king is slain!
'Arthure, allace! for evir now art thow gone!
'And slane this da oure nobillis ar ilkone.   *each one*
'Is no remeid to all the laif bot flie,   *remedy, living*
'Or doutles all ilk man heir man we die.'   *each*
Full mony Brit quhen that tha hard that cry,
27890 Tha kest fra thame thair harnes haistelie,   *cast*
But ony stop or tha wald langar stynt,   *longer stay*
Syne fled als fast as fyre dois out of flynt.   *then*
The lawe[56] that knew that cry wes for ane trane,   *trick*
Still in the feild ay fechtand did remane,   *always fighting*
Suppois that tyme thair power wes bot small,   *realise*
Quhill syne on force tha wer confoundit all,   *thus*
And slane ilkone for all thair senyeorie: *nobility*
To Scot and Pecht so fell the victorie.
This battell wes richt bludie to thame baith,
27900 Wes none that da that chapit but greit skayth;   *escaped, harm*
Of Scot and Pecht that da into the feild,
War tuentie thousand and king Modred keild.
King Arthure als upoun the tother syde,
And schir Gawane with mony uther gyde,
With threttie thousand best wat of the Britis,
Wer slane that da, as that my author writis.

How Ewgenius held the feild that nycht, and on the morne partit the spulze [spoils] amang his men

27907 Eugenius he held the feild that da,
Syne on the morne quhair all the Britis la,   *where*
Richt mony nobill fra the feild that fled,

27910 Within thair tentis lyand in thair bed,
 Thair with thair quene, Gwanora hecht to name, *called*
 And hir ladeis unmaculat of fame, *unblemished*
 Eugenius, thair sleipnand quhair tha la
 Into thair bed he tuke thame lang or da, *long before*
 And all the riches in the tyme tha had.
 Syne haistelie on to the feild him sped,
 And all the spulze in the feild he fand, *spoils*
 Richt quietlie, without stop or ganestand, *hindrance*
 To everie man into the tyme he gaif,
27920 Efter his deid as he hes wrocht to haif.[57]
 Arthuris wyffe was callit Gwanora,
 That in hir tyme was fair as dame Flora,
 Onto the Pechtis quhilk plesit thame to haif, *which*
 This ilk princes Eugenius to thame gaif,
 And ladeis all, suppois tha had bene may,
 With mony uther presoner and pray. *booty*
 Syne all the laif, quha lykis for to heir, *since, living*
 In Scotland brocht baith pray and presoneir.
 Siclike the Pechtis with the quene Gwanoir *thus*
27930 And presoneris that tha had les and moir,
 Tha send to keip into Orestia,
 Quhilk callit is now Angus at this da. *day, time*
 Into ane castell callit Doun-bervie,
 Quhairof the fundament restis yit to se, *of which, foundations*
 Quhilk biggit wes richt weill with lyme and stone, *built*
 Tha presoneris war kepit thair ilkone,
 Remanand thair ilkone quhill tha war deid. *until*
 Thair graifis yit apperis in that steid, *graves, place*
 By Megill toun, ten myle above Dundie,
27940 Thair graifis yit remanis for to se:
 Off quene Gwanoir all tyme amang the laif,
 Be the scriptour weill knawin is the graif.

PART 3

ARTHUR IN EARLY FRENCH ROMANCE

CHRÉTIEN DE TROYES, Erec and Enide (c. 1170)

While the Arthur of Geoffrey of Monmouth's History *and the 'chronicle' tradition is an epic warlord and hero, Chrétien de Troyes introduces the Arthur of chivalric romance, an apparently middle-aged ruler who is more inclined towards peace than war.*

Writing over a period of about twelve years at the court of different French nobles, Chrétien composed a total of five Arthurian poems, most of them dealing principally with the relationship between men and women, and in each of these he focuses his attention on a young Arthurian knight.

In Chrétien's first Arthurian romance, Erec and Enide, *a young Arthurian knight sets off in response to a challenge to royal authority. His first task is to defend the queen's honour, and thus that of Arthur. Winning a bride is an integral result of his success, but the remainder of the story recounts his attempts to regain the loss of reputation which results from his neglecting chivalric exploits in order to spend all his time with his beloved.*

The first extract is taken from the opening scene, where Arthur decides to revive the custom of hunting the white stag, despite Gawain's warning that it could cause rivalry among the young knights. This episode produces the first of many instances in French romance where Arthur is portrayed as a weak and possibly inadequate ruler, while Guenevere and Arthur's nephew, Gawain, appear as much stronger characters than the king himself.

The Hunt for the White Stag

One springtide, on Easter Day, King Arthur held at his stronghold of Cardigan a court more lavish than had ever been seen; for it was attended by many good, bold, brave and proud knights and rich ladies and maidens, fair and noble daughters of kings. Now before that court disbanded, the king told his knights he wished to hunt the white stag and renew the worthy observance of that custom. My lord Gawain was far from happy to hear his declaration. 'Sire,' he says, 'this hunt will bring you no thanks or gratitude. For a long time we've all well known what the custom of the white stag is: whoever can kill this white stag must by right kiss the fairest of the maidens in your court, come what may. This could lead to very great trouble, for here there are no fewer than five hundred high-born damsels, attractive and intelligent daughters of kings, all with knights as lovers – bold, valiant men, each of whom would wish to claim, rightly or wrongly, that the one he favours is the most attractive and beautiful.' The king replies: 'I am aware of this; but I shall not give up my intention on that account, for when a king has spoken, his word should not be retracted. Tomorrow morning we shall all derive great enjoyment from going to hunt the white stag in the forest where adventures abound. It will be a truly marvellous hunt.' Thus the matter is arranged for daybreak the following morning.

The next day, as soon as it grows light, the king gets up and dresses, putting on a short tunic for riding in the forest. He has the knights wakened and the horses made ready for the hunt. Without more ado they are all mounted and on their way, equipped with bows and arrows. Behind them mounts the queen accompanied by an attendant maiden, a king's daughter riding a white palfrey. Spurring hard after them comes a knight named Erec, who was of the Round Table and enjoyed a very high reputation at court.

While Arthur and the other knights are involved in the hunt, Erec remains with the queen, who is insulted by an unknown knight's dwarf. Arthur himself kills the stag, but cannot decide on whom to bestow the kiss. Meanwhile, Erec goes off on adventure in pursuit of the unknown knight (Yder), whom he defeats in the Sparrowhawk contest. In this adventure, Erec also obtains a beautiful bride, Enide, whom he brings back to Arthur's court.

Erec Brings Enide Back to Court

Together they rode along until, about midday, they approached the fortress of Cardigan, where they were both awaited. The leading nobles of the court had gone to the upper windows to watch for them. Queen Guenevere hurried there, and the king himself came, and so did Kay and Perceval of Wales, followed by my lord Gawain and Tor, the son of King Arés, together with Lucan the cup-bearer: many fine knights were there. They spotted Erec coming, bringing his beloved with him, and all recognized him easily the moment they saw him. The queen is overjoyed and the whole court delighted at his coming, for they are united in their love for him. On his arrival in front of the hall, the king goes down to meet him, and the queen in turn; and all greet him in God's name. They warmly welcome him and his maiden and praise and applaud her great beauty. Then the king himself took her and helped her down from her palfrey, showing very great courtesy and being in the best of spirits at that time. He did the maiden much honour, leading her by the hand up into the great stone hall.

After them, Erec and the queen went up hand in hand; and he said to her: 'My lady, I bring you my maiden and sweetheart, dressed in poor attire. Just as she was given to me, I have brought her to you. She's the daughter of a poor vavasour. Poverty degrades many a worthy man. Her father is of fine, courtly character, though endowed with little wealth; and her mother is a most noble lady, for she has a brother who is a rich count. I should not refuse to marry the maiden on grounds of beauty or lineage. It's because of poverty she has worn out this white shift so that both sleeves are torn at the elbow. Yet, had I wished, she would have had plenty of good dresses, for a girl, her cousin, wanted to give her a robe of ermine and spotted or grey silk; but on no account did I wish her to wear any other dress until you had seen her. Now think about it, my dear lady! As you well see, she's in great need of a fine, becoming dress.' And the queen immediately replies: 'You've acted quite properly. It's right that she should have one of my robes, and I shall at once give her an excellent one: beautiful and brand-new.'

Without more ado, the queen takes her off to her private apartment and orders that the new tunic be quickly brought along with the greenish-purple mantle embroidered with little crosses that had been made for herself. The person she had sent brought her the mantle and the tunic, which had white ermine trimmings down to the sleeves. At the wrists and neck-band there was, without a word of a lie, more than half a mark's weight of beaten gold; and set everywhere in the gold were very precious stones of indigo, green, blue and dark brown hues. The tunic was very rich, but I fancy the mantle was worth every bit as much. As yet no fastening had been put on it, for it was, like the tunic, absolutely brand-new. The mantle was of fine, excellent quality: at the neck were two sable-skins, and in the tassels was more than an ounce of gold; on one side was a hyacinth, and on the other a ruby that shone more brightly than a burning candle. The lining was of white ermine: none finer or more splendid was ever to be seen or found. The purple cloth was superbly worked with little crosses, all different, in indigo, vermilion, violet, white and green, blue and yellow. The queen asked for a pair of bands, four ells long, made of silk thread and gold. These beautiful, well-matched fastenings are handed to her. She at once had them attached quickly to the mantle by a man who was a true expert at the work.

When there was nothing more to be done to the mantle, that noble, distinguished lady embraced the maiden in the white shift, with the generous words: 'My young lady, you must change that shift for this tunic, which is worth more than a hundred silver marks: that's a favour I should like to do you. Then put this mantle on over it! I shall give you more on another occasion.' She did not refuse it, but took the dress with thanks. Two maids led her into a room apart, where she took off her shift, not having the slightest regard for it any more, with the request that it be given in charity for the love of God. Then she puts on the tunic, fastening a belt of gold brocade tightly round her waist; and after that she dons the mantle. Her expression was now far from dejected, for the dress suited her so well that it made her look much more beautiful than ever.

The two maids bound her fair hair with a golden thread; but her locks shone brighter than the thread, though it was of very fine gold. On her head the girls place a circlet made of flowers of many different colours. They do their utmost to adorn her in such a fashion that no room for improvement could be found. One of them placed round her neck a ribbon to which were attached two small brooches of enamelled gold. Now she was so graceful and lovely that her equal, I think, could not have been found in any land, seek and search as one might, so excellently had Nature fashioned her.

Then she left the room and came to the queen, who welcomed her very warmly, liking and greatly approving of her because of her beauty and fine manners. Taking each other by the hand, they came before the king, who, on seeing them, rose to his feet to receive them. As they entered the hall, so many knights rose to greet them that I cannot name one tenth, or thirteenth, of fifteenth of them; but I can tell you the names of some of the best nobles among those of the Round Table, who were the finest in the world.

Before all the good knights, Gawain should come first, Erec the son of Lac second, and Lancelot of the Lake third. Gornemant of Gohort was fourth, and fifth was the Handsome Coward. Sixth was the Ugly Brave, seventh Meliant of Liz, eighth Mauduit the Wise and ninth Dodinel the Wild. Let Gandelu come tenth for his many good qualities. I shall tell you the others in no particular sequence, because

I find it difficult to put them in order. Eslit was there with Briien and Yvain son of Urien. Yvain of Loenel was also there and Yvain the Bastard. Beside Yvain of Cavaliot was Garravain of Estrangot. After the Knight with the Horn was the Youth with the Golden Ring. And Tristan who never laughed sat beside Blioblaheris, and next to Brun of Piciez was his brother Grus the Wrathful. The Armourer, who preferred war to peace, was seated next, and after him Karadués the Short-Armed, a knight of very cheerful disposition; and Caveron of Robendic and King Quenedic's son, the Youth of Quintareus and Yder of the Dolorous Mount, Gaheriet and Kay of Estraus, Amauguin and Gales the Bald, Grain, Gornevain and Carahés, and Tor the son of King Arés, Girflet the son of Do, and Taulas who never tired of arms; and a young man of great merit, Loholt, King Arthur's son; and Sagremor the Impetuous should not be forgotten, nor Bedoiier the Marshal who was an expert at chess and backgammon, nor Bravaïn, nor King Lot, nor Galegantin of Wales, nor Gronosis, well versed in evil, who was Kay the Seneschal's son, nor Labigodés the Courtly, nor Count Cadorcaniois, nor Letron of Prepelesant, whose manners were so polished, nor Breon the son of Canodan, nor the Count of Honolan who had such a fine head of fair hair and was the one who received the ill-fated king's horn and never had regard for the truth.

When the lovely stranger maiden saw all the ranks of knights who were gazing steadily at her, she bowed her head low: it was not surprising that, in her embarrassment, her face turned scarlet; but her confusion was so becoming that it made her look more beautiful still. When the king saw her embarrassment, he would not have her leave him. Gently he took her by the hand and seated her beside him on his right. The queen sat down on the king's left and said to him: 'Sire, I truly believe that a man who can win by deeds of arms such a beautiful wife in another land is entitled to come to a royal court. We did well to wait for Erec. Now you can bestow the kiss on the fairest in the court. I doubt if anyone would stand in your way or anybody but a liar ever claim that this is not the most attractive of the maidens present here or in the whole world.' The king replies: 'That's no falsehood. Upon her, unless any challenge me, I shall bestow the honour of the white stag.'

Then he addressed the knights: 'My lords, what do you say? What is your view? In face and body and whatever features are proper to a maiden, this one is the most charming and beautiful, I think, to be found this side of where earth and sky meet. I say that it is right and proper that she should receive the honour of the stag. And you, my lords, what have you to say? Is there any objection you can raise? If any man wishes to contest this, let him speak his thoughts here and now. I am king and must not lie or be a party to any baseness, deception or high-handedness. I must safeguard right and reason. It's the business of a true king to uphold the law, truth, good faith and justice. I would not wish in any way to commit disloyalty or wrong any more against the weak than the strong. It is not right that any should have a complaint against me, and I do not wish the traditional custom to lapse which my family habitually observes. You would doubtless be unhappy if I wished to introduce for you customs and laws other than those kept by my father the king. Whatever may become of me, I must safeguard and uphold the practice of my father Pendragon, the just king and emperor. Now give me your full opinions! Let no one hesitate to say truly if this maiden is not the fairest in my household and should not rightly receive the kiss of the white stag: I wish to hear the truth.'

They all cry out with one voice: 'Sire, by the Lord and His cross! you may well kiss her in all justice, for she is the fairest one there is. In this maiden there is more beauty than there is brightness in the sun. You are free to give her the kiss: we agree to it unanimously.' When the king hears that they are all content, he will not delay in kissing her, but turns towards her and embraces her. The maiden was not foolish and truly wanted the king to kiss her: it would have been unbecoming of her to take it amiss. In the sight of all the nobles the king kissed her in courtly fashion with the words: 'My sweet friend, I give you my love in all honesty. I shall love you with all my heart without baseness or impropriety.' Those were the circumstances in which the king observed the rightful tradition associated at his court with the white stag. So ends the first part of the story.

CHRÉTIEN DE TROYES, Cligés (c. 1176)

This story is probably the first in a series of French romances wherein an unproved hero seeks knighthood and honour at Arthur's court. The romance falls naturally into two sections: the first part dealing with Cligés's father, Alexander, and the second concentrating on Cligés himself and his love for Fenice, who is forced to marry his uncle. Although his father finds honour and a bride at Arthur's court, Cligés, since he is already bound by love, leaves court after proving his prowess in a tournament against Arthur's followers, refusing to join their ranks.

In the extracts included here, Alexander, eldest son of the Greek emperor, decides to visit Britain with twelve companions in order to acquire fame. He has heard about the great renown of King Arthur and his court.

Cligés's Father Visits Court

Because of their extremely sick state they spend that night at Southampton, but in the best of spirits, and make enquiries as to whether the king is in England. They are told he is in Winchester and that they can get there very quickly, so long as they are prepared to set out early in the morning and take the direct road. This news delights them; and at daybreak the next morning the youths wake early, dress and equip themselves. Once ready, they left Southampton and, following the direct route, came to Winchester where the king was staying. Before six o'clock in the morning the Greeks had arrived at court.

They dismount at the foot of the steps; and their squires and horses remain in the courtyard below while the youths go up into the presence of the best king who ever was or ever may be in the world. And when the king sees them coming, their appearance greatly pleases and delights him. But before approaching him, they unfasten their cloaks from their necks so as not to be considered ignorant. In this way, with their cloaks removed, they went before the king. All the nobles fell silent, very pleased at the sight of these handsome, well-mannered young men and not doubting they were all sons of counts or kings. So indeed they were: all of a most attractive age, good-looking and well built; and the clothes they wore were all of the same cloth and cut, of identical design and colour. There were twelve of them apart from their lord, of whom I will merely tell you that none was better than he. But it was modestly and without presumption that he stood before the king without his cloak, very handsome and of fine physique as he was. He knelt before him; and all the others knelt as a mark of honour beside their lord.

Alexander, his tongue well schooled in wise and eloquent speech, salutes the king. 'King,' he says, 'unless accounts of your fame are false, since God created the first man there never was born a God-fearing king of your might. King, your widespread fame has brought me to your court to serve and honour you; and, if you approve my service, I should like to stay here until I'm made a new knight by your hand and no other; for unless it is through you, I shall never be called knight. If you appreciate my service enough to wish to knight me, then keep me with you, noble king, and also my companions here.' The king immediately replies: 'My friend, I turn neither you nor your company away, but bid you all welcome. For you seem, and I think you are, the sons of high-born men. Where are you from?' – 'We come from Greece.' – 'From Greece?' – 'Yes indeed.' – 'Who is your father?' – 'The emperor, sire, I assure you.' – 'And what is your name, my good friend?' – 'Alexander was the name given me when I received the salt and holy oil and Christianity at my baptism.' – 'Alexander, my dear good friend, I will retain you with me very willingly, and I'm most pleased and delighted to do so, for you have done me great honour in coming to my court. I am most anxious for you to be honoured here as noble, wise and well-conducted vassals. But you've been on your knees too long: I bid you rise, and be from now on members of my court and my confidants, for you have found a good haven.'

At that the Greeks rise to their feet, happy that the king has so kindly made them welcome. Alexander is well off, for he lacks nothing he wants; and in court there is no noble, however high his rank, who does not receive him kindly and welcome him. He is not foolish and does not give himself airs or behave in a self-important, swaggering manner. He makes the acquaintance of my lord Gawain and of the others, one by one, becoming very popular with each of them; and my lord Gawain is even so fond of him that he calls him his friend and companion.

The Greeks had taken the best lodging they could have with one of the citizens of the town. Alexander had brought great wealth from Constantinople, being anxious above all to heed the emperor's entreaties and advice to have his heart set on generous giving and spending. To this he devotes much attention and effort, living very well in his lodgings and giving and spending liberally as befits his wealth and his heart dictates. The whole court wonders where his resources have come from; for he gives to all and sundry valuable horses he had brought from his own country. Alexander has made such great efforts and excellently performed his service to such good effect that he gains the great love and esteem of the king as well as of the nobles and the queen.

At that time King Arthur wished to cross into Brittany. He summoned all his lords together to advise him, asking to whom he can entrust England until his return, to hold it in peace and security. On their unanimous advice, I believe, it was placed in the charge of Count Angrés of Windsor; for it was their opinion that there was no more trustworthy lord in all the king's territory. The following day, with the land placed under the count's control, King Arthur set out, together with the queen and her maidens. In Brittany they hear that the king is coming with his lords; and the Bretons rejoice greatly at the news.

Aboard the ship in which the king made the crossing there was no young man or maiden other than Alexander and, accompanying the queen, Soredamors, who was scornful of love. She had never heard tell of a man, however handsome, valiant, noble or highly born, whom she might condescend to love. Yet the damsel was so charming and beautiful that she really should have learnt something of love, had she wished to turn her attention to it; but she was never willing to give it a thought. Now Love will make her suffer, intending to take full vengeance for the great arrogance and reluctance she has always displayed towards him. Love has taken good aim and, with his arrow, pierced her to the heart. She often turns pale and frequently perspires, being forced to love despite herself. She can hardly restrain herself from gazing at Alexander, but has to be on her guard against my lord Gawain, her brother. She pays dearly to make amends for her great pride and disdain.

Love has warmed for her a bath which she finds very hot and scalding. Now she likes it and now it is painful for her, now she wants its and now rejects it. She accuses her eyes of treason, saying: 'My eyes, you have betrayed me! Through you my heart, which used to be so faithful, has come to hate me. Now I'm distressed at what I see. Distressed? But no – rather it pleases me. And if I do see anything that distresses me, are not my eyes under my control? I should really have lost my authority and should have a poor opinion of myself if I cannot rule my eyes and make them look elsewhere. In that way I can easily guard against Love, who wishes to control me. What the eye doesn't see, the heart doesn't grieve over: if I don't see him, he means nothing to me. He asks or requests nothing from me. If he loved me, he would have made some approach; so as he does not love or have any regard for me, shall I love him when he doesn't love me? If his beauty lures my eyes and my eyes respond to the lure, should I say I love him because of that? No, for that would be a lie. So he has no claim on me, and I have no more or less of a claim on him. One cannot love with one's eyes. And what crime, then, have my eyes committed against me, if they look where I wish? What wrong are they guilty of in that? Should I blame them for it? No. Whom then? Myself, who am in charge of them. My eyes gaze at nothing unless it suits and pleases my heart; and my heart should not wish for anything that might grieve me, but it is its wish that makes me suffer. – Suffer? Then I am indeed foolish when through it I'm wanting something that upsets me. I should, if I can, banish any desire that brings me pain. – If I can? Foolish girl, what have I said?

I should not be able to do much at all, if I had no control over myself. Does love think he can put me on the right road, when he usually leads others astray? He had better guide others, for I'm not at all dependent on him, nor ever will be nor ever was; nor shall I ever cherish his friendship."

While Alexander, who accompanies King Arthur to Brittany, falls in love with Gawain's sister, Soredamors, Count Angrés of Windsor plots rebellion during Arthur's absence.

The Rebellion of Count Angrés

At the very beginning of October, messengers came from London and Canterbury by way of Dover, bringing the king news that filled him with dismay. The messengers told him he risks staying in Brittany too long; for the man to whom he had entrusted his land is intending to rebel against him, having already summoned a great army of his own men and his friends and established himself in London in order to hold that city against the king whenever he might arrive.

On hearing the news, the king, angry and incensed, calls together all his lords. To goad them better into bringing the traitor to grief, he says that all the blame for his trouble and strife is theirs, for it was on their advice that he placed his lands in the hands of that criminal who is worse than Ganelon. There is not one of them who does not admit that the king is absolutely right, for that was the advice they gave him; but they say the man will be utterly destroyed, and he may be quite sure that no castle or city will afford him protection against their hauling him out by force. Thus they all reassure the king, solemnly pledging and swearing to deliver the traitor to him or never again hold a fief. And the king proclaims throughout Brittany that no one fit to bear arms in battle shall fail to come at once to follow him.

The whole of Brittany is on the move, and never was there seen such an army as King Arthur assembled. When the ships set sail it seemed the whole world was at sea, for the waves were so covered by ships that nothing of them could be seen. This will be a real war! From the commotion on the sea it seems the whole of Brittany is under way. Already the ships have made the crossing, and the assembled host is quartered along the coast. Alexander had the idea of going to beg the king to knight him; for if he is ever to win renown, he will win it in this war. Fired by a determination to put his plan into effect, he took his companions with him, and they went to the king's tent.

The king was seated in front of his tent; and when he saw the Greeks coming, he called them into his presence. 'Sirs,' he says, 'don't keep from me the reason for your coming here.' Alexander spoke for them all, telling him of his desire. 'I've come', he said, 'to beg you, as I should entreat my lord, on behalf of my companions and myself, to confer knighthood on us.' The king replies: 'Very gladly, and there shall be no delay in doing it, since you've requested it of me.' Then the king orders equipment to be brought for thirteen knights. The king's bidding is done. Then each asks for his own equipment, which is given to one and all, fine arms and a good horse. They all took their own gear. That for each of the twelve, arms, robes and horse, was of equal value; but Alexander's own outfit, should anyone wish to value or sell it, was worth exactly as much as all the other twelve. At the sea's edge they undressed, washed and bathed themselves. Not wishing or consenting that any other bath be heated for them, they made the sea serve as bath and tub.

These events are known to the queen, who does not dislike Alexander: on the contrary, she is very fond of him, praises and thinks highly of him, and wishes to do him a real favour, which is far greater than she realizes. She rummages through all her chests and empties them until she takes out a white silk shirt, splendidly made and of very fine, delicate quality, sewn with nothing but gold or, at the least, silver thread. From time to time Soredamors had taken a hand in the stitching; and in places, on the two sleeves and the collar, she had worked in beside the gold a hair from her own head, as a test to see if she could ever find a man who would examine it so closely as to tell the one from the other; for the hair was just as bright and golden as the gold itself, or more so. The queen takes the shirt and has it sent to Alexander.

Ah God! How great Alexander's joy would have been had he known what the queen was sending him! And she, too, who had worked her hair into it would have been very joyful had she known that her beloved was to have and wear it. She would have been able to take great comfort from that; for she would not have cared so much for the rest of her hairs as for the one Alexander had. But they are both unaware of this; and it is a great pity they do not know. The queen's messenger came to the port where the young men were bathing and, finding the youth in the sea, presented him with the shirt. He is delighted with it, especially as it has come from the queen. But had he known the rest, he would have cherished it far more and would not in exchange have accepted the whole world; rather he would have treated it, I think, as a holy relic and adored it day and night.

Alexander waits no longer, but dresses himself at once. When he was dressed and equipped, he returned to the king's tent along with all his companions. The queen, it seems, had come to sit in the tent, wishing to see the new knights arrive. One might think them handsome; but the fine figure of Alexander was the most handsome of them all. Now they are knights; and I shall say no more of them, but speak of the king and the army which came to London. Most of the people joined with him, but he also had a large number against him. Count Angrés gathers together on his own side as many as he could win over by promises and gifts. Once he had mustered his men, he fled secretly at night since, as he was hated by many, he was afraid of being betrayed. But before he made off, he plundered London of all the foodstuffs, gold and silver he could, and distributed everything among his men. The king is given the news of the traitor's flight together with his entire force, and told that he has taken from the city so much wealth and provisions that the townspeople are impoverished, made destitute and ruined. And in response the king declares that he will never take a ransom for the traitor, but will hang him, if he can catch or lay hands on him.

At once the whole army moved off and came as far as Windsor. In those days, whatever it may be like now, the castle was far from easy to take from anyone who wished to defend it; for the traitor, as soon as he planned his treachery, fortified it with triple walls and moats, and had the walls buttressed behind with heavy logs, so that catapults could not bring them down. He had spent a great deal on the fortifications, taking all June, July and August to build walls and palisades, moats and drawbridges, ditches, barriers and barricades, iron portcullises and a great keep of dressed stone. Never was a gate closed there from fear or against an assault. The castle stood on a high hill, with the Thames flowing beneath. The army encamped on the river bank, and that day they were fully occupied in preparing their quarters and erecting the tents.

The army has pitched camp beside the Thames, and the whole meadow is covered with green and scarlet tents. The sun strikes down on the colours, making the riverbank blaze with them for a full league and more. The men from the castle had come to amuse themselves by the waterside, with just their lances in their hands and their shields held against their chests, but otherwise unarmed. By coming without their armour, they showed those outside the castle that they had little fear of them. On the other bank, Alexander noticed these knights duelling with each other in front of them. He would like to come to grips with them, and so calls to his companions by name, one after the other. First there was Cornix, who was very dear to him, then the bold Licorides, then Nabunal of Mycene, Acorionde of Athens, Ferolin of Salonica and Calcedor from Africa, Parmenides and Francagel, mighty Torin and Pinabel, Nerius and Neriolis. 'Sirs,' he says, 'I should like to go and try conclusions with shield and lance against those people who've come to joust in front of us. I can see they have a poor opinion and think little of us, or so it seems when they've come to joust here, unarmed, under our very noses. We're newly dubbed and haven't yet favoured any knight or quintain with our attentions. We've kept our first lances intact far too long. What were our shields made for? They're still not holed or broken. They're useless things to have except in a fight or attack. Let's cross by the ford and set about them!' They all say: 'We'll not fail you!' And each adds: 'So help me God, anyone who lets you down now is no friend of yours!'

They immediately gird on their swords, secure their saddles and tighten their girths, mount and take their shields. Having hung the shields at their necks and grasped the lances painted with their individual colours, they all gallop as one to the ford; and those on the other side lower their lances and charge to strike at them. But they knew how to give as good as they got, and without sparing or avoiding them or yielding as much as a foot against them, each strikes his opponent so hard that there is not a knight good enough to stay in the saddle. They did not mistake the Greeks for mere lads or cowards or idiots! Their first blows were not wasted, for they unhorsed thirteen of their enemies. The news of the great blows they dealt reached the army. There would soon have been a fine set-to had the others dared to wait for them. The men in the army rush for their arms, then dash into the water with a great clamour; and the others turn to flight, thinking that is no place for them to linger. And the Greeks go after them, keeping them company with blows from lances and swords, lopping off plenty of heads, but without any of their own number being wounded. That day they gave a good account of themselves; but Alexander took the main credit, capturing four knights by himself, trussing them up and leading them away. And the dead lie on the sand, for there were many decapitated, others wounded or maimed.

Alexander courteously presents to the queen the gift of his first spoils as a knight, not wanting the king to have them in his power, for he would quickly have them hanged. The queen has them taken and held prisoner on a charge of treason. Throughout the army they talk of the Greeks, and everyone says that Alexander is very courtly and sensible not to have surrendered the knights he had captured to the king, for he would have burned or hanged them. But the king does not find that amusing and sends at once for the queen, telling her to come and speak with him and not keep custody of his traitors; for she must either hand them over or displease him by keeping them. The queen came to the king, and they duly had their discussion about the traitors. All the Greeks had remained in the queen's tent with her maidens, the twelve talking a great deal with them, but Alexander not saying a word. Soredamors, who had sat down close to him, noticed this. With chin in hand, he appears lost in thought.

They sat for a long time like this until Soredamors saw at his arm and at his neck the hair she had used in her stitching. She drew a little closer to him, having now found an opportunity to speak with him; but first she wonders how to open a conversation with him and what word she should begin with, whether she should call him by his name. So she turns it over in her mind. 'What shall I say first?' she asks. 'Shall I address him by name, or call him friend? – Friend? Not I. – What, then? – Call him by name! God! "Friend", though, is such a beautiful, sweet word to utter. If I dared call him friend! – Dared? What stops me? – The fact that I think that would be lying. – Lying? I don't know what will come of it, but if I lie, I'll be sorry. So it's best to admit I wouldn't want to lie. God! Yet he'd tell no lie if he called me his sweet friend! And would I be lying about him? We both ought to speak the truth. But if I do lie, the fault will be his. And why is his name so hard for me to say that I want to use a second name for him? It seems to me to have too many letters, and I'd stop in the middle. But if I called him friend, that's a name I could say very quickly. Because I'm afraid of not getting through the other, I'd gladly shed my blood for his name to be "my sweet friend".'

She remains immersed in these thoughts until the queen returns from the king who had summoned her. Alexander sees her coming and goes to meet her, asking what the king orders to be done with his prisoners and what their fate is to be. 'My friend,' she says, 'he requires me to hand them over to him at his discretion and let him bring them to justice. He's very angry that I've not already surrendered them to him; so send them to him I must, for I see no way out of it.' Thus they spent that day; and on the next the good, loyal knights gathered before the royal tent to pronounce legal judgment as to the punishment and torture by which the four traitors should die. Some say they should be flayed, others that they should be hanged or burned. And the king himself maintains that a traitor should be drawn apart. Then he orders them to be fetched. When they are brought, he has them bound and says they are to be drawn all round the castle in full view of those inside.

After this sentence had been passed, the king addresses Alexander, calling him his dear friend. 'My friend,' he says, 'yesterday I saw you attacking and defending splendidly, and I wish to reward you for it. I increase your company by five hundred Welsh knights and a thousand men-at-arms from my own land. When I've brought my war to an end I shall, in addition to what I've given you, have you crowned king of the best kingdom in Wales. There I shall give you towns and castles, cities and halls until such time as you inherit the land held by your father, of which you are to be emperor.' Alexander expresses to the king his deep gratitude for this gift, and his companions add their own thanks for it. All the nobles in the court say that Alexander fully deserves the honour the king confers on him.

No sooner does Alexander see his men, his companions and men-at-arms that the king is pleased to give him, than bugles and trumpets are duly sounded throughout the army. All without exception take up arms: good men and bad, those from Wales and Brittany, Scotland and Cornwall, for indeed the army was greatly reinforced from all quarters.

The level of the Thames was low as there had been no rain all summer, and the drought was such that the fish in it had died, the boats were stranded in the port, and it was possible to ford the river at its widest point. The army crossed the Thames, part occupying the valley and part climbing on to the higher ground. Those in the fortress observe them and watch the arrival outside of this amazing army, which is making its preparations to destroy and seize the castle, while they for their part make ready to defend it. But before any attack is launched, the king has the traitors drawn round the castle by four horses, through the valleys and over the hills and fallow ground. Count Angrés is furious at the sight of those he held dear being dragged round his castle; and the rest are very dismayed, but despite their alarm they have no wish to surrender. They need to defend themselves, for the king openly displays to all his anger and wrath, and they see plainly that if he captured them he would put them shamefully to death.

When the four had been drawn, and their limbs were strewn over the field, then the assault began. But all the attackers' efforts are in vain, for however much they hurl and shoot their missiles, they can achieve nothing. Nevertheless they try their hardest, casting and shooting great numbers of javelins, bolts and darts. On all sides there is a great din from the crossbows and catapults, and arrows and round stones fly as thick and fast as rain mixed with hail. They struggle like this all day, some defending, some attacking, until night separates them. And on his side, the king has a proclamation made telling the army of the gift he will bestow on the man responsible for the taking of the castle: he will give him an extremely valuable cup of gold weighing fifteen marks, the most costly in his treasury. The cup will be very fine and rich, and, to tell the ungarbled truth, should be admired more for its workmanship than the material. The craftsmanship of the cup is excellent; yet, if the truth be told, the stones on its sides are worth more than either the workmanship or the gold. If the man who has the castle taken is a foot-soldier, he shall have the cup; if it is taken by a knight, then whatever reward he may ask as well as the cup, he shall have it, provided it can be found in the world.

It is, of course, Alexander and his followers who succeed in capturing Windsor castle for Arthur, by disguising themselves as Angrés's men in order to enter the castle.

CHRÉTIEN DE TROYES, Lancelot, or the Knight of the Cart (c. 1177)

This story, which may be associated with the earlier abduction of Guenevere by Melvas, recounts her rescue by the young unknown knight who subsequently becomes her lover. While there is no direct source for Chrétien's Lancelot *extant, the theme of Queen Guenevere's abduction was apparently already well known, occurring in Caradoc of Llancarfan's* Life of St Gildas *(see above, p. 20), and depicted in the carving at Modena Cathedral by the early twelfth century.*

Introducing the figure of Lancelot and his love for Queen Guenevere into the Arthurian story, Lancelot *was undertaken by Chrétien at the request of his patroness, Marie de Champagne. However, he deliberately left the poem incomplete for Godefroi de Leigni to finish, so it is quite probable that Chrétien did not enjoy the subject matter.*

The extract is taken from the opening scene at Arthur's court, which contains the first known reference to Camelot, the elusive place that most people today consider to have been the location of Arthur's court.[58] The motif of an unknown knight arriving at Arthur's court to deliver a challenge becomes a standard theme of Arthurian romance. Kay the seneschal, a heroic figure in early Welsh poetry and one of Arthur's earliest followers, has, by this

time, already acquired his conventionally poor reputation.[59]
Another topic seen in this work which frequently recurs in sub-
sequent Arthurian romance was the don constraint: here Arthur,
when blackmailed by Kay, readily promises to give his seneschal
whatever he desires.

King Arthur, one Ascension Day, had left Caerleon and held a most
magnificent court at Camelot with all the splendour appropriate to
the day. After their meal, the king did not leave those in his company.
In the hall there were many nobles; and the queen was there too and
with her, I believe, numerous beautiful courtly ladies conversing easily
in French. Kay, who had waited at the tables, was eating with those
who had served with him; and as he was sitting there at his meal, all
of a sudden here is a knight arriving at court well equipped and fully
armed. And, thus arrayed, the knight went right up to the king where
he sat among his nobles. He gave him no greeting, but said: 'King
Arthur, I hold in captivity knights, ladies and maidens from your land
and your household. However, I give you this news of them not
because I intend to return them to you: on the contrary, I wish to tell
and inform you that you lack the strength and resources to be able
to get them back. And you may be sure you'll die without ever being
in a position to help them.' The king replies that he must put up with
this, if he can do nothing about it, though he is deeply grieved on
that account.

The knight then makes as if he wishes to leave and turns away, not
staying before the king, but going as far as the hall door. Yet he does
not go down the steps, but stops there, with the words: 'King, if there
is in your court so much as one knight whom you trust enough to
dare hand over to him the queen, to be taken after me into those
woods where I'm heading, I'll promise to wait for him there; and, if
he can win her from me and manage to bring her back, I'll return to
you all the prisoners held captive in my land.' Many in the palace
heard this, and it set the court in a turmoil.

Kay, hearing this news as he was eating with the servants, leaves
his meal and comes straight to the king and, with every appearance
of anger, addresses him thus: 'King, I've given you very long, faithful
and loyal service. Now I take my leave and shall go away, for I'll not
serve you any further. I have no intention or desire to serve you from
now on.' The king is saddened by what he hears; and as soon as he
is able to reply, he at once says to him: 'Do you mean this, or are you
joking?' And Kay replies: 'My good lord king, I've no mind to joke
now, but am quite definitely taking my leave. I don't ask from you
any other reward or wages for my service. That's what I'm determined

to do now: to be off, without delay.' – 'Is it out of anger or defiance that you want to leave?' asked the king. 'Seneschal, stay at court as usual, and you may be sure that I have nothing in this world I would not give you without hesitation just to keep you here.' – 'Sire,' says Kay, 'it's no use: I'd not accept a bushel a day of the purest gold.' Imagine the king's great despair as he then goes off to the queen. 'My lady,' says he, 'you've no idea what the seneschal wants from me! He's asking for his leave and saying he won't be at my court any longer – I don't know why. What he refuses to do for me he'll readily do if you ask him. Go to him, my dear lady! Since he doesn't deign to stay for me, beg him to do so for your sake, even if it means falling at his feet; for I'd never be happy again without his company.'

The king sends the queen away to the seneschal, and off she goes to him. Finding him with the others, she went up to him and said: 'Kay, you may be quite sure that I'm extremely upset at what I've heard about you. I've been told, to my sorrow, that you want to leave the king's service. Where did you get this idea? What is your motive? I don't now think of you at all as sensible and courtly, as I used to. I want to beg you to stay. Stay, I beseech you!' – 'My lady,' he says, 'I thank you; but I wouldn't remain here.' Again the queen pleads with him, joined by the whole company of knights. And Kay tells her her efforts will be quite fruitless. Then the queen falls full length at his feet. Kay begs her to rise, but she refuses: she will never get up again until he agrees to do as she wishes. Kay then promised her to stay, provided the king will first agree to what he will propose and that she will herself consent to it. 'Kay,' says she, 'whatever it is, both I and he will agree to it. Now come along, and we'll tell him you will stay on this condition.' Kay goes with the queen, and they come before the king. 'My lord,' says the queen, 'I've kept Kay here after a great deal of trouble; but I bring him to you on the understanding that you will do what he proposes.' The king sighed with joy, saying that whatever his request to him may be, he will do as he wishes.

'Sire,' says Kay, 'this, then, is what I want and the nature of the favour you've promised me; and I think myself very fortunate that I shall have it, thanks to you: you've agreed, sire, to hand over to me my lady here, and we shall go after the knight who is waiting for us in the forest.' This saddens the king, yet he makes her over to him, for he never went back on his word; but the distress and grief it caused him were clearly evident on his face. The queen too was extremely dejected; and everyone throughout the building says that what Kay had asked and sought was arrogant, outrageous and absurd. Then the king took the queen by the hand with the words: 'My lady, it is inevitable that you must go away with Kay.' And Kay says: 'Hand her over to me now; and have no fear at all, for I'll bring her back, quite happy and unharmed, without fail.'

The king entrusts her to him, and he leads her away. Everybody follows them out, all very troubled, without exception. You may be sure the seneschal was fully armed; and his horse was brought into the middle of the courtyard, and beside it a palfrey fit for a queen. The queen comes to this palfrey, which was neither fiery nor impetuous. Miserable and depressed, the queen sighs as she mounts. Then, softly so that no one might hear her, she said: 'Oh! If only you knew, you would never, I think, allow me to be led away a single step without opposition!' She thought she had said that very quietly; but Count Guinable, who was close to her when she mounted, did hear. When they left, every man and woman watching grieved as bitterly as if she lay dead in her coffin, not believing she would ever come back again in her lifetime.

The seneschal in his recklessness leads her to where the other knight awaits him. But no one was sufficiently concerned to take the trouble to follow him until my lord Gawain said openly to his uncle the king: 'Sire, you've done an extremely silly thing which astonishes me. But if you take my advice, while they're still close at hand you and I and anyone else who wants to come will follow them. Nothing could keep me from going after them immediately: it would not do at all if we didn't follow them at least until we knew what will happen to the queen and how Kay will acquit himself.' – 'Ah, good nephew,' said the king, 'now that's a very chivalrous suggestion. And since this is what you're set on doing, order our horses to be brought out, bridled and saddled, so that it only remains to set out.'

At once the horses are brought and saddled with all their trappings. The king is the first to mount, followed by my Lord Gawain and all the others, just as fast as they can. Anxious to be in the company, everybody sets out as he pleases, some of them armed and many without arms.

CHRÉTIEN DE TROYES, Yvain, or the Knight of the Lion (c. 1177)

In Yvain, *which was written at about the same time as his* Lancelot, *Chrétien de Troyes continues the theme of established Arthurian knights setting off on quest in response to challenges of Arthur's authority. Here, the first task of the hero is to defeat a knight who refuses to accept Arthur's authority as overlord; in this case he assumes the lordship in dispute, and defends it for his lady against the king. Persuaded to return to court by his cousin Gawain, he forgets his wife so that, like Erec before him, the object of his later adventures is the re-establishment of his identity and the regaining of the lady's respect.*

Again, as in Chrétien's earlier poems, this work provides Arthur with only a small role and does not leave a good impression of his character. In fact, although Arthur's fine qualities are held up for emulation in the opening lines of the poem, the king's only action on this occasion is to irritate his vassals by leaving the feast and retiring to his room, where he falls asleep! Meanwhile, his knights entertain themselves by listening to a story, significantly an account of failure rather than success, and something of the character of Queen Guenevere is revealed in an argument with the unruly Kay.

Arthur, the good King of Britain, whose noble qualities teach us that we ourselves should be honourable and courtly, held a court of truly regal splendour for that most sumptuous festival that is properly called Pentecost. The court was at Carlisle in Wales. After the meal, throughout the halls, the knights gathered where they were called by the ladies, damsels and maidens. Some related anecdotes; others spoke of love, of the torments and sorrows and of the great blessings that often come to the members of its order, which at that time was powerful and thriving. Nowadays, however, it has few adherents, since almost all have abandoned love, leaving it much debased. For those who used to love had a reputation for courtliness, integrity, generosity and honour; but now love is made a laughing-stock, because people who feel nothing of it lie by claiming to love; and they make a deceitful mockery of it when they boast of it without having the right. But let us leave those still alive to speak of those who once were! For, in my view, a courtly man who is dead is still worth more than a living churl. Therefore I am pleased to relate something worth hearing concerning the king who was of such repute that he is spoken of near and far; and I agree with the people of Britain that his name will live on for ever. And through him are remembered those fine chosen knights who devoted all their efforts to honour.

That day, however, they were quite astonished to find the king rise and leave their company; and some of them were very offended and did not spare their comments, having never before, on such an important feast-day, seen him retire to his room to sleep or rest. On this day, though, he came to be detained by the queen and happened to stay so long at her side that he forgot himself and fell asleep. Outside the door of his room were Dodinel and Sagremor, Kay and my lord Gawain and with them my lord Yvain; there too was Calogrenant, a very good-looking knight, who had begun to tell them a story that was not to his honour but to his shame. As he was telling his tale, the queen could hear him; and she got up from the king's side and came upon them so stealthily that she had landed in their midst before anyone caught sight of her, except that Calogrenant alone jumped to his feet to greet her.

Then Kay, who was extremely abusive, wickedly sarcastic and sneering, said to him: 'By God, Calogrenant, I see you're very gallant and sprightly now, and indeed I'm delighted you are the most courtly of us; and I know very well you think so – you're so completely devoid of sense. So it's only right for my lady to suppose that you possess more courtliness and gallantry than the rest of us. Perhaps it was out of laziness that we failed to rise, or else because we didn't deign to? I assure you, sir, that wasn't our reason, but the fact that we didn't see my lady until you had stood up first.' – 'Really, Kay, I do believe you'd burst', says the queen, 'if you couldn't empty yourself of the venom you are full of. You're tiresome and churlish to insult your companions.' – 'My lady,' says Kay, 'if we don't gain from your company, take care we're not the worse for it! I don't think I said anything that should be counted against me, so I beg you to speak no more of it. It's neither courtly nor sensible to quarrel over a trifle. This argument should go no further, and no one should make any more of it. But have him carry on with the story he'd begun to tell us, for there shouldn't be any squabbling here.'

At this Calogrenant speaks up in reply. 'Sir,' says he, 'I'm not greatly worried by the quarrel: it's of small concern or importance to me. If you've wronged me, I'll never be harmed by that; for you, my lord Kay, have often insulted more worthy and wiser men than I, as indeed is your usual practice. The dung-heap will always stink, the gad-fly sting and the bee buzz, and a pest pester and plague. But, if my lady doesn't press me, I'll tell no more of my story today; and I beg her kindly to refrain from asking me to do anything I don't wish to.' – 'My lady,' says Kay, 'everybody here will be grateful if you do insist, as they will be glad to hear it. Don't do anything for my sake; but by the faith you owe the king, your lord and mine, you'll do well to tell him to go on.' – 'Calogrenant,' says the queen, 'take no notice of the attack of my lord Kay the seneschal! He's so used to uttering abuse that no one can talk him out of it. I would beg you urgently not to harbour any resentment on his account or to refrain because of him from telling us something we'd like to hear. So, if you want to enjoy my affection, begin again from the beginning!' – 'Really, my lady, I find what you ask me to do very irksome: I'd rather have one of my eyes plucked out than tell any more of my tale today, were I not afraid of annoying you. But I shall do as you please, however much it may hurt me. Listen, then, as this is what you wish!

A later scene from this poem, where a judicial combat is fought between Ywain and his cousin Gawain, is recounted in Ywain and Gawain, *the poem's English version.*

CHRÉTIEN DE TROYES, Perceval, or the Story of the Grail (Le Conte du Graal) (c. 1182)

The incomplete Perceval *was dedicated to Philip of Alsace, Count of Flanders, perhaps suggesting that Chrétien de Troyes had left Champagne by this time. Introducing the French technique of interlacing, this poem recounts the adventures of two heroes: the first is an unknown youth, Perceval the Welshman, a rustic bore who seeks to win honour at Arthur's court; set in sharp contrast to him is the courtly and sophisticated Gawain, who is Arthur's favourite nephew and already a prominent member of Arthurian society.*

This, Chrétien's last Arthurian romance, may in fact have been intended as two separate poems on Perceval and Gawain. Here, the Holy Grail is introduced to Arthurian legend, a spiritual quest to be achieved in some later works by Perceval or another chosen knight, such as Galahad or Gawain,[60] but which has little directly to do with King Arthur himself.

The following extract involves a common Arthurian theme: the arrival of a defeated knight at court to submit to Arthur's mercy. Defeated by Perceval for mistreating his mistress because of his jealous nature, the Haughty Knight of the Heath has been ordered to treat her more considerately, and sent by the hero to Arthur's court. Pleased by Perceval's fine service on his behalf, Arthur determines to set off in search of the hero, and the whole court accompanies him.

That evening the knight has his beloved bathed and richly dressed;

and he takes such good care of her that she has regained all her beauty. After that they take the direct road together for Caerleon, where King Arthur was holding court, though on a very intimate scale, for only three thousand knights of repute were there! The newcomer, leading his damsel, went to King Arthur to constitute himself a prisoner in the sight of all; and when he had come before him, he said: 'Good lord King, I am your prisoner to do whatever you wish. And this is only right and proper, for those were my instructions from the young man who asked and obtained from you crimson arms.' The moment the king hears this, he understands very well what he is referring to. 'Disarm yourself, good sir,' he says; 'and may joy and good fortune attend the one who has presented you to me! And be welcome yourself: for his sake you'll be cherished and honoured in my house.'

'Sire, there's one thing I want to tell you before I'm disarmed. Only I'd like the queen and her maidens to come and hear the news I've brought you; for it will never be told until the one has come who was struck on the cheek merely for uttering one laugh – that was her only misdeed!' Thus he finishes what he has to say, and the king hears that he is to summon the queen before him. He does call her; and she comes, and with her all her maidens, holding each other by the hand. When the queen was seated beside her lord King Arthur, the Haughty Knight of the Heath said to her: 'My lady, a knight I esteem highly and who vanquished me in armed combat sends you his greetings. I don't know what more I can say of him; but he sends you my beloved, this maiden here.' – 'I'm very grateful to him, my friend,' says the queen. Then he describes to her all the disgrace and shame he had inflicted on her for a long time, and the suffering she had endured, and his reason for his action. He told her everything, concealing nothing.

They then showed him the girl struck by Kay the seneschal; and he said to her: 'Maiden, the one who sent me here asked me to greet you on his behalf. And I was never to remove my leggings and boots from my feet until I had told you that he would forfeit God's aid should he ever on any account enter a court held by King Arthur before avenging you for the slap, the cuff you were given because of him.' Then, on hearing him, the fool jumps to his feet and cries out: 'Kay, Kay! God bless me, you'll really pay for that, and very soon!' The king for his part follows the fool in saying: 'Ah Kay, it was really courtly of you to mock that young man! With your mockery you've taken him from me, so that I don't expect ever to see him again.' The king then had his prisoner sit down in front of him. He excuses him from captivity, and after that orders him to be disarmed.

My lord Gawain, who was sitting at the king's right hand, asks: 'In God's name, sire, who can that be who, in a single armed combat, defeated such a good knight as this? For I've never heard any knight named in all the Isles of the Sea, or seen or known one who could compete with this one in arms or chivalry.' – 'Good nephew,' says the king, 'I don't know him, yet I've seen him. But when I did see him, it didn't occur to me to ask him about anything. He told me to make him a knight on the spot; and, seeing his handsome, attractive appearance, I said to him: "Gladly, brother; but dismount for a while until you've been brought a set of entirely gilt arms." Then he answered that he would never take them or dismount until he had red arms. And he added another amazing thing: that he would accept no arms other than those of the knight who was making off with my golden cup.

'Then Kay, offensive as he was, still is and always will be, ever reluctant to say a good word, told him: "Brother, the king grants you those arms and freely gives them to you, so go and get them at once!" The young man, not understanding the joke, thought he was telling the truth: he went after the knight and killed him with a javelin cast. I don't know how the fight and skirmish began except that the Red Knight from the Forest of Quinqueroi struck him very arrogantly with his lance, I'm not sure why; and then the young man pierced him right through the eye with his javelin, and so killed him and obtained the arms. After that he's pleased me so well with his fine service that, by my lord Saint David whom they worship and pray to in Wales, I shall never lie for two nights together in chamber or hall until I know if he's alive on land or sea, but will set out at once to go in search of him!' As soon as the king had made this vow, everyone was in no doubt that it only remained to start off.

Then you might have seen sheets, bedspreads and pillows packed into chests, coffers filled, packhorses loaded and carts and wagons laden, for they are not sparing in taking with them tents, pavilions and awnings. A learned, well-lettered clerk could not write a list in a whole day of all the harness and other equipment that was immediately made ready; for the king leaves Caerleon as though he is going on campaign, and all the nobles follow him. Not even a maiden is left there without being taken by the queen in a show of opulence and splendour. That night they encamped in a meadow beside a forest.

In the morning there was a good snowfall, and the countryside was bitterly cold. Early that day Perceval had risen as usual with the intention of seeking adventure and deeds of chivalry; and he headed straight towards the frozen, snow-covered meadow where the king's host was encamped. But before he reached the tents, a flock of wild geese, dazzled by the snow, came flying over. He saw and heard them; for they were honking as they went on account of a falcon that came swooping swiftly at them until it found one of them on its own, separated from the flock. It struck at this one and caught it so hard that it knocked it to the ground. But it was too early in the morning, so it flew off without bothering to pounce and secure it. Perceval begins to spur in the direction he had seen the flight. The goose was wounded in the neck, and from it came three drops of blood, which spread out over the whiteness to look like natural colouring. The goose was not injured or hurt enough to remain on the ground until Perceval arrived shortly after, by which time it had already flown.

When he saw the disturbed snow where the goose had lain and the blood that was visible round it, he leant on his lance to gaze at this sight; for the blood and snow together have for him the appearance of the fresh colouring on his beloved's face. By these thoughts he becomes carried away; for in her face the flush of crimson on the white resembled the appearance of these three drops of blood on the white snow. As he continued to gaze he thought, to his delight, that he saw the fresh complexion of his fair love's face.

Perceval spends all the early morning musing on those drops until squires came out of the tents and, seeing him in his reverie, supposed he was dozing. Before the king, who was still sleeping in his tent, awoke, the squires encountered outside the royal pavilion Sagremor who, because of his rashness, was called the Impetuous. 'Tell me,' he says, 'without hiding anything: why have you come here so early?' – 'Sir,' they say, 'outside this camp we've seen a knight dozing on his charger.' – 'Is he armed?' – 'Yes indeed.' – 'I'll go and talk to him,' says he, 'and bring him along to the court.' Sagremor runs at once to the king's tent and wakes him. 'Sire,' he says, 'there's a knight outside dozing on the heath over there.' The king then orders him to go, asking urgently that he should bring him back and not leave him there. At once Sagremor called for his arms to be produced and asked for his horse too. His orders were promptly obeyed, and he quickly had himself well armed. In full armour he left the camp and rode until he reached the knight.

'Sir,' he says, 'you must come to the king!' The other does not move and appears not to hear him. He repeats his words and is met with silence. He grows angry and says: 'By Saint Peter the Apostle, you'll come there, like it or not! I'm very sorry I ever asked you to; for that was a waste of my words.' Then he unfurls the pennon wound round his lance, and the horse beneath him springs forward as he takes his distance opposite the knight, then shouts to him to be on guard, because he will strike him unless he defends himself. Perceval glances towards him and sees him coming at the charge. Then he comes quite out of his reverie and in turn spurs forward at him. As they clash together, Sagremor shatters his lance. Perceval's does not break or bend, but he drives it with such force that he topples him in the middle of the field. And his horse proceeds to take flight, head in air, making for the encampment. Then those who were getting up in their tents saw it; and whoever did was most upset.

Thereupon Kay, who could never stop himself from making wicked comments, made a joke of it and said to the king: 'My good lord, see how Sagremor's coming back! He's holding the knight by the bridle and leading him here against his will!' – 'Kay,' says the king, 'it's unkind of you to mock at worthy men in this way. Now you go there, and we'll see how you'll do better than he.' – 'Indeed,' says Kay, 'I'm delighted that you'd like me to go; and I'll bring him back without fail – by force, whether he wants it or not. And I'll make him give his name.' He then has himself properly armed. This done, he mounts and goes off to the one who was gazing so intently at the three drops of blood that nothing else concerned him. Kay shouts to him from some distance: 'Vassal, vassal, come to the king! You'll come now, by my faith, or else pay very dearly!' Perceval, hearing himself threatened, turns his horse's head and digs in his steel spurs to make for Kay, whose own approach is far from slow. Each of them wants to do well, and there is nothing half-hearted about their encounter. Kay strikes and, as he puts all his strength into the blow, his lance breaks and crumbles like bark. And Perceval does not lack resolution: he strikes him above the boss of his shield and knocks him down so hard on to a rock that he dislocates his collar-bone and breaks the bone between his right elbow and armpit like a dry twig, just as predicted by the fool, who had often foretold it. The fool's prophecy had come true.

In his agony Kay faints; and his horse takes flight and heads for the tents at a fast trot. The Britons see the horse returning without the seneschal. Then youths mount, and ladies and knights set out and, finding the seneschal in a swoon, are convinced he is dead, whereupon they all, men and ladies alike, began to mourn him bitterly. And Perceval leans once more on his lance, contemplating those three drops. The king, however, was deeply worried about the wounded seneschal. His grieving and sorrow continued until he was told to have no fear, for he will make a complete recovery provided he has a doctor who knows how to go about putting his collar-bone back into place and setting his broken bone. Then the king, who is very fond of him and, in his heart, loves him well, sends him a very expert doctor and two maidens trained by him; and they put back his collar-bone and bandage his arm, having joined the shattered bone. They then carried him to the king's tent and did much to comfort him, telling him he will get quite well again and must not worry about anything.

My lord Gawain then says to the king: 'Sire, sire, so help me God, it's not right, as you know well and have yourself always quite properly said and maintained, that one knight should, as these two have done, distract another from his thoughts, whatever they may be. I don't know if they were in the wrong; but what is certain is that they've come to pay for it. The knight was brooding over some loss he's suffered; or his love has been stolen from him, so he's upset and dejected about it. But if that were your pleasure, I would go to see how he's behaving; and should I find him in the situation of having come out of his reverie, I'd ask and beg him to come here to you.'

These words enraged Kay, and he said: 'Ah, my lord Gawain, you'll lead that knight by the bridle, even if he objects: that will be done if you can manage it and you don't have to fight. You've taken many a captive that way! Once the knight is exhausted and has had enough of the combat, that's when a worthy man should ask permission and have the opportunity to go and gain the victory! Ah, Gawain, a hundred curses on my neck if you're at all so foolish that there isn't a great deal to be learnt from you! You're very good at finding a buyer for your words, extremely fair and polished as they are. Will you ever say anything quite outrageous, wicked or arrogant? A curse on anyone who has thought that or thinks it now! I don't! You really could do this job in a silk tunic: there will be no need for you to draw a sword or break a lance. You can pride yourself that he'll do what you want, so long as your tongue doesn't fail you before you've said: "God save you, sir, and give you joy and health!" Not that I'm trying to teach you anything. You'll know well enough how to smooth him down like stroking a cat; and people will say: "Now my lord Gawain's fighting fiercely!" ' – 'Ah, Sir Kay,' says Gawain, 'you might have put that more politely. Do you want to take out your anger and bad temper on me? I swear I'll bring him back, my dear good friend, if I possibly can. I'll never have my arm damaged or my collar-bone put out of joint, for I don't fancy that kind of payment.'

'Now you go there, nephew,' said the king. 'That's a very courtly thing you've said. Bring him back if at all possible. But take all your arms, for you shall not go unarmed.' That man who has a name and reputation for all the virtues had himself armed straight away and, mounted on a strong, agile horse, came directly to the knight who was leaning on his lance, still not tired of the reverie that gave him great pleasure. However, the sunshine had made two of the drops of blood lying on the snow vanish, and the third was fading away; and so the knight's concentration on them was not as deep as it had been. Then my lord Gawain approaches him at a very gentle amble without any appearance of hostility and said: 'Sir, I would have greeted you were I as sure of your feelings as of my own. But I can venture to tell you that I'm a messenger from the king who, through me, desires and requests you to come and speak with him.' – 'There have already been two,' says Perceval, 'who were after my life and wanted to lead me off like a captive. I was so engrossed in a very pleasurable thought that anyone forcing me out of it was simply asking for trouble. For just here on that spot were three drops of fresh blood bright against the whiteness; and as I gazed at them it seemed to me that I was seeing the fresh colour of my fair love's face; and I would never have wished to relinquish that thought.'

'Truly,' says my lord Gawain, 'that was no base thought, but a very courtly, tender one; and whoever turned your heart away from it was wicked and stupid. But now I'm very anxious and eager to know what you would like to do; for I'd be delighted to take you to the king, if that would not displease you.' – 'Now tell me first, my dear good friend,' says Perceval, 'if Kay the seneschal is there.' – 'Yes, indeed he's there. And let me tell you he was the one who jousted with you just now. But the joust cost him so dear that you shattered his right arm, though you don't know it, and dislocated his collar-bone.' – 'Then I think I've well recompensed the maiden he struck.'

When my lord Gawain heard that, he started with astonishment and said: 'God save me, sir, you're just the one the king was looking for! What is your name, sir?' – 'Perceval, sir; and what's yours?' – 'Sir, you may be quite sure that I was baptized with the name of Gawain.' – 'Gawain?' – 'Yes, truly, good sir.' Perceval was overjoyed and said: 'Sir, I've indeed heard people speak of you in many places, and I would like us two to become friends, if that's pleasing and agreeable to you.' – 'Indeed,' says my lord Gawain, 'that pleases me no less than you – more, I think.' And Perceval replies: 'Then, by my faith, I'll go gladly where you wish, for that's only right; and I have a much higher opinion of myself now I'm your friend.' Then they go to embrace each other and set about unlacing helmets, coifs and ventails, and they pull down the mail. So they come rejoicing on their way.

Then some youths, seeing them making much of each other, run at once from a low hill where they were standing and come before the king. 'Sire, sire,' they exclaim, 'my lord Gawain really is bringing the knight, and they're making a great fuss of each other!' There is nobody hearing the news who does not dash out of his tent and go to meet them. Then Kay said to his lord the king: 'Now my lord Gawain, your nephew, has the distinction and the honour. The combat was very hard and perilous, unless I'm lying! He's returning just as cheerful as he left, for he never took a blow from anyone else, and no one felt any blow of his, and he hasn't given the lie to anybody. So it's right that he should have the distinction and credit for it, and that people should say he's accomplished what we others couldn't, though we put all our strength and effort into it.' So as usual Kay spoke his mind, right or wrong.

My lord Gawain has no wish to take his companion to court in his armour, but wants him completely disarmed. In his tent he has him stripped of his armour; and from one of his own chests a chamberlain of his takes an outfit, which he offers him as a gift. Once he was elegantly dressed in the tunic and mantle, which went admirably on him and suited him well, they proceed together, hand in hand, to the king where he was seated in front of his tent. 'Sire,' my lord Gawain says to the king, 'I'm bringing you the person whose acquaintance, I believe, you would gladly have made a full fortnight ago. I present him to you. See, here he is!'

'Many thanks to you, dear nephew,' says the king, who goes so far as to jump to his feet to greet him with the words: 'Welcome, good sir! Now I beg you to tell me what I should call you.' – 'By my faith, I'll never keep that from you, my good lord king,' says Perceval. 'My name is Perceval the Welshman.' – 'Ah, Perceval, my dear good friend, now you've been brought to my court, you'll never leave it if I have my way. Since I first saw you I've grieved over you a great deal; for I didn't know the advancement God had in store for you. Yet it was accurately predicted to the knowledge of my whole court by the maiden and the fool struck by Kay the seneschal; and you've proved their prophecies entirely true. There's now no one in any doubt of the fact that the report I've heard of your chivalry is true.'

As he spoke the queen arrived, having heard the news of the young man's arrival. No sooner had Perceval seen her and been told who she was, and had seen coming after her the damsel who had laughed when he had looked at her, than he at once went up to them and said: 'May God grant joy and honour to the fairest, the best of all ladies alive, as witness all who see her and all who have seen her!' And the queen replies: 'And welcome to you too as to a knight proven in high and splendid prowess!' Then Perceval greets in turn the maiden who had laughed for him; and embracing her, he said: 'My fair one, should you need me, I would be the knight whose aid would never fail you.' The damsel thanks him for that.

It was with great rejoicing that the king, the queen and the nobles took Perceval the Welshman to Caerleon, where they returned that day. They spent the whole night in celebration and the following day too before, on the next day, they saw a damsel approaching on a tawny mule, holding a whip in her right hand. The damsel's hair was plaited in two twisted black pigtails; and if what is said and related in the book is true, there was never any creature so completely hideous, even in Hell. You have never seen iron as black as were her neck and hands, and yet that was the least part of her ugliness. For her eyes were two holes as small as those of a rat; her nose was like that of a monkey or cat and her lips like a donkey's or bullock's, whilst her teeth were so yellow that they looked like egg-yolk; and she was bearded like a billy-goat. She had a hump in the middle of her chest, and her spine was crook-shaped. Her loins and shoulders were splendid for leading a dance! She had a lump on her back and hips twisted just like two osiers: splendidly made for leading a jig!

The damsel dashes up on her mule in front of the knights: never before had any such damsel been seen in a royal court! She gives a general greeting to the king and all his nobles, except for Perceval alone; but to him, as she sat on her tawny mule, she said: 'Ah, Perceval! Fortune is bald behind, but has hair in front; and a curse on anyone who greets you or calls down any blessings on you! For when you met Fortune, you did not welcome her: you entered the Fisher King's house and saw the bleeding lance; yet you found it so hard to open your mouth and speak that you were unable to ask why that drop of blood issues from the tip of its bright head; nor, when you saw the grail, did you ask or enquire what worthy man was served from it. He is a wretch indeed who sees as fine an opportunity as could be wished, yet goes on waiting for a better one to come. You are that wretch who saw that it was the time and place to speak, yet held your tongue, though you had every chance. It is unfortunate for you that you remained silent; for had you asked, the rich king, now in distress, would at once have had his wound quite healed and would peacefully rule his land, of which he will now never hold any part. And do you know the fate of the king who will hold no land or be healed of his wounds? Through him ladies will lose their husbands, lands will be laid waste, maidens left orphaned and helpless, and many knights will perish: all these evils will be of your doing.'

Then the damsel said to the king: 'Don't be offended, O King, if I leave now, for I must take my lodging far from here tonight. I don't know if you have heard tell of the Proud Castle, but that is where I have to go tonight. In that castle are five hundred and sixty-six eminent knights, and there is none of them, you may be sure, who is not accompanied by his beloved, a noble, courtly, beautiful lady. I give you this information because none who go there fail to find a joust or a combat. Whoever wants chivalric action will not be disappointed if he seeks it there. But if anyone wants to gain the high esteem of the entire world, I think I know the place and locality where it could be best achieved, if there were someone of sufficient daring. On the hill below Montesclaire a damsel is besieged: whoever could raise that siege and rescue the damsel would gain great honour and win universal praise; and the one to whom God granted such good fortune would be able to gird on quite safely the Sword with the Strange Baldric.' With that the damsel fell silent, having said all she wished, and departed without another word.

At that my lord Gawain leaps up, saying he will go there and do all in his power to rescue the damsel. And Gifflet the son of Do said that for his part he would go with God's aid before the Proud Castle. 'And I shall go and climb the Dolorous Mount,' says Kahedin, 'and won't stop until I get there.' Then Perceval spoke quite differently, saying that as long as he lived he would not spend two nights in a single lodging, or hear news of any adventurous passage without going by way of it, or of any knight worth more than one or two others without going to fight him, until he discovered who was served from the grail and had found the bleeding lance and been told the certain truth as to why it bleeds. He will not give up, whatever the hardship. Thus up to fifty of them rose, pledging and declaring and swearing to each other that they will not learn of any marvel or adventure without going in search of it, however dreadful the land it was in.

The First Perceval Continuation (c. 1190)

This is the first of a number of continuations of Chrétien de Troyes's unfinished work, which picks up the story at the point where he left off. The First Perceval Continuation, a fairly substantial work, concentrates on the adventures of Gawain rather than Perceval, although it also contains episodes on other heroes, such as Caradoc.

The following extract begins at the point where Chrétien's text finishes – where Arthur, grieving for the absent Gawain, hears news that his nephew is in good health and has won a fine lordship. In this episode, Arthur is reunited with his long-lost mother, Queen Ygerne, who fled to a remote place of refuge after Uther's death.

*The passage sheds further light on the characters of Guenevere and
Kay: while the queen, like her lord, is anxious for Gawain's safety,
Kay is usually overcome with his jealousy of the hero's superior
prowess and popularity, although on this occasion he manages to
speak favourably of his rival.*

The king recovered from his faint, and the boy came up to him
and said:

'God bless you, king, and all your good company. I bring you such
greetings as befit a king from your nephew, Gawain.'

Hearing this, the king leapt to his feet; he had never been so happy
as he was at this news. It was so welcome and such a joy to him that
he took the boy in his arms and swept him from his hunting-horse:
and all the court, seeing this, longed to know what the boy had told
the king. And the king said to him:

'Friend, may God guard and aid my dear nephew Gawain and you.
I love him no less than myself. Tell me, how is Gawain? Is he in good
health and spirits?'

'God give me joy, sir, I left him well and happy in a castle that he's
conquered far from here; there's none in all the world more splendid
or more finely situated. He requests and summons you, as his uncle
and his lord, to aid and honour him as his great need requires. He
needs your help, for he has accepted a challenge to single combat,
and he begs and summons you to come without fail and guard him
against treachery. He wants to rebut Guiromelant's boast that he'll
dishonour him. I tell you truly, neither you nor Gawain, nor any of
your friends, have a more mortal enemy. In time of need a man sees
who his true friends are: Sir Gawain has sent me to the one who
supports those in need against the proud.'

I can tell you in all truthfulness, never was a court so beset by grief
so soon restored to joy. Everyone's heart, without exception, exulted
at the news. They no longer felt any cause for grief, now that they
knew that the one held to be the most courteous of the age, unsur-
passed by count or king, the most great-hearted, the most valiant and
the finest at arms, was alive. Then you would have seen a jubilant
court, as harps sang and hurdy-gurdies played and the whole hall
rang with music. No man alive could describe the sweet melodies
they made. They celebrated endlessly, and they had the best cause in
the world: happiness and love inspired them – a splendid cause for
rejoicing; I can't think of a finer one.

Lady Ysave of Carahet heard the rejoicing in the hall, and from
the gallery where she was sitting, she ran straight to the queen and
said:

'My lady, I think we're about to hear good news! The king is filled with happiness and has greeted the messenger with joy; it's a most reassuring sign. I think you'll hear good and pleasing news of Sir Gawain today; so says the sweet music that's ringing in the hall. My heart tells me that we'll soon have cause to rejoice for the nephew of my lord king!'

'Dear lady, may God hear your prayer; it's my wish, too, and the wish of all these ladies and maids and these courteous girls.'

The queen rose, and was in such a hurry that she did not think of donning a mantle. She ran to the hall without a mantle or a cloak, and hurried in. All the ladies and maids and noble girls threw off their mantles and raced after her. No ladies ever left their chambers in such a rush as these, or ever entered a king's hall in such a state of disarray.

The king leaned towards the boy and said:

'Go to the queen quickly, friend, and tell her the news that's delighted me. I'd rather she heard it from you than from anyone else, even me.'

The boy went to her without more ado and said:

'May God who dwells above and sets the good at His right hand protect you and your dear company, lady; so Sir Gawain wishes.'

The fair-faced queen replied:

'God save you and give him joy and happiness! Is he safe and in good health?'

'Yes, lady, and full of joy. And as your good, dear friend he bids you through me, his messenger, to go to his aid by the faith you owe him. Go to him with all the girls and maids and ladies who have come to this court; bring them all in your company. Shame upon those who are friends in word alone; a true friend is as one with you, backing up his words with deeds. Gawain hasn't known before if he's any true friends, but now he will. No-one knows as well as a man in need whether his friendship is returned, for true friends are revealed when they see you in distress. God save me, a man who lacks nothing can never know if he's loved or hated.'

When Kay the seneschal heard this he replied in courteous words; but often before he had spoken scathingly and mockingly of Sir Gawain. But what of that? An abrasive man can be worth twenty-two of pleasant speech who are faint-hearted and worthless and weak when it comes to action; for a man whose custom is to flatter melts away like foam when help is needed urgently; there are friends of that kind near and far.

'My lords,' said the seneschal, 'I think, without question, we should all thank God that Sir Gawain is alive; we were more anguished and dejected and dispirited at losing him than joyful at the presence of the rest. Let us thank Almighty God for keeping him safe and sound so long. We can truly see that a worthy man brings many great gains and great profit; that's why the fear alone that he might have died by some mischance caused us such dismay. As God's my witness, it's true what they say: no-one knows what a worthy man is worth until he's gone. God has done our lord King Arthur, and all of us, a great honour, it seems to me; for there were a good thirty thousand of us grieving and downcast, but God has brought light and day to us, now that the one who's full of courtliness is alive and happy. We'd never known such anguish, but our happiness and joy have been restored by the good, fair, noble and worthy one who is so kind to all men that no-one knows his equal in the world.'

With that he bade that two trumpets be sounded. Then you would have seen the squires, all noble, fair and handsome youths, with white towels at their shoulders. There was no place for villains or for fools, for they would not have been allowed to serve there. And I can tell you, without a word of a lie, the wash-basins were worth a fortune, for most of them were of fine gold, and the rest of bright silver, and they served the ladies and knights with them handsomely, and happily and willingly. Then everybody sat down in the hall.

There were so many dishes that I shan't try to describe them; but I tell you, never has such a splendid feast lasted a shorter time or been received with such joy in any court; none so swift has ever been seen. Their love for Gawain drove them to finish their feast with speed. And then God! you'd have seen so many pennons laced on straight after, and so many fine Spanish mules, so many chargers and palfreys saddled! Everyone was terrified of not being packed in time. Never, I think, have people been so eager for a journey. You'd have seen so many chests and splendid coffers loaded that day. And the king delayed no longer; he mounted and rode from the city, with fully thirty thousand knights and fifteen thousand ladies and girls and maids. No man has ever seen such an army raised as rode that day from Orguenie. There were many splendid waggons to carry the king's equipment, his provisions and his pavilions; his baggage-train was of an astounding length. The line stretched out across the plains, and those at the rear had to camp a league from the place where the foremost lodged, in a meadow beside a river.

They set out again early the next day; and the boy led them and guided them joyfully and with great delight, through forests and across fair open land, with plenty of feasting all the way, straight to the castle where Sir Gawain now was lord. The king reached there on the seventh day, and the boy came up to him and said:

'There is the castle, dear sir, that your good nephew has won.'

The king stepped down; and then you would have seen them all dismount and pitch their tents and pavilions. And the Welshmen among them, most skilled in the craft, built a great number of lodges in the Welsh manner: of interwoven branches; and they made shelters for their horses, and for other purposes, too, by taking boughs from the forest and stripping off their leaves. Then the cooks were provided for with the smaller twigs and branches. Yvain, King Urien's son, and Gifflet, the son of Do, arrived with the queen, whom they were escorting. And I tell you, in their company, which was well endowed with ladies, came three thousand knights, and none of them lacked a fine warhorse; and behind them came the great convoy of waggons – you never saw one so great. The queen dismounted at her tent, pitched for her.

Queen Ygerne was in the upper chambers of the hall, and saw the great host stretching all along the meadow. She was terrified at the sight, and her heart was faint and trembling. She took her daughter by the hand and said:

'Norcadet, my daughter, we've lived a long while, and now our time has come, for we're besieged! I've never seen so many men amassed, so many shining helmets and shimmering shields. Look at all the swords and lances! Are they ladies or fairies down there on the riverbank?'

'God help me, I don't know, dear lady. But I've never seen such girls or ladies or maids in such a throng, either leading an army or going off to war, and it troubles me most terribly.'

Just then Sir Gawain and his sister Clarissant came from a chamber, and as soon as she saw him Ygerne rushed to him and said:

'My good, dear friend, look at the mighty army besieging us down there, all along the meadows. And look, dear friend, on that side there are only girls and ladies. Sir, you asked a favour of me for love's sake: that I shouldn't ask you your name for seven days, or enquire about your lineage. I refrained completely, and didn't say a word. But now, you know, the seventh day has passed, and I'd like to know your name.'

'I shall indeed tell you, lady, for I've never hidden my name from anyone. I am called Gawain.'

She embraced him on the instant, and kissed his eyes and lips and face. And her daughter was beside herself, her heart leaping and soaring for joy, such joy as had kept her wide awake on the day when he was born, and she kissed his face and breast.

'My good, dear friend,' said Queen Ygerne, 'by the faith I owe almighty God, I am the mother of King Arthur, and this is my daughter: she is your mother.'

But when Gawain's sister Clarissant, who was also there, heard this, she rushed to her chamber and began to grieve desperately, because her brother knew all about her love for Guiromelant, who had challenged him to battle.

'Gawain, dear grandson,' said Queen Ygerne, 'you can see our plight: they're besieging us without doubt. For the love of God, what are we to do?'

'My lady, there's no danger. That's King Arthur, your son.'

'Is that true?'

'Yes, lady. It's he, have no fear.'

'I can't wait to see him! I've never been so happy in my life!'

And Gawain said:

'By your leave, my lady, I would like to cross the river and speak to him.'

She could not help kissing him. He had many a willing kiss from his grandmother and from his mother; then he left the ladies and mounted a swift horse, and took ten worthy and able knights with him across the river.

Kay was the very first to see him, as he came from the tent of King Do. He galloped with all his might to King Arthur's pavilion and joyfully announced:

'Here comes your nephew, good sire!'

And he dismounted before the king. The king mounted a palfrey, in too much haste to wait for another horse, and rode to meet his nephew with all the speed the mount could summon. And as soon as he reached him he kissed him as fast as he could, twenty times on the lips and face before he had said a word. You may be sure he was not displeased to see his nephew! And Sir Gawain said:

'Great joy awaits you, sir, for your mother is longing to see you and wants to speak to you, and rightly so.'

The king smiled at the knights and then said:

'My good, dear, sweet nephew, by the faith I owe my father's soul, I haven't had a mother for fifty years.'

'With respect, sir, yes, you have – I can say so in all truthfulness. When Uterpendragon died, Ygerne fled with a great treasure, seeking the loneliest land there was, until she found this place. And with the great wealth she'd brought she had this castle built and made it her home. I know of no finer or better one. And when my father King Lot, who held Orguenie, lost his life, my mother – your sister – came to this castle and lived with her mother and yours, giving up and abandoning all our land. She was left pregnant, and bore a daughter who's there in the castle, a beautiful, comely, and most worthy girl.'

The king and all those present were overjoyed at this astounding news. And the queen kissed Gawain sweetly, and so did a hundred other ladies and girls of worth. He would happily have done without many of those kisses, but when some good thing is desired, it is taken by whoever can take it, not according to the bestower's will. All the king's host were filled with joy. And as for the great king's mother, who was still up in the hall, listen now to what she did that night.

With her in the castle she had five hundred newly dubbed knights, all of high lineage, of excellent families, and wise. She gave orders that all their arms – which were wonderful, full of precious stones – should be placed at all the windows of the chambers and the hall and on the battlements, so that the jewels, truly, threw as brilliant a light on King Arthur's host as if it had been noon. They were astounded by the light, and thought a spell had been cast on them; and the king was stricken silent, thinking he had been bewitched, and greatly fearing that Gawain had been tricked by sorcery. But Gawain managed to convince the king that he should set off and go with four companions, secretly summoned, and take the queen and three of her maids – no more than that.

They came down to the river and passed across, and went straight on to the castle. And Queen Ygerne, her head crowned with flowers, received her son King Arthur with indescribable joy, and welcomed the gracious Queen Guinevere, too, with the greatest happiness.

The Second Perceval Continuation

(c. 1190–1200)

This work, which continues the Perceval story from the point where The First Perceval Continuation *ends, gives more attention to Perceval than the former poem, although it also continues Gawain's adventures. In the following extract, Gawain meets his son, Giglain,*[61] *and they return together to Arthur's court to assist him in a punitive attack against King Carras of Recesse. On the way, Gawain informs his son about his experiences at the Grail Castle.*

As soon as day broke and the sun was bright, Gawain remounted at once and rode hard until midday. In the distance, on open ground, he noticed a knight, fully armed, well furnished and equipped, mounted on a great, swift charger. And he had, I believe, a shield painted gold and blue. He seemed a most assured knight, strong and bold and alert. Gawain saw him and headed towards him, and he likewise rode down to meet Gawain. As soon as they were within earshot of each other, the knight greeted Gawain and asked his name at once.

'I have never concealed my name,' he said, 'and shall not do so now. I was baptized, my good dear sir, with the name of Gawain.'

When the knight heard this he seemed overjoyed, and Gawain immediately asked him his name.

'Sir,' the knight replied, 'I am Giglain, your son, whom King Arthur named the Fair Unknown.'

Hearing this, Gawain was filled with joy and said:

'Dear boy, I truly did not recognize you and was certainly not expecting you. When did you last see my lord?'

'Sir,' he said, 'a fortnight ago tomorrow, I think.'

'How is the king? Is he well?'

'Yes indeed, sir. And he bids you, no matter what your business, to return to him without delay, for he is troubled and enraged by King Carras, lord of Recesse, who never ceases, day or night, to attack and capture his men and reduce his towns to ashes. The king is in dismay, and has sent people in search of you throughout the land, for he needs your aid. He has assembled a great army, and I know that if you were there he would move against King Carras and wage war on him and capture all his land. He hates him deeply, and is warning him that he isn't after bulls and cows – only Carras himself.'

When Gawain heard this his heart burned with grief and rage. And he began to tell Giglain that he would go to his uncle's court, but first he would strive to find the Fisher King.

'I shall never rest,' he said, 'until I have returned from there and learned the truth about the knight who rode past the tent of my lady the Queen, and whom Kay tried to bring back by demands and high-handedness. But his force and insolence were to no avail, I assure you! Instead I led the knight back with gentle words, and promised him without hesitation that if he could not fulfil the quest he had undertaken, then I would mount his horse and complete it for him. Then we returned to the Queen's tent, but before we could enter he fell dead from his horse. So I mounted without delay and rode on until, around midnight, I came across a chapel in the middle of a wood. I went in as fast as I could, for the night was so dark, so pitch, so stormy, that it seemed as if the sky were being torn apart and the great forest crumbling.

'So I entered the chapel, and it was most beautiful and pleasant. There was an altar in the middle with a single candle burning on it, shedding a brilliant light. I had not been there long when, I promise you, I saw a man's hand appear from the altar, blacker by far than ink, and it snuffed out the candle immediately. I left the chapel at once, for it had terrified me, and rode on until, on the third day, I came to a rich castle, where all the walls and battlements were most handsomely designed. I could not find a living soul, but in a splendid hall, all hung with cloth from Thessaly, I found a body lying on a bier, covered with a sumptuous purple cloth. I gazed at it for a little, and then saw a brilliant light all around it, and a crowd of people crying and lamenting wondrously. They did not say a word to me or address me in any way, and they disappeared so suddenly that I didn't know what had become of them or which way they had gone. I stayed there in bewilderment until a knight suddenly appeared from a chamber. There were three servants with him who welcomed me with the greatest honour and stripped me of my arms and took care of my horse. I have never been treated with such honour at any court.

'They led me to a chamber painted with flowers, that's all I know, and knights rose as I entered, and so did their lord – who was a king, I can assure you: his countenance made that clear. And then, without more ado, we all sat down to dine. I dined with the king himself, for he insisted. I saw a boy carrying a lance with an iron head, and from the tip sprang a drop of blood. Another boy came holding a naked sword which was broken across the middle, and he presented it to the king. The king commanded me to put the pieces together; I did so, but I couldn't make them join. The king shook his head and said that I could not achieve the task for which I'd come. I was filled with shame, as you can imagine, and my face turned red; but I saw something else which comforted me greatly, because there was also a Grail, the like of which was never seen. It was carried by a girl, most elegant and beautiful; and it served the whole table and set bread before the king. I watched this in delight. Then the king said:

' "My good, dear friend, ask me whatever you like about what your eyes have seen, and I shall tell you the truth."

'So I asked him why the lance bled so profusely; and he told me at once that it was truly the lance with which Our Lord was struck when He was set upon the Cross. But I enquired and asked no more, for I was all preoccupied, and I began to feel sleepy after eating. And the king had a bed made for me, where I slept most sweetly until daybreak the next morning. Before the sun was fully up I found

myself upon a rock along with my arms and my horse. I armed at
once – I had no desire to dally – and set off, for I wanted to find out
about everything I've told you. God bless me, that's why I left my
land – and also to seek Perceval, who I heard had gone to the Pillar
on Mont Dolorous in search of adventure.'

Giglain replied directly that it was less than a year since he had
spoken to Perceval in the forest of Monbrehan.

'And he asked me a great deal about King Arthur and his men, and
also about you. And he told me that, if he could, nothing would stop
him coming to see you and the king before the dispersal of the court
which is to be held at Christmas.'

And Gawain replied:

'I wish he would, so help me God! Then I'd return with him to
seek the king of whom I've spoken. And I'm certain that through
Perceval I could learn and hear and understand something of the
lance and the Grail.'

With that they set off along a forest path, wide and well beaten.
They followed it, day and night and morning and evening, until, I tell
you truly, at the very end of the week they came at last to the castle
of Cardigan. They were received most splendidly, but King Arthur
was not there; he had gathered all his knights at Escavalon; there
were many kings, many princes, and many barons of great power in
his company. So before day dawned Gawain was on the road again,
and he journeyed on by day and night until he reached Escavalon.
King Arthur and the queen and his knights were overjoyed at his
coming, and the king explained the reason for assembling his people.
Gawain replied:

'Truly, King Carras has committed a great outrage, and so has his
brother King Gaudras, who used to be Lord of the Desert. They won't
escape without loss unless they surrender, I promise you. Let your
men be armed and your battalions arrayed; then let us ride at once
to your enemies' lands. We'll reduce their towns and castles to flame
and ash, and if King Carras can be caught, then do with him what
you will.'

The king vowed to do so. He called for the trumpets and the great
silver horns to sound; and the army made ready and drew up and
deployed, and as the sun rose they struck camp and set off through
the forest, riding straight on, across good ground and bad, not holding
back with bridle or reins, until they all reached the land of their
enemies. What else should I tell you? They set fire to all their castles,
destroying many, and cast down many high towers, which were
poorly defended, and trapped their quarry everywhere. There is no
need to say any more; they laid waste all the land.

King Carras had assembled a great band of men and knights, but when he heard that Arthur was burning his land, he could not think of any way of defending himself; and he was well aware that if Arthur caught him he could expect no mercy. So he retreated with all his forces to a castle he had overlooking the sea, most rich and strong; and there King Arthur laid siege to him. He besieged him for two months or more, I believe, but still he could not take the castle. Arthur was enraged, and swore to God and all his saints that he would not leave the castle until he had captured and destroyed it. This was announced to King Carras inside the castle, and he was far from happy, but he made no outward show of it. He sent word to Gawain, asking him to come, if he would, to the gate, which was splendid and strong, and Gawain went at once. King Carras then spoke to him, and begged him to help him, that he might make peace with his uncle, King Arthur; thenceforth he would always be at his command and serve him faithfully. Sir Gawain replied that he would gladly do all he could to help him, and returned to the king and told him what Carras had said. When King Arthur heard this he said:

'Dear nephew, I agree to it, but first I would like the advice of my knights and yourself.'

'Sire,' said Gawain, 'we say that you should accept this offer of peace and homage and amends he has made. What one thinks is winning can often be losing, as you have seen yourself many times. If we had done battle, someone would have been killed in combat for whom your heart would have grieved all the days of your life. One should not give folly so much free rein that it cannot be restrained when necessary to avoid heavy loss. You'll have complete power over King Gaudras of the Desert.'

'Dear nephew,' said the king, 'let it be just as you wish.'

Then the worthy Gawain summoned King Carras, and he came at once and fell at Arthur's feet, but he was promptly raised up again by the king's own hand: he forgave him his ill-will and allowed him to keep his land.

Then the army withdrew, all returning to their own lands; and King Arthur and his household returned to Escavalon. But as he dismounted at the mounting-block he was sad and downhearted, for he now had only three hundred knights left in his company. He swore to God that he had never in all his days had so few knights, even when his court was dispersed. And so Gawain stayed with him.

GERBERT DE MONTREUIL, Perceval Continuation
(c. 1210–25)

There are two works which continue the Perceval story from the point where The Second Perceval Continuation *leaves off: one by Gerbert, and the other written at about the same time by Manessier; apparently neither of them had any knowledge of the other's work.*

Gerbert is generally accepted as being Gerbert de Montreuil, the author of the Roman de la Violette. *In Gerbert's poem, after failing at the Grail Castle, Perceval returns to Arthur's court, where the king is again hunting the white hart. This episode contains another version of the Siege Perilous, but it is rather different from that found in the* Didot Perceval.

He [Perceval] journeyed on all day long and all the following week, and encountered many hard and fearsome adventures, and passed through many lands, and many dire and evil passages. Then he entered the forest of Carlion, and pressed on until nearly three o'clock, when he heard the sound of a horn and the loud baying of dogs. Perceval spurred his bay horse in the direction of the horn, rejoicing at the sound; and he rode on until he caught sight of a man who blew his horn three times, and he headed towards him and called to him, saying:

'In whose service are you, my friend?'

'King Arthur's, sir,' he replied. 'And he is coming up behind, and his knights with him; they're hunting the white hart of the Black Knight. And my lady the queen is coming, too, with many other ladies. But I tell you, upon my soul, the hart cannot be caught, which has made the king all sad and pale, for he had promised it to the queen and sworn to hunt it down.'

And while he was talking the king rode up, and with him came the king of the Irish and the king of Rodas, and the king of Dinas Clamadas, and also the king of Duveline. And Perceval saw many girls and young ladies coming with my lady the queen; he was delighted by the sight of the beautiful company. But when the king saw Perceval sitting armed upon his horse he did not recognize him; for his arms were so battered and rusty that he could not identify them, and no wonder. When Perceval saw the queen he rode straight towards her and said like a well-bred and worthy knight:

'Welcome indeed to my lady! She is the jewel of them all in honour, wisdom, beauty, courtesy and goodness.'

And the queen replied:

'Good sir, may it please God to send you all that your heart cherishes and desires; but I would very much like to know your name and who you may or may not be, for I do not recognize you by your arms.'

'Lady, it shall not be kept from you. My correct name is Perceval the Welshman.'

When the queen heard this she reached towards him and threw her arms around his neck, saying:

'What a joy to have found you, my good, dear friend, a knight of proven worth and high and splendid prowess!'

And all the girls and ladies greeted him most nobly. King Arthur rode swiftly up to him, and all the others on horseback; and when the king heard who he was he was overjoyed, and embraced him over and over. The knights were filled with joy and all were eager to see Perceval, as the king had him recount the troubles and hardships and obstacles he had encountered in the quest for the Grail which he had twice seen at the house of the Fisher King. But Perceval explained how he was denied the right to hear who was served from the Grail, and had been plainly told that he was not worthy to know the Grail's secrets, and could not on any account know why the lance bled, though he had asked most earnestly. But he had repaired a sword which was broken in half, though imperfectly, for a notch remained in the blade; and until the notch was mended no-one would know anything about the Grail. Kay, hearing this, said to Perceval:

'You don't know much about forging! You, sir, have undertaken a quest which will cost you your skin, I think! You've suffered a lot of humiliation this summer, and gained very little. You're chasing after dreams and fancies; you're like a man who fools around all day, skipping and dancing, just to get attention. Yes, that's your game! Because people would talk about it you go out looking for what can't be found. What foolishness! Do you think you're better than other men? No, you'll be old and grey before you've learned the slightest thing. Take my advice and stay here quietly with my lady this winter. The hundred devils of Hell have made you set your sights on what can't be seen or known.'

When the king heard this he was deeply upset and angry in his heart, for Kay had heaped reproach upon the knight he loved most in all the world; and he said to him at once:

'Sir Kay, your foolish tongue and your insolence are always troubling you. I think your heart would burst if you didn't let out your bitterness.'

'Sire,' said Perceval, 'his broken arm has healed, I see.[62] If he suffers for his evil tongue he needs some strong advice. He got a harsh reward when his collar-bone was broken.'

When Kay heard Perceval's retort he was filled with shame and his face fell. And the king embraced Perceval whom he cherished dearly, and abandoned the hunt.

They returned to Carlion. The cooks had prepared dinner and everything was ready: meat and poultry and fresh fish beyond count. And there were many kings and dukes and counts and many rich barons, and many ladies of renown in the queen's company. My lady the queen sent a gown of costly cloth, lined with ermine, for Perceval to wear, which he did most gladly, having already disarmed. And as soon as he was dressed the king took him by the hand, and after washing they sat down at the table, and the queen and her girls and the ladies and knights all sat down together. They were all dressed in short mantles, as was their custom at court. But Sir Gawain stood before the table and did not move. With him were Lancelot of the Lake, Ywain, and Erec the son of Lac, and a good twenty of the finest knights to be found there or anywhere, and they did not sit down. Suddenly Perceval looked up, and at the head of one table he saw a chair of strange appearance, which seemed to be very valuable. It was made of gold, inlaid and studded with many stones and richly enamelled; and it sat empty. Perceval gazed at it and imagined it must have been placed there for the king, and that he would sit in it. But since the king was already seated, Perceval wondered why it was that no-one went to sit there. He called to the king and asked him to tell him, if he would, why nobody was sitting in the magnificent seat.

'Are you expecting a king or a prince to come and take the chair? I would love to know why it remains empty. I can see so many knights standing with nowhere to sit; I've been watching them for a long time. So why? How is it that they daren't sit in the chair?'

And the king replied:

'Perceval, good sir, don't worry about that. It's of no consequence.'

But Perceval said:

'Now I'm sure that you don't love me very dearly. So that God may keep you from harm in this world, both by word and deed, and that your soul may end in Paradise, tell me at once, without deceit, the truth about that chair; for you may be sure of this: I will never eat in this house until I know why it is that no-one comes to sit there.'

When the king heard this he sighed deeply, and wept, and all the barons with him. And the queen, it seems, and all the girls wept and tore their robes with grief. Even Kay, who had mocked Perceval, was grieving so much that it seemed he would surely die. He dismayed many men with his bitter grieving:

'Oh!' he cried. 'It was an evil day when that chair was brought here, for it has cost us many worthy men!'

Perceval was amazed at all this grieving, and said to the king:

'If I've done something wrong I'm quite willing to make amends, but I still want you to tell me why no-one sits in that chair.'

And the king, still weeping tenderly, said in a mournful voice:

'Oh, Perceval, I thought you would bring me comfort and joy; now I'm to have only grief and pain.'

But Perceval urged him to tell at once. And the king said:

'Perceval, my friend, the one who sent me that chair had little love for me or my honour. The fairy of Roche Menor sent it to me by a messenger – and may God send that messenger shame and misfortune! Before he would tell me anything he made me swear, upon my crown and by my life, that the chair would be placed as it is now on every high feast-day, and said that one man would be worthy to sit in it; the one who was to win the praise and esteem of the whole world and learn what no-one else would ever know – the secret of the Grail and the lance; he could sit there without fear. Now I've told you the truth.'

When Perceval had listened to this, he said:

'By Saint Leger, sire, just tell me this: has any man ever sat there?'

'Yes,' replied the king, 'as many as six good knights of my court. But if they sat there it was briefly, for the earth swallowed them up. May ever-truthful God keep you from sitting there.'

But Perceval said:

'I tell you, I'm going to sit there right away, no matter who tries to stop me. I shan't desist for anyone, and may God give me honour and joy.'

The queen heard this and fainted, and Sir Gawain railed against death for not devouring him instantly. At the same time Perceval went and sat down in the chair. The king stood up in floods of tears and everyone fell back. The chair let out so loud a groan that it was heard throughout the hall and everyone shook with terror; and the ground beneath the seat cracked and split so wide apart that it no longer touched the chair at all – by two yards or more on every side the earth had split away. The chair hung motionless as if suspended in the air, moving neither back nor forth; but Perceval did not stir or pale, and felt no fear of anything. And before the earth closed up again and the cavernous pit was covered up, out came six knights who had been swallowed there. All six rose at Perceval's feet, and thereupon the earth closed up to cover the abyss. The adventure was completed. The king ran to Perceval, and all the knights of the court raced up to see him without delay. Kay the seneschal was so jubilant that he was singing for joy and laughing, and before the whole court he declared that he would not be so happy for a thousand pounds as he was at seeing Perceval safe and sound after sitting in the chair and the six returned to earth.

'In faith,' said Ydres the son of Nu, 'you've now done two courteous acts which should certainly be noted: first you wept and were beside yourself with grief when you thought that Perceval would be lost, I think; and now you've rejoiced and sung because he's still alive. This must be counted to your credit! I tell you truly, it doesn't often happen that you say anything about anyone but baseness and offence, but now you have behaved most courteously.'

When Kay heard this banter he replied angrily, saying:

'Sir Ydres, you've reproached me very rudely. You thought everyone would be freely yours when you went to claim the sparrowhawk for some wrinkled, wizened hag.[63] You thought the world of her when you gave her your love and took her to the sparrowhawk to claim and prove that no fairer girl could be found. But what happened when Erec and Enide arrived? You left the sparrowhawk with them!'

Ydres, hearing this reproach, said:

'This has taught me again to keep my mouth shut.'

The king, who had no time for this, bade them end their argument, and they did so without dispute. Then the king asked the knights who had returned from the pit how they had fared beneath the earth. And they told him that they had suffered much pain and hardship; and as for those wicked souls who preferred young men to girls:[64] 'Truly, it's a wonder that the earth doesn't swallow them all at once; they'll burn most terribly on the Judgement Day. You may be sure that the fairy who sent you the chair did so solely to make known what reward is in store for anyone tainted with that vice. Know that on the great day of judgement they will be in the deep pit of Hell, blacker than ink or iron. But the fairy knew very well that the one who was to complete the Grail quest and know its outcome has such a true and fine heart that he would free us from the abyss. No-one could express one tenth of his goodness and his valour. He is the one who will learn about the lance, and why the iron head bleeds. Perceval, dear friend, you have freed us from the foulest suffering and restored us to the greatest joy, and we would never have been set free had it not been for your goodness.'

King Arthur was overjoyed at hearing the words of these knights, returning to tell what they had seen; and he said:

'Those who are stained with such a horrible sin may well be

dismayed. I myself was dismayed when I heard it spoken of just now. Whoever is taken in such a sin will be damned at the end, and may his body be burned by a terrible fire, for I abhor that kind of carnal pleasure. Blessed be the man who cares for his wife or his sweetheart, and loves her dearly, and can call himself a loyal friend: blessed be that kind of loving.'

With that my lord King Arthur sat down again beside Perceval, and all the knights together, and the queen and her girls; and they all had whatever dishes they wished. And you may be sure indeed that Perceval was most honourably and nobly served with everything that took his fancy, and handsomely and at leisure.

MANESSIER, Perceval Continuation (c. 1210–25)

Manessier's poem finally concludes the lengthy story of Perceval and the Grail with Arthur attending Perceval's coronation as the Fisher King. In this extract, Perceval has just returned to Arthur's court after defeating Partinial and healing his uncle, the Fisher King.

The feasting lasted for eight days, and throughout the eight days King Arthur wore his crown. It was a joyful time indeed. And during those festivities a young lady arrived at court, riding a swift hunting-horse. She dismounted at once beneath a pine and climbed up to the hall. She greeted King Arthur first out of respect for him as lord, and then she greeted Perceval, and all the rest of the assembled company together. Then she came up to Perceval and handed him a letter. He read it and learned that his uncle had died in his joy, and had wanted him not to stay at Cardueil but to return to be crowned and to rule his land and uphold his kingdom. He had entrusted it to him in the name of his soul and of God and of the lady who had borne God as her son. Perceval was deeply upset at this news, but the king and all the company were overjoyed for him, and Arthur happily declared that he would go and attend his coronation. They packed and prepared their baggage with all speed and set off, for Perceval summoned them, every one, by name; and they rode straight on until they reached Corbrie, where they were received most fittingly by the people of the land, who honoured Perceval unstintingly. And at the feast of All Saints the good Welshman was crowned. That day fourteen kings were present in honour of him, and all were of high renown. The kings sat together round the high table, and all the worthy company were seated together, too; and it was not long before they saw the Holy Grail, completely uncovered, come through an open door, carried by a girl most elegantly. Behind it, straight afterwards, there came a boy who held a lance with a white head from which there sprang a drop of blood. And after that, in view of everyone, there came a silver trencher, carried by a girl most gracefully. They passed three times before the tables; and thereupon they were all laden with delectable dishes; the tables were filled so splendidly that there was no dish any man could name but it was there before his eyes, along with wines of every kind. Then the boy and the girls returned to the chamber, and the good King Arthur began to ask about what he had seen. Perceval the Welshman told him the truth at once, from start to finish, omitting nothing; the king quite forgot his eating, as did all the others who could hear, and what they heard delighted them.

The plenary court remained there for a month, and every day the Grail served them in its customary way. At the end of the month the court broke up and King Arthur departed with all his companions, riding on until he reached his land.

The Didot Perceval[65] (c. 1200–12)

This early thirteenth-century French prose work combines a version of the Perceval story with Arthur's war against the Romans and Mordred's usurpation. While in most Arthurian stories Merlin disappears soon after Arthur becomes king, he remains an important advisory figure for both Arthur and Perceval throughout this work. It is Merlin who instructs Blayse to write down accurately everything that has happened during Arthur's reign, after Arthur is conveyed to Avalon.

In the Didot Perceval, *King Arthur's fame has spread so far and wide, and his court is so brilliant, that no knight is held in esteem unless he has served in it. Perceval's father, Alain le Gros, had intended to send his son to court once he grew to manhood, and the youth now honours his dead father's wishes, departing without his mother's knowledge. On his arrival at court, Arthur makes him a knight, and he quickly learns about chivalry and love-service.*

Eager for adventure, Perceval demands Arthur's permission to let him sit in the empty thirteenth seat at the Round Table, which

Merlin has expressly forbidden anybody to do. This precipitates the Arthurian knights into the search for the mysterious Holy Grail, by now associated with Christ and Joseph of Arimathea.

When his mother heard that Perceval had departed, she was very grieved, and believed in her heart that the wild beasts of the forest would devour him; she was, indeed, so distraught that she died of grief. Unaware of this, Perceval rode until he arrived at the court of the wealthy King Arthur; he came before the king and greeted him most respectfully in the presence of all the nobles. Perceval declared that it would give him great pleasure to stay with Arthur as a member of his entourage. The king retained and knighted him, and at court Perceval learned much wisdom and courtesy, since you should know that when he left his mother he knew nothing. Indeed, he proved his worth so well to the other barons that he became a member of the Round Table, and was much loved among his peers.

After this there arrived at court Sagremors and Ywain, the son of King Urien; and another Ywain, he of the White Hands; and Dodinaus, the son of the Lady of Malehaut; and Mordred, the nephew of Arthur, who later did him great damage, as you shall hear; and Guirres his brother, and Garries and Gawain. These four knights were the sons of King Lot of Orkney, and King Arthur was their uncle. Later on, Lancelot of the Lake, who was of very great worth, arrived at court. So many other knights came to court that I cannot recall them all; but I must stress to you that there were so many good knights at the court of King Arthur that no one throughout the world spoke of any chivalry except that of the Round Table which the rich King Arthur maintained. Arthur thought a great deal about certain matters of which Merlin had spoken. Therefore he went to his nobles and knights and addressed them thus:

'Gentlemen, you must all return at Pentecost, for I wish to hold the greatest feast ever held by any king in any land on such a day. Moreover, if you wish to do so, each of you may bring your wife with you, since I desire to honour the Round Table, which Merlin established in the time of Utherpandragon, my father. I intend to seat at the table the twelve best knights of my court. All those who attend my feast and wish to remain shall for evermore be members of the Round Table, and every man that attends shall have a badge with the symbol belonging to the Round Table.'

At these words there arose a great shout; all the nobles of the court were delighted, since they all desired to be renowned members of the Round Table. Each departed to his own land, and Arthur remained in Logres, since he was deeply occupied in contemplating how he would re-establish the Round Table.

When the time of Pentecost arrived, knights from every land assembled to attend the feast which King Arthur held. For Arthur had such a high reputation that even those who did not hold land from him would consider themselves shamed and would never dare attend any fine court, nor any place where a man of prowess might see them, if they had not been present at Arthur's Pentecostal court. They all came from so many lands that no one could remember them all, until the day of Pentecost arrived when Arthur brought them to the Round Table at Cardueil, and had Mass sung before all the people present. After Mass was over, the king took aside his nephew Gawain, and with him the best knights whom he could find at court, and seated them in the twelve places at the Round Table; the thirteenth seat remained empty to signify the place where Judas sat. During the reign of Utherpandragon, Merlin left this seat empty, and for this reason the king did not dare fill it.

The feast which Arthur held on the day of Pentecost was very grand; those seated at the Round Table dressed the king in regal garments and placed the crown on his head, so that the king was honoured as he should be. More than seven hundred incense-burners of fine gold perfumed the whole scene, and they threw gladioli and mint before him, and showed him as much honour as they could. Then the king commanded that all who were present at his feast should be given identical new robes, each bearing an emblem, and as soon as the command was given it was obeyed. There were so many knights and squires present that the king gave away 5,400 robes and badges of the Round Table.

Now the king commanded the arrival of water to be heralded by a hundred trumpets, and the knights all sat down to eat. Arthur himself served, wearing his crown and a robe of gold; he was highly regarded by those who have never previously seen him, and his bearing was prized by all those who saw him that day. After dinner the king commanded the tables to be removed, and they all went into the fields to joust.

Then the ladies and damsels climbed up into towers and peered through the crenellations of the walls or gathered at windows to watch the knights joust. For on that day all the members of the Round Table took part in the jousting and were eagerly watched by the ladies and damsels, and for that reason they strove very hard, since there was scarcely a knight who had neither a sister, a wife or sweetheart present. That day the knights of the Round Table earned the prize, for Sir Gawain the son of King Lot jousted most splendidly, as did Kay the seneschal, son of Entor, a brave knight called Urgans, Sagremors, Lancelot of the Lake, and the very chivalrous Erec. All these jousted so well that by evening they overthrew the opposing team and took the prize. The most valiant King Arthur sat on a palfrey that day, with a baton in his hand, and rode between the ranks to maintain peace, that none might dispute among themselves. With him rode Perceval, son of Alain le Gros, who was very upset at being unable to joust, since he was wounded in the hand, and spent the whole day with Arthur, Guirres and Garries, the sons of King Lot and brothers to Sir Gawain. These three knights spent the entire day with the king, visiting the ladies and damsels and watching the jousts which took place.

The daughter of King Lot of Orkney, Sir Gawain's sister, who was called Elaine, was the most beautiful damsel at that time; seeing Perceval the Welshman she fell in love with him. Why should she not do so, since he was the most handsome knight in the retinue of King Arthur? That evening when the tournament ended, the knights and damsels began to sing and celebrate, but Elaine, Sir Gawain's sister, thought a great deal about Perceval the Welshman, whom she dearly loved. When night fell the knights went to their lodgings and pavilions; but Elaine, unable to rest, called a servant and sent him with a message to Perceval, informing him that Elaine, sister of Sir Gawain, sent him her best wishes and greatly desired to see him joust at the Round Table. She commanded him, by the faith which he might owe her,[66] that he joust before her in the morning, wearing the red armour which she would send him. When Perceval heard this message he was very surprised and his heart was filled with joy that such a worthy damsel as King Lot's daughter should command that, for the sake of her love, he should arm himself and joust against the Round Table knights. He told the messenger that there was nothing that the damsel could command him that he would not do for her love: 'I will joust most willingly.'

When the messenger heard this, he was very pleased and, returning to the damsel, repeated every word of Perceval's reply. The delighted damsel took the armour and sent it to Perceval, who was very pleased with it, and slept very little that night. The next morning the king, accompanied by his barons, rose and went to hear Mass; afterwards the twelve peers went to eat at the Round Table, where they were served well. Arthur honoured them to the utmost of his power; he commanded the water to be announced and the other knights seated in the hall were also properly served. The story does not inform us which dishes they ate, but I can assure you that they had whatever they desired, and King Arthur himself served them.

After the meal, they all rose and went into the fields to joust, while the ladies and damsels went to watch. Gawain's sister Elaine was among them, most eager to see Perceval bearing the armour which she had sent him. The knights who wished to compete for the prize left Cardueil, came to the Round Table tournament and began to joust, and thus recommenced the greatest festival which had ever taken place. Lancelot of the Lake, with Gawain and Urien's son Ywain, out-jousted all those of the opposing team. Then Perceval the Welshman arrived, well armed in the armour sent to him by the damsel, and challenged Sagremor by striking his shield at full gallop.[67] When Sagremor heard this, he came out against Perceval, allowing his horse to gallop as fast as possible; they exchanged such great blows on each other's shields that both lances broke. Perceval, who was a good and very experienced knight, struck so hard using the weight of both horse and rider that he stunned Sagremor who, unaware of how it had happened, flew from his horse and hit the ground so heavily that everyone who watched thought that he was dead. Perceval took Sagremor's horse and presented it to Elaine, who displayed great joy.

Perceval performed such feats of arms that day that he surpassed all the Round Table knights, defeating Kay the seneschal, Ywain son of Urien, and Lancelot of the Lake, so that everyone who beheld him said that he was the best knight in the world and should fill the empty place at the Round Table. The king, who was very worthy and wise, approached Perceval and said to him, 'Sir knight, henceforth I wish that you should join my retinue and the Round Table fellowship, and remain with me, and I wish you to know that from now on I greatly desire to honour you.' Perceval replied, 'Thank you, sire.'

Then Perceval removed his helm, and the king recognized him, and he marvelled greatly and demanded to know why Perceval had taken up arms since yesterday, and why he had disguised himself. Perceval said to the king, 'Sire, I would hasten to your aid if required, but I must explain that I acted thus for the sake of love; and you should know that even if I were given the same choice again, I would still act as I have done.'

When the king heard and understood this, he began to laugh, and pardoned Perceval willingly, telling him that what one did for love should be easily forgiven. Sir Gawain, Ywain, Lancelot and all the members of the Round Table also forgave Perceval, who then informed the king that he wished to see the Round Table and those who sat at it, to which Arthur replied, 'Good friend, you can see it tomorrow.' Perceval answered, 'Sire, I would most willingly see them seated there.'

Then they spent the night in festivity, and the next morning the barons assembled to hear Mass; afterwards they all went to the place where the Round Table was situated, and the king bade them sit down. When they were seated, there remained the empty place; Perceval asked the king about the reason for the empty seat. King Arthur answered, 'Dear friend, it has great importance, since it is destined for the best knight in the world.'

In his heart Perceval thought that he should sit there, and said to the king, 'Sire, grant me the gift of sitting in that place.' The king replied that Perceval should not sit there, since great harm could come from this, for in the empty place once sat the false disciple, so that whoever sits there is swallowed up into the ground. 'Even if I were to grant you such a request, you should not sit there.'

When Perceval heard this, he became angry, and said, 'Lord king, as God is my witness, if you don't grant me leave, I warn you that I will no longer remain in your household.' When Gawain heard this, he was very grieved, for he was very fond of Perceval, and he said to Arthur, 'Sire, grant him his desire.' Lancelot then begged the king, as did all the twelve peers, and they all pleaded so strongly that finally the king was persuaded to agree, saying, 'I grant you your request.'

When Perceval heard this, he was most delighted and, going forward, crossed himself, calling upon the Holy Spirit, and sat in the empty place. As soon as he was seated, the stone beneath him split open so violently that it seemed to all those present that the world was falling into the abyss, and accompanying the rumbling noise that the earth made there rose thick smoke and darkness which spread for more than a league, so that it was impossible to see. Then came a voice speaking the following words:

'King Arthur, you have committed the greatest error of judgement ever conceived by a king of Britain, for you have broken the commandment given to you by Merlin. You know well that Perceval has performed the rashest exploit ever attempted by man, which will earn the greatest hardship in the world, for him and for all members of the Round Table. You should also know that if it were not for the goodness of his father Alain le Gros, and the bounty of his grandfather Bron, who is called the Fisher King, Perceval would have been thrown into the abyss and died the grievous death which Moys experienced when he falsely sat in the place which Joseph of Arimathea had forbidden. You should also know, King Arthur, that Our Lord intends you to be aware that the Holy Vessel which Our Lord gave to Joseph in prison, called the Grail, is in your country. The Fisher King has fallen ill and is very infirm, and you should be aware that this king will never recover, nor will the stone beneath the vacant seat where

Perceval sat at the Round Table be rejoined, until a knight has achieved such deeds of arms, bounty and prowess that he is the best knight in the world. When this knight has achieved all these things, Our Lord will send him to the house of the Fisher King, and when he has asked who made the Grail and what its function is, then the Fisher King will be healed, the stone reunited, and all the enchantments which exist today in the land of Britain overthrown.'

When the king and those seated at the Table heard the voice, they all marvelled greatly and vowed that they would never rest until they had found the house of the Fisher King and asked about the Grail. Perceval the Welshman swore that he would never spend more than one night in any place until he had found the Fisher King; Sir Gawain, Erec, Sagremors and all those seated at the Round Table swore the same oath. When Arthur heard this he was very grieved and wished he had not granted Perceval the boon. Yet he was also delighted that Merlin's prophecy had been fulfilled.

Arthur now dismissed his court, and, while many returned to their own country, many others remained in their lodgings, attending the king. Perceval and his Round Table fellows departed as quickly as possible and armed themselves at their lodgings, and when fully equipped they reappeared mounted before the king, in the presence of the nobles at court. Then Gawain spoke in the hearing of the nobles present: 'My liege, we must now go as the voice of Our Lord has commanded us, although we do not know where or in which direction this adventure will take us.' When the king and his barons heard this, they began to weep, since they believed that the knights would never return.

Perlesvaus, or The High Book of the Grail
(c. 1200–12)

This is another French prose version of the story of Perceval (Perlesvaus) and the Grail, although in this version the adventures of various knights are interwoven and Arthur himself takes an active role. In the following episode, King Arthur accompanies Gawain in quest of the Fisher King, first of all encountering the Damsels of the Tent whom Gawain has visited before, on whose behalf they take part in a three-day tournament.

On the first day of the tournament (Arthur wearing the gold and

Gawain the red arms presented to them by the ladies) they perform splendidly and receive everyone's admiration. But on the second day, Gawain's lady orders him to wear his own arms and to do his worst, earning everyone's scorn. On the final day, the damsels tell Arthur and Gawain each to wear the arms that the other had worn on the first day and perform their best. The prize, a circle of gold, is presented to Gawain at the end of the tournament, although he would have preferred Arthur to have received it.

After leaving the tournament, they get into a fight at the Waste Manor, where Lancelot had previously killed a knight, and meet up with Lancelot and Meliot de Logres, who requires Gawain's assistance against Nabigan of the Rock. Meanwhile, back in Arthur's kingdom, everyone believes that the king is dead, and Arthur's enemy, Brien of the Isles, has joined Kay in destroying the land.[68]

Here the story leaves Lancelot and tells of King Arthur and Sir Gawain who were greatly afraid for him, and would gladly have heard some news. They met a knight galloping towards them, and Sir Gawain asked him where he came from; he said that he was from the land of the Queen of the Circle of Gold, who had suffered a great misfortune, for the son of the Widowed Lady had won the Circle of Gold by killing the Knight of the Dragon, and she was to keep it for him until such time as he wished to collect it. But Nabigan of the Rock had seized it from her and commanded a maiden to take it to a tournament which was to be held in the meadow where the tent of the two maidens stood, where Sir Gawain had broken the evil custom; and the maiden would present it to the knight who won the tournament, for Nabigan was determined to win it in combat. The knight departed, and the king and Sir Gawain rode on until they came to the tent where the evil custom had been, which Gawain had broken by killing the two knights. He found the tent adorned both outside and inside as it had been before; and he seated the king upon a rich mattress of brocaded silk, and bade the squire take off the king's armour while he disarmed himself. Then they bathed their faces and hands because they had been bruised by their iron mail. Sir Gawain found the coffers beside the couch unlocked, and he dressed the king in the fine white cloth which he found inside, and adorned him in rich gowns of silk and gold; and he dressed himself likewise, for the coffers were far from empty: the tent was well stocked with rich garments. And when they were thus attired you could have sought far and wide before finding two knights so fair. Just then, in came the two maidens of the tent, and Sir Gawain said:

'Welcome, damsels!'

'Sire,' they replied, 'we wish you both good fortune. It seems that you take our belongings most boldly, but for neither of us would you do as we requested.'

'Sir Gawain,' said the elder, 'there is no knight in this kingdom who would not rejoice if he thought I loved him, but I once begged for your love because of your great chivalry, and you refused. How is it that you dare to trust in my good will and take my possessions so confidently, when I cannot trust in you?'

'Damsel, I dare because of your courtesy and because of the customs of this tent, for you told me when the evil custom was broken that all proper honours and respects would be paid to any knight who came here to take lodging.'

'You speak true, Sir Gawain, but one must refrain from being courteous and reward discourtesy with discourtesy. In this fair glade the tourney will begin tomorrow. There will be a good number of knights here, and the prize will be the Circle of Gold. We shall see who will perform best. The tournament is to last for three days, and you and your companion can boast that you have the finest and most pleasant lodging of all the knights.'

The younger maiden looked at King Arthur, and said:

'And you, sire, will you be as cold towards me as Sir Gawain, intimate though he is with other ladies?'

'Damsel,' replied the king, 'Sir Gawain will do as he likes, and so will I. I shall never be cold towards you or any maiden, but will honour them as long as I live. I shall be at your command.'

'Great thanks, sire,' she said. 'Then I pray you, be my knight at the tournament.'

'That request I should not refuse you. And it would gladden my heart if I could perform some feat which would please you, for knights should always strive to please ladies and maidens.'

'What is your name, sire?' she asked.

'My name is Arthur, damsel, and I am from Tintagel.'

'Are you related to King Arthur in any way?'

'Damsel, I have been to his court many times, and if he did not love me and I him, then I would not be in the company of Sir Gawain. But he is the king I love most in all the world.'

The maiden gazed at King Arthur, not thinking that it was he, and his bearing and appearance pleased her greatly. The king could have been quite sure of having a lover if he had wanted; but there was a great difference between his appearance and his mind: he was raising the maiden's hopes with his behaviour, but his thoughts, wherever he might be, were always with Queen Guinevere.

The maidens had the horses stabled and the knights bedded most finely that night: they lay on two rich couches there in the tent with their arms at hand before them, and the maidens would not leave until their guests had fallen asleep. Next day the equipment of the knights who were going to be at the tournament arrived from all around. Their lodges and pavilions were pitched there in the glade, and when King Arthur and Sir Gawain awoke that morning they saw knights coming from every direction. The elder maiden came to Sir Gawain and said:

'Sire, out of love for me I would have you bear this day the red arms which I shall give you, and make sure that they are put to good use. And I do not want you to be recognized by your arms: it will be put about that you are the Red Knight, and you must confirm that it is so.'

'Great thanks, damsel,' said Sir Gawain. 'I will perform as well as I can out of love for you.'

The younger maiden came up to King Arthur, saying:

'Sire, my sister has presented her token, and I shall now give mine. I have some arms of gold, the finest that any knight could bear, and these I will give to you, for I believe that you will put them to better use than any other knight. And I beg you to remember me by them in the tourney, just as they will remind me of you.'

'Great thanks, damsel,' said the king, 'no knight who ever beheld you should fail to remember you in his heart.'

The knights had now arrived and donned their armour. The king and Sir Gawain were armed, too, and had decked their horses most richly. The maiden who was to present the Circle of Gold had also arrived, and Nabigan had come with great companies of knights. On all sides the tourney began. The younger maiden cried out to King Arthur, saying:

'Sire, you have the finest arms at the tournament: I have never seen a knight better armed! Now be sure to fight like a good knight today out of love for me.'

'Damsel,' said the king, 'may God grant that I fight like a good knight, here and everywhere.'

'And you, Sir Gawain,' cried the elder maiden, 'make sure that people speak well of you but do not recognize you, and when you return, see that you fulfil my wishes.'

'Damsel,' he said, 'I thank you deeply for your words.'

With that they cantered away from the tent, and then sent their horses leaping forward. At their necks hung shields, strong and new, and new shield-covers they had, and lances they held and they had swords girded on. The maidens watched them eagerly as they rode forward, and said that they looked fine knights indeed.

'Damsel,' said the younger, 'do I not have a good champion?'

'Yes, indeed,' said the elder, 'but Sir Gawain will not fulfil my wishes – though I believe I will pay him for that yet.'

Now the knights assembled on all sides and the companies met. The king and Sir Gawain fought in the tourney like two lions; as they charged in they felled two knights, and Sir Gawain seized their horses and bade the king's squire present them to the maidens. After that they did not trouble to take spoils that day, but they vanquished every company they met: no-one could last long in combat with them. Suddenly Nabigan of the Rock caught sight of Sir Gawain, and Gawain saw him. They came charging towards each other, and Sir Gawain struck him full in the chest with such force that he sent both him and his horse crashing down in a heap. Nor was King Arthur idle: most fled before him; and although there were a good number of other knights who performed well, none could rival the feats of the king and Sir Gawain, who gave and received many blows that day.

When evening fell the tourney broke up. The knights went to their lodges to take off their armour, and said to each other that the knight with the gold arms and the knight with the red arms had fought better than any others, and that the one with the red arms was a fine knight indeed.

King Arthur and Sir Gawain had taken off their armour, and the maidens were making much joy of them, when in came a dwarf who was in the service of the maidens, and he said:

'Damsels, you may indeed rejoice, for all agree that your knights performed best of all!'

Then the king and Sir Gawain sat down to dine with the maidens at a rich table of ivory inlaid with gold and precious stones, and there were plates of venison in great plenty; and wines were served to them, and spiced wines, too, in rich vessels of gold and silver. King Arthur dined with the younger maiden, and Sir Gawain with the other.

After they had eaten they wanted to sleep and rest, for they were very tired from the blows that they had given and received; and so they slept until the morning when day rose, fair and clear. In their pavilions the knights began to wake, and many had already donned their armour in their eagerness for combat. The king and Sir Gawain had just risen from their couches when the two maidens came in.

'Sir Arthur of Britain,' said the younger maiden, 'may God grant you a good day and good fortune!'

'I wish you joy and honour,' replied the king.

'Sir Gawain,' said the other, 'do you remember the King of the

Watch with whom you took lodging after you had won the sword with which Saint John was beheaded? He wanted to keep it, which grieved you deeply, but he returned it to you on condition that you would do the first thing that a maiden asked of you, without objection.'

'Damsel,' said Sir Gawain, 'I remember that well.'

'Are you now opposed to your promise?'

'Damsel, if it please God and if God permit, I will do whatever I have to do.'

'Sir Gawain, so that we may see whether you are as true to your word as people say, I beg and entreat you to perform worse than anyone at the tournament today, and to do all the cowardly deeds that a knight can do, and bear none but your own arms so that you may be more clearly recognized. And if you fail to do so, you will have broken the promise that you made to the king, and I shall personally go and tell him.'

'Damsel,' said Sir Gawain, 'I have never failed to keep a promise to which I could be faithful, and I shall not break this one, if such is your wish.'

'By my life, it is!' she said. 'And let no-one implore me to change my mind, for I shall not.'

That day the younger maiden gave King Arthur azure arms, praying and entreating him to bear them out of love for her. The tourney began. Sir Gawain had no arms to bear but his own, and thus he was recognized by everyone. The king and he rode up to the tournament, which was already very big, and companies were coming from all around; the ranks formed up, and King Arthur spurred forward and felled two knights as he charged. Then Sir Gawain rode out between two ranks so that he might be more clearly recognized, and many said:

'There is the good knight Sir Gawain, the nephew of King Arthur.'

Nabigan of the Rock charged at him, lance in hand, and Sir Gawain saw him galloping towards him and threw down his lance and fled away as fast as he could; forty or more knights saw him, and were all astonished, and Nabigan said that he would never pursue a vanquished knight or a knight of his kind, for it would be no great honour to take him prisoner or win his horse. Another knight wanted to joust with Sir Gawain, but he avoided him and fled as fast as he could, pretending that he did not dare face an attack from anyone. He rode back to King Arthur for protection, and the king was deeply ashamed by what he had seen him do, and had to forget about fighting well that day. And he had great difficulty in defending and protecting Sir Gawain, for he was clinging as close to him as a magpie to a bush when falcons are trying to seize it. In this disgrace Sir Gawain remained throughout the tournament, and the knights all said that he had a far greater reputation than he deserved, for they had never seen so cowardly a knight at any tourney, and never would they fear him as much as they had done before; now many of them would be able to avenge kinsmen and friends whom he had killed in the forests.

When evening fell the tournament broke up, much to the delight of King Arthur and Sir Gawain; the knights went to their lodges to disarm, and the king and Gawain went to the maidens' tent. Just then the dwarf came in, saying:

'By my life, your knights are going from bad to worse. The one with the azure arms did passably, but Sir Gawain is the most cowardly knight I have ever seen. If he attacked me tomorrow and I were armed like him, I think I could defend myself against him very well! Devils must make him go forth amongst other knights, for the more people there are around, the more his cowardice is known. And you, sir knight,' he said to the king, 'why do you endure his company? You would have performed well today if it had not been for him. He clung as close to you to avoid blows as a hare to a thicket to escape the hounds. It is not right that a good knight should keep the company of a coward. I say this because I wish that he were even worse than he already is, because of the two knights whom he once killed outside this tent.'

The maiden listened to what the dwarf said, and it made her smile; for she realized that Sir Gawain had earned much reproach. The knights said that they did not know to whom they could give the Circle of Gold now, for the knight with the gold arms and the knight with the red had not been there, and they had fought best on the first day. The next day the tourney was to begin once more.

'Gawain,' said the king, 'you earned much reproach today, and I myself was put to shame because of you. I never believed that so fine a knight as you could behave so much like a coward. You have done a great deal for the maiden, and she has gained her revenge upon you. But if you are as cowardly tomorrow as you were today, you will be in disgrace for ever more.'

'But truly,' said Gawain, 'I must do as the maiden wishes, since we are at her command.'

They lay down to rest that night after they had dined, and when they rose the next morning the maiden came up to Sir Gawain and said:

'I want you to don the arms that your companion wore on the first day, and I would have you fight today as well as you have ever fought, or better. But I command you, by the promise that you made to the King of the Watch, to reveal your identity to no-one; if anyone asks you your name, you will say that you are the Knight of the Golden Arms.'

'Great thanks, damsel,' said Sir Gawain. 'I will gladly do as you wish.'

The younger maiden came up to the king, and said:

'Sire, I wish to change your arms. You will carry red arms today, as Sir Gawain did on the first day, and I would have you be as good a knight today as you were then, or better.'

'Damsel,' said the king, 'it will please me greatly to change my arms and my ways, and I thank you deeply for choosing to say so.'

Their horses were now decked in their trappings, and the king and Sir Gawain mounted, fully armed, and charged into the tournament with such fury that they smashed right through the biggest companies, felling horses and knights and whatever they met. Then the king caught sight of Nabigan who was riding forward in all his finery; the king struck him such a furious blow that he sent him crashing from his horse and broke his collar-bone, and he presented Nabigan's horse to the younger maiden, who was filled with joy. Sir Gawain was seeking opponents all over the field, fighting so well that hardly anyone could withstand his blows. Everyone gazed in wonder at the king and Sir Gawain; and the story says that the king would have performed even better, but he held himself back because Sir Gawain had done so badly the day before, and he wanted him to win the prize.

The maiden who bore the Circle of Gold was there at the tournament. She had placed it in a rich vessel of ivory inlaid with precious stones, and was guarding it with all honour. When the tourney came to an end she bade all the knights draw up and give their true decision on who by his fighting had most deserved the Circle of Gold. And they all declared in all truthfulness that the knight with the golden arms and the knight with the red ought to have the prize before all the others; and of those two the prize should go to the knight with the golden arms, for he had performed on the first day so well that no-one could surpass him, and on the last day likewise; and if the knight with the red arms had not held himself back on the last day, he would have done just as well, or better. The Circle of Gold was brought to Sir Gawain, though no-one knew that it was he, and Gawain would gladly have had them present it to the king. Then the knights left the tourney, and the king and Sir Gawain came back to the tent bearing the Circle of Gold, which brought the maidens the greatest joy. Just then the dwarf returned, and said:

'Damsels, these guests of yours are more worthy of lodging than Gawain, the base, the cowardly, who was so disgraced at the tournament. You were greatly reproached for having given him lodging for so long. But this knight has won the Circle of Gold by his fine combat.'

The maiden laughed at what the dwarf said, and commanded him by the eyes in his head to be gone. The king and Sir Gawain took off their armour, and the maiden said:

'Sire, what will you do with the Circle of Gold?'

'Damsel,' replied Gawain, 'I will take it to the knight who first endured mortal danger to win it, and free from blame the maiden who was to keep it for him, from whom it was stolen.'

The king and Sir Gawain lay that night in the tent. The younger maiden came up to the king and said:

'Sire, I have been told that you performed many great feats of arms at the tourney out of love for me, and I am ready to reward them.'

'I thank you, damsel,' said the king. 'Your reward and your service are most dear to me, and your honour even more: I would wish you to have as much honour as any maiden can have, for no-one should trust in a maiden who honour lacks. May God grant that you keep yours.'

'Damsel,' she said to the other, who was sitting before Sir Gawain, 'this knight and Sir Gawain have been conspiring together: there is no comfort or courtesy in them. Let us leave them to sleep, and henceforth may God save us from such guests.'

'By my life,' said the elder, 'were it not for the Circle of Gold and the duty from which he must free the queen who was to keep it, who is my lady, they would not leave this tent as they will; but although Sir Gawain may be shy with maidens, I know that he is loyal in other ways and will not break his word.'

The maidens departed that night, and the king and Sir Gawain did likewise when they saw the day break; and Nabigan was carried away in a litter, for he had been wounded at the tournament.

Meliot of Logres was out in search of Sir Gawain. He met the knights with all their equipment returning from the tourney, and he asked many of them if they had any news of Sir Gawain, and they said yes, very bad. They asked him why he was looking for him, and he said:

'My lords, I am his liege vassal, and he has a duty to defend my land against all men, and Nabigan, who is being carried there in that litter, seized it from me unjustly. And so I was looking for Sir Gawain so that he could help me to win back my land.'

'In faith,' said the knights, 'we do not see how he can be of any use to others when he cannot even help himself. Sir Gawain was at the tournament, and we can tell you in all truthfulness that he performed worse than anyone.'

'Alas!' cried Meliot of Logres, 'then I have lost my land.'

And he turned away downcast.

The king and Sir Gawain left the tent and rode on with all speed towards the land for which they were heading, dearly hoping that Lancelot would come. On they rode until they came one night to the Waste Manor to which the hound had led Sir Gawain, where he found the body of the knight whom Lancelot had killed. They lodged there that night, and there were knights and maidens there who recognized them. The lady of the Waste Manor called for help and sent word that King Arthur, who sheltered knights who killed others, was there with Sir Gawain; and she would have dearly loved Lancelot to be there with them, for it was he who had killed her brother. A great number of knights came, intent on doing harm to the king and Sir Gawain, but the lady was so courteous that she would not permit them to do them any injury in her house. Seven knights, burning with courage, had ridden up from the forest to guard the bridge, so that the king and Sir Gawain could not leave without facing the points of their lances.

This high story tells us that Lancelot left the Waste City, and rode on until he came to a forest where he met Meliot of Logres, who was much disturbed by what he had heard about Sir Gawain. Lancelot asked him where he had come from, and he replied that he had been seeking Sir Gawain but had heard news which grieved him deeply.

'What?' said Lancelot. 'Has some ill befallen him?'

'Yes, so I have been told; he used to be a good knight, but now he has turned to shameful ways. He was at the tournament, and I met the baggage-train and the companies on their way back, and they told me that no knight had ever shown such cowardice, although a knight who was with him had fought well. But whatever they may say, I cannot believe he has turned coward.'

'Sir knight,' said Lancelot, 'I am going to look for him, and you may come with me if you wish.'

Meliot of Logres set off with Lancelot, and they rode on until they came to the Waste Manor where the king and Sir Gawain had taken lodging.

They had donned their armour and were about to leave when they found the seven knights guarding the exit, fully armed. The king and Sir Gawain saw that it would do no good to stay, and galloped over the bridge to where the seven knights were guarding the way, fully armed; in they charged, and the knights met them with the heads of their lances. Just then Lancelot and Meliot appeared; Lancelot caught sight of the king and Sir Gawain and cried out to the knights like a sparrow-hawk to a lark, sending them scattering in all directions. As he charged in he caught up with one of them and thrust his lance right through him, and Meliot killed another. The king recognized Lancelot and was overjoyed to see him safe and well, and Sir Gawain rejoiced with him. Lancelot and Meliot thus secured their passage, and the knights fled away, not daring to tarry longer.

The lady of the castle was holding a boy of great beauty by the hand; she recognized Lancelot as soon as she saw him, and cried out to him:

'Lancelot, you killed this boy's father, but if it please God he or another will take vengeance.'

And hearing the lady speak, Lancelot fell silent.

They left the Waste Manor. Meliot and Sir Gawain recognized each other and rejoiced at their meeting, and Meliot said:

'Sire, I came to appeal to you against Nabigan of the Rock, who is trying to seize my land for which I pay you homage, and says that he will fight for it with no-one but you. The day is now near, sire, and if you do not come on the day my cause will be lost.'

'I will come most willingly,' said Sir Gawain; and so he departed by the leave of the king and Lancelot, saying that he would return as soon as he could.

Arthur and Lancelot set off with all speed towards the land which had belonged to the Fisher King, while Sir Gawain rode on until he came to the land of Nabigan of the Rock. Meliot informed him that his advocate Sir Gawain had come and was ready to defend his rights for him. Nabigan was now healed of the wound he had received at the tourney, and had little respect for Sir Gawain after the cowardly performance he had seen of him; and he told his knights not to interfere in their combat, for even if four men had challenged him he felt that he could have vanquished them. He rode out of his castle, fully armed. Sir Gawain saw him coming and drew up on one side, and the bold Nabigan lowered his lance and charged at him without another word; he struck him on his shield and his lance flew into splinters, but Sir Gawain was on target and thrust his lance clean through his heart; Nabigan fell to the ground, dead. His knights now came charging at Sir Gawain, but he staunchly fought them off, and Meliot did likewise. Sir Gawain forced his way into the castle, battling with the knights, and extracted justice from them, making them pay homage to Meliot of Logres and return the keys of the castle.

Having secured for Meliot all the land that had been taken from him, Sir Gawain departed and rode off after King Arthur and Lancelot. In the forest he met a maiden riding swiftly along.

'God guide you, damsel,' he said. 'Where are you going in such a hurry?'

'Sire,' she replied, 'I am going to the greatest tournament that you will ever have seen.'

'Where is it to be held?' he said.

'At the Field of Silks, sire. But I am looking for the knight with the golden arms who won the Circle of Gold at the Field of the Tent. Have you any news of him, fair sire?'

'Damsel,' said Sir Gawain, 'what do you want with him?'

'Truly, sire, it would give me great joy to see him. My lady, who was guarding the Circle of Gold for the son of the Widowed Lady, who won the Circle first, has sent me out in search of him.'

'Why?' asked Sir Gawain.

'Sire,' she said, 'she send him word and begs him through me that, for the sake of the Saviour of the world, if he ever had pity on a lady or a maiden he take vengeance on Nabigan, who has been killing her men and destroying her land; for she has been told that he who won back the Circle of Gold is to take vengeance on him.'

'Damsel,' said Sir Gawain, 'you need toil no more in your quest, for I can tell you that the knight who won back the Circle of Gold has killed Nabigan.'

'How do you know, sire?'

'I know the knight well, and I saw him kill him; and to prove it here is the Circle of Gold: he gave it to me so that I might take it to the one who has conquered the Grail, and thus absolve your lady of her duty.'

The maiden was overjoyed, and turned back to tell her lady the joyful news. Sir Gawain set off towards the tournament, because he knew that if the king and Lancelot had heard about it they would be there. And so he set as straight a course as he could, and had ridden but a little way when he met a boy who looked tired indeed, and his mount looked very weary, too. Sir Gawain asked where he had come from, and the boy replied:

'From the land of King Arthur, where a great war is being waged; no-one knows what has become of him, and many people are saying that he is dead, for never since he left Cardueil with Sir Gawain and Lancelot has news been heard of him. And the queen is grieving so deeply for him and for the death of her son that it is said she is going to die. Brien of the Isles has Sir Kay the seneschal in his company and is burning the king's land and stealing the cattle outside his castles.

Of all the knights of the Round Table only thirty-five remain, and ten of them are badly wounded. They are in Cardueil, defending the land as well as they can.'

Sir Gawain's heart was filled with pity at this news. He rode on towards the tournament as fast as he could, and the boy with him, weary though he was, and there he found the king and Lancelot. Knights had come to the tourney from many kingdoms, because a knight had arrived leading a white war-horse and bearing a rich golden crown, and it had been announced through all the neighbouring lands and kingdoms that the knight who performed best at the tourney would win the horse and the crown, which had belonged to a queen who was now dead; but he would have to guard and defend the land of which she had been the lady. And because of this news many knights had arrived: it was a great tournament indeed.

The king and Sir Gawain and Lancelot took up their positions on one side. The story says that at this tourney King Arthur bore the last shield that the maiden had given him, the red; Sir Gawain bore his own, the one he always carried; and Lancelot had a green shield, which he bore out of love for the knight who was killed while aiding him in the forest. They charged into the tournament like unchained lions, bringing down three knights as they came. They sought opponents all over the field, and toppled knights and felled horses, and the king smashed the shield of every knight he met right down to the boss; all the knights feared his blows. Nor were Sir Gawain and Lancelot idle, for each held his own most well; but it was the king that most knights were watching in awe, for he was making a stand like a lion whom the dogs dare not approach. The tourney continued like this for two days, and when it ended the knights declared and judged that the knight with the red shield had performed best. The knight who had brought the crown came up to King Arthur, not recognising him, and said:

'Sire, you have won in combat this golden crown and this war-horse, for which you should rejoice indeed, so long as you are valiant enough to defend the land of the finest lady on earth, who is now dead. It will be a great honour for you if you have strength enough to protect that land, for it is great and rich and powerful indeed.'

'To whom did the land belong?' asked the king. 'And what was the name of the queen whose crown I see?'

'Sire, the king's name was Arthur, and he was the finest in the world, but many people say that he is dead; and the crown belonged to Queen Guinevere, who is now dead and buried, which is a grievous pity. Their knights will not leave Cardueil lest Brien of the Isles seize the city, but they have sent word by me to the kingdom of Logres, entrusting to me the crown and the horse because I know the isles and the strange forests; they begged me to go to all the tournaments to find news of King Arthur and Gawain and Lancelot, and to tell them, if I could find them, that their land has fallen into great suffering.'

The king heard this news and was filled with grief. He drew away to one side, while his knights uttered the bitterest lament in the world. Lancelot did not know what to do; and through clenched teeth he said that now his joy was over and his knightly deeds were ended, for he had lost the noble queen, who gave him heart and comfort and stirred him to great deeds. Tears flowed from his eyes and down his cheeks and chin, and he would have lamented even more if he had dared. Of the king's grief it is not proper to speak. He held the golden crown and kept gazing at the white horse out of love for the queen, for it was he who had given it to her. Sir Gawain could not stop weeping, and he said:

'Truly, I now know that the noblest and wisest queen who ever lived is dead. Never will there be another of her worth.'

'Sire,' said Lancelot to the king, 'if it please you and Sir Gawain, I will go now to Cardueil and do what I can to defend your land until you return from the Grail, for it is in grave need of help.'

'Truly,' said Gawain, 'Lancelot has spoken well, if you will give your consent.

'I am very grateful to him,' said the king, 'and I pray him to go and guard my land until such time as God leads me back.'

Lancelot took his leave of the king and rode away, filled with grief and anger.

Branch Ten

Here the story leaves Lancelot, and another branch of the Grail begins, in the name of the Father, Son and Holy Spirit.

You have heard of the king's great sorrow. He had the white horse led along behind him, but kept the golden crown very close to him, and he and Gawain rode on until they came to the castle which had belonged to the Fisher King. They found it as rich and beautiful as you have often heard it described, and Perceval, who was there at the castle, rejoiced at their coming, and so did the priests and the aged knights. When King Arthur had been disarmed, Perceval led him to the chapel where the Grail was kept. There Sir Gawain presented the Circle of Gold to Perceval and said that the queen had sent it to him, and told how Nabigan had seized it from her and how he had been killed. Then King Arthur offered him the crown which had belonged to Queen Guinevere, and when Perceval heard that she was dead his heart was filled with sorrow. King Arthur was shown the sepulchre of the Fisher King, and was told how the tomb was placed there by Our Lord's command alone; and they showed him a rich silken cloth which lay upon it, and said that each day a new cloth was found there, as rich as that one. The king gazed at the tomb and said that he had never seen one so fine; and from it rose a sweet and gentle fragrance.

The king stayed at the castle and was highly honoured, and saw the richness and plenty that had returned there, for it lacked nothing in the world that worthy people should have. Perceval had had the bodies of the dead knights laid in a burial-place beside an old chapel in the forest, along with the body of his uncle who had so basely killed himself. Behind the castle, the story says, there was a river, by which the castle was supplied with all good things; it was a beautiful river indeed and rich in fish, and Josephus tells us that it came from the Earthly Paradise and ran all around the castle and flowed on into the forest to the house of a worthy hermit. There its course ended and it vanished into the earth, but wherever it flowed there was a great abundance of all good things.

In the rich castle that Perceval had conquered nothing was lacking, and it had three names, the story says. Eden was its first name, another was the Castle of Joy, and another was the Castle of Souls. It was called the Castle of Souls, says Josephus, because the soul of anyone who died there went to Paradise.

One day King Arthur was leaning at the windows of the castle with Perceval and Sir Gawain, and as he gazed out before him he saw a great procession of people coming, one in front of another, and they were all dressed in white. The one at their head bore a huge cross, and all the others carried small ones, and many were bearing lighted candles; on they came, singing in the sweetest voices, and the one at the rear carried at his neck a bell and its striker.

'Ah, God!' cried the king. 'What people are these?'

'Sire,' said Perceval, 'I know them all except the last. They are the hermits of this forest who come here to sing before the Holy Grail three days each week.'

When they neared the castle the king and the knights went down to meet them, and worshipped the crosses and bowed to the holy men. And as soon as they entered the chapel they took the bell from the one at the rear and offered it to the altar, and then laid it on the ground. Then the holy and glorious service began.

Now, the story tells us that at that time there was no chalice in the land of King Arthur. The Grail appeared at the consecration in five forms, but they should not be revealed, for the secrets of the sacrament none should tell save he whom God has granted grace. But King Arthur saw all the transubstantiations, and last appeared the chalice; and the hermit who was conducting the Mass found a memorandum upon the consecration cloth, and the letters declared that God wanted His body to be sacrificed in such a vessel in remembrance of Him. The story does not say that it was the only chalice anywhere, but in all of Britain and the neighbouring cities and kingdoms, there was none.

The king was filled with joy by what he had seen, and he bore in his heart the memory of the name and form of the holy chalice. Then he asked the hermit who had brought the bell where such a thing came from.

'Sire,' he said to Sir Gawain, 'I am the king on whose behalf you killed the giant, through which deed you won the sword with which Saint John was beheaded, which I see upon the altar. I had myself baptized before you, and had all the people of my kingdom turn to the New Law, and then retired to a hermitage overlooking the sea, far from any people, and there I have dwelt for a long while. I rose one night at matins and looked down from my hermitage, and saw that a ship had anchored there. I went down when the tide had gone out and found on board the ship three priests and their clerks. They told me their names, and said that they had been baptized Gregory, all three of them, and came from the Earthly Paradise; and they told me that Solomon had cast three bells with which to honour the Saviour of the world and His sweet mother and His saints, and by his command they had brought this one to this island because there was none here. And they said that if I were to bring it to this castle, they would take all my sins upon themselves, so that I would be absolved of them, and so would they. And so I have brought it here as they commanded, for God wishes it to be the model for all those that will be made in the kingdoms of this island, where there have never been any before.'

'Truly,' said Sir Gawain to the hermit, 'I do remember you, and you are a good man indeed, for you kept your promise to me most faithfully.'

King Arthur and all the people in the chapel were greatly pleased by the bell, and the king thought that its sound resembled the bell that he had heard ringing since he left Cardueil. After they had worshipped the service, the hermits returned to their dwellings.

The Bridleless Mule *(La Mule sans Frein)* *(c. 1190)*

This short French Arthurian poem, like its contemporary The
Knight With Two Swords, *has Arthur's nephew Gawain, as the
hero. Composed at about the time that Chrétien de Troyes was
writing, or shortly afterwards, both these poems make allusion to
the master of romance: in* The Bridleless Mule *there is a reference
to a* Pagan of Maisieres *(Pagan of Mycenae), which is probably a
parody of Chrétien de Troyes. It has been suggested that these
works may even be by Chrétien himself.*[69]

*Displaying Arthur's standard method of protecting the inherit-
ance of his vassals by sending a knight on quest, the poem provides
one of the fullest examples of the custom of a Round Table knight
relating his adventures on his return to court. In the following
extract, the hero gives a detailed summary of his victorious exploits.*

King Arthur and the queen had gone out to enjoy themselves,
accompanied by many of their knights, from the hall and the rooms
above it. Gawain continued to approach, and the queen was the first
to see him, pointing him out to the knights. Both the knights and the
ladies went out to meet him, and the damsel, that is she who ought
to possess the bridle, when she heard that Gawain was coming, was
elated at the news. Now Gawain had arrived, and the damsel went
to meet him.

'Sir,' she said, 'God give you a splendid welcome, and all the delight
that anyone could possess, both by day and by night.' 'And may you
have good fortune,' replied he, as he dismounted from the mule by
the silver stirrup to the ground. The maiden took him in her arms
and kissed him more than a hundred times. 'Sir,' she said, 'it is
appropriate that I should place myself totally in your service, as I
know well that no other man whom I have sent inside the castle for
the bridle has ever obtained it for me, since many knights have died,
having had their heads cut off and so lacking the power to obtain it.'

Then Gawain related the adventures which he had encountered: of
the deep valley and the wood, of the fountain beside the prickly
bushes, and of the water which was black, and of the rotating castle,
and of the lions which he slew, and of the knight whom he had
defeated, and of the rustic's pact, and of the combat against the
serpents, and of the dwarf who had greeted him (although he did not
choose to say more), and how afterwards he returned, and how he
was obliged to dine in the room of the damsel who was the maiden's
sister, and how the bridle was handed over, and, when he left the

castle, how he had seen the rejoicing in the streets, and how he was able to depart without impediment or inconvenience.

When Gawain had recounted this, and the maiden had sought leave of the barons of the court to depart, Queen Guenevere ran up, and the king and the knights came up to entreat her to remain there with them, and to take one of the Round Table knights as her beloved.

'Sir, may the mother of God confound me,' she said, 'if I did not remain willingly if I dared, but I cannot stay for anything.' She asked for her mule, and when it was brought to her, she mounted by the stirrup, and the king went to see her off, but she said that she did not wish to have an escort, so as not to trouble them, and also since it was quite late. She took her leave and, putting her mule into a trot, she departed.

ROBERT BIKET, The Lay of the Horn (Le Lai du Cor) (c. 1175–1200)

Robert Biket's The Lay of the Horn *is probably the earliest account of a chastity test at Arthur's court; several similar examples involving drinking-horns and mantles are recounted elsewhere. Another version of the story of Caradoc and the horn is found in* The First Perceval Continuation, *while the test reappears as the 'Tankard Episode' in Heinrich von dem Türlin's* The Crown *(Diu Krône). The related story of the mantle is found in* Le Mantel, My Lord Gawain, *or the* Avenging of Raguidel *and* La Cote Mal Tailiee, *which is retold by Malory in the* Book of Sir Tristram, *and the Middle English tale* The Boy and the Mantle.[70]

The whole of Biket's fairly short poem is included here. Caradog is the hero of the poem and Arthur is depicted as a violent man who has to be restrained from attacking the queen when the horn proves her disloyalty (or his jealousy) by spilling wine over him.

Of an adventure which occurred at the court of the good king who held Brittany and England free of homage, as the storyteller found written:[71]

King Arthur was holding a very extravagant feast on the day of Pentecost at Caerleon. As the story told, the feast was very grand: twenty thousand knights sat down to eat there, with twenty thousand maidens, ladies and damsels. This was a great wonder: each of the knights had a female companion with him; the man who had no wife ate with his girlfriend, his sister or his sweetheart; this was a very courteous custom. The king had summoned all his barons from Esparlot in Bretaingne[72] as far as Germany, from the city of Holland down as far as Ireland. In a spirit of fellowship the king had sent word to his nobles that they should be at Caerleon on this day of public absolution.[73]

All came on that day, both the great and the lesser people, but before they had eaten they would all be angered. For you might have seen a young nobleman, who was very comely and handsome, who came quickly to the palace on a fast horse. In his hand he held a horn which had four bands of gold around it. The horn was made of ivory, finely carved. There were stones set in the gold: beryl, sardonyx and rich chalcedony; it was made from elephant ivory; never was such a fine example seen, either so strong or so beautiful. On it was a ring which was inlaid with silver, and it had a hundred small bells made of pure gold. In the days of Emperor Constantine the Great a fairy who was skilful and wise had made the horn and given it a special property, as you shall hear now: whenever anyone placed his finger on the horn (however lightly), its hundred little bells rang more sweetly than a harp or hurdy-gurdy; neither the merry voice of a maiden nor the song of the Sirens[74] had such an effect on the listener. A man might go a league on foot before he ceased to hear them; whoever heard the sound, forgot everything else.

The messenger entered the palace, carrying the horn. He saw the great assembly of barons, all full of valour. He took the horn, which hung from his neck, into his hand, then he lifted it on high. He was dressed in a long-sleeved tunic with an embroidered hem.[75] He blew on the horn; the place echoed with the sound, while the bells rang and produced such harmony that all the knights stopped eating. There was not a young man present who looked after the dishes, nor such a well-trained cup-bearer who served the wine, whether he carried a wooden bowl or a massive goblet of fine gold, containing brandy, spiced wine, spiced mead or herbal drinks, who could proceed – the men who held them spilt them – no seneschal was so strong, however skilful or worthy, who did not fall or stumble as he carried the plates. The squire who was cutting the bread paused to listen. They were all enthralled by the horn's music, and everything else was forgotten; everyone stopped talking to hear the horn. The noble King Arthur was so silent for the horn's sake, and the counts and kings kept so quiet, that not a soul present spoke.

The messenger went to the king, moving quickly towards him,

holding the horn in his hand. He recognized the ten kings by their extremely rich garments; they were surrounding King Arthur, dumbfounded by the horn. The messenger, a comely youth, addressed the king, greeting him politely with a smile: 'King Arthur, may God who dwells on high, preserve you and all your barons whom I see assembled here.' Arthur replied to him, 'May He also give you joy.' 'Sire!' the messenger said to him. 'Listen to me for a little while: the king of Morraire, who is noble and courteous, sends you this horn which he took from his treasure, with the single condition – hear his intentions that you will neither be grateful to him nor wish him ill from it.' The king spoke thus: 'Friend, your lord is courteous, and I will accept the horn with four bands of gold and will neither thank him nor wish him any ill from it.'

King Arthur took the horn, which the youth held out to him. From his cup of fine gold he ordered wine to be given to the youth, then Arthur said to him: 'Take this plate; sit before me, eat and drink. When I have eaten I will make you a knight, and in the morning you shall have one hundred pounds of fine gold.' The other laughingly replied: 'It is not seemly that a squire should eat at the knights' table. I shall go to my lodgings and rest. When I am properly equipped, dressed and attired, I shall return to you and take my promised reward.' With this the messenger left the king and departed from the hall. He went from the town, declaring that he should not be followed.

The king remained in the palace; he had never been so thoughtful before; his barons were gathered around him. He held the horn by the ring – he had never seen such a beautiful object. He showed it to Gawain, Giflet and Ywain. The four sworn followers and all the barons round and about looked at the horn. The king took back the horn and saw that there were letters engraved in silver on the gold, then he spoke to his chamberlain: 'Take this horn in your hand; show it to my chaplain, who shall read these words to me; I wish to know what is written there.' The chamberlain took the horn, and gave it to the chaplain, who read the letters; when he saw them he began to laugh. He addressed the king: 'Sire, listen to me. I will whisper right now in your ear a wonder greater than any heard in England or in any other land, but this is not the place to tell it to you.'

The king did not delay, but rather affirmed and swore that the chaplain should tell it in everybody's hearing, so that his barons would hear it, and also the ladies, damsels and sweet maidens who were all gathered there from foreign lands. 'Such a desirable thing,' said the king, 'should not be concealed.' Everyone present was overjoyed when they heard the king declare that they should all hear whatever the letters might say; but the great joy there was later regretted, and the great pleasure would turn to anger. So the chaplain, who was neither foolish nor wicked, declared: 'If I had been believed, I would not have read the inscription which is written on it today, nor what the letters say. But since you wish it, you shall hear it publicly:

This Mangoun sends to you, from Moraire the blond:[76] *a fairy made this horn, jeering and full of resentment; she cast a spell that no man might drink from it, however wise or foolish he might be, if he were a cuckold or jealous, or if he possessed a wife who had foolishly given a thought towards another man. Never shall anyone, even someone of high rank, be permitted to drink from the horn without its spilling its contents on him, however grand he may be, both on himself and his clothes, even if they are worth a thousand marks. Whoever shall drink from this horn will need to have a wife who has never thought, through disloyalty, either to win wealth or for anything on earth more beautiful, that she might ever wish to have a better lord. If his wife is completely faithful, then he will be able to drink. However, I do not believe there is a knight from here to Montpellier that has married a woman who will be able to drink a single drop; and thus whoever wrote these letters speaks truthfully.*

My God, how many a happy lady was angry that day. None of them was so loyal that she did not lower her gaze in embarrassment; even the queen hung her head, and all the barons round and about who had wives knew where they stood. The maidens chattered amongst themselves and whispered; looking at their menfolk, they gave them polite smiles, saying: 'Today you shall see the jealous, the acquiescent cuckolds, and the unwitting ones.'

Arthur was very angry but attempted to pretend that he was pleased. He called to Kay: 'Fill this rich horn for me, for I will endeavour to find out if I may drink from it.' And Kay the seneschal hurried to fill the horn with spiced wine and held it out for the emperor. King Arthur took hold of the horn and raised it to his mouth, for he expected to drink, but it overturned on him, spilling the wine as far as his feet, which made the king furious. Arthur said, 'Now this is the worst thing possible.' He took a small knife, with which he intended to stab the queen to the heart, but Gawain, Kadoains and Ywain seized the king – between the three of them, with the help of Giflet, they took away the knife, pulling it out of his hand, and rebuked him severely. 'Sire,' said Ywain, 'you should not be so wicked, for there is no married woman here who has not had one foolish thought. I am not surprised that the horn spilled the wine!

All here will try, for those who have wives wish to know if they will be able to drink; then you may blame the queen of the fair countenance. You are a great nobleman, and my lady is loyal. Never have I heard any man speak of her committing an offence.'

'Ywain,' said the queen, 'now I might make a fire of hawthorn to embrace my lord, and throw myself on it. May I burn my hair or tear my clothes; you may drag me, or pull me apart by horses, if I have ever loved or will ever love a man save only the body of my lord. This horn is very truthful; by one small fault I was open to attack. A year ago, I gave a ring to a young nobleman, a young man little more than a child, who killed a giant, a ruthless malefactor who with great treason accused Gawain at court here, the youth's first cousin.

'The youth defended Gawain and fought the giant; with the blade of his sword he cut off his opponent's head. As soon as the giant was dead, he took leave of this court. I offered him my love to keep him at court, and gave him a ring which I believe he kept; but if he should return he would not be loved by me. Certainly,' said the queen, 'since the time when I was given to you as a maiden, I have been happy; never did I commit any further wickedness in my entire life. There is no man under heaven who is so powerful – not even the King of Rome – whom I could love more than you, for all the gold in Pavia, neither any emir or count. Whoever sent this horn has brought me great shame at this feast – no lady will ever love him. I shall never be happy until I am avenged.'

Then King Arthur spoke: 'Do not speak of this any more. If I have any powerful neighbour, either relation or cousin, who makes war on him, I will never love him in my heart. I have sworn before all my people that as long as I live I will not wish him ill. It is not right that I should go back on my word, for that would be a crime; as a king I am bound to keep my word.'

'Sire,' replied the queen, 'since I was a maiden and was given to you, I have been blessed. A lady of high birth would commit a great sin if, when she had a good husband, she took another man as a lover. He who deliberately seeks better wine than that of the grape, or better bread than that from wheat, such a man should be hanged and his ashes scattered. Without a doubt, I have the best of the three kings whom God ever made; why, then, should I seek anyone finer or worthy? I tell you well, sire, that you bear anger towards me wrongly: a man should never give this horn to a noble knight to hold, in order to shame his wife.'

The King said: 'This they all shall do – all shall try the horn, both king, duke and count; I shall never bear shame alone!' King Arthur gave the horn to the King of Snowdon, and it spilled wine over him as soon as he had accepted it. Then King Nut took the horn, and wine was spilled over him; and King Aguisans of Scotland was determined to drink from it by force, but it completely emptied itself over him, which made him very angry. The king of Cornwall desired to drink from it without fail, but it was all spilled over him, for which reason he was very annoyed; and the horn was spilled over King Gohors. It spilled very well on King Glovier; as soon as he held it in his hands it spilled over Kadoains. Then King Lot, who considered himself very wise, took hold of it, and it again spilled over his moustache; it soaked Cararours and two kings of Ireland. There was not one of them over whom it did not spill; nor among the thirty counts, who were thence very ashamed. There was never a baron around or about that might try the horn who was ever pleased: it overturned on each king, who became angry. They passed it on, for they were very upset; they declared that this horn should be sent to the Devil, and with it the man who brought it and the one who sent it, for each believed that this horn shamed his wife!

When King Arthur saw how the horn spilled over them all, he was no longer angry, but began to laugh and showed great joy. He addressed his barons: 'My lords, listen to me. I am not alone in being mocked; the man who gave me this horn presented me with a great gift. By the faith which I owe to all those whom I see here, I would not give it away for all the gold in Pavia; nor in the future shall I accept any follower who does not drink from the horn.' The queen is blushing for this great wonder of which she does not dare speak. She is more beautiful than a rose: the king looked at her, and she appeared very lovely to him. He drew her towards him and kissed her three times. 'Lady, I freely withdraw my anger towards you.' And she replied, 'I thank you, sire!' 'Then take the horn, both great and small.'

A knight seized the horn and smiled at his wife. He was the member of the court who displayed the greatest happiness and spoke the least mockery, and was the most courteous; and when he was armed he was feared the most, for there was no better knight in Arthur's court, nor anyone who accomplished more with his hands, except my Lord Gawain. He had blond hair and a reddish moustache, clear and laughing eyes, a comely body, arched and well-made feet: he was a true knight. His name was Caradog, and he was highly renowned. He had a very faithful wife, King Galahal's sister, born in Cirencester. She sat beside him on his left, a very beautiful and well-dressed lady with a well-made body and long golden hair. There was not a more beautiful lady present, except for the queen. Caradog looked at his wife – her colour never altered but, rather, she spoke to him saying,

'Good sweetheart, do not ever doubt that you shall drink from the horn at this high feast; so lift your head and do me honour. I would not take as my lord any man, however powerful, even if he were an emir, to leave you, my love – I would not take any other as a husband, but would rather become a nun and clothe myself in a nun's habit. For each woman should be faithful like the turtle-dove who, once she takes a mate will never have another. Thus should a lady behave if she is of noble birth.'

Caradog was very happy, and leaped to his feet. He was good and handsome, a true knight. He put the horn to his mouth – well might I say that he touched it! When a servant had filled it, it held a measure and a half; it was full of red wine; to the king he said, 'Wassail.'[77] He was both broad and tall, and he completely drained the horn. He was greatly overjoyed; he leaped over the table, and came at once before King Arthur, and said in mid-stride, but not speaking in a low voice, 'Sire, I have drunk in full, of that you may be sure.' 'Caradog,' said the king, 'you are valiant and courteous. Truly you have drunk it; more than one hundred people have seen you. You look after Cirencester, which I entrusted into your care more than two years ago: I will never take it from you; you shall have it throughout your life, and your children after you. Moreover, for your wife's sake, who is very worthy of praise, I shall give you this horn, which is worth one hundred pounds in gold.' Caradog replied, 'I thank you, sire.' Then he sat down at dinner beside his wife, with the clear complexion. When they had dined, each person took his leave; they returned to their own lands, from whence they had come; they took with them their wives, whom they loved most.

Epilogue

Lords, this song was composed to tell of the deeds of Caradog. Truly, whoever was at Cirencester on a high-feast day could see this horn there. Thus said Robert Biket, who knew a great deal about tricks. He said that he had written this story from the narrative of an abbot, who stated that the horn was won thus at Caerleon.

BÉROUL, The Romance of Tristan (c. 1190–1200)

While Arthur is not a central figure in any version of the Tristan story, occasionally he is introduced into an episode. In later versions of the story, for example in some manuscripts of the Prose Tristan, *the Tristan story is incorporated into the Arthurian legend. Here, in Béroul's account, there is an episode in which Yseult appeals to Arthur, as King Mark of Cornwall's overlord, to make judgement concerning her adultery with Tristan. Yseult's squire, Perinis, arrives at Arthur's court with her request. In the following extract, Arthur gives his judgement about Yseult's guilt.*

Arthur rode on the queen's right, and their journey seemed to him very short. [The edge of the forest was on their left] and the path continued to the right. They dismounted at their lodgings, of which there were plenty on the heath. Tent-ropes were at a high price. In place of reeds and rushes, they had all carpeted their tents with flowers. By roads and by-ways people came to the Blanche Lande until it was crowded. Many a knight had brought his lover. The knights who were in the meadow found many a stag to pursue. That night they stayed on the heath. Each king sat to hear the requests of his people. Those who were rich were quick to exchange presents. After his meal King Arthur went to the tent of King Mark to pay his respects, taking his private household with him. Little coarse cloth was worn there, almost everything was of silk! Of the clothes what shall I say? There were garments made of the finest wool, dyed scarlet; many people were richly clad. No one ever saw two richer courts. Nothing that they needed was lacking. They made great joy in their tents. That night they discussed the matter in hand, how the queen was to vindicate herself against the accusation in the presence of the kings and their barons. King Arthur went back to his bed with his barons and friends.

Anyone who was in the wood that night could have heard the sounds of flute and horns coming from the tents. Before daybreak there was thunder, a sure sign of heat. The watchmen sounded their horns at daybreak, and everywhere people woke up and rose without delay. The sun was already hot soon after dawn and the mist and hoar-frost had dispersed. The Cornish people had gathered in front of the tents of the two kings. No knight in the whole kingdom had failed to attend this court with his wife. A cloth of dark grey silk, embroidered with small animal figures, was placed before the king's tent and spread out on the green grass. The cloth had been bought in

Nicaea. Not one holy relic was left anywhere in Cornwall in a treasure-chest, in a casket or a phylactery, in reliquaries or boxes or shrines, not even those that were set in gold or silver crosses or amulets, for they had all been placed on the cloth and arranged in their order. The kings drew to one side. They wanted to come to a fair decision. King Arthur, always quick to speak, spoke first:

'King Mark,' he said, 'whoever advised you to make this accusation did you a terrible wrong and certainly acted disloyally. You are easily influenced, but you must not believe false words. The man who made you convene this meeting was preparing a bitter sauce for you. Whoever brought this about deserves to be severely punished. The noble, good Yseut has not asked for any delay. I want those who have come to hear her trial to know this for sure: I will see them hanged if they make any spiteful accusations of wickedness after her trial. They will deserve their death. Now listen, King Mark: whoever is to be proved wrong, let the queen come forward so that everyone can see her. She shall swear to the Heavenly King, holding her right hand over the holy relics, that there was never love between her and your nephew which was in any way shameful, and that she has never loved anyone wrongfully. My lord Mark, this has been going on too long: when Yseut has sworn that oath, tell your barons to hold their tongues.'

'My lord Arthur, what can I do? You reproach me and you are right, for only a fool believes an envious man; yet I believed them against my will. If the queen is vindicated in this meadow, no one will ever be so bold again. If anyone, after the trial, speaks of the queen otherwise than to her honour, he will suffer for it. Arthur, noble king, know that this has been done against my will. From now on let them take heed!'

Then the counsellors separated. Everyone sat down in rows except the two kings, for Yseut was between them holding their hands. Gawain stood near the relics, and the household of Arthur was seated round the cloth. Arthur, who was nearest Yseut, began to speak:

'Listen to me, fair Yseut, and hear what you are accused of. You must swear that Tristan never loved you wickedly or wrongfully, and only bore you the love he owed to his uncle and his wife.'

'My lords,' she said, 'by the mercy of God I see holy relics here before me. Listen now to what I swear, and may it reassure the king: so help me God and St Hilary, and by these relics, this holy place, the relics that are not here and all the relics there are in the world, I swear that no man ever came between my thighs except the leper who carried me on his back across the ford and my husband, King Mark. Those two I exclude from my oath; I exclude no one else in the world.

From two men I cannot exculpate myself: the leper and King Mark my lord. The leper was between my legs [as everyone who was watching could see]. If anyone wants me to do more, I am ready here and now.'

All those who heard her oath could bear no more.

'God,' said everyone, 'that would be a cruel wrong! She has done everything that justice demands, and she put more into her oath than the villains required her to. She needs to make no defence concerning the king and his nephew beyond what all of us have already heard. She swore in her oath that no man ever came between her thighs, except the leper who carried her across the ford yesterday morning and King Mark, her husband. A curse on anyone who mistrusts her now!'

King Arthur rose to his feet and addressed King Mark so that all the barons could hear:

'King, we have seen and heard the queen's defence. Now let the three villains Denoalan, Ganelon and the evil Godwin, take care never to speak of it again. As long as they remain in this land, we shall be ready to come swiftly to defend the rights of the fair Queen Yseut as soon as she sends a message.'

'Sire,' she said, 'I thank you.'

The three villains were greatly hated by all the court. The courtiers separated and made their departure. The lovely, fair-haired Yseut thanked King Arthur deeply.

'My lady,' he said, 'I am your surety. As long as I am alive and healthy, you will never again find that anyone says anything that is not to your honour. The villains have had evil thoughts. I have begged the king your lord, in loyalty and friendship, never to believe what the villains say about you.'

King Mark said: 'If I do from now on, I shall be greatly to blame.'

Then they parted from each other and each returned to his own kingdom. King Arthur went to Durham and King Mark stayed in Cornwall. Tristan remained where he was, with few worries.

RAOUL DE HOUDENC, My Lord Gawain, or the Avenging of Raguidel (Messire Gauvain, ou La Vengeance de Raguidel) (c. 1200–20)

(This work is usually referred to merely as Vengeance Raguidel [The Avenging of Raguidel].)

Raoul de Houdenc wrote two Arthurian poems in the early thirteenth century: Vengeance Raguidel *and* Meraugis de Portlesguez. *While Chrétien de Troyes is sometimes critical of Arthur, Raoul depicts an Arthur of lesser stature than previously seen, heedless of royal duties in his childish petulance at being deprived of excitement during his festivities.*

In this poem there is a strong challenge to Arthur's honour and reputation. As in many works, the poem opens at King Arthur's court where, according to his custom on great feast-days, he waits until hearing of an adventure before eating. The frequent application of the title 'Messire' to Gawain (Gauvain) in this and other French works – an honour sometimes shared with his cousin Yvain – denotes his rank and royal blood. In the absence of a son, Gawain, as Arthur's eldest and closest nephew is heir apparent, holding a rank which in contemporary terms is equivalent to that of HRH the Prince of Wales. Lancelot and the other knights are of lower social status, as is apparent in the seating arrangements at feasts such as that in Sir Gawain and the Green Knight, *where Gawain and Ywain sit on the high dais with Arthur and Guenevere.*

It was in the early summer, and King Arthur had spent the whole of Lent at Rovelant. Now he came, with a great number of followers, to hold his Easter court at Caerleon; for the king desired to maintain his custom at that time. With him was King Enquenors, and King Aquissait was also there, but I could never recount for you the number of princes which he had there, at that court. Thus, as the story tells, the king held court at Caerleon. All the nobles and princes were assembled at court, so that by comparison there were more people than usual, for there had never been previously so many knights present.

King Arthur had a custom that he never ate on a feast-day until news of an adventure had arrived at his court. So then it was a mishap when the day passed and night came without anything happening there. The whole court was dark and confused. They all awaited the adventure, until the hour of dining had passed. The king was silent and deep in thought at the lack of any event. He held this desire so dear to his heart that he almost died of anger, and the nobles came to him and spoke:

'Sire, for God's sake abandon this thing; you cannot gain anything by grieving: come and eat. You should see that your knights are amazed, ten here, twenty over there.' 'Never,' said the king, 'has it happened to me before, that on such an important day nothing has occurred before I have eaten; rather, an adventure has come from some direction! God, who gives and takes away all good things, has upheld the tradition for me. If the time ever comes when no more occurred, then I would lose my dignity, and I would lose my right to rule. I would rather die than lose this custom, I tell you all this plainly.'

Afterwards, when the nobles had heard this, they waited for a long time to see if an adventure would occur. When the king realized that no adventure was going to happen, he was so grieved that he wished he might have died there, he was so disappointed with what he saw. 'Order the tables to be set straightaway,' he said. 'Then go and eat!'

'Sire,' answered the knights, 'what have you said we should do? Certainly, may it please God, without you we will not eat on this occasion.' 'My lords,' replied the king, 'do this, since I wish it, and beg you to do so.' Then my lord Gawain came out of a room, and went there immediately. When his uncle the king saw Gawain, he spoke to him: 'Good nephew, by the faith that you owe me, go and eat with this company of lords.' My lord Gawain heard the king's words and, since he never contradicted him in anything, he replied: 'Sire, most willingly.'

My lord Gawain sat at the high table to eat, and all the other knights who wished to dine also seated themselves; however, most of those present were discontented, and I will tell you why: they had come there to attend the king at the feast, so they ate and drank very little. They were properly served with various courses, since there were plenty of dishes, but you should realize that they were annoyed that the king had not joined them at the meal, as he was accustomed to do, and each of them was grieved in his heart.

The king was silent and climbed up into a room beside the tower; there he remained thinking all day. When night fell, he lay in bed, but did not sleep all night; he tossed and turned from one side to the other, so tormented that he could not rest, and although he desired to do so, he was unable to sleep. He could not sleep because no adventure had happened. He pushed off the cover with his feet; in an instant he dressed himself in his shirt, riding breeches and shoes and, taking a surcoat, he donned it as quickly as possible. Going to a window, he put out his head to look outside.

The king glanced down towards the sea; there he saw a ship sailing towards him, which was rapidly approaching, although he could see no one in it, either steering or sailing it, and the wind drove with such a force on the sail that the mast was bent. In such a manner the ship arrived, striking against a stone which it pushed on to the shore.

When the king saw the noble vessel arrive, he could hardly contain himself from going to see the ship, so he went to learn the truth; all alone, without any company, he went to the place where the ship had beached. When he had reached it, he entered the ship. In the central part of the boat he found a chariot with four huge wheels. To see better he went closer, and inside the chariot saw a knight lying on his shield; he had been struck through the body by a lance, of which the broken stump protruding from his body measured more than six feet. The king looked at this wonder. A rich girdle encircled the dead man; from it hung a beautifully worked alms-purse. The king speedily opened this and took out a letter from it. Then he said between his teeth, 'God has sent me an adventure, which will make my court happy and rejoice; and I am happy also, as I should be.'

After this, he saw five rings on the four fingers of the knight's right hand. Each of the five he pulled and twisted more than four times, but since he could not remove them, he left them in place. After a while, the king returned and went back to the place which he had left, the room under the tower, which was very richly equipped. The chamberlains were up; since they had not found the king in the bed where he had spent the night, they were very alarmed, anxious and surprised. From the room they had raised the alarm. Then the king returned; they did not know where he had been. He spoke to them: 'Good lords, be quiet; be joyful, leave your grief, and listen to some news which is good and most pleasing. Out there a ship has arrived, and such a beautiful one was never seen before. I found there no man born of woman, except a body, which lies murdered on his shield. The corpse is placed inside a chariot, which is beautiful and well made. The knight wears on his fingers five rings, which I could not remove, either by strength or by force, whatever I tried. However, I found these letters in his alms-purse, which are in my hand; call my chaplain to me.'

At the king's command, the chaplain came quickly and the king ordered him: 'Tell us everything that these letters say.' 'Sire,' he answered, without refusing, 'I will tell you as well as I can. The knight who was murdered has been brought to you in order that you may avenge his death; since he was wrongfully killed, he was sent here to you. However, I am unable to say who he is and who killed him: I cannot name him or his land. The message addresses the knight whose task it is to avenge him: whoever can remove the broken lance which he has in his body. Nobody but this knight will be able to achieve vengeance; and he will do so with the broken section of the lance which he will pull from the body. Vengeance must be gained by whoever is able to do this; and he who removes the lance will not be able to take revenge unless he has another knight with him; and the death of this man will be avenged with the aid of the man who can remove the rings, for without the help of the knight who knows how to remove the rings, the man who has the broken part of the lance will not be able to achieve revenge. Sire,' he ended, 'the letter tells no more.' 'Then I command,' declared Arthur, 'that my barons should come with me.'

When Kay heard the news, he came before the king. 'Sire,' he said, 'give me this quest of vengeance. For my service, you have always promised that I should have honour: if you allow me this thing, I swear you are free of all other claims. Great king, grant my request, that I may pull forth the broken lance which is in the knight's body. Thus I shall go to avenge him against whoever treasonably killed him.' The king granted him his request, and then said, 'Lord seneschal, you are very brave and valorous to have demanded such a boon from me: there is no knight in my household so bold, who has not hesitated about this thing which you have requested from me. Pull the lance from the corpse.'

Then immediately the king set forth from the hall with his followers. They went to see this dead man in the chariot, who had arrived there in the ship. First the broken lance was seized by Kay, as though he knew how to remove it, but he was quite unable to tear it away. When he realized that he could not pull it out, he placed his foot on the body, to see if he could move it by force. He tried so often and with such effort that he caused the blood to flow forth from the dead man's wound. 'Sir seneschal,' said the king, 'you are not behaving courteously: take care that you pull it no more! Go, return your foot to the ground: for you have done a very shameful deed!' Then Sir Kay went away, very angry and ashamed. Then came Blioberis, one of my lord Gawain's comrades. He took the broken lance in his hand and tried hard to pull it forth, but was quite unable, so he left it there. Lancelot of the Lake came next: he took hold of the lance, and pulled with great force, but was unable to draw it forth.

'A great marvel is to be seen!' said all the nobles. 'Lancelot of the Lake cannot achieve it.' They were all very surprised, since Lancelot had failed there; and many other good knights came to try after him. Tristran, he who never laughed, took the lance fragment in both hands, but could not attain it by any means. The revenge would have been well trusted to him, for he was a very fine knight; but the broken lance held itself in the body, as firm as a church, as though nothing could draw it forth. I will not make a long story of this: in the court there was no king or count who did not come there to try, but there was never a knight who could pull it out, it was so strongly held in place. So they greatly wasted their efforts, until right at the end came Sir Gawain. He took hold of the lance quite gently, and did not use such force as the others had done. He drew it towards him: all his friends were very delighted when they saw that he had withdrawn the lance.

Then all the squires and knights came to attempt to remove the rings: not a single man could be found who had not come to try for the rings, but none of the household could find out how to do so, and each in turn failed. The king regarded himself as ill-served; he commanded his men that there should be no more delay before the murdered knight was brought from the ship. Along the way, they should carry him with his body exposed, so that any man who saw him might try to take off the rings. They obeyed the king's order, and it was done as instructed. The king departed, and returned to the hall below the castle; there he had fine and rich food prepared in the kitchens. At his bidding, squires brought water for people to wash. The king sat down to eat, and all his knights after him. Great joy filled the palace: they had plenty of fine dishes; both high and low had venison and fresh fish.

The king told one of the servants that he should hurry up with the side dishes; he did not wish to waste time sitting there all day. So the servant, without any delay, went running into the kitchen, but the smoke and heat there hit him in the face. Then, so I am told, the servant went to a window, since he could no longer stay in the smoke, which greatly troubled him. For coolness he placed his head through the window; on the ground beneath he saw a knight on a war-horse: he was very handsome and well-armed, and was holding all the rings, which he had removed from the dead knight.

The servant, so I am told, rose from the window and ran in fright to the king. There he would have told his news, if he had not met Kay, who said to him, 'Boy, where are you going?' 'Sir, I have seen a marvel!' And he told Kay: 'The young man of the chariot, he has no rings now; for they have all been taken from him by the armed knight whom I saw there on his Gascon horse.' The seneschal lifted his fist and gave the servant a great blow, which he did repeatedly: he gave him a good beating. Then the servant cried for mercy; and Kay told him that if he did not swear that he would not speak of this to the king, he was a dead man: he would not escape! The servant, who was greatly afraid, promised to obey Kay's wishes. 'Sir,' he said, 'for God's sake, have mercy!' Kay told him: 'Don't utter a word about this before the king has finished dining.' 'Sir,' he replied, 'I will not do so.'

Kay went to his lodging to arm: he ordered his hauberk to be brought. With him he had a squire who took great trouble to arm him. When he had brought all the parts of his armour, he laced them all in a very short time. Afterwards, Kay put on his hauberk, then girt on his sword and took his shield. When he had laced on his helm, the squire prepared his horse, which was led to the door, where the seneschal mounted, hung his shield on his neck and took the reins in his fist. His helm was very elegant, with a circle of purified gold. When armed, he was a fine knight, and sat well on his charger; he rode along the road, reached the gate and passed through. He wished to ride after the man who carried the rings belonging to the dead knight, whom my lord Gawain should avenge, since he had removed the lance: Kay desired to achieve the revenge without the king's bidding. Thus Kay rode out alone, without asking leave of the king to depart.

Kay, as in many other works, is defeated ignominiously by the strange knight, Yder, who eventually joins Gawain in a successful quest for vengeance.

During his quest for the murderer, Gawain rescues his brother Gaheriet and then they encounter a beautiful heiress called Ydain. Gawain falls in love, and determines to take her back to court, since he must return to obtain the broken lance, without which he cannot achieve his quest. On the way back to Arthur's court they meet a squire who has just come from there and has important news to tell them. The mantle story which the squire relates is a familiar one in Arthurian literature, and is similar in theme to Robert Biket's The Lay of the Horn. After they arrive at court, an ugly dwarf appears and demands a boon from Arthur: Ydain.

They travelled through woods and open meadows, over mountains and valleys, until, still on horseback, they arrived at an open heath-land. It was evening, and Ydain was weary and tired of riding.

Suddenly they saw a squire hurrying towards them, riding at a gallop on a packhorse. My lord Gawain, as soon as he saw the squire, called out to him, 'Stop! stop!' At which the squire immediately stopped. Gawain asked him: 'Who are you? Where are you going? From whence have you come? Tell me this.' 'Lord,' said the servant, 'in truth, I am from the Lord of the Moor; I have come from Carduel, and am returning to Rovelant. King Arthur is staying there with a great number of people, and has been there for the past twelve days.' 'Squire, if you bear news from there, tell me it.' 'My lord, yesterday morning, about midday, an adventure happened at court, which has greatly disturbed and darkened the court.' 'What was that?' 'It was a mantle of marvellous richness and beauty; but it became shorter whenever a damsel who was disloyal to her lover wore it.

'The man who brought this mantle to the king has many enemies: for the queen wore it, and it became short on her body. Thus, she was tested first of all, and all the ladies of the palace, more than a hundred in number, donned the mantle one by one, and it did them ill. By my life! The king would not have wished, for a thousand marks, as he himself said, that it should shorten or draw higher on anyone, either in front or behind. All the ladies were shamed, save one, the lady of Caraduel Briebras: on her the mantle hung low, and her lover was very proud.'

'Squire, who else wore it? Tell me, if you know.' 'By my faith, there were many people to whom it did great harm there. The seneschal, Sir Kay, had a very grieved heart for his lady, since the mantle showed him a truth which he could never conceal there later; shamefully he was placed last. Kay was driven almost out of his senses.' 'Go along, squire, it is time; go now where you have been sent.'

Thereupon each of them moved off, for one departed and the other came on. However, the news which they had heard, which the squire had told, was not entirely forgotten. It greatly grieved my lord Gawain that the mantle was not shared between him and the lovely Ydain, since he believed very sincerely, without a lie, that his lady would have been the most honoured. They rode on through the evening, as day passed and night came, until by chance they met a vavassor,[78] who took them with him and lodged them as finely as he could. He and my lord Gawain had known each other for a long time. The vavassor, who was well educated, showed them great honour that night. Early in the morning, at daybreak, they took leave of him, and set off. They rode and travelled so hard that they soon arrived at Rovelant, where there were many people. The king was there, and had brought a huge following with him. The news soon reached the king that my lord Gawain had arrived, and Gaheriet with him, leading a lady on a mule. The rumour quickly spread through the court; everyone found out, and, displaying great joy, ladies and knights went out to see Sir Gawain and accompany him back.

My lord Gawain, with pleasure, disarmed himself in his lodging. The beautiful Ydain, whom he brought with him, dressed herself very appropriately. Gawain presented himself at court straightaway, and with him Ydain. The king saw Gawain coming and was very delighted. Gawain greeted the king, who rose to return his greeting; he embraced his two nephews, kissing them one after the other. The king saw Ydain, who came before him in the palace, and thought her very beautiful. 'Good nephew,' he said, 'this maiden is most worthy. Does she belong to you?' 'Yes, by my faith! She is my lady and my sweetheart.' The king replied, 'I do not dislike her myself; since you love her, I shall love her.' 'Sire, I love her and will serve all those who will love her for my sake, and those who show her honour know well that thus they honour me.'

The queen, who was sitting near the king, took Ydain by the hand: 'My lady,' said Sir Gawain, 'this is my sweetheart, so I beg you to treat her just as you do myself, if you are willing, since you love me more than any knight whom you know.' The queen replied, 'Willingly, I will love and serve her, my good lord, and I will treat her equally with any lady who is here.' 'So, may I entrust her to you at once, since I trust you completely?' The queen replied simply, 'You know well, I shall honour her for your sake, as much as I can.'

It was the end of Pentecost when King Arthur and his barons were staying at Rovelant; there were plenty of princes present with their lady loves. My lord Gawain arrived thus, as I have told you; then the king asked him, 'Good nephew, have you achieved vengeance? The knight who had the broken lance in his heart, which you pulled out – tell me, since you last saw me, have you learned his name?' 'May God help me, no, sire. Although I have sought and searched. I forgot the lance with which I should avenge him; nor do I know its whereabouts. I gave it to the queen, who was present, as soon as I obtained it.' The queen replied, 'I have it, I have protected it in my safe-keeping.'

'Sire,' interrupted Kay, 'may God protect me, you would do wrong to thank God. Since Sir Gawain is here he cannot but remain. Here he has brought on his right arm this maiden whom you see here. Certainly he has arrived here at the right time, and has conquered this castle. He will avenge the knight next summer, I know that without fail; he and Ydain have taken up the battle of love: for which reason this quest is delayed. I do not say this to disdain him, neither for his harm nor to shame him.' 'Kay, I know well where this is leading; never will you desist for my good!' Gawain continued, 'You are quite wrong, Kay; yet I know your argument too well: for tomorrow morning I shall leave to seek revenge for the knight.'

'Then, when you go to avenge the injury,' said Kay, 'I advise you to leave her here. Otherwise, if you see a beautiful manor-house, the pair of you will stay there.' 'Kay, be quiet, you are being foolish; we have no intention of staying. Early in the morning, at dawn, we shall depart, myself and my sweetheart, Ydain.' 'Certainly,' said Kay, 'I do not grumble; indeed, it greatly pleases me. You have loved her long enough: I do not ask when you will become tired of loving her; however much I grumble, the engagement is all that matters.' 'I will lead her away immediately!' 'Gawain, may God give you speed!' Thus Kay replied to him with this speech. 'For your sake, she would face Wihot, as long as you were the right partners for each other. Love has made you an ass; it gives nothing in return. If you had been here the other day, you might never have loved anyone again, for you would have seen us all shamed. Moreover, since women shame all men, the same thing which happened to us would have befallen you.'

My lord Gawain concealed his thoughts, for he had no desire to quarrel; and Kay tried to enrage him, always as much as he could, more and more. Gawain remained quite silent, not speaking a single word, while Kay continuously insulted him, until everyone there was angry. King Arthur, who was leaning on his elbow, on the dais, spoke: 'Kay, be silent; you are wicked and sinful, for you have reminded us of our shame. Now be quiet, and speak no more of it.' 'I promise that I will never speak again,' replied Kay, 'for I have nothing to do here. One cannot undo the shame; everyone knows it, you are well aware of this.' 'Kay,' replied the king, 'go! Go and order the table-clothes to be laid.' Those whose business it was quickly set the tablecloths and brought water for everyone. Then the king and all the knights sat to eat. There were plenty of dishes, of that I am sure; I will not give you a long sermon on the food, since I do not know more; nor do I wish to.

The king, who sat at the high table, was well served and it is said that he held a court suitable for such a day, and for the high annual feast; the ladies ate in the hall in front of the king. The queen sat the beautiful Ydain beside her, among her retinue: to honour my lord Gawain she held her dearer than all her other ladies. They had plenty of wine and good conversation, and there was great joy among those at table. Kay, who had such an evil tongue, was serving before the king: one man he hit, another he pushed back, some he threw outside, others he chased; this man he hated, another he threatened, this man he watched closely, that one he knocked; one man waited, another fled. Kay acted in this manner, speaking rudely to everyone: one man hated him and another spoke ill of him, one flattered him and another kept silent. One replied, 'Sir, if it pleases you', whilst wishing that he might be burned. However, they so feared his wicked words, that none dared to speak against him.

The seneschal ordered a side-dish to be carried before the king; all their dishes were now there, except one which was still to come. My lord Gawain, who was seated before the king at the meal, looked at Kay and, as he watched him for a long while, he remembered what the servant had told him about the mantle. 'Kay,' asked Gawain, 'how did it go with the mantle which came to court? Tell me what happened, and if your sweetheart wore it.' When he heard this, Kay turned round, very thoughtful, and with bowed head; anger and indignation overwhelmed him, so that he could scarcely speak. Then he allowed his tongue its freedom: 'What is that? How? What is this?' said Kay. 'Are you content, Sir Gawain? You may love! You may love! For I shall never love again, never at any time shall I have a sweetheart, and I will not love anyone while pillows last. They are all shameful: all women in the world can be described with one word!'

Sir Gawain held himself in check, while Kay, who had gone too far, went away. My lord Gawain pondered about Ydain: he thought her true, I know for sure, since he believed that he had the best and most courteous lady. However, he was concerned and very irritated by Kay's words: most willingly he would have contradicted Kay, since he had not spoken courteously, but he believed he might hear more slander; thus he remained quiet, but it grieved him greatly. The king rose from the table, and so did all the others; they called for water and washed.

Then, when they had finished the meal (which for you was cut short), an armed knight on a war-horse entered the hall, shield on his neck, lance in hand. Such a knight as this had never been heard of before. The horse on which he sat was a sorrel with white feet, from Castile; the knight had fine, straight legs and well-shaped feet, and sat his horse as though he had been born in the saddle. From his breeches to his spurs, a better-made man had never entered court; but he had such a short body, which was flat and protruding with a curved spine; he had a hump in the centre of his chest, which looked horrible: no man who had not seen this hump could have believed that such a thing was possible; another similar lump was positioned against his heart.

His body was no longer than a span and a half; the man was exactly as I have described, and I believe that he was even shorter.

However, he had beautiful hands, with square fists and huge arms, well built with muscle and bone, strong, hard and bare. His hair was blond and fine, with beautiful long fair tresses; his neck was as white as that of a maiden, his beard large and his face proud. In a single phrase I can describe him to you: he was well-made in all his limbs, but his body was small and ugly, and more ill-favoured than that of any other man. Anyone who had seen his raised head, legs and arms, and then looked at his ribs, which were very ugly and small, would not have thought, I truly believe, when he saw the strong limbs, that they could be attached to such a body: he would not have believed, or imagined it possible. For whoever deemed the body ugly might be more grieved by one of his legs, if he jested about it. The knight was made in such a manner.

This knight came before King Arthur; he stopped close beside Kay; he greeted the king and all the noblemen who were present. Then King Arthur replied, 'God save you, friend, you are welcome; dismount, wash yourself and eat.' 'Sire,' the knight spoke thus, 'I do not desire to eat. I have come here to discover if you practise such great generosity as I have heard recounted, for it is said that you never refuse a man a favour who does not inform you what the request is in advance: I require that you should grant me such a boon. You cannot refuse me this favour since, if I do not receive it, your court will lose its renown this very day.'

When the knight had spoken thus, all the nobles who were present around the king were silent, and he waited no longer but continued to speak: 'This is the end; today *this* king will be finished, since thus I have been refused here!' My lord Gawain, hearing these words, declared, 'Go on! Speak to us; the king has not been undone by you yet, and the court shall not lose its reputation. I believe that you shall have your wish granted.' Then he spoke to the king: 'Promise him.' 'I will promise him. Now then, tell me knight, what do you wish to have?' 'Sire, sire, you must know well, before I name it, all the barons who are here must swear, my lord Gawain first.'

The king told him, 'I will command them to promise, and thus I ask.' 'Sire,' he answered, 'thank you; you have said enough, it seems to me.' Then they all shouted together aloud; each one said, 'I wish it! I promise it!' Then the knight spoke again to the king: 'Sire, sire, that is enough. The gift which you have promised me is the damsel Ydain, the sweetheart of my lord Gawain. You must seize her for me, I demand it!'

The knight drew himself forward: then he took hold of the silken mantle and said: 'I will take this with me, for it is mine. Ydain, mount behind me quickly.' When he heard this, my lord Gawain was very angry and infuriated. He said to the knight: 'By my faith! You have demanded an outrageous thing of the king; you yourself will be shamed: even if you might win her by force of arms, you would be dishonoured.' The other turned his bridle back and spoke: 'Gawain, you know for certain, that although you may believe that I have disgraced myself here, none, however great or small, shall find blame or injustice in this place. The king has no man in his household, however grand he is, who wishes to arm himself here, to declare that I am wrong, and fight face to face, since none may fight as strongly as myself, except you, and for this reason I refuse to do battle against you here, in this court, since here your strength is stronger than my own. Since it does not suit me to be shamed, if you will take the combat to another court, I will go there; I am already mounted, and there I will do battle against you where, at a gallop, I will fight the bravest man straightaway. You should accept completely one of these two things which I say, or I will lead her away at once. What do you say, Sir Gawain?'

Then my lord Ywain, Tristran, Perceval, Cahadin, Giflet, Governal, Amangins and all the other knights at court rose from their seats. Each one stood up and ran to plead with Sir Gawain. Each of them offered to defend his lady there against the knight. 'Sire,' said Lancelot, 'I am your companion, you tell me that often enough; I will fight him here, grant this to me: you must take care lest he lead her away!' The others made many similar offers, but Gawain wished to accept none of them. Thus he replied: 'My lords, you know truly, I will put no champion in my place. I will defeat him; if I should lose, if it came to losing, you should not speak of this: you should not believe that I would allow you to defend my honour and my sweetheart. If I thus abandoned the fight through lack of courage and put a companion in my place, he would not be able to defend me, however valiant he might be, against the worst enemy whom he could find throughout the entire world! Thus I shall go there over the sea to fight against the strongest man who might be found in Welshport. Speak no more of this matter, I beg of you.'

'How?' the dwarf knight said. 'Is it thus? Do you wish to fight me wherever I go?' 'Yes, by my faith! Go! I will come, without delay. Name which court and on what day.' 'You will go there?' the other asked. 'Without fail? The battle shall be held, a month from today, at the court of King Baudemagus. There we shall go most eager to fight for the damsel; but who wishes to pledge on your behalf that you will be there as promised? I do not wish to leave here before I have made quite sure of this.' 'Friend,' King Arthur addressed the knight, 'I pledge by my hand that he will go.' 'Do you pledge that he will take the damsel there, without fail?' 'Yes.' 'I will demand no more,' the knight said, as he turned to depart. 'My friend,' said the king, 'come back. Before you leave, tell us, what is your name?' 'I am Druidain, the son of Druilas, and I am called Druidain, since I should be Ydain's lover: she is my love [*drue*] and I am hers.'[79]

Then he cried joyously and vigorously, 'This can never be altered: no man who is born can alter this truth! The talking Lion, which never lies, has told me that I shall have her,' he said. He spoke truthfully, since he had heard it virtually every day of his life. It was destined, as soon as he was born.

Then the knight departed, and Kay leapt up from the other side. He had heard all, and could not keep silent; Kay declared, 'Now we have much to do; now it is time to begin again seeking vengeance for the knight! It seems to me that respite has been given! This interruption, this despised hunchback, has come to save the day! Now, Gawain, you have even more to accomplish, before you follow the adventure. Certainly, one who leads such a life must abandon plans every day; I do not wish to remain here to wait for you to seek vengeance. You should take on your burden, and leave the quest for vengeance, for you can never achieve anything except shame, villainy and pain. A knight who leads his sweetheart should not begin any exploits.'

'Sir Kay, you should stop seeking a quarrel either with words or with fighting. I will lead her, for my solace, to the court of King Baudemagus, against Druidain, who is in a hurry to challenge me there; certainly I shall take her with me! Never will I go anywhere without her, neither here, nor there, near or far.' 'Gawain,' replied Kay, 'I give you a promise. Whenever it happens that the smoke flies upwards, you shall have a portion of shame; otherwise you would never leave here.'

'Kay,' said Lucan, 'you are lying: the Lion lied and so did Druidain, who thought by this argument to seize the beautiful Ydain by force. Indeed, he will not fight against my lord Gawain here under any circumstances. If this creature, this rock, could live in the sea, and his entire heart was not just a hump, and if his heart were not borne in his hump, I would not see a battle there. Certainly, he has said very little!' Then the argument ended, and Kay, who was miserable, kept quiet.

Night came, the day had ended, and in the morning, on a Monday (it was true, and I heard it told), my lord Gawain rose, and both he and Ydain, whom he greatly loved, dressed themselves for the ride. My lord Gawain was armed on a carpet of expensive silk; all those by whom he was loved had come to his house. Whoever had good weaponry, either a good lance or fine sword, now brought it to Gawain, and he chose from them at his pleasure. Someone had now brought him the fragment of the broken lance, with which he must obtain vengeance, and he took this and hung it, by a thong, from his right arm, between his body and his shield. Then he took leave, first of King Arthur, then of all the knights. With him he led two greyhounds, while Ydain carried a sparrowhawk. There was not a single lady or knight present who did not commend Gawain to God's safe-keeping. Then, without further delay, they went forth; the couple went on their journey, and the courtiers returned to Rovelant.

RAOUL DE HOUDENC, Meraugis de Portlesguez (c. 1200–20)

This is another romance concerned with the adventures of a young knight who arrives at Arthur's court to seek his fortune. In Merau-gis two young knights, Meraugis de Portlesguez and his best friend, Gorvain Cadruz, spend their time entering tournaments in friendly rivalry until the day they both fall in love with Lidoine, the fair lady of Landamore. Unable to decide between them, but unwilling to allow them to do battle for her hand, Lidoine bids her two suitors attend Arthur's Christmas court at Carduel for their case to be judged. Guenevere displays her determination to be the 'Queen of hearts', making judgement in all cases concerning love.

Meraugis, drawn to Arthur's court to win his lady, sets off on a quest for Gawain, whose prolonged absence Arthur has failed to investigate. In this poem, as in numerous other Arthurian romances, it is love-service which often motivates the chivalric exploits of Arthur's followers.

When everyone had arrived at court, Lidoine waited no longer, but went before the king and told him of the two young men and their love for her; and when King Arthur had heard this, he was very surprised, and commanded that she should have judgement as she had requested, for he wished to know which of the two suitors most deserved her love. When the barons heard this, they did not wait, but all came to judge the case. Kay spoke first before them all: 'Sire, I think that each should have her for a month.' 'Master Kay,' said Count Quinables, 'that is not a sensible decision, but your mockeries will never end.' 'Sire, I did not speak mockingly, but spoke thus to make peace, which will never happen if each does not have his wish. If it is agreeable to them, it would be sensible for them to share her thus.' 'Kay,' answered the count, 'what you suggest will never bring them to agreement.' 'I do not know how that will be obtained,' said Kay, 'but meanwhile I shall keep quiet.'

Then after this everyone voiced his opinion, and when they had spoken for some time, the queen came and demanded to hold her court and, although the king bade her be quiet, she would not do so. Very proudly she demanded her right, saying, 'My lord king, it is well known that all the judgements concerning love are mine, and you have no right to make a decision.' And Kay, who could not contain himself any longer, said, 'My lady speaks truly.' With this, all the barons followed Kay's example, saying all together that the queen should hold her court. Now when the king heard that she had the right, he gave in. Then the queen declared, 'Sire, leave this palace! Then my ladies will assist me in forming judgement here.' At this the barons left the palace, and the ladies entered it.

After the queen and her ladies have heard the two lovers plead their cases they unanimously declare themselves in favour of Meraugis, recalling the king to announce their decision. Gorvain denounces their judgement as false and challenges Meraugis to trial by combat.

Then there would have been no more rest, nor any delay for armour or horses, but it would soon have been decided which was most valiant, had not the king declared that neither should be bold enough to strike a blow or begin a mêlée at court, since he did not wish this. The queen went straight to the two knights and spoke to them thus: 'May God help me, sir vassals, it is unworthy that you should think to do battle here.' 'Why, my lady?' enquired Meraugis. 'May God help me, this annoys me greatly! I tell you, without fail, that I would rather do battle and conquer him by my sword than gain lady Lidoine without any action. Why? Because this concerns my honour.'

'I do not know what praise it brings,' she replied, 'but I can tell you that if you desire to do battle lest you suffer shame, you should begin the fight elsewhere, not in this court.' 'How,' asked Gorvains, 'does this court have any honour, when one cannot do battle here?' 'Sire, I see no problem if the quarrel had not originated in another place; but battle cannot take place here since the judgement was made here.'

'Lady, I did not come here in order to argue, but to prove that the damsel should accept me as her lover. If Meraugis wishes to continue this feud, he shall have a quarrel; I will not stay for the sake of the king, for you put his court to shame. Certainly, he holds a fine court, but I shall not trouble myself to come before you again, since I have been misjudged here, but I wish you to know that you have miscalculated my behaviour. You may well treat me as a puppet if you repay me thus. I will not tolerate receiving nothing. Thus I complain, and I have the right, for in this court they conceal the truth.'

King Arthur then intervenes to prevent the duel. While Gorvain leaves the court in anger, the joyful Meraugis remains behind. However, Lidoine declares that she will not accept him as her husband for a year, during which time he must prove his knightly worth. An episode at court soon provides him with the opportunity to do so.

The king called for water and addressed his nobles: 'Come and wash.' Then you might see squires and well-dressed damsels hurrying about. It was a custom that on such a high feast-day young damsels served at the king's table, and the highest-born ladies of the household were chosen. Squires of high renown served before the queen.

Then there was no more delay: the king was seated, the dinner arrived; there were more than twenty courses served. They loaded and covered all the tables. What more need I tell you? The king was served at dinner just as a king should be. Before they desired to rise from the table – he would stay there for a long time – you could have seen a dwarf, as ugly as he could possibly be, riding on a white-footed horse. What was he, then? He was flat-nosed: that is my word for being ugly, for before this dwarf was born God had made nothing so flat-nosed.

The dwarf, who always played the fool, stopped before the king and spoke: 'King, listen to me for a while. Hear me, make your people be quiet! King, how can you be joyful? I am amazed. I wish to tell you that nobody should laugh in this court.' 'Should he not?' 'No, king, and there is a good reason why. Look all around you: Gawain, your nephew, is he present? He is not to be seen! Now, is it for nothing that your court is famous? No! Your court is deprived of the best knight in the world. King, you descend from the mountain when you should be climbing higher. Why should I say this? I wish to speak to you about him. Will it be for your good? No. Tell me, king, do you not remember that it is a year since my lord Gawain left here to conquer for the honour of your court? King, you know very well that he went to seek, for your fame and to flatter you, the wonderful sword with the strange scabbard-ring, and I am amazed that you took no other advice; for I tell you, since I have come from him, that he should be here today, if he were safe and well. King, you must know very well that he is no longer free, since he has not returned. Therefore I am very surprised when I find that this court can rejoice.'

'Ah!' said the king. 'Dwarf, you undoubtedly speak the truth: he should return today!' The king could not contain himself now but sighed and seemed to change, for he was full of concern for the man whose voice could not be heard. Everyone else, who had been happy and light-hearted, became full of anger. The king, who was more concerned than all the others, addressed the dwarf in these words: 'Friend, tell me at once, is Gawain alive or in prison? Hide nothing from me!'

'Whether he is alive or dead you shall not learn from me,' said the dwarf, 'only this single fact: if, in this court, there is a single knight who so dares to value himself that he might go on quest to search for Sir Gawain, he may hear news of him.' 'Where?' 'At Merlin's dwelling: if he is not there, this is the end, for you will never hear of him again. However, before any knight dares undertake this quest, I emphasize this to him: if he does not feel himself to be the bravest, I advise him never to contemplate this adventure.' 'Why?' 'He should think that there is no better knight in the world: otherwise, I would not dare promise that he could ever enter that land; but he may only do so to achieve the honour and the good which is spoken of him. However, I have heard of him who will be chosen to go in search of news of the ladies' knight.'[80]

When the king had heard the dwarf speak, he saw that the knights around him were silent, and he thought about this; for after the dwarf had spoken nobody showed any response except Meraugis, who said, 'Sire, if it pleases my lady, her knight will go on this quest: I beg her leave.'

The lady [Lidoine] replied, 'Thank you, my friend, I am quite ready to agree, for it pleases me and I am very happy with this undertaking of yours. Moreover, since it will assist your task, it pleases me, and I am determined to go with you on this journey as a token of my affection, if you so wish.'

Then the knight replied, 'You honour the truce and the peace. What more could you demand? It is right that you should command, and I will not contradict you in anything.' 'These words are most agreeable,' said the king, who had not the least objection. 'The lady speaks very courteously, and he talks like a true knight. I declare this because I am most willing for him to go: may only good come of it.'

'It shall never be lacking on my part,' said Lidoine, 'to show kindness, but yet I would be more pleased if the prowess which he possesses should be seen through me than through another. It is true, and one can only repeat the saying: to know something is worth more than to hear it stated. For this reason, his companionship pleases me.'

When the dwarf had heard the lady speak, he tugged on his bridle and turned about. Then Kay, who turned towards the dwarf, looked at him and said, 'Flat-nosed thing, since you are here, dismount, rest and await your company.' The dwarf, who was not in the least bit dismayed, returned and said, 'Sir Kay, you have always been thus, and always will be: your tongue is always ready to give many evil blows, but your mockeries are so very trivial that the whole world thinks little of you. You play a game: what do you wish to do? If you love to quarrel more than [to have] land, I am here and quite ready to dispute.' Then Kay, who dared mutter no more, kept silent, and the dwarf departed. It is true that the king called after him, but he had no desire ever to return. Then the knight [Meraugis], as quickly as he could, prepared to leave. What more can I tell you? To speak the truth, they were soon mounted, and took their leave.

Meraugis is successful on his quest, finding that Sir Gawain, who has won a jousting contest, has been honour-bound to remain to defend the land of the lady whose knight he has defeated. By a ruse, Meraugis helps Gawain escape this bondage, but Lidoine believes her lover to be dead. She is captured and held in a castle which is besieged by Gorvain Cadruz, from where she is finally rescued by Meraugis, with Gawain's assistance. The following extract contains the final judgement, by battle, between Meraugis and Gorvain at Arthur's court at Canterbury.

Before they had arrived at court, a damsel who was noble and wise brought them a message from Gorvain Cadruz. You shall hear what she said. In everyone's hearing, she spoke thus to Meraugis: 'Meraugis, I have been sent here to you by Gorvain, who informs you through me that he has gone to capture Cavalon; but the war may be concluded if you are brave enough to desire to defeat him in single combat, since he seeks nothing more. He was misjudged at Christmas by your plea at the king's court. Never will he make peace with you, but he demands battle. Will you fight him?' 'Yes, without fail,' said Meraugis. 'To me it is very pleasing that this war should be decided by his body and mine. Once the day of battle is determined, I would

set off the following day with no more delay.' The girl replied, 'He
appoints the day of Pentecost, and bids you to demand battle in no
other court than that of King Arthur. He wishes to prove himself
against you at Arthur's court, since he was misjudged there.'

Meraugis said, 'Although he is in the wrong, tell Gorvain that I
shall be there.' She replied, 'Good, I will tell him.' Then she left, while
Meraugis remained behind; he showed his joy, like a man who
believed in rejoicing, and all the nobles demonstrated their delight;
that night was devoted to happiness. What more need I tell you? In
the morning Meraugis set off on his way, accompanied by his lady.
He led a very noble company of knights; the nobles accompanied him
to his combat. They travelled until at Pentecost they found King
Arthur holding his court at Canterbury. It was known throughout
Arthur's empire that the combat would take place there...

Meraugis had arrived at court – and what of Gorvain Cadruz? Did
he come? Yes, the next day. He led such a great company of people,
with more than a hundred ladies. As soon as he dismounted, Gorvain
demanded of the king his right to do battle. 'Sire,' said Meraugis,
'you see I am here, quite ready to engage him in combat.' King Arthur
said, 'It seems to me that this battle is a judicial one, and through me
there is no more respite. To the field!'

At last the knights were together in the field. Like mortal enemies
they rode against each other as fast as the wind. At the first strike,
their lances crashed together with such great force that both were
completely shattered; they attacked at full gallop, but in a very short
time they were fighting together with swords.

What more should I tell you? Their battle was, without doubt, the
fiercest ever fought on a tourney-ground, and when the struggle was
finally over, Meraugis had defeated Gorvain. Since he had previously
been his friend, he said to Gorvain, 'My friend, for the sake of
fellowship, I beg you to accept that she is my lady. Since you were
my companion, I am ready to swear a renewed fellowship, on holy
relics, rather than that you should lose your head by my hand;
since I should be heavy with sorrow.' Then Gorvain, who had no
alternative, cancelled his claim to both the damsel and her kingdom,
in favour of Meraugis. Their fellowship was completely restored, and
thus I tell you all was renewed and they were friends and companions
again.

PSEUDO WILLIAM OF MALMESBURY, Concerning the Ancient Church of Glastonbury (De Antiqitate Glastoniensis Ecclesiae) (1229–39)

The T. Hearne 1927 edition of Concerning the Ancient Church of Glastonbury *in* Arthur of Britain, *ed. Sir E. K. Chambers (London: 1927) was written by William of Malmesbury, and contains numerous later interpolations in later twelfth- and early thirteenth-century hands. The insertions in this monastic chronicle replace William's cautious and scholarly conclusions with unverifiable details about connections of the Celtic saints Gildas and Patrick with the abbey. They also call Glastonbury the Isle of Avalon and devote the following sections specifically to Arthur, although William himself never connected the king with this place. These references provide the first association of the river Camel in Cornwall as the site of Arthur's fatal battle against Mordred, with the improbable claim that Arthur was almost a hundred years old at the time! The second passage is a brief account of how Ider, a newly dubbed Arthurian knight wishing to prove his valour, dies after fighting three giants at Brent Knoll in Somerset.*[81]

Among the many British princes, one should not forget to mention Arthur, the renowned king of the Britons, buried with his wife between two pyramids in the monastic cemetery at Glastonbury. This same Arthur in the year of Our Lord 542 was mortally wounded by Mordred beside the river Camel in Cornwall and was carried thence to the Isle of Avalon to heal his wounds, and there died in the summer around Pentecost when he was nearly a hundred years old, or thereabouts.

About the famous Arthur

One may read in the deeds of the most illustrious King Arthur that he decorated with the Order of Knighthood a most vigorous youth, namely Ider, the son of King Nut, at a certain festival celebrating the birth of Our Lord at Caerleon. Arthur, wishing to initiate this untried youth, included him in a small force which he led to Toads' Mount, now called Brentecnol [Brent Knoll], where three giants lived who were infamous for their evil deeds. Going ahead without the knowledge of Arthur and his companions, Ider bravely attacked the said giants and killed them with an incredible slaughter.

Arriving after this had been achieved to find Ider completely worn out by his labour and lying incapable of any action, Arthur and his companions lamented the youth's impending death. Therefore, returning to his camp with unspeakable grief, Arthur left the body there, realizing it to be lifeless, while he organized a vehicle to recover the body, blaming himself for the youth's death because he had arrived too late to help him. When Arthur at length arrived at Glastonbury, he ordered eighty monks to pray for Ider's soul, providing them with property and land for their sustenance, and a substantial gift of gold and silver goblets and other vessels for the church.

Yder (c. 1210–25)

The Old French romance of Yder *was probably composed by a French poet living in England during the early years of the thirteenth century. The poem, the start of which is missing, opens at the point where Yder has just helped King Arthur by killing two knights who attacked him while out hunting. Safely back at court, Arthur forgets to reward Yder for his services, and disgusts the young hero when he fails to give assistance to one of his vassals, the Lady of the Maidens' Castle.*

In this poem, Arthur goes to Pontefract Castle, a place not associated with him in other works, but a royal castle at the period when the poem was composed. By this reference, the poet indicates to his audience that his 'Arthur' should be identified with the present English king, almost certainly the despotic King John.[82]

He prepared his horses and took his stick of meat in his hand. Yder spoke to his lord: 'My lord,' he said, 'I think those huntsmen are sounding their horns for the chase.' He stopped and listened. 'Young man,' he said, 'wait a moment. I think I can hear a horn I know very well.' 'Lord,' said the young man, 'answer them with the horn which hangs round your neck. Yesterday you lost your retinue; it is certainly some of your men you can hear, sounding their horns to call you.' The lord did as he suggested until his friends heard the horn and were close by; they rushed straight up to him. They displayed great joy when they found their lord. It made all of them, without exception, very happy, especially the one who loved him most; that was Queen Guenevere. He embraced her and lifted her up on to the neck of his charger. Yder asked one of the huntsmen who it was that they had welcomed so warmly. When the huntsman heard him he thought he was joking because he saw that he was accompanying him, and he said: 'What! aren't you with him?' 'Yes,' he replied, 'but only since yesterday evening late. I don't know his name and am asking you to tell me who it is.' 'That is King Arthur,' said the huntsman. 'Is it really, young man?' said Yder. 'Yes, indeed; it is King Arthur renowned for his valour and his wisdom and his courtliness, whose honour surpasses all other things, past and present: all who come after him will be inferior to him; I am not exaggerating for he is so endowed with valour and courtliness that nobody who speaks well of him can lie.'

Yder was extremely happy at what the young man had told him. He had come into contact with a lord from whom he hoped to find advancement. He was only seeking advancement in one respect, to be able to prove his prowess in arms before leaving Arthur's land: and after that he would not want to stay one day longer provided he could manage it so that his beloved should hear of it and recognize that he was worthy of her love.

The King came to Pontefract. He paid no attention to the young man. When he had put the different pieces of meat in the store, he went to look after the horses, but he could not find anywhere to stable them. He left them beneath a tree. His lord had forgotten him which surprised Yder very much. The meal was prepared.

The King sat at his meal. Yder kept his horses at rest. He was standing beneath the tree. Soon a young girl came along, riding on a tawny mule. She was pretty and of noble bearing, with a bright face and a beautiful body; she had a fine harness and was richly equipped; she was dressed in silken cloth. She dismounted in front of the hall, went up the steps and greeted the King and his companions courteously. 'Good King,' she said, 'listen to me and I shall tell you my news: I come from the Maidens' Castle; my lady sends you this message: when she received her castle from you, you undertook to protect her. Now her fine castle is besieged; the Black Knight wants to take her captive; she can defend herself against him all right. The castle is well-fortified and strong and my lady has such forces that the besieging troops could not resist if she let them meet in battle; even if the Black Knight had two armies, they could not resist our men. Yet, since my lady is your vassal, it brings shame on you that he has besieged her. King, come to her and rescue her, I only ask it for your own honour. I have come to you at her command to ask you to keep your pledge.'

After a little the King said: 'I recognize my pledge; but those who are here know that I have to go and lay siege to Rougemont. Talac does not want to accept me as his liegelord and I want to make him repent of that. I shall besiege him, you may be sure, within three days. I have said I shall, and I don't want to go back on it.' The girl replied angrily: 'If you go back on your promise to my lady, it is a greater disloyalty because you promised that first. Let my lady benefit from the advantages of putting herself in someone's service. Originally, she held her inheritance from no-one but God. Now she deservedly has what she desired! If God brings me back to her, I shall make it very clear that she has failed here in her intentions. If she seeks help elsewhere, she cannot be blamed for it.' With such words she left. Yder stood on the other side; he had listened to the messenger. Then he went back to his horses; he was greatly grieved about his lord when he heard about the promise and realized that he was breaking his word. 'May God never help me,' he said, 'if I stay with this man any longer even if it means being without a lord. I have served him well in a short time, and he has forgotten me so quickly, he neither remembers me nor keeps any promise.' He met a young man as he was going down the steps. Yder asked him his name. 'I am a noble man,' he replied, 'but I am poor and have no friends. My father was killed this year. He was a knight, of high birth; my relations have my inheritance, and they chased me away without my being able to resist.' Yder was very sorry for him. He gave him the two horses whose riders he had killed. Now Yder had made him a rich man. He took his leave and went on his way.

The young man took the chargers and put them in a stable. Then he came to the hall. For a time he had been penniless and destitute, but now he was extremely happy. He told his companions about his adventure.

The King was thinking about the message he had received and noticed that they were talking and laughing. 'What is it?' he said and they told him. He asked who the young man was. The young man came forward and told him that he had come across a youth who had given him two horses worth two hundred marks or more. When the King heard this, he was very embarrassed. 'Tell him,' he said, 'to come to me.' 'My lord, he is leaving,' the young man told the king. 'Leaving?' said the King. 'I have been brought to great shame; never was a king so well served by a hundred youths as I was by him alone last night. He won the two chargers, killed the two who assailed me and saved me from death. I have given him poor thanks; I had forgotten him completely.' While everyone listened, the King related exactly what had happened to him. He got about twenty of his young followers to mount their horses and promised them generous gifts if they found the young man and brought him to him. They would not be successful; they exerted themselves for nothing.

In a later episode in the poem Arthur has sent Kay to investigate the fortified dwelling place inhabited by two ferocious giants. When the seneschal fails to return, Gawain offers to go in search of him. Arthur refuses the offer, however, deciding to send Yder instead.

'My lords,' said King Arthur, 'I'm not very confident about Kei, I'm afraid he has been taken prisoner; he could easily have been back by now if he were a free agent.' Gawain said: 'He's been a long time; he left here a long while ago but since then we haven't heard a shout or any noise and if you would like me to I'll willingly go after him.' 'I want to send someone else; I've chosen my lord Yder for it.' Yder was filled with joy when he heard that and thanked him. He went into the lonely courtyard; at the steps he dismounted from his horse; when he could not find anywhere to tie it up, and he had no squire or servant, he put the reins over the pommel of the saddle, then he had no fear that the horse would go away. He went up into the palace and found the two giants side by side; the smaller of the two was fifty feet tall, fifty or more. They had their backs turned to the door. The two of them were cooking a huge boar: one was turning the spit which was made of an enormous branch over the fire, and the other was raking the coal towards the pig which his companion was turning. It was complete with the skin and hair. Two strong men would have found it difficult to lift their spit, if they had lifted it.

The one looking after the fire saw Yder who was amazed at their height and breadth. Yder shouted at them, and that one jumped up and raised his poker above his head; it would knock Yder to pieces; normally a horse-drawn cart would be weighed down by it. He made a thrust down from on high; it completely shattered the shield which Yder held out when he saw the blow coming; he did not want to hold his ground for it could have killed him. It made his shield fly from round his neck. Yder saw clearly that if the giant struck again he would soon be in a terrible pass. Yder attacked him valiantly, he could only wound him from underneath: with his sword which he had drawn he inflicted a big wound a foot long on him below his waist; he would have struck him higher up if he could. The giant roared as he felt the blow, and he bent down angrily; as he was about to close his arms around him, Yder hit him with his steel blade; he cut his shoulder from his neck. The King heard the clatter from the hall of the falling foe. Gawain and Yvain were ready to join in if the King wanted; but they were not to go he told them. Yder saw the giant wounded, he saw his body lying wide open, looked at the wound and plunged his sword in up to the hilt. No sooner had the point reached the heart than the other giant rushed upon him.

Yder stood his ground and the giant came at him; Yder was dead if he got him. He aimed a blow at Yder which should have wounded him but a rope hanging down deflected the blow and protected him, but not enough to prevent his falling stretched out on the ground. The giant tried to pick him up, but Yder jumped to his feet unhurt; he had a bold spirit and a good sword, and anger redoubled his strength: he thrust high up to injure the giant but he was furious when he did not manage to injure him with a high thrust; the blow was weak or failed altogether. It was weak for he did not have enough strength to be able to see, low down as he was, how he could hurt him; he made a thrust at his thigh, he made his thrust and turned it in such a way that he cut through his thigh.

The giant tried to pick him up and bent down; Yder saw him, charged at him, and as he stood up again he struck him so that he severed his head from his body. Immediately he took off his armour, put his arms on a table which stood on pillars at the side of the hall and removed from it a fine knife he saw there; it was the one his beloved had spoken of. Before he took it away he would suffer misfortune. When Yder had put it in its case, he sat down on a bench by the fire and with the embers he wiped the blood from his sword which he held very dear. When he had put it back in his scabbard, he lay it down on the bench beside him; there Yder waited for the King.

The King and his companions did not move when they heard the noise and nor did Kei who started up inside the house; they had heard and listened to the cries of the giants and the mighty, terrible roars they uttered and the sword which resounded with the blows he dealt them. They heard all the noise cease; the King told them he was quite sure the battle was over, whoever had the upper hand. Gawain who was very anxious said to the King: 'What shall we do? We shall have acted wrongly; we've heard clearly that there was a fierce battle up there. I'm afraid ill has befallen our companions since neither of them has come back to us.' 'And what can we do?' said the King. Yvain replied: 'We'll go in and free our companions if the two giants have taken them prisoner, or else we'll avenge them if they've been killed.' They all three went into the bailey. Kei had been extremely alarmed; he heard the noise in the palace and when he heard that peace reigned, he stuck out his head; the King saw him and went straight over to him in the hiding place and his two companions with him. The King asked what he was doing there. Kei replied quietly: 'I'm very frightened. I can't deny it, and I concealed myself in this hiding place; there's no man on earth who would not have trembled with fear if he had had to face those monsters without lots of troops; and I tell you that the man you sent in is dead, I swear it for certain.' 'Oh! God!' said Gawain, 'what a terrible loss! God! What a sad end his courage has come to! Oh! my lord Yvain, this is dreadful, we have done him a great wrong. The friendship pledged between the three of us has not lasted long.' The King replied: 'Gawain, fair nephew, if something dreadful has happened, it would have been much worse if you had gone with him.' 'There are only two giants,' said Yvain, 'and there are four of us; he went all alone to fight with them; it's true that he undertook a tremendous task. If we don't go in now, we'll never be able to defend ourselves from the accusation of cowardice, since one man dared to undertake so much.' 'God forbid,' said the King, 'that there should be any thought of cowardice while you three are with me; may my life be spared no longer if I ever think of it. All of you protect yourselves as best you can for I'm going to dismount first.' Gawain dismounted with the King; Yvain dismounted; Kei was already on foot; they climbed the steps in a line, put their shields over their heads and held their bared swords in their hands.

They walked into the palace and found Yder sitting by the fire; he had no armour on and was quite at his ease. King Arthur and the others with him were very alarmed by the monsters lying in the palace. Yder stood up to meet them; the King thought he was wounded and so did Kei, but they would have liked him to be dead; they would have grieved for him at once. The two who loved him loyally asked him how he was; that was Yvain and Gawain. Yder replied that he was unhurt. They took their armour off at once and put their arms on the table; they rejoiced in the palace. 'Let's not have any laziness,' said Kei: 'we're in complete possession of the house, let's find out if there's anything to eat. There's no-one to prevent us.' Yder replied: 'That's a good idea, and it's time; it's evening, the sun is setting, so I accept your suggestion. I'm ready to go with you.' They unlocked a door and went into a room; they found plenty of cakes, fresh clear wines and big pies made of capons and pieces of meat, so they enjoyed sumptuous hospitality. That night they amused themselves there. They made the fire big and bright; a bed was made for King Arthur. He slept and the others stayed awake and kept watch for fear of the giants; they would have dragged them outside but their bodies were so heavy that they could not move them. One could kill a packhorse if it were loaded with just one of the heads. Then a great misfortune ensued.

They amused themselves by the fire for so long that it was past midnight, I think; Yder was struck by a great thirst. 'What shall I do, Kei?' he said. 'What about?' 'I'm very thirsty.' 'Drink then.' 'How can I quench my thirst then?' 'The spring will cure you; I'll give you some water from it.' 'Now we'll see,' said Yder who did not know what Kei who held him in mortal hatred had in mind. On a large pinewood table, Kei saw a white maple cup lying upside down; Kei went and took it and went down the palace steps; he came down into the courtyard beneath a tree, and under it there was a slab of marble and beside a spring bubbled up with clear healthy water; there was a wooden cup in it from which people could drink. But there was another spring on the other side which Kei knew of because he had heard about it from those who fled the land, for it was a fact that anyone who drank from it would die. It was poisoned with a strong poison, the grass around was all withered by it and the approach to it was difficult because it was forbidden.

But if Kei could, he would devise a means to reach it; he would not give it up for anything. The spring was surrounded with stakes, but Kei was full of treachery: with his sword he cut through the bar in which the pegs stood firm, he attacked the stakes and knocked down a whole pathway; he filled the cup and went back. He put the deadly drink in Yder's hand; he wanted nothing else and had been suffering for it. He emptied the cup; the poison attacked his veins at once, they were full of the venom. The venom was terrible, his body trembled inside and burned; he went to lie down, he was in torment, his skin swelled away from his flesh because it was becoming infused with the venom; his neck was up by his temples, his face no longer showed any sign of his ever having a nose; there was no place where his pulse was beating. Why should I give a long description? The fact is, he no longer showed any sign of a human form.

At daybreak the King awoke and called Kei to make preparations so that he could start on his way back. 'My lord,' said Kei, 'that's a good idea; we've been here long enough.' The horses were prepared; the King, Gawain, Yvain and Kei put on their armour in front of the table. 'It's extraordinary,' said Kei, 'that Yder can't wake up.' 'I'll wake him,' said Gawain. The traitor, certain that Yder was completely dead replied: 'He shouldn't do it: the King's waiting for him, tell him to hurry up for he's delayed too long.' Gawain went where Yder lay but he could not say what it had been; not what it had been but what it was, for he had been quite different from how he looked now. Gawain saw him disfigured, he said how wretched he was and that his death was a great misfortune, he beat his breast and wrung his hands and greatly lamented Yder's prowess. 'Yder,' he said, 'it was unfortunate that I ever knew you: now I'll never love this life again, it's too full of wickedness; God! what shall I do? Alas! I can't stay here, yet how can I leave my friend?'

The King was down in the courtyard; when he heard the great grief he came running. 'Is something wrong with him now?' he said. Gawain replied: 'Indeed it is: we're leaving too great a payment here.' When the King saw Yder, he crossed himself and then stepped back; he was completely overcome. Yvain wept bitterly; Kei said to them: 'My lords,' he said, 'as God help me, my lord Yder fought valiantly against the two giants he killed; they were strong and fierce and wicked, but he couldn't live after them. They bore poison which has killed him, no-one can fail to see that; the poison has already overwhelmed him so that one can't see where his face was; I can see his skin is full of it and blackened. Now let's pray God to have mercy on his body and his soul. We can't give him any more help; but we can stay here so long that we finish up by having further cause to weep. I've told you the truth; I've no confidence in our situation, I feel very sad for the King and for you too, but specially for myself; I'm not trying to deceive you: it's too late to be sorry when one is overwhelmed by death.' 'Kei,' said the King, 'you're quite right.' He blessed the body and left; he prayed to God to protect his soul from the suffering and torment of Hell. Gawain approached Yder's body and beat his breast and wrung his hands. 'Yder, I should never have met you,' said Gawain. Yvain rushed up, weeping bitterly; they both fainted on top of him. The King could hardly pull them away, but he managed to lead them off and made them mount and they left with him, but they were consumed with great grief.

GUILLAUME LE CLERC, Fergus of Galloway
(c. 1210–25)

The poem opens with Arthur and his knights hunting a white stag.[83] On their return to Carlisle, they are observed by the young Fergus, whose father is a wealthy peasant and whose mother is a noblewoman. Eager to join Arthur's retinue, Fergus sets off for Arthur's court at Carlisle, dressed in his father's rusty armour and fighting some robbers on the way. Granted a quest by Arthur, Fergus proves his worth and wins a bride.

The following extract reveals Arthur's willingness to accept the services of an inexperienced and rather rash man on condition that

he undertakes a seemingly impossible quest proposed in mockery
by Kay. The conventional contrast between Gawain's courtesy and
Kay's boorish behaviour is a prominent feature of the passage.

By daily stages he rode over mountains and through valleys until he
came to Carlisle in Wales.[84] In the halls after dinner that day was
King Arthur and with him a thousand and more knights who had
suffered many hardships. Then along the streets here comes the young
man on a chestnut horse that was worth a good thousand pounds in
gold. He did not stop until he reached the great hall, where the king
was sitting peacefully, surrounded by his noble company. The naïve
youth came directly into that hall where the mighty king was seated
and greeted him in courtly fashion. The king said to him, very good-
naturedly: 'Welcome, friend! What is your native land, and what do
they call you in your country? And what have you come for? Tell me
at once!' The young man said: 'I've no wish to avoid disclosing my
name to you. I'm called Fergus by those who know me in my land.
I've come a long way to look for you here. On account of your high
renown I've left my own region and come here to serve you. If you
deign to keep me, I'll be your counsellor along with these other
knights I see sitting round you.'

Sir Kay, unable to restrain himself, said to him: 'By my faith, lad,
you really look the part of a counsellor to a king! A blessing on
whoever sent you here! We were completely at a loss. We desperately
needed, may God preserve us, this advice that we now have. It's true
that God doesn't forget those who always serve Him well. Now,
thanks be to Him, He's sent us great and splendid aid! For you seem
to be a valiant, courtly knight well trained in arms. Never in any
country have I seen one so handsome or better built. That helmet
with the gold shining in it becomes you very well, and so does the
shield slung at your neck. That fine, white lance in your hands suits
you even better. The truth is, and far be it from me to lie about it,
that you're very good at striking great blows with both lance and
sword: you've lopped off many a head that way. What the jester used
to say is true: that a knight would arrive here who would go to the
Nouquetran, where Merlin passed many a year; and he would take
the horn and the wimple hanging from the neck of the gentle lion,
then blow the horn three times and afterwards fight with the knight
who is as dark as a blackberry. Tell me this instant whether you have
the heart for it! If the king took my advice, he would retain you on
the understanding that tomorrow, at the crack of dawn, you'll go
alone, quite unaccompanied, to the Nouquetran and bring us that
wimple and the horn hanging with it. You'll bring back with you the

knight vanquished and bloody; and then you'll have properly avenged all those he has beheaded.'

My lord Gawain almost went out of his mind with sorrow to hear Kay's despicable words to the simple-minded young man. He said: 'Sir Kay, it's always said that the mouth is somewhat tainted by the foul poison that infects the heart; and, make no mistake, I'm referring to you. You'd have burst here and now if you hadn't got rid of it. Have you sobered up now? Begin again: you've not said much! By the faith I owe the Holy Spirit, I never saw your equal for insulting and mocking people. You speak more like a base lecher than a knight. That's a most unpleasant habit of yours.' My lord Kay burns with shame but does not dare to let it show for fear of crossing my wise lord Gawain. He hid his anger and kept it to himself: 'Ah, truly I didn't mean any harm with what I said but was simply pulling the young man's leg.'

The youth had heard very plainly how Kay had mocked him; and that really put his back up. He glared at him and said: 'By the faith I owe Saint Mungo, if I wouldn't be thought an idiot, sir vassal with the braided hair, you'd pay very dearly for your gibes at my expense! If you weren't in the king's presence, I'd let fly at you to such effect that I'd slice through all your ribs.' – 'Come now, good sir,' said the king: 'don't start such a squabble in my great hall in front of these people! Rest assured that you shall have such amends made as will quite satisfy you, I think. But tell me, if you don't mind, where you got those two heads hanging behind your back.' – 'Sire, I've no wish to lie to you about that. The day before yesterday four wicked robbers attacked me in the woods back there, though it wasn't sensible of them, wanting to have my horse and threatening more besides. By Saint Mungo at Glasgow, they didn't know me very well: if they had known anything about me, they would never have assaulted me. They were as stupid as animals. I lopped the heads off two of them. Once I'd knocked them to the ground, and the other two had seen that and spotted that their two companions were dead, they didn't fancy attacking me. I didn't care to go in pursuit, but took a path that led me to the main road where I'd stopped following the tracks. Now I've come here before you. Tell me, lord king, if I shall be retained as your counsellor on condition that tomorrow I go to avenge your knights on the Black Mountain, whoever may lament over it. And so I'll have the wimple and horn.'

'My good young man, may it not please Saint Victor that I should retain you on these terms! I don't wish you to come to any harm on my account. You'd be in for trouble if you went to the Nouquetran, searching on the Black Mountain. I don't advise either you or anyone else I can see to go looking for that lion.' The youth says: 'I'll not be put off for any mortal man. I don't want your seneschal to be thought a liar in the matter: no, I'll be off at dawn tomorrow, if you're prepared to have me in your service.' – 'As you please then, friend!' says the good-natured king, who was able to tell clearly from his appearance that he came from a good family. Now the young man is more joyful and jubilant than ever before because King Arthur has thus retained him in his household. Now nothing he sees displeases him. Then he approached the king for his leave to go and find quarters in the town. This was readily granted him by the king, for he had no doubt that he would be given lodgings within the stronghold; and for that reason he gave him leave.

The youth leaves the court, on his face a glad, happy expression, not that of someone plunged in gloom: he thinks himself just as good a man as Roland! He goes riding about the town, but without finding a living soul to speak to him or take him to his house, or there being anyone he could ask. A light rain began to fall, a very fine drizzle; and the water seeped right through his hauberk to his bare skin. With his lance erect he goes up and down the streets like an idiot. In the end he plants the lance under a laurel-tree, leans there in the wind and rain, and begins to doze off.

In a room on the upper floor of a house, an attractive, shapely and well-mannered maiden looked down through the window and saw that handsome, well-built young gentleman asleep. Going down as quickly as she could, she approaches him with a greeting and asks him what he is about, on watch there at such an hour. He is not taken aback, but answers the maiden: 'I'm looking for a lodging, my fair one; and if you're happy to do so then put me up, and you'll be doing a good deed. You'll certainly lose nothing through me.' The girl laughed and said: 'I'm afraid, sir, that it's not up to me to give you lodging. My father is the king's chamberlain, and he's the master of this house. No one takes lodging in here. Even so, I'll go so far as to put you up here for the night on condition that my father agrees when he gets back from court. If he shows the least annoyance or displeasure on your account, then you'll do well to go away again: I couldn't take your part if he disapproved of you.' – 'Damsel,' said Fergus, 'I ask no more than that of you tonight: give me lodging until he comes. I'll never be ungrateful to you for that; and if he should show you the sharp end of his tongue, I'll leave his house and go to look for lodgings somewhere else.' With that he dismounted and walked into the house.

Here then is the young man lodged in quarters where, you may be sure, he will be shown much consideration and honour before he leaves. The girl runs into the bedroom and fetches a very rich mantle, which she put on the young gentleman once she had had his armour removed. Then she had his horse installed in a fine, handsome stable. Having removed its saddle, two grooms rubbed its back well down. But they are highly alarmed to find the heads hitched on behind the saddle. They promptly take to their heels in fright and, running straight up to him, ask him directly what that is under his cloth. Then he gave them an account of all his activities since he left his country and a detailed description of the robbers he had killed. And when the damsel hears him, she thinks wonderfully highly of him for this, saying it was most courageous of him to dare wait for the robbers. She orders the heads to be taken and dumped somewhere out of the way where they would cause no trouble or alarm.

The young man has fine quarters: never since he was born was he lodged better, more to his liking or more comfortably, for he sees nothing that displeases him. Wearing a grey mantle, he took his seat beside the maiden by the blazing, sparkling fire. He would have been very handsome had his face not been bruised from wearing armour; and had he known how to fit himself out in the English fashion, one could not have found in any land a knight more handsome than he. Conducting himself in the manner of his own region, he nevertheless greatly pleases the beautiful, sensible maiden, who is favourably impressed by his spirit and physical charm. She could see nothing about him that did not utterly delight her, apart from the ugly accoutrements he was wearing: he had on a pair of rawhide shoes, white breeches and a shaggy jerkin as when he went ploughing, never having changed his apparel after his father armed him.

They spent a long time in this fashion, speaking of one thing and another, until it was time for supper. Two handsome serving-lads from Lothian, who were extremely capable and courtly, hurried to bring in the water. The young man washes, as does the girl, who could easily have been a queen. At the meal they sat together side by side on a rich, grey-brown fabric. Over a white dining-table was spread a cloth for the two of them alone, the household and servants eating at another table. I have no wish to talk at length of the courses, but they had many of them to their hearts' content. If I did now want to tell the facts about their dishes, as I could, I should make my matter that much longer and might spoil the work with it. So I do not want to toil over that, preferring to concentrate on composing something better, if I am able to turn my mind to it. I am not keen to put in inferior matter, but should like to devote myself to a quite different subject.

They sat for a long time over supper until, it seems, the chamberlain returned from court. He sees his daughter and, at her side, the young man who had been given lodging. Not being used to that, he was much taken aback. The maiden sitting beside Fergus jumped up to greet her father, her face flushed. The young man too, on seeing him, leapt straight to his feet. But her father tactfully said to them: 'Stay as you are: don't bother to move. I'm going to sit beside you.' With that they each sat down. The chamberlain was good-hearted, prudent and courtly and well versed in all customs. He goes to recline next to them and then begins questioning the young man as to whether he has been given lodging (a highly surprising thing to him), or whether he has been foolish enough to appropriate quarters and a lodging.

'Not I, sir, so help me God! I'm not like that, good sir!' says the good-looking youth. 'I've been given lodging on the understanding with your daughter here that if you grant me hospitality, I shall be put up for the rest of the night, and that if you're unwilling to do so, I'll go on to look for lodgings somewhere else.' – 'May it not please God on high,' says the genial chamberlain, 'that my house should be exchanged for another, now that you've been given lodging. What's more, I'm very grateful to my daughter and think all the better of her for having taken you in; and I'm most anxious for her to show you honour. Are you the man who was at court before the king a little while ago?' – 'Indeed I was, sir, I assure you: never doubt it. But that person who mocked me today isn't at all in his right mind, I give you my word on that. He'll pay for it some time when he least expects it. He's extremely foolish and ill-mannered; and I'd very much like you to tell him from me, if you please, to beware of the peasant's son.' Those were the words he spoke to his host.

At that a young gentleman removes both cloth and table for them. After the meal two serving-lads bring them the water; and then, having washed, they asked for the wine. In a silver goblet they were served with good wine, both honeyed and spiced, for of that the host had a plentiful supply. They went to recline on a couch – the chamberlain along with Fergus and the maiden: just those three, as I understand it. There they had a discussion, the three of them, on various matters. The master of the house, a very courtly man, said to the youth: 'My dear good sir, are you a knight yet?' He replied that he thought he was: 'I am a knight, by my head, because the good peasant dubbed me when he sent me to serve at court. And he gave me his good horse (there's none better this side of Galloway) along with a shield, hauberk, lance and helmet as good, I warrant, as any here in your king's realm. I've been dubbed to my liking. If I were armed on my charger, there's no knight in your court who would put a scrap of fear in me so long as I had my axe and six javelins hanging at my saddle.'

It is plain to his host that he is a simpleton, full of monstrously foolish ideas. Drawing towards him, he puts his arm round him with a noble, kindly gesture and says: 'I presume, dear friend, that you would not be averse to kindly granting me a favour I should appreciate. And I would truly like you to know that it will bring you great honour and far greater profit; and you would never arrive in any place where you'd not be held in greater affection for it.' Hearing him talk like this to the effect that, should he grant him such a favour, it must redound to his honour, he is not justified in refusing him – on the contrary, he freely consents that he should do and say what he likes regarding him and all he has, agreeing to everything. 'Now you've replied as I would wish,' said the chamberlain at once with gentlemanly courtesy. 'The granting of this favour will bring you high honour. Tomorrow at morning Mass you are to be a newly fledged knight, and you shall have equipment that is richer and more handsome than this. You shall stand as a knight tomorrow before the best king in the world, for he himself with his own hand will gird your sword at your side and give you the accolade as is the custom of this country. Be careful not to look bewildered, but conduct yourself in a courtly, civil fashion, for I shall fit your spurs to your feet myself. That much I shall do for your honour.'

At that Fergus is very distressed, since he is to lose his accoutrements that he brought from his land. Had that favour not been granted, he would not have renewed or changed his equipment for anything. He is left quite glum and disconcerted; yet he did just say: 'By the faith you owe me, my good host, shall I be made a knight twice? Wasn't I then dubbed by Soumillet, the peasant who loved me well?' – 'Good brother, I have no wish to lie to you: nobody can make a knight unless he also is a knight: know that for a fact. And you have pledged me to do as I wish: take care not to break your word, for that would be the height of folly.' When the young man hears and understands that there will be no other outcome, he promises his host everything he has asked of him.

Thereupon the lord ordered that the beds be prepared for them to retire to rest and sleep; so the attendants hastily made them ready. The youths proceeded to take the rawhide shoes off the young man's feet. The chamberlain, at great pains to give him worthwhile instruction, goes to take him by the right hand and leads him into a bedroom. I fancy I have still to hear tell of a more luxurious one; for, according to the account I have heard, both sun and moon were painted there, and there is no single star you would not have seen in that room. The man who carried out this work was amazingly expert, bringing everything together in a small space. The room contained a single bed, in which they put Fergus to lie on a sheet of rich brown material as fine as any this side of Thessaly. In no time Fergus was asleep.

The chamberlain left and came straight to his daughter, who was sitting with the others, and said: 'My sweet daughter, when you get up in the morning have some breeches and a shirt ready for the young man. I don't imagine you're so short of them that you don't have a good supply.' – 'I'll have what clothes you wish brought, dear sir, and he shall have them when he gets up tomorrow.' The beds are made, and they retire to them until it grows light the next day.

Early in the morning the chamberlain rose and called his household, his daughter being already up, fully ready and supplied with what he had asked her for. With the maiden, the master of the house came as quickly as he could to the bedroom, going up to the young man and calling him. Fergus rises quickly, and the damsel hands him the splendid clothes, which were of fine quality. These he puts on immediately; so he was dressed and rigged out, complete with hose and shoes laced on. As he left the room he looked most handsome, with a complexion like fine crystal. So radiant was he that you might have expected him to light up the district and entire country: such was the great beauty bestowed on him by the Lord God who, with deliberate care, had fashioned him with His own hand.

Then he is anxious to get to the court. At once a lad runs up bringing him his charger, though without having been to harness it with all the trappings Fergus had when he arrived. He brought him nothing of this, but left behind everything except his good steed. That Fergus was not willing to change, for it was just to his liking. Straight away he asked his leave of the maiden and took it, as she gladly granted it.

At that, without more ado, Fergus departs with the chamberlain; and they go at once to speak to the king and request arms and equipment. The king had come from church and asked for a chessboard, to play with one of his lords. Before there had been a checkmate, Fergus and his host arrived in court. They dismounted at the foot of the staircase, then climbed it to come before the best king in the world. Fergus strides straight into the middle of the hall. The people sitting there stare hard at him and, seeing how handsome and good-looking he is, murmur a great deal among themselves. They say: 'Never before has Nature formed so handsome a being!'

He hurried through the great hall and came before the king. Putting his hand to the cloak hanging from his neck, he took it off; for his host had taught him that, and he remembered his lesson well. The frank, noble-hearted man remained in just his tunic. He would not have known what to do, had his host not told him to prostrate himself at the king's feet and ask him for arms. The young man was not backward, but promptly knelt down, seized the king by the legs and feet and saluted him; and after that he asked him without delay for equipment appropriate to a knight.

The king looks at Fergus and, seeing him well-mannered, wishes to raise him up. But his response is: 'No more of that! If you don't give me equipment, I'll never budge from here.' The king said to him: 'I shall give you some. But tell me where you come from and what your name is.' – 'Don't you recognize me? I'm the young man who was here yesterday and was mocked by the seneschal. But you may be sure that the way he spoke was not very sensible: I've not forgiven him for the wrong he did me, and he'll pay for it yet. He'd better beware of me!' – 'My friend,' said the king, 'by my faith, don't be so bad tempered! If my lord Kay has done wrong, don't doubt that he'll make you amends for his misdeed to your satisfaction.'

Just then my lord Gawain arrived, holding in his hand a knife, with which he was whittling a small stick. He said to the king, having clearly heard the youth ask him for equipment: 'Listen to me, sire. My lord Kay's in the habit of speaking offensively to all knights, intimates and strangers alike. He has a very rough, sarcastic tongue. But let all that be. It's quite right that you should give the young man arms and a horse. Remember Perceval, of whom Kay deprived you. He took him from you by his hurtful talk, as you well know. But forgive him this time, and I don't think he'll do it again. Be quick and give arms and gear to the young man, who seems very worthy; for he's been on his knees too long. If it didn't displease him, I should very much like to propose to him that from now on we should be companions, he and I, in all friendship and sincerity.' – 'Good nephew,' the king replied, 'then I too beg him most urgently to agree.'

Fergus was quick to reply: 'Good sir, I in no way refuse either your friendship or your companionship, and am most willing to be entirely yours to do whatever you wish. But I would first like to have such equipment as is appropriate. After that I'll set off, perhaps, in search of the wimple and horn and will also fight the knight who guards the horn. If I can find him on his look-out hill, either he'll kill me or I him: one of us won't manage to come out of it unscathed. Then, when I've fought the combat, I'll come back and hope to get to know you and make friends: I don't look for any better than yourself.' When my lord Gawain hears that Fergus has no intention of failing to go directly on that dire adventure, he is extremely heavy-hearted, as are all the others. With one accord they curse, execrate and call on

Tintagel Castle, Cornwall: Legendary site of Arthur's conception (see pp. 27–30). The extant fortifications, which date from the mid-thirteenth century, were built by Richard Duke of Cornwall, brother of Henry III (1216–72).

il a meine oie. il sen leuerene
tout maintenant en son pa
les. et saffiet ala table. se a
uenture aunit ruoue en e
son ruiserueil iuuqu ele nu
aunt asilalrer feste. com e
le estoir gene uos encont
neus.Car ge men uoull reto
ner sor vn grane conte.

inonier qui vorga) ne etlou
apellee uisoit le cliant. et ail
larpoit. et la ou ele se vouier
entel maniere com ge uos r
cont. atant es uos teins ue
nir miffinc yuarn qui ame
noit auce soi le clir ve loeno
rs. quane les vames virene
renur miffinc yuarn. qui a

OPPOSITE PAGE, ABOVE
AND BELOW:
*South Cadbury Castle,
Somerset*: Commonly thought
to be the site of Arthur's
legendary Camelot since the
sixteenth-century antiquarian
Leland identified Cadbury as
Camelot.

THIS PAGE, ABOVE:
Arthur Enters Camelot: Parade
portrayed by an Italian artist at
the time of Edward III. Note
the bagpipe, which was a common instrument in England as
well as Scotland at this time.

RIGHT: *The Green Knight
Shows Arthur His Head*: The
Green Knight's (and Morgan la
Fay's) aim is to frighten
Guenevere to death (see pp.
438–56). In this illustration and
in the text itself, Arthur,
Guenevere and the knights are
not sitting at a round table but
on a raised dais, according to
contemporary practice.

la ueille de la pentecou
ſte que tour li conpaig

LEFT: *Arthur at a Feast*: The
Round Table companions assemble at Arthur's court on the eve of
Pentecost. (North French manuscript *c.* 1316.)

BELOW: *Brent Knoll, Somerset*:
The legendary site where the
young Arthurian knight, Yder, the
son of King Nut, fought three
giants (see p. 240).

THIS PAGE: *The Archivolt of the North Door of Modena Cathedral (c. 1105):* An early depiction of the abduction of Guenevere. See pp. 20–21 for the earliest written account.

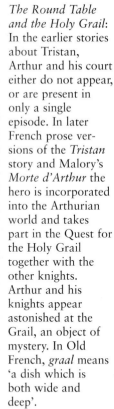

The Round Table and the Holy Grail: In the earlier stories about Tristan, Arthur and his court either do not appear, or are present in only a single episode. In later French prose versions of the *Tristan* story and Malory's *Morte d'Arthur* the hero is incorporated into the Arthurian world and takes part in the Quest for the Holy Grail together with the other knights. Arthur and his knights appear astonished at the Grail, an object of mystery. In Old French, *graal* means 'a dish which is both wide and deep'.

The Round Table and the Holy Grail: Here, the Holy Grail has become a magical dish which supplies Arthur and his knights with their favourite food, according to individual tastes (see pp. 187–8).

BELOW LEFT: *Arthur Single-Handedly Slays the Giant*: The giant of Mont-Saint-Michel in Brittany had devastated the duchy and abducted Helena, niece of Duke Hoel of Brittany (see pp. 89–95).

BELOW RIGHT: *Arthur Fights in Single Combat*: Apparently with the Roman tribune Frollo on an island in the middle of the river Seine, for control of Paris (see pp. 50–51).

Arthur on the Wheel of Fortune: Although appearing in French works, the finest 'Wheel of Fortune' episode occurs in the alliterative *Morte Arthure*, shortly after Arthur's victory over the Romans (see pp. 114–22). (North French manuscript *c.* 1316.)

LEFT *Arthur's Last Battle Against Mordred*: Mordred has usurped Arthur's throne and married Queen Guenevere (see pp. 37; 124–5).

BELOW *The Site at Glastonbury*: Identified as the Isle of Avalon, where Arthur's tomb was reputedly discovered in 1191 (see pp. 517–23).

FOOT *Detail from an Italian Mosaic*: Arthur is associated with Sicily in several texts in this anthology (see, for example, pp. 523–5).

the Lord God in Heaven to confound the tongue of Kay the seneschal.

Fergus pays little heed to them, for his heart is kindled by Prowess, and Valour counsels him, saying in his ear that he should go to the fight and take no account of their pity. Thus prompted, he pressed the king insistently to make him by his grace and favour a new knight. The king realizes and sees very plainly that no pleading will influence the youth with the fair locks. He calls for a good set of arms for the dubbing of the young gentleman, and is speedily brought the hauberk and steel helmet, with many knights looking on.

On the flagged floor of the great hall sat Fergus, a fine figure. He was not inept at arming himself. First he drew on a pair of leggings of iron chain-mail, after which he took the fine hauberk and put it on his back. The courtly lord Gawain placed the pointed helmet upon his head. Here now comes Perceval the Welshman making his way down the middle of the hall. In his hand Perceval held a sharp sword presented to him by his good host who had given him lodging. Perceval was no boor: he placed it in the hands of King Arthur, who then girt it on the young man. The chamberlain busies himself with fitting the right spur, and the Knight with the Lion goes to attach the left one. Never before, I think, was such honour done in the court of any emperor to any knight as to Fergus; and rightly so, noble and of excellent character as he was. And thereafter he was the finest warrior ever born of mother, though I would make exception of Gawain, who never found his equal or was overcome by any man. That is why I would except him. Nevertheless, apart from him, Gawain, there is none better than he.

Fergus is handsomely armed. From the stables they brought for him the charger, a fine steed, but he was not prepared to exchange the one he had brought and which was at the foot of the staircase. A squire quickly goes down and leads his own horse to him. Fergus seizes it by the bridle and, with my lord Yvain holding the stirrup, throws himself onto its back. They bring him a great quartered shield, which he takes and at once hangs at his neck. In his hands they have placed the lance, which was strong and stout as he would wish. Once he was armed on horseback, he would not have been so delighted, I fancy, had anyone given him four cities. He braced himself in the stirrups with such wonderfully fierce pride that he all but burst the good horse on which he was seated.

'God,' said the king on seeing this, 'how my heart may grieve when Kay through his wicked talk has deprived me of such a very valiant young man! It's a mockery and an outrage against me.' The jester sitting by the hearth began to call aloud: 'Don't be dismayed, sire, for no man will be able to stand against his chivalry! In no time you'll see the knight arrive here from the Black Mountain promptly delivering the wimple and horn; and he will make you what amends you wish. But as for the seneschal, you may be sure that the wicked things he was guilty of saying to the young gentleman will bring great harm and disgrace on his head.' My lord Kay goes almost beside himself with rage. Had it not been for the shame he would have incurred, he would have given the jester a sound drubbing and hurled him right into the fire. However, for the shame of it he leaves him on this occasion, not wanting to let his feelings show.

Fergus thereupon took his leave of the king and the distinguished lords; and first and foremost he asked and took his leave of my gallant lord Gawain, who was as reluctant to grant it as he could be. They repeatedly pray that Jesus Christ may preserve him from all difficulty and let him return to them. Fergus remains there no longer, but sets off with all possible speed.

Gliglois (c. 1210–25)

Following in the footsteps of other untried youths, the young hero Gliglois, hearing of Gawain's reputation for prowess and courtesy, goes to Arthur's court to become Gawain's squire. There he quickly falls in love with the proud Lady Beauty, whom Gawain had unsuccessfully wooed. The lady appears to spurn Gliglois but sends him to her sister. She makes him a knight and provides him with rich armour and an entourage of knights, some of them crusaders, enabling him to challenge Arthur's followers in a tournament. There the prowess won through his love earns him victory, and the approval of all present, and at the ensuing banquet his future as Beauty's lord and Arthur's vassal is determined.

Gliglois returned to his lodging and gave all the horses which he had won in the tourney to his companions; of all the knights taken prisoner, he kept nothing of their belongings for himself, not even a pack-horse, dividing the spoils between them, so that all departed happy, both the captured knights and the crusader-knights who had fought on his side in the tourney.

At the palace everyone awaited his arrival, and the ladies especially were eager for Gliglois to appear, but he could not do so until he had divided the spoils so that each might depart at his own pleasure. All the entertainers were rewarded; then, when dinner was ready, the tables were set and they sat to eat. When dinner was over, Gliglois spoke to them all: 'Gentlemen, we must now go to keep my promise.' Each knight called for his horse, mounted, and rode honourably to court. There, dinner was over, but everyone awaited the arrival of Gliglois, which was desired by all, including King Arthur.

As soon as Gliglois entered the palace, Gawain went to meet him and very affectionately greeted him, and all the other knights went out to welcome him. The knights accompanying Gliglois were very politely greeted, which pleased them greatly. King Arthur himself came out to meet Gliglois, first greeted him, then kissed him. Gliglois did not know what to think but knew how to behave; he took the king by the hand, who called his nephew Gawain to join and advise them. Gliglois then addressed the king: 'Sire,' he said, 'I ask that you and your nephew should assist me by interceding with the queen, for I am sent to her as prisoner at her mercy. I beg you to aid me.' 'God help me,' said the king, 'it is very right and proper that one should assist you energetically, for you are a valiant knight, and I will willingly take you with me everywhere I go and retain you in my household.' 'Sire,' he replied, 'you will love me, God willing, or so in truth I believe, when you discover who I am.'

At this the queen emerged from her rooms with her head bowed; a knight had informed her that her prisoner had arrived. Gliglois moved to meet her, and the queen seized him by the right hand and led him into her chamber. Gliglois called in after him the provost,[85] who loved him greatly. The other knights remained outside, while Gliglois entered the room. They sat on a bed of white ivory. Of those three who entered, Gliglois sat beside Beauty, and the provost on her other side. She greeted Gliglois with an embrace, and showed him great affection.

Gliglois addressed the queen, saying, 'My lady, I surrender myself to you and will do your command. The king of Wales, who captured me, sent me here to ask for your mercy, if you do not consider it improper; I have given him my pledge that I will tell you without fail that he sends you the knight who performed best at the tourney today. Give me your command.' He blushed with shame, and the queen saw that he was embarrassed. 'Sir,' she said, 'what is the purpose of your speech? Why are you ashamed? Truly, we all know that you performed best today. Since you gave your word, it is not surprising that you speak thus. No one has heard it except the three of us, and now you have kept your word, so I release you from your bond, on condition that you tell me who you are, and hide nothing from me. Reveal everything, for you may be sure that I already have a good idea who you are. Tell me, are you Gliglois?' 'Yes, truly, I am indeed,

I will hide nothing from you.' 'By my faith, I hold you very dear. Tell me, Gliglois, who made you a knight?' 'Lady Beauty is responsible for everything you see.' The queen asked Beauty to tell her the truth. 'Lady,' she said, 'I will tell you, for you are such a great lady that no evil will come of it for me.'

Beauty then recounted the life which Gliglois had led, how he had loved her and all the misfortune he had suffered, and how he had run after her and would not return to court. 'My lady, I wanted to test him, for I loved him more than any other, but did not wish to reveal it to him. I sent him to my sister, with a short letter commanding her to make him a knight, which she did willingly. Lady, I love him more than anything, and am sure that he loves me; I will have no other lord. Sweet lady, by your honour, I beg you to intercede with the king to think kindly of both Gliglois and myself.'

The queen replied, 'I am delighted that you do not lie; I am well aware of the love between you two, since Gliglois is good and worthy and you are a noble maiden; I do not believe there is another such damsel on earth. If you tell me your desire, I will give you a good fief, with land and inheritance, but Gliglois must do me homage for it, and my lord king will restore your land on the day that you marry. Gliglois may expect a large inheritance from both his father and his mother, and you will receive substantial land. Indeed, you will be wealthy people. You make a good pair, but now let us send for the king, and let him hear of your proposal.'

Beauty was not foolish, and thanked the queen greatly, curtseying low before her. The queen delayed no longer, but sent for the king, who came, with Gawain, in whom there was no trace of villainy. They all sat on the bed, and the queen told the king and Gawain that this was Gliglois. 'God help me,' said the king, 'I knew him as soon as I saw him.' Gawain was happy when he heard this; indeed there never was a happier man. He drew near to Gliglois and embraced him, greeting him joyfully. 'My friend,' he said, 'I never dared to say that you might be Gliglois; I am delighted with your success. You shall always be my companion, and I yours. I give you my hand in pledge that while I possess a single penny, I will never refuse it to you. As is proper, I shall love you as a friend.' 'Gliglois,' said King Arthur, 'you shall remain in my retinue, and I will find you plenty of horses and armour.' 'Sire,' answered Gliglois, 'my humble thanks.'

The queen called the king aside. 'Sire,' she said, 'listen to me. Do you know why I have sent for you? Gliglois and Beauty, whom you see, love each other dearly, and he came yesterday morning to the tourney, for her sake. At her command, her sister dubbed him knight, for she loves him above all things, and he loves her, as I know well.

There are none in the land better suited for each other. Now, if you are willing, Beauty requests your love and permission, for she has already pledged her love.'

Gawain heard this and was overwhelmed with grief, sighing when he heard the queen talk of love, for he believed himself to be in love with Beauty. Yet, on the other hand, he was also happy, since he greatly admired Gliglois; Gawain never committed any misdeed, and so he spoke to the king, requesting that he permit the marriage and increase their inheritance. In reply the king said, 'I will do so most willingly, since Gliglois is a good knight and I value his homage highly.'

Huth Merlin (c. 1210–25)

This work is one of several French versions of the Merlin story. It contains material which will be familiar to readers of Malory, who condensed the Huth Merlin *in Book I of his work. In the first extract, Arthur's sword (which he had taken from the stone) has proved inadequate in combat, so Merlin promises the king a sword befitting his rank and prowess. Merlin takes Arthur to visit the Lady of the Lake, who presents him with a fine sword in exchange for his promise to grant her request, whatever it is, at a later date.*

'I warned you,' said Merlin, 'that your sword would not last. However, I know there is a fine sword in this land, in a lake inhabited by fairies. If you could obtain this sword, it would last your lifetime.' 'Ah! Merlin my good friend,' replied the king, 'how can you arrange for me to have it?' 'I can lead you to the place where the sword is, but I cannot give it to you myself since it is not in my power. Nevertheless, I am certain that you shall have it, and in such a manner that you will be amazed. Now let us go to a nearby hermit, where you may rest tonight. Tomorrow, when your wounds have been treated, we will go together to the place where I have told you the sword is, if you are able to ride, although I am afraid that you may be so seriously wounded that you will find travelling difficult.'

The king replied that he had no wound that would affect his ability to ride. Then the king mounted the defeated knight's horse and rode off with Merlin, who led him to a hermitage on a mountainside, where a very noble hermit led a saintly life; he had been an excellent knight in his youth and knew a lot about healing wounds.

When the king had dismounted and disarmed, and the hermit had examined his wounds, he told Arthur that he was certain that he would heal very easily, since he had no really dangerous wound. The king and Merlin remained in the hermitage both that day and the next; then they departed, travelling until they came almost to the sea. Merlin turned right, towards a mountain, and they travelled until they reached a lake; then he said to the king, 'Sire, what do you think of this water?' 'Merlin,' replied the king, 'it seems very deep, and of such a nature that if any man entered it, he would perish.' 'Most certainly,' said Merlin, 'you are quite right. No one who enters without the permission of the fairies can survive, and you may be sure that the good sword which I spoke about is in this lake.' 'In this lake?' enquired the king. 'How could this be?' 'That you shall see soon enough, if it please God.'

While they were thus speaking, they looked into the middle of the lake and saw a sword appear out of the water, in a hand, with an arm visible to the elbow; the arm was clothed in white samite, and the hand was holding the sword out of the water. 'Now you can see,' said Merlin, 'the sword which I have said you shall have.' 'Oh God!' said the king. 'How can we obtain it? For no man may enter this lake without perishing.' 'God will give you some good advice,' said Merlin. 'Let us wait awhile.' Whilst they were talking about the sword, they saw a damsel coming towards them along the seashore. She was riding a small black palfrey and seemed excited, since she was travelling at a great speed.

When the damsel came near the lake, she greeted the king, and when Merlin returned her greeting, she addressed them thus: 'I am aware that you are waiting until you can find a means of obtaining that sword. However, it is foolish to aim to possess it, since there is no manner in which you can secure it except through me.' 'Indeed, lady,' said Merlin, 'I know well that without you he could never possess the sword. You have so enchanted this lake that no other magic has any power to overcome it. Since I respect your magic, I beg of you, as a gift, that you should fetch the sword and give it to my lord the king. For we are both well aware that there is no one else in the world at this time by whom it would be better employed.'

'I am aware of this,' she answered, 'and therefore I have ridden swiftly so that I could be here in time for your arrival; if you swear that he will promise to grant me the first gift which I require of him, I will go and fetch the sword and give it him. Then the king gave his promise that he would grant her request, provided that it was in his power. 'I require no more of you,' she replied.

Then she hurried into the water and passed across dry-shod, in such a manner that neither her feet nor any other part of her became wet, and, reaching the sword, she took it. The hand which was holding the sword disappeared under the water and was no longer visible. The damsel returned to the king and said to him, 'Sire, here is the sword; you may be sure that I believe there are not two of this quality in the whole world. Certainly, if I did not believe that it would be well employed by you, you should not have it, for it is a much richer treasure than you might imagine.'

The king took the sword and thanked the damsel profusely. She told him, 'Sire, I must leave now, since I have much to do elsewhere. Remember well that you owe me a favour; for perhaps I shall demand it of you sooner than you imagine.' He replied that he would indeed do so; she might come to ask for it whenever she liked, for he would fulfil it if it was within his power. Then she left them, and Merlin commended her to God's care and thanked her greatly for her generosity.

King Arthur examined the sword and, perceiving that the scabbard was marvellously intricate, he prized it highly. Then he drew forth the sword and, examining it, saw that it was so fine and splendid that in his opinion it was the finest in the whole world. Merlin asked the king, 'Sire, what do you think of the sword?' 'I prize it so highly,' said the king, 'that there is not a castle in the world for which I would exchange it. I believe that, in the hands of a skilled warrior, there is no armour which could resist it.' 'Tell me, which do you esteem most, the sword or the scabbard?' 'I think the sword is better than a hundred such scabbards,' said the king. 'Nevertheless, this is the finest and most beautiful scabbard I have ever seen, and I do not believe there is a better one in all the world.' 'Indeed, sire,' said Merlin, 'now I can tell that you hardly understand the extent of the damsel's generosity towards you. You should realize that the scabbard is worth ten such swords, for it is made of leather which possesses such a property that no man who wears it will lose blood or receive a mortal wound, as long as he is reasonably well armed.'

(Such were the words that Merlin spoke about the sword's scabbard, and he spoke truthfully, but the book does not explain more at this time, although later it describes how Morgan, Arthur's sister, stole the scabbard and gave it to her lover, so that he could fight Arthur.[86] Since she took it from Arthur, he would have been killed, had it not been for Merlin's foresight. It is only at this point that the story explains that the scabbard possessed such a nature.)

When the king heard how highly Merlin praised the scabbard, he said to him: 'Merlin, is what you tell me true?' 'You will not appreciate it fully,' replied Merlin, 'until you have lost it; only then will you realize its value.' 'How then, Merlin, will I lose it?' 'It will be stolen from you,' answered Merlin. 'Don't ask me any more about it, for I shall tell you nothing else.' Then they both left the lake, carrying the sword; the king girt it about him, very happy that fortune had sent him such a rich present.

Accompanied by Merlin, Arthur arrives at the pavilion of a knight whom he must fight. Afterwards, when Arthur asks Merlin how the damsel was able to walk on the water, he explains that she used an invisible bridge. Arthur returns to the city and gives his sister Morgan in marriage to King Urien.

When one of the Lady of Avalon's damsels arrives at Arthur's court, seeking assistance to remove a sword chained about her, a strange knight called Balain the Savage, who is exiled from the king of Northumberland's court, succeeds in the task.

While they were inside the palace discussing this event, a damsel entered on horseback and, still mounted, rode up to the king and addressed him familiarly: 'King, you owe me an obligatory reward: fulfil it before all these worthy men here.' The king looked at the damsel and, recognizing her as the lady who had given him the sword, answered, 'Indeed, damsel, I do owe you a gift, if I have the power to fulfil it. But please tell me something which I forgot to ask.' 'And what is that?' she asked. 'It is the name of the sword that you gave me.' 'Now know,' she replied, 'that the sword is properly called Excalibur.' 'Now ask,' he said, 'whatever you desire, for I will grant it to you if I am able.' 'I demand of you,' she said, 'the head of that damsel who has just brought a sword in here, or that of the knight who now has it. Do you know,' she continued, 'why I request such a strange gift? You should be aware that this knight killed one of my brothers, a valiant and worthy knight, and this damsel caused my father's death. It is for this reason that I would be revenged on either one or the other.'

When the king heard this demand, he drew back in utter astonishment and replied, 'Damsel, before God I beg you to ask for a different boon, for with such a gift I would certainly be fulfilling my obligation to you evilly; indeed, it would be nothing less than criminal wickedness for me to have either of them killed, since neither has done me any harm.' When the strange knight heard that the damsel had demanded his head, he came up to her and said: 'Ha! Damsel, I have been searching for you for a long time: indeed, for more than three years. It was you who poisoned my brother, and for this reason I hate you so violently that, since I could not find you, I killed your brother. However, since I have now found you, I need seek no further.'

Then he drew his sword from its scabbard; when she saw this, the damsel attempted to flee from the hall to escape his clutches. He cried, 'That will avail you nothing; instead of your demanding my head from the king, I will give him yours.' Then he leapt towards the damsel and struck her so hard with his sword that her head flew to the ground. Then, holding the sword and her head, he approached the king, saying: 'Sire, know that this is the head of the most treacherous lady who ever entered your court. Much worse would have befallen you if she had remained longer in your court, and many evil things would have occurred; I must tell you that the greatest joy ever known will fill the land of Northumberland when news of her death is known.'

When the king witnessed this event, he was furious and replied to the knight, 'Certainly, sir knight, you have performed the greatest villainy that I have ever seen perpetrated by the sort of knight I believed you to be. I did not believe that any knight, either a member of my household or a stranger, was so foolhardy that he would dishonour me as you have done. For certainly nothing more shameful could have been done to me than to kill, in my presence, a damsel under my protection, whom I should have safeguarded; for since she was in my palace, she should have had nothing to fear in any way, since while she was in my court she should have been protected against everything. Such is the law and custom of my court, which you have broken and contravened through your pride; I tell you plainly that even had you been my brother, you would have repented of such a deed. Leave my court immediately and go away, and know that I shall not be friendly towards you until this haughty deed has been avenged.'

Arthur's barons are anxious for him to marry and he consults Merlin on the choice of a bride. The prominence of the Round Table in Arthur's list of Guenevere's qualities suggests that the urge to possess this object may have influenced his choice of her as his bride. In contrast, in the later Of Arthour and of Merlin *it is clearly love which motivates him. Interestingly, in* Perlesvaus *the ownership of the Round Table is disputed upon Guenevere's death, since it was part of her dowry.*

When Merlin had arrived at court, he found plenty of people who greeted him joyfully, for everyone was very pleased at his arrival. The king said, 'Merlin, what shall I do? My barons are criticizing me every day, and blaming you, and are ashamed that I have not taken a wife. How would you advise me? For without your guidance I won't do anything, since I wish to act in everything by your advice, just as my father did.' 'Sire,' replied Merlin, 'they are right if they advise you, since it is very sensible that you should have a wife from now on. Now, tell me if you know of any woman who takes your fancy more than any other, for such a powerful man as you are certainly should be able to have a woman who satisfies him.' 'Yes,' said the king, 'I know one who pleases me very much, and I love her: and if I don't have her, I will not take a wife.'

In the name of God,' said Merlin, 'since you love her, if you don't obtain her, Merlin has never been able to achieve anything. Now tell me who she is, and I will go and fetch her; but you can keep me company.' 'It is,' he said, 'Guenevere, the daughter of King Leodigan of Carmelide, who maintains in his household the Round Table which you and my father, King Utherpendragon, established. Moreover, this Guenevere is the most worthy damsel, and the most beautiful, and the most praised of all those whom I know of in the island. So, for this reason, I wish to have her; and if I don't have her I won't ever take a wife.'

'Indeed,' said Merlin, 'you are quite right about the damsel's beauty, for she is the most beautiful that I know of in the world at this time. But if you did not love her so much I would have you take another woman whom I would recommend to you more, for such great beauty as Guenevere has could well be harmful in the future. Nevertheless, there will come a day when her beauty will assist you to such an extent that you will acquire land in a situation when you will believe that everything is lost.' [Merlin was referring to Galehot, who would become Arthur's liege man and hand over his land when he had won everything; he would do all this for love of Lancelot.][87] The king did not understand what Merlin said at this time, since it was too obscure; nevertheless, it happened just as Merlin had predicted, as the story of the Holy Grail relates.

Then Merlin spoke again to the king: 'Sire, since you desire Guenevere so much, you need only accompany me if I go to seek her in Carmelide.' And the king said that he would take with him a company as great as he dared and knew how to assemble: he chose a hundred of his household knights, and took numerous squires and valets, and Merlin, having changed his appearance, joined this company. They travelled by sea and land until they came to King Leodegan's land.

Merlin requested that his daughter should become King Arthur's wife, and she would be made queen of the kingdom of Logres and of many other lands.

King Leodegan was very pleased at this news, and he replied quickly to Merlin, even though he still did not recognize him: 'May God do honour to King Arthur, for he has done me such a great honour that I do not dare ask him for anything. He can take my daughter and myself and do whatever he wishes with my realm, for indeed I have never had such great joy of anything in my life than I have of this news. I shall give him my land, if he desires, but I know well that he has no need of it for, thanks be to God, he has plenty of other lands. However, I shall send him that which I love best: that is my Round Table, although it is not complete, as there are fifty knights lacking, who have died since King Utherpendragon left this world. I would have chosen fifty knights already, but a wise hermit told me that I should not concern myself with replacing the fifty. "Why?" I asked. He replied: "Since it will fall next into the hands of a man of such prowess that he will maintain it better than you have done. Moreover, he will possess fifty of the best men of prowess whom you would not find in your land."

'The wise man told me this, and for this reason I have left the table in such a situation that there are now only a hundred of the one hundred and fifty knights which it should have.' 'Indeed,' said Merlin, 'it is true; this is as it should be, and it will be fulfilled soon enough, if it pleases God. For now it will come into the hands of such a man as will maintain it in greater power and force than it has hitherto enjoyed. Moreover, he will place it in such a high position and give it such renown that after his death no one will be bold enough to dare undertake to preserve it.' 'May God give him it to maintain,' replied King Leodegan, 'since he has prowess and honour!'

Then all the hundred knights who were companions of the Round Table were summoned. When they had arrived, the king said to them, 'My lords, your company around me is lacking fifty knights, and, I believe, I lack the considerable prestige and power to dare complete their number. However, since I esteem you all so much that you should be complete, and I have one engendered of my body, I wish that your honour should grow and increase. Henceforth, I shall send you to such a man as is well able to maintain you; I know well that he will do this willingly, and that he will love you just as a father loves his son. Moreover, there are so many men of prowess in his household, and so many attend his court, that he will easily be able to find fifty worthy men to choose as knights, whom he will add to your company, so that the right number of the Round Table, which should be one hundred and fifty knights, will be complete in his household, which I am unable to achieve in all this land.'

'Sire,' they answered, 'who is this man whom you praise so much, and what is his power?' He replied, 'It is King Arthur.' Then they all raised their hands to the sky and exclaimed, 'Oh, God! Blessed be Thy name, since Thou hast provided such a father for us! He will indeed be a good father and will maintain us as his sons. Indeed, we thank God that He has placed us in His hands. Now we shall go, right away, if it pleases God. May God grant him the force and the power that he is able to maintain us, both to his honour and to ours.'

Merlin remained there for three days, both he and his companions. When it came to the time for departure, the king wept more for the Round Table companions than for his daughter: he embraced each one individually, and his daughter afterwards; and if he had any fine youth or beautiful female entertainer, you should know that he sent them to King Arthur. Then the messengers who were conducting the damsel departed from the king, and in their company each one of the Round Table fellowship. They travelled until they reached the realm of Logres, and they heard that the king was residing in London, so they rode towards there.

When they were nearby, Merlin instructed the king to come with a large company: he should take care that he should come to meet them happily and with a grand feast. When the king heard the report that the companions of the Round Table had come to his court to remain with him, he was extremely pleased, for he desired nothing in the world so much as that they should be in his company. Then he left London with a numerous entourage and went to greet them. He received them all with considerable honour and gave them such a welcome and so splendid a feast that he made them very happy that they had come to that place.

The wedding apparel was made, the terms drawn up, and the day appointed for the wedding. Then Merlin said to the king, 'King, choose the fifty best knights you know from throughout your kingdom, and if you know any poor knight who is valiant of body and prowess, do not overlook him on account of his poverty. Moreover, if anyone of noble birth and high lineage wishes to be a member and he is not an excellent knight, take care that you do not permit him to join, since a single one, if he is not an excellent knight, will dishonour and discredit all the chivalry of this company.' 'Merlin,' said the king, 'you know each one better than I do, both the good knights and the bad ones. You chose those yourself whom you believe are most worthy.' 'Now let it be,' replied Merlin, 'and since you have given me all the responsibility for this matter, I will perform it in such a manner that I shall never be blamed. I will have chosen them all so that they shall all be placed in their seats on the day of your wedding, and so the high table will be complete.' ...[88]

Then the king sent through his realm to all the worthy men who held lands from him, that they should come on the day appointed to the land of Camelot to the marriage feast, and that they should come if they could possibly manage it. When they had arrived, the king said to Merlin, 'Consider about the Round Table.' 'Yes, I will do so,' replied Merlin, who then began to choose the knights whom he knew to be the most worthy. When he had appointed forty-eight, he took them aside and then said, 'Henceforth, it is necessary for you to be closely bound in affection and to hold each other as dear as brothers, since, for the love and sweetness of this table where you are seated, you will give birth in your hearts to such a great joy and such a great fellowship that you will leave your wives and children to become one with each other, and to employ your youth together.

'Nevertheless, your table will not be complete in my lifetime, nor until the excellent knights will come to this place, the best of the good, who will achieve the dangerous adventures of the kingdom of Logres in which all the others will fail.' Then he came to the hundred and fifty wooden seats, all new, which King Arthur had constructed; he approached the seat in the middle and showed it to King Arthur and to all the others who were present, both knights and ladies, and said to them, 'Here is the Perilous Seat; you should remember well after my death that I have called it thus.' Then the king asked Merlin, 'Merlin, why have you called it perilous?' 'Sire, because there is such a great danger that no knight will sit there without being altered or harmed, until the time when the best knight comes who will put an end to the most marvellous adventures of the kingdom of Logres. He will sit there, and remain unharmed, but that will not happen for a long time.'

PART 4
THE VULGATE CYCLE

Around 1220, a prose story recounting in detail the life of Lancelot – a character already depicted by Chrétien de Troyes – became the centrepiece of a vast compilation of material depicting the Arthurian world from an entirely new viewpoint. This group of works, called The Vulgate Cycle, *owes little to Geoffrey of Monmouth's* History. *The central characters of Arthur, Guenevere and his principal followers, Gawain and Kay, remain virtually unchanged from that of romance tradition. But the addition of the French hero Lancelot, descended from Arthur's vassal King Ban, introduces a new dimension to the legend, since he and his followers constitute a new faction within the Round Table. It is the conflict arising between this group and the Orkney clan, led by Gawain, which eventually divides Arthur's kingdom, even before the treachery of Mordred destroys Arthur. It is* The Vulgate Cycle *that forms the basis for Malory's* Le Morte d'Arthur. *The first volume of the cycle is concerned only with the early history of the Grail and is not discussed here.*

The Story of Merlin *(Lestoire de Merlin) (c. 1210–25)*

The early part of The Story of Merlin *is about Merlin, whose magical powers are derived from his devil father. His service to Arthur's immediate predecessors – his uncle Aurelius Ambrosius and father Uther – is taken from Geoffrey of Monmouth's account. The story changes following the death of Uther. His successor is undecided and civil war threatens until, in answer to the archbishop's prayer, God sends the test of the sword in the stone to reveal the true king. In the civil war which follows Arthur's accession, King Lot and his four allied kings are defeated by the young squires led by Lot's son, Gawain. After Gawain has defeated his father in single combat, peace is restored when Lot submits to*

Arthur, who accepts the rebel king's homage for his nephew Gawain's sake.

Despite the title of this work, Merlin does not always figure prominently in the narrative. He does not appear in the extract presented here, which is concerned with the vows of Arthur and his knights.

King Arthur was in Logres in joy and delight, as you have heard; and when the mid-August festival came,[89] all the knights came to court dressed and decked out in their finest garments, and both the queen and her damsels were apparelled as richly as was appropriate for such a feast. When High Mass was rung, they went to the church and heard the service, which the archbishop celebrated for them. On that day the king wore his crown and his wife, Queen Guenevere, and King Ban and King Bohors wore their crowns out of respect for him.

After Mass, they returned to the hall, where the tables and the tablecloths were set, and the barons sat down as they should, each one in his place. On that day, my lord Gawain served at the high dais where the four kings sat, with Kay the seneschal, Lucan the butler and my lord Ywain, son of King Urien, and Girfles and the other Ywain, and Sagremor and Dodinal the Savage; and so many others served that there were twenty-one serving at the high dais, and forty young bachelors at the other tables. All were so well served that no people had ever been better attended.

At the end of the meal, when all the dishes had been served, King Arthur spoke aloud so that everyone in the hall heard him: 'Listen, my lords, one and all, you who have come to my court to honour me; I give you my gratitude and thank God for the joy and honour which you have shown me. Know, moreover, that, to enhance my reputation, I wish to establish a custom at my court every time I wear my crown: I vow to God that I shall never sit to eat before some adventure has arrived here, from wherever it might be.

'By observing such a custom as this, which is a good one, I shall attract those knights to my court who wish to assemble here to acquire renown and honour, and who will be my friends, companions and my relatives.'

When the Round Table knights heard the vow which King Arthur had made, they talked amongst themselves and declared that, since the king had made the vow at court, it was appropriate that they also should make a vow. After they had taken counsel and agreed about something, they gave Nascien the burden of relating it to the king, loud enough that all the barons could hear.

Then all the companions of the Round Table came before the king, and Nascien started to speak and spoke aloud so that everyone in the hall could hear. 'Sire,' said Nascien, 'the Round Table companions who are present vow before God in the presence of you and all the barons who are gathered here that, since you have made your vow, they will make another: that never, for as long as the world lasts, if a maiden in need of help should come to your court for assistance, or require any aid which could be achieved by single combat of one knight against another, would they not willingly go wherever they were led to deliver her from whatever danger she was in, and they would do whatever was necessary to redress the wrongs which had been done to her.'

When the king heard this, he asked the companions if they pledged to perform what Nascien had said, and they replied, 'Yes': they promised to do everything in their power to maintain it, even unto death. Then the joy was greater than it had been before, and when my lord Gawain heard and saw the delight and the celebration which they were enjoying there because of the vows which they had established, he approached his companions, well aware that each one of them would approve of what he would say, since he would make an offer from which they would derive great honour all the days of their life. They replied that they would agree with everything that he would say. 'Pledge me, then,' he said, 'to bear me company.' And they all gave their promise; there were eighty companions in total.

When my lord Gawain had taken his companions' pledge, he came before the queen and said, 'Lady, my companions and I come before you to beseech and request you to retain us in your household as your knights, since when we go into a strange land to acquire prowess and renown, and some gentleman asks us whom we serve and from what land we come, we can tell them that we are "of the land of Logres, and are knights of Queen Guenevere, the wife of King Arthur".' When the queen heard this, she stood up and replied, 'Good nephew, thank you very much, both yourself and your companions, for I will retain you most willingly as my lords and my friends. Moreover, just as you wish it, so I desire it myself with pure and loyal heart, and may God grant me strength and ability, and permit me to live long enough to be able to reward you for the honour which you have promised me to perform, and for your courtesy.'

'Lady,' replied Gawain, 'so, since we are your knights and you have retained us through your great mercy, now we will make a vow among ourselves that never shall anyone come among us seeking assistance against a knight without finding a champion ready to enter into single combat against him, and prepared to be led wherever they please, however far off it might be. Moreover, if it should come to pass that this champion does not return within a month, each one of us will search for him for a year and a day without returning to court until he brings back true news of his companion, either of his life or of his death; and when they have returned to court, each one will relate, one after another, all the adventures that have occurred, whatever they might be, whether good or ill, and they should swear on holy relics that they do not lie in anything, either in their outward journey or in their return. All this we wish to perform.'

When the queen heard the vow which my lord Gawain had made, she was very happy, and the king was happier than all the knights in his court; and, since the king saw that the queen was more at ease, he said to her, 'Lady, since God has given you such a good company, it would be better if you should receive it from me; and, for the love of them and of you, you should know that I assent and grant it. I give my treasure totally into your power in such a manner that you shall be mistress of it, and shall disperse it among those whom you please.'

When the queen heard this, she knelt before the king and said: 'Sire, thank you very much.' Then the queen called my lord Gawain and said to him, 'Good nephew, I wish that four clerks should be appointed here who shall concern themselves with no other thing except to put in writing all the adventures which befall you and your companions, so that after our deaths the prowess of the worthy men in this place shall be remembered.' 'Lady,' replied my lord Gawain, 'I agree.' So four clerks were chosen to put in writing all the adventures as they were recounted at court from thenceforth. After this, my lord Gawain said that he would never hear of an adventure which he would not undertake; so he and his companions agreed to bring back true news to court; and, as his companions promised, so likewise did those members of the Round Table. Moreover, henceforth my lord Gawain and his companions were called 'the Knights of Queen Guenevere'.

The Prose Lancelot (c. 1210–25)

This long prose version of the Lancelot story begins with the hero's upbringing and education by the Lady of the Lake. It recounts his arrival at Arthur's court at Camelot where, although the king knights him, it is Guenevere who presents him with his sword, so that he may be considered to be her knight, rather than Arthur's. Lancelot's love for the queen inspires him to seek adventure away from court, and he rescues Gawain and his companions from imprisonment at Dolorous Garde.

Arthur, hearing of the young knight's prowess and regretting his prolonged absence from court, frequently sends his knights in search of the hero. However, it is not until he hears of Gawain's terrible injuries received defending Arthur's land against Galehot that Lancelot is persuaded to return; disguised as the Black Knight, he defeats Galehot and they become great friends.

It is through Galehot that the first secret meeting between Lancelot and the Queen takes place, ending with the kiss made famous by Dante.[90] Lancelot leaves court again to visit the territory of his new friend, Galehot, and only reappears when Guenevere is in danger.

In the following extract, Guenevere's position as queen is challenged and Arthur is kidnapped.

The story tells how King Arthur had arrived at Cardueil in Wales, and with him a great number of barons from throughout his kingdom. Sir Gawain and other companions were also there, because the king did not wish that anyone should leave his presence, since Christmas was approaching, for he intended then to hold a very splendid and formal court.

One day the king was seated at dinner, and when the meal had ended, an extremely beautiful damsel entered the hall, and with her came a very old knight, white-haired with age. They both came before the king, and the knight spoke so loudly that everyone throughout the hall heard him, saying to the king:

'Sire, we are sent here by the person whom you should love most dearly in the world: that is Guenevere, the daughter of King Leodegan of Camelide, who should have been crowned queen of Britain if God had preserved her honour. You married her legally and loyally and promised God, as the sacred and anointed king, that you would treat her as honourably as a king should treat a queen. Thus you have done much wrong both towards God and the world, so much that if all men knew this equally well as I do, you would never find a loyal or worthy man who loved you in his heart, for there is no such man who honours and holds dear anyone who is disloyal towards his Creator. Since you are such a disloyal person, you have abandoned and deserted the law given to you by Holy Church, through which we might achieve the great joy of Paradise. Nevertheless, I have heard witness that you are a great man, so I truly believe that, if you knew the truth about this matter, you would not delay in amending it.' 'Certainly,' said the king, 'if I had known of such a thing as you have here revealed to me, I would hate myself wholeheartedly.'

'Sire,' said the knight, 'I will reveal to you that you are soiled by all these things, and will tell you how. It is true that when you married the king of Camelide's daughter she was a young damsel, as you yourself should know. There is nobody, be it either a nobleman or lady of high birth, who does not have many enemies in the world who hate them in their heart and, indeed, eagerly wish for them to suffer misfortune and sorrow. Thus it befell my lady, for when you were bedded with her the first night, as you lay there it so happened that you got up again. Then enemies of my lady came, who seized her and carried her from the bed where she had been lying with you, and, since she believed that this was at your command, she dared not protest. Thus *that* damsel there,' (with which he pointed at the queen), 'who calls herself Guenevere, was placed in bed in place of my lady by those who had perpetrated this treason. Then they carried the real Guenevere out of the country and imprisoned her in a convent, where she has been treated so badly until now that if they had buried her the traitors could not have been more sure of her. However, praise God, she is released from prison, and wishes you to know that this Guenevere who is here has no right to wear the crown, and thus deserves to die shamefully. Moreover, if there is any knight present who wishes to deny the truth of what I have spoken, I am ready to prove it true with my body against his, and this shall be either right now or on any day which may please him.'

Now when the queen heard this speech, she was very anxious and looked about her for help; and then my lord Gawain leapt up first and said that he would defend his lady the queen of this accusation of treason which the knight had placed her under. 'So help me God,' said Dodynal the Savage, 'if God wills, my lord Gawain, you shall not dishonour yourself so much as to fight him. But my lord the king should send in search of Do of Cardueil, who is as old as this man, and they shall fight each other, for it would not be honourable for you to fight such an old man.'

Then Berthelai replied that there was no knight in the whole world who was so worthy that he would not fight bravely against him, for in defending loyalty a noble man would never be shamed. Then the damsel who came with Sir Berthelai spoke again, and gave the king some letters which she declared her lady had sent to him; and the king took the letters, gave them to one of his clerks and commanded him to read them. The clerk began to read aloud, saying:

'Sire, Guenevere the queen, daughter of the king of Camelide, salutes you and wishes you to know that first she was thrown from her royal throne by you, and afterwards, by the traitors whom you maintain in your household, has for a long time been cast out from her rightful place. But now, she begs and requests that you will here amend that error by which you previously transgressed. Since she cannot write all that she wishes you to amend, she wishes that you should believe what this damsel tells you by word of mouth.'

Then the damsel took up his speech and said: 'Sire, my lady bids you, as the man whom she holds as her lord by the bond of marriage, that you take her back as you should. However, if you do not wish to take her as your wife, you should send her the Round Table, as well supplied with good knights as you took it from her on marriage. For since the day that you received her hand from her father, King Leodegan, there has been only that Round Table in all the world, nor should there be any other. Moreover, my lady is very distressed since she is deprived of the flower of chivalry, which should by right be in her power. Therefore, my lady requests that you either restore her inheritance, or take her back as your queen. If you should be unwilling to do either of these things, my lady is prepared to show her claim by this knight, who is here at her command. You should know well that, if she was not in the right, she would not have sent here a man of such age, for she could have found plenty of young knights, who would willingly have fulfilled this need if she had wished so to command them. Also, she sends you,' the girl ended, 'as a sign of faith, the ring with which you married her.'

Then she drew from her purse a very fine ring and gave this to the king, who took the ring and gazed at it for a long time. Then he showed it to the queen and declared that he was quite certain that this was the ring with which he had wed her. But the queen knew well that this was untrue, so she rose and went to find her own ring. When she brought hers there, all the knights looked at it in amazement, for the two rings were of the same workmanship and design. Then the damsel took back her ring and told the king that she wished to leave, and that the knight had offered adequately to uphold his lady's right by arms.

'And yet,' she said, 'I tell you on behalf of my lady that you should ensure that she shall not be condemned hastily in your court; thus you should arrange a day for the battle, so that judgement may be given to her.' The king said that he would do this most willingly, but did not wish to end this matter at present. Thus he gave the day after

Christmas at Camelot as the day: 'For,' said he, 'all the nobility of my land will be present, and I wish this matter to be brought to a conclusion in their presence.'

'Sire,' said Berthelai, 'I tell you truly that I will come on that day to do battle for my lady's honour; and you should be well aware that if no one wishes to contest it against me, we will claim that my lady has won her quarrel.'

The king said that this was reasonable, and agreed in this manner. Then both the knight and damsel took their leave and departed from court, leaving the king very bemused with the news which they had brought. However, the queen was the most grieved of all those present, although Sir Gawain and the other knights comforted her with all their power, telling her not to be dismayed, because she had plenty of knights to defend her against the charge of disloyalty made against her.

The story tells how Berthelai and the damsel returned to Camelide, where they informed the false Guenevere of events. Realizing that his lady is not powerful enough to make war on Arthur, Berthelai plans to use trickery to deceive him. With a retinue of knights, they all leave for Cardueil, where they are pleased to find Arthur still in residence.

That night they slept in a religious house which was at the edge of the forest. They took the best precautions in their power, that no one might discover their hide-out. In the morning they rose as soon as day broke and went straight into the forest as Berthelai ordered them; they travelled until they came to one of the most wild places existing on earth. Then Berthelai made them all dismount there and said that he would send a message to Cardueil. 'And I will conceive it in such words that it shall be given only to the king when he is alone, without any company. And you,' he said to the knights, 'arm yourselves, and seize him as soon as he encounters you.' They told him that he should have no fear of that, unless he failed to come. 'Certainly,' he replied, 'I know truly that he will come as soon as he hears the message which I shall send to him.'

Then he called a squire and told him to go in great haste to King Arthur's court. 'And tell him,' he continued, 'that in this forest there is the largest boar in the world, which is so fierce and frightening that no one dares to approach this area, for it has attacked and killed many men. Moreover, if this animal remains here much longer, everything will be destroyed by its ravages. For this reason, all those of this country send to him, begging him to deliver them from the beast, or they must leave the land. And I am certain,' he said, 'that Arthur will come as soon as he hears this news; and you shall lead him straight towards us. Tell him, when you are near, that the boar is hiding in this valley and that you will show him where it is. But tell him that if he wishes to see the animal it is necessary for him to come alone, since the boar will not stay if there are more than two men together.'

'Willingly, sire,' said the squire. He went to his horse, mounted, and spurred the mount until he reached Cardueil; he found the king, who had just heard Mass, greeted him and said, 'King Arthur, I come to you in great need to seek help in a matter in which you should not refuse me.' 'What is that?' asked the king. 'There is,' said the squire, 'a savage boar in this forest, the largest which has ever been seen. The land around where he dwells is so destroyed that no one dares live there. Therefore, the people of this region have sent me to you, begging you for God's sake that you will bring succour, since we have found the place where the boar hides. If you will come there with me, I will lead you to the place where we have left him lying.'

'Certainly,' said the king, 'I will go most willingly.' Then he called my lord Gawain, my lord Ywain, Kay the seneschal, Bedevere the constable, and as many others as he pleased, and told them that he wished to go into the woods and that they should accompany him, and they replied that this was a good idea. They immediately sat down to dinner, and when they had eaten, the king with his knights set off on their way. The squire went in front of them, leading them to the place where they expected to find the boar. They travelled until they came to a distance of less than three bows' lengths from those who were awaiting them in the forest. Then the squire said to the king:

'Sire, it is not much further to the place where the boar is, and you must know that it is the most marvellous beast that you might ever see with your eyes. If you wish to see the animal, it is essential that you should leave your companions, for it will not stay if many people are together.' The king replied that this might well be the case. Then he took his bow and arrows and went off with the squire, commanding his knights that none of them should leave the place where they were until they returned, which they agreed to. However, they would have been there for a very long time if they had waited for his return, for the squire led the king on until they reached the valley where Berthelai and his companions lay in ambush. When they saw the king and the squire coming, they were delighted, for they knew well that escape was impossible. Moreover, the king followed the squire everywhere, as one who was quite unaware of the situation until he was already among them and ensnared.

They leapt out at the king from all sides, and he was quickly seized before he realized what was happening; and when he did understand, he was very astonished and begged them, for God's sake, not to kill him. They said that he must give his word that he was a prisoner, which he gave; then they all mounted their horses and started on the way to their own country, having achieved what they had set out to do.

King Arthur's knights waited until it was almost night; they marvelled greatly as to what had become of the king and worried that he had been led into danger by his guide. Then they started out to look for King Arthur in the direction in which they had seen him leave and searched for him high and low. When they realized that they could not find him, they returned, very distressed, and that night there was great grief among the ladies and knights in King Arthur's hall. However, the damsel who had captured the king was not sad, but the happiest of all those who had ever known joy, for she believed that she had achieved so much that she would become crowned queen of Britain, since she had the king a captive.

In this way they rode on until they arrived at the abbey which the damsel had come from. It is not necessary to ask if the king was honoured there that night, for everyone did whatsoever they believed was good. When it was time to eat, they sat down, but the king ate very poorly, since he was too disturbed by what had happened to him. Between them, the damsel and Berthelai had concocted a poison which they gave the king to drink at the meal, and as soon as he had drunk it the anger which had heated his whole body became reduced, and he became as joyful as the happiest person present. Then the damsel was very happy and said to herself that she might win, and if she did all in her power she might ensnare the king in love. When they had eaten and it was time for bed, they led the king into a room where they had prepared his bed as richly as was suitable for such a man. Then the damsel, who was very beautiful, came before the king and said that in this bed they should lie together, and the king, who had fallen in love with her through the drink which she had given him, replied that this would greatly please him.

'Certainly, sire,' she said, 'if you are a noble man, it should please you greatly. And in your heart you should be very joyful, since God has brought us together, although for a long time you have lived in adultery. But, if it please God, soon she who parted us shall receive her just deserts, and if she shall not pay in this world, she shall pay in the next, if God gives judgement as the Holy Scripture promises us. For, if a man despises with his power the Holy Church established by God, he is an enemy to Jesus Christ and should lose all honour, while we shall have great joy.'

The king said that, if he could learn the truth, he would take such great vengeance that it would be remembered for ever. Then they went to bed together, and passed a very good time that night. Before it was day the damsel had so pleased the king that he loved her more than anyone else living. However, he did not yet wish to disclose his feelings, for it was too soon; thus he concealed his thoughts until the next day dawned, and then they arose and went to hear Mass. After Mass was sung, they returned to the damsel's room and sat together on the bed where they had made love during the night. The king gazed at the damsel happily, and the more he looked the better he felt, for she was very beautiful. Nevertheless, he thought always about those who had been in his company a long time, and who were so courteous and valiant, both my lord Gawain and the other knights of his household, whom he believed he would never see again, so that his heart was very grieved, and he was unable to show good cheer at any time. However, the damsel comforted him and said that he had no fear of being dishonoured or reduced: 'For, if it please God,' she said, 'you shall again be honourable in the sight of God and mankind, more than you ever were before.'

The king stayed there for fifteen days in this manner with the damsel, and was well served and honoured by one and all. Every day the damsel gave him to drink some more of the potion which she and Berthelai had made between them, so that before the fifteenth day had passed he loved her more than anything living, and said that, because of the great love which he had for her, truly he had married her, and that from now on he wished that she should be considered queen of Britain: 'For,' he said, 'the Crown has been dishonoured for a long time, since she who has worn it secured her position through murder and treason.'

'Certainly, sire,' said the damsel, 'you should know that well, since I have for a long time been in great sorrow since I knew truly that I was dispossessed from the highest worldly honour, and another was in my position, given the lordship to which she had no right. However, I have never found until this hour anyone who wished to do so much for God or for pity's sake that he made a complaint to you; for I knew very well that you were such a noble man that you would amend this willingly when you were aware of the truth.'

The king replied that he would not have been in such a vile state of sin for so long if he had known anything of what he now knew. 'But know well,' he said, 'that I did not believe that any lady in the world might be as worthy as she who has so shamed me in this land by her trickery and disloyalty towards my Creator, which has caused me great anguish of heart. For no lady,' he said, 'was ever of such great intelligence as she, or had such great courtesy, or was so sweet and debonair. Moreover, her generosity is known among all those who ever lived, and she was so full of good qualities that by her great virtue she won the hearts of rich and poor throughout the entire kingdom of Britain, so that they say she is the emerald of all ladies alive. But I believe,' he said, 'that she has done all these things to deceive me and others, so that no one should perceive her felony and disloyalty.' 'Sire,' said the damsel, 'it is always the way that those who practise evil are more deceitful than other people.'

'Truly,' said the king, 'that is so; but I marvel greatly that a disloyal heart could be so full of good virtues, as is hers. Nevertheless,' he continued, 'I will say no more, for the love which I have for her, although she has done me such great shame that I can never be happy while she has life in her body; for what I have lost in body and soul cannot be replaced.'

Thus the king spoke about the queen and praised her goodness in front of the woman who with all her power sought the queen's shame and disgrace. The king remained in this mood until the damsel realized that he truly loved her; then she was very light-hearted, and all those who held land from her were joyful. Then Berthelai came to the king, and spoke thus:

'Sire,' he said, 'there is great joy since it pleases Our Lord to place in your heart a desire to repent of your sin and leave the evil life which you have led. And if you are willing, my lady will send her knights throughout her land and make known the peace and love that exist between you and her, for they have waited too long to know the honour which has befallen her.'

The king replied that this greatly pleased him and that from henceforth he wished that she should be his lady and be honoured in all places where he had any power. Then Berthelai took leave of the king and his damsel and went to the highest noblemen in the kingdom of Camelide and told them how the king was reconciled with their lady, and he achieved so much that he led some of them with him to the place where the king and the damsel were. When the nobles saw Arthur, they showed great joy and were at pains to serve and honour him, because until that time they had not seen him in their land since he had married Queen Guenevere. They said that he should not have hidden himself thus, but he replied that he had been so busy that they would not blame him if they knew the great trouble which he had faced since he left Britain.

The nobility of Camelide were delighted with King Arthur, and he left the place where he had stayed and travelled through the land, riding with a great company of knights, and with him went the damsel, for he could not bear to be separated from her. All the ladies of the country came to meet her, and all truly believed that she was their lady, since King Arthur himself was reconciled with her. She was well received in all the fine towns that she visited, and those who wished to honour her gave her many expensive gifts.

When the king had been in many places around the kingdom, he then returned to stay in the place where the damsel had first taken him, for the house was very comfortable and delightful. He told the knights who were with him that he wished to send in search of his nephew, my lord Gawain, and the other companions of his retinue: 'For I fully realize,' he said, 'that they will be very concerned if they believe that I have perished.' Then he called Berthelai and demanded that he should send word to his own land; the old knight sent Arthur a squire, whom the king charged with his message, having written certain signs by which his message would be believed. When the king had given him his message, the squire departed on his way, whilst the king remained in great joy and delight with the ladies and knights.

However, the queen whom he had left in Britain had no reason to be joyful, but showed such great sorrow every day that it was marvellous that she could so endure. Moreover, all the knights of the king's household were very disconsolate and declared that they would never be happy until they heard news of him; they searched for him in many places and frequently returned to court to know if the queen had heard any news yet.

Now the squire who had left the king travelled on his way until he came to Bretaigne, and asked for news of the queen, who was in Camelot, where she had travelled to spend Christmas, which was approaching. She wished to keep the promises made by Arthur to the knights from foreign lands, since he ought to hold his court, and he had commanded that they attend him from all his territories. The queen said that she would always honour men of worth with all her power and hold court on behalf of her lord, for whom her heart was very heavy, and to preserve the honour of Britain, for she would have great sorrow if she saw it fall into decay in her lifetime.

When the squire who was bringing news from the king knew that the queen was in the town, he travelled there as quickly as he could, and there with the queen he found my lord Gawain, who had only that day returned from his quest, also Kay the seneschal, and several other knights. When Gawain saw the squire coming, he told the queen that soon they would have news. The squire came before them, and did not greet the queen, whom he stared at most insolently, but spoke to my lord Gawain: 'Sire, at the command of the king your uncle, I greet you.' As soon as the squire had said this, Gawain leapt up and embraced him, and then enquired where his uncle was.

'Truly,' he replied, 'he is in Camelide with my lady the queen, and commands you, by the faith which you owe him as his liegeman and his nephew, that you should go to him and bring with you all the nobles of the kingdom of Logres, for he intends to wear his crown and hold a most formal court in the land of my lady this Christmas. He wishes that my lady shall be anointed and sanctified before all his nobles, and receive the honour of the crown of Britain.'

'What?' asked my lord Gawain. 'Is this the damsel who recently sent here the old knight to my lord the king to ask him that he should accept her?' 'Sire,' he said, 'it is indeed her, and undeniably she has both sought and obtained, through the will of God, and the king is reconciled with her and knows truly that she is the lady he married and through whom he should hold the Round Table and the whole land which belonged to King Leodegan. And you must bring with you,' continued the servant, 'as your uncle demands, this lady here, who has sought and gained so much by evil. And she will receive her just deserts for her treason against my lady, by which she has enjoyed such high honour until now.'

When my lord Gawain saw the signs which the king had sent, and knew him to be safe and well, it was not necessary to ask if he was joyful, for he had never been so happy about anything before, and all the others felt the greatest joy possible. However, the queen's grief was doubled, since she was very frightened that for a single sin which she had committed in the past, Our Lord wished that she might be shamed and dishonoured on earth. She showed such great grief that no one was able to comfort or quieten her. The squire took his leave of my lord Gawain, saying that he wished to go, but Gawain said that he should not yet depart. 'But,' he continued, 'stay with me until the nobility of this country have arrived here, and then you shall lead us all together to the place where my lord the king is staying.'

'Sire,' he replied, 'I will stay as long as you please, for I know very well that I shall not be blamed for anything which I do for you.' Thus the messenger remained with my lord Gawain, who sent to all the barons of the kingdom, commanding them all to come to him as quickly as they could, and that he had certain news of the king. Then many people were overjoyed, who had been very sorrowful.

The queen, who was very grieved in her heart, thought that she would send in search of Galehot and Lancelot, for she knew well that they could relieve her in her trouble, as no one else might give her advice. Then she took aside one of her damsels and sent her to them, begging her to hurry; the girl went as quickly as she could, and travelled for several days until she arrived at the place where Galehot and Lancelot were, and she gave them her message face to face.

'And you should be aware,' she said, 'that if you wait until Christmas to come, you will never see my lady. Thus I beg and request that you will help her in this need, if ever she did anything to please you, for there is now great necessity that all should give their service. And as to you, sir knight,' she said to Lancelot, 'you above all men should devote great labour and exertion to protect the honour of my lady the queen, for if she is dishonoured before you, unless you should defend her, then you would rightly lose all honour.'

'Truly,' he replied, 'she shall never be dishonoured whilst I live, for I would gladly lose my life if I could arrive at the place of justice where she might be defended by the body of a single knight. Never will I spend a second night anywhere until I reach the place where she is.'

'Sir,' said the damsel, 'she has great faith in you, for although all the world might fail her, she knows well that you will face death to help her.' 'May God help me,' he replied, 'that I will do; and I should do well, for I shall never have joy unless through her.'

Galehot and Lancelot were both very grieved by this news and strongly felt that they should wait to know the truth more fully when they were with the queen. They set off the next morning as soon as they saw day approach and travelled continuously until they arrived at Camelot. When the queen saw them, she became more at ease than before, whilst my lord Gawain and all the other knights were very pleased. The queen led them into her chamber, since she wished to reveal her trouble to them, and told them first how the damsel had sent Berthelai to court and how he had left, and by what snare the king had been captured.

'Now,' she said, 'he loves the damsel, and has ordered my lord Gawain, his nephew, and all the nobles of his kingdom to go to meet him, for he wishes to hold court this Christmas in Camelide and crown the damsel who has thus deceived him by her trickery. Also, he has commanded that I be seized and taken to this great feast to be destroyed before all the people by the judgement of the traitors who have achieved this infamy. Therefore,' she concluded, 'I have sent for you, and beg that you will advise me what to do, for I am very frightened.'

'Lady,' said Galehot, 'do not dismay yourself, but control your behaviour, for otherwise it will seem that you might be guilty of the disloyalty of which you are accused. But I will tell you,' he continued, 'what you must do. You will go there with my lord Gawain, your nephew, and the other gallant men who love you greatly and who will suffer deeply if you should come to harm. Lancelot and myself will also go there with you, and know that I will bring with me all my forces. And if they decide that there should be a trial by battle, he is prepared to fight for you; if they decide to put you to death by some other means, we will have there sufficient men to rescue you easily, snatching you away by force, and they will not dare to oppose this. And then,' Galehot ended, 'I shall lead you into my country and give to you and Lancelot, my companion, the kingdom of Sorelois, which is sufficiently rich and beautiful; he shall be king and you queen, and you shall lead a happy life together, as people who dearly love each other.'

'Sir,' she said, 'many thanks for your promise; nor will I refuse it, for, after Lancelot, you are the man on this earth in whom I have the greatest faith that you will save my honour and my life.' 'Lady,' replied Galehot, 'you know that I will protect you with all my power and will be on your side against all men, even though I should have to commit a misdemeanour against King Arthur, who is my overlord.'

The Grail Quest (La Queste del Saint Graal) (c. 1210–25)

The story opens at the feast of Pentecost. The Round Table knights are assembled at Camelot when a beautiful damsel hastens into the king's hall and asks if Lancelot is present. When she leads Lancelot off into the forest, Arthur and his knights are very curious, but they do not follow. The damsel takes Lancelot to a convent, where he finds his cousins Bors and Lionel. Then three nuns bring in Galahad – the child of Lancelot and the daughter of the Fisher King – destined to be the perfect knight who will achieve the Grail. When Lancelot and his cousins return to court, they look at the seats of the Round Table on each of which is written the name of the person who sits there. When they come to the Perilous Seat, they find that there are new letters engraved on it, stating that at the following Pentecost the seat will be filled.

The king decided it was time to dine and ordered the cloths to be spread.

'Sire,' objected Kay the steward, 'in my opinion, if you sit down so soon to dinner you will infringe the custom of the court. On high feast-days we have never seen you seat yourself at table before some adventure has befallen the court in the presence of all the barons of your household.'

'Kay,' said the king, 'you speak the truth. I have always observed this custom and I will do so as long as I may, but in my great joy at seeing Lancelot and his cousins safe returned I had quite forgotten the practice.'

'You stand reminded,' retorted Kay.

Even as they talked a page came in and said to the king:

'Sire, I bring you news of a great wonder.'

'What is it? Tell me quickly.'

'Below your palace, Sire, I saw a great stone floating on the water. Come and look for yourself for I know it signifies some strange adventure.'

The king and his barons went down at once to see this marvel. When they came to the river bank, they found the great stone lying now by the water's edge. Held fast in its red marble was a sword, superb in its beauty, with a pommel carved from a precious stone cunningly inlaid with letters of gold. The barons examined the inscription which read: NONE SHALL TAKE ME HENCE BUT HE AT WHOSE SIDE I AM TO HANG. AND HE SHALL BE THE BEST KNIGHT IN THE WORLD. When the king saw the lettering he turned to Lancelot and said:

'Good, sir, this sword is yours by right, for I know you without a doubt for the best knight in the world.'

But Lancelot answered abruptly:

'Indeed, sire, this sword is not meant for me, neither have I the courage nor the audacity to lay hand on it, for I am in no way worthy or fit to wear it. Wherefore I will refrain from putting my hand to it: such presumption would be folly.'

'Nonetheless,' said the king, 'try whether you can withdraw it.'

'Sire, I will not. For I know full well that none shall fail in the attempt but he receive some wound.'

'How came you by such knowledge?'

'Sire, suffice it that I know. And I will tell you more: I would have you know that this day shall see the beginning of the great adventures and the marvels of the Holy Grail.'

When the king saw that Lancelot would not be prevailed upon, he addressed himself to Sir Gawain:

'Good nephew, you try your hand.'

'No, sire,' said he, 'saving your grace, since my lord Lancelot will not attempt it, neither will I. Nothing would be gained by my laying hand to it, for you are well aware that he is a far better knight than I.'

'You shall try all the same,' he insisted, 'not to win the sword, but because I ask it.'

Sir Gawain thrust out his hand and grasped the sword by the hilt, but tug as he would, he could not move it.

'Leave it be, good nephew,' interposed the king, 'you have done my bidding loyally.'

'My lord Gawain,' said Lancelot, 'know that you will see the day when you would not have touched this sword for a castle, for it will cut you to the quick.'

'Sir,' said Gawain, 'what is done, is done; were I to die of it here and now, I was only obeying my lord's command.'

When the king heard these words he repented his part in what Sir Gawain had done.

King Arthur then bade Perceval try his fortune. Perceval agreed readily in order to keep Sir Gawain company. He took hold of the sword by the hilt and strained but could not shift it. The assembled knights were certain now that Lancelot spoke the truth and that the writing on the hilt was no fable, and there was none so bold that he dared touch the sword. Thereupon Sir Kay said to the king:

'Sire, sire, upon my oath, you may surely sit down to dine at your pleasure, for I hardly think you have wanted for an adventure.'

'Then let us go in,' said the king, 'for the hour indeed is late.'

The knights returned to the palace leaving the stone on the river bank. The king had the trumpets sounded for water to be brought, and took his seat at his high table while the companions of the Round Table went each one to his place. That day saw four crowned kings serving at table, together with such a company of noblemen of rank that one might well have marvelled at the sight. When all were seated it was found that the fellowship of the Round Table was complete and every seat filled, excepting the one that was known as the Seat of Danger.

The first dish had just been served when a most extraordinary thing occurred: for all the doors and windows of the palace where the companions sat at meat closed of themselves without anyone setting hand to them; and yet the hall was not a whit the darker. This spectacle dumbfounded both the simple and the sage. King Arthur, who was the first to speak, exclaimed:

'In God's name, gracious lords, we have witnessed wonderful events this day, both here and at the river's bank, yet I think that before nightfall we shall see stranger still.'

As the king was speaking there appeared in the hall a man robed in white, of venerable age and bearing, yet not a knight there knew the manner of his entry. He came on foot leading by the hand a knight in red armour who carried neither shield nor sword, and as soon as he stood within the palace he said:

'Peace be with you.'

Then turning towards the king, he addressed him, saying:

'King Arthur, I bring you the Desired Knight, he who stems from the noble house of King David and the lineage of Joseph of Arimathea, and through whom the enchantments lying on this and other lands are to be loosed. Behold him here.'

This news rejoiced the king exceedingly and he answered the good man:

'Sir, if your words are true we wish you welcome here, and welcome too to the knight! If he be indeed the one for whom we have waited to bring to a close the adventures of the Holy Grail, no man has ever met with greater joy than he shall have of us. And whether he be the one whom you announce or another I wish him well, since on your testimony he is of most noble birth and ancestry.'

'Upon my faith,' said the old man, 'you shall see presently your hopes take fair departure.'

With that he had the knight unarm till he stood in a tunic of red sendal; then he handed him a red mantle to wear on his shoulder, woven of samite and lined with whitest ermine.

When the youth stood robed and ready the old man bade him follow and led him straight to the Seat of Danger, alongside Lancelot. He raised a corner of the silken cloth that Bors and Lionel had placed there and uncovered an inscription reading: THIS SEAT IS GALAHAD'S. The good man studied the letters, finding them, as he thought, fresh-traced, and he was familiar with the name they spelled. Then he said to the youth in a voice so clear that the assembled company heard each word:

'Sir Knight, be seated, for this place is yours.'

The knight sat down with impunity and said in turn:

'Sir, you may return now for you have carried out your orders faithfully. Greet all at the blessed castle on my behalf, especially my uncle, King Pellés, and my grandsire, the Rich Fisher King, and tell them from me that I will visit them as soon as I have the means and the occasion.'

The Death of Arthur (Mort Artu) (c. 1225)

This French prose text, as part of The Vulgate Cycle, *incorporates the figure of Lancelot into Geoffrey of Monmouth's basic account of Arthur's death. In fact, whereas Geoffrey's version is only a few pages long, this is a romance of several hundred pages, containing much more than just the final battle against Mordred. In the following extract, Arthur's sister, Morgan the sorceress, decides to inform him about Lancelot's adultery with Queen Guenevere.*

Morgan thought a great deal about King Arthur, because she intended him to know the whole truth about Lancelot and the queen, and yet she feared that if she told him everything and Lancelot heard that the king had found out from her, nothing in the world could guarantee that he would not kill her. That night she pondered over the question, whether to tell him or to remain silent; because if she told him she would be in danger of death should Lancelot find out, and if she kept the affair secret, she would never again have such a good opportunity of telling him as now. She kept thinking about this until she fell asleep.

In the morning, as soon as it was light, she arose and went to the king, greeted him very courteously, and said:

'My lord, I beg you for a reward for all the services I have rendered you.'

'I shall grant you it,' said the king, 'if it is something in my power to give.'

'You can certainly give it to me,' she said, 'and do you know what it is? It is that you stay here today and tomorrow. You can be sure that if you were in the finest city you possess, you would not be better served or more at ease than here, because there is no wish you could express that would not be satisfied.'

And he said he would stay, because he had promised her her reward.

'My lord,' she said, 'of all the houses in the world, you are in the one where people were most longing to see you; I can tell you that there is no woman anywhere who loves you more than I do, and so I should, unless human love did not exist.'

'My lady,' said the king, 'who are you that you love me so much, as you say?'

'My lord,' she said, 'I am the person closest to you in blood. My name is Morgan, and I am your sister. You ought to know me better than you do.'

He looked at her and recognized her, and jumped up from the bed as joyful as it was possible to be. He told her that he was very happy about the adventure that God had granted him.

'You see, my sister,' said the king, 'I thought you were dead and had left this world; and since it has pleased God that I should find you alive and well, I shall take you back to Camelot when I leave here, and from now on you will live at court and will be a companion for my wife Queen Guinevere. I know she will be very happy and joyful when she hears the news about you.'

'Brother,' she said, 'do not ask that of me, because I swear to you that I shall never go to court, for when I leave here I shall most certainly go to the Isle of Avalon, which is the dwelling-place of the ladies who know all the magic in the world.'

The king dressed and sat down on his bed. Then he asked his sister to sit beside him, and he began to ask her how she was. She told him a part, and kept a part secret from him. They remained talking there until Prime.

That day the weather was very fine; the sun had risen splendid and brilliant and its light penetrated all parts of the room, so that it was even brighter than before. They were alone, because they took pleasure in talking together, just the two of them. When they had asked each other many questions about their past lives, it happened that the king began looking around him and saw the pictures which Lancelot had painted long before, when he was a prisoner there. King Arthur knew his letters well enough to be able to make out the meaning of a text, and when he had seen the inscriptions with the pictures that explained their meaning, he began to read them. So he found out that the room was illustrated with all Lancelot's deeds of chivalry since he had been made a knight. Everything that Arthur saw he remembered from the news that had constantly been brought to court about Lancelot's chivalry, as soon as he had accomplished each of his acts of prowess.

Thus the king began to read of Lancelot's deeds in the paintings he saw; and when he examined the paintings which related the meeting arranged by Galeholt, he was completely astounded and taken aback. He looked again and said under his breath:

'In faith, if these inscriptions tell the truth, then Lancelot has dishonoured me through the queen, because I can see quite clearly that he has had an association with her. If it is as the writing says, it will be the cause of the greatest grief that I have suffered, since Lancelot could not possibly degrade me more than by dishonouring my wife.'

Then he said to Morgan:

'My sister, I beg you to tell me the truth about what I am going to ask you.'

She replied that she would be pleased to, if she could.

'Swear that you will,' said the king.

And she swore it.

'Now I am going to ask you,' he said, 'by the faith you owe me and have just pledged me, to tell me who painted these pictures, if you know the truth, and not to refuse for any reason.'

'Ah, my lord,' said Morgan, 'what are you saying and what are you asking me? Certainly, if I told you the truth and the man who did the paintings found out, no one except God could guarantee that he would not kill me.'

'In God's name,' he said, 'you must tell me, and I promise you as a king that I shall never blame you for it.'

'My lord,' she replied, 'will you not spare me from telling you for any reason?'

'Certainly not,' said the king. 'You must tell me.'

'In that case I shall tell you without lying about anything,' replied Morgan. 'It is true, though I do not know whether you know it yet, that Lancelot has loved Queen Guinevere since the first day that he received the order of chivalry, and it was for love of the queen that he performed all his acts of prowess when he was a new knight. You could have known this at the castle of the Douloureuse Garde when you first went there and could not enter because you were stopped at the river; each time you sent a knight he was unable to go inside. But as soon as Kay went, since he was one of the queen's knights, he was allowed in, and you did not notice this fact as well as some people did.'

'It is true,' said the king, 'that I did not notice it, but all the same it did happen exactly as you say. However, I do not know whether it was for love of the queen or of me.'

'My lord,' she replied, 'there is more to come.'

'Tell me,' said the king.

'My lord,' she said, 'he loved my lady the queen as much as any mortal man can ever love a lady; but he never revealed the fact himself or through anyone else. His love spurred him on to perform all the deeds of chivalry you see depicted here.

'For a long time he only languished, just like anyone who loves and is not loved in return, because he did not dare to reveal his love. Eventually he met Galeholt, the son of the Giantess, the day he bore black arms and won the tournament organized by the two of you, as you can see related in these pictures here. When he had made peace between you and Galeholt in such a way that all honour fell to you, and when Galeholt saw that Lancelot's strength was declining daily because he could not eat or drink, so deeply did he love the queen, he kept pressing him until in the end he admitted that he loved the queen and was dying for her. Galeholt begged him not to despair, because he would arrange matters so that Lancelot could have what he desired from the queen. And he did just as he promised; he implored the queen until she gave in to Lancelot, and, with a kiss, granted him her love.'

'You have told me enough,' said the king, 'because I can clearly see my shame and Lancelot's treachery; but tell me now who painted these pictures.'

'Indeed, my lord,' she replied, 'Lancelot did them, and I shall tell you when. Do you remember two tournaments held at Camelot, when the companions of the Round Table said they would not go to a joust where Lancelot was on their side, because he always carried off the prize? And when Lancelot knew, he turned against them, making them leave the field and forcing them to retreat into the city of Camelot. Do you remember that?'

'Yes,' replied the king. 'I can still see that tournament in my mind, because never in any place that I have been to have I seen a knight carry out so many feats of arms as he did that day. But why do you speak about that?'

'Because', she replied, 'when he left court on that occasion he was lost for more than a year and a half, and no one knew where he was.'

'Yes,' said the king, 'that is true.'

'In fact,' she said, 'I held him prisoner for two winters and a summer, and during that time he painted the pictures you can see here. I should still be keeping him in prison, and he would never have escaped all the days of his life, if it had not been for what he did, the greatest sorcery that a man ever carried out.'

'What was that?' asked the king.

'In faith,' she replied, 'he broke the bars of that window with his bare hands.'

And she showed him the bars, which she had had repaired since. The king said that it was not the work of a man, but of a devil.

He looked carefully at the paintings in the room, and he thought deeply about them. For a long time he did not say a word. After he had thought for some time, he said:

'Agravain told me about this the other day, but I did not believe him, as I thought he was lying. However, what I have seen here makes me far more certain than I was before. For that reason I can tell you that I shall never be satisfied until I know the whole truth. If it is as these pictures witness, that Lancelot has brought me such great shame as to dishonour me through my wife, I shall never rest until they are caught together. Then, if I do not inflict such justice on them as will be spoken of for evermore, I promise that I shall never again wear a crown.'

'Indeed,' said Morgan, 'if you did not punish them, God and the whole world should certainly hold you in shame, because no true king or true man can tolerate being dishonoured in this way.'

The king and his sister spoke a great deal about the matter that morning and Morgan kept urging him to avenge his shame without delay; and he promised her as a king that he would do it with such vigour that it would always be remembered, if he should manage to catch them together.

'It will not be long', said Morgan, 'before they are caught together, if you go about it carefully.'

'I shall make sure', said the king, 'that ı. one loves the other adulterously as you say, I shall have them caugh together before the end of the month, if Lancelot should return to coṵrt by then.'

That day the king remained with his sister, and the next day and the whole week; she hated Lancelot more than any other man because she knew the queen loved him. All the time the king was with her she never stopped urging him to avenge his shame when he returned to Camelot, if he had the opportunity.

'My sister,' said the king, 'you do not need to ask me, because not for half my kingdom would I fail to do what I have resolved.'

The king stayed there the whole week, since the place was beautiful and pleasant, and full of game which he spent all his energy hunting. But now the story stops telling of him and Morgan, except to say that he did not allow anyone to enter his room while he was there, save only Morgan, because of the paintings which made his shame so evident, and he did not want anyone else apart from himself to know the truth, because he feared the dishonour too much, and feared also that the news would spread.

The following extract covers the well-known episode in which Arthur's sword, Excalibur, is thrown back into the lake and the mortally wounded king is carried away in a ship by his sister Morgan.

King Arthur spent the whole night in prayer. The next day it happened that Lucan the Butler was behind him, watching him and noticing that he did not move. Then he said in tears:

'Ah! King Arthur, how great is your grief!'

When the king heard him say this, he stood up with difficulty because of the weight of his arms; he took Lucan, who was unarmed, and embraced him, holding him so tightly that he burst his heart inside him. Lucan was unable to say a word before his soul left his body. When the king had been in that position for some time, he released his hold, because he did not realize he was dead. Girflet looked at Lucan for a long time and, seeing that he did not move, he knew that he was dead and that the king had killed him. Then he began grieving once again and said:

'Ah! my lord, what a bad thing you have done in killing Lucan!'

When the king heard this, he gave a start, looked round him and saw his butler lying dead on the ground. Then his grief became even greater and he replied to Girflet, obviously in great anger:

'Girflet, Fortune, who has been my mother until now, but has become my step-mother, is making me devote the remainder of my life to grief and anger and sadness.'

Then he told Girflet to put the reins and saddles on their horses. This he did. The king mounted and rode towards the sea until he arrived there at noon. He dismounted on the shore, ungirded the sword he was wearing, and drew it from its scabbard. After he had looked at it for some time, he said:

'Ah! Excalibur, you fine rich sword, the best in the world except the one with the Strange Belt, now you will lose your master. Where will you find a man who will put you to such great use as I have, unless you come into Lancelot's hands? Ah! Lancelot, the noblest man in the world and the finest knight, would to Jesus Christ that you could hold it and that I would know! My soul would certainly be at greater ease evermore.'

Then the king called Girflet and said:

'Go up that hill, where you will find a lake, and throw my sword into it, because I do not want it to remain in this kingdom, in case our wicked successors gain possession of it.'

'My lord,' he said, 'I shall carry out your commandment, but I would rather, if you please, that you gave it to me.'

'I shall not,' replied the king, 'because it would not be put to good use in you.'

So Girflet climbed the hill, and when he came to the lake, he drew the sword from the scabbard and began to look at it. It seemed so fine and beautiful that he thought it would be a great pity to throw it into the lake as the king had commanded, because it would be lost. It would be better for him to throw in his own and tell the king he had thrown it. So he ungirded his sword and threw it into the lake, and laid the other one in the grass. Then he went back to the king and said:

'My lord, I have carried out your commandment and thrown your sword into the lake.'

'And what did you see?' asked the king.

'Nothing, my lord,' he replied, 'except good.'

'Ah!' said the king, 'you are trying me. Go back and throw it in, because you have not done it yet.'

So he returned to the lake and drew the sword from its scabbard; he began to have great regrets about it and said that it would be a great shame if it were lost in that way. Then he thought he would throw in the scabbard and keep the sword, because he or someone else might have need for it. He took the scabbard therefore, and straight away threw it into the lake. He then took the sword, put it down under a tree, and went back to the king, saying:

'My lord, now I have carried out your commandment.'

'And what did you see?' asked the king.

'My lord, I saw nothing that I should not have seen.'

'Ah!' said the king, 'you have not thrown it in yet. Why are you annoying me so? Go and throw it in, and you will see what happens, because it will not be lost without a great marvel.'

When Girflet saw that he had to do it, he went back to where the sword was. He picked it up and began to gaze at it and to have regrets about it, saying:

'You splendid and beautiful sword, what a great pity it is for you that you will not fall into the hands of some noble man!'

Then he hurled it into the lake as deep and as far from him as he could, and as it fell near the water, he saw a hand come out of the lake which revealed itself up to the elbow, but he saw nothing of the body to which it belonged. The hand seized the sword by the hilt and brandished it in the air three or four times.

When Girflet had clearly seen this, the hand disappeared back into the water together with the sword. He waited there for some time to see if it would show itself again, but when he saw he was wasting his time he left the lake and returned to the king. He said he had thrown the sword into the lake, and told him what he had seen.

'By God,' said the king, 'I thought indeed that my end was very near.'

Then he began to think, and as he thought the tears came to his eyes. After he had been deep in thought for some time, he said to Girflet:

'You must go from here and leave me; from now on you will never see me again as long as you live.'

'If that is the case,' said Girflet, 'I shall not leave you for anything.'

'You will,' said the king, 'or else I shall hate you mortally.'

'My lord,' said Girflet, 'how could I possibly leave you here alone and go away, especially when you tell me I shall never see you again?'

'You must do what I say,' said the king. 'Go quickly, because you must not delay. I am asking you to go, by the love there has been between us.'

Hearing that the king was asking him to go so tenderly, Girflet replied:

'My lord, I shall do what you command, as sadly as can be; but please tell me if you think I shall ever see you again.'

'No,' said the king, 'you can be sure of that.'

'Where do you expect to go, my dear lord?'

'I cannot tell you,' said the king.

When Girflet saw that he would learn no more, he mounted and left the king, and as soon as he had left him, very heavy rain began to fall, and continued until he reached a hill a good half-league away from the king. When he had reached the hill, he waited under a tree for the rain to stop. He looked back to where he had left the king, and saw a ship entirely occupied by women coming across the sea. When the ship had come to the shore opposite where Arthur was, they came to the side, and their lady, who was holding King Arthur's sister Morgan by the hand, called to Arthur to come aboard. As soon as Arthur saw his sister Morgan, he arose from the ground where he was sitting, and went aboard ship, taking his horse and his arms with him.

The Book of Arthur (Livre d'Artus) (c. 1250–75)

While included in H. O. Sommer's edition of The Vulgate Cycle, *this lengthy prose romance, which survives in a single manuscript, does not quite seem to form part of the* Cycle. *Despite the title, the principal hero of this romance is Gawain. Nevertheless, the exploits of various other Arthurian heroes are celebrated, and much time is devoted to recounting Arthur's adventures as a knight-errant.*

Setting off from London, Arthur goes hunting with Gawain and Sagremors. When a storm disrupts their sport, they separate at a crossroads in search of adventure. After relating the individual adventures of Gawain and Sagremor, the story returns to Arthur.

The story tells how after leaving Sagremor and his nephew Gawain, for a long time King Arthur was so tormented by the wind and rain that he continued on incessantly until nightfall, when he arrived at a hermitage, very disappointed that he had encountered no adventure worth recounting. When he reached the hermitage, it was already late at night; the hermit did the best he could to wipe the king dry, because he was very wet, and battered by the foul weather. He offered Arthur such welcome as he could provide and, since the hermit gave the guest his own bed, he was comfortable and slept easily, as one who had been greatly tormented all day by the wind.

A little after midnight, when it drew towards day, the moon began to shine clear and bright and the weather became mild after the storm; then the king began to sleep more fitfully and wake often. Once, as he was waking up, a damsel riding a mule passed close by the hermitage and she was lamenting very grievously, speaking so loudly that the king clearly heard her say, 'Ah, my beautiful sister, countess of Orofoise, I have brought you death and shame although, when I left you, I promised to bring you such a knight from King Arthur's court that you should be delivered by him from the tyrant who has destroyed and wasted your land. Woe is me! I do not know where else I may go, since I have failed to obtain help in the place where all men and women without counsel shall have advice, and all those who need assistance shall be aided and comforted. I shall be a feeble captive, distressed, as also will you, who have been so honoured in your lifetime. What can I do, or how can I avoid the truth, when I cannot bring help to the lady who needs it.' Then the damsel dismounted from her mule and sat beneath a tree, grieving as no lady or damsel had ever done before, weeping and sobbing with regret.

While she remained there lamenting, four debauched highway robbers passed by, mounted on strong, swift horses and well armed, as such men usually are. As soon as they heard the damsel, they galloped towards her and found her to be quite alone. Then their leader spoke thus: 'It's a good thing we came to this prize first; I wish to take this mule, which is very fine.' The other three said, 'We will remove the girl's clothes and do with her as we please.' 'By God,' said the leader, 'I will have my way with her first, before any of you.' They replied that it was fine by them, and all four moved towards her.

When the damsel saw them, she leapt up in fright and cried out, 'Leave my mule, good sirs, since she is mine.' Three of them moved nearer, and took hold of her in several places, declaring that she would never be released until she had given them her robe. When she heard this, she was so distraught that she fell to the ground, trembling with fear like a leaf on a tree. The villains seized her and tore off her clothes, down to her chemise, and then the chief robber grabbed her and said that he would have his way with her. The girl defended herself and cried out in a loud voice, 'Blessed Mary, help me, Lady; help me, most high and glorious queen!' Although she cried as loud as she could, the man did not release her, but attacked her more and more. Yet she defended herself so well that he could not have his way with her, and he became so angry that he took hold of her beautiful hair and dragged her about, beating her as hard as he could, while she cried out, 'Vile and disloyal traitor, you may beat me and kill me, but my body will never be yours; nor, whilst I live, shall you violate me.'

When the traitor saw that he could do no more, he took thorny branches and began to beat the girl so badly that all her flesh was bleeding. She wept and cried in great anguish, with loud high shrieks, so that King Arthur, who was in bed, heard the torment which she suffered, and realized that she was being brutally attacked. He was so overcome with pity that, almost unaware of what was happening, he angrily leapt from his bed, dressing and fastening his spurs in a very great hurry. The hermit came and, finding him already risen, said, 'Sir, did you hear that wretched lady whom some wicked man is mistreating?' 'Indeed,' said the king, 'fetch me my arms and my horse, for I believe that he will kill her before I can reach her.' The hermit fetched King Arthur's armour and then ran quickly to saddle and bring his horse. The king, who had armed himself, took his sword, hung his shield around his neck, quickly mounted his horse and took his lance in hand. Departing by the gate which the hermit opened, he spurred towards the place where the damsel cried and screamed as the wicked man abused her.

The king travelled very energetically and arrived to find the robber grasping the damsel with one hand by her hair. As soon as the lady saw the armed knight, she began to call out, 'Ah! Noble knight, aid an unhappy wretch whom this evil-doer is going to kill. For God's sake remember that without you there is no pity, compassion or generosity.' Then the king hastened as fast as he possibly could, shouting, 'Villain, release the damsel, for, if you kill her and if you do not free her, you are dead.' And when the bully heard the knight call out to him, he let go of the damsel as he beheld the king rushing towards him to do battle.

When the robber saw the knight thus advancing he called to his companions, who leapt up and ran to aid him, but the king acted so quickly that he had already thrust their leader through the body with his lance before they reached him; then he rushed at the other three, and in a short while had killed them all. He made a rope from pliant branches which he tied to each of their bodies, and he hung all four of them from a great oak, declaring that such justice should be dealt to robbers and murderers. Then he went to the damsel, who was weeping bitterly, returned her dress, and waited while she dressed herself as she had been before, although she was so sorely beaten that she could scarcely stand unaided. The king then took the mule by the reins and led it with them; he took the four horses which had belonged to the robbers and gave them to the hermit, bidding him to sell them and use the money to repair his dwelling; the good man thanked the king most humbly.

Afterwards the king returned to the damsel and asked where she was going at such an hour; she replied that she was returning from Logres, where at Arthur's court she had sought help for her sister, whom a giant had dispossessed, destroying all her land. 'And I do not know which way to turn, for I was unable to find either the king or any of his companions, who had set off in search of the king, since he is lost and there is no news of him, my lord Gawain his nephew, or Sagremor the Desree, who were all lost in a single day. All the other royal companions have left to search for them, and the court is so deserted that I could not find a single person; thus I return grieved and dispirited, as one who has totally failed. Since it was such terrible weather yesterday I was unable to travel and, although I waited to hear if there was any news, I left court as soon as the weather improved. The queen begged me to stay long enough to know if the king would return, but I had promised my sister that whatever happened at court I would not delay there; now I know that we are both deprived of our inheritance and dead.'

The king enquired who her sister was, to which she answered, 'The countess of Orofoise.' Then the king asked why this giant was making war on her. 'Sire,' said the damsel, 'there is a castle four miles from Orofoise where this robber, who is of the lineage of Hanguis, dwells; however, he has such a small amount of land that he could not survive without robbing his closest neighbours. Since we have very fine lands, he is so envious of my sister that he secretly ensnared my sister's husband, seizing him in this forest and killing him. Then he commanded my sister that she should place herself at his mercy and present him with her land by such a contract that he might hold her in his castle as his lady. My sister conveyed to him that she would rather be dead; nor, if it please God, should he ever possess her. When the robber heard this, he attacked her land very violently and ravaged it, since he is such a cruel and fierce man that no one can withstand his great strength. He has so destroyed the land that all the peasants have fled, until not a single one is left; whilst the knights of the land who remain do not dare oppose him.

'When my sister realized that she could not resist him, she promised that if he fought and defeated all the knights that she sent against him for a year, she would agree to all he asked; if, however, he was defeated, he would place himself at her mercy. He sent word that he could not ask for better terms, and until now he has defeated all those who have come against him; he is so huge and strong that he overturned them all with one of his arms, whilst he is so well armed that any blow given against him is powerless; and there are only eight days left of the year which my sister agreed with him, so you may well understand that we have lost all our land.'

'Damsel,' asked the king, 'where is Orofoise?' 'Sire,' said the damsel, 'it is near Sorelois, on the boundary of the kingdom of North Wales.' 'I wish to go there,' said the king, 'for I have much to do there if you will lead me thither; grant me but one request, and I will spend one night in your castle and wait until midday to fight against this giant of whom you so loudly complain.' 'Ah, sir!' said the damsel, 'many thanks. I swear that it will be evil for him if you will fight for us against him, for you have already done me so much good that, whatever you may ask for from either myself or my sister, you shall not be refused, and I promise to give you it whenever you please to ask.' 'Then you have given your promise,' said the king, 'that while I am in your company or that of your sister, no one, either you or any man or woman in your service, shall ask my name until after I have fought the battle with the giant.' She agreed to this, since she had no other choice.

Now the damsel mounted her mule, and the king took leave of the hermit, each commending the other to God's care; then Arthur and the damsel set off on their way, journeying for several days without meeting any adventure, until they reached level country in front of a castle called Levezerp, which belonged to Duke Escaut of Cambenic. As soon as the king and damsel entered the plain, Arthur beheld a great tournament, which was attended by at least a thousand men, for the duke had knighted his son and the people of that land and the surrounding country were celebrating, whilst the duke himself was there since he wished to lead all his followers in a battle to be fought on the hill of Malohaut against King Sorionde (of whom the story has told you).

As soon as King Arthur had entered the tourneying ground, he bade the damsel ride ahead; she obeyed his command, since she dared not refuse, and rode in front of him, while he remained a little distance behind her, so that all the people of that place could see him; but not a soul knew his identity. Then a knight detached himself from the ranks of those present and called out to the king, 'Turn back, sir knight, for you must joust with me, since this is the rule of this castle.' The king turned as soon as he heard, and spurred his horse against the man who had made the challenge; with his lance he struck the knight on the shield so fiercely that it shattered into pieces; and the king, who was an expert, struck his opponent so hard on the pennon of his helm that he overturned him from the saddle and threw him to earth so violently that the knight thought that heaven and earth were revolving. Then Arthur took his opponent's horse by the reins and presented it to the damsel; she took the bridle and continued smoothly on her way, impressed by his actions and regarding him favourably in her heart.

King Arthur then took up his position behind her, but the duke's knights, who had witnessed him joust against their companion, declared that he should not leave thus, and six of them detached themselves from the company and followed him. The first of these, a bow-shot in front of his companions, called out to the king, 'Sir knight, return; you may not leave so soon. Turn, for you must fight, or I shall strike you from behind.' The knight set his lance under his armpit, and the king turned to meet him, striking him with such success, that his opponent's lance flew into pieces, and the king thrust him so hard in the neck area of his hauberk that he fell to the ground, so bemused that his wits were lost. The king took the horse and gave it to the damsel, who accepted it, but the other knights were in hot pursuit, their lances poised against him, and the king, whose lance was still undamaged, turned back again and galloped against the other five whom he saw approaching.

The first he encountered he struck with such a blow that his lance entirely pierced the shield and entered the knight's left shoulder, striking him to the ground, the iron still in the wound; and Arthur pulled the lance out, striking the next to approach him with such ferocity that he knocked the opponent from his horse, the knight's right arm broken by the blow on his shield. Then the other three broke their lances against him and drew their bare swords, attacking him from all sides. When the king saw that they were all attacking, he threw himself into the affray, lance under his arm. He struck the first so purposefully that his lance passed through the knight's side and he was thrown bleeding to the earth; then Arthur's lance broke, able to endure no longer, and he drew from its scabbard the iron sword which had belonged to King Rion. With it he struck the first opponent on the shoulder, cutting it to the bone, so that he fell senseless from his horse to the ground. Then Arthur struck the other knight such a blow on the helm that he split it in two to the neck of his hauberk: if the sword had not been diverted to the left he would have split the knight to the teeth; the man was so stunned that he flew from his horse to the ground. Not forgetting the damsel, Arthur captured all the horses save the last, which had taken cover in the wood; the king recovered this one too, and then returned to the damsel with them all.

When the other knights who wished to participate in the tourney saw that a single knight had thus unhorsed seven of their comrades, at least ten wished to gallop after him, but the duke, who was present, went before them and swore his oath that anyone brave enough to do so would be unlucky, for the knight carried himself well, 'And truly, so help me God,' he said, 'to me this is a good thing, since it was an unfortunate incident, for you saw that he is a foreign knight, weary and battered, who did not wish to stop here, yet he did what was required of him, as you saw. Surely if you had all been captured and kept prisoner, you would have more shame than honour. But you should allow that man to go, whom God guides and defends from evil, for truly, so help me God, he is a brave man: as you know he has dealt with these seven, unhorsing all those of whom the worst believed yesterday morning that single-handedly he might capture this man and hold him by force.' Thus the duke restrained his followers by command[91] and sent them to enquire about their comrades who were seriously wounded, ordering that they be carried to Levezerp Castle. Then, however, he stopped the tourney; no more was performed there since the duke was very angry, as his nephew had been very badly wounded there.

King Arthur had followed the damsel into the forest, where they travelled until about three o'clock in the afternoon, when they entered a very deep valley, where the wood was so thick that they could not see far and, when they emerged from the valley, the hills began to climb on all sides; so they entered a great wasteland. Suddenly they heard a great and marvellous noise which was very terrifying and unpleasant to hear, and it seemed that someone was very grieved. The king stopped as soon as he heard this, wondering greatly what it might be, and then he went forward a little. Then the voice cried again, so loud that it seemed certain that whoever the voice came from was burning; and then the king realized that the voice was that not of a man or woman, but of a dumb beast. He wondered greatly where the voice came from and whose it was; so he told the damsel to wait a little, since he wished to go and find out from whom the voice came. The damsel said, 'Willingly, sir,' and the king spurred his horse through the wood, straight towards the cry, which became neither weaker nor louder; he continued until eventually he saw a lioness which was showing the greatest grief ever made by a beast, for she was biting the ground with her teeth, scratching, rolling about, and crying so loudly that all the air around vibrated with the noise.

When the king saw the beast which was creating such a disturbance he stopped and looked closely at it; when the animal saw him it moved its tail and, appearing pleased to see him, stopped its crying; and then it came towards the king and welcomed him, rubbing his horse with its tail. Then she moved forward a little, calling him in the way of a mute beast; and, having gone a little way, she looked to see if the king was following her. She behaved in such a manner that the king realized that she was in need of help and assistance and said to himself that he would follow until he found out what she wanted. So he followed the beast, and they continued, the lioness ahead and him behind, until they came to the very depth of the wood, which was thick with pines and other lesser trees.

As soon as she approached this covered place, the lioness left the path and went inside. The king followed on foot, since he was forced to dismount and, tying his horse to a tree, he removed the shield from his neck and drew his naked sword from its sheath, preparing to defend himself if the lioness attacked him. When the lioness had entered the deep wood, she began to make an even greater uproar than before, and, after crying for a while, she reappeared from the covered place and looked to see if the king was coming, for he was delaying greatly. When the king saw the lioness return, he went in her direction, and the lioness entered in front of him.

When King Arthur entered the thick wood, he saw that the lioness had stopped on the edge of a little ditch which was full of moss. In this ditch was a small cub which had two serpents entwined around its lower back; they were pressing it so closely that it had no more power to cry out, but lay on the ground as if dead. When the mother approached to lift it, and put out her paw just once, the serpents spat fire and venom mixed together so that she dared not approach. Then the lioness drew back a little, scratching the ground with her feet, gnashing her teeth and demonstrating her sorrow. The king, whose eyes were so wet with sadness that they produced enough water to wash his hands, now realizing the reason for the beast's cries, placed his shield between himself and the serpents and thrust his sword between the cub and the snakes. When he had thus drawn them away from the cub, he cut and thrust at the serpents with his sword until they were divided into small pieces, and threw them out of the ditch with his sword. Then the cub stirred and began to cry, like an animal which had endured much trouble. After this, the king returned to his horse and mounted, while the lioness showed him great respect.

Then the king wiped his sword and replaced it in its scabbard before retracing his steps the way he had come, while the lioness walked beside him, as though reluctant to leave him so soon. Thus the king returned to the damsel who awaited him. When she saw the lioness, she marvelled greatly in her heart and asked the king what had happened. When he told her of his adventure and how he had rescued the cub, 'Ah,' said the damsel, 'that is why the mother shows you such great devotion.' And he agreed that this was true.

Then King Arthur and the damsel continued on their way until they had climbed a high hill; when they reached this, the lioness decided to go no further. She stopped and watched the king until she could see him no longer and then returned to her cub as quickly as she could. (The story told of this adventure here, since Arthur's good deed to the lioness was later rewarded on his return, when both the mother and cub helped him, as shall be told later at the right time, for it is not now the correct place.)

When King Arthur had left the lioness, he and the damsel continued their journey all day until nightfall without food or drink, and travelled on for a great part of the night, since they found no manor where they might seek shelter. A little before first light, when men were at rest, they saw the light of a far-off fire, to which they made their way in great haste, since they hoped to find help and advice there, and arrived after some difficulty. Then the king saw twelve very well-dressed robbers just beginning their dinner, seated at a table in front of a large, bright fire, for there were plenty of bushes available for firewood. They had good venison to eat, seasoned with pepper, with fine, clear wine which they drew from a cask close beside them in a cavern where they stored the things which they stole from the populace.

When the king saw these men seated at dinner, he dismounted and removed his helm, allowing it to hang behind his shoulders, suspended by the strong straps. Going to the damsel, he lifted her down from the mule in his arms. Together they went to the men eating, first ensuring that their mounts were securely tied, so that they could not bolt. When Arthur reached the robbers, he greeted them with the hope that God might give them good evening, and they replied that they happily accepted both his arrival and hers, to which the king answered that he was well aware of this, and they would receive no trouble from him provided they offered him none. Then he took the damsel and made her sit in the best place at the centre of the table opposite their leader, telling her, 'Damsel, eat, since it is a fortunate man who easily wins such a meal.'

Then the robbers said that on that day they had almost everything they needed, and the only thing they lacked was a woman. The king heard their talk but kept quiet, not saying a single word in reply as he sat beside the damsel, who was terrified at these words. The king nudged her, and told her to eat; he himself ate a great amount and then took a cup full of wine which was before the chief robber and drained all the wine. When the leader saw this he cried, 'The Devil drinks thus to God's death. Eat and drink your fill, sir knight, for you know well that the meal is good when someone else is paying.' 'I believe,' said the king, 'that you should not say that I will give you double, since it cost you nothing, but eat freely and then we will count the cost.'

Then the king took the food which was close to them and ate vigorously, bidding the damsel do likewise, but she was too frightened and did not dare. Then the king desired to drink from the main cup, and attempted to take it, but the leader said that if the stranger put his hand on the cup, he would pay dearly. The king would not give way, but lowered his arm to take the cup; the robber lifted up a leather bottle which was full of wine and threw it, intending to hit King Arthur on the head, but he dodged and it passed over him. Then the other robbers threw whatever was available, knives, bread, or plates, but none did him any harm. Then, sword in hand, the king struck the leader such a blow that he split him to the teeth, and with a second thrust he made his head fly from his shoulders. At this, all the other robbers leapt up and rushed for their weapons; the king placed his helm on his head, quickly lacing it, and moved to attack them. He struck so successfully that, in a very little time, ten were lying dead and bleeding on the ground, whilst the remaining two, not daring to remain, turned and fled. Then the king mounted his horse in pursuit, and quickly killed them both, before returning to the terrified damsel.

There, he found also a man-servant who had waited on the robbers; he had begged the damsel to have mercy and save his life. As soon as the king saw this man he rushed to attack him, but he begged for his life, and the damsel added her pleas for mercy, so the king agreed and dismounted with the assistance of the servant, who said, 'Sir, you should not doubt me, since truly, so God help me, I would never do anything which might cause you annoyance or grief.' Then he took the king's helm and shield but did not remove any of his other armour. Then they sat down in front of the fire in full view of those whom he had killed, and then he and the damsel washed and sat down to dine anew, whilst the valet served them to the best of his ability; thus they ate and drank at their leisure.

After the meal, when the tablecloths were removed, the servant made up very lovely couches beside the fire, beneath the tables on which they had dined; the king and the damsel lay beside the fire, remaining awake for a long time. The king gazed at the damsel by the firelight and beheld that she would have been very beautiful if she had not been so distressed. He drew nearer to her, and lay as close as he could beside her, and she touched and caressed him, scratching him most sweetly, because she regarded him to be such a brave man, until he fell asleep in her arms, while she remained awake as long as she could, since she blamed herself as a weak woman. But eventually, because she was a very weak and travel-tired woman, she also slept.

A little before day, the king awoke and, looking about him, perceived that the servant was lying some distance away, near the horses, and sleeping heavily. The king rose and, going to relieve himself, saw that the damsel was asleep; on his return he felt such a strong desire for a woman that he began to twist and turn about. He lay down beside the damsel, but was quite unable to sleep, and he twisted about so much that the damsel awoke and, realizing that he was in great discomfort, enquired, 'Sir, what ails you, that you are in such trouble?' And he replied that he was feeling ill, which caused him distress; then she asked him what was the problem. He answered that if he should tell her, he believed that she could help him, to which she replied that there was no cure which she would not seek out, were it within her power, until he was healed. 'Damsel,' he said, 'if you must know, if I do not enjoy the company of a woman I shall die. Never have I felt such distress before.' 'Thank God, sir,' replied the girl.[92] 'I believe that I have caused you this pain since I have been so close to you.' 'Damsel,' he answered, 'I do not know the cause, but I have been kept awake by the distress I have endured. Do not think that I would say this for any dissimulation or ruse, for there is no worthy lady in the world with whom I would wish to make love if her desire to do so was not as great as my own. But, for God's sake, I beg that if you are not a virgin I may enjoy your favours.'

'Sir,' she answered, 'you seem to me to be a noble knight, and it would be very sad if you obtained either harm or evil from me in any way when I might help you. Here I am, a damsel with whom you may do whatever you please, for there is nothing you might wish to do which would be against my will.' Then the king thanked her most sweetly and, taking her in his arms, embraced and kissed her tenderly, and she returned his caresses, since she desired this as much as he, if not more. Then the king lay with her twice without stopping, before withdrawing himself a distance from her, as he was a man who had great desire and great appetite. He found the damsel of such charming nature that he had never found any woman that pleased him so much; thus they played and amused themselves, the two of them together for a long time in front of the fire in a forest clearing, since the servant could not see them. They played and amused themselves and did whatever they pleased, and their delight lasted until they saw the day break.

When the king saw that it was day, he told the damsel it was time to move on, because they could travel well in the cool morning, and she replied that she was ready to mount whenever he pleased. Then the king went to the servant, who awoke and saddled both the horses. Then the servant asked, 'Sir, what will become of the spoils that are below in this cave, because you cannot carry them away?' The king replied that he was not interested in the clothing, but he would take with him any money and silver vessels which might be there. Then the servant replied, 'Yes, I will load two pack-horses.' The king took these, and had the money placed in coffers and loaded on the horses which he had led there, and arranged that these should follow the damsel, who rode ahead on the road; everything else he gave to the servant, ordering him to take everything he wished and to go wherever he pleased. The servant answered, 'Many thanks, sir.'

Now the king and the damsel left the servant, carrying with them plenty to eat and drink, and loading one of the horses with as much as possible, since they had many strange countries to pass, most of which were at war. The damsel avoided all the dangerous paths of which she knew, and they often amused themselves together whenever they were seized by desire, and they passed an enjoyable time through-out the journey. However, I intend to tell you no more of their travels, or how they took advantage of each place they visited, until they arrived at Orofoise after eight days. The king found the countryside wild, uninhabited and everywhere despoiled, where it used to be beautiful, rich and full of all delights.

As soon as the king and damsel arrived at Orofoise, the countess went out to meet them, showing great happiness, with all the inhabi-tants of the city. When they arrived at the principal castle, the king was disarmed and provided with everything which was considered fine. Then the damsel who had led him to Orofoise sent for warm water and personally washed his neck and face, which were quite blackened by the armour which he had worn. Then she placed a mantle around his neck, and they both went to sit beside the countess at a window facing the river, before an abundant supper was provided. Then, on her sister's advice, the countess sent a messenger, ordering her enemy to be prepared to do battle in the morning at the hour of prime [6 a.m.]. He replied that he was never so happy and was quite prepared; but that it would little avail her, and she could have no guarantee that she would not be in his power within two days. 'Tomorrow, I am still bound by her terms, but after tomorrow...'

The countess had made these terms with her enemy as her sister had advised her, and for this reason she could not retain the knight until the following midday. Afterwards, her sister told her that she should take care not to ask her champion his name or whom he served until after the battle had ended. 'For I have promised him,' she said, 'before he agreed to come here.' The countess declared that she would not do so since it was agreed. Then the damsel recounted how the knight had rescued her from the four evil attackers, how at Levezerp she had seen him joust against seven knights, whose captured steeds might be seen here, and how he had killed the twelve robbers in the forest. Then the countess looked closely at the stranger, and the more she gazed at him, the more he pleased and interested her, for she saw how handsome and capable he was. Then the countess sat beside him at the window, and they spoke long enough together, while she complained to him incessantly about the giant and how much he had pestered and annoyed her. The king then said, 'Do not be dismayed, lady, for he shall soon have his reward, for Our Lady is so powerful that she can deliver you when she pleases.' 'Truly, sir,' she said, 'I have waited long.'

Thus the king and the countess talked together until the meal was prepared; the damsel who had guided the king ordered the tables to be set, for she knew well how to organize the lodging of a valiant and noble knight. Soon the water for washing was brought: first to the king, then to the two sisters, and, finally, to those knights who were present; the king sat between the damsel and her sister, and they dined together. They were very well served, for the two sisters were very courteous and wise, and they showed him all the honour possible. And when they had eaten and the tablecloths were removed, and they had washed, they went outside to amuse themselves, the king with the two sisters, followed by the knights. When they had thus enjoyed themselves there, the beds were prepared; they led the king into a very beautiful room, in which he was to sleep, which contained only his bed and that of the damsel who had travelled there with him; her bed was prepared at some distance from his, and much lower. The countess slept in her own room in another part of the castle.

When the king was in bed, the sisters brought him wine, a little of which he drank; the damsel informed him that she would lie there alone in the bed beside him. Then she went to the countess's room with her, where she undressed until completely naked, and showed her sister where the robber had beaten her with the thorn-branch; at which her sister wept most tenderly, and said that she would have a bath prepared. The damsel answered that she would never allow herself to be comfortable or have a bath until she saw how the battle would go. 'And may it please God that tomorrow we will be quite delivered, for this knight is both brave and of great prowess.' 'It is in the hands of Our Lady,' the damsel replied; then she dressed herself again, in a white chemise. The countess went to her own bed to rest, while the damsel went to her room as quietly as she could; she fastened the door behind her with a sliding bar and then went to her bed. The king remained asleep, since he was very tired, but it grieved the damsel that he did not come to speak with her; it was not long, however, before she too was asleep.

When the king had slept for a little while, he awoke and rose to relieve himself in a hidden corner. There was a lighted candle in a sconce at the foot of his bed, so he looked about the chamber to see where the damsel was sleeping, and saw the truckle-bed on which she lay. He placed his hand on her face, her breasts and stomach, and caressed her white and tender flesh, where the wounds which she had received in the forest from the robber still showed. The damsel awoke when she felt him touch her, and embraced him round the neck, saying, 'You are very welcome, sir.' 'Get up,' he replied, 'and come to my bed.' 'Ah, sir,' she said, 'I may not do so, for the marks of my wounds will be seen on your sheets, and then I shall be betrayed to my sister.'[93] Then the king realized that she spoke sensibly, so, going to the candle, he extinguished it and went to sleep with the damsel. They had a very happy time together that night, for he pleased and satisfied her; they lay together until it was almost day. Then the king returned to his own bed and fell asleep, since he was tired from staying awake.

When morning came, the countess arose and, donning her chemise, a surcoat and a short mantle, with a fine veil over her head, she went to the room where the knight was lying and found him still asleep, and likewise her sister, who was well covered with her robe. The countess left again without a single word, and without delay returned to her own room and slept a little until Mass was rung. Then the king, who had also slept, rose and went to the church to hear Mass; in his company were the two sisters, neither of whom wished to be a single step away from him. After the morning Mass was sung, they returned to the hall and looked out from the windows in the direction from which the giant would come. When the king realized that the giant had not arrived, he became very angry, commanded his horse to be saddled and his armour brought, and declared that it was time for him to go. When the countess heard this, she was very concerned, for she had a great fear that he might leave without doing more. The damsel who had travelled there with him announced that the meal was almost ready, and as he looked at her and she at him, he began to smile. So she brought the meal, and the three of them ate, without any others, in a private room. When they had eaten, the king looked up at the sun and said that it was almost midday, so he rose and demanded his armour.

Then both the countess and her sister began to weep most tenderly, so the king took pity on them and asked, 'Ladies, why do you weep? I shall be prepared with my armour, so that it will be better if the tyrant summons me out when he arrives.' 'Sir,' said the damsel, 'you speak truthfully, but I beg you for God's sake that you will stay as long as you can.' He said he would undoubtedly do this.

As soon as his armour was brought the king began to arm himself, the damsel aiding him as best she could; and when he was totally armed except for his helm, he sought her advice, asking, 'Damsel, is there anywhere nearby, any lodge three or four miles away, where I might stay if the need arises? For you know well that I cannot stay more than one night in any lodging while I am on quest, since I have sworn not to do so unless I am captured or ill, or besieged by people wishing to take me by force. For the sake of your love, if the tyrant does not come before night I must go and lodge elsewhere and wait until prime tomorrow, and he will have to come and find me.'

Then the damsel fell at his feet weeping and implored him for mercy; and the king lifted her up and begged her that she would not speak of this to anyone, which she promised. 'Sir,' said the girl, 'how will you take the harness, horses and wealth which we brought here?' 'My dear, sweet love,' said the king, 'it is all yours, for I do not want a single penny of it. For you have treated me so well that I should give you a lot more than this; but you shall be rewarded another time if I am ever able to do so.' 'Sir,' she said, 'I have enough, since I have the love of a brave man like you; but one thing upsets me greatly, that I do not know who you are or where I may find you if you should leave without telling me.' 'Damsel,' he said, 'if you enquire which arms I bear, I need tell you no more.' To which the damsel answered that he had spoken well.

While they were in discussion, the countess approached the king to beg him to wait a little while, for if the enemy was coming he would soon arrive. When the king saw her coming, he rose to meet her, took her by the hand and led her to the window. They spoke of many things, until finally the king said, 'Lady, this country here, do you hold it from anyone?' Then the countess, weeping, told him that she held it from a man who was so powerful that he should help her and guarantee her safety, but by chance he knew nothing of these events.

When the king asked who this was, 'Truly, sir,' she said, 'he is Arthur of Britain, but he is so busy with many people that even if I send to him he cannot come to aid me. I should not blame him for this, since I have only sent to his court once, and on that occasion he was not found there; thus I have not known what to do until this day. And truly, so help me God, if you should go, then I shall have to flee, I know not where, for I would rather seek my bread from charity in another land than allow the giant to hold me here in bondage like a common slut, the most disloyal thing which ever was, the most ugly and shameful, especially since he is a pagan and I a Christian. Just look at my plight.' Then she began to be so upset again that she almost fainted, at which the king was filled with such pity that tears came to his eyes; he comforted her as best he could, bidding her not to be dismayed, for God was still able to help her.

While he was thus listening to the countess recounting her sorrow, he saw the people of the country fleeing from the woods and all parts of the town towards the castle, crying at the top of their voices, 'Run, run! The tyrant is chasing us, and is so angry that he is killing anyone he meets.' When the countess heard this noise and the people shouting, she was so terrified that she went as white as a sheet. The townsfolk rushed to the gates to close and bar them, barricading them with wood so that the giant would not be able to enter the town, since, if he did so, they would all be lost and killed. Then they mounted the walls and defence points, for they still did not feel safe even with the gates barred.

Then King Arthur looked towards the woods and saw the giant coming, a great club on his shoulder, chasing two men in flight, whom he seized in one hand, as easily as another man might hold an olive branch. He was armed to his toes with a serpent's skin which came from India and was so strong that no weapon could penetrate it, however sharp and pointed it might be. This giant was so very enormous that the Shepherd's Story[94] relates that he was eighteen feet high, and so broad that it required two men to reach around his shoulders; he was so strong that he could wrench a tree from the ground. He had a head as large as an ox, great black eyes which burned like glowing coals, and a voice as loud as a trumpet, and when he raised his voice he could easily be heard half a mile away. His face was altogether so ugly when he was angry that nobody had ever seen an uglier: there was a good half-foot between his eyes. On his head he wore a helmet of cured leather and serpent's skin, which hung down to his shoulders; it was so strong and hard that no weapon could penetrate it.

The giant, who was just as I describe, came to the gate on foot, for no horse was strong enough to carry him when he was fully armed. When he reached the gate, he beat on it so violently with the edge of his club that the whole structure shook. Then he called out in a loud voice, 'Countess of Orofoise, the day has arrived, the day when I shall have at my mercy both you and that disloyal harlot, your sister, who has daily been at such pains to annoy me. But it will avail her nothing, for I shall reward her well: I have no boy in my following, no matter how vile, to whom I shall not give the freedom to use her as he desires. And you shall be given to the squires if you do not guarantee, by your God who allowed himself to be crucified and wounded, or by King Arthur your overlord, that you will honour your promise.'

When the king heard the giant speak so fiercely against God and holy faith and put his trust in Satan, he looked at him, saying, 'Then this villain is a devil from hell, for cursed was the hour he was born. Bring here my helm and my horse, for I have delayed too long, and I cannot wait until the time when he breaks down this gate.' Then the damsel brought his helm, which the two sisters laced on his head, and then they led out his saddled horse. He quickly hung his sword in place; then the damsel gave him a marvellously strong lance, while the countess handed him his shield, which was not complete, since it was pierced with I know not how many lances. 'Sir,' said the countess, 'this shield is not as strong as I would wish.' 'Lady,' answered the king, 'I cannot help that, but if it pleases God, it will be changed for a better, that of this great villain, which I will carry while I live.' He explained that the giant's shield was very strong, since it was totally covered with serpent's skin.

When the king had mounted his horse, he left, commending the two sisters to God, as they did him, weeping heavily. Then with short strides he rode along the castle road towards the gate, which the giant was still beating like a demon, shouting threats at the two sisters and calling them roving whores, and also using abusive language to the townspeople, all of whom he threatened to destroy and send into captivity. The gate remained closed against him, for they were all terrified. When the king arrived at the gate, he made them open it so that he could pass through, but as soon as he was outside it was quickly closed behind him. The king crossed the bridge and rode straight towards the giant, who had withdrawn a little to dispute with the citizens.

When King Arthur saw the giant he challenged him, saying,

'Infamous giant and evil-doer, what do you want from the countess of Orofoise? You have no claim on either her or her land, for she holds it from King Arthur, on behalf of whom I am here to defy you and demand that you should depart and leave the countess and her land in peace. And if you do not wish to leave, I defy you and am prepared to show against your body in combat that you are wrong and she is in the right.' Then the giant said that he did not value either him or King Arthur a button; 'And you would have done better to be in Egypt than come here.' Then he rushed against the king, club in hand, for he did not care a penny for his opponent, since he saw he was small. When the king saw him approaching, he spurred his horse, placed his lance in position, and gave the Saxon[95] as strong a blow on his covered shield as the impetus of the horse would allow, but the serpent-skin with which it was covered was so strong and hard that the lance could not pierce it but was shattered in pieces by the impact.

The giant was so strong that he was quite unaffected and unmoved by the blow, but the horse, which was strong and hardy, returned again, and the king gave the giant such a blow in the chest that he threw him to the ground, so stunned that he was badly wounded. The horse went so close to the giant that his four feet went over the giant, who was so huge and fat that the horse was overturned, and the king fell off, but did not wound himself, God be thanked; but, leaping to his feet, he drew his sword from its sheath and prepared to defend himself if attacked. The giant, who was still lying on the ground, was very angry that he had fallen and that the king's horse had fallen on his body; he lifted one of his feet in anger and kicked the horse so hard that it landed in the middle of the field, whilst he picked himself up and leapt to his feet, the club raised in his right hand, and attacked the king, declaring that his enemy was as good as dead.

When the king saw this devil coming against him, he was doubtful of the outcome but crossed himself and called on God, covering himself with his shield. The giant lifted his club, intending to hit his opponent on the head, but the king, who was very skilful, dodged the blow, and the mace hit the buckle of the shield so hard that a great fragment broke off, hitting the ground with such force that it was driven into the earth a depth of over two feet. The king raised his sword and struck the Saxon, who was unprotected by his shield, hitting his right arm with such force, just as he drew the club towards himself, that he cut off the arm, so that the giant's fist, still holding the club, flew to the ground.

When the Saxon saw how he was maimed, with his fist lying on the ground, he was so furious that he almost lost his reason; he rolled his eyes and foamed at the mouth like a boar, twisting and turning in fury and pain, and while he raged in this manner the king recovered and, coming close to the giant, struck him so heavily on the head that he made his eyes see stars, although the coif and helmet which he wore on his head were so strong that they did not yield anywhere. However, the blow was so heavy that the Saxon staggered, and while he was stumbling the king struck him so hard that he forced the giant to his knees, who beat on the ground with his left fist. Then a shout rose from the castle, and loud voices called out, 'God, give this knight the strength and power to overcome and kill the giant.'

The two sisters, who had come to watch the fight from the wall above the gate, wept most tenderly and sent prayers to Our Lord to give their champion the strength he needed to defeat this enemy; the damsel said to the countess, to comfort her, 'Sweet sister, with God's help you may be certain that the giant will be defeated; do you not see that he has lost his right hand.' The knights and people around said that the giant was already doomed, whatever might happen.

When the giant saw what had happened to his right fist, and how Arthur was ill-treating him, he leapt to his feet in anger and, taking his shield in his left hand, he rolled it towards the king with such speed that it made a great noise. When Arthur saw this coming, being very dexterous he jumped to one side, allowing it to pass him; and the shield passed without touching him. When the king saw that the giant was unprotected, he rushed at him, with his naked sword in his hand, and struck him a great heavy blow on the shoulder, but did no damage. Then the giant ran at the king and attempted to seize him with his left hand, but King Arthur drew back and avoided him; the giant chased him more and more, and after the king had used this ruse to avoid him several times, he could anticipate when the giant was next about to lunge at him, and struck on the unprotected arm so heavily that he made it fly across the ground.

Then the giant was so furious when he saw how he had been fooled that he almost became mad; he raised his head against his enemy and kicked so hard on the king's shield that he almost knocked it to the ground. The king approached again and gave his enemy great blows to left and right but was unable to cut, break or damage the serpent-skin which protected his body down to the feet. The giant was still fierce, lifting his head again, intending to kick the king on the helm with his foot, but the king struck him on the exposed leg below the knee, with such a blow that he amputated the foot, with all the leg-muscles, like a shin of beef. Then the giant gave such a cry that the castle, the river and the woods about echoed with the noise, but he retained in one foot so much pride and conceit that he would not submit. The king returned to his enemy and struck him such a fierce blow that he threw him to the ground, and a cry rose from the castle, such a great roar from men and women that the air trembled and shook; shouting that with God's help the tyrant was dead, they rushed down from the walls to open the city gates.

As soon as he saw that the giant was defeated, King Arthur went to fetch the giant's shield and placed it about his neck, leaving his own, which was badly damaged. Then he went to his horse and, quickly mounting, turned the animal towards the forest and disappeared into the trees as fast as his horse would go, travelling away from that place as quickly as he could, not caring where he went.

When she cannot find Arthur, the damsel sets off alone and seeks him fruitlessly for a long time.

PART 5

LATER FRENCH ROMANCE

The Knight With Two Swords (Chevalier as Deus Espees) (c. 1235)

This complex French romance is set in the peaceful period after Arthur has defeated the Saxon invaders and before his war against the Romans. It incorporates the exploits of the young unproven knight Meriadeus on behalf of Arthur's vassal with the adventures encountered by his mentor, Gawain, who has to restore his reputation. The poem is further complicated by the interlaced story of Meriadeus's quest to avenge his father, slain by Gawain in judicial combat on behalf of another of Arthur's vassals.

The poem opens at Arthur's court, and the poet develops the story of King Rion's[96] beard, first mentioned in Geoffrey of Monmouth's History. *In the following extract, the poet praises Arthur's splendid court and generosity towards his knights.*

The king held his land for a long time, without departing for war, and had kept all his enemies under his control, so that he and his queen were happy and his court was greatly envied. The good king, who was of such great worth, decided that he would hold the best and largest court that had ever been held, although he was accustomed to hold very grand ones; this was the thing which he most wished to do, and what gave him the greatest pleasure was to reward and draw to himself the hearts of his knights. He loved these men and held them dear, so that he allowed none of them to leave his entourage if he could prevent it. Rich, great and noble were the gifts which they were given daily by him, for he was never sparing or mean. In aspiring to be wealthy, he had no other motive than to honour his knights. Thus King Arthur's hand was never empty but always ready to provide large gifts, while he, the generous and courteous king, although he gave much, gained even more. Therefore his generosity could not impoverish him, I well assure you, but by all accounts it increased his wealth.

King Arthur was so worthy and so honourable that nothing done for the sake of honour ever seemed to him to be any trouble or hardship. The least important days of the week, when he dined most privately, seemed like the Easter celebrations of another king. One day he summoned his bailiffs and clerks, of whom he had plenty, and when he saw them gathered before him, he commanded them to inform all those who held fiefs or lordships from him, that they should not fail to come to Carduel at Pentecost to keep him company. For if anyone did not come, truly he would forfeit both the king's friendship and his fief, without pardon or pity.

When the day of the feast arrived, the nobles of many lands assembled, as was right and proper: all of them came to keep the king company as they ought to. The king heard High Mass sung in the cathedral, with the queen and all the knights, ladies and damsels, of which there were many beautiful ones present; then the king returned to his palace and declared that, since it was time, the water should be brought, which was done without delay. There was not a squire present who did not leap to fetch either a basin or a towel.

The king washed first, as did the queen, who was very lovely; then they sat side by side at the high dais in the great palace. They wore their grandest crowns, as was appropriate for such an important feast. Owing to the splendour and honour of the festival on this important day, ten kings wore their crowns, and I will name all ten as I should: first in great lordship sat King Lot of Orkney, the father of my lord Gawain, whilst King Uriel, the father of my lord Ywain came next. King Ares, the father of Tor sat next to him, then King Yder, in whom there was great and clear wisdom. Then sat King Amangons of Greenland, who, as all the court knew, was the father of my lady Guinloie, the loyal sweetheart and mistress of my lord Gawain. For this reason, her father, who knew this well, loved her harshly. Karados, the king of Vanes, who was very noble, sat next in rank; then sat King Aguisiaus, the most valiant and courteous king and lord of Scotland; then King Baudemagus, from whose land there is no return: no strangers come back from there.[97] After him, if I remember correctly, sat King Estrangares, who held the city of Pelle. King Bruans, whose surname was 'Four-Beards', the lord of the Lost City sat below these others, in the humblest seat. All these ten kings wore crowns and sat at the king's table, just as I have described to you.

Three hundred and sixty-six knights sat at the Round Table, except for three who were journeying throughout the world in search of adventure, so that they might prove themselves and become famous, although this caused the king to be very pensive. My lord Gawain was one of the three, Tors was another, and the third knight was Gierfles.

The dinner was now ready, and that day Kay served at the tables, with Bedevere the constable and Lucan the butler; these three were in charge of serving the meal. Kay had declared and made it known that nobody could sit in the hall to eat, however proud he might be, save only the knights, high clerics, maidens, ladies and damsels; but these he allowed to remain there peaceably. On this fine day the least number of menials serving in the palace was ten thousand.

All were seated nobly and in great comfort, and they dined with considerable pleasure. I do not believe that I have ever seen so many fine people together. After Kay had served the first course to everyone, both well and finely, in the manner of one who did many things well, the king hung his head low and suddenly began to meditate. He became very angry when he saw the dais covered on all sides, with such beautiful people, for there were many damsels, ladies and knights all joyfully waiting to dine, as he could see, and he beheld the ten kings seated there, all wearing their crowns in his honour, who had come to be with him. Therefore he felt even more upset, for he had never before seen so many fine people at any court that he had held where no adventure had occurred, since he had never before held a great court at which no adventure had happened. This caused the king to ponder deeply and entirely ignore his food, as he kept watch.

Now you might see a knight galloping up on a large palfrey; he was entirely unarmed, and dressed in scarlet cloth, which greatly suited him. He wore a well-made surcoat and mantle, both lined with fur and in truth trimmed with a very expensive black sable. The knight did not enter the hall mounted, but stopped his horse outside and dismounted. A squire ran to meet him at the threshold, and the knight told him to wait there for a while to guard his horse; then he looked at all those present, both high and low, and thought in his heart that the man to whom all these people belonged had plenty of noble vassals. Then he looked upwards to the head of the table and saw the dais where the king, the queen and all the crowned kings sat, and he recognized which was King Arthur. Although he had never seen him before, yet he knew of him through his deeds, for he was aware that Arthur was honoured more than any other man, and he seemed to be such a good lord that he was not feared at all.

The knight entered the hall and was stared at by one and all: he was tall, handsome, comely and bore himself well. He went straight to the king and did not delay until he had announced his complete message: 'King,' he said, 'I do not greet you; I am the messenger of King Ris of the Netherworld.' Since the king was so deep in thought, he looked up at this man, since he had spoken so proudly, and told him that he should not desist from delivering the message which he had been given, for he would listen to it in full. This man was not nervous when he heard the king command him thus, and he replied:

'Sire, King Ris informs you that he, who is capable of achieving plenty, has already spent nine years since he left his country, and in these nine years he has conquered, entirely by force, nine kings, who have paid him homage to become his vassals, and he has seized the fief of each king. They do not leave his entourage, but they and their followers serve him, and he has shaved the beard of each king and from them he will make a mantle and give this to his sweetheart, to whom he has promised it. She has requested that the fur trimming facing [the mantle] should be made from your beard; he has promised her that everything shall be as she wishes. Therefore, he bids you, through me, because he considers you to be the highest and best king in the entire world after him, that as a mark of honour he wishes to make the tassel of this mantle from your beard. For this reason, he wishes that you should attend him and should hold your land from him, and he will entrust it to you. If you refuse to do this, he will never cease until he has deposed you and taken your entire kingdom for himself, to be under his control according to his wish, and until he has seized the queen and given her to the king of Northumberland, who has asked him for her. And above all he informs you, as one who makes war against him, that he has entered your land with as many as ten thousand knights, well-chosen plunderers who make war as they please, and he is besieging the queen of Cardigan, and he will not leave that place, for fear of any man born, until he has captured all the land.'

When the king heard this message, he was very angry at what the messenger had said, and he felt shame and amazement at the manner in which he dared to suggest such villainy. He was extremely ashamed on account of the nobility who were present with him. The messenger urged him that he should announce his intention, and the king said to him:

'Knight, I have heard very well the outrageous things which you have said to me here today in the presence of all my vassals. You may inform your lord that he should busy himself accomplishing other things, and that he will have to wait a long time to place my beard on the mantle. And if he has besieged the Castle of Cardigan, this would annoy me greatly. Tell him, that unless he leaves, I will lead such a company against him, so many standards and so many banners, that he will have nothing left except his name, for there would be no strife between us if he should see what power I have. Truly, I shall never be happy until I have avenged the very shameful message which he has sent me, this great pride and massive affront.'

The messenger went out, mounted his horse and set off on his way at once. Nobody from the hall accompanied his departure, you must realize, or went after him, but all declared that never before had anybody sent to such a great king a message of such great pride, or showed such ill-conceived conduct, without it being corrected. The king said that all his followers should be summoned without delay, and he sent messages to every place where he had any power, that no man should dare to stay away if he knew how to fight, but should be at Carduel within forty days, completely prepared for war. The seneschal, who was greatly angered, sent the order out everywhere, as the good king had commanded him.

Arthur is saved the trouble of going to war against his challenger, since Meriadeus overcomes King Ris in single combat, sending him and his vassal kings to do homage to Arthur. Later in the story, Gawain returns to court, but when out riding one morning unarmed, he is attacked and left for dead by Brien of the Isles, the suitor of the Queen of the Isles, who has set him the task of fighting Gawain to win her love. In this extract Arthur declares that he would be unable to maintain his rule without the assistance of his nephew Gawain.

The day was clear and sunny, a pleasant morning with the birds rejoicing. The king and queen had already risen and were dressed, and they were wondering where my lord Gawain might be, for he was accustomed to rise earlier than the other knights every morning and was usually the first to come to court, unless he was ill or if he had ridden off on some new adventure.

Now the queen called before her Lore de Branclant and Faukain of Hopeful Mountain, who were nearby. 'Damsels,' she said, 'go to the lodging of my lord Gawain, and tell him that he will be the last to arrive at court; tell him that he must arise and prepare himself, for he should not lie in bed so long. The knight who yawns during the day shall not have the love of his sweetheart. Tell him that he should not stay abed any longer, for the king and I have sent for him, and we have been up for some time and wish to go to church.'

The damsels went to Gawain's lodging without delay; they enquired of the chamberlain where Gawain lay, and he told them. They went there at once, knelt before his bed and spoke: 'Are you still sleeping, good lord?' 'Damsel Lore, you and your companion are very welcome,' he said. 'I am not asleep, nor have I been since daybreak.' 'Lord, you should be aware that the king has already risen, and also my lady, and they command you, through us, that you should go to them quickly, and my lord Ywain also. You should not delay for any reason; you have been a long time in coming; this they may well say, truly, that at this hour you should no longer be in bed, and that you always rise before those knights who are already there. No man should be asleep on such a lovely morning; it is getting late, and the king is waiting for you at court.' When my lord Gawain heard what the maiden said to him, he paused, gave a sigh, and then replied in a weak voice: 'Today it cannot be otherwise, damsel, but you must go immediately to court and tell my uncle that I am unwell and that I do not wish to trouble either him or my lady.'

The damsels went back to court and reported to the king what Gawain had told them. When the king heard and realized that his nephew was disheartened and ill, he was upset, for there was a very strong love between them. He said to the queen, 'My lady, let us go to see my nephew; for a long time now I have never known him to be so ill that he lay in bed; I well believe that he must be very sick, for nothing else would keep him there.' 'Sir, that may well be so,' she replied. 'Let us go to see how he is.'

Then the king mounted and went, accompanied by the queen, knights and ladies, for all the court held Gawain equally dear: he did not cause any quarrels or trouble there. My lord Ywain had now arisen, as had many other knights who had slept there [in Gawain's lodging], and they were very surprised when they saw the king arrive there so humbly. Without speaking to anyone, the king went straight to the bed where his nephew lay, and so did the queen; he sat down, had a window opened, looked closely at his nephew, saw that he was badly off colour, and said to him, 'How are you, good nephew? You seem to me to be very ill, and you must tell me all about it.' Gawain weakly replied: 'Sire, it is an evil enough hour.' Now the king uncovered him and saw that my lord Gawain was wounded and that his bed was full of blood, and he was lying in his own blood; and he demanded to know who had done such an outrageous and wicked deed. Then my lord Gawain told him everything as it had occurred, and that he had not known what to do except pretend to be dead, since his attacker had shown great joy when he believed that he had left Gawain for dead. He related how he had covered his body with a mantle and how he had returned to his lodging. Then the king felt faint and displayed great grief, and no man could describe the sorrow which the queen showed, tearing her hair and pulling it out, so that she almost killed herself with grief. All the knights wished to die of grief, as did the ladies; thus the sorrow was shared by all commonly, and I promise you that there was no one present who did not weep or show their grief.

'Ah, good uncle, stop this!' said my lord Gawain. 'Desist, for nothing will be gained by making such grief, but send for the doctors and bid them come to take care of me. I can give you no better advice than to take comfort. You should delay such a display until you know what will happen.' The king, who was unable to reassure himself about anything, showed considerable grief without being able to control himself, but when he realized that his nephew wished to comfort him, he said, in the manner of one who has great apprehension and cannot expect to receive any consolation, 'My dearest nephew, how could I be joyful and how could I replace you, and how could I hold my land if you should die? You whom all the world honours, you who perform such deeds above all others, you who pacify the angry, you who are the shield of the world, you who live to help poor ladies every day, you who are accustomed to support disinherited maidens, you who have always overthrown the evil-doers. In whose valour could I ever entrust my kingdom? Who would bear shield or helm any day for the honour of Britain? Ah God, may you grant that he will be healed again, he on whom I depend, for never will I believe in you any more, if he is not healed. The heart of the man who did this to you should be otherwise; we know well that he committed treason either by ruse or by surprise. May God grant that the man who committed this crime shall have his payment very soon; he shall have it without a long delay, and I vow this.'

When he had mourned the injury to the valiant lord who was his nephew, the king immediately sent for his doctors, those whom he believed to be the most knowledgeable, and begged them to go there to take care of his nephew, and that they should not lie to him but tell him the truth accurately and in detail, whatever they might find wrong with Gawain. They promised to do this, for, after the king, Gawain was the man in whom they had most faith and whom they should serve best. 'But you should leave us here to care for him, and you should draw a little aside.'

Then the doctors tarried no longer, but immediately removed Gawain's robe and then washed his wound with warm water and inspected it, and when they had examined it well, they declared, 'Do not dismay, good lord, it is certain that you will be quite healed within a month.' When my lord Gawain heard this, he said, 'Thanks be to God, that I shall be able to bear arms again. Go and tell the king, who grieves so much in his heart.' The doctors did so, and when everyone received the news, they were all so happy that nobody had ever seen such grief completely changed into such great joy. However, the doctors ordered Gawain's room and the whole house to be kept quiet, and they told the king that it would be best if the courtiers departed, and that two damsels should remain with Gawain to care for him, for he had no need of anything else.

The king and queen left my lord Gawain, and everyone, both great and small, returned to his lodging. Then the doctors returned to Gawain and busied themselves a great deal with him, giving him all their attention so effectively during that week that, responding to their attention, in eight days he was so much better that he was able to leave his bed and go about his lodging to amuse himself as he pleased; from which sprang great joy in his heart, for he had feared that he might die.

One day the king visited Gawain to see how he was, and as soon as he realized that his nephew was recovering, he was overjoyed and said: 'Good nephew, I am most anxious to know who did this to you.' 'I am not sure, but when he believed that he had killed me, he said that now he knew for certain that without doubt the most wonderful good luck which had ever befallen a knight had come to him; for he would now, without hindrance, become the King of the Isles, he would win his sweetheart, the most beautiful lady in the world, through whom he would hold the lordship. However, what angered me most when he said this was the great joy which he showed when he thought me dead. That certainly upset me more than the fact that I was wounded.' 'Good nephew, forget about this; we shall have our vengeance soon enough; now I have no other desire except that you should recover without delay, and that you should not think of this any more.' 'Good uncle, I have thought little about it,' replied Gawain.

Then the queen spoke to the king and drew him on one side: 'Sire, it is very proper that your nephew should be guarded better than before; he will get up before his time and will steal away. For he is so very angry that he will never be happy until he has avenged this evil deed, and if it happened by chance that he should arrive at a place where he might find his attacker, and they fought together and his wounds re-opened, if he was inflamed through any action, he might easily be killed, and then you would hear terrible news.' 'You speak the truth.' Then the king called to him my lord Ywain, Gerflet, Garahet and Garehiet, Tor, Dodinel and Eslit, since he saw them nearby, and with them Carados Short-Arms, and he said to them, 'My lords, I put you in charge of Gawain, and for God's sake, if he wishes to go anywhere, you should not allow him to do so unless you have informed me of this.' 'Willingly, sire.' Then the king left the knights, took leave of his nephew, and left him with his companions.

When fully restored to health, Gawain departs from court to avenge himself against Brien of the Isles. Subsequently the hero, Meriadeus, hears from his mother how the cowardly Brien de la Gastine (of the Wasteland) has taken advantage of Arthur's generous habit of granting all his followers' requests, in order to contrive the death of Meriadeus's father, against whom Brien has been at war. Although peace has now been agreed upon, and ratified by Brien's marriage to Meriadeus's sister, within three weeks Brien raids his father-in-law's lands and the two sides reassemble their forces.

When all the people on both sides were assembled, the wicked cowardly Brien was afraid and dared not join battle, but called out to my lord and made the suggestion that if he dared fight against him in single combat they would avoid the conflict, and whichever of them was the victor should have the lands of them both, and if he agreed on a day, he should come without delay. When my lord heard Brien speak of this, he had the greatest joy that a Christian ever felt. When Brien requested this, he agreed, for he believed that he would undoubtedly win Brien's land. The day was fixed, without delay, to be in six months' time; those who were present on Brien's behalf requested this. The people then began to leave, and the host was disbanded.

Brien, who did not forget about this agreement, did not delay, but mounted and rode off alone, and in nine days arrived at Karehes, where King Arthur was holding court, and he went to request a boon of the king, saying that he should not refuse this, since Brien was his vassal and held his land from King Arthur. On his knees and in distress, he declared that he would not move until the king had agreed completely. The king did not think about the request for very long, but said that Brien could have what he wished.

Then Brien told King Arthur that he had granted him that my lord Gawain his nephew, the good and worthy knight, who was renowned everywhere, should go with him wherever he might lead him! Gawain should always obey his instructions and do whatever Brien wished, without disputing or refusing; and the king agreed to all this completely. Immediately, they started on their journey, my lord Gawain and Brien, who was happy that he had in his power, and ready to do his bidding without question, the finest knight and greatest warrior who had ever lived. Finally, he led Gawain into a prison, where he kept him until the appointed day arrived when he must keep his pledge.

The two parties gathered their people together, who came in great numbers from all parts. Brien led his prisoner with him, already completely armed so that no one but the two of them might know that he was my lord Gawain. My lord, who was full of joy and eager for the fight, came to that place and hurried to arm, for he was very late; and Brien came from the opposite side, armed save for his helm, and asked my lord if he requested battle, and he made it known that the covenant which they had made was ensured; they would be safeguarded on all sides when they met: this was agreed in an evil hour. Then Brien declared that he would go to his tent and lace his helm and come forth mounted. With that, he entered his tent and immediately summoned my lord Gawain to keep Arthur's promise, and bade him take up the battle on his behalf. Gawain agreed to this, and Brien very quickly gave him all his armour, his horse, and accoutrements, to disguise his identity, and Gawain mounted.

Unaware of this exchange, Meriadeus's father jousts against Gawain and is unhorsed, being fatally wounded by his opponent's lance. On hearing Gawain's voice, the dying man begs him to reveal his identity and forgives him on learning who he is. Meriadeus proves less forgiving than his father. Gawain is only able to secure Meriadeus's forgiveness after he has rescued the hero's mother and avenged her husband's death by defeating her enemy Brien. Eventually the two heroes are reconciled and return to Arthur's court, where they are welcomed triumphantly with a procession led by the rejoicing king.

The Perilous Cemetery (L'Atre Périlleux) (c. 1250)

This mid-thirteenth-century French poem which, like many works, both opens and closes at Arthur's court, is one of several to contain an identity crisis for Gawain. In the following episode, the importance of courtly etiquette is displayed in Gawain's hesitation to leave Arthur's table without his permission before the meal has ended. The damsel's request to be Arthur's cup-bearer is a more sophisticated type of don constraint than Druidain's blunt demand in My Lord Gawain, *or the* Avenging of Raguidel. *Unknown to Arthur and his court, this is a device to ensnare Gawain, for the lady is the mistress of her abductor, Escanor, who plans to kill Arthur's nephew. The figure of Escanor reappears in Girart d'Amiens's* Escanor, *where he accuses Gawain of murder.*

On the Saturday afternoon, when the king was just setting off on a hunt, he observed a beautiful damsel enter the hall and ride towards him, without using her reins to slow her horse until she had reached the king. She travelled alone, but was dressed in rich garments, including a dress of rich red samite; I shall not describe her saddle and the other trappings of her horse, since they were of such high quality that it would be very difficult.

'King,' she said, 'may the Lord who rules both high and low in heaven, sea and earth, protect you. I have come from my country to ask you a boon: I will not seek from you anything unjust, shameful or evil.' The king happily agreed that he would willingly grant her request. 'Tell me,' he said, 'what it may be, and you shall have it without argument, provided it is in my power.' 'Thank you, sire,' she replied, 'then you shall hear what I desire of you: I wish to be your butler at the feast tomorrow, to have charge of your cup and serve at your meal. Therefore, I wish that a knight of your court, the one who is considered the best and the most highly regarded, should guard, honour and defend me while I am at your court, so that no evil may befall me; for I would not dare to stay without a very efficient protector.'

The king looked benevolently at the damsel: 'Beautiful lady,' he said, 'all shall be as you desire; but I am not able to decide who is the best knight among all those of my retinue. You are so wise and intelligent, and have said that you wish for one; do please name someone, whoever you wish it to be. I will ensure that he will guard and defend you and will know how to serve you well, while you remain here.' 'Sire,' she replied, 'it is not seemly that I should grant all the honour to one man; thus I must put the burden of decision upon you, since you have promised me the boon. I fear I will make a bad choice if I do so alone.' 'By God,' said the king, 'I do not see how I can determine the best; but I wish you to agree with me on my choice, if you see that it is good. Without choosing, you wish to place yourself in the care of a knight who is handsome, worthy, courteous and wise; if he were not related to me, I would speak highly of a certain person.'

The maiden, who was not stupid, replied: 'Sire, please name him, before I agree.' 'Lovely lady,' said the king, 'it is Gawain, under whose protection you shall be tomorrow, and for as long as you please.' 'Sire,' she answered, 'before I came here, I had heard Gawain greatly praised; I will remain here as you wish, for I demand of you no one else but him.'

So he granted the request, just as I have related. Gawain led her to his lodging with great joy, and behaved towards her in such a manner that no one could find any fault with him; for it is clearly understood that a maiden served them, and Gawain's lovely sister kept them company. They all passed a very pleasant time that night until the following morning. Gawain got up very happy, as did all three maidens. Then he went in armour to hear Mass in the monastery, for the king was already in the church, as were the queen and her maidens. When Gawain and the damsels arrived there from their lodgings, the service was already ended, so they all returned to court together.

There, it seemed to me, as she had been promised, the principal cup was given to the damsel, for the tables were already set; then began the service of the meal, which was very grand, splendid and appetizing, since King Arthur was not miserly, but wished there to be abundance; but I have no need to tell you any details of the meal, only what happened there.

The girl served from the cup. The queen sat beside the king, with the king of Wales next to her; Gawain, Tors the son of Ares, and Erec sat on the other side of the king, while Carados Briesbras made the fourth. All the others sat lower. There were many knights of prowess present, and many intelligent damsels; before them were many napkins and dishes of gold and silver.

They had not long begun the meal, and had only completed one course, when a knight was seen entering the main door in haste, and, believe me, although he was not very large, there was no one under heaven more handsome. Yet he was a very great nuisance, since he was a fine knight and well armed. He entered the hall thus in armour, apart from his lance, which he had left outside, leaning against the wall. This fellow was so proud that he did not restrain his horse until he had reached the king, and he came so quickly that his bridle struck the table; there was no usher or constable who dared oppose him in any way. When he had studied them with great insolence, but without uttering a single word, he turned towards the maiden, seized her by the shoulders, then lifted her up on to the horse's neck in front of him.

'King,' he declared, 'I do not seek to hide it from you that this damsel is my lady friend; I have sought her in many courts since I undertook to love her. I have never been able to find her in a court where I might dare to seize her; but I know that your court is so soft and so empty of good knights that I can lose nothing because of them, and thus I will take her away without any trouble, unless a knight from among those seated here is prepared to take up his shield against me.' (I say this to annoy them, and since I have already seized her from them.) 'My lord king,' he continued, 'I have seen the highway through this wood which leads to my country. Do you know why I tell you the road by which I must travel? If there is any knight here who, through wisdom or folly, despite what I have told you, desires to dispute by battle, I would not flee, going by any other route. Before all those present I boast that I shall take this road and travel slowly until evening; I intend that whoever may follow me should have an easy task, if he does not turn back through cowardice before I reach the wood!'

With these words he set off, picking up his lance on his way, for he had no desire to leave it; his horse passed through the door at a walking pace; thus easily he carried the damsel away towards his land. Seated beside the king at table, Gawain was grieved and deep in thought; he did not know which was the most honourable action: whether to leap up from the table in pursuit of the knight, or to remain seated until the meal was over. He thought for a long time, neither eating nor drinking; finally, he decided that it was best to suffer the delay, since he knew his horse was so fast that he could soon overtake the stranger.

Kay, who had perceived all that took place, addressed his companions: 'Gentlemen,' he said, 'now you may learn how to serve this court well, for I shall immediately follow the knight who has committed such an outrage in the presence of all the nobles. With rash pride, he has seized the damsel from the king's presence at table; never before has any knight behaved in such a manner. Of one thing you may be sure: such a thing has never happened to the king before, since he held his first feast; this was such a great disturbance, since the man in whose care the king placed this damsel failed to prevent her from being snatched away. A hundred curses on whoever first declares that Gawain is a good knight.'

With this, Kay rushed to his lodging and armed himself magnificently. As soon as he was armed, he mounted a fine horse, then set off along the high road by which the knight had departed. He studied the country around him, to see if the stranger's horse had left tracks; then he broke into a great gallop in order to reach his target quickly. He had not ridden far when he saw his quarry climbing a hill. Then Kay began to call out: 'There you are, sir varlet! I shall lead the damsel and your horse along with me, and deliver your body to the king for his justice to be done. It was wicked to take the lady from his presence so insolently; if you do not surrender through death or capture, I shall not consider myself worth a prune.'

The knight lifted the damsel down from his horse, and replaced his bridle, then asked, 'Is this Gawain who follows me so rashly?' 'Oh, no,' he replied, 'I am Kay, King Arthur's seneschal.' 'Well now,' the other answered, 'it is an evil hour for you to demand this: the reputation of your chivalry is not very high in my country.' Then each charged against the other, for there was no further wrangling. Kay struck his opponent below the boss of his shield, which broke with the blow, but the knight's hauberk protected him, and none of the mail was damaged; Kay struck so hard that his lance broke. His opponent hit Kay so hard that he overturned both the seneschal and his horse. Falling down, Kay was seriously shaken and wounded; his right arm was broken between the shoulder and the elbow. His horse jumped up, and returned home the way it had come. His enemy took no further interest in Kay, but left him lying there; he quickly returned to the damsel and lifted her back on the horse in front of him. 'My beauty,' he said, 'as I thought, *Sir* Kay will not take you back.' Then he set his steed towards the woods, rejoicing greatly with his lady.

Now I must return to the king and his company, who were still sitting at table; Arthur was very thoughtful about the adventure. In full view of everyone he took a knife, which had been fixed in a loaf of bread; then he bent the knife in his hand until it broke in two. There was not a single one of the knights present who dared to enquire of the king the direction of his thoughts; Arthur realized this, and knew full well that they had seen how the knife had been broken. 'My lords,' he said, 'I am very angry about the enmity shown today; I have even greater annoyance about the misconduct of Gawain. I believed it certain that I would never be bothered by the presence of a single knight while Gawain defended me. If by chance another knight had the damsel in his care and, for whatever fault he possessed, he had not dared protect her, Gawain should have undertaken to defend her for the sake of my honour. It upsets me greatly that such annoyance has befallen me on such an important day.'

Then Yder the son of Nu spoke: 'Sire,' he said, 'do not worry yourself; the seneschal has gone, and will adequately avenge this shame.' The king replied, 'That is not the point: it increases and doubles my annoyance. There is such great prowess in that knight, and he is so fierce and proud, that if Kay is not already injured, he may well be conquered; never in all my life have I seen anyone more outrageous than him.'

Then Gawain said: 'Thank you, sire! You have spoken as you please; but I did not wish to leap up from your table during the meal. I feared to be reproved, if I had offended by departing in such a manner. You possess such great lordship, and God has made you such a prominent man, that if the emperor of Rome himself came here to threaten you while you were seated at dinner, it would be the worst he could do to you, since whatever he might do should not disturb you here. After the meal, he who wished to please you, and to whom the business belonged, would depart to avenge your honour and his own. I know that my horse is so swift that I may quickly overtake this fellow. You must not believe that he can abduct the damsel with impunity. God would never give me honour if I left this task unfinished. If I have done any wrong, I am quite ready to make amends.' With these words, Gawain rose from the table and demanded his arms, which were brought by two squires; he was very quickly armed, then mounted his good horse, which never failed in battle; and when he had seized his shield, and his lance had been handed to him, he hurried off on his mission.

Gawain is not able to overtake the abductor, Escanor, for several days, for various reasons. Throughout this romance he is at pains to regain his reputation and undertakes many tasks disguised as 'the Nameless Knight', in pursuit of Escanor, whom he eventually defeats. In the concluding scene, the nuptials of two young knights who have assisted Gawain in redeeming his reputation provide an opportunity for a splendid display of Arthur's gratitude. This demonstration of magnanimity to those knights who, while not Arthur's followers, have rendered services to him or his knights is commonplace; often they subsequently become Arthur's vassals.

The Romance of Hunbaut (c. 1250–75)

This story, which opens in King Arthur's court at Caerleon, reveals the king's power and wealth, but also sheds light on his character. In this extract, Arthur is revealed to be an aggressive ruler, eager to extend his overlordship by force. He is also shown to be rather rash and unmindful of the basic requirements of his own followers in order to fulfil his commands. Thus Arthur sends Gawain to confront a foreign king who refuses him homage, with only the hero's sister to accompany him.

King Arthur had a great deal of wealth and a large treasury of gold and silver; he also had many fine people from all over the world, since he was a king possessed of all riches. It was at Caerleon, I believe, that the good king spent most of his time in a fine abode; but one joyful, happy and fine day, Hunbaut (for whom the king had considerable affection) came back to court. He was a knight who had been away from court for a year or two and had never been seen at court during this time, since he had been wandering about to increase his renown, like a courteous and well-informed man who was endowed with fine qualities. He was a member of the Round Table, to which no bad man could belong.

The king asked him about his situation and how he had fared. They spoke together from the time they got up until the moon had risen, and when the night was pitch-black, the king, who was very anxious to hear what Hunbaut recounted of his adventures, commanded (so the story tells) that a bed should be prepared in front of his own in his chamber, since he had such a strong desire to hear Hunbaut speak, and he very much wished to converse during the night while he was awake. So when they had spent enough of the night awake, they went to sleep for a while, for they had little enough time, as it was the end of May. They were not troubled about anything, but slept until the morning.

The birds sang in the morning, since they were happy and joyful that it was day. Then the king called out to Hunbaut, who answered him at once. 'Hunbaut,' the king said, 'now tell me, you who have travelled through the world, is there then nobody, either in a valley or on a mountain, who does not hold his land from me? There is no one so clever in England, France or Constantinople, that he would not be grieved, however noble he might be, if he should break my command.' Hunbaut replied after a short while that, between the isles, there *was* a king who had immense pride, 'since he holds his kingdom independently; he lives and reigns in great splendour, since his realm is free.' King Arthur replied immediately, without seeking anyone's advice, that his nephew Gawain, who was very valiant, should make this king come to court.

'Hunbaut,' he said, 'since you are wise, I will explain why I have undertaken such an enterprise. Gawain my nephew is very worthy, as many people know, and he is valiant, good and noble, a fine speaker, courteous and wise: I wish to entrust him with my message; I will send him beyond the isles to that king who is so very proud that he does not accept me as his overlord. Gawain, who knows how to behave well, will tell him what I have sworn: I vow before God that, if he does not come to receive his land from me and render me homage, he may be assured that I will move against him on the first day of summer.'

'Sire, I've been in that land,' replied Hunbaut. 'Sire, I do not believe that anyone could capture any of his castles by assault, or could send ships across the sea in an attack; and I assure you, so help me God, there are many wicked men to overcome.' The king said, 'Don't say this, if you wish to have my affection, for I will not give up my undertaking for a tower full of wealth.'

So Gawain, he whom the whole world admires, is commanded to come to court. One of the king's chamberlains hastens to inform him of the king's order, and my lord Gawain asks for his robe of ermine, of which there is no equal, and he puts it on. Stories have informed me that he has no equal in the world for prowess and valour.

When he had climbed up the stairs to the chamber whither his uncle had summoned him, Gawain immediately asked him, 'By God, sire, what do you require?' The king commanded him at once to go and take the message, and he replied like a wise man, 'Sire, I will do it, if I am able.' Then he added very courteously that, if it did not displease the king, he would very much like to have a companion who could give him some assistance.

Then the king was very astonished that Gawain, who was so highly regarded that it was hard to find his equal, thought of having a companion. The king was really amazed that he had a need for any companion, and replied, 'I have too few knights, for which reason I'm very concerned. I don't mind if you take my niece, who is here; you can take her with you, if you don't mind: she's your sister, a fine friend to assist you, if anyone attacks you.' Gawain replied, 'So God save me, I am satisfied with this offer, and well paid by her company.' When Hunbaut heard this, he was astonished that the king had said such a strange thing, and why he had thought so little about it.

Gawain took his sister by the hand, and they went together to the lodging, both the girl and he who had such a reputation that nobody could take it from him [...].[98] ... except for a surcoat, without any other garment. No man shall say that I steal the fine expressions of Chrétien de Troyes, who threw out ambushes and snares to achieve mastery of the game, and we use much word-play for this reason.

In this way, it appears to me, they arrived at the lodging together: these two about whom I have been telling you. Gawain's sister, who came with him, had a beautiful body and an even more beautiful face: it is clear that Nature forgot nothing in whatever she had done. The king displayed the poverty of his character in his behaviour towards Gawain, in sending him into such a country where there was so much peril and uncertainty.

The Romance of Laurin (Le Roman de Laurin)
(c. 1250–75)

This French prose work is concerned mainly with the chivalric exploits of Laurin and other non-Arthurian characters, but there is a fairly substantial Arthurian episode. In fact, Laurin's visits to Arthur's court are linked with his friendship to Gawain, who appears as the White Knight since he is involved in a crisis over his reputation and supposed death.

The first extract describes the arrival of Baudemagus and his friends at Arthur's court, which is here located at Winchester. The king is anxious for news of his nephew, Gawain, who has been absent from court for a long time and is depressed when he fails to hear anything.

They did not stop riding until they arrived at Winchester, where King Arthur and all his barons were. They saw that the town was so full of banners that there could not possibly be any more. They entered the court and dismounted. Arthur was at the hall window, with his closest friends around him. He looked out and saw the companions [of the Round Table]. He could not wait for them to climb up, so he descended the steps. He greeted them and called each one by his name and recognized him, and then he embraced them all and asked them how they were. They told him that they were all well and in good spirits, thank God.

Perceval and the other companions gave them a hearty welcome. After they had gone upstairs, Arthur called the five companions and asked them if they knew any news of his kinsman Gawain. They all comforted him as well as they could, but none of them had any accurate news to relate. Then the king began to weep most heavily. 'What?' said Lancelot. 'You should hold a feast for Baudemagus and the companions who have come, and yet you make a worse appearance at their arrival than if they had stayed away.' 'Lancelot,' said the king, 'I expected to hear better news from them than I have; this makes my heart afflicted, which is not surprising.' Then Baudemagus spoke, and said, 'Sire, if I dared criticize you for the welcome which you have given me, know that I blame you for it willingly, for I tell you that soon you shall hear such news as will make you very glad.' 'Indeed,' said Mordred under his breath, 'he will see with his eyes who has murdered his kinsman, so he will avenge him, if he is able.'

It was time for supper, and Kay had ordered the horn to be blown

which announced that the water was ready for the diners to wash
their hands before eating.[99] After the king had washed and was
seated at supper, Lancelot began to speak to Baudemagus and his
companions, and everyone seated themselves, one after another. The
supper lasted a long time, and everybody was getting annoyed that
the king was sitting so long, but it was not surprising, for the king
was pensive and grieving: thus the supper continued for a very long
time. Why should I make a long story of it? The tables were removed.

Lancelot du Lake took Baudemagus by the hand and led him aside
and asked him about his adventures. Baudemagus told Lancelot what
had befallen him, and how he had been accompanied by a knight
from Greece called Laurin, and explained how he had parted from
this knight, and how the three of them had set off on a quest to find
him. When Lancelot understood this, then he did not cease to ask
about Laurin, for he had a great desire to see him and make his
acquaintance. Baudemagus related to him first how he had met
Laurin, and afterwards everything in the order in which it occurred
right to the end. 'By my faith,' said Lancelot, 'I know well that he
has great virtue. Now, may God guard him in whatever place he is.'

It was bedtime, so the beds were prepared and they went to sleep.
When it was morning, the king got up early and went to church. The
barons had come from the whole realm, and I tell you that the town
was so filled with people that nobody could find lodgings. Why
should I draw out the story? The tourneys were to be held on the
second day after Baudemagus's arrival at court.

*The following passage contains an interesting episode in which a
lady, dressed as a knight, arrives at Arthur's court and unhorses
Kay for his insolent language, throwing him into the river at
Winchester.*

On the third day after the hour of Vespers it happened that King
Arthur and a large number of his barons were at court, and while
they were there a fully armed knight entered the court, bearing before
him[100] a woman's robe which was very rich, and beside him came an
unarmed knight riding on a palfrey. They entered through the door.
Those who were there left their amusements and came towards them.
They dismounted and came before King Arthur and greeted him most
nobly, and the king told them that they were welcome, and then asked
them without further delay who they were.

'Sire,' he said, 'a knight who left your court three days ago who is
called Laurin sends us to you to do your will; since by my serious

affront I insulted him, he conquered me by force of arms. He told me that I should come to you and do your will.' 'In what direction did the knight go?' asked the king. 'For you should inform me!' 'Sire,' he said, 'he went after a knight and a maiden, whom he has now overtaken, as far as I know, since we passed them shortly after we encountered him.' Then the king asked him whose dress it was that he carried. 'Sire,' he said, 'it is mine.' 'Yours?' he said. 'Do you then wear women's clothes?' 'Sire, why should I wear any other clothes than those which pertain to me?' 'Are you a knight?' asked the king. 'Indeed,' the knight replied, 'I am a woman when I am dressed in my robe, but whoever has dealings with me when I am dressed as I am now will find me a knight.' Then when she had said this and the barons had seen her, they were very surprised and laughed heartily.

Sir Kay himself came forward and said, 'By God, lady, a knight who has conquered you by force of arms should prize himself highly, for, if you were clad in your robe, you could conquer all those in this place, one after the other.' Then the damsel was highly incensed, and said, 'By God, son of a whore, slave, if I did not believe I would commit a fault against another, rather than merely against you, I would make you drink of this river so that you will have enough of it, whether you like it or not.' 'Kay,' said the king, 'your tongue is very venomous. Can't you be quiet? Believe that if she is a woman, then she is a gentlewoman.' Kay said, 'Before she makes me drink of that river she will have her skin wet, and she can put it to the test whenever she likes.' 'Sire,' said the damsel to the king, 'I ask you, since he wishes it, that you will give me permission. Then you will know who is right or wrong.'

Then the barons said to the king, 'Sire, permit this thing. Neither of them will get injured.' Then the king said, 'Damsel, do whatever you wish.' Then she came towards Kay, and when he saw her coming he did not refuse, but jousted with her (and believed that he would overthrow her), but he might just as well have jousted against a pillar, since she was not weak; instead she struck him so hard that she made him cry out. She did not wish to stop there, so she carried him to the river and threw him in. He was soon rescued, but there was never such a noise as was made at that time.

The damsel was now disarmed and appeared in her robe, and was one of the most beautiful creatures who could be wished for. She came before the king and said to him, 'Sire, here is the knight whom Laurin sent you.' The king looked at her very closely, then he sat down beside her and said, 'By God, damsel, I'm very pleased to retain you. Moreover, you should know well that if you had killed one of my men, it would have been your right, and if I should see you as you are now, it would be pardoned.' 'Sire,' said the damsel, 'thank you very much.'

The maiden was made much of and welcomed by all. Then the king asked her name. She replied that she was called Maligne, and her friend was Celidos. When the king heard this he was pleased with the adventure, and said that he wished that they would join his retinue. Then the damsel said that she would do so willingly. Afterwards, the knight said to the king: 'Sire, Laurin wished me to greet Kay.' Then Kay was called and when he came, she said to him: 'Sir Kay, Laurin greets you and informs you that he was never so hard-pressed by a knight as he was by me.'[101] 'Lady,' said Kay, 'the knight had good adventure, and you were happy when you were next to him.' 'Indeed,' said the damsel, 'if I do not avenge that remark of yours before the year is out, if I have the time and place, may I never wear a hauberk.' Then Kay was greatly blamed for this remark, but it was left for now as it was time for supper. Then the tables were set and the water announced by horn and they sat to supper; and when it was time to rise they washed and went to play, some here and others there.

In the tournament which follows, Laurin fights the mysterious White Knight, afterwards discovered to be Gawain, who then recounts how an evil knight had misused his identity to deceive a damsel who was in love with the hero. As the White Knight, Gawain had killed this villain and wooed the damsel before re-establishing his reputation.

The Rise of Gawain (De Ortu Walwanii) (c. 1250–75)

This mid-thirteenth-century Latin work relates the early life of Arthur's famous nephew Gawain, who had been sent to Rome at the age of twelve to be brought up in the household of Pope Sulpicius, by whom he is knighted.[102] Another version of this story is extant in the fragmentary thirteenth-century French poem Les Enfances Gauvain *(Gawain's Childhood).*

The following extract opens at the point in the story where Gawain, who is known in this work as the Knight of the Surcoat, has returned in triumph to Rome after defeating a pagan champion. He is honoured by the emperor and senate and, since he has now secured peace for the Roman Empire, he is eager for further opportunities to display his prowess. He takes leave of the emperor in order to visit the court of King Arthur, whose fame is known throughout the world.

In this work, Queen Gwendoloena (Guenevere) is a sorceress who is able to foretell the future. She informs Arthur of the hero's arrival. Arthur himself is an active figure, maintaining a joust custom, rather than the more usual customs of not dining before hearing of an adventure or the hunt for the white hart. Arthur's manners resemble those of his companion Kay in this story, and his treatment of the hero is rather harsh, even after he becomes aware of Gawain's identity. It is only when Gawain has rescued the young lady of the 'Castle of Maidens' and defeated her pagan oppressor, after Arthur and his knights have failed, that the king recognizes him as his nephew and bestows on him the honour he deserves.

Once these deeds had been accomplished, as no one was presuming to move against the Roman Empire by sword, the Knight of the Surcoat, disdaining the peaceful life and desiring military action where his courage and prowess could be constantly exercised, eagerly enquired what region might be torn by the tumults of war. When the name of Arthur, the famous King of Britannia (his uncle, though he did not know it), acclaimed for prowess around the world, was brought to his attention, unmoved by all the emperor had given him, the Knight of the Surcoat humbly petitioned [to leave] time and again. The emperor, though he had already decided to promote him to the highest position, and he had no doubt that the departure of so worthy a man would be to his own loss, gave assent to the petition in order that the knight might learn from whom he traced his lineage, and also because he felt confident that through him the Kingdom of Britannia, so long separated from the Roman Empire, would be regained for himself. The emperor bestowed on him rich, sumptuous, and priceless gifts and delivered to him the coffer in which the proof of his parentage remained, with orders that it must be presented to King Arthur, adding his own letter as testimony that everything the documents of record stated was established and confirmed. Further, he forbade him to look inside the coffer before he entered the presence of King Arthur. He ordered, then, that the first citizens of the Gauls through whose lands the knight must pass should receive him with honour, serve him, provide him with necessities, and escort him safely through their territories all the way to the sea. So, farewells spoken, the knight departed, leaving the ruler behind.

With everyone grieving over his departure, the Knight of the Surcoat began the journey as planned. He crossed the Alps; and having made his way through Gaul, he arrived safely in Britannia. Enquiring where at that time King Arthur was in residence, he learned that he was staying at the city of Caerleon in Demetia, where he was accustomed to spend more of his time than in his other cities. That charming city, laid out with groves, abounding in animals, rich in treasures, pleasant for its green meadows, and watered by the Usk River and, not far away, the Severn, offered a dwelling place of the utmost delight. Here was the metropolitan city of the province of Demetia, here the legions of Rome used to spend the winters, here King Arthur celebrated the high feasts, wore the crown, and convened all the princes of Britannia for his assembly. As soon as the knight found out where Arthur was residing, he made his way in that direction, travelling swiftly in high spirits, pressing on day and night without a break. He was almost there; it was the last night before he expected to reach Caerleon, and he was just outside the town of Usk, six miles away, when a sudden violent storm struck with driving rain. Everyone with him either left the high road or was unable to keep up.

The same night, King Arthur and Gwendoloena, his queen, were talking to each other about many things while resting in bed. (Because of the length of night they had had enough sleep.) Queen Gwendoloena was indeed the most beautiful of all women, but she was initiated into sorcery, so that often from her divinations she would read the future.

Among the other things she discussed with the king, she said, 'Lord, you boast and greatly extol your prowess, and you assume that no one is your equal in strength.'

Arthur replied, 'It is so. Doesn't your own heart feel the same about me?'

The queen answered, 'Of course it does – but there is at this very hour of the night a knight from Rome who is passing through the town of Usk on his way here. Have no doubt that you will find him pre-eminent in courage and prowess. He is mounted on a steed to which no other can be compared in vigour, value, or grace. His armour is impenetrable, and no one withstands the blow of his right arm. And lest you think I declare this to you lightly, look for the sign: he will send to me a gold ring and three thousand-pieces as well as two horses by mid-morning.'

Arthur, aware that she had never deceived him in any prediction whatever, still decided to test this information without her knowledge. For it was his custom that whenever he heard of any strong man presenting himself, he would challenge that man, so that by single combat he could display the greater worth.

So a little later when the queen had drifted off to sleep, he got up, armed himself, mounted his horse, and took as his companion for the encounter only Kay, his seneschal. He came upon the Knight of the Surcoat halting at some little stream flooded by the run-off of the storm; he was looking for the crossing of the ford and cursing the delay. Actually because he was confused by the foul fog of the night, he had decided on the deep channel of the river.

Sighting him by the gleam of his armour, Arthur shouted, 'Where did you come from, you who wander over this countryside in the dead of night? Are you a fugitive, a bandit, or a spy?'

To him the knight replied, 'I wander because I do not know the roads. No flight of an exile drives me, no pillage of a bandit tempts me, nor does deceit cover any trickery.'

Arthur answered, 'You rely on your quick tongue. I see your game. I know too well that you have to be one of those three I named. So without more ado, lay down your arms. Unless you give yourself up to me utterly, you will learn immediately that I am the scourge of your wickedness.'

The knight responded, 'Anybody is foolish and fainthearted who starts to run before the fight, or who gives in to his enemy before he must. If, however, you still want my arms, I swear to their power; I'll match you for them, blow for blow.'

So words exchanged between them erupted into threats and abuses, and Arthur, goaded to fury, made ready to cross the river, spurred his horse to the encounter, and rushed blindly at him. The Knight of the Surcoat, waiting for him with drawn and couched lance, drove at him in the ford itself and knocked him into the middle of the river. Backing up, he caught hold of his struggling horse by the reins. Kay the seneschal, wanting to avenge his lord, spurred his horse and met the Knight of the Surcoat, but just as before, with the first blow he was piled on top of Arthur in a single heap. The knight, using the point of his lance, pulled the horse toward him. The darkness of the night had saved Arthur and Kay from being harmed. Those two who had come to this place as knights returned home as foot-soldiers with no little disgrace.

Arthur, in fact, climbed back into bed. Queen Gwendoloena asked him, stiff as he was with cold, soaked not only by the rain but also by the river water, where he had been for so long and why he was so wet.

Arthur replied, 'I thought I heard some sort of commotion outside in the courtyard; I figured it might be some of my men fighting, so I went out. It took a while to settle, and I was drenched in the rain.'

The queen answered, 'Whatever you say. Truly, wherever you went and what took place my messenger will tell me in the morning.'

The Knight of the Surcoat, having crossed the shallowest part of the water and not realizing with whom he had done battle, turned towards the nearby village and found lodging. At the first light of day, he hurried on towards Caerleon. About two miles down the road he noticed a boy and asked who employed him.

The boy told him, 'I am a messenger of the queen, whose personal instructions it is my duty to carry out.'

And the knight said, 'Will you do what I shall require of you?'

The boy replied, 'I am at your service.'

The knight said, 'Take these two horses and lead them for me to the queen as my gift so that she may accept gladly the proof of my prowess in pledge for requesting friendship.'

Handing him the gold ring and the three pieces of gold to be carried to her as well, he told him his name and declared he would follow him on the road. The messenger did what had been asked of him. He accepted the gold items and led the horses with him.

Meanwhile, Queen Gwendoloena, aware of what was going to happen, stood on the wall of the castle watching the road that led to the town of Usk. When she observed from a distance her messenger returning, leading two horses with all their trappings, she understood the situation, and, descending quickly, met him as he entered the hall. The boy transacted the business gracefully, revealed his instructions, delivered the things sent, and announced that the Knight of the Surcoat was about to arrive. The queen, smiling at the name, accepted the gifts and thanked him. She ordered that the horses should be led into the bedroom right to the couch of the king, who was still resting since he had spent the whole night awake and active.

Having roused him from his sleep, she said, 'Lord, lest you accuse me of fabricating what I know, see the ring and the gold which yesterday I promised must be sent to me today. Moreover, the knight I foretold last evening has presented to me these two horses which, having overthrown their riders at that river, he commandeered for himself.'

King Arthur, recognizing his own horses and seeing disclosed what he had hoped to be kept secret, was consumed with shame.

Then Arthur went out to the assembly of nobles he had ordered to come together on that day for pressing concerns. As he sat before the hall under the shade of an ash tree with his people, the same Knight of the Surcoat entered the gates on horseback. Approaching the presence of King Arthur, he greeted him along with the queen and knights sitting nearby.

Arthur, not unaware of who he was, turned a grim face towards him and responded quite bluntly. He asked about his origin, where he travelled, what he sought in these regions. The man replied that he was a Roman knight, and that since he had heard Arthur was pressed by war and in need of knights, he had come to offer his services, and that furthermore he had brought imperial mandates. He then handed the sealed coffer and document to the king. When Arthur had received the letter, he withdrew from the assembly and ordered it to be read. On receiving the testimony of the document along with the records of proof and the pallium and signet ring offered in evidence, he was greatly astonished. All this he strove with every desire to regard as truth. Out of immense joy he simply could not believe the fact that this man was indeed his nephew. He remained incredulous of the matter till both parents had been summoned – Loth, King of Norway, and Anna, the Queen – who, it happened, were there, summoned along with the other nobility. He exacted the truth from them and rigorously tested the facts. They confessed that it was all true, that he was indeed their son, and their testimony was witnessed and attested by special oaths. Arthur was exhilarated with incredible joy that the man upheld in so many ways by the emperor's commendations and by a great reputation for exalted prowess was, as a final surprise, related to him by close kinship. Nevertheless, he purposely ordered that none of this should be revealed to the knight till he had accomplished some outstanding exploit in his presence.

So returning to the assembly and calling the knight before everyone, Arthur said, 'Your help, friend, I do not need at the present time; I do not know precisely whether prowess or awkwardness flourishes more in you. I have a band of knights of such incomparable prowess, endowed with such strength and courage, that to include a clumsy and cowardly one among the skilful and daring is to risk weakening their spirit from its customary boldness and aggressiveness. An enormous number of knights like you serve me voluntarily without stipend, among whom, unless you should first show you deserve it, my decision stands that you should not even be enrolled.'

To this the Knight of the Surcoat, goaded by his words, replied, 'By offering to serve you, I have incurred from you a grave rejection and an unexpected injury – I, who heretofore was deemed worthy to offer to come to your aid inasmuch as I was not dissuaded by numerous entreaties nor influenced by great wealth. I do not doubt that I will find someone whom I may serve; yet even if I try, I will not easily find your equal. Indeed, since a desire for military challenge brought me here, and if I should depart from here it could be ascribed to cowardice and clumsiness, on the following condition you might consider me worthy to be one of your band of knights: that I alone accomplish something in which your whole army shall have failed.'

Arthur answered, 'My reply is this decree: If you should accomplish what you have bargained, I shall not only enrol you among them but indeed set you to be loved above them all.'

The plan pleased the king and all his nobility as well, and he kept the knight at his court for the present under the agreed condition.

Not twice six days had passed when an occasion of this sort compelled Arthur to set forth an expedition. In the northern part of Britannia was a certain castle called 'Castle of the Maidens', which a young woman, who was noted as pre-eminent for her grace and nobility, governed by right of lordship. She was allied to Arthur by the deepest obligations of friendship. A certain pagan king, captivated by her graceful bearing and great beauty and having in turn been rejected by her, had besieged her in her own fortified town. Already, since the siege machinery had been constructed and transported to the site and the mounds to support it built up, he was threatening to storm the castle and seize her. Since she knew she could not bear up under the remitting attacks and daily assaults, she sent a messenger and begged Arthur to come to her aid. As she was barricaded in her tower and the farther wall had already been breached, she deemed it necessary to surrender very soon to the enemy unless he brought up reinforcements immediately.

So Arthur, fearing the peril of the young woman in her castle, at once mustered, armed, and drew up the ranks of his knights; and fully prepared, though consumed by great dread, he began the march to the place where he had been summoned. Many times, it is true, he had encountered and fought this very king, but it had always resulted that he was repulsed and beaten. As he was approaching the siege, a second messenger arrived, running with hair loose about his cheeks, who reported that the pagan king had razed the city and had seized and carried off the lady. The messenger continued to plead for his mistress that the love King Arthur had held for her in prosperity he would now show her in adversity. Arthur pursued the enemy burdened with plunder. He fell furiously upon their rear guard where he thought them least protected, but because of an unfortunate omen, he was intercepted by them. Having been thus warned of his approach, they repulsed him armed and in battle order. To protect the line they had placed the more experienced warriors in the rear guard, which would not then be easily thrown into confusion by sudden attack.

His front ranks, instead, were brought to confusion by the unexpected strength of the enemy's rear guard; and they, surrounding Arthur's men on all sides, contained them, pressed them, and shattered them. Here the bitterest battle was fought and bloody slaughter was inflicted on both sides. And Arthur, having been in the very lap of the enemy, was being pressed back most strongly, demoralized and exhausted; and unless by cutting his way out he could immediately retreat, he would be slain and his entire army cut down. He therefore gambled on the deliverance of flight, calculating it wiser to run to safety than to succumb to the disaster hanging over him.

At the beginning of the engagement, the Knight of the Surcoat had withdrawn to a high, remote lookout in order to see what might befall the fellowship of knights during the course of battle. When the retreat revealed the disaster to him, he confronted Arthur fleeing with the first wave, and laughing at him, shouted bitingly, 'Tell me, O King, do you pursue deer or perhaps rabbits that you go scattered this way along the paths?'

To him Arthur replied indignantly, 'I have sufficient proof of your great prowess that you, while others are involved in battle, have removed yourself to some secret hiding places of the forest.' Without further words he rode off, the enemy in pursuit.

The Knight of the Surcoat, taunting with jeers and slurs every single one of the knights he encountered, turned to attack the pursuing enemy. He rushed raging upon the advance patrols, penetrating through the tight and strong formations into their very midst like a winter storm – he injured no one except those who offered him resistance.

When he saw the royal guard, he instantly spurred his horse forward; with lance couched, the unexpected assailant ran the gleaming point into the hollow of the king's chest. Having thrown the dying man to the ground, he seized the young woman by her horse's bridle and at once set out to return the way he had come.

But the guard which surrounded the king, thrown into disorder on seeing their lord struck down in their midst, with a shout cut the invader off; and swords drawn, they charged and set upon him. They rush at him together, and he at all of them. From a distance some throw spears at him; from all sides others strike at him ceaselessly with their blades. Like a rain storm the multitude of blows beat upon him. Still, he continued on his way, leaving them cut down. But he was greatly hampered because he had to defend not only himself but his lady. Not far distant was a broad and deep fosse marking the boundary between two provinces. By this was the limit and division of their boundaries decreed. It had only a narrow access and its bridge allowed only one person to cross at a time. To this place, then, the Knight of the Surcoat raced, and arriving there, he sent the lady to safety within the fortifications of the fosse, ordering her to remain hidden from sight until he returned. Once more plunging into the ranks of the pursuing enemy, he turned them back, put them to flight, and dispersed them. Roaring like a lion bereft of its cubs, he raged cruel slaughter upon them without mercy. Not one of them bore up under the attack nor did any who came in contact with the massive power of his right arm go away uninjured. Wherever he turned, they were scattered as from the blast of a tempest.

The powerful one continually slashed them to death without pity. Not withdrawing until all of them had been routed, he marked all for death: some flung themselves from the steep banks, some by choice threw themselves into the obstructing waters, and the remainder he himself cut to pieces in a massacre.

The Knight of the Surcoat, having gained victory without injury to himself, cut off the head of the pagan king with the royal diadem still in place, fastened it on his standard and, raising it on high, returned to King Arthur with the lady by his side. Exulting, he entered the hall where King Arthur, depressed and grieving at the misfortune of war, was seated.

He cried out, 'Just where, O King, are your famous champions of whom so long you boasted that no one is their equal in courage? See the head of the man I alone conquered and laid low, along with the entire force of his knights. He was the king who with a handful put to flight and terrified so many thousands of your men so often that it is shameful! Do you consider me worthy to be your knight?'

Arthur, joyous, recognizing the head of the king hateful to him beyond all others and the young woman so dear to him rescued from the hands of the enemy, ran to embrace him and replied, 'You are truly worthy to be chosen as a knight, and you must be granted special honours! Nevertheless, since till now we have been uncertain who you are who have come to us, I ask you to explain more in detail where your native land is, from whom you trace your lineage, by what family name you are listed?'

And the other replied, 'The truth of what I have told you holds. I was born in the region of Gaul, fathered by a Roman senator. I was educated in Rome, and "Knight of the Surcoat" is what I happen to be called.'

Arthur returned, 'You are plainly mistaken and what you have thought true cannot be confirmed; you must learn that, in a word, you have been deceived in this information.'

The knight asked, 'How so?'

Arthur explained, 'I shall show you your lineage. Knowledge of this fact shall be the reward for your deeds.'

Thereupon, with both of his parents present, to wit, Loth, King of Norway, and Anna, the Queen, he ordered the letter written by the emperor brought to him and, when it was brought, to be read in the hearing of the multitude of people and of nobles. When all the people were informed and all the documents read, amazement and incredible joy arose with the comprehension of it all, and they proclaimed the parents blessed for such an offspring.

Then King Arthur, gazing at him with joy, spoke: 'I acknowledge you, dearest one, my nephew. You are the son of my sister to whom ought to be ascribed the good fortune to have borne such a child not for any disgrace but for the greatest honour.' He added, 'Indeed at an early age you were called "Boy with no Name", and from the time you entered knighthood till the present, "Knight of the Surcoat". From now on you will be known as "Gawain", your real name.'

When Arthur announced this, three times, four times from the entire assemblage 'Gawain, nephew of King Arthur' was repeated and echoed.

The son, having been acknowledged by his father, the nephew by his uncle, the magnitude of joy is doubled, not only for the recovery of a lost loved one but also for this man's incomparable courage and strength. What other outstanding exploits fall to the share of Gawain, he who desires to know must demand by request or payment from one who knows. Realizing that just as it is more decisive to take part in a battle than to record a battle, even so it is more difficult to compose a history in eloquent style than it is to present it orally in the words of common speech.

ROBERT DE BLOIS, Biausdous
(mid-thirteenth century)

Perhaps written in response to the honour given to Galahad, Lancelot's son, in The Grail Quest, *popular stories were composed about Gawain's son, usually called Guinglain, who arrives unidentified at Arthur's court to win honour and claim his place in society. The first of these works is* Li Bel Inconnu *(The Fair Unknown), which is represented in this anthology by its English derivative,* Libaeus Desconeus.

Claimed by the poet to have been translated from a Latin text in the church of St Martin at Tours, Biausdous is another adventure involving a son of Gawain, but with a slight difference. Here, the young knight wins honour and the love of a beautiful heiress before attending court to claim his position as Arthur's close relation and vassal.

The poem opens at Arthur's Pentecostal court, where the news of King Lot's death is followed by a discussion of the forthcoming wedding of his son, Gawain, to Darling, the Princess of Wales, and his coronation as King of Ireland.

The story then turns to the hero who, although unaware of his father's identity, being merely called 'Biausdous' by his mother, desires to become a member of the Round Table. The young man is knighted by his mother, who orders him to conceal his identity until he has won honour. On his way to Arthur's court, the hero, known as the 'Knight with Two Shields', encounters a damsel returning from court after a fruitless visit to find a valiant knight to save Beauty, the Princess of the Isles, from the unwanted attentions of King Madoine. After Biausdous has defeated the unwanted suitor in single combat, he sends him prisoner to Arthur's court.

When the king [Madoine] had given his promise, Biausdous returned to the castle, while the king departed with his army, taking thirty knights with him on his journey. They rode for five whole days, and on the sixth came to Montagu, where they found King Arthur with a great gathering of nobles. On that very day Biausdous's mother had arrived there from Wales. You might have seen (if you were there) King Madoine visible to all in such armour and with such equipment as when he left the battleground. For it was a custom at that time, however valiant a man was, of whatever renown or reputation, that when he was conquered in battle, and if the knight who defeated him sent him to surrender to another person, he give himself up in this manner, just as he had departed from the fight.

King Madoine entered the hall at Montagu in such armour. He greeted King Arthur politely, and all the others in a similar manner. Then he spoke so that all could hear: 'King Arthur, the Knight with Two Shields commands me to salute you, as he who every day is eager to enhance your honour, for he greatly prizes you and holds you very dear. Owing to his valour, I must surrender myself to you and await his arrival, for without doubt he will come to court.'

King Arthur listened very attentively to this news and then replied, 'I thank you, but who are you, and what is your name?' 'I shall not hide that from you,' he answered. 'I am called Madoine.' Then immediately the king and barons rose up to meet him and greatly honoured him; as soon as his identity was known, he was received with great joy. They knew well that he was one of the best knights in all the world, so they did him great honour and showed great pleasure. The knights who had set off with Biausdous, when they heard the news, left the hall and entered the room where Biausdous's mother was; this lady had been very grieved when she had not found her son at court. They told her the news privately, and when she heard it, she was comforted at once. She left the room immediately and went straight up into the hall, where both the king and at least seven earls rose to meet her.

Gawain, who was very concerned because he did not know what had become of his son, had expected that he would have wanted to come to court with his mother, while Biausdous's mother had believed that she would undoubtedly find her son at court with his father. There was nobody, of either high or low rank, at court who was not sorrowful for Gawain's sake, except those who knew that his son was the Knight with the Two Shields, whom they were all talking about and whose prowess had been so tested in many places throughout the land.

When this lady entered the hall, the whole place was illuminated with her great beauty; King Madoine was amazed to behold how lovely she was. When she recognized King Madoine, she placed both her arms around his neck and kissed his eyes and face more than seven times without stopping. Afterwards she implored him in these words: 'Gentle, debonair king, do not conceal from me any detail about the Knight with Two Shields. Is he safe, and well, and loved? For God's sake tell me the truth! When did you leave him? I love him so much that for his sake you shall have a splendid stay at court. I myself wish to protect you on his behalf, and I will serve you well, if you and the other knights whom he has sent as captives will be my prisoners, if you do not scorn my prison. But I do not believe that my prison will annoy you, either by day or by night.'

Then they all sat down together, and King Madoine replied very courteously, as one who is well bred: 'Lady, you should know for certain that I shall consider myself more highly if I may be your prisoner, which I shall be while it pleases you; I shall tell you the whole truth about the knight, without a lying word. When he had defeated me in arms (today is the sixth day since then), whether I wished it or not, in the sight of many people, I swore that I would surrender myself to King Arthur and remain with the king until he should arrive, for he ought to come to the high court. With him will come a maiden, and I tell you truthfully that her beauty will surpass that of all women who were ever born save only yours, for you are certainly her equal! All the islands of the ocean shall be his through this lady; for her father, who was a crowned king of great wealth, has no other heir, and this knight has proved himself, and men know well that he has achieved honour and renown above all other knights, through his beauty and courtesy as much as by his prowess, so that no one could be declared superior to him. I do not know what more I can tell you: there is no knight who can match his worth.'

The lady was very delighted when she heard this news, while Gawain was not only happy but completely amazed at this; he showed great delight in the king and was completely absorbed by the king's news. Since he was so happy, he declared: 'My lady, by the faith which you owe this knight whom you love so much, who is he? Tell us about him, whom we are all eager to know and honour, if he wishes to come to us. You should know that, for love of you, we will honour him even more.'

She answered, 'Since you have asked me, I will tell you the truth, for I should not conceal it from you any longer. He is the man whom you should love the most, for he is your son, I assure you.' Afterwards, she told Gawain how she had sent Biausdous off to court, and how she had instructed him to allow no one to discover his real name; nor should he refrain from undertaking exploits until he had proved himself in arms, and gained a reputation for prowess. 'Also, I made him carry two shields so that he should be known as the Knight with Two Shields, until he became better known.'

Then she called his companions, who recounted how they had encountered a damsel wearing a sword which was wrought in such a fashion and made with such mastery that it could never be drawn from its scabbard: through his expertise, Biausdous had drawn forth the sword, which nobody else could do. They related how they had left him there, with the damsel to guide him, since he told them that he would meet them at court as soon as possible.

The happiness which Gawain showed, when he heard this reliable news of his son, cannot be described. King Arthur was also very joyful, and all those who were present at court showed great happiness out of love for him, all declaring: 'God! When shall we see the knight whom we all most desire to behold, and when can we serve and honour him, and rejoice with him? He is worthy of great lordship, through both his prowess and his parentage; the whole world talks about him; I do not believe that the best of those whom a man might know nowadays is worth as much as he. By God! How miserable the evil-doers are, who do not wish to be chastised, when they hear the valiant praised and valued, those who through their goodness are honoured both when they are alive and when they are dead. Good deeds will never die while heaven and earth endure.'

When all those at court were sure that Biausdous was the son of Gawain, they showed great delight; but this joy would be redoubled as soon as he came to court. Often he was remembered by them, and he was talked about a lot by many people there. The king, who very much wished him there, said, 'My lords, listen, and when you have heard me, give me your advice. In my heart I am very happy, since I know that it is my nephew who is valued above all others. However, I am certainly very disappointed that I have never seen him, and do not know whether or not I will ever see him. For this reason, I beg you, my lords, for God's sake, that you consider how he might come before I hold a great court, for, if we fail to receive him beforehand, we could not provide him with a good enough welcome, since it is a custom at court that I honour everyone equally when I hold a formal court: then I must demonstrate goodwill to all, for I must not honour one man more than the others, but should welcome one and all. Therefore, it would please me very much if he might arrive here before the great court is gathered, for there are enough people here, of one sort and another, that one will be able to show him such happiness as he deserves and as I wish.'

'For my part,' said Gawain, 'I advise you to announce that a tournament will be held at Winchester or at Caerleon on the fifteenth day of Ascension. When he hears this news, he will go there if he is able, and if we do not find him at the tourney, we will never see him at court.' This pleased the king and all the others, and the tournament was announced to attract Biausdous; the day was appointed for its opening at Winchester.

The news spread so quickly that it soon reached Biausdous, who said that he must attend the tourney without fail, since he wished most eagerly to show his prowess there. He assembled all the princess's nobles and addressed them thus: 'My lords, what do you advise? I desire to go to this tournament which has been proclaimed, but in truth I know that I shall not be able to return before King Arthur has seen me, and that if I go there the king will wish to retain me, whether I desire it or not; I shall not be able to leave there, at least until the court disbands. I will not leave my lady to go there. To guard against this, if you think it a good idea, we will go there together. If you believe that it is too soon for you to go at once, I will go ahead and you shall find me at court when you reach there.'

The barons agree that those who wish to attend the tournament should depart with Biausdous, while the princess should meet him in London with the rest of her retinue.

At the tournament, Biausdous fights incognito, unhorsing Kay, Lancelot, Cliges, Yvain, Calogrenans and Erec. On the third and final day he jousts against Gawain, who is delighted when both are unhorsed, since he is certain that the unknown stranger must be his son. After the tournament, Biausdous hastily departs for London, without revealing his identity.

King Arthur was very surprised to learn that the victor of the tournament had departed. When the squires who had found Biausdous's shield showed it to Gawain and the king, everyone declared, 'This was Biausdous; we have all been totally deceived. It was he, most definitely: one might know this by the shield, for no other knight save he ever bore two shields.'

At once the tournament was terminated, and King Arthur, with all his equipment, left for London in the morning by the fastest route. However, Biausdous had already arrived there and had dismounted at his lodging, ordering everyone to keep his arrival secret. That night, Biausdous and his lady bathed together and were provided with every comfort. The king arrived in London on the following day, and when Darling saw Gawain she immediately asked him where Biausdous was. He replied that he did not know, but told her how their son had been present at the tournament, how he had departed thence, and that nobody knew where he had gone. 'By God, my lord,' answered Darling, 'I do not believe that you should have any doubt that he has gone whither I am going, for the lady whom he intends to marry has arrived here [in London]; you should be aware that she is prized above all other women for her beauty and wisdom.'

At this Gawain was quite delighted, and between them they then told the king, who had been depressed and rather angry since he did not know what had become of Biausdous; they sent for Beauty to comfort King Arthur. However, Biausdous had already secretly commanded Beauty to remain concealed at the lodging upon her arrival there, and had bidden her to prepare herself for court. She had not delayed in doing this; she was richly clothed, and her damsels also were richly attired to take the news to the king. Forty knights were sent on ahead; then he and the princess started on their way a little later, without more than thirty other gentlemen, each of whom led a beautiful damsel or lady by the hand.

The news that Biausdous was coming had spread, so that people gathered at windows on his route, all crying out, 'He is the best! By God, what a fine knight is he!' Nobody could, however hard they tried, ever describe completely the great beauty of the damsel whom he was leading. If Darling were also in this procession, a man could find there all the good qualities that God bestows on women.

Thus they proceeded until they arrived before King Arthur, with whom there were a thousand knights: in my opinion, none so fine could be found if one searched the entire world. The queen was present, and so also was Darling, who lit up everything around her with her beauty, as the sun lights the day. There was no one there, young or old, who did not hurry into the hall, for every one of them desired to see the knight arriving; and when he entered, before he greeted them all, his weeping mother threw herself around his neck to welcome him; then the king took Biausdous in his arms and kissed him more than seven times. Gawain embraced his son very lovingly, showing such joy as none had ever seen him demonstrate before; the queen's joy could not be described. The knights who had accompanied Biausdous from Wales were the most delighted of all; those who expressed most happiness did not forget the damsel. All showed such delight in the others that it was a marvel, and all were very happy and joyful when they learned the truth about Biausdous: when they were all told how he had been at the tournament, and that it was he and the duke who had carried the black shields. Never did any man achieve or behold such prowess as was shown by Biausdous.

Now Biausdous had arrived at court, King Arthur showed great delight in him; he found others there who were also very happy. There, at court, he discovered all the prisoners whom he had sent to surrender to the king, who now released them all from their captivity but would not allow them to leave until the formal court had ended. They remained there joyfully together and prepared for the coming festival, whilst Gawain arranged that he and his son should be crowned together, so there should be three noble kings at this court, and soon there would be a fourth there, for he was not a coward in matters of honour, nor did he forget either largesse or courtesy.

The Romance of Claris and Laris *(1268)*

A substantial late French verse romance, Claris and Laris *incorporates many of the ideas found in earlier works. Here, the two young heroes establish their reputation for prowess before arriving at Arthur's court and subsequently assist the king in his various wars. Little time is spent at Arthur's court, since the king is depicted in warlike mood.*

Like the Didot Perceval, Claris and Laris *introduces Arthur's war against the Roman emperor into a romance, although here it is merely a short episode in the lengthy poem. Evidently known in England in the fourteenth century, since it is mentioned in the* Chandos Herald's Life of the Black Prince *(M. K. Pope and E. C. Lodge, eds [Oxford: Clarendon Press, 1910], l. 4100), the poem may have given Malory the idea of transferring the Roman War to an earlier part of Arthur's reign.*

While relating the adventures of the titular heroes, the poem includes those of several established Arthurian heroes, especially Gawain and Ywain. The various episodes are interlaced in a complex manner, providing themes of chivalric combat, love stories and hospitality in almost all possible combinations. In the following passage, various Round Table knights inform the king and court of the assistance which they have received from Claris and Laris during their adventures. After hearing everything, Arthur summons a clerk to write down an accurate account, so that their deeds will be remembered.

They rode on until they reached Cardigan, where King Arthur was spending the entire winter until summertime. They told him about those whose prowess they had heard of, their news, and how they had learned it. They were willingly listened to by both ladies and knights, for at court were Gawain, Carados and my lord Ywain, who recounted his adventure to the king: how the dwarf had evilly led him into his castle, where he had exerted himself in tormenting him, how the thieves had imprisoned him and how the two young heroes, who bore identical arms, had freed him. The king and his chivalric followers listened eagerly to Ywain's news, and did not consider it to be an exaggeration, but an account of wonderful prowess and hazardous action.

The White Queen had arrived at court, but when she had heard this explanation, she was very pleased. She rose to her feet at once, and told the king her adventure: about all the trouble and irritation which King Nador had caused her, and how she had been rescued by Claris and the courteous Laris; the king and all those present laughed at this account. Then those who had been compelled to perform dangerous and laborious work in the tower where the goblin had imprisoned them immediately recounted how they had been freed by the efforts of two knights who bore exactly the same arms; this adventure was praised enthusiastically by all.[103] My lord Gawain then truthfully and most willingly began to tell how, when four knights had attempted to take his life and then to shame his sweetheart, the two companions had found them and delivered them both. King Arthur was very pleased at this story.

Carados then appeared and told the king in complete honesty how King Ladas had wickedly desired to possess and conquer his sweetheart, and would have succeeded if the kind companions had not arrived in that land. The two of them and just himself had fought nine knights; yet, in truth, the three of them had been victorious.

The marvellous enchanter, who held the Perilous Castle, recounted to the king the great wonder which no other could achieve: how the two knights had passed through the entrances which they found: first of all the tower of fire; and then he recounted, truthfully, their fight with the leopards and the two giants. King Arthur was very happy at this and said that it was a very brave deed; but the enchanter did not rest, and told how he and his nephew had been conquered when they attempted to avenge the giants, who had been killed by those who had crossed the threshold [i.e. Claris and Laris].

Matiadas of the Lost Rock, without delay, told the king about the joust against ten knights: how the companions had speedily taken away their chargers, and how he had truthfully seen three lions in the forest killed by the two companions. Then King Lot quickly told how Thoas had captured him and his companions and how they were freed by Claris and Laris, who had dealt their captors many blows.

When the king had heard everything, without delay he sent for a clerk, and ordered it all to be written in a document. I will tell you truthfully why: since he began ruling in Britain, it was customary for a record to be written, so that the deeds of the good should be for ever renowned, and the wickedness of evil-doers should be known through this account, so that after their death those who might hear of their deeds would amend their ways.

The king made it known throughout his land that nobody, unless he was prepared for war, should cause the two companions any trouble, either by day or by night: they were to be safeguarded by all and worthily served. Now what I have told you about the courteous companions, whose hearts were completely dedicated to serve chivalry attentively with a pure heart, is the complete truth.

In this extract King Arthur meets Claris and Laris for the first time, although they are already known to him through the assistance which they have given to various Arthurian knights. The two heroes feel embarrassed by the excessive attention Arthur shows them in his desire to secure them as members of the Round Table. The following little-known account of the Roman War and its aftermath is quite different from the familiar one recounted by Geoffrey of Monmouth and his literary successors.

That night they sang and danced together for a long time, and then they went to bed until the next day; when it was dawn, King Arthur arose, as indeed did the queen and all the other courtiers. Then they rode out together until they approached the town where the two companions were staying; they had recovered completely from the illness which they had suffered, although they had lain ill for a long time.

Then the king arrived there and took the provost by the hand. Gawain was leading the queen, who had a rosy complexion. Their company was very elegant, and enriched with beautiful ladies, knights and maidens, ladies and damsels. As soon as they entered the town, the companions went straightaway to meet the provost at the gate. The king dismounted first; when he saw the two companions, as soon as he recognized them, he went towards them and embraced them, gallantly wrapping his arms around both their shoulders; then he greeted them most honourably.

They returned his greeting in a manner appropriate to their rank. Then they asked, 'Who are you, lord?' And the king began to talk to them. Then the queen arrived, and Gawain helped her dismount; she went to embrace the two companions without delay. Immediately, they returned her embrace, and then asked her name. She told them most sweetly that she was the wife of the king himself. Then they bowed deeply to her.

Then, without further delay, you might have seen the flower of chivalry and the foremost beauties; each and every one of them greatly endeavoured to honour the two knights, whom they led to a lovely meadow near the town, for I tell you without any deception that such a large number of people had arrived there that they could not leave the town by the main road and had to go secretly through the gardens to leave the town, for it was feared that people might be killed, so closely would they have pressed forward to see the two companions.

The king made Claris and Laris sit beside him high in the meadow, so that all, both near and far, might clearly see them. Then the king commanded that the meal should be prepared; in a very short time it was ready. The king and barons washed their hands and then dried them. Laris, who had a fine complexion, sat between the king and queen, and Claris his companion with him, but they were greatly bored by the honour which the king showed them; it embarrassed them excessively, and they would have preferred the company of the young knights, which would have given them solace and delight. Moreover, what most upset them was that in front of the royal seats were more than a thousand vassals who were watching them from the narrow streets. They were greatly ashamed that below them sat my lord Gawain, Sagremors, lord Ywain, Gaheriet and Brandaliz, Karados and Laiz Hardiz, all members of the Round Table who were the most renowned knights in the world.

The meal was both suitable and good, for no king or queen had ever given a better, since the food was delicious. When the tables were removed, King Arthur stood up and then, without delay, spoke politely to the two companions: 'My lords,' he said, 'if God leads me, I have great need of assistance, but if you are willing to help me, I shall show you much goodwill and I will do your bidding, for the Roman emperor in his country has no man capable of bearing arms whom he has not brought with him; he wishes to drive me from Britain: I beg you to remain with me and lead my companions.'

Claris answered, 'Dear good sir, you have so many fine knights that we would commit a sin if we accepted lordship over them, but we wish to be their good companions, share their deeds and their way of life; if you wish to retain us, great good shall come to us from this.' Then the king replied, 'This will suit me very well, as long as it does not trouble you.'

Then the knights mounted and returned to Cardigan, where they were received royally, and the entire British army was assembled; the good did not flee, although the wicked hid themselves, because they feared the battle. However, so many brave men, of one sort or another, came there that the total number was truly remarkable. King Arthur strove very hard to welcome these brave men, but above all he wished to honour Claris and Laris highly. My lord Gawain graciously led them to his lodging. You must realize that these three well-endowed heroes will bring much grief to the emperor, with many fine blows!

Thus the king prepared his people, for he did not wait until the time when the Romans had arrived; he was very willing to take measures to encourage his supporters. From all parts of the country he had weapons brought to arm his men, so that they would be better able to defend themselves. (For I have often heard it reported that nobody could increase his renown if he was not prepared on many occasions; whoever is prepared is never shamed: thus the wise man speaks truthfully.) Thus King Arthur proudly awaited the arrival of the Romans, but he did not know when they would come.

When the day of Pentecost arrived, the Roman army assembled at Rome, the fortified city which was so powerful. Emperor Thereus, when he saw his barons arrive, was very happy and joyful; then he made his forces set off, and they went straight towards France. The senators travelled well; they passed through valleys and mountains, both the rough terrain and the plains; they travelled on, riding until they entered the land of the king who held Britain in his possession.

Arthur, who had assembled his people in the meadow below Cardigan, heard the news. Then he made it known that all should arm themselves the next day and not remain unprepared, for they would be marching against the Romans, who had entered his land. Then you might have seen hauberks whitened[104] and iron blades sharpened; straps were replaced on shields by those who know how to fight in close combat; horses were gathered together and shod by those who wished to fight on horseback; during the whole day they prepared themselves, and a great number stood watch that night in order to prepare their equipment properly and organize their needs.

The next day, as dawn broke, the army was on the move; Gawain led the advance guard with Claris, Laris, Ywain, Lucan, Kay the seneschal, Gaheriet and Gales li Chaus. These rode in front with ten thousand heavily-armed knights under their command who would never flee for fear, but delighted in fighting; thus they rode towards France. They travelled and exerted themselves until they approached the Roman army, and they stopped at least two leagues from the enemy. There, they camped beside a river which was very wide and had a strong current; that night they were watchful, since they did not wish to be attacked by surprise. For their part, the Romans kept guard, watched, and posted many sentinels; and they wished for daylight to come, since they greatly feared the British.

In the morning, at daybreak, the Roman army prepared to fight; they dressed in hauberks of fine mail, laced their helms, took up shields; swords and lances were sharpened, and then they girded themselves with swords. The emperor himself organized them into seven battalions ... the emperor himself led the seventh, and with him were the senators.

On the opposite side, King Arthur did not behave as a coward, but arranged his forces in battalions to fight in good order: the advance guard was led by Claris, the valiant Gawain, Ywain, Laris, Lucan and Kay the seneschal, with Gaheriet and Gales li Chaus. These formed the first advance guard. After them, in the noise of battle, rode King Carados, Cador, lord of Iroys, Perceval, Brandalis, Bedevere and Laiz Hardiz; these led the second battalion; I do not believe that they fled the fight, but they gave many blows with the lance before the Romans had left France.

In the third battalion was King Cadiolans, a very valiant king, King Mark and Gawain's brother, Agravain, Giflet and Do son of Nu, who suffered many great troubles; these would make the Romans tremble when it came to the affray. In the fourth was Baudemagus and the well-known Erec, King Brangor and Sagremor the Savage; those would surprise the Romans if they joined in the fight. King Urien, with his followers the good King Lot of Orkney and the king of Northumberland and Elidus the king of Ireland, formed the fifth battalion; they were drawn up in front of King Arthur, who commanded the sixth battalion. He had few with him of a delicate nature, for the men of his household were all there, except for those whom I have already named as leading other battalions.

After three days of fighting, in which Claris, Laris and Gawain excel in creating havoc among the enemy, King Arthur's army is finally victorious. Interestingly in this account, the Roman emperor survives.

Thereus watched his people die, and he had no remaining hope; whether he wished it or not, it was necessary to flee, since he saw that he could not save the day. Leaving the standard, he turned in flight, realizing that he had stayed too long already; he fled in great anger, together with the four kings left alive; behind him he left ten of his senators, which grieved his heart. In this battle he had lost fourteen kings, to say nothing of a great number of the chivalrous knights whom he had led into battle, of whom he had less than a third remaining; his heart almost stopped with grief.

The British pursued them for a long time, and then returned to the camp which the Romans had abandoned. God! How they were well satisfied with bread, wine, salted meat and wheat-bread. There were fine cattle, fine fat pigs, ewes, sheep and lambs, gold and silver and silken cloths! The British were overjoyed with the spoils which they had found. Without delay, King Arthur ordered all the treasure to be collected together: the silver and gold valuables. Then he divided them among his people, and shared them fairly, with each man having an equal share; however, for himself he only retained the enemy standard and nothing else, saying that he was going to give it to his beautiful wife Guenevere, who would be delighted at the news, when she heard that they had been victorious.

As soon as this was completed, they stirred themselves and set off towards Britain; they rode hard until they reached Cardigan, where the king was held very dear. The queen led the celebrations, exerting herself to honour the king and both Claris and Laris, as Arthur had instructed her. However, King Lador had sent for Claris and Laris, ordering them to go to him, and that no impediment should prevent them.

This was in the joyful summertime that King Arthur had been fighting the Romans in France, and had delivered many great blows with his hands. The king, who was very noble and courteous, stayed at Cardigan now, and beside him sat the queen. Many a lady of high rank could be seen throughout the hall, and none lacked beauty. With the ladies sat Gawain, Laris, Claris and Ywain, and many knights of great worth, who were skilled at courting ladies. They spoke among themselves of love, quoting sonnets and love-songs; but Claris kept completely silent, thinking only of his sweetheart, and was so deep in thought that he heard nothing around him.

Now you might see a messenger coming on a fast horse! He dismounted in front of the hall, then climbed the steps without delay and entered the hall. He greeted the king courteously, and then the rest of the company; after this, he made his way towards the two companions, who were sitting among the ladies, talking with them of love, happiness and celebrations. The messenger did not stop but greeted the ladies who were assembled there, and then went to the nobles, not concealing his message: 'My lords, King Lador greets you and begs and commands that you, for love's sake, go to see him in Gascony! This should not displease you, Claris and Laris, for he has generously nurtured you.'

When they heard the messenger, they both leapt to their feet without further ado; they showed great joy at this message and said, as wise and valiant men, that they would most willingly go to the king; it was only right, since it was their duty. Thus they prepared to depart and return to their own land; but this greatly upset the knights of Britain, who would have liked it better if the two companions had spent their lives in their company. King Arthur, the queen and the nobles all strongly begged them to stay in Arthur's household and join their fellowship. They replied that they could not stay any longer, but would like to see them again in their own land. Thus they set off on their journey, promising to return.

King Arthur had lent them ten of his knights to help them on their

way. I will name right now those who went in their company, who
were faithful and honourable towards them: Gawain was the first,
then Gaheriet, Lucan and Kay the seneschal; the fifth was Gales li
Chaus, then Bedevere, and the seventh I am told was Brandalis,
Sagremor the eighth, Agravain the ninth and Girflet the tenth. Thus
these nobles rode out; King Arthur watched them depart, then
returned immediately to Cardigan.

*Later, Arthur meets Claris and Laris again. A substantial section
of the romance is concerned with Arthur's expedition against the
Danish king, and the two heroes share many exploits with Round
Table knights. The story culminates in the marriage of Laris to his
sweetheart when Arthur holds a great feast to honour his ally.*

GIRART D'AMIENS, Escanor (c. 1266–1300)

Escanor, *another massive Old French verse romance dating from
the end of the thirteenth century, was presented to King Edward
I (1272–1307), who modelled himself on Arthur,*[105] *and whose
ambition was to control the whole of Britain. In this work, where
the relationship between Arthur and his vassals is of particular
relevance, the subjugation of unruly princelings is an important
theme.*

While this story is as long as Claris and Laris, *there are fewer
interlaced plots and accounts of the adventures of different knights.
Here, Gawain is again undoubtedly the principal hero. His identity
crisis involves Escanor, the opponent encountered earlier in* The
Perilous Cemetery.

*During Gawain's absence, Escanor visits Arthur's court and
wrongfully accuses Gawain of treason, since he wishes to test
himself against the finest knight. Returning from Brittany, where
he has subdued a revolt by Arthur's barons, Gawain is distressed
by the accusation but prepares to fight, refusing his friends' offers
to represent him.*

*As Escanor approaches court, Gawain's squire, thinking that his
master requires protection, attacks Escanor and severely wounds
him. Believing Escanor to be dead, Arthur is very distressed, since
the knight was travelling to court under his safe conduct. Arthur's
court becomes less well attended as he is depressed by the failure*

*to discover the identity of Escanor's attempted murderer. Arthur
seeks the advice of his baronial council, and summons his vassals
to a Pentecostal court. Kay the seneschal, a lover and an important
hero in this romance, has just returned to court after undertaking
chivalric adventures.*

King Arthur, who was not resentful at Kay's arrival, told him that he
had kept his promise this time. 'Sire,' Kay replied, 'remember that
there has never been a day when I have forgotten to undertake your
command.'

In this manner, Kay returned to the court and remained with the
king, who held him very dear. However, nobody alive could cheer up
the king, because of the knight [i.e. Escanor]. Why? Since he had been
vilely mistreated while under Arthur's protection. The king was so
deeply despondent that he did not know what he should do, and Kay,
who could not refrain from speaking, said: 'Sire, whatever shall
happen, you should know it is not appropriate for a man as important
as yourself to lead such a life. If you could restore health to the
knight, it would be another matter; but each one of your followers,
even the most valiant, however fine and noble, is talking about this
grief of yours, and is saying that it is a considerable insult that the
greatest assembly of nobles who have ever gathered is undone. Thus,
I tell you well, there has never been such a folly as you have done.'

The king, who understood Kay very well, realized that what he said
was sensible and observed that the time for Pentecost was returning, a
festival which he willingly honoured with great solemnity. Then he
explained how he had been anxious because of the knight who was
wounded, and he was so badly overcome with anger and melancholy
that he had allowed himself to act foolishly. For this reason, he wished
to summon the highest barons of his land: they should join him at
Caerleon a month before Ascension to take counsel about what he
should do; nor, henceforth, did he wish to remain in this depression
and anxiety, for all his court was distraught.

Then he sent off messages to the important barons and to the wisest
people, that they should come to him without making excuses. Since
many worthy men had attended, they were angry because of his grief.
King Arthur called them after the meal to a secret meeting, then he
spoke to them, and they fell silent. He said, 'Lords, now listen to me:
I will tell you why I have sent for you and what I wish to say to you.
You know well that I am very upset because of the mishap which
befell the knight who came here the other day to accuse my lord
Gawain.

'I have made a detailed search and enquiry in all the places where

I believed that news might be obtained. I have searched thoroughly, and explored most of the country to discover the truth. However, in whatever place anyone has been, nothing in the world has been learned by which I could discover whom to arrest. I do not know on whom I should take vengeance. I tell you well, I have such a great heaviness because he was thus snatched from me that never before in my life have I known such grief, so that I am unable to have joy or take part in entertainments.

'However, it would be neither good nor fine to be always in such uncertainty, in such grief and such sadness, as we have been in. For this reason, I would willingly lead another life again, for nobody should take pleasure in always being in such despondency; for my part I am totally overwhelmed. Moreover, it has been known before this that many men are deceived by envy and falsehood, for which reason I have been made to suffer this disloyalty: but it has happened in this way, since it couldn't have turned out better.

'My intention in saying this is not to cause grief, nor because I believe that the knight could be revived (for you have seen me grieving all this year); but I should have even greater agony, and I would have much more to overcome, if I should dishonour my court completely, which is already badly disturbed. For this reason, I no longer wish to remain in such grief: henceforth I wish to endeavour to encourage my barons, for there is no more need for such misconduct, either for them nor for myself, since, I see well, up till now my court has been totally dishonoured: for there is nobody in my household, neither lady, maiden, girl nor damsel, neither knight nor youth, who has joy or pleasure: thus they are all entirely reduced in spirit. For this reason, I do not wish anyone here to be so bold as to continue in this mood of depression; but if anyone does so, it will not cause them pain, for they will not be rebuked by me, since I understand such grief: thus, I will have patience and comfort my people.'

Everyone said to him, 'Sire, you should know that the injury to the knight was very severe, but, since nothing can be discovered, you have done what you ought to; for, if you were his brother, you need not have done so much. For no king of such noble estate, if he had either sense or reputation, would submit his heart to grief, or remain in such a wretched state; on the contrary, every man who is wise rouses himself out of such melancholy. Good Lord, put on a cheerful face and forget about this misfortune! Thus you will make us recover our tranquillity, for there is no man in this land who will not be utterly astonished and who will not say in retrospect that a king should never change his manner so foolishly. For this reason, it is necessary that your people recover their joy swiftly. You, who should give us joy, have disturbed us all: if everyone is comforted, your court would be restored to good shape, where there is no happiness at the moment. Thus your people are so disheartened that your court is confounded.

'Therefore, if it is seen in your face that you have either the heart or the courage to put your court in order again, you will see how each one of your barons would involve himself and make an effort. Moreover, the queen, she who is not uncourtly, will be most joyful, for almost a year has passed since this grief began. Also you should know well that since then you have seemed so confused to us that everyone is as hot as fire with utter boredom and every illness: for this reason, it would be very agreeable for everybody if they saw you with a cheerful appearance. The best of your men, and we ourselves who are here, ought to speak frankly to you.'

The king replied, 'Good lords, I know well that no king ever found a greater allegiance in his people; nor could he have tested them as much as I have done all of you; for which reason, I have no doubt that you would advise me in anything where you can protect my honour. I wish to act loyally towards you, and I desire to hold a fine festive court this Pentecost, which will be outstanding, whatever the cost; and I wish henceforth that the news should be spread around my land, so that no baron, king, count or queen, damsel or girl who has beauty or bearing, or anyone who is worthy, should fail to come to me on that day. Also, there should be no delay in sending for them straightaway, and a great effort should be made, as is appropriate for such an occasion. So now without making an excuse, I will go and speak with the queen, who most sweetly and without anger will help me to arrange this feast; for she will send through my land for the ladies who should be summoned, and command them to attend.'

After this, he went to the queen and told her that it was necessary for her to send messengers throughout the land to summon ladies and damsels, and that she should send for them immediately, as he wished to hold a fine court at Pentecost, if it were possible. The queen was so delighted that she leapt for joy and said, 'Sire, so help me God, you will greatly increase your honour, for there is nobody, either great or small, throughout your land, who will not put great effort and care into doing their duty at the feast; moreover, you should be aware that there isn't an honest lady in your land who will fail to attend. It is sufficient for you to concern yourself with your knights, I shall look after the ladies, and I will send for them at once.'

The queen, who was very wise, as soon as she had heard the king's intention, had letters written, and made them as fine as she was able, to inform all the noble ladies and damsels of the realm about this news. King Arthur sent out in search of all those whom he could summon, and Kay worked hard to prepare the necessary provisions; but he was unable to cast from his thoughts the beautiful lady who had so sweetly given her love to him, wondering how he might aid her.

Arthur prepares for war against Escanor. He travels through North Wales in order to rescue Giflet, one of his knights who is being held in captivity by Escanor's ally, the Queen of Traverses. The following passage opens with Arthur leaving the castle of Brien of the Isles, where he had been staying, and returning to his own lands.[106]

The king would not wait any longer, but took his leave and returned to his own land, where as soon as he could he organized his affairs, ordering letters and legal documents to be written, with which he summoned his followers and friends. Meanwhile, he ordered provisions to be prepared and everything else which was necessary. He organized his provisions well, and sent victuals by sea; and when it was time to set off, he instructed that his host should be led by those who knew the country well. There one could see armour glittering, and war-horses prancing and whinnying, and the companies coming into formation as soon as they entered the area where they expected to encounter opposition.

Moreover, the king, who was never negligent in demonstrating his love for his people, hurried his host forward and pushed on to rescue Giflet from Traverses. You should be aware that there were several roads existing through North Wales, and the people of the Isles were wicked and aggressive whenever they dared; but since they could not fight against the king, they left his army in peace. They passed through many diverse tracks, but, since the weather was as bad as in winter, the king's force could not cross the marshes or rivers. Indeed, there were so many vast boggy areas and so much rough terrain, which was so deep and dangerous, that in winter the inhabitants did not guard the land, for they had so little need to protect it.

In winter, they had no fear of strangers, however bold or valiant, however great their power to make war, for no one was so knowledgeable about their land that he knew all their paths. For this reason, people who attempted to pass through there suffered great injuries, since in winter the inhabitants of these isles never tired of doing wickedness to their neighbours on the plain whom they attacked from above.

However, when summertime returned, the people of the Isles were repaid in full for the great misdeeds which they had committed in the surrounding hamlets, villages, castles and towns, and in the lands outside the Isles: they suffered great damage, unless they had friends or feudal connections on account of whom people might prefer to leave them in peace, or unless one of them could enforce law in the land through his power, or if they could make an alliance.

King Arthur rode on until he encountered these wicked people, entering the passages and marshes and woods, since it was necessary. Since he was leading such a great army, he could not go by a direct route every day, but hither and thither due to the baggage train which followed after them, by which the army was sustained; they sought springs (for drinking water), of which they found many of very high quality, which was most beneficial for the king's army.

You should know that neither the king nor his men approached Brien's lands; they travelled by another route, which they had not used before, passing along the edge of North Wales as much as they could, since the inhabitants, who knew well that they did not have sufficient power or strength to oppose King Arthur, did not dare to annoy them in anything. Whether from force or fear, they showed him such indications of affection, as though he were their true lord, for which reason they suffered the anger of the king of North Wales for some time to come.

Arthur's enemies make preparations to resist him, so the king sends Ywain with a message for Escanor, who has been assembling his allies. Accused of imprisoning Giflet and attempting to murder Gawain, Escanor refuses Arthur's offer of peace if he releases Giflet and makes amends for his wrongdoing. Arthur's army therefore camps before Traverses and prepares to besiege the town, although the king forbids his army to pillage the country or molest the inhabitants.

The king had decided to camp between two small towns, about three leagues from Traverses, beside the sea. No man could count the great numbers of ships, barges and other vessels which King Arthur had assembled, with which (as you should know) he could provide the army with food and whatever else they required.

Arthur had commanded his army not to rob or despoil the people of the Isles, or commit any crime against them; instead, they should pay generously for everything which they bought, so that they might be seen to behave well. Never did Arthur allow his soldiers to do wrong in any place where they went; thus the inhabitants of the country did whatever King Arthur wished, so that no evil might come to them. On the other hand, they did as he wished, because they dared not act otherwise for fear of being punished by death or loss of property.

Nevertheless, they were perturbed that the queen might treat them maliciously, and they were very concerned about this. On the other hand, they comforted themselves that, since the war was only against her, they would not fight on her behalf; indeed, a good half the land supported the king and would most willingly assist him, on account of the benefits which they would receive if he had need of their help. They would serve him and his men, and they prayed to God that he would protect their country. Arthur knew well that they would do him no injury; in fact, they sustained the greater part of his army with supplies until it departed.

King Arthur was so noble, so generous, so courteous and concerned not to dispossess the poor people in any place where he intended to do battle, he never did harm in any place unless it was impossible to avoid it, because he listened to their prayers, and ordered that no knight, sergeant or other follower should commit any sin or crime against anyone, during either the army's advance or its retreat; for any country which surrendered to him should not be maltreated, and while it was friendly he would protect it from harm. However, you should realize that they did great service to the king and his men with food and supplies; each day they brought many goods to the host, according to whatever was available.

JEHAN, The Marvels of Rigomer (Les Merveilles de Rigomer) (c. 1266–1300)

Like other works of similar great length, the poem describes the adventures of various Arthurian knights who set off in response to a request. The Marvels of Rigomer concentrates on the exploits of Gawain and Lancelot. Lancelot's inability to resist the sorceries of Rigomer makes him a willing prisoner, working in the castle kitchens at the command of its chatelaine, whose ring he wears to denote his love-service.

Lancelot and his fellow Round Table companions who are kept in similar bondage have to await the arrival of Gawain, the only

*knight able to resist the temptations and overcome the marvels. In
fact, this very earthly hero, despite his possession of a fairy mistress,
is treated as an almost Messianic figure, whose success is frequently
predicted throughout the episodes preceding his arrival at Rigomer.
As in many French romances, the poem opens at Arthur's court,
where the king remains while his knights set off on adventure.*

Jehan, who in many things is well versed and who has created many
a beautiful rhyme, has begun here for us a romance by very briefly
putting the Matter of Britain into a form which I believe can rival the
best of all those other stories. The romance we shall read is about
King Arthur and his company. Arthur was the kind of knight in
whom more sense than foolishness could be found (only my lord
Gawain matched him with as much sense and less confusion). I
likewise shall tell you something about Lancelot of the Lake here, in
the telling of *The Marvels of Rigomer*, that I now propose to begin
without further ado:

When, on a fine Sunday afternoon in the springtime month of May,
the king had spent some five days at Carlion, in the company of his
knights and barons, they should have sat down to dine but, either for
pleasure or from caprice, they delayed doing so until some adventure
or other might manifest itself. As the tale explains, it was customary
for them to take their places at the dinner table but refrain from
eating until some worthwhile, beautiful adventure was announced.
Nor would they ever have broken this custom of the king's court, not
even for a thousand marks of gold. So, without any fuss at all, the
knights decided to go above the palace eaves and stick their heads
out of the windows to scout the plain below and see if they could
spot any novel thing from there.

Just then, they saw a damsel coming towards them, quite alone
and unescorted, riding a beautiful and costly palfrey. It appeared that
the mantle and a tunic of silk she was wearing protected her well
against the heat, as did her cotton chemise, which was whiter in
colour than any snow. Indeed, her skin, sides, flanks, bosom, neck,
and face were even whiter than a lily of the valley. Thus, as she came
ever closer to the court bearing her message, she impressed everyone
there as being both courteous and wise.

It was only fitting, therefore, for each of them to point at her with
his finger and exclaim, 'That maiden is bringing us some news.' Then
all at once, the knights and all the vassals ran down to the castle's
entrance and managed to arrive there at the very same time she did.
When they had courteously helped her dismount, my lord Gawain
took her by the right hand and accompanied her into the great

hall. She conducted herself in a very courtly manner, as would any accomplished maiden who was neither simple nor overly fussy. So, she very elegantly presented her greetings to the king and then turned to salute the queen and all the knights assembled there. It seems to me they all responded by telling her, 'Beauty, you are truly most welcome.'

Not feeling the least uncomfortable, she began to speak and they all quieted down since they were expecting her to tell them some pleasant story or other. But in a little while, all those who just happened to be there to see her then would become displeased by what she would say.

'Noble king,' she began, 'to you and to all those who are here I say: None of you should ever be given even a single cherry blossom worth of respect or honour! You are all slothful wretches who give little thought to matters of honour any more and are just becoming fatter and fatter and lazier and lazier! Do you all believe that you would debase yourselves by seeking reputable quests of honour in other lands? Great and daring adventures which will last even as long as the very sky and earth await you over the sea in Ireland! There are no other adventures of comparable beauty like them in the land I have come from. Thus, on behalf of my lady, do I enjoin all you brave, jolly fellows to set out now and seek her! She instructs me to tell you that she invites any and all who desire fame and honour, winsome maids and great wealth, and the favours of the most desirable ladies that may be found in any kingdom from the Western Isles to the Orient. The place may be reached in a mere two months. Once there you will have the possibility of acquiring a great deal of wealth – all that my lady has put aside – (her lands and her country) which she has joyfully agreed to commit and spend, up to the very limit they can yield. Whoever hopes to find a fair lady will do so without fail; and there too everyone will have the means of acquiring a great and powerful reputation. I shall return there now since there is nothing else that compels me to stay here. Therefore, I would like to mount my palfrey again.'

They were so dumbfounded by her words that not one of them was smart enough to ask the lady's messenger more about her mistress or her land, or even the name they might use to search for her in order to find her keep more readily. Every single one of them truly felt they were plain fools that day.

The Knight of the Parrot (Le Chevalier du Papegau)
(c. 1300)

This late French work is the only romance to have King Arthur himself as the hero. The story, which contains many features which by now have become conventional, is set right at the beginning of Arthur's reign, on the very day on which he is crowned. In some works Lot is Arthur's enemy, but in this work Arthur entrusts his realm to Lot's safe-keeping during his absence on adventure.

He who delights in hearing fine adventures and stories of prowess and chivalry, listen to hear the first adventures which befell the good King Arthur when he first wore his crown, and which began in this manner.

On the day of Pentecost, the very day on which King Arthur was crowned, there was great joy and happiness in the city of Camelot. When the Mass had been sung with due ceremony, as befitted such a festival, the king and his barons all went up into the palace. Then you might have seen a damsel, alone and without any companions, riding in great haste on a mule; she rode until she reached the court, where the feast was being held. When she had dismounted at the mounting-block and had tethered her mule, she went up into the hall, and as soon as she saw the king, who was sitting at the high table, she greeted him most politely, saying to him, 'Good sir, a lady who is the most beautiful, most deserving and most courteous that is known anywhere, has sent me to you, asking you and begging that you should send her a knight of your court who is brave and valorous, that he may succour her against the knight who has crossed the sea and daily goes about destroying her people and her land. He has already killed sixty of the best knights of her land, so that she can no longer find anyone brave enough who dares fight against him. Moreover, if it is the first adventure to occur in your court, she begs you, for the sake of God and your honour, that you will do this.'

Then King Arthur, after he had returned the damsel's greeting, replied to her most gently, 'My lady, I have eagerly listened to what you have said. Good luck shall come to your lady who sent you! For I will most willingly do as she requests.' Then Arthur commanded a squire who was in front of him, a most noble young man, to take care of the damsel and help her as much as he could, and, when there was time, he would think of all her needs. The squire did exactly as King Arthur bade him, for he conveyed her to the lodging of one of the richest and most courteous townsmen of the city of Camelot; the citizen received her very willingly and ensured that all her commands were honoured and that she was well attended, and the damsel remained at his house while the court lasted, which was eight whole days.

A week after Pentecost, when the king had completed his official rich and formal court, the nobles of foreign countries took their leave of him, and the king gave to each of them, according to their rank, gold, silver and silken cloths, for Arthur knew well how to give largesse. Each person left to return to his own land, delighted and happy by the foreign custom, and they each offered their services to the king, should he require them at any time. The king remained at Camelot with the nobles of his household, and then the damsel who had announced her lady's distress returned. All the knights and nobles offered to go to serve the lady, but King Arthur did not wish to grant permission to any of them but said, 'This adventure is mine, by right; for this is the first which has happened at my court, and, since I am a newly crowned king, I do not wish that anyone but myself should go into the service of this lady.'

It will never be known how much the barons begged the king that he might stay at Camelot; at once he gave his court and kingdom into the charge of one of his nobles, who was called my lord Lot, and he ordered it to be announced throughout the land that everyone must obey Lot's orders until the king returned. After he had done this, King Arthur was armed with all his armour, he mounted his war-horse, and he and the damsel left the city. All his nobles also rode out to accompany him, riding together until they came to the forest of Camelot, when King Arthur commanded all his barons to go back. When they saw that this pleased the king, they all returned to Camelot, grieving and upset to see their lord, such a young knight and so sensitive, although experienced in arms, departing for far-off lands about which they knew nothing. Without doubt he was the best knight of his age who was known of anywhere.

When the king had left his nobles, he rode alone with his damsel, speaking of one thing and another as they pleased. After they had ridden for a while, they heard a voice crying very loudly, which indicated that someone had need of assistance, since it said, 'Good, sweet Lord God, have mercy on me!' It cried thus three times, and when the king heard this voice, he looked around and saw a lady, who was very beautiful and richly attired, fleeing on a mule from an armed knight on a warhorse, who pursued her with naked sword in hand. When this lady saw the king riding beside the damsel, she hastened towards him and addressed him thus: 'Ah, noble knight, have mercy on me, for God's sake! Succour me, so that I am not murdered, and do not allow this knight to kill me; he has wrongfully killed my lover and desires to murder me!' She had scarcely finished this speech when the knight arrived, his sword raised to strike the lady, but the king moved forward and cried to the knight, 'Sir knight, for courtesy do not touch this lady, for it is not honourable for a knight ever to kill a lady or damsel in such a manner!'

When the knight saw that the king wished to defend the lady, he spoke to him very unpleasantly: 'Sir vassal, if you should wish to defend her, you must beware of me, for I believe that you will defend both yourself and her badly.' Then the knight replaced his sword in its sheath and retraced his path to regain his lance, which he had left at the foot of a tree. When he had found his lance, he spurred his horse with great force and galloped towards the king, and the king prepared to defend himself against the knight. The strange knight, who was coming from a distance, struck the king so hard on the shield with his lance that the lance pierced both the shield and the hauberk on his right side, and if the lance had not broken, he would have wounded the king very severely. However, the king returned the blow with such force that neither shield nor hauberk protected the knight, whom he threw swiftly to the earth, so ferociously that the man was too stunned to know where he was. After a while, when he had recovered his senses, he beheld the king, who had dismounted and was coming towards him with his sword drawn and eager to strike him. As soon as he was able, the knight cried, 'Noble knight, for God's sake do not kill me and do not consider my villainy!'

When the king heard his opponent beg for mercy, he answered him, 'If you wish me to have mercy on you, I desire that you shall place yourself at the mercy of this lady, so that she may do with you as she wishes.' 'Ah, good sir,' said the knight, 'for God's sake, I would wish that you might kill me, rather than that she should have me in her power!' Then the king demanded why he had killed the lady's lover, and the knight answered him thus: 'Lord, I will tell you truthfully. It is a fact that she is the most beautiful lady in the world, as you yourself may see, and her beauty has caused me to love her; thus I have loved her more than any knight ever loved a lady, and she loved another more than myself, and thus I desired to destroy her, since she did not wish to be with me. I also killed her lover, since he served her despite me, and against my challenge.' 'Ah, knight,' said the king, full of anger, 'what is your name?' And the other replied that he was called the Knight of the Waste Land. Then the king spoke to him again: 'You must place yourself at the mercy of this lady, in her prison, or I shall kill you; and I believe that she will show you mercy, for love of me.' 'Ah, lord,' said the knight, 'the mercy of a lady is too dangerous; but, since you must have your will, I will do as you bid me.'

Then the lady, who had heard all these exchanges, said to the king, 'My lord, I do not have any desire to keep my enemy in prison, since then I cannot take my revenge; for prison is the refuge of a wicked man, and I will tell you how: for if the wicked man is not kept in prison he uses all his life evilly, so that he is killed and overthrown by his own deeds. For that reason, good sir, I leave this man to you, to do with as you please.' Then the king made the knight swear that he would go to Camelot and there surrender himself to lord Lot, on behalf of the young knight who rode with the damsel, and remain there at Lot's mercy until King Arthur should return to court.

When King Arthur had sent the Knight of the Waste Land to court, as you have heard, he enquired of the lady which way she wished to travel, and she answered him, 'Good sir, I would like to lead you, if you please, to one of the most beautiful courts you have probably ever seen, which is quite close to this place. There are at least three hundred ladies and damsels there who are the most beautiful and courteous whom you might ever see anywhere. Moreover, there are at least five hundred of the best knights in the country, who have arrived there to see the court, which is devised in such a manner that the man who has the most beautiful sweetheart and can prove this by battle shall have a parrot which is brought there every year by a dwarf. He is the best bird in the world for singing sweet and pleasing love-songs and for speaking so well that it pleases the hearts of both men and women to hear him.[107] However, a knight attends this place, who has defeated all the others of the country in battle, and there he performs the worst wrong and greatest injustice ever done by a knight.'

'What wrong does he do them, lady?' enquired the king. 'Sire,' said the lady, 'once every month he causes all the knights and ladies, damsels and squires of the entire land to attend him on the meadow of Causuel, where he forces them, without cause or reason, to pay him homage; he also has a sweetheart, the most ugly creature that you might ever have seen, and he forces these people to declare her the most beautiful, most courteous and best-mannered lady in the world. Good sir, it would be a very great courtesy to deliver the knights, ladies and damsels from the servitude by which they are wronged, and you might easily deliver them if you so wished, and indeed I will explain how. Since you have defeated the Knight of the Waste Land in the joust, I will place myself on your shield against the knight,[108] and you shall easily and rightfully show him that I am much more beautiful, and of higher birth and richer than his sweetheart; nor shall you know who I am or by whom you will have been helped.'

'Certainly, lady,' said the king, 'especially since you are, in my opinion, the most beautiful lady and the most agreeable that I have ever seen, so that Love invites me to be under your command and to do everything which you desire. If this damsel of mine, in whose guidance I have placed myself, agrees, there is nothing which I will not do to obey your every wish.' Then the lady turned towards the damsel and spoke to her thus: 'Damsel, I beg you to come to this court with this knight, and you should be aware that you could never make a better journey if he may conquer the knight.' 'Lady,' replied the damsel, 'if the decision was mine, I would do everything as you wish, since I see that you are so courteous and well-mannered. However, I am in the service of a lady who sent me to seek this knight in the place where I found him, so that I have no right to order him, only to show him the way; and if it pleases him to go, it will not displease me at all, so that I may not say yes or no, but I will go wherever he wishes.' When the king perceived that the damsel would not deny him, they all set off together to go to the court.

They had not ridden far when they saw in a beautiful meadow tents and pavilions and cloths of silk, most richly worked with strange devices, and they saw ladies and damsels on mules and palfreys richly adorned, who were watching knights joust on their warhorses in the meadow making a great noise in a strange manner. When the king and his companions approached them, the knights stopped their jousting and began to shout at the king, since they perceived that he was a stranger, 'Sir, you have come in an evil hour, sir, evilly come! Here you shall display your valour.' Meanwhile others mocked his companions. When the king heard them mock and insult in this manner, he spoke to them: 'Ha, caitiff and evil people, without courtesy or control, who are in servitude through your cowardice! I have come here to deliver you from the servitude in which you live, and you dare to show me dishonour? Certainly, no one should help you.' When they heard what the king had said, the knights were very ashamed and repented of the wrongful way in which they had so wickedly greeted the king and his companions.

Then the king asked them where was the knight to whom they had to give homage. He had hardly finished speaking when he saw a very well-armed knight coming on a black charger, causing a great noise. With him he led a damsel on a very richly embellished mule, but of the lady's beauty I am unable to tell you, since she did not have any at all, nor do I wish to tell of her ugliness, for I cannot describe it all, since she had so much. Accompanying them came ladies and damsels playing very joyfully on harps and viols, and behind them followed a dwarf who was dressed in scarlet lined with fur, who drove before him a palfrey carrying a cage in which sat the parrot of which I have already told you. When the knight saw the king speaking to the knights and ladies, since the stranger was armed, he at once realized that he had come to fight him. Then, without any further delay, he took his shield and lance, full of anger and evil intent, and commanded the place to be cleared, and immediately his command was obeyed. After, when the area was evacuated, the king, who realized that he was bound to partake in a joust, placed his shield before his chest and seized his lance, as did the knight.

Then they spurred their horses and clashed together, striking each other's shield so violently, with such great force, that everything was broken and scattered in pieces. Nevertheless, their hauberks were so strong that they protected both from death, and the chargers crashed together so violently that they both fell dead under their masters as they jousted. The two knights were strong and swift and quickly rose; they seized their shields and, placing their hands on their swords, rushed against each other with great ferocity.

The battle between King Arthur and the knight who fought against him was very fierce, and it lasted for a long time without it being possible to decide who had the worst of it. However, all the men and women who were present marvelled greatly that the king, who was so young, had lasted so long against their lord; and because of the courage which they saw he possessed, and owing to their wish to be delivered from the servitude in which their overlord wrongfully held them, they all prayed in their hearts that he might defeat their lord and then kill him.

The two men fought together for such a long time that the knight who fought against the king became very annoyed that his opponent stood against him so long, and he was very ashamed at this since he realized how young the other man was. Then he leapt forward, full of anger and evil intent, and struck the king a blow on the top of his helm with such hatred that he split the helm open, and badly wounded the king in the face. When the king felt himself wounded and saw the blood running down below his visor, he was very angry; and his great anger doubled his strength, for through anger the strength to endure of a brave man is increased, while in the wicked it causes cowardice and worthlessness. Thus, full of anger and strength, Arthur rushed at the other knight and struck him with all his might between the helm and the shield, such a great blow that he completely severed the left arm, which fell to the ground still holding the shield. When all those present saw this blow, they all cried with one voice, 'Our lord has found an equal and master!' And the knight, when he had lost his arm, fell to the ground in great agony.

Then the king went to his fallen opponent and wrenched the helm from his head, and the knight, as he should, begged for mercy, that for God's sake his victor should not kill him. Since the king had found him to be such a fine knight, he took pity on him, but the ladies and knights, and each and every one of his followers, begged with one voice that the king should kill their lord, so Arthur did not know what to do. Meanwhile, he spoke to the knight: 'Before I have mercy on you, I wish you to tell me your name and parentage; then I shall know what honour you deserve.'

The knight replied, 'Willingly, since it pleases you. Good sir, my father was a poor vavassor with a small fief, possessing nothing in the world except the castle which you see before you, which men call Causuel. Since I was so unruly when I was a child, he called me 'the Wicked Boy', and I did not lose the name until I became a newly made knight, and then my name was changed, and I was called 'the Merciless Lion', since I overthrew all the knights who jousted against me. Moreover, when I had conquered them, I made them swear themselves prisoners, and thus I made them place all their honour in subjection to me, without any mercy.' 'And those who refused to submit in this way, what did you do to them?' asked the king. 'Sir,' replied the knight, 'I killed them; then I took their wives, children and their possessions, whatever they had, and kept them in servitude, so that they would never oppose me as their overlord.' 'And those,' said the king, 'who placed themselves entirely at your mercy, what did you do to them?' 'Lord, I took away from them half of what they possessed at the time when I defeated them, and made them and their wives, and their children, both young and adult, come here once a month to do me homage, so that they have been under my command until this day.' 'And how long have you maintained this lordship?' enquired the king. 'Good sir, I have held it fifteen years and more, and have found no knight who could stand against me for long, save you, who have conquered me. These people are now under your command, and I beg you, good sir, that you will not kill me.'

'Lion,' said the king, 'you have very badly represented the order of chivalry; for chivalry desires to bring reason and law to all people; you would have done better to keep the name which your father gave you than the name which you were given as a new knight, and I will explain why. You have taken away the possessions of knights who were unable to defend themselves against you, a shameful deed, and then without right or reason you have kept them and their people under your control, and thus you have deserved the name of 'Wicked

Boy' but never that of 'Lion'. For a lion is the most worthy beast in the world: for he never feels such great hunger that he is very angry towards another beast, so that if it lies on the ground and shows him humility, he does not wish any longer to attack it. Thus you have maligned the name of lion.

'But since I do not wish your evil to contaminate my goodwill, I will have mercy on you, such as you deserve; and do you know what I desire of you? That you should free from bondage all the people who are here, great and small, and that you should restore to them all their possessions which you have taken, if you still have them, and turn to good the evil which you have wrongfully done to them through your pride. Furthermore, I wish that you should remain in this place in a prison which you shall make, and you should know that all these people, great and small, who used to do you homage, shall come to visit and behold you once a month until King Arthur of Britain commands that you go to speak to him at court in the way I shall describe. You shall then dress in the best clothes which you possess and ride in a richly decorated cart, suitable for a knight who cannot ride, and you should command all the knights whom you used to keep in servitude that they should pull you to court, helping each other. And this punishment I wish them to have on account of their cowardice and worthlessness.'

Thus the king made the Merciless Lion and the other knights there promise to do as he had decreed. The knights and all the nobles were amazed that such a young knight as the king should know how to wreak such vengeance on the Merciless Lion, and they were all very pleased, swearing to obey his wish and do his bidding; but no one could describe the noise made by the parrot, who spoke, in the highest voice he was capable of, to the dwarf who led him, exclaiming, 'Dwarf, dwarf, carry me to see the best knight in the world! This is he about whom Merlin spoke in his prophecy, when he said that the Son of the Ewe should subdue the Merciless Lion, who was full of pride, felony and anger. Ah, dwarf, do not delay any longer! Carry me to him, for he has won me.' When the parrot approached the king, he began very sweetly to tell all the events which had occurred from the days of Merlin until that present time, so that the king and all the others present wondered greatly at what he said.

Then the parrot asked the king, 'Sire, why do you not take hold of me? I am yours by right, for you are the best knight in the world and also you have with you the most beautiful lady known of anywhere, although you do not know her name or her parentage.' 'Sire,' said the Lady Without Pride, 'I am the sister of Morgaine the fairy of Montgibel.' The king was overjoyed when he heard the speech of the parrot and then the words of the lady. Then he came forward and took the parrot, the dwarf and all his accoutrements. Then he thanked the Lady Without Pride because she had led him to this court, and all the people of the land together showed him great honour and besought him most sweetly that he would remain at Causuel for as long as he pleased. He replied that he could not stay, since he had undertaken an adventure which he was required to complete for the love of a lady. Then Darsenois the Greek, who had arrived at court, presented a fine broad charger to the king which was very well-trained, as was fitting for such a knight. The king accepted the mount very willingly, but not as one who needs to be rewarded for his service.

Then the king mounted, followed by the damsel and the dwarf, who drove the palfrey carrying the parrot. The Lady Without Pride and all the other ladies and damsels who were present, with all the nobles and the other people, together mounted to accompany the man who had freed them from servitude. They rode along in great joy, to the sound of viols and harps, and when they had travelled an English mile,[109] the king asked them all to return. When they saw that this would please him, they asked who they should say had delivered them from their state of servitude, and the king answered, 'The Knight of the Parrot.' Then he commended them to God, and asked his damsel, who rode with him, that she should not call him anything else.

Then the Lady Without Pride took her leave of the king, offering him her service, if he should need it, and she returned to Causuel with the others, who were happy and overjoyed by the wonderful adventure which had befallen them. Thenceforth, both they and the Merciless Lion acted as the king had bidden them.

Arthur, now known as the Knight of the Parrot, continues his adventures. In this episode, he is entertained in the Amorous City by the Lady with Golden Hair, who possesses a magnificent chamber which seems like Paradise.

'Damsel,' said the Knight of the Parrot, 'I will do your will, since I have promised you, and I shall be delighted if I can achieve your lady's request. Now, mount, and we will go with these people to the Amorous City, until it is time for us to continue our journey.' And the damsel did as he bade her.

The Knight of the Parrot was highly praised because he had promised to help the damsel, except by the Lady with Golden Hair. She did not agree with his decision, but was so sorrowful when she heard him promise to go with the damsel that she felt herself enraged with grief. Nevertheless, she hid her feelings so well from all her people that nobody perceived them, and she behaved more pleasantly to the Knight of the Parrot than she had formerly done; and she had good reason to do so, since he well deserved it.

They rode on until they entered the city, and dismounted at the principal palace. When they had dismounted, the lady called a tournament to be announced for a week's time. This was devised so that the winner of the tourney might kiss her once in front of all the nobility, and she would accept him as her lover for a year. Then she begged the damsel Flower of the World to stay with her and the Knight of the Parrot until the tournament had finished, which the damsel readily agreed to do.

The barons were all delighted that the lady had sworn to kiss the man who would be judged the best in the tournament, and they believed that she would take the man who kissed her as her husband, so that each of them prepared as extravagantly as they could, with fine chargers and good arms. Then nobles and knights arrived there from all parts, to enter the tournament for love of the lady, and love of her made each believe in his heart that he would be the best knight in the tournament and would receive the kiss before all the nobles, and that none of them except him would have a reputation. Until the period of the tourney arrived, the Lady with Golden Hair and the Knight of the Parrot led a very pleasant existence, and often dined together in private rooms and in gardens.

The day before the tournament was to take place, all the nobility of the country assembled together on the meadow outside the Amorous City. There, the lady had already ordered a heated room to be prepared in a part of the meadow from which she and her damsels could watch the tournament, so that the knights would become stronger and braver when they saw her. On this same day, the eve of the tourney, the lady had a bed prepared, with silken curtains and precious stones which shed great light, in a chamber which philosophers had created by their craft, made in such a fashion that no one who was outside would be aware why it was so white and clear, and nobody could see it except with difficulty. Within, it was high, airy and vaulted; there was no sort of stone in the world possessing any value which was not used in the ceiling of the room, worked with beasts, birds and flowers, and with many stories of ancient deeds. Also, in the middle of the room, there was a stone carved in the shape of a falcon, which bore in its beak a golden chain which hung a good span's length, to which was attached a precious carbuncle, which shone with such great splendour at night that it seemed the room was entirely ablaze. Inside the falcon's chest was a glass phial full of balm which spread a wonderful perfume from the falcon's beak, in such profusion that the whole chamber was pervaded, so that it seemed to those within that this was a paradise. On the other side the falcon held in its feet a marble tablet a good ell[110] long, and a good span wide, on which were raised letters painted with gold, which could be read easily.

The Lady with Golden Hair commanded the Knight of the Parrot to come to her chamber to talk; he went there very happy and joyful, since that was the thing that he most desired in all the world. When she saw him coming, she went to the door of her room to welcome him, then laughingly took him by the bare hand and welcomed him, bowing to him most sweetly and regarding him lovingly. Then they sat on the bed, gazing at each other in such a manner that their hearts caught fire, and they spoke of whatever pleased them both. 'Sir,' said the lady, 'Love has wounded me to the heart and commanded that I should do all Her[111] bidding, but I do not know if you would do her will or not.' 'Sweet lady,' answered the knight, 'I do not know if Love has touched you on my behalf or for another, despite all that you say. But if Love advises you that you should commit any shame for me, she would not do so because I may not command her in anything (for I have never done so much for her that I might deserve her to do anything for me), only what she might do through her courtesy and mercy, because I have placed my whole heart at her command and pleaded night and day that she might give me and say the thing which might please her, otherwise nothing.' 'Sir,' said the lady, 'what do you ask of Love? Do you beg her to teach you how to speak to me?' 'Lady,' he said, 'I beg that she might turn your heart in my favour, so that you might take pity on the way I feel for you.' 'My heart, sir, by my faith! I no longer have one,' she replied. 'And to whom have you given it, lady?' asked the Knight of the Parrot.

Then the lady spoke no further word, but she leaned against him, looking at him so lovingly that he became inflamed with passion and held her so close to him that they both fell on to the bed, where they kissed and embraced at their pleasure, without restraint. You may well believe that the lady would have lost the name 'chaste' if they had not heard a damsel coming towards the door of the room, so they quickly arose, in order that they would not be seen. Then the lady asked the knight if he could read, and he answered, 'Yes.' 'Then read,' she said, 'the letters written on this tablet here at the feet of the falcon.' He read them, and when he had done so, the lady demanded that he should speak them aloud. 'Lady,' he said, 'they say this: "You knight, who stand before me, faithfully promise to do whatever the lady whom you speak to may tell you." ' 'Sir,' the lady said, 'do you wish to promise as the letters bid you? Then you shall have my heart at your command.' 'Yes, lady,' replied the knight, 'there is nothing in the whole world that I would not do in exchange for this promise which I can make.' 'And then I shall be certain?' 'Yes, lady,' replied the knight. 'Say whatever you please, and I will do your bidding if I possibly can.'

'Sir,' she answered, 'I wish that you shall fight on my behalf in the tournament tomorrow, and there, for my sake, you shall perform as the worst knight-at-arms in the entire world, for I wish that your failure may be seen by all the world, in contrast to the good reputation which you have enjoyed.' 'Ah, my lady, have mercy, for God's sake!' said the knight. 'Allow me to serve you tomorrow as the best knight there, if you please, rather than as the worst!' 'I do not wish that,' said the lady, 'but I desire that you should keep your covenant.' 'Certainly,' said the knight, 'I will do so, since I have promised you, but it would give me greater pleasure to serve you as the best knight than as the worst. But I will say no more than that I wish to do whatever pleases you; for none could better serve his lord than by doing whatever pleases him.' With that he left her room and returned to the hall deep in thought; but he continued to appear joyful, so that no one would realize his true feelings.

In the tournament the following day, Arthur fights badly, as his lady ordered him. That night she is confronted by Love, who persuades her to invite Arthur to her room again.

She did exactly as Love had advised her, for she led him into her room, where she showed him the greatest display of love that any woman could show a man, and she quite abandoned herself to obey his bidding and act at his pleasure. When the Knight of the Parrot saw that he could have his will with the lady, without opposition, he seized her roughly by the hair with both hands and threw her to the ground. Then he spoke to her: 'Wicked whore, full of every evil, be quiet! This is the service which I have promised you, for I promised to serve you today as the worst knight in the world. I wish to keep your commandment well, for today you have stolen my honour and reputation, for which I shall be shamed all my life. And you now abandon yourself before me, so that I may have my way with you, so you still take me for the worst knight in the world. It would have been better for you if you had taken me for the best, because if you wish it I will this day give you such service as the worst knight in the world, which you deserve.'

Then he pulled her all around the room by her hair, beating and kicking her with his feet, while she kept on crying, 'Mercy, for God's sake!' and weeping, pleading with him to take pity on her, lamenting softly in a low voice, so that she would not be heard in the hall, or by her damsels in the other rooms. After the knight had beaten and kicked her enough, he left her and, going from the room, he returned to the hall, where he found the knights and nobles playing chess and backgammon. They greeted him merrily and he tried to appear as calm as possible, so that they would not perceive that he was angry about something.

The next day the lady is overwhelmed with love for the Knight of the Parrot, who encounters his opponent of the previous day, the lady's suitor, Count Doldois.

Now when the place was cleared of spectators, the two knights moved apart to take their places, then rode towards each other, using their spurs to make their horses charge as fast as possible, and then hurtled against each other with all their power and strength. Count Doldois, who was full of anger and malice, struck the Knight of the Parrot so violently that neither shield nor hauberk prevented him from receiving a great wound in the left side, but he never left his saddle. Then the Knight of the Parrot thrust his lance through the shield and hauberk of Count Doldois, so it entered his body a good three fingers and hurled his opponent to the ground, legs in the air, very badly wounded, though not mortally. When the Knight of the Parrot saw the count on the ground, he dismounted and stood over him with drawn sword to prevent him rising again; but his opponent had no strength left, but begged for mercy from the Knight of the Parrot, asking that he should not kill him, but would pardon the evil things that he had said and done to him.

When the Knight of the Parrot saw the count lying on the ground, unable to move and begging for mercy so gracefully, he took pity on him, knowing full well that it was not honourable for a knight who valued anything to kill another knight who had asked for mercy. Then he said to his opponent, 'I wish that you should know, sir count, that there are three types of fool in the world. The first is the man who so threatens his enemy that he does not fear him in any degree. The next is the man who boasts so much that he is never believed, whether he speaks the truth or a lie. The third is the man who gives so much to another that he keeps nothing for his heir. Sir count, if you had known this wisdom yesterday when you left the tournament, you might not have boasted of those things which still remained to achieve, of which I shall say no more. However, since you ask me for mercy, I desire that you should be bound by such a covenant that you shall place yourself at the mercy of the Lady with Golden Hair, and declare that I have won the fight.' The count agreed, as befitted a man who had no choice.

Then Count Doldois arose as best he could, and went to place himself at the mercy of the Lady with Golden Hair; but this lady would have so well repaid his malicious behaviour to the Knight of the Parrot that he would never have had the desire to wrong another knight of whom he knew nothing, had it not been for the Knight of the Parrot, who begged the lady to spare the count. Since the court was full of joy and happiness, the lady agreed with him. Then the count left, with his followers and rode off to his lodgings to be healed of the wound he had received in the battle. Without further delay, the Knight of the Parrot went up to the lady and kissed her in front of the nobles, as the best knight in the tournament. Then they went into the city with great joy and happiness, and all dismounted at the principal palace, which the lady had ordered to be entirely curtained off with silken draperies which were richly embroidered with gold.

The tables were already set, and as soon as they entered the hall, water was brought. Then the lady sat at the highest table and, taking the Knight of the Parrot by the right hand, sat him beside her, and the duke of Valfort on the other side. Why should I make a long story of it? When they had eaten as they pleased, in great comfort and delight, and the tables had been removed, a great many carols were begun throughout the hall, to the wonderful sound of viols, harps and other instruments which the jugglers played sweetly throughout the palace. The marshal, eager to obey the commands of his lady, had spread tapestries and silken hangings throughout the chamber, as she had desired.

Then the Knight of the Parrot arose and took the Lady with Golden Hair by the hand, and the two went to sit alone together in another part of the hall. There they talked together about one thing and another, and with happy hearts they readily forgave each other for their anger and malicious behaviour, turning their hearts completely towards other desires: each wished what the other desired, and they planned to spend that night together in mutual pleasure, greatly wishing that the night might quickly come.

Elsewhere in the hall, ladies, damsels and knights were talking, speaking as they pleased, each of them desiring to possess a sweetheart since the Knight of the Parrot had found their lady. Thus they passed their time until supper was prepared, and they dined in great happiness. After they had supped it was time to retire to bed; they all left the hall, each person going to their own lodging. Then the Lady with Golden Hair went to her room, with two of her damsels, who lay down as comfortably as they could. The Knight of the Parrot found that he was well attended right until bedtime.

When everyone throughout the court was in bed and asleep, the Knight of the Parrot arose and threw a mantle around his neck, and went to the door of the room where the Lady with Golden Hair was sleeping, as they had arranged the day before. Finding the door open, the knight entered and closed the door behind him; at the entrance he smelt such a wonderful aroma, from the balm which the falcon had in the glass phial in its chest, that it seemed that he was entering Paradise. Then he came to the bed of the lady, who could not sleep, but waited for him in great eagerness, and she received him into her arms with great solace and delight. Then the Knight of the Parrot had great joy and pleasure with the Lady with Golden Hair. They enjoyed each other with great bliss, without any constriction of their desires, as young people will do when they are happy and relaxed. What else should I tell you? They spent the best night that young people could ever have, and well they might wish that the night could have lasted for a year; but that could not be.

When it was a little before day, the Knight of the Parrot returned to his own bed, so no one should know; there he slept well enough, as a man who had not slept all night, and was asleep until it was almost tierce [9 a.m.]. Then he rose and dressed himself, wonderfully joyous and happy, as a man who had spent the day and night in all the delight and relaxation which any mortal man could describe. He stayed for eight whole days, in such joy and delight, during which time he thought of nothing else in the world, except spending his time with the Lady with Golden Hair, so secretly that no one perceived their behaviour.

PART 6
GERMAN AND ENGLISH
ROMANCES

HEINRICH VON DEM TÜRLIN, The Crown
(Diu Krône) (c. 1210–25)

Heinrich von dem Türlin's The Crown (Diu Krône) is a lengthy German verse romance which draws on Chrétien's works and other French Arthurian material for inspiration. While some episodes are derivative, other sections present a more original interpretation of King Arthur.

Arthur wishes to learn the identity of an unknown knight, but the stranger refuses to tell him, so they fight each other. Finally, the knight says that he will reveal his name, and much more besides, to just one person: King Arthur himself. While this episode has parallels in various other works, the treatment of the theme is original.

'If it is true that you are seeking Arthur, Dame Fortune has been kind to you, for I am he. I am called Arthur and am lord of this country. Now there is no reason why you can't say who you are. Since I have told you my name and my homeland, it is only proper that you tell me yours, even though it may mean nothing to me.'

'I would gladly reveal all you want to know,' answered the knight, 'if I could be sure that what you say is true. But unless this can first be confirmed beyond doubt so that there can be no mistake, I can't believe it. You must give me some proof.'

'Such talk only causes delay,' declared the king. 'Let us do as I suggest: if you know of any trait by which you could see that I am the right Arthur, I hope to convince you. You will not be disappointed here, of this I am sure. If what you have heard is correct, you will find that I have been truthful.'

'I would be able to tell in the daytime,' said the knight, 'for I have heard that Arthur has a scar the width of a finger running down his forehead. Could I but touch it, I would have fewer doubts; indeed, they would vanish.' In reply, Arthur bent his head down and asked him to untie his helmet and look for the proof. The truth would thus reassure him and the conflict be ended. The knight felt about for the scar, and when he had found it, he could no longer refuse to give his name.

'King Arthur,' he said, I am willing to tell you who I am because I am happier than I can say: Dame Fortune has supplied the proof. The day has come to which I have looked forward for a long time. People call me Gasozein de Dragoz. Now, since I have complied with your request, I should be able to assume that you too will act in a knightly and honourable manner; it would be noble and would befit you. I ask that you treat me justly in the matter that I wish to present, and if I am not greatly mistaken, you will do so. With your permission I shall tell you about it, because there is nobody else to whom I can complain. You, King Arthur, are the only one who is able to help me.'

'You must reveal it, then. Whatever you say, you will find friendship and justice, and since I can satisfy your claim, I shall give them readily. So do not be dismayed but tell me everything you wish concerning the matter.'

The knight thanked Arthur with a bow and said: 'In your castle you hold prisoner someone who belongs to me. More than seven years have passed since she first went there, mainly because of your power. You are keeping her against my will, and this injury to me that has lasted so long does not add to your fame.'

'Tell me, Sir Knight,' replied the king, 'whom have I taken from you as a prisoner? Unless something has happened that has been kept from me, I have done nothing of the kind and am quite innocent. I would think you had made a mistake except that I do not know of anybody else named Arthur, so I must be the lord you mean. But there is no prisoner in all my retinue, unless one has been taken since yesterday. As far as I know, I've never seen one.'

'Yet I am certain, king,' declared Gasozein, 'that whether you believe it or not, you have her who was stolen from me. It is Ginover, the queen, whose true love I have always been, for she was assigned to me at her birth by the night spirits. And their promise was not forgotten, because Cupid later saw to it that things went as had been destined for her. You should not think my words stem from mere presumption, because I shall support them with evidence that would enable even a child to see clearly the truth of what I have said, and you should not be greatly displeased.

'If you were to bring us together, I would prove it to you at once by her own words. At least grant me one request: take her this belt, which is known only to her, Gawein, and me, and ask her to come soon and speak with me here for my love's sake. When she sees the belt, she will know that your report is true. Gawein won it for her and she gave it to me when I last parted from her. The belt has such power that the wearer is adored by both men and women and cannot be defeated in battle, for his virtues and strength are greatly increased. Fortune never fails him but watches over him day and night and aids him in all he does; no one ever enjoys her favour more than he. A mighty fairy called Giramphiel, helped by her sister, made it to bring good luck to her lover, Fimbeus of Sardin.'

Arthur was much distressed at hearing this; indeed, the burden of his grief almost broke his heart. It was the queen's unfaithfulness, as revealed by the knight, that pained him so – just as many men suffer today who hear something unbecoming or shameful about their dear wife and are overcome with great sorrow. No one ever bore a stronger chain than that which binds an honourable man to a beloved woman; how sweet is her kindness when one faithfully cares for her! But he who has been vanquished by worry because of his love for a woman is weighed down by a load of sorrow that is far greater than the joy she brings him. So I have been told by those who have known both.

Yet however much he was troubled, this did not happen to Arthur. And he was wise enough not to answer any statement with abuse or give insult for insult. Instead, he only said courteously: 'I must find it annoying, sir, that you should make such a false charge against my wife and for no reason except arrogance. I am certain that as long as I have known her no one could reproach her with any sin or dishonour or maintain that she had not remained upright and free of any man except me to this day.'

'King,' replied Gasozein, 'I did not intend to discredit my lady; indeed, I would rather add to her fame and esteem than accuse her of any wrong. I have spoken only of honourable conduct on her part, for I am her rightful husband, and you have no right to be with her. She pledged me her love as soon as she began to talk, for Amor long before had kindled in her the flame of love; there is no mistaking it. One cannot deny that she was always in my care from the cradle on until you took her from me. Now I have come, but this need not trouble you, since I shall show that her feelings have not changed and that she loves me more than she ever loved you, for that is the proper thing to do. She would rather look at me for a year than at you for a single day.

'It is a shameful blow for a man to live thus, who still must remain what he is even though he seals up his heart and buries it in a woman. Unfortunately, if she sometimes greets him with false warmth, he believes that she holds him in her heart: the poor man is struck by Cupid's leaden dart but will never receive an honest reward from her. Many different kinds of tents have been set up on Venus's field.

'Since you do not believe that you have robbed me of my heart's beloved, I give up my claim to her to the extent of making a request that is fair and honourable. I ask you to bring the lady here today so that we can settle this manifold dispute by seeing who can win her in knightly combat. Should I be the lucky one, I promise to give up all claim to her if within a year you find a man who can gain fame by taking her from me in a second joust. Then the queen would be yours without objection and I would never pursue her again. And hear this, too: the noble lady would be carefully guarded from all harm and untouched by me until my right to her was beyond question. Now tell me what you are going to do about it. I am so happy in her presence that it is hard to be without her.'

When Arthur, the child of Fortune who always knew how to do what was best and to whom this was most fitting, heard these words, he replied politely: 'If your request were proper, I should grant it, but he who asks for what is unseemly loses also the right that by custom would be his. I would have agreed to single combat even if you had not spoken as you did. But since you lay claim to my wife and her love by this means, I shall nevertheless let you have your wish. Still, we must postpone the time for the final settlement of our dispute, when your complaint and my defence will be completed. It would be a disgrace were two brave knights to fight who were not equally prepared, and our present conditions are uneven, since I am wearing armour and you are not. Yet it would not be just if you were spared the shame of defeat because of this, for then I would be the loser.

'It would be best if we were to fix a certain day for the combat and wait; at the appointed time I myself shall fight. Should you prove your contention against me, you will not need to answer to another. And you will never again have to be concerned about me, for I shall let you be her husband without further interference.' The knight agreed and also accepted the date proposed. It was decided that the trial by combat should take place at Karidol in six weeks; each kept his promise.

The knight at once gave Arthur the horses and departed joyfully. The king, on the other hand, was unhappy. The report about his wife filled his heart with bitterness, and he was eager to settle the matter. 'I'll bring disgrace on her if I can,' he thought. 'She shall pay dearly for having shamed me so, I'll think of something that will be painful for her. I wonder how best to get revenge for the dishonour I have suffered: should I ban her to a desert island, or hang her, or have her burned? That's it! It shall be done as soon as I see her.' But then his thoughts took another turn: 'If I did that, I might be judged unstable. I could lose my reputation and have to be ashamed wherever it was known. I would do better to swear that the knight lied about her without cause to gain renown and let no one convince me that she is not faithful and honourable. The one thing that distresses me is that she would rebuke me because of him. This makes me believe him. She is caught in her own snare.'

This extract completes the story of Arthur's dispute with Gasozein of Dragoz. First they fight a duel, which is abandoned before either is victorious when they decide to allow Ginover (Guenevere) to choose between them.

It therefore seems to me that you should allow the matter to be settled in another way. Since we both believe the lady loves us dearly, let us take a solemn oath to permit her to decide as she wishes and to allow him who gets the prize to be her companion and rightful husband. Give her a chance to choose the one her heart desires, without deceit or threats. I shall take such an oath, although you have not yet said whether you will join me, provided that we swear to each other to keep it; that it is not to become void however much one of us may regret it and, breaking his word, wants to renounce it; and even though afterthoughts often cause an affair to be brought up anew when there has been no firm commitment, for a deceitful heart will so advise if it is not well restrained.'

'Knight,' answered the king, 'it is true that I said she preferred me to you, and since you make this proposal, I'll settle the matter thus and, for my part, will gladly leave it to her: let him of whom she is fondest have her and be happy.'

Their dispute having ended with this agreement, Gasozein and Arthur rode back at once to Karidol Castle with reversed banners like knights who come in peace, since they had granted it to each other. The story quickly flew about that the kind Arthur had become reconciled with Gasozein, and all the retinue fell to frivolity and gaiety, for they were greatly pleased at the favourable outcome for their lord. The two quickly rode up to the castle gate, dismounted, and without removing their armour walked hand in hand to the courtyard, where they were received by the knights who had gone there to meet them. Remembering their oath, the king sent for Ginover to come with her maids-in-waiting. Her beauty ensnared and wounded many hearts whose owners were unsparing of furtive glances, for sorrow is a goad to the eyes.

When she appeared before the king, he welcomed her and the knight bowed. Then, without further delay, Arthur addressed the company. 'You lords, kinsmen, and vassals whom I have summoned,' he said, 'listen carefully to a matter that I must make public here. You know I am telling the truth when I say that I fell in love with the queen here seven years ago, that we have always lived together as is usual in marriage, and that I believed her to be my lawful wife. Now this knight has come here with the claim that she would vouch for the fact that her love rightly belongs to him, and he offers himself as her advocate. It has been decided and confirmed with oaths that we would put aside the trial by combat and leave the matter up to her. She shall today resolve the conflict between us as she wishes, but in this manner and no other: she is to accept as her lord the knight or me. We shall thus learn where the truth lies. Lady, I also want to tell you that we shall all be at your disposal if you are better pleased with this warrior and choose him over me – truly he is worthy of it and you will be well rewarded with him – but should you want to remain with me, you will be as highly regarded as any woman ever was. You will therefore not be dishonoured however you decide.'

On learning that she was to choose between the two, the queen's heart almost burst with trouble and pain. She did not reveal her thoughts, but one could see that she was greatly distressed at having to declare openly before the whole assembly whether or not she had been keeping such a secret. She just stood there among them and didn't know what to do or whom to take. Gasozein tensely awaited her decision, for he was overcome with the pangs of love and suffered much anxiety because of this bitter punishment. 'Sir King,' he exclaimed spitefully, 'you are taking an unfair advantage of me! You have her surrounded on all sides so that she can't even walk. How long must she stand there before you let her go where her heart longs to be? Truly, you will merit little praise by cheating me with such tricks. You should remember your oath and treat me justly.'

In reply, Arthur told the queen to go wherever she wished and bade the knights move back. She became pale, then quickly turned red, for secret anguish greatly oppressed her in this choice. I don't know whether her heart struggled to be near or far. 'Lord and king,' she said, 'if my reward for always having served you well is that I am now to ask leave to depart, you have repaid me very poorly. This cannot be: I must remain with you. Do you want me to go away in shame to his country with a man I have never known – I can prove it – just because you are angry? How can I stop him if he wants to swear a thousand oaths that he loves me more than anyone else? That gives him no claim on me.' Hearing this, Gasozein was so wounded that he departed in a rage without asking leave. Nevertheless, Arthur did him the courtesy of riding a ways with him and offering him a friendly escort. The knight thanked him.

Of Arthour and of Merlin (c. 1270–1300)

While Lawman attributes the establishment of the Round Table to Arthur, The Story of Merlin *(Lestoire de Merlin) describes its foundation by Uther for his Pentecostal feast at Carduel, where Merlin chose fifty knights and asked them to seat themselves at that table and dine there.* Of Arthour and of Merlin, *one of several Middle English versions of* Lestoire, *retains Uther's foundation of the table, stressing the prowess required for membership, but does not mention the topic of equality. The rules of conduct for Uther's Round Table knights in* Of Arthour and of Merlin *appear to resemble those of the Knights Templar, who were established in London, the region of the poem's dialect, by 1128.*

2196	Our king bigan the Rounde Table –	
	That was thurth Merlines hest.	*through, advice*
	Of knightes that men wist best	*knew*
	In this warld thurthout	
2200	That table schuld sitte about,	
	At that table non sitt might	
	Bot he were noble and douhti knight	
	Strong and hende hardi and wise	*noble*
	Certes and trewe withouten feyntise,	*truly, lack of eagerness*
	Her non other schuld faile	*none of them*
	No never fle out of bataile	
	Whiles he on fot stond might	
	Bot if hem departed the night.[112]	
	At bataile and at bord also	*table*
2210	Bi hemselve thai schuld go –	
	So monkes don in her celle	*their*
	Bi hemselve thai eten ich telle.	*I*
	Wher wer were alder mast[113]	
	Thai wer thider sent on hast.	
	This table gan Uter the wight	*began, worthy*

Ac it to ende hade he no might		*but*
For thei alle the knightes under our Lord		
Hadde ysiten at that bord		*sat*
Knight bi knight ich you telle		
2220 The table no might nought fulfille		*none*
Til he wer born that schuld do al		
Fulfille the mervails of the greal.		*Grail*

*Guenevere admires Arthur from the safety of the city walls, while
he and his followers assist her father, King Leodegan, against his
Saxon enemies. The celebrations which follow Arthur's victory are
the occasion of his first meeting with Guenevere, who, with her
maidens, washes the weary battle-soiled warriors. The existence of
her illegitimate half-sister, also called Guenevere (who in some
works causes a rift between Arthur and his queen) is here explained
by the poet.[114] When the princess later serves him at the banquet,
Arthur, smitten by love, wishes to relieve her of this duty, but
Guenevere declares that she considers it an honour to serve such a
hero. In response to Ban's question about his daughter's unmarried
state, Leodegan, aware of Arthur's reaction to her beauty, declares
that he is merely awaiting a suitable suitor.*

6375 Gueneoure sat on the cite-walle		
And the other leuedis alle		*ladies*
Of Arthour seighe justing this		*saw*
On him thai laiden al the priis. [...]		
After this bataile amd scumfite		*defeat*
Our men bothe gret and lite		*small, unimportant*
Togider gaderd hem comonliche		*themselves*
And comen hom nobleliche		
And biforn hem driven al the pray		*spoils*
6450 Of XXC cartes y say		*I*
And com to Carohaise that riche toun		
With joie and with processioun;		
King Leodegan tho hete		*ordered*
His men nimen that pray skete		*to take, without delay*
That in the twenti C cartes was		
Taken it Arthour more and las		
So deden the kinges knightes,		*did*
Arthour nome it anon rightes		*took*
And parted it wel curtaisliche		*shared it out*
6460 Bi Merlins conseil sikerliche		*truly*
And so miche gaf his ost Blaise[115]		

That riche hem made and wele at aise.   *ease*
Ac Arthour no Ban no forth his host   *but*
No lenge with Blasie soiourne most
Ac to court thai were yfeched rathe   *quickly*
And ydon in riche bathe;   *placed*
Gueneour wesche the King Arthour
And Ban and Bohort with honour,
Guenore another damisel
6470 And other maidens fair and fel   *excellent*
Weschen alle her gentil feren –   *companions*
Here ye schul now yheren   *hear*
Hou the other Guenour was bigete
Y wil that ye it alle wite.   *know*
Tho Leodegan spoused his quene
A burmaiden he hadde fair and schene,   *chambermaid, bright*
On fair maner and gentil wise
That served the leuedi of heighe prise,   *lady, esteem*
The kinges steward Cleodalis
6480 Seighe this maiden of gret prise   *saw*
And spac so fair to the king
That he wedded that swete thing.
After a yer other to ywis   *two, indeed*
That gentil knight Cleodalis
Went ther him hete the king   *where, ordered*
And left his wiif in the quenes yeming   *care*
And ich you sigge par ma fay   *tell, by my faith*
In the quenes chaumber sche lay.
Ich night it was the quenes maner   *each*
6490 To chirche gon and matins here,   *to go, hear*
Also the quen herd matines   *while*
The king aros bi wrongful lines   *behaving wrongfully*
And what bi love and what bi striif
He forlay the stewardes wiif   *committed adultery with*
And bigat a maide of gret mounde   *power*
That was Guenour the secounde,
And fram that time al afterward
He binam the wif his steward   *took away/abducted*
And hadde hir fer in on trist   *far away, secret place*
6500 Whiderward the steward nist   *was unaware*
Natheles Cleodalis
That gentil knight of michel priis   *much/great*
Noither in servise no in bataile
No feined ogain the king saun faile;   *against, without fail*

	This Guenour was the other so liche	*like*
	So pani is other sikerliche.	*penny, truly*
	These weschen this gentil man	
	And leyd tables after than.	
	Leodegan nam yeme wich onour	*took, care*
6510	Alle the other born king Arthour,	*respected*
	King Arthour sat withouten fable	*lying*
	Midelest at the heighe table	
	King Ban at his right half sat	
	Ac the other half king Bohort at	
	Afterward her compeinie	*their*
	Was yset thritti and neie	*nine*
	And next hem withouten fable	
	Sat the knightes of the Rounde Table,	
	After that ysett were there	
6520	Al tho other after thai were.	
	In halle thai hadden riche servise	
	Whereto schuld y that devise?	*describe in detail*
	Ac Gueneour withouten les	*lying*
	Served Arthour of the first mes;	*dish*
	Leodegan that wele y say	
	Biheld his douhter and Arthour noblay	
	So michel on her he thought	*much*
	That of mete no drink he no rought,	*took*
	A noble knight Hervi de Rivel	
6530	Undernam his semblaunt wel	*perceived, expression*
	And seyd 'Sir thi thought lete be	
	And make thine ostes gamen-gle,	*guests, merry entertainment*
	Eten and drink men schal on benche	
	And after mete in chaumber thenche,'	*deliberate*
	The king this tale understode	
	And made his gestes semblaunt gode.	
	Ac on Gueneour biheld Arthour	*gazed*
	And was al nomen in hir amour	*captured by love*
	Ac he tempred so his blod	
6540	That no other it understode;	
	Guenoure on knewes oft gan stoupe	*knees*
	To serve King Arthour with the coupe	
	And he seyd to hir saun faile	*without fail*
	'Crist lete me yeld the thi travaile,'	*thank you for your labour*
	And sche seyd to him 'Sir gramerci	*if you please*
	It nis nought to yeld Sir, je vus dy,	*I tell you*
	Ac swiche a thousand so y be	*such*

Sir no might it yeld the
The help and the travail and the honour
6550 That ye han don to mi lord and your socour,
Yherd be Ihesus Cristes sond *message*
That you sent into this lond' –
Gueneour was ever tofor Arthour *before/in front of*
And served him with gret honour
And bifor everi gentil man was
Maidens to serve with gret solas.
Ther were trumpes and fithelers *viol-players*
And stivours and tabourers *bagpipers*
Thai eten and dronken and made hem glade *cheerful*
6560 And tho thai were al glad made
The clothes weren up ydrawe
And thai weschen so it was lawe. *customary*
After mete asked King Ban
To the King Leodegan
Whi Guenour his douhter precious
To sum gentil man nere yspouse *never*
Seththen he no hadde non airs, *since, heirs*
'Certes Sir' quath Leodegan vairs *in truth*
'If were ner so mot y live *as I may live*
6570 Sche were mani day ygeve, *given in marriage*
Wist ich owhar ani bacheler *if I knew anywhere*
Vigrous and of might cler *flawless*
And he were of gode linage
Thei he nadde non hirritage *even if he had no inheritance*
Mi douhter ich wald him give
And al mi thing with to live' – *wealth/property*
For King Arthour that he seyd.
Merlin tho toforn hem pleyd *before*
And cleped up King Arthour and Ban *called out to*
6580 And her feren fram Leodegan *their followers*
So that Leodegan might of nothing
More wite of her being; *learn*
Ther seyd Merlin anon right *straightaway*
To King Arthour al the sleight *slaughter of men*
That Wawain and his feren of mounde *worthy followers*
Hadde ydon biside Lounde *London*
And al that therwhiles schuld falle *happen*
He told ther biforn hem alle,
Wherthurth blithe in that toun *for which reason, happy*
6590 Thai bileft til the Assensioun. *stayed*

Lete we now here King Arthour
And his feren with gret honour
And hereth of the chaunces ille   *harsh fortune*
Therwhiles in Inglond bifelle.

The Fair Unknown (Lybeaus Desconus) (c. 1330–40)

*Thomas of Chestre's Middle English translation of the Old French
Biaus Descouneus of Renart de Beaujeu survives in two manu-
scripts: London, British Library, MS Cotton Caligula A., and
London, Lambeth Palace, MS 306. The poem, which places
Arthur's court at Glastonbury, was known to Chaucer.*[116] *The
passage here selected recounts the arrival of the unknown young
hero at Arthur's court and his request to receive knighthood at
Arthur's hand, and undertake the first adventure which arises.*

1   Jhesu Criste oure Savyour
      And his moder, that swete ffloure,
      Spede hem at her nede   *help them in their need*
      That lysteneth of a conquerour,
      Wise of witt and a wight wereour   *brave warrior*
      And doughty man of dede.
      His name was Sir Gyngelayne,
      Gotten he was of Sir Gaweyne,
      Under a forest syde;
10   A better knyght was never prophitable
      With Arthur at the Roun Table:
      Herde I never of redde.

      Gyngelayne was fayre of sight,
      Gentyll of body and of face bryght,
      Bastard though that he were;
      His moder hym kepte with hir myght
      That he shulde se no knyght
      I-armed in no maner,
      For he was full savage
20   And gladly wold do oute-rage
      To his ffellaves in fere;   *companions*
      And for all dred of wycke loose   *evil report*
      His moder alwey kepte him close

As dughty childe and dere.   *doughty*

And for he was so fayre of ffyce,   *face*
His moder clepte him Bewfiz,   *called*
And none other name,
And this childe was so nyse   *naive*
He asked never, i-wysse,   *indeed*
30   Whate he hight off his dame.   *was called*
Tyll hit be-fell uppon a day,
The childe wente him forthe to playe,
Off dere to have som game;
He fond a knyght there he lay,
In armes stoute and gaye,   *colourful*
Slayne and made ful tame.

He toke of that knyghtis wede;   *armour*
Hym-sylffe therin well fayre can shrede,   *dressed*
All in that bryght armour.
40   Whan he had do that in dede,   *done*
To Glastynbury the childe him yede,   *youth, went*
Ther lay Kyng Arthure.
And whan he came to Arthurs hall
He fond him there and all his lordis all;
This childe knelyd downe on his kne:
'Kyng Arthure, Criste the save and see!
I am come oute of fer contre   *a distant land*
My mone to make to the.   *request*

I am childe unkowthe
50   And come out of the Southe
And wolde be made a knyght;
Lorde I pray the nowthe,   *now*
With thi mery mouthe,
To graunte me anone right.'   *right now*
Than saide Arthure the kynge,
'To me childe, with-out dwellinge: *delaying*
Whate is thi name aplight?   *called*
For never sethe I was born,   *since*
Sawe I never me be-forne
60   So semely to my sight.'
Sayde Gyngelayn, 'Be Seint Jame!
I ne wote whate is my name: *know*
I am the more nyse;   *foolish*
But while I was at home,

My moder, on hir game,   *playfully*
Clepped me Bewfice.'   *called*
Than sayde Arthur the kyng,
'This is a wonder thinge,
Be God and Seint Denyce,   *by*
70   Whan that he wold be made a knyght
And wote not whate his name heght   *is called*
And hathe so fayre a vice.   *face*

I shall if hym a name,   *give*
Amonge you all in same,   *together*
For he is fayre and fre;   *noble*
Be God and be Seint Jame,   *by*
So clepped him never his dame,   *gave him a name*
Whate woman so she be.
Clepeth him in your use,
80   Lybeus Disconeus,   *the Fair Unknown*
For the love of me;
Than mowe ye wit, on a rowe,   *Thus you may all together know*
That the better ye mowe knowe
Certis so hight hee.'

Kynge Arthur anone right   *straightaway*
Con make him a knyght,   *made*
In that sylffe daye.   *same*
'Now Kyng Arthur hathe made me knyght,
I thanke him with all my myght:
90   Bothe by day and nyght
With my fomen I will fight   *enemies*
Them to say with stroke of myght   *assay/put to the test*
And to juste in feer.'   *together*
Whan he was a knyght made,
Off Arthur a bone he bade   *he made a request*
And sayde, 'My lorde fre: *noble*
In hert I were full glad
The first fyghtinge that ye hadde
That men will aske of the.'
100 Than saide Arthur the kynge,
'I graunte the thine askynge,
Whate batayll so it bee;
But me thinketh thu arte to yonge
To do a gode ffyghtynge,
Be ought that I can see.'   *by*

With-outen eny more reyson,   *discussion*
Duke, erle and baron
Wesshed and went to mete.
Volatyle and venyson,   *fowl*
110   As lordis of grete renon,
I-now they had to ete.   *enough*
Nade Arthure syt but a while,   *Arthur had not*
The mountence of a myle,   *the time it takes to walk a mile*
Att his tabyll sett,
Ther con a mayde in ryde
And a dwerffe by hir syde,
All be-swett for hete.   *covered in sweat, due to the heat*

The may hight Ellyne,   *maiden, was called*
Gentyll, bryght and shene: *polished*
120   A lovely messengere.
Ther nas countes nor quene   *there was no countess*
So semely on to sene   *attractive to look at*
That myght be hir pere.   *peer/equal*
She was clothed in tarse,   *cloth made in Tarsus*
Rownd and nothinge scarse,
I-pured with blawndenere;   *trimmed with ermine*
Hir sadill was ovir-gilt
And with diamondis ffyltt: *inlaid*
Milke white was hir destere.   *horse*

130   The dwerff was clothed in ynde,   *Indian cloth*
By-fore and eke be-hinde;   *also*
Stoute he was and pertte.   *pert/lively*
Amongis all Cristyn kyng
Suche sholde no man fynde:
His surcote was so ryche bete.   *embroidered*
His berde was yelewe as wax,
To his girdyll hange his fax: *hair*
The sothe to say in sertente.   *to tell the truth*
Off gold his shone were dight   *shoes, adorned*
140   And coped as a knyght: *wearing a cape*
That signyfied no povert.   *poverty*

Theodeley was his name;
Wyde wher spronge his fame,
By Northe and eke by Southe;   *also*
Mekyll he couthe of game,[117]
Sotill, sawtrye in same,   *both psaltery and other strings*

Harpe, fethill and crowthe.   *fiddle*
He was a gentill boourdour   *jester/trickster*
Amonge ladyes in boure: *chamber*
150 A mery man of mouthe.
He spake to the mayde hende,   *noble*
'Foe-to tell thine erende,
Tyme hit were nouthe.'   *now*

The mayde knelyd in hall
Be-for the knyghtis all
And sayde, 'My lorde Arthur,
A casse is nowe beffall,
A worsse with-in wall
Was never yitt of doloure: *grief*
160 Mi lady of Synadowne
Is brought in stronge prison,
That was of grete valure,
And pray you sond hir a knyght   *send*
That is of wer wyse and wight,   *war, valiant*
To wynne hir with honoure.'

Uppe startte that yonge knyght,
With hert mery and light,
And sayde, 'Arthur my lorde,
I shall do that fight
170 And wyn that lady with myght,
If ye be trewe of worde.'
Than sayde Arthoure, 'That is sothe,   *true*
Certeyn with-outen othe,   *oath*
Therto I ber recorde.
God yf the strenthe and myght   *give*
To holde that ladyes right
With dynte of sper and swerde.'   *blow*

The mayde be-gan to chide
And sayde, 'Alas that tyde   *time*
180 That I was heder i-sentt!
Thy worde shall sprynge wide:
For-lorne is thy pryde
And thi lose shentt,   *reputation, destroyed*
When thou wilt send a childe
That is witles and wylde
To dele eny doughty dent,   *blow*
And haste knyghtis of renon:

Syr Persyfale and Syr Gawyn,
That ben abled in turment.'   *experienced in tournament*
190 The dwerffe with grete erroure   *misjudgement*
Went to Kynge Arthowre
And saide, 'Kynde kynge:
This childe to be weroure   *warrior*
And to do suche labour
Is not worthe a fferthinge!
Or that he that lady see,
He shall do bataylles thre,
Wyth-oute eny lesynge;   *lying*
At Poynte Perilowse,
200 Be-syde the Chapell of Awntrous,
Shal be his begynynge.'

Syr Lybeus than answerde,
'Yett was I never a-ferde
For dred of wordys awe.
To fyght with spere and swerde
Somdell have I lerned,   *something*
Ther many man hathe be slawe.
That man that fleyth by wey or strete,   *flees*
I wolde the devyll had broke his nek,
210 Wher-ever he hym take;
Also I wolde he were to-drawe   *pulled apart by horses*
And with the wyne to-wawe,   *to be drowned in wine*
Till the devill him take.
The batayll I undir-take
And never none for-sake,
As hit is londis lawe.'   *the law of the land*

The kynge said anone right,   *straightaway*
'Thou gettist here none other knyght,
By Him that brought me dere!
220 Iff ye thinke the childe not wyght,   *sturdy*
Get the another wher thou myght,
That is of more power.'
The mayden for ire and hete
Wolde neyther drynke ne ete,
For none that there were;
She sate downe dismayde
Tyll the table was raysed,
She and the dwerffe in fere.   *together*

Kyng Arthour, in that stounde,   *time*
230 Comaunded of the Tabill Rownde
Foure of the best knyghtis,
In armys hole and sownde,   *whole*

To arme him anone rightis;   .
And sayde, 'Throwe the helpe of Criste,
That in the fflome was baptiste,   *water*
He shall holde uppe all his hightis,   *promises*
And be gode champyon
To the lady of Synadon
And fellen hir foon in fyghtis.'   *overcome, foes*

240 To armen him the knyghtis were fayne: *glad*
The fyrst was Syr Gawayne,
That othere, Syr Persyvale,
The third was Syr Iwayne,
The fourthe highte Agfayne: *was called*
Thus telleth the Frensshe tale.
They kestyn on him of sylke   *placed*
A sorkett white as mylke,   *surcoat*
That semely was in sale;   *hall*
Ther-on an haubryk bryght   *coat of mail*
250 That richely was dyght   *adorned*
With mayles thik and smale.   *interlaced rings of iron*

Syr Gawyn, his owe syre,   *father*
Henge aboute his swyre   *hung, neck*
A shelde with one chefferon;   *chevron/V-shaped design*
And an helme of rich atyre
That was stele and none ire   *not iron*
Sir Percyvale sett on his crowne;
Lawncelett brought him a spere,
In armes him with to were,
260 And a fell fauchone;   *lethal falchion[118]*
Iwayne brought him a stede
That was gode at nede
And egir as eny lyon.

The knyght to hors gan sprynge
And rode to Arthure the kynge
And sayde, 'My lorde hende: *noble*
Yeff me thy blessynge,   *give*
With-oute eny dwellynge: *delay*

My will is nowe to wende.'   *depart/go*

270   Arthur his honde up-haffe
And his blessyng him yaffe,
As curteys kynge and kynde,
And sayde, 'God yf the grace,   *give*
Off spede and eke of space,   *also*
To brynge that byrde oute of bonde.'   *danger*

Sir Percyvell of Gales *(c. 1330–40)*

*This is a Middle English version of the Perceval story, from which
the Grail is completely omitted. The English poem is substantially
shorter and less sophisticated than Chrétien's* Perceval, *from which
it may have been derived. The source of* Sir Percyvell of Gales *may,
however, be a more primitive, perhaps oral, version of the story.*[119]
While much of the material in Chrétien's version is omitted, Sir
Percyvell of Gales *introduces some new elements into the story,
including the detail about Perceval's father being Arthur's brother-
in-law, so that Perceval is now Arthur's nephew. Perceval also has
an encounter with a witch, the mother of the Red Knight; another
notable addition is the reappearance of Perceval's mother (here
called Acheflour) towards the end of the poem, where she is
defended by Perceval against the Black Knight.*

*In the following extract, the young Perceval arrives at Arthur's
court and avenges his father by killing the Red Knight.*

485   He come ther the kyng was
Servede of the firste mese,   *course*
To hym was the maste has   *(see) him, chief purpose*
That the childe hade.
And thare made he no lett,   *did not delay*
490   At yate, dore ne wykett,   *any entrance*
Bot in graythely he gett   *promptly*
(Syche maistres he made).   *threats*
At his firste in comynge,
His mere, withowtten faylynge,
Kyste the forhevede of the kynge –   *forehead*
So nerehande he rade.   *close (to him)*

The kyng had ferly thaa,   *was astonished*

And up his hande gan he taa,   *raised*
And putt it forthir hym fraa –
500   The mouthe of the mere!
He saide, 'Faire childe and free,
Stonde still besyde mee,
And tell me wythen that thou bee   *from where*
And what thou will here.'   *you want*
Than saide the fole of the filde,
'I ame myn awnn modirs childe,
Comen fro the woddez wylde
Till Arthure the dere.   *To, noble*
Yisterday saw I knyghtis three –
510   Siche on sall thou make mee   *such a (knight)*
On this mere byfor the,
Thi mete or thou schere.'   *before you carve*

Bot than spak sir Gawayne
(Was the kynges trenchepayne)   *cutter of bread*
Said, 'Forsothe is noghte to layne –   *hide*
I am one of thaa.
Childe, hafe thou my blyssyng,
For thi feres folowynge;   *fellows*
Here hase thou fonden the kynge,
520   That kan the knyghte maa.'   *make*
Than sayde Percyvell the free,
'And this Arthure the kyng bee,
Luke he a knyghte make mee:
I rede at it be swaa!'   *order him to do this*
Thofe he unborely were dyghte,   *roughly, dressed*
He sware by mekill Goddes myghte,
'Bot if the kyng make me knyghte,   *Unless*
I sall hym here slaa!'

All that ther weren, olde and yynge,
530   Hadden ferly of the kyng: *Were amazed at*
That he wolde suffre siche a thyng   *behaviour*
Of that foull wyghte.   *base creature*
On horse hovande hym by,   *standing*
The kyng byholdez hym on hy –   *looks up at him*
Than wexe he sone sory,
When he sawe that syghte;
The teres oute of his eghne glade   *streamed*
(Never one another habade):   *stopped for*

'Allas,' he sayde, 'that I was made,
540 Be day or by nyghte;
One lyve I scholde after hym bee,   *survive him*
That me thynke lyke the;
Thou arte so semely to see,   *handsome*
And thou were wele dighte.'   *If only, turned out*

He saide, 'And thou were wele dighte,
Thou were lyke to a knyghte
That I lovede with all my myghte,
Whills he was one lyve.
So wele wroghte he my will,   *carried out, wishes*
550 In all manere of skill,   *competence*
I gaffe my syster hym till
Forto be his wyfe;
He es moste in my mane –   *remembrance*
Fiftene yere es it gane,
Sen a theffe hade hym slane   *villain*
Abowte a littill stryffe!
Sythen hafe I ever bene his fo,
Forto wayte hym with wo;   *lie in wait for*
Bot I myghte hym never slo:
560 His craftes are so ryfe!'   *powers, manifold*
He sayse, 'His craftes are so ryfe,
Ther is no man apon lyfe,
With swerde, spere, ne with knyfe,
May stroye hym allan;   *destroy, unaided*
Bot if it were sir Percyvell son
(Whoso wiste where he ware done):   *If only one knew*
The bokes says that he mon   *must*
Venge his fader bane.'   *murder*
The childe thoghte he longe bade   *had been waiting*
570 That he ne ware a knyghte made,   *Without being*
For he wiste never that he hade
A ffader to be slayne!
The lesse was his menynge: *grief*
He saide sone to the kynge,
'Sir, late be thi jangleynge –   *drivelling*
Of this kepe I nane!'   *don't want any of it*

He sais, 'I kepe not to stande
With thi jangleyn[ge] to lange: *(Listening) to*
Make me knyghte with thi hande,

580 If it sall be done!'   *you're going to!*
     Than the kyng hym hendly highte   *promised*
     That he schold dub hym to knyghte,
     With thi that he wolde doun lighte   *Provided, dismount*
     And ete with hym at none.
     The kyng biholdez the vesage free,   *noble features*
     And ever more trowed hee
     That the childe scholde bee   *must*
     Sir Percyvell son;
     It ran in the kynges mode   *mind*
590 His syster Acheflour the gude –
     How scho went into the wodde
     With hym forto wonn.   *live*

     The childe hadde wonnede in the wodde
     He knewe nother evyll ne gude;
     The kynge hymselfe understode   *could see*
     He was a wilde man!
     So faire he spakke hym withall,
     He lyghtes doun in the haulle,
     Bonde his mere amonge tham alle   *Tied up*
600 And to the borde wann.   *went to*
     Bot are he myghte bygynn
     To the mete forto wynn,   *get to*
     So commes the Rede Knyghte in
     Emangez tham righte than.   *In the midst of*
     Prekande one a rede stede   *Thrusting forward*
     (Blode rede was his wede):
     He made tham gammen full gnede,   *very short of mirth*
     With craftez that he can.   *powers, had*

     With his craftes gan he calle,
610 And callede tham recrayhandes all: *cowards*
     Kynge, knyghtes inwith walle,   *within*
     At the bordes ther thay bade.   *remained sitting*
     Full felly the coupe he fett   *fiercely, snatched*
     Bifore the kynge that was sett:
     Ther was no man that durste hym lett,   *stop*
     Thofe that he ware ffadde.   *However bold*
     The couppe was filled full of wyne;
     He dranke of that that was therinn:
     All of rede golde fyne
620 Was the coupe made.

He tuke it up in his hande
(The coupe that he there fande)
And lefte tham all sittande,
And fro tham he rade.

Now fro tham he rade
(Als he says that this made);   *wrote*
The sorowe that the kynge bade   *endured*
Mighte no tonge tell.
'A, dere God,' said the kyng than,
630 'That all this wyde werlde wan,   *redeemed*
Whethir I sall ever hafe that man *Shall I, any knight*
May make yone fende duelle?   *put a stop to*
Fyve yeres hase he thus gane   *behaved*
And my coupes fro me tane,
And my gude knyghte slayne,
Men calde sir Percyvell.
Sythen taken hase he three
And ay awaye will he bee,   *he gets away*
Or I may harnayse me,   *arm myself*
640 In felde hym to felle.'

'Petir!' quod Percyvell the yynge,
'Hym than will [I] down dynge,   *knock flat*
And the coupe agayne brynge,   *back*
And thou will make me knyghte.'
'Als I am trewe kynge,' said he,
'A knyghte sall I make the,
Forthi thou will brynge mee   *As long as*
The coupe of golde bryghte.'
Up ryses sir Arthoure;
650 Went to a chamboure
To feche doun armoure
The childe in to dyghte;   *array*
Bot are it was doun caste,   *before, got down*
Ere was Percyvell paste,   *had gone*
And on his way folowed faste
That he solde with fyghte.   *The one that*

With his foo forto fighte,
None othergates was he dighte   *In no other way*
Bot in thre gayt skynnes righte –
660 A fole als he ware [...][120]

He cryed, 'How, man on thi mere!
Bryng agayne the kynges gere,   *property*
Or with my dart I sall the fere   *terrify*
And make the unfere!'   *disable you*
And after the Rede Knyghte he rade,
Baldely withowtten bade;
Sayd, 'A knyght I sall be made
For som of thi gere!'   *In exchange for*
He sware by mekill Goddez payne,
670   'Bot if thou brynge the coupe agayne,
With my dart thou sall be slayne
And slongen of thi mere!'
The knyghte byhaldez hym in throo,   *angrily*
Calde hym fole that was hys foo –
For he named hym soo   *gave such a name to*
The stede that hym bere.

And forto see hym with syghte,
He putt his umbrere on highte   *raised up, visor*
To byhalde how he was dyghte
680   That so till hym spake.
He sayde, 'Come I to the, appert fole   *manifest*
I sall caste the in the pole,   *pond*
For all the heghe days of Yole,   *In spite of*
Als ane olde sakke!'
Than sayd Percyvell the free,
'Be I fole, or whatte I bee,   *Whether or not*
Now sone of that sall wee see
Whose browes schall blakke.'   *turn pale*
Of schottyng was the childe slee;   *throwing, skilled*
690   At the knyghte lete he flee:
Smote hym in at the eghe,
And oute at the nakke.

For the dynt that he tuke,   *received*
Oute of sadill he schoke   *jerked*
(Whoso the sothe will luke)
And ther was he slayne.

Ywain and Gawain (c. 1350)

Although considerably shorter and less contemplative than its French original, this poem is much closer to Chrétien de Troyes's Yvain *than* Sir Percyvell of Gales *is to his* Perceval. *In the following episode, a great lord has died, leaving his two daughters as heiresses. Wishing to obtain the whole inheritance, the eldest daughter travels to Arthur's court and secures Gawain as her champion. The younger daughter then also goes to court, but Gawain tells her that he cannot help. She obtains a forty-day respite from King Arthur and decides to seek the assistance of the Knight of the Lion (Ywain). The extract opens with the ensuing trial by combat, over which Arthur presides.*

3385 Als sone als the day was sent,	*it was dawn*
Thai ordaind tham and forth thai went;	*got themselves ready*
Until that town fast gan thai ride	
Whare the kyng sojorned that tide,	
And thare the elder sister lay	
3390 Redy forto kepe hyr day.	*day appointed to her*
Sho traisted wele on Sir Gawayn,	
That no knyght sold cum him ogayn;	*oppose*
Sho hopid thare was no knyght lifand,	*thought*
In batail that might with him stand.	*against*
Al a sevenight dayes bidene	*For, altogether*
Wald noght sir Gawayn be sene,	
Bot in ane other toun he lay;	
For he wald cum, at the day,	
Als aventerous into the place	*knight errant*
3400 (So that no man sold se his face).	
The armes he bare war noght his awyn,	
For he wald noght in court be knawyn.	*recognized*
Syr Ywayn and his damysell	
In the town toke thaire hostell,	
And thare he held him prevely,	
So that none sold him ascry.	*recognize*
(Had thai dwelt langer by a day,	
Than had sho lorn hir land for ay.)	
Sir Ywain rested thare that nyght,	
3410 And on the morn he gan him dyght;	
On slepe left thai his lyowne	
And wan tham wightly out of toun.	*made their way swiftly*

(It was hir wil and als hys awyn,
At cum to court als knyght unknawyn.)
  Sone obout the prime of day,
Sir Gawayn fra thethin thare he lay   *from where*
Hies him fast into the felde;
Wele armyd with spere and shelde.
Noman knew him, les ne more,   *humble, noble*
3420 Bot sho that he sold fight fore.
The elder sister to court come,
Unto the king at ask hir dome;   *judgement*
Sho said, 'I am cumen with my knyght,
Al redy to defend my right.
This day was us set sesowne,   *time fixed*
And I am here al redy bowne;
And sen this es the last day,
Gifes dome and lates us wend oure way.
My sister has al sydes soght,   *everywhere*
3430 Bot, wele I wate, here cums sho noght;
For sertainly sho findes nane
That dar the batail undertane,
This day for hir forto fyght –
Forto reve fra me my right.   *take away*
Now have I wele wonnen my land,
Withowten dint of knightes hand;
What so my sister ever has mynt,   *intended*
Al hir part now tel I tynt.
Al es myne to sell and gyf:
3440 Als a wreche ay sal sho lyf!   *beggar*
Tharfore, sir king, sen it es swa
Gifes yowre dome and lat us ga.'   *ruling*

The king said, 'Maiden, think noght lang.'
(Wele he wist sho had the wrang!)
'Damysel it es the assyse,   *custom*
Whils sityng es of the justise,
The dome nedes thou most habide;   *wait for*
For, par aventure, it may bityde,   *possibly happen*
Thi sister sal cum al bityme –   *soon enough*
3450 For it es litil passed prime.'   *first hour*
When the king had tald this scill,   *made, point*
Thai saw cum rideand over a hyll

[3438] I now consider that she has lost the whole of her share.
[3443] don't be impatient.

The yonger sister and hir knyght –
The way to town thai toke ful right
On Ywains bed his liown lay,
And thai had stollen fra him oway;
The elder maiden made il chere
When thai to court cumen were.
The king withdrogh his jugement,   *withheld*
3460 For wele he trowed in his entent   *believed, mind*
That the yonger sister had the right,
And that sho sold cum with sum knyght.
Himself knew hyr wele inogh;   *perfectly well*
When he hir saw, ful fast he logh.
Him liked it wele in his hert
That he saw hir so in quert.   *calm*
    Into the court sho toke the way,
And to the king thus gan sho say:
'God, that governs alkin thing,
3470 The save and se, syr Arthure the kyng;
And al the knyghtes that langes to the,   *are your vassals*
And also al thi mery menye!   *company*
Unto yowre court, sir, have I broght
An unkouth knyght that ye knaw noght.   *strange(r)*
He sais that, sothly, for my sake,
This batayl wil he undertake –
And he haves yit in other land
Ful felle dedes under hand.   *bold, in*
Bot al he leves, God do him mede,
3480 Forto help me in my nede!'
    Hir [elder] sister stode hyr by
And tyl hyr sayd sho, hastily,
'For hys luf that lens us life,   *grants*
Gif me my right, withouten strife,
And lat no men tharfore be slayn.'
The elder sister sayd ogayn,
'This right es noght, for al es myne,
And I wil have yt, mawgre thine!
Tharfore, if thou preche alday,   *even if*
3490 Here sal thou nothing bere oway.'   *take*
The yonger mayden to hir says,

3481 *elder: yonger* written over erasure (British Library MS Cotton Galba E. ix. Hereafter
    'G'. RDW)
3484 what is legally due to me ... contention.
3488 in spite of anything you can do.

'Sister, thou ert ful curtays,
And gret dole es it forto se   *pity*
Slike two knightes al[s] thai be,
For us sal put thamself to spill.
Tharefore now, if it be thi will,
Of thi gude wil to me thou gif
Sum thing that I may on lif.'
        The elder said, 'So mot I the,
3500 Whoso es ferd I rede thai fle!   *advise them to*
Thou getes right noght, withowten fail,
Bot if thou win yt thurgh batail.'
The yonger said, 'Sen thou wil swa,
To the grace of God here I me ta;   *commit myself*
And lord als he es maste of myght,   *greatest*
He send his socore to that knyght,
That thus, in dede of charité,   *as an act*
This day antres hys lif for me.'   *risks*
        The twa knightes come bifor the king,
3510 And thare was sone ful grete gedering;   *assembly*
For ilka man that walk might
Hasted sone to se that syght.
Of tham this was a selly case,   *amazing situation*
That nowther wist what other wase;   *who*
Ful grete luf was bitwix tham twa,
And now er aither other fa.   *each of them is*
Ne the king kowth tham noght knaw,
For that wald noght thaire faces shew:
If other of tham had other sene,
3520 Grete luf had bene tham bitwene.
Now was this a grete selly –   *marvel*
That trew luf and so grete envy,   *hatred*
Als bitwix tham twa was than,
Might bath at anes be in a man.   *at the same time*
The knightes, for thase maidens love,   *sake*
Aither til other kast a glove   *challenged*
And, wele armed with spere and shelde,
Thai riden both forth to the felde.
        Thai stroke thaire stedes that war kene –
3530 Litel luf was tham bitwene!

3494 *als: al* G.
3495 they are prepared to destroy each other.
3529 spurred on their fearless horses.

Ful grevosly bigan that gamyn;   *contest*
With stalworth speres strake thai samen.   *together*
(And thai had anes togeder spoken,   *If, once*
Had thare bene no speres broken;
Bot in that time bitid it swa,   *it so happened*
That aither of tham wald other sla.)
Thai drow swerdes and swang obout,   *brandished*
To dele dyntes had thai no dout.   *were not afraid*
Thaire sheldes war shiferd and helms rifen –   *split*
3540 Ful stalworth strakes war thare gifen;   *mighty*
Bath on bak and brestes thare
War bath wounded wonder sare:
In many stedes might men ken   *places, see*
The blode out of thaire bodies ran.
    On helmes thai gaf slike strakes kene   *such*
That the riche stanes, al bidene,   *jewels, every one*
And other gere that was ful gude   *armour*
Was over coverd al in blode.
Thaire helmes war evel brusten bath,   *badly broken*
3550 And thai also war wonder wrath;   *enraged*
Thaire hauberkes als war al totorn,   *cut to pieces*
Both bihind and als byforn;
Thaire sheldes lay sheverd on the ground –
Thai rested than a litil stound   *short while*
Forto tak thaire ande tham till   *recover, breath*
(And that was with thaire bother will).
Bot ful lang rested thai noght,
Til aither of tham on other soght.
A stronge stowre was tham bitwene;   *hard battle*
3560 Harder had men never sene.
    The king and other that thare ware
Said that thai saw never are
So nobil knightes, in no place,
So lang fight bot by Goddes grace!
Barons, knightes, squiers and knaves
Said, 'It es no man that haves
So mekil tresore, ne nobillay,   *princely wealth*
That might tham quite thaire dede this day.'
Thir wordes herd the knyghtes twa –

3556 they both agreed to that.
3558 Before they would both attack each other (again).
3568 (properly) recompense them for.

3570   It made tham forto be more thra!   *resolute*

       Knightes went obout, gude wane,   *many of them*
       To mak the two sisters at ane;   *reconcile*
       Bot the elder was so unkinde,
       In hir thai might no mercy finde;
       And the right that the yonger hase,
       Puttes sho in the kinges grace.
       The king himself, and als the quene,
       And other knightes al bidene,   *together*
       And al that saw that dede that day,
3580   Held al with the yonger may;   *Sided*
       And to the king al thai bisoght
       (Whether the elder wald or noght)
       That he sold evin the landes dele,   *equally, divide*
       And gif the yonger damysele
       The half, or els sum porciowne
       That sho mai have to warisowne;   *in her possession*
       And part the two knightes in twyn:
       'For sertis,' thai said, 'it war grete syn,
       That owther of tham sold other sla,
3590   For in the werld es noght swilk twa.'   *their equals*
       When other knightes said thai sold sese,
       Thamself wald noght asent to pese.   *agree*
          Al that ever saw that batayl
       Of thaire might had grete mervayl;
       Thai saw never under the hevyn
       Twa knightes that war copled so evyn;   *matched*
       Of al the folk was none so wise,
       That wist whether sold have the prise,   *which (of them)*
       For thai saw never so stalworth stoure –   *valiant combat*
3600   Ful dere boght thai that honowre!
       Grete wonder had sir Gawayn
       What he was that faght him ogain,
       And sir Ywain had grete ferly   *marvelled greatly*
       Who stode ogayns him so stifly.
       On this wise lasted that fight,
       Fra midmorn unto mirk night,   *dark*
       And, by that tyme, I trow thai twa   *am sure*
       War ful weri and sare alswa.
       Thai had bled so mekil blode,
3610   It was grete ferly that thai stode:

3610 great wonder that they could stand on their feet.

So sare thai bet on bak and brest,   *grievously, smote*
Until the sun was gone to rest;
For nowther of tham wald other spare,
For mirk might thai than na mare,   *lack of light*
Tharfore to rest thai both tham yelde   *agreed*
(Bot or thai past out of the felde,
Bitwix tham two might men se
Both mekil joy and grete peté).
    By speche might no man Gawain knaw –
3620 So was he hase and spak ful law,   *hoarse*
And mekil was he out of maght   *greatly enfeebled*
For the strakes that he had laght;   *received*
And sir Ywain was ful wery,
Bot thus he spekes and sais in hy: *loudly*
He said, 'Syr, sen us failes light,
I hope it be no lifand wight   *am sure*
That wil us blame, if that we twin;   *break off*
For of al stedes I have bene yn,   *places*
With no man yit never I met
3630 That so wele kowth his strakes set!   *lay on*
So nobil strakes has thou gifen,
That my sheld es al to-reven.'   *split in pieces*
    Sir Gawayn said, 'Sir, sertanly,
Thou ert noght so weri als I;
For if we langer fightand were,   *even if*
I trow I might do the no dere.
Thou ert nothing in my det
Of strakes that I on the set.'   *In respect of*
Sir Ywain said, 'In Cristes name,
3640 Sai me what thou hat at hame.'
He said, 'Sen thou my name wil here   *wish to*
And covaites to wit wha[t] it were –
My name in this land mani wote:
I hat Gawayn, the king son Lote.'
Than was sir Ywayn sore agast: *appalled*
His swerde fra him he kast;
He ferd right als he wald wede,
And sone he stirt down of his stede.   *promptly leapt off*
He said, 'Here es a fowl mischance,

3617-8 They would express between them great joy and pitiful concern at once.
3640 you are called in your own land.
3642 [ ] obscured.
3647 behaved exactly as if he were losing his wits.

3650 For defaut of conisance!   *failure to recognize*
      A sir,' he said, 'had I the sene,
      Than had here no batel bene;
      I had me yolden to the als tite,   *immediately*
      Als worthi war for descumfite.'   *one defeated*
          'What man ertou?' said sir Gawain.
      'Syr,' he sayd, 'I hat Ywayne,   *am called*
      That lufes the more, by se and sand,
      Than any man that es lifand,
      For mani dedes that thou me did,
3660 And curtaysi ye have me kyd.   *shown*
      Tharfore, sir, now in this stoure
      I sal do the this honowre:
      I grant that thou has me overcumen
      And by strenkyth in batayl nomen.'   *captured*
          Sir Gawayn answerd, als curtays,
      'Thou sal noght do, sir, als thou sais;
      This honowre sal noght be myne,
      Bot sertes it aw wele at be thine.
      I gif it the here withowten hone   *forthwith*
3670 And grantes that I am undone.'   *acknowledge, defeated*
      Sone thai light, so sais the boke,   *At once*
      And aither other in armes toke,
      And kissed so ful fele sithe: *very many times*
      Than war thai both glad and blithe!
      In armes so thai stode togeder,   *Embracing thus*
      Unto the king com ridand theder,   *Until*
      And fast he covait forto here   *desired*
      Of thir knightes what thai were,
      And whi thai made so mekil gamyn,
3680 Sen thai had so foghten samyn.   *When, together*

      Ful hendli than asked the king
      Wha had so sone made saghteling   *Who, reconciled*
      Bitwix tham that had bene so wrath,
      And aither haved done other scath.   *injury*
      He said, 'I wend ye wald ful fain
      Aither of yow have other slayn –
      And now ye er so frendes dere!'
      'Sir king,' said Gawayn, 'ye sal here.
      For unknawing, and hard grace,

3679 And why they were so very cheerful.
3689 lack of recognition and evil fortune.

3690 Thus have we foghten in this place.
  I am Gawayn, yowre awin nevow,
  And sir Ywayn faght with me now;
  When we war nere weri, iwys,
  Mi name he frayned, and I his.   *asked*
  When we war knawin, sone gan we sese.
  Bot sertes, sir, this es no lese:
  Had we foghten forth a stownde,   *lie*
  I wote wele I had gone to grounde; *been defeated*
  By his prowes and his mayne,   *Through, might*
3700 I wate for soth I had bene slayne.'
   Thir wordes menged al the mode *troubled, mind*
  Of sir Ywayn als he stode:
  'Sir,' he said, 'so mot I go,
  Ye kn[a]w yowreself it es noght so!
  Sir king,' he said, 'withowten fail,
  I am overcumen in this batayl.'
  'Nai, sertes,' said Gawayn, 'bot am I.'
  Thus nowther wald have the maistri; *supremacy*
  Bifore the king gan aither grant *each acknowledged*
3710 That himself was recreant.   *vanquished*
  Than the king and hys menye
  Had bath joy and grete peté;
  He was ful fayn thai frendes were,
  And that thai ware so funden in fere. *at one*
   The kyng said, 'Now es wele sene
  That mekil luf was yow bitwene.'
  He said, 'Sir Ywain, welkum home'
  (For it was lang sen he thare come)
  He said, 'I rede ye both assent *advise, agree*
3720 To do yow in my jujement,   *put yourselves*
  And I sal mak so gude ane ende
  That ye sal both be halden hende.' *esteemed noble*
  Thai both assented sone thartill, *to that*
  To do tham in the kynges will –
  If the maydens wald do so.
  Than the king bad knightes two
  Wend efter the maydens bath,   *both*
  And so thai did, ful swith rath. *very quickly indeed*

3695 As soon as we recognized each other, we stopped at once.
3704 *knaw: knw* G.
3721 resolve matters so well.

Bifore the kyng when thai war broght,
3730 He tald unto tham als him thoght:
'Lystens me now, maydens hende,
Yowre grete debate es broght til ende;   *quarrel*
So fer forth now es it dreven   *has gone so far*
That the dome most nedes be gifen,
And I sal deme yow als I can.'
The elder sister answerd than,
'Sen ye er king that us sold were,   *protect*
I pray yow do to me na dere.'   *injury*
He said, 'I wil let for na saw
3740 Forto do the landes law:
Thi yong sister sal have hir right,
For I se wele that thi knyght
Es overcumen in this were.   *(judicial) battle*
(Thus said he anely hir to fere,   *solely, overawe*
And for he wist hir wil ful wele   *intention*
That sho wald part with never a dele.)   *bit*
'Sir,' sho said, 'sen thus es gane,
Now most I, whether I wil or nane,
Al yowre cumandement fulfill,
3750 And tharfore dose right als ye will.'
The king said, 'Thus sal it fall:
Al yowre landes depart I sall;   *divide*
Thi wil es wrang, that have I knawin,
Now sal thou have noght bot thin awin –
That es the half of al bydene.'   *together*
Than answerd sho ful tite in tene   *promptly, anger*
And said, 'Me think ful grete outrage
To gif hir half myne heritage!'
The king said, 'For yowre bother ese,
3760 In hir land I sal hir sese,
And sho sal hald hir land of the   *from you*
And to the tharfore mak fewté;   *do homage*
Sho sal the luf als hir lady,
And thou sal kith thi curtaysi.   *show her*
Luf hir efter thine avenant

3735 judge your case to the best of my ability.
3739–40 no entreaty will prevent me from imposing.
3754 but what is due to you.
3759 *ese: esse* G; the peace of mind of both of you.
3760 put her in legal possession of.
3765 in a manner proper to you.

And sho sal be to the tenant.'
(This land was first, I understand,
That ever was parted in Ingland.)
Than said the king, withowten fail,
3770 For the luf of that batayl,   *On account of*
Al sisters that sold efter bene
Sold part the landes tham bitwene.

The Stanzaic Morte Arthur *(c. 1350)*

This is a mid-fourteenth-century translation of the French Mort
Artu *(The Death of Arthur) but, as with many Middle English
versions of French works, it is substantially shorter, being only
about one-fifth of the length. The English poet concentrates on
the main plot, omitting anything which he considers superfluous.
Malory used the stanzaic* Morte Arthur *as a main source for the
final part of his work.*

While the extract taken from the Mort Artu *deals with Arthur's
discovery of Lancelot's affair with Guenevere and the return of
Excalibur to the lake, the following extract from the stanzaic*
Morte Arthur *opens at the point when Arthur has just learned of
Mordred's treachery. In this version of the story, Mordred wins
over the support of many people by giving splendid feasts and gifts,
so that they prefer his rule to Arthur's.*

2946 Such message was them brought.
There was no man that thought it good.
The king himself full soon it thought –   *very*
Full muche morned he in his mood
2950 That such tresoun in Yngland sholde be wrought –
That he moste needes over the flood.   *needs to go*
They broke sege and homeward sought;
And after they had much angry mood.

3771-2 should come after them, should divide (in this way).

That false traitour, Sir Mordred,
The kinges soster son he was
And eek his own son, as I rede   *also*
(Therefore men him for steward chese),
So falsely hath he Yngland led,
Wite you well, withouten lees,   *know, doubt*
His emes wife wolde he wed,   *uncle's*
That many a man rewed that rese.   *regretted, deed*

Festes made he many and fele,   *numerous*
And grete giftes he gave also;
They said with him was joy and wele,   *prosperity*
And in Arthurs time but sorrow and wo,
And thus gan right to wronge go;
All the counsel, is not to hele,
Thus it it was, withouten mo,   *more ado*
To hold with Mordred in land with wele.

False lettres he made be wrought,
And caused messengeres them to bring,
That Arthur was to grounde brought   *dead*
And chese they moste another king.   *must*
All they said as them thought:
'Arthur loved nought but warring
And such thing as himselfe sought;
Right so he took his ending.'

Mordred let cry a parlement;   *proclaimed*
The peple gan thider to come,   *assembled there*
And holly through their assent   *wholly*
They made Mordred king with crown.
At Canterbury, fer in Kent,
A fourtenight held the feste in town,
And after that to Winchester he went;
A riche brid-ale he let make boun.   *bridal feast, prepared*

In sommer, when it was fair and bright,
His faders wife then wolde he wed
And her hold with main and might,   *force*
And so her bring as bride to bed.
She prayd him of leve a fourtenight –
The lady was full hard bestedde –   *pressed*
So to London she her dight,   *prepared*
That she and her maidens might be cledde.   *clad for the wedding*

2960

The queen, white as lily flowr,
With knightes fele of her kin,   *many*
She went to London to the towr
And sperred the gates and dwelled therein.   *bolted*
Mordred changed all his colour;
Thider he went and wolde not blinne;   *delay*
3000 There-to he made many a showr,   *shower (of arrows)*
But the walles might he never win.

The Archebishop of Canterbury thider yode   *went*
And his cross before him brought;
He said: 'Sir, for Crist on Rood,   *cross*
What have ye now in all your thought?
Thy faders wife, whether thou be wode,   *mad*
To wed her now mayst thou nought.
Come Arthur ever over the flood,   *if Arthur ever comes*
Thou mayst be bold, it will be bought!'

3010 'A nice clerk,' then Mordred said,   *naive*
'Trowest thou to warn me of my will?   *Expect, forbid*
By Him that for us suffred pain,
These wordes shalt thou like full ill!
With wilde horse thou shalt be drayn   *ripped apart*
And hanged high upon an hill!'
The bishop to flee then was fain,   *eager*
And suffered him his follies to fulfill.

Then he him cursed with book and bell   *i.e. excommunicated*
At Canterbury, fer in Kent.
3020 Soon, Mordred herde thereof tell,
To seech the bishop hath he sent   *seek out*
The bishop durst no lenger dwell,
But gold and silver he hath hent;   *taken*
There was no lenger for to spell,   *speak*
But to a wildernesse he is went.

The worldes wele there he will forsake;
Of joy keepeth he never more,
But a chapel he lette make   *had built*
Between two highe holtes hore,   *rough woods*
3030 Therein wered he the clothes black,
In wood as he an ermite were;
Often gan he weep and wake   *keep watch*
For Yngland that had such sorrows sore.

Mordred had then lien full long,   *laid siege*
But the towr might he never win,
With strengthe ne with stoure strong   *fight*
Ne with none other kinnes gin;   *type of trick*
His fader dredde he ever among;
Therefore his bale he nill not blinne;   *evil deeds*
3040 He wend to warn them all with wrong   *thought to deny*
The kingdom that he was crowned in.

Forth to Dover gan he ride,
All the costes well he kend;   *coasts, knew*
To erles and to barons on ilk a side   *every*
Grete giftes he gave and lettres sent
And forset the se on ilk a side   *blockaded*
With bolde men and bowes bent;
Fro Yngland, that is brode and wide,
His owne fader he wolde defend.   *deny entry*

3050 Arthur, that was mikel of might,   *great*
With his folk come over the flood,
An hundreth galleys that were well dight.   *prepared*
With barons bold and high of blood;
He wend to have landed, as it was right,   *planned*
At Dover, there him thought full good
And there he fand many an hardy knight
That stiff in stour again him stood.   *strong in battle*

Arthur soon hath take the land
That him was levest in to lende;[121]
3060 His fele fomen that he there fand   *many enemies*
He wend before had been his frend;   *believed*
The king was wroth and well-nigh wode,   *mad*
And with his men he gan up wend;
So strong a stour was upon that strand   *beach*
That many a man there had his end.

Sir Gawain armed him in that stound;   *place*
Alas! too long his hede was bare;
He was seke and sore unsound;
His woundes greved him full sore.
3070 One hit him upon the olde wound[122]
With a tronchon of an ore;   *oar*
There is good Gawain gone to ground,
That speche spake he never more.

Bolde men, with bowes bent,
Boldly up in botes yode,   *went*
And rich hauberkes they rive and rent   *cleave*
That through-out brast the redde blood.
Grounden glaives through them went;   *Sharpened, spears*
Tho games thought them nothing good,   *those*
3080 But by that the stronge stour was stent,   *finished*
The stronge stremes ran all on blood.

Arthur was so much of might
Was there none that him withstood;
He hewed on their helmes bright
That through their brestes ran the blood.
By then ended was the fight;
The false were felld and some were fled
To Canterbury all that night
To warn their master, Sir Mordred.

3090 Mordred then made him boun,   *ready*
And boldly he will batail abide
With helme, sheld, and hauberk brown;
So all his rout gan forthe ride;   *army*
They them met upon Barendown,   *Barlam Down in Kent*
Full erly in the morrow tide;
With glaives grete and gonfanoun,   *pennons*
Grimly they gonne togeder ride.

Arthur was of rich array
And hornes blewe loud on hight,
3100 And Mordred cometh glad and gay,
As traitour that was false in fight.
They fought all that longe day
Til the night was nighed nigh;
Who had it seen well might say
That such a stour never he sigh.   *battle, saw*

Arthur then fought with herte good;
A nobler knight was never none.
Through helmes into hede it yode   *his sword went*
And sterred knightes both blood and bone.[123]
3110 Mordred for wrath was nighe wode,   *mad*
Called his folk and said to them one: *alone*
'Releve you, for Cross on Rood!   *recover yourselves*
Alas! This day so soon is gone!'

Fele men lieth on bankes bare,   *many*
With brighte brandes through-oute borne;   *swords, stabbed*
Many a doughty dede was there,
And many a lord his life hath lorne.   *lost*
Mordred was full of sorrow and care;
At Canterbury was he upon the morn;
3120 And Arthur all night he dwelled there;
His freely folk lay him beforn.   *noble, before him*

Erly on the morrow tide
Arthur bade his hornes blow,
And called folk on every side,
And many a dede buried on a row,   *dead body*
In pittes that was deep and wide;
On ich an hepe they laid them low,[124]
So all that ever gon and ride   *go by*
Some by their markes men might know.

3130 Arthur went to his dinner then,
His freely folk him followed fast,
But when he fand Sir Gawain
In a ship lay dede by a mast,
Ere ever he covered might or main,   *before, recovered*
An hundreth times his herte nigh brast.   *broke*

They laid Sir Gawain upon a bere,
And to a castle they him bore,
And in a chapel amid the quere   *choir*
That bold baron they buried there.
3140 Arthur then changed all his cheer;
What wonder though his herte was sore!
His soster son, that was him dere,
Of him sholde he here never more.

Sir Arthur he wolde no lenger abide;
Then had he all manner of ivil rest;
He sought ay forth the South side,
And toward Wales went he West.
At Salisbury he thought to bide,
At that time he thought was best,
3150 And call to him at Whitsuntide
Barons bold to battail prest.   *eager*

Unto him came many a doughty knight,
For wide in world these wordes sprong,

That Sir Arthur had all the right,
And Mordred warred on him with wrong.
Hidous it was to see with sight;
Arthures host was brode and long,
And Mordred that mikel was of might,   *great*
With grete giftes made him strong.

3160 Soon after the feste of the Trinitee,
Was a batail between them set,
That a stern batail there sholde be;
For no lede wolde they it let;   *man, prevent*
And Sir Arthur maketh game and glee,
For mirth that they sholde be met;
And Sir Mordred came to the countree
With fele folk that fer was fette.   *numerous, fetched*

At night when Arthur was brought in bed
(He sholde have batail upon the morrow),
3170 In strong swevenes he was bestedde,   *dream*
That many a man that day sholde have sorrow
Him thought he sat in gold all cledde,   *he imagined*
As he was comely king with crown,
Upon a wheel that full wide spredde,
And all his knightes to him boun.   *ready by him*

The wheel was ferly rich and round;   *marvellously*
In world was never none half so high;
Thereon he sat richly crowned,
With many a besaunt, brooch, and bee;   *coin, ring*
3180 He looked down upon the ground;
A black water there under him he see,   *saw*
With dragons fele there lay unbound,
That no man durst them nighe nigh.

He was wonder ferde to fall   *frightened*
Among the fendes there that fought.   *fiends*
The wheel over-turned there with-all
And everich by a limm him caught.   *each (of the dragons)*
The king gan loude cry and call,
As marred man of wit unsaught;   *troubled, disturbed mind*
3190 His chamberlains waked him there with-all,
And wodely out of his sleep he raught.   *madly, awoke*

All nighte gan he wake and weep,   *remain awake*
With drery herte and sorrowful steven,   *voice*

And against the day he fell on sleep.   *just before*
About him was set tapers seven.
Him thought Sir Gawain him did keep,   *attend*
With mo folk than men can neven,   *name/count*
By a river that was brode and deep;
All seemed angeles come from heven.

3200   The king was never yet so fain,   *glad*
His soster son when that he sigh: *saw*
'Welcome,' he said, 'Sir Gawain,
And thou might live, well were me.
Now, leve frend, withouten laine,   *dear, deceit*
What are tho folk that follow thee?'
'Certes, sir,' he said again,   *indeed*
'They bide in bliss there I mot be.   *may*

'Lordes they were, and ladies hende   *noble*
This worldes life that han forlorn;   *lost*
3210   While I was man on life to lende,   *remain*
Against their fon I fought them forn;   *foes, for them*
Now find I them my moste frend;   *best friends*
They bless the time that I was born;
They asked leve with me to wend,   *go*
To meet with you upon this morn.

A monthe-day of trewes most ye take   *truce*
And then to batail be ye bain;   *prepared*
You cometh to help Launcelot du Lake,[125]
With many a man mikel of main;   *of great strength*
3220   To-morn the batail ye moste forsake,
Or elles, certes, ye shall be slain.'
The king gan woefully weep and wake,
And said, 'Alas, this rewful regne!'   *pitiful realm*

The Anturs of Arther *(c. 1375–1400)*

The Anturs of Arther *opens with Arthur setting out from Carlisle
on a hunt beside the Tarne Wathelan with his nobles and knights.*[126]
*It is common for a hunt to initiate an adventure in Arthurian
literature, particularly in those short Middle English works which
are not closely derived from a known French original.*[127] *However,*

the practice also occurs in several French texts and assumes a variety of different forms. Sometimes a hunt is employed as a suitable opportunity for revenge or treacherous conduct, as in Malory's Accalon episode.

In the first section of the poem, Sir Gawain accompanies Queen Gaynour (Guenevere) on the hunt, and they become separated from the rest of the hunters during a blizzard.[128] An apparition comes out of the lake to curse Gaynour. It is the ghost of Gaynour's mother, who warns her to take pity on the poor, for their prayers can win her salvation. The ghost then continues, in the following extract, by informing Gawain about Arthur's covetousness, Fortune's wheel and the approaching fate of the Round Table fellowship. After the ghost's departure, Gawain and the queen return to Rondallsete Hall in Cumberland for supper.

The second part of the poem opens with the interruption of supper that evening by the arrival of a lady leading a knight. When Arthur asks the knight why he has come, he replies that he is Sir Galrun of Galway, whose lands Arthur has stolen from him and given to Gawain. Galrun wishes to fight one of Arthur's knights to determine ownership of the lands, and Gawain tells Arthur that he will undertake the duel.

260   'How schall we fare,' quod Gauan, 'that foundus to these
            fightus
        And defoules these folk in fele kyngus londus:
        Riche remus orerennus, agaynes the ryghtus;
        Wynnes wurschip and wele throghe wyghtenes of
            hondus?'   *power*
        'Yaure king is to covetus and his kene knyghtus;
        Ther may no strenghthe him stir quen the quele stondus.
        Quen he is in his magesté most in his myghtus,
        Then schall he lighte full lau bi the see sondus.   *shore*
        Thus your chiualreis kynge chefe schall a chaunse;
        [Felle] Fortune in fyghte,   *Cruel*
270   That wundurfull quele-wryghte,   *wheelwright*
        That lau wille lordis gere lighte: *cause to fall*

[260] seek out battles.
[261] oppress the people of many kingdoms.
[262] Overrun great kingdoms, contrary to justice.
[264] *Scho sayd* before *Yaure.*
[265] no power can displace him while the wheel (of Fortune) is at rest.
[268] endure (mis)fortune.
[269] *Felle: Felles* (Robert H. Taylor collection, Princeton. Hereafter 'P'. RDW)

Take wittenesse be Fraunse!

For Fraunse have ye frely with yaure fighte wonnen   *wholly*
Frol and his farnet ful [fey] have ye levyt   *vassals, doomed*
Bretan and Burgoyn is both in your bandum   *control*
And all the duseperis of Fraunse with your dyn devyt.
Now may Gian grete that evyr hit was begonn –
Ther is noghte lede on leve in that lond levet;   *alive, left*
Yette schall the rich Romans be with you aure runnun
280   And atte the Roun Tabull the rentus schall be revet.
Hit schall be tynte as I troue and timburt with tene.
Gete the wele sir Gauan:
Turne the to Tuscan,   *Go back*
[F]or lese shall ye Bretan
Thrughe a knyghte kene.

A knyghte schall kenely croyse the croune   *shatter, monarchy*
And at Carli[l] be crounet for king;
That segge schall ensese him atte a session,   *man*
[That] mykill barette and bale to Bretan schall bring.
290   Ye schall be told in Tuskan of that tresun,
And be turnut agaynne with that tithing;   *turned back, news*
Ther schall the Roun Tabull lese the renownn,   *its glory*
Besyde Ramsay the riche atte a ryding.
In desese schall dee the dughty[est] of all –   *anguish*
Gete the wele, syr Gauan,
The baldest of Bretan:
For in a slac thou schall be slayn,   *hollow*
Seche ferles schyn falle.

Seche ferles schall [fall], withouten any fabull,
300   Opon Corneuayle cost, with knyghtus full kene;

---

[274] *fey* D: *fery* (Bodleian Library Oxford, MS Douce 324. Hereafter 'D'. RDW): *fery* P.
[276] deafened by your clamour.
[277] Guienne lament.
[280] revenues will be taken away from.
[281] lost, I believe, and encompassed with harm.
[284] *For* DT (Lincoln Cathedral Library, MS 91. Hereafter 'T'. RDW): *Or* P.
[287] *Carlil*: *Carlit* P.
[288] take possession (of the land) at a parliament.
[289] *That*: omitted P; strife and harm.
[293] an armed encounter near the splendid (town of) Romsey.
[294] *d* above *desese*; *dughtyest* DTL (Lambeth Palace Library, MS 491. Hereafter 'L'. TDW): *dughty* P.
[298] wonders must come about.
[299] *fall*: omitted P.

Ther Arthore [the] avenant, onest and abull,   *courteous*
Schall be woundut i-wis, wothelik I wene;   *disastrously*
All the riall route of the Roun Tabull,   *company*
Thay schall dee that day, tho dughti bedene,   *together*
Sussprisut with a subjette that bere schall of sabull
A sauter engralet of silver so schene –
He berus hit of sabull, quo sotheli will saye.
In kyng Arthers halle
The child playes atte the balle,
310 That outray schall yo alle   *destroy*
Derfely that daye.'   *Cruelly*

Ho sayd, 'Have gode day, syr Gauan and Gaynour the gode!
I have no lengur tyme yo tithinges to telle,
For I mun walke on my way throgheoute yondur wud
[Unto] my wunnyng place i[n] wo for to welle!   *boil*
For him that [ryghtewisly rose and rest] on the rode,
Thenke quat dounger and dele that I inne duelle;   *Remember*
Funde to grete my saule with sum of thi gode,   *Take pains*
And myn me with massus and matyns imele.   *remember, together*
320 For massus ar medesins for us in bales bides;
Us thing a masse als squete,   *seems, sweet*
As any spyce that evyr thou ete –'
Thus with a gryliche grete   *hideous wailing*
The gost away glidus.

Noue with a griseliche grete the gost away glidus,
And a sore gronyng, with a grym bere.   *outcry*
The wynd and the welkyn, the wethur [unhides];
The cloude unclosut, the sune wex clere.   *open*
The kynge his bugul con blau [and] opon the bent bides;
330 His fayre folk on the fuilde, thay flocken in fere, *together*
And all the rial route to the quene ridus,
Meles to hur mildely opon thayre manere.   *Speak, usual way*

---

301 *the*: omitted P.
304 all those valiant (knights) together.
305 Taken unawares by ... black (arms).
306 A: preceded by *With* P; A Saint Andrew's cross with scalloped edges.
315 *Unto* TL: *For in* P; *in* DTL: *is* P.
316 *ryghtwisly rose and rest* D: *ryghtewis rest and rose* P.
320 salves for those of us who dwell in torment.
325 terrifying wailing.
327 *unhides* D: *in that tide* P; sky ... clears up.
329 *and*: omitted P; remains in the open field.

Tho wees of the wederinges forwondret thay were;
Princys pruddust in pall,   *silk*
Gay Gaynoure and all,
Thay wente to Rondallsete hall
Unto thayre sopere.

Quen he to sopere was sette and servut in his sale,   *hall*
Undur a seler of sylke, with dayntethis dighte,   *canopy*
340 With all welthis to wille, and wynus to wale,
Briddes bacun in bred on brent gold bryghte –   *refined*
So come in a seteler with a symbale,   *player on citole*
A lufsum lady ledand a knyghte:
Ridus to the he dese before the riall
And hailsutte king Arthore hindely on heghte.   *greeted*
Sayde to the soveran, wlonkest in wede,   *most splendid*
'Thou mon makeles of myght,   *unequalled*
This is an ayre and a knyght –   *heir*
Thou do him resun and ryghte
350 For thi monhed.'   *As you are a man*

Monli in his mantill he sate atte his mete,
With pall puret in poon was prudlich pighte,   *adorned*
Tro[felyte] with trulufes and trave[r]ste betuene;
The tassellus were of topeus that was therto tighte.   *topaz*
He gly[fte] up with his ene, that gray were and grete,
With his beveren berd opon the birne bryghte:
He was he semelist soveran sittand in his sete,   *throne*
That evyr segge hade soghte or seen [with] syghte.   *knight*
Thenne oure comelich king carpus hire tille   *speaks*
360 And sayd, 'Thou wurlych wight,   *excellent creature*
Lighte and leng all nyght;   *Dismount, remain*
Quethun is that ayre and that knyght,   *Whence*
And hit were thi wille?'

[333] knights were greatly astonished by the (changing) weather.
[339] served with delicacies.
[340] As abundant as they could wish, with great choice of wines.
[341] baked in pastry.
[352] silk trimmed with fur.
[353] *Trofelyte* T: *Trowlt* P; adorned with ornamental knots; *traverste* T: *trauest* P; crossed
with stripes.
[354] attached to it.
[355] *glyfte* T: *glysset* P; glanced; eyes.
[356] reddish-brown beard over the shining mail-shirt.
[357] *on*: before *sittand* P.
[358] *with* DTL: him P.

Ho was the wurliche[st] wighte that any wee wold: *knight*
Hir gide that was glorius was of a gresse grene;   *robe*
Her belle was of blenket with briddus ful bold,
Beten with besandus and bocult ful bene.
Her fax in fyne perré was frettut in fold,
Hir counturfelit and hur kell were colurt ful clene,

370   With a croune cumly, was clure to behold;   *splendid, dazzling*
Hur kerchefes were curiouse with mony a proud prene.   *pin*
Hur enparel was apraysut with princes of myghte: *esteemed*
Bryghte birdus and bold   *maidens*
Hade inughhe to behold
Of that freli to fold,   *embrace*
And the kene knyghte.

Than the knyghte in his colurs was armit ful clene,
With a crest comely – was clure to behold;   *bright*
His brené and his basnet was busket ful bene,

380   With a bordur aboute all of brent gold;
His mayles were mylke quyte, enclawet ful clene,   *white*
His stede trapput with that ilke (so true men me told),
With a schild on his shildur of silver so schene,
With bore hedis of blakke and brees ful bold;   *brows*
His stede with sandell of [Tars] was trapput to the hele;
Opon his cheveronn beforn   *head armour*
Stode as an unicorn,
Als scharpe as a thorn,
An anlas of stele.   *spike*

390   In stele was he stuffut, that sterne on his stede,   *clad, bold*
With his sternes of gold stanseld on stray;
His gloves an[d] his gamesuns gloet as the gledes,
Arayet aure with rebans, rychist of raye;   *material*
With his schene shinbaudes scharpest in schredus

---

364   *wurlichest* (most excellent): *wurliche* P.
366   cloak was woollen strikingly (adorned) with birds.
367   Inlaid with gold ornaments and neatly fastened.
368   With precious stones in the plaits of her hair.
369   ribbon and headdress were bright of colour.
379   mail-shirt and helmet were beautifully polished.
381   neatly riveted.
382   trappings to match.
385   *Tars: trise* P.
391   Profusely adorned with stars of gold.
392   *and: an* P; (quilted) tunics shone like live coals.
394   bright leg armour, the pieces most cleanly cut.

His polans with his pelidoddes were poudert to pay.
Thus launce opon lofte that lovely he ledus,   *erect*
A fa[wnt] on a fresun him folut, in fay;   *Friesan (steed)*
The freson was afrayet and ferd of that fare,   *noise*
For he was syldun wunte to se
400   A tablet flourré:
Sech game and sich glee   *revelry, music*
Seghe he he nevyr are.   *before*

Then the king carput him tille on hereand hom all:
'Qwethun art thou wurlich we, and hit were thi will?   *if it*
Telle me quethun thou come and quethir thou schall;
Quy thou stedis in that stid and stondus so still.'   *stop, place*
Then he avaylet uppe his viserne fro his ventall,
With a knyghtelich countenaunse he carpes him till;
Sayd, 'Quethir thou be cayse[r] or kyng here I the becall
410   Forto fynde me a freke to feghte on my fill;   *knight*
For feghting [to] fraest I foundut fro home.'   *seek, departed*
Then speke the kynge opon heghte,
Sayd, 'Lighte and leng all nyghte;   *stay*
As thou art curtase knyghte,
Thou tell me thi name.'

He sayd, 'My nome is syr Galrun, withouten any gile,
The grattus[t] of Galway of grevys and of gillus   *woods, glens*
Of Carrake, of Cummake, of Conyngame, of Kile,
Of Lonwik, of Lannax, of Laudonne hillus,
420   That thou hase wonun on were with thi wrang wiles: *deceit*
Gifhen hom to syr Gauan – that my hert grillus!   *angers*
Yette schall thou wring thi hondus and wary the quiles
Or any we schild hom weld atte my unnwilles:
Atte my unnwilles, i-wis, he schall hom nevyr weld,
Qwil I the hed may bere,   *As long as*

395 knee-armour pleasingly adorned with green gems.
396 *he ledus*: repeated P.
397 *fawnt* (lad) L: *fauyn* P.
400 table decorated with fleurs-de-lis.
403 *thenne*: after *Then*: spoke to him so that all might hear.
404 Where do you come from noble knight.
407 lifted the visor from his neck-armour.
409 *cayser* (emperor) DTL: *caysell* P; I demand of you.
411 *to*: *thus am* P; *and*: after *fraest* P.
417 *grattust*: *grattus* P; most powerful.
422 curse the day (that you did so).
423 Before any knight should possess them without my consent.

Butte he may wynne hom on were,
With schild and with scharpe spere,
Opon a fayre fylde.

For in a fyld will I feghte – therto I make faythe –
430   With any freke opon fuld that is fre born;   *on earth*
To lose such a lordschip me wold thinke laythe,   *repugnant*
And ich lede opon lyve wold laghe me to scorne.'
'We are in wudlond,' cothe the king, 'and walkes on owre wayth
Forto hunte atte the herd-with hounnde and with horne;
Gyf thou be gome gladdest, now have we no grayth –
Yet may thou be machet be mydday tomorne;
Forthi I rede, rathe mon, thou rest the all nyghte.'   *hasty*
Thenne Gauan, graythest of all,
Lad him furthe thrughh the halle
440   Untylle a pavelun of palle,
Was prudlych i-pyghte.   *splendidly appointed*

Hit was prudlych y-pighte of purpure and palle
With beddus brauderit o brode and bankers y-dyghte;
Therinne was a schapell, a chambur and hall,
A schimnay of charcole to chaufen the knyghte.   *warm*
Thay halen uppe his stede, had him to stall;   *lead away*
Hay hely they hade in haches [o]n highte.   *nobly, racks*
[B]rayd up a burd and clothes couthe calle;   *Set up, called for*
With salers and sanapus thay serve the knyghte
450   With [torches] and broches and stondartis bitwene.
Forto serve the knyghte
And the wurlich wighte,
With rych dayntethis dyghte
In sylvyr so schene.   *silver dishes*

Thus in silvyr so schene thay serve of the best

426–7 in reverse order P.
432 every living person.
433 *Ye*: before *we* P; and are engaged in hunting.
435 However much you may wish it, we are unprepared at this time.
436 an opponent may be found for you.
443 supplied with bed(-spread)s embroidered all over and tapestries.
447 *on*: *vn* P.
448 *Brayd up*: *Prayd vp with* P.
449 salt cellars, napkins.
450 *torches*: *troches*: and candlesticks small and large.

With vernage [in] verres [and] coupus ful clene;
With lucius drinkes and metis of the best,   *delicious*
Rych dayntes endoret in dysshes bidene.   *glazed, completely*
As tyde as that riall was rayket to his rest,
460 The kinge callut his councelle, the doghti bedene,
And bede: 'Umloke yo lordinges, oure lose be notte lost!
Quo shall countur with yondur knyghte cast yo bituene.'
Thenne sayd syr Gauan, 'Hit schall us noghte greve:
I will countur with the knyghte,
Forto maynteine my ryghte:
Therto my trothe I the plyghte,
Ye, lord, with thi leve.'

'I leve wele,' quod the kinge, 'thi lates ar lyghte;
But I wold notte for no lordschip se thi life lorne.'   *estate*
470 'Lette go,' coth sir Gauan, 'God stond with the ryghte!
For and he scapette scatheles hit were a gret scorne.'
And in [the] dayng of day the doghty were dyghte: *prepared*
Herd matyns [and] mas myldelik on mornn.
Inmyd Plumtun L[and] hor paveluns were pighte, *Plumpton Wall*
Quere nevyr frekes opon fulde hade foghtun beforne.
Thay sette listes on lenthe, olong on the lawnde;   *clearing*
Thre soppus of demayn
Wos broght to sir Gauan,
Forto cumford his brayne,
480 The king gart cummaunde   *gave orders (for this)*

The kinge commawnndet kindeli the erle of Kente,
For his mecull curtasy, to kepe the tother knyghte;   *entertain*
And made him with dayntethis to dine in his tente,
And sythun this riall men arayut hom oryghte;

---

456 white wine in glasses; *in, and* DTL: *and, in* P.
459 By the time that that noble knight had gone to bed.
460 convoked his council of valiant knights.
461 commanded, 'Be careful ... our renown'.
462 do battle with ... decide.
463 cause us any difficulty.
468 believe ... you are eager for action.
471 if he were to get away scot-free.
472 dawning; *the: ther* P.
473 *and*: omitted P.
474 Within; *Land* DL: *lone* P; tents were set up.
475 (bold) warriors on earth.
476 marked out the extent of the jousting area.
477 pieces of fine bread soaked in wine.
484 armed themselves fittingly.

And aftur quene Waynor warly thay wente,   *discreetly*
And beleves in hur warde that wurlych wighte.   *leave, keeping*
Sethun the hathels in hie hor horses have hente;
Inmydde the lyste of the lawnde the lordus doune lighte –
All butte the stithest in steroppus that stode.
490   King Arthur schayer was sette   *throne*
     Obone his chaselette,   *Above, dais*
     And thenne dame Gaynour grette   *wept*
     For Gauan the gode.

Gawain and Galrun fight, dealing each other terrible wounds so that Gaynour becomes anxious for Gawain. Finally, Gawain gets the upper hand and Galrun's lady cries out to Gaynour to stop the fight.

617   Thenne sir Gauan bi the coler clechis the knyghte –   *grips*
     Thenne his lemmon on lofte ho scrilles and scrikes   *loudly*
     And sayd to dame Gaynour, with grones full grille,   *painful*
620   'Thou ladé makelest of myghte,   *unequalled*
     Haue pety of yondur nobull knyghte,
     That is so dilfully dyghte –
     And hit were thi wille.'

     Thenne wilfull Waynour to the king wente,   *impetuous*
     Keghte of hire curonall and knelit him tille;   *snatched*
     Sayd, 'As thou art ray richist and riall in rente,
     And I thi wedut wife atte thin one wille,
     Yondur byrnes in batell that bidus on the bent
     Thay ar weré, i-wisse, and woundut full ille,   *weary*
630   Throghgh schildus and schildures schomfully shente:
     The grones of sir Gauan hit dose my hert grille;
     The gronus of sir Gauan the gode hit grevis me sore!
     Wold ye, luflych lord,   *gracious*
     Make yondur knyghtes at acord,   *Reconcile*

[487] quickly taken their horses by the reins.
[488] At the edge.
[489] (two) strongest.
[493] *a fitte*: written to the right of his line.
[626] king most powerful and magnificent in wealth.
[627] to command in all things.
[628] continue to fight in the field.
[630] shoulders disastrously hurt.
[631] makes me suffer in heart.

Hit were a grete cumford,
For all that [here] ware.'

But thenne speke sir Galrun to Gawan the gode:
'I wende nevyr we yette hade bene so wighte.
And sayd, 'Here I make the relesch, [renke], bi the rode,
640   Before this riall route resigne the my righte;   *company*
And sithin I make the monraden, mildist of mode,
As mon on this mydlert that most is of myghte.'   *man, earth*
He stalket touward the king in stid quere he stode,
And bede the burlych his brand that burneschit was bright:
And sayd, 'Of rentis and of richas I make the relesche.'
Doune knelis the knyghte
And speke these wurdis opon highte;
The king stode uppe ryghte
And cummawnndut pese.

650   The king cummawnndut pese and stode up ryghte,
And Gauan godely he sesutt for his sake;
And then these lordus so lele thai lepe up lighte:
[Yvayn ffys] Uryayn and Arrake [fys] Lake,   *son of*
Sir Meliaduke, [sir] Marrake, that mekill wasse of myghte.
These toe traueling men truly uppe thay take –   *toiling*
Unnethe myghte these sturnn men stond uppe ryghte;   *Hardly*
So forbrissutte and forbled – thayre blees were so blake:
All blake was thayre blees, forbetun with brandis!   *battered*
Withoutun any hersing,   *(need for) repetition*
660   There dighte was thayre saghtenyng;
Before the comelich king
Thay heldun uppe thayre hondus.   *gave their promise*

'Now here I gife the,' quod the king, 'Gauan the bold,

---

636 *here: ther* P.
638 never imagined until now that (any) knight could be.
639 relinquish to you; *renke* (knight) DL: *rength* P.
640 surrender my title to you.
641 will do you homage.
643 moved quietly to where the king was standing.
644 offered the noble (king).
649 ordered all to be silent.
651 graciously left off.
652 faithful sprang to their feet.
653 *Yvayn ffys: Huaya ffus* P; *fys: fy* P.
654 *sir* L: *the* P.
657 So badly bruised and so drained of blood ... faces were so pale.
660 reconciliation was brought about.

Glawmorgan londus with grevys full grene;   *woods*
The wurschip of Wales to weld, and thou wold –
Kirfre castell, with colurs ful clene,
Iche [Ulstur halle] to have and to hold;   *Also*
Wayifforthe and Waturforth, wallet I wene,
Toe baron[rees] in Bretan with burgesse full bold,
670   That [ar] batelt aboute, and biggutte full bene.
Here I doue with as duke and dub the with my hondus,   *endow*
Withthi thou saghtun with yondur knyghte,
That is so hardi and so wighte,
And resingne him thi ryghte
And graunte him his londus.'

'Nowe here I gif the, Galrun,' quod Gauan, 'withoutyn any
       gile,
All the londus, forsothe, fro Logher to Layre –'
Carrake, Cummake, Conyngame and Kile –
Sir, to thiselvun and sithun to thine ayre.   *after that*
680   [The Lother, the Lemmok, the Loynak, the Lile;
With frethis and forestes and fosses so faire,]   *woods, moats*
Witthi tille oure lordschip thou leng in a qwile,
And to the Round Tabull to make thi repare: *journey*
Here I feffe the in fild frely and fayre.'   *enfeoff*
Bothe the king and the quene
(And other dughti bidene)
Throghghowte the grevis so grene
To Carlille thay kayr[e].   *make their way*

[The king to Carlele is comen with knightes so kene],
690   Throgh grevis so grene held the Roun Tabull with riall aray;
These wees that were wothely woundet, I wene,   *dangerously*
Thenne surgens hom savyt quo sotheli wynne say;
Cumfordun hom kindely, the king and the quene,   *lovingly*

665 feudal domain of.
667 *Ulstur halle* D: *Hulkers home* P.
668 with their walls ... intend.
669 *baronrees* DTL: *baroners* P.
670 *ar* DT: *is* P; have battlements around them ... pleasingly built.
672 Provided that you are reconciled.
680–81 omitted P; supplied from D.
682 you remain here for a time in our household.
688 *kayre: kayrit* P.
689 omitted P, supplied from D.
692 healed them, whoever will speak the truth.

And sithin dubbut hom dukes bothe on a day.
And thenne he weddutte his wife, wlonkest I wene,
With giftus and with gersums, sir Galrun the gay.
Thus Gauan and Galrun gode frindes ar thay;
Qwen thay were holle and sownde,
Thay made Galrun, in that stounde,
700　A knyghte of the Tabull Rounde,
Untill his ending day.

Thenne gerut Dame Waynour to write into t
To all the religeus, to rede and to sing;
Prustes, provincials to pray were full pres
With a meliun of massus, her modur mynnyng.
Boke-lornut byrnus and bischoppus of the beste　　*Scholars*
Thro-oute Bretan so bold these bellus con ring.
And this ferli befelle in Ingulwud forest,　　*took place*
Beside holtus so hore, at a hunting.
710　Such a hunting in a holt aw noghte to be hidde:　　*ought*
These knyghtus stalewurthe and store　　*valiant, powerful*
Throghh the forest thay fore:　　*journeyed*
In the tyme of king Arthore
This anter betidde.

Sir Gawain and the Green Knight (c. 1385–90)

The poet's structural use of Arthur's court as a starting-point for an adventure and the centre of civilization to which the hero will eventually return to relate the outcome of his quest is commonplace in French Arthurian romance, occurring in most works from Chrétien de Troyes's Erec onwards. While the poet appears to have been familiar with the traditional elements of French romance, his originality is such that this poem might be regarded as the only English Arthurian romance with no identifiable French source.

The discussion of Arthur's custom of awaiting an adventure is

694　created them ... at the same time.
695　the most splendid, to my judgement.
702　had (letters) written to (all parts of).
705　in commemoration of her mother('s soul).
710　(The story of) such.
714　*ffinis*: to right of line.

particularly interesting and by itself suggests that, despite the archaic English and alliterative style employed, the poet may well have been familiar with this French Arthurian custom since this is its first appearance in an English poem. The silence with which the knights respond to the rather awesome intruder's challenge is reminiscent of that which greets the dwarf's speech in My Lord Gawain, *or the* Avenging of Raguidel. *While Arthur's personal reaction to the giant's challenge is very unusual, the behaviour of his nephew Gawain closely follows that traditionally exhibited by his French counterpart: he immediately shows concern for his uncle's safety, offering to take his place.*

A prominent aspect of Arthur's festive court at the start of the poem is its emphasis on revelry and courtly pleasure, rather than on knightly prowess. Although Christmas is an appropriate occasion for enjoyment, some critics believe that the frequency with which the poet refers to the celebrations, and the precise language he employs, imply that the lavish festivities should be regarded as excessive. An association has been made between Arthur's feast in Sir Gawain and the Green Knight *and that of Balzassar in* Cleanness, *by the same poet.*[129] *However, it is difficult to believe that the* Gawain-Poet *wished to draw a close link between the two monarchs and thus condemn Arthur's court as blasphemous.*

25	Bot of alle that here bult of Bretaygne kynges	*lived, Britain's*
	Ay was Arthur the hendest, as I haf herde telle.	*ever, noblest*
	Forthi an aunter in erde I attle to schawe,	
	That a selly in sight summe men hit holden,	
	And an outtrage awenture of Arthures wonderes.	
30	If ye wyl lysten this laye bot on littel quile,	*a little while*
	I schal telle hit astit, as I in toun herde,	*at once*
	with tonge,	*(recited) aloud*
	As hit is stad and stoken	*set down and fixed*
	In stori stif and stronge,	*bold and strong*
	With lel letteres loken,	
	In londe so has ben longe.	

This kyng lay at Camylot upon Krystmasse
With mony luflych lorde, ledes of the best,   *fine, men*

[27-9] And so I intend to unfold a real adventure, such that some men consider it a supreme marvel, and a most strange adventure amongst the wonders of Arthur.
[35-6] Linked with true letters, as it has long been in the land.

Rekenly of the Rounde Table alle tho rich brether,
40   With rych revel oryght and rechles merthes.
Ther tournayed tulkes by tymes ful mony,
Justed ful jolilé thise gentyle knightes,   *jousted, gallantly, noble*
Sythen kayred to the court, caroles to make.
For ther the fest was ilyche ful fiften dayes,
With alle the mete and the mirthe that men   *food*
      couthe avyse;   *could devise*
Such glaum ande gle glorious to here,   *noise, merriment*
Dere dyn upon day, daunsyng on nyghtes.   *cheerful din*
Al was hap upon heghe in halles and chambres
With lordes and ladies, as levest him thoght.
50   With all the wele of the worlde thay woned ther samen,
The most kyd knyghtes under   *renowned*
      Krystes selven,   *Christ Himself*
And the lovelokkest ladies that ever lif haden,   *loveliest*
And he the comlokest kyng that the court haldes;
For al was this fayre folk in her first age,
      on sille,
The hapnest under heven,
Kyng hyghest mon of wylle.
Hit were now gret nye to neven
So hardy a here on hille.

60   Wyle Nw Yer was so yep that hit was nwe cummen,
That day doubble on the dece was the douth served.
Fro the kyng was cummen with knyghtes into the halle,   *after*
The chauntré of the chapel cheved to an ende,

39-41 All those noble brethren of the Round Table, in fitting fashion, with splendid revels indeed and carefree pleasures. There knights on many occasions took part in tournaments.

43-4 Then they rode to the court to dance carols. (The 'carol' was a ring dance with singing). For there the feasting was continuous for fully fifteen days.

48-50 Good cheer was fully abroad in halls and chambers, amongst lords and ladies, to their perfect contentment (lit. as seemed dearest to them). With all the joy in the world they dwelt there together.

53-9 And he who holds court (is) the handsomest king; for this fair company in the hall were all in their first youth, the most favoured (people) in the world, the king a man of the noblest temperament. It would now (i.e. in the poet's own time) be very difficult to identify so brave a company in a castle (lit. on a castle-mound).

60-1 While New Year was so new that it was only just arrived, that day the company on the dais was served with double portions (of food).

63-7 The singing of Mass in the chapel having come to an end, loud cries were uttered there by clerics and others, Christmas (was) celebrated anew, called out by name again and again (i.e. 'Noel' was used as a greeting, equivalent to 'Merry Christmas'). And then nobles ran forward to give presents, cried aloud 'New Year's gifts', offered them by hand.

Loude crye was ther kest of clerkes and other,
Nowel nayted onewe, nevened ful ofte.
And sythen riche forth runnen to reche hondeselle,
Yeyed 'yeres yiftes' on high, yelde hem bi hond,
Debated busyly aboute tho giftes.   *eagerly*
Ladies laghed ful loude, thogh thay lost haden,   *had*

70   And he that wan was not wrothe, that may ye wel trawe.
Alle this mirthe thay maden to the mete tyme.   *until, meal*
When thay had waschen worthyly thay wenten to sete,
The best burne ay abof, as hit best semed;
Whene Guenore, ful gay, graythed in the myddes,
Dressed on the dere des, dubbed al aboute –
Smal sendal bisides, a selure hir over
Of tryed Tolouse, of Tars tapites innoghe,
That were enbrawded and beten wyth the   *embroidered, set*
     best gemmes
That myght be preved of prys wyth penyes to bye
80   in daye.
The comlokest to discrye
Ther glent with yyen gray;
A semloker that ever he syye,
Soth moght no mon say.

Bot Arthure wolde not ete til al were served,
He was so joly of his joyfnes, and sumquat childgered;
His lif liked hym lyght, he lovied the lasse
Auther to longe lye or to longe sitte,
So bisied him his yonge blod and his brayn wylde.

90   And also another maner meved   *consideration moved*
     him eke,   *as well*

---

70 And he who won was not angry, that you may well believe.

72–7 When they had washed (their hands) politely they went to their seats, the man of highest rank always more highly placed (i.e. they were seated in order of degree), as seemed best; Queen Guinevere, most beautiful, was placed in the midst, seated on the high dais, (which was) decorated all round – fine silk to the sides, a canopy over her of choicest Toulouse (i.e. a rich red fabric associated with Toulouse), many tapestries of Tharsian silk.

79–84 That ever money could buy (lit. that might be proved to be of value by buying them with money, on any day). The loveliest to behold looked (about her) with grey-blue eyes; no man might truthfully say that he had ever seen a more beautiful lady.

86–9 He was so light-hearted in his youthfulness, and somewhat boyish; his life pleased him (when it was) light, the less he liked either to lie for long (lit. longer) or sit for long, his young blood and restless brain stirred him so much.

That he thurgh nobelay had nomen he wolde never ete
Upon such a dere day, er hym devised were
Of sum aventurus thyng an uncouthe tale,
Of sum mayn mervayle that he myght trawe,
Of alderes, of armes, of other aventurus;
Other sum segg hym bisoght of sum siker knyght
To joyne wyth hym in justyng, in jopardé to lay,
Lede lif for lyf, leve uchon other,
As fortune wolde fulsun hom the fayrer to have.

100   This was kynges countenaunce where he in court were,
At uch farand fest, among his fre meny
      in halle.
    Therfore of face so fere   *proud*
    He stightles stif in stalle;
    Ful yep in that Nw Yere,   *youthful*
    Much mirthe he mas with alle.   *makes, everyone*

Thus ther stondes in stale the stif kyng hisselven,
Talkkande bifore the hyghe table of trifles ful
      hende.   *courteous*
There gode Gawan was graythed Gwenore   *good, seated*
    bisyde,
110   And Agravayn a la dure mayn on that other syde sittes,
Bothe the kynges sister sunes and ful siker   *sister's, true*
    knightes.
Bischop Bawdewyn abof bigines the table,
And Ywan, Uryn son, ette with hymselven.
Thise were dight on the des and   *seated*
    derworthly served,   *sumptuously*
And sithen mony siker segge at the sidbordes.
Then the first cors come with crakkyng   *course, came, flourish*
    of trumpes,

91-102 (Namely) that he in his nobility had undertaken that he would never eat on such a holiday until he had been told a far-fetched tale of some adventurous exploit, of some great marvel which he might believe in, of princes, of (feats of) arms, of other adventures, or else (until) some man had asked him for a true knight to join with him in jousting, to place themselves in jeopardy, stake life against life, each to allow the other to have the better as fortune favoured them (i.e. they were each to accept the outcome of the joust). This was the king's custom wherever he held court, at every great feast, amongst his noble company in hall.

104 He stands upright in his place.

107 And so the bold king himself stands there in his place.

112-13 Bishop Baldwin sits at the head of the table, and Ywain, Urien's son, ate with him. (The courtiers were served in pairs; see line 128.)

115 And afterwards many true men at the side-tables.

Wyth mony baner ful bryght that therbi   *from them*
   henged;   *hung*
Nwe nakryn noyse with the noble pipes;
Wylde werbles and wyght wakned lote,
120   That mony hert ful highe hef at her towches;
Dayntés dryven therwyth, of ful dere metes;
Foysoun of the fresche, and on so fele dische
That pine to fynde the place the peple biforne
For to sette the sylveren that sere sewes halden
   on clothe.
     Iche lede as he loved hymselve
     Ther laght withouten lothe;
     Ay two had dische twelve,   *each pair*
     Good ber and bryght wyn bothe.   *beer*

130   Now wyl I of hor servise say yow no   *their (table-) service*
   more,
For uch wyye may wel wit no wont that ther were.
An other noyse ful newe neghed bilive,
That the lude myght haf leve liflode to cach.
For unethe was the noyce not a whyle sesed,
And the fyrst cource in the court kyndely served,   *duly*
Ther hales in at the halle dor an aghlich mayster,
On the most in the molde on mesure hyghe,
Fro the swyre to the swange so sware and so thik,
And his lyndes and his lymes so longe and so grete,
140   Half etayn in erde I hope that he were;
Bot mon most I algate mynn hym to bene,

118-27 (There was) a new noise of horns with the noble pipes; wild and vigorous trillings wakened echoes, so that many hearts soared high at their strains; dainties (were) brought in with it (i.e. the music), made up of most excellent foods; (there was) an abundance of fresh meats, and on so many dishes that it was difficult to find room in front of the people to set on the cloth the silver that held the various stews. Each man as he desired helped himself (to food) there without restraint.

131-4 For everyone (i.e. in the poet's audience) may be sure that there was no lack of anything. Another quite new noise approached suddenly, so that the prince might be free to take food. For the noise (of the music) was scarcely at an end.

136-50 (When) there comes in at the hall door a fearsome lord, the very biggest in the world in his tall stature, from the neck to the waist so square and so thick-set, and his sides and his limbs so long and so large, that I believe he may have been half giant indeed; but at any rate I consider him to be the biggest of men, and the handsomest of his size who might (ever) ride horse, for although in back and breast his body was strong, both his stomach and his waist were becomingly small, and all his parts (were) in keeping with his shape, without exception (lit. most completely). Men wondered at his colour, plain to see in his face; he bore himself like a man of battle, and he was bright green all over.

And that the myriest in his muckel that myght ride,
For of bak and of brest al were his bodi sturne,
Both his wombe and his wast were worthily smale,
And alle his fetures folwande in forme that he hade,
    ful clene.
    For wonder of his hwe men hade,
    Set in his semblaunt sene;
    He ferde as freke were fade,
150   And overal enker-grene.

Ande al graythed in grene this gome and his wedes –
A strayt cote ful streght that stek on his sides,
A mere mantile abof, mensked withinne,
With pelure pured apert, the pane ful clene,
With blythe blaunner ful bryght, and his hod bothe,
That was laght fro his lokkes and layde on   *thrown back from*
    his schulderes;
Heme, wel-haled hose of that same grene,
That spenet on his sparlyr, and clene spures under
Of bryght golde, upon silk bordes barred ful ryche,
160 And scholes under schankes there the schalk rides.
And alle his vesture verayly was   *clothing indeed*
    clene verdure,   *bright green*
Bothe the barres of his belt and other blythe stones,   *fine gems*
That were richely rayled in his aray clene   *set*
Aboutte hymself and his sadel, upon silk werkes,   *embroidery*
That were to tor for to telle of tryfles the halve
That were enbrauded abof, wyth bryddes and flyyes,
With gay gaudi of grene, the golde ay inmyddes.
The pendauntes of his payttrure, the proude cropure,

151-5 And all arrayed in green (were) this man and his clothes – (he wore) a straight coat, very tight, that fitted his sides, a splendid cloak over it, adorned on the inside, with close-trimmed fur exposed, the edging most elegant, very bright with beautiful ermine, and his hood as well.

157-60 Neat, tightly-drawn hose of that same green, that clung to his calves, and elegant spurs beneath of bright gold, on most richly barred bands, and no shoes on his feet (lit. under his legs) where the man rides (in the stirrups).

165-74 So that it would be too hard to tell of half the details that were embroidered on it, with birds and butterflies, with bright ornamentation of green, gold everywhere amongst it. The pendants of his horse's breast-harness, the splendid crupper (i.e. saddle-strap passing under tail of horse), his bit studs and all the metal (fittings) were enamelled (green) also; the stirrups that he stood on were coloured similarly, and his saddle-bows (were) all matching and (also) his splendid saddle-skirts, that ever gleamed and glinted all with green stones. The horse that he rides on (was) bright with the same (colour), unquestionably.

His molaynes and alle the metail anamayld was thenne;
170 The steropes that he stod on stayned of the same,
And his arsouns al after and his athel skurtes,
That ever glemered and glent al of grene stones.
The fole that he ferkkes on fyn of that ilke,
     sertayn.
    A grene hors gret and thikke,   *big, thick-set*
    A stede ful stif to strayne,   *strong, curb*
      In brawden brydel quik   *embroidered, restive*
      To the gome he was ful gayn.   *man, obedient*

Wel gay was this gome gered in grene,
180 And the here of his hed of his hors swete.
Fayre fannand fax umbefoldes his schulderes;
A much berd as a busk over his brest henges,
That wyth his highlich here that of his hed reches
Was evesed al umbetorne abof his elbowes,
That half his armes therunder were halched in the wyse
Of a kynges capados that closes his swyre.
The mane of that mayn hors much to hit lyke,   *great*
Wel cresped and cemmed, wyth knottes ful   *curled, combed*
  mony
Folden in wyth fildore aboute the fayre grene,
190 Ay a herle of the here, an other of golde.
The tayl and his toppyng twynnen of a sute,
And bounden bothe wyth a bande of a bryght grene,
Dubbed wyth ful dere stones, as the dok lasted,
Sythen thrawen wyth a thwong, a thwarle-knot alofte,
Ther mony belles ful bryght of brende golde rungen.
Such a fole upon folde, ne freke that hym rydes,
Was never sene in that sale wyth syght er that tyme,
     with yye.
    He loked as layt so lyght,

179-86 Truly handsome was this man attired in green, and the hair of his head matched
that of his horse. Beautiful hair, fanning out, enfolds his shoulders; a great beard like a
bush hangs over his breast, which together with his splendid hair reaching down from
his head was clipped all round above the elbows, so that half his arms were enclosed
underneath in the manner of a king's cape that fits round his neck.

189-99 Plaited in with gold thread round the beautiful green, always one strand of the hair,
another of gold. The tail and the forelock (were) plaited to match, and both bound
with a band of a bright green, adorned with most precious stones, to the end of the
tuft, then tied tight with a thong, an intricate knot at the top, where many very bright
bells of pure gold jingled. Such an extraordinary horse, or man riding it, was never seen
in that hall before that time, by (any) eye. His glance was as swift as lightning.

200   So sayd al that hym syye;   *saw*
         Hit semed as no mon myght   *as though*
         Under his dynttes dryye.   *bows, survive*

         Whether hade he no helme ne hawbergh nauther,
         Ne no pysan, ne no plate that pented to armes,
         Ne no schafte, ne no schelde, to schwve ne to   *spear, thrust*
               smyte,
         Bot in his on honde he hade a holyn bobbe,   *one, holly spray*
         That is grattest in grene when greves ar bare,   *most, woods*
         And an ax in his other, a hoge and unmete,   *huge, monstrous*
         A spetos sparthe to expoun in spelle, quo-so myght.
210   The lenkthe of an elnyerde the large hede hade,
         The grayn al of grene stele and of golde hewen,
         The bit burnyst bryght, with a brod egge   *blade, edge*
         As wel schapen to schere as scharp rasores.   *fashioned, cut*
         The stele of a stif staf the sturne hit bi grypte
         That was wounden wyth yrn to the wandes ende,
         And al bigraven with grene in gracios werkes;
         A lace lapped aboute, that louked at the hede,
         And so after the halme halched ful ofte,
         Wyth tryed tasseles therto tacched innoghe
220   On botouns of the bryght grene brayden ful ryche.
         This hathel heldes hym in and the halle entres,   *man goes in*
         Drivande to the heghe dece – dut he no wothe.
         Haylsed he never one, bot heghe he over loked.
         The fyrst word that he warp: 'Wher is,' he sayd,   *spoke*
         'The governour of this gyng? Gladly I wolde   *ruler, company*
         Se that segg in syght, and with hymself speke
               raysoun.'
               To knyghtes he kest his yye,   *cast, eye*

203-4 Yet he had no helmet or coat of mail either, nor any throat-armour, nor any plate
   that had to do with armour.
209-11 A cruel battle-axe to describe it in words, whoever might try to do so. The great
   axe-head was an ell-rod (i.e. 45 inches) in length, the stock (i.e. the upper part of the
   axe-head) entirely forged out of green steel and of gold.
214-20 The stern knight gripped it by the handle of a strong shaft that was wound round
   with iron to the shaft's end, and all carved with pleasing designs in green; a cord was
   wrapped round it that was fastened at the (axe-)head, and so looped along the shaft
   again and again, with many splendid tassels attached to it (i.e. the cord) on buttons of
   the (same) bright green, most richly embroidered.
222-3 Pressing forward to the high dais – he feared no danger. He greeted no one, but
   looked high above (them).
226-7 Set eyes on that man, and have speech with him.

And reled hym up and doun.
230   He stemmed, and con studie
Quo walt ther most renoun.

Ther was lokyng on lenthe, the lude to   *for a long time, man*
    beholde,
For uch mon had mervayle quat hit mene   *everyone wondered*
    myght
That a hathel and a horse myght such a hwe lach   *colour, take*
As growe grene as the gres and grener hit   *as to grow, grass*
    semed,
Then grene aumayl on golde glowande bryghter.
Al studied that ther stod, and stalked hym nerre,
Wyth al the wonder of the worlde what he worch   *would do*
    schulde.
For fele sellyes had thay sen, bot such never   *many marvels*
    are;   *before*
240   Forthi for fantoum and fayryye the folk there hit demed.
Therfore to answare was arwe mony athel freke,
And al stouned at his steven and stonstil seten
In a swoghe sylence thurgh the sale riche;
As al were slypped upon slepe so slaked hor lotes
       in hyye.
    I deme hit not al for doute,   *think, fear*
    Bot sum for cortaysye;   *courtesy*
    Bot let hym that al schulde loute
    Cast unto that wyye.

250   Thenn Arthour bifore the high dece that
       aventure byholdes,   *strange event*
And rekenly hym reverenced, for rad was he never,
And sayde: 'Wyye, welcum iwys to this place,   *sir, indeed*
The hede of this ostel Arthour I hat.   *house, am called*

229-31 And his eyes looked quickly up and down (the hall). He stopped, and examined carefully to see who had the greatest renown there.

236-7 Glowing brighter than green enamel on gold. All who stood there stared, and moved cautiously closer to him.

240-45 And so the people there took it for illusion and magic. For that reason many a noble knight was afraid to answer, and all were dumbfounded at his voice and sat still as stone in a dead silence throughout the rich hall; as though all had slipped into sleep, so their noise died away suddenly.

248-9 But let (imperative) him to whom all must defer (i.e. Arthur) address himself to that man.

251 And greeted him courteously, for he was not at all afraid.

Light luflych adoun and lenge, I the praye,
And quat-so thy wylle is we schal wyt after.'   *whatever, learn*
'Nay, as help me,' quoth the hathel, 'he that on hyghe
    syttes,
To wone any quyle in this won, hit was not myn ernde.
Bot for the los of the, lede, is lyft up so hyghe,
And thy burgh and thy burnes best ar holden,
260 Stifest under stel-gere on stedes to ryde,
The wyghtest and the worthyest of the worldes kynde,
Preve for to play wyth in other pure laykes –
And here is kydde cortaysye, as I haf herd carp,   *shown, tell*
And that has wayned me hider, iwyis, at this   *brought, indeed*
    tyme.
Ye may be seker bi this braunch that I bere here   *sure*
That I passe as in pes, and no plyght seche.   *peace, trouble*
For had I founded in fere, in feghtyng wyse,
I have a hauberghe at home and a helme bothe,   *coat of mail*
A schelde and a scharp spere, schinande bryght,
270 Ande other weppenes to welde, I wene wel, als.
Bot for I wolde no were, my wedes ar softer.
Bot if thou be so bold as alle burnes tellen,   *men say*
Thou wyl grant me godly the gomen that I   *graciously, game*
    ask
        bi ryght.'   *as of right*
    Arthour con onsware,   *answered*
    And sayd: 'Sir cortays knyght,
    If thou crave batayl bare,
    Here fayles thou not to fyght.'

'Nay, frayst I no fyght, in fayth I the telle;   *seek*
280 Hit arn aboute on this bench bot berdles chylder;
If I were hasped in armes on a heghe stede,   *buckled*
Here is no mon me to mach, for myghtes so wayke.

²⁵⁴ Kindly dismount and stay (with us), I pray you.
²⁵⁶⁻⁶² 'No, so help me God (lit. He who dwells on high)', said the man, 'it was not my
    mission to stay any length of time in this place. But because your renown, sir, is lifted
    up so high, and your castle and your men are held to be the best, the mightiest in
    armour who ride steeds, the bravest and the worthiest of the world's creatures, fit to
    contend with in any noble sports.
²⁶⁷ For had I travelled in (warlike) company, in fighting fashion.
²⁷⁰⁻⁷¹ And other weapons to wield, as I well know, besides. But since I want no war, my
    clothes are softer.
²⁷⁷⁻⁸ If you crave battle without armour, here you will not fail to get a fight.
²⁸⁰ There are only beardless children (sitting) about on these benches.
²⁸² Here is no man to match me, their strength is so weak.

Forthy I crave in this court a Crystemas gomen,　　*and so, game*
For hit is Yol and Nwe Yer, and here ar　　　　　　*Yule*
　　yep mony.　　　　　　　　　　　　　　　　*many young men*
If any so hardy in this hous holdes hymselven,
Be so bolde in his blod, brayn in hys hede,
That dar stifly strike a strok for an other,
I schal gif hym of my gyft thys giserne ryche,　　*battle-axe*
This ax, that is hevé innogh, to hondele as　　　*heavy, handle*
　　hym lykes,
And I schal bide the fyrst bur, as bare as I sitte.

290

If any freke be so felle to fonde that I telle,
Lepe lyghtly me to, and lach this weppen;
I quit-clayme hit for ever, kepe hit as his auen.
And I schal stonde hym a strok, stif on this flet,
Elles thou wyl dight me the dom to dele hym an other,
　　　barlay.
　　And yet gif hym respite　　　　　　　　*(I) give*
　　A twelmonyth and a day;
　　Now hyye, and let se tite
300　　Dar any herinne oght say.'

If he hem stowned upon fyrst, stiller were　　*stunned, at first*
　　thanne
Alle the heredmen in halle, the hygh and the lowe.　　*courtiers*
The renk on his rouncé hym ruched in his sadel,
And runischly his rede yyen he reled aboute,
Bende his bresed browes, blycande grene,
Wayved his berde for to wayte quo-so wolde ryse.
When non wolde kepe hym with carp he coghed ful hyghe,
Ande rimed hym ful richly, and ryght hym to speke:
'What, is this Arthures hous,' quoth the hathel thenne,　　*man*
310　'That al the rous rennes of thurgh ryalmes　　*talk, realms*
　　so mony?

285-7 If any in this house considers himself so bold in his temperament, so hot-headed, as to dare to strike fearlessly one stroke (in return) for another.

290-96 And I shall endure the first blow, unarmed as I sit (here). If any man is so bold as to put to the test what I propose, let him run quickly to me and seize this weapon; I give it up for ever, let him keep it as his own. And I shall stand a stroke from him, firm on this floor, provided that you will give me the right to deal him another, by agreement.

299-300 Now hurry, and let us see quickly if any here dare say anything.

303-8 The man on his horse turned in his saddle and fiercely rolled his red eyes about, wrinkled his bristling brows, shining green, swept his beard from side to side (i.e. turned his head) to see whoever would rise (from his seat). When no one would engage him in talk, he coughed very loudly, and drew himself up most grandly, and proceeded to speak.

Where is now your sourquydrye and your conquestes,   *pride*
Your gryndellayk and your greme and your   *fierceness, anger*
    grete wordes?
Now is the revel and the renoun of the Rounde   *revelling*
    Table
Overwalt wyth a worde of on wyyes   *overthrown, one man's*
    speche,
For al dares for drede withoute dynt schewed!'
Wyth this he laghes so loude that the lorde greved;
The blod schot for scham into his schyre face   *shame, fair*
    and lere.   *cheek*
He wex as wroth as wynde;   *grew, angry*
320   So did alle that ther were.   *who were there*
The kyng, as kene bi kynde,
Then stod that stif mon nere.

Ande sayde: 'Hathel, by heven thyn askyng is   *sir*
    nys,   *foolish*
And as thou foly has frayst, fynde the behoves.
I know no gome that is gast of thy grete wordes.   *man, afraid*
Gif me now thy geserne, upon Godes halve,
And I schal baythen thy bone that thou boden habbes.'
Lyghtly lepes he hym to, and laght at his honde;
Then feersly that other freke upon fote lyghtis.   *man*
330   Now has Arthure his axe, and the halme grypes,   *handle*
And sturnely stures hit aboute, that stryke wyth hit
    thoght.
The stif mon hym bifore stod upon hyght,   *stood upright*
Herre then ani in the hous by the hede and more.   *taller*
Wyth sturne schere ther he stod he stroked   *expression, where*
    his berde,
And wyth a countenaunce dryye he drow   *unmoved, drew*
    doun his cote,
No more mate ne dismayd for hys mayn dintes

315-16 'For all cower in fear without a blow being offered.' With this he laughs so loudly
    that the lord (i.e. Arthur) took offence.
321-2 The king, as one brave by nature, then stood near that formidable man.
324 And as you have asked for folly, you deserve to find it.
326-8 'Give me your battle-axe now, for God's sake, and I shall grant you the boon that
    you have asked for.' Quickly he runs to him, and took hold of his hand (i.e. to help
    him dismount).
331 And grimly swings it about, intending to strike with it.
336 No more daunted or dismayed by his great blows (i.e. by Arthur's brandishing of the
    axe).

Then any burne upon bench hade broght hym to   *than if, man*
    drynk
        of wyne.
    Gawan, that sate bi the quene,   *sat*
340   To the kyng he can enclyne: *bowed*
    'I beseche now with sawes sene
    This melly mot be myne.'

    'Wolde ye, worthilych lorde,' quoth   *if you would, honoured*
    Wawan to the kyng,
    Bid me bowe fro this benche and stonde by yow there,   *go*
    That I wythoute vylanye myght   *so that, discourtesy*
      voyde this table,   *leave*
    And that my legge lady lyked not ille,
    I wolde com to your counseyl bifore your cort   *to advise you*
      ryche   *noble*
    For me think hit not semly, as hit is soth knawen,
    Ther such an askyng is hevened so hyghe in your sale,
350   Thagh ye yourself be talenttyf, to take hit to yourselven,
    Whil mony so bolde yow aboute upon bench sytten,
    That under heven, I hope, non hagherer of wylle,
    Ne better bodyes on bent ther baret is rered.
    I am the wakkest, I wot, and of wyt feblest,   *weakest, know*
    And lest lur of my lyf, quo laytes the sothe.
    Bot for as much as ye ar myn em, I am only to prayse;
    No bounté bot your blod I in my bodé knowe.   *virtue*
    And sythen this note is so nys that noght hit yow falles,
    And I have frayned hit at yow fyrst, foldes hit   *asked, it falls*
      to me;
360   And if I carp not comlyly, let alle this cort rych,
        bout blame.'
    Ryche togeder con roun,   *nobles, whispered*

341-2 I implore (you) now in plain words that this quarrel might be mine.
346 And provided that my liege lady was not displeased.
348-53 For it seems to me not fitting, as is manifestly evident, that where such a request is
voiced so loudly in your hall you should take it upon yourself, even though you yourself
may be willing, while many most bold men sit around you on the benches, such that
under the heavens, I believe, there are none of readier courage, nor better men on the
field where battle is done.
355-6 And my life would be the smallest loss, to tell the truth (lit. whoever wishes to know
the truth). I am only to be esteemed inasmuch as you are my uncle.
358 And since this business is so foolish that it is not at all proper for you.
360-61 And if I do not speak fittingly, let all this noble court decide (the matter), without
blame.

And sythen thay redden alle same:
To ryd the kyng wyth croun,
And gif Gawan the game.

Then comaunded the kyng the knyght for to ryse,
And he ful radly up ros and ruchched hym fayre,
Kneled doun bifore the kyng, and caches that weppen;   *takes*
And he luflyly hit hym laft, and lyfte up his honde
370   And gef hym Goddes blessyng, and gladly hym biddes
That his hert and his honde schulde hardi be bothe.   *bold*
'Kepe the, cosyn,' quoth the kyng, 'that thou on kyrf sette,
And if thou redes hym ryght, redly I trowe
That thou schal byden the bur that he schal bede after.'
Gawan gos to the gome, with giserne in   *man, battle-axe*
    honde,
And he baldly hym bydes, he bayst never the helder.
Then carppes to Sir Gawan the knyght in the grene;   *speaks*
'Refourme we oure forwardes er we fyrre passe.
Fyrst I ethe the, hathel, how that thou hattes,
380   That thou me telle truly, as I tryst may.'
'In god fayth,' quoth the goode knyght, 'Gawan
    I hatte,
                                                      am called
That bede the this buffet, quat-so bifalles after,
And at this tyme twelmonyth take at the another
Wyth what weppen so thou wylt, and wyth no wyy elles
    on lyve.'
That other onswares agayn: *answers (back)*
'Sir Gawan, so mot I thryve,   *may, prosper*
As I am ferly fayn
This dint that thou schal dryve.'   *blow, strike*

390   'Bigog,' quoth the grene knyght, 'Sir Gawan, me lykes

363-4 And then they gave advice with one accord: to relieve the crowned king.
367 And he rose up most promptly and duly prepared himself.
369 And he graciously gave it up to him, and lifted up his hand.
372-4 'Take care, kinsman,' said the king, 'that you steady your blow, and if you manage him rightly, I fully believe that you will survive the blow that he will offer later.'
376 And he boldly waits for him, he was none the more dismayed.
378-80 Let us restate our agreement before we go further. First I entreat you, sir, to tell me truly how you are called, so that I may be sure (of you).
382-5 Who offers you this blow, whatever happens after, and who at this time twelve months hence shall take another from you with whatever weapon you desire, and from no one else on earth.
388 I am exceedingly glad.
390-91 'By God,' said the green knight, 'Sir Gawain, it pleases me that I shall take at your hand what I have asked for here.'

That I schal fange at thy fust that I haf frayst here.
And thou has redily rehersed, bi resoun ful trwe,   *in words*
Clanly al the covenaunt that I the kynge   *correctly*
   asked,   *put to*
Saf that thou schal siker me, segge, bi thi trawthe,
That thou schal seche me thiself, where-so thou hopes   *think*
I may be funde upon folde, and foch   *earth, take for yourself*
   the such wages
As thou deles me to-day bifore this douthe ryche.'   *company*
'Where schulde I wale the,' quoth Gauan, 'where is   *seek you*
   thy place?
I wot never where thou wonyes, bi hym that me wroght,

400 Ne I know not the, knyght, thy cort ne thi name.
Bot teche me truly therto, and telle me howe thou hattes,
And I schal ware alle my wyt to wynne me theder,
And that I swere the for sothe, and by my seker traweth.'
'That is innogh in Nwe Yer, hit nedes no more,'
Quoth the gome in the grene to Gawan the hende: *noble*
'Yif I the telle trwly, quen I the tape have
And thou me smothely has smyten, smartly I the teche
Of my hous and my home and myn owen nome;   *name*
Then may thou frayst my fare and forwardes holde.

410 And if I spende no speche, thenne spedes thou the better,
For thou may leng in thy londe and layt no fyrre –
      bot sokes!   *enough*
   Ta now thy grymme tole to the,   *take, weapon*
   And let se how thou cnokes.'   *strike*
   'Gladly, sir, for sothe,'   *indeed*
   Quoth Gawan; his ax he strokes.

The grene knyght upon grounde graythely hym dresses,
A littel lut with the hede, the lere he discoveres;
His longe lovelych lokkes he layd over his croun,   *handsome*

---

394 Except that you must assure me, sir, by your word.

399 I do not know at all where you live, by Him who made me.

401-4 'But direct me faithfully to it and tell me how you are called, and I shall use all my
   wits to find my way there, and that I swear to you truly, and on my word of honour.'
   'That is enough (talk) for New Year, no more is needed.'

406-7 If I assure you that when I have received the blow and you have duly struck me, I
   shall (then) promptly inform you.

409-11 Then you may try my hospitality and keep the agreement. And if I say nothing, then
   you will fare the better, for you may stay in your own land and look no further.

417-18 The green knight at once takes up his stance, bent his head a little, (and) exposes
   the flesh.

420   Let the naked nec to the note schewe.   *in readiness*
       Gauan gripped to his ax and gederes hit on hyght,   *lifts, high*
       The kay fot on the folde he before sette,   *left foot, ground*
       Let hit doun lyghtly lyght on the naked,
       That the scharp of the schalk schyndered the bones
       And schrank thurgh the schyire grece and scade hit in
            twynne,
       That the bit of the broun stel bot on the grounde.
       The fayre hede fro the halce hit to the erthe,   *neck*
       That fele hit foyned wyth her fete, there hit   *many, kicked*
            forth roled;
       The blod brayd fro the body, that blykked on the grene.

430   And nawther faltered ne fel the freke never the helder,
       Bot stythly he start forth upon styf schonkes,
       And runyschly he raght out, there as renkkes stoden,
       Laght to his lufly hed, and lyft hit up sone;   *seized, at once*
       And sythen bowes to his blonk, the brydel he   *then goes, horse*
            cachches,
       Steppes into stel-bawe and strydes alofte,   *stirrup*
       And his hede by the here in his honde haldes.
       And as sadly the segge hym in his sadel sette
       As non unhap had hym ayled, thagh hedles nowe
            in stedde.

440   He brayde his bluk aboute,   *twisted, trunk*
       That ugly bodi that bledde;
       Moni on of hym had doute,   *a one, fear*
       Bi that his resouns were redde.

       For the hede in his honde he haldes up even,   *plainly*
       Toward the derrest on the dece he dresses the face;
       And hit lyfte up the yye-lyddes, and loked
            ful brode,   *with a broad stare*
       And meled thus much with his muthe, as ye may now here:

423-6 Let it come down swiftly on the naked flesh, so that the sharp blade shattered the
    bones and sank through the white fat and cut it in two, so that the blade of bright steel
    bit on the ground.
429-32 The blood spurted from the body, shining on the green (flesh and clothes). And yet
    never the more for that did the man falter or fall, but strongly started forward on firm
    legs, and reached out roughly (*and* weirdly), as men stood there.
437-9 And the man sat himself in his saddle as steadily as though no mishap had afflicted
    him, though he was now headless there.
443 By the time he had had his say.
445 He turns the face towards the noblest (one: i.e. Gaynour) on the dais.
447 And spoke with his mouth to this effect, as you may now hear.

'Loke, Gawan, thou be graythe to go as thou   *ready*
    hettes,   *promise*
And layte als lelly til thou me, lude, fynde,
450 As thou has hette in this halle, herande   *in the hearing of*
    thise knyghtes.
To the grene chapel thou chose, I charge the, to   *go*
    fotte   *receive*
Such a dunt as thou has dalt – disserved thou   *blow, dealt*
    habbes   *have*
To be yederly yolden on Nw Yeres morn.   *promptly, repaid*
The knyght of the grene chapel men knowen me mony;
Forthi me for to fynde, if thou fraystes, fayles thou never.
Therfore com, other recreaunt be calde the behoves.'
With a runisch rout the raynes he tornes,   *rough jerk, reins*
Halled out at the hal-dor, his hed in his hande,   *went*
That the fyr of the flynt flawe fro fole hoves.
460 To quat kyth he becom knwe non there,   *land, went*
Never more then thay wyste from quethen he was wonnen.
    What thenne?
    The kyng and Gawen thare   *there*
    At that grene thay laghe and grenne;
    Yet breved was hit ful bare
    A mervayl among tho menne.

Thagh Arther the hende kyng at hert hade wonder,   *noble*
He let no semblaunt be sene, bot sayde ful hyghe   *sign, loudly*
To the comlych quene, wyth cortays   *comely, courteous*
    speche:
470 'Dere dame, to-day demay yow never;   *do not be dismayed*
Wel bycommes such craft upon Cristmasse,
Laykyng of enterludes, to laghe and to syng,
Among thise kynde caroles of knyghtes and ladyes.
Never-the-lece to my mete I may me wel dres,   *meal, proceed*
For I haf sen a selly, I may not forsake.'   *marvel, deny*

---

449 And search for me as faithfully, sir, until you find me.
455-6 And so if you ask, you will never fail to find me. Come, therefore, or you deserve to be called a coward.
459 So that the flint-sparks flew from the horse's hooves.
461 Any more than they knew where he had come from.
464-6 Laugh and grin at that green man; yet it was openly spoken of as a marvel amongst the people.
471-3 Such doings are entirely fitting at Christmas time, playing of interludes (i.e. dramatic entertainments between courses at a banquet), laughing and singing, amongst the pleasant carols of knights and ladies.

He glent upon Sir Gawen and gaynly he sayde: *looked, courteously*

'Now sir, heng up thyn ax, that has innogh hewen.'   *hang, enough*
          hewn

And hit was don abof the dece, on doser to henge,

Ther alle men for mervayl myght on hit loke,   *as a marvel*

480   And bi trwe tytel therof to telle the wonder.

Thenne thay bowed to a borde thise burnes togeder,   *went, table, men*

The kyng and the gode knyght, and kene men hem served   *bold*

Of alle dayntyes double, as derrest myght falle,

Wyth alle maner of mete and mynstralcie bothe.   *kinds of food*

Wyth wele walt thay that day, til worthed an ende in londe.   *in that place*

Now thenk wel, Sir Gawan,

For wothe that thou ne wonde

This aventure for to frayn,

490   That thou has tan on honde.   *undertaken*

Syre Gawene and the Carle of Carelyle *(c. 1400?)*

While out hunting, Gawain and his companions are forced to seek shelter with the Carl of Carlisle, who beats Kay and Bishop Baldwin for their mistreatment of their host's foal. Gawain, on the other hand, is rewarded for his courteous obedience to his host's commands by being given the Carl's beautiful daughter. Afterwards, Gawain is told to return to Arthur and bring him to dine with the Carl.

565   He gaf syr Gawen, sothe to say,

His doughter and a white palfray,

A somer ichargid wyth golde.   *pack-horse, laden*

---

[478] And it was placed above the dais, to hang on the wall-tapestry.

[480] And on its true authority (i.e. with it as incontrovertible evidence) tell of the wondrous event.

[483] A double portion of every delicacy, in the best manner.

[485] They passed that day in enjoyment, until it came to an end.

[488-9] That you do not shrink because of danger from pursuing this adventure.

Sche was so gloryous and so gay
I kowde not rekyn here aray,   *could*
570 So bryghte was alle here molde.   *head*
'Now ryde forthe, Gawen, on my blessynge,
And grete wel Artyr, that is your kynge,
And pray hym that he wolde,
For his love that yn Bedlem was borne,
That he wulle dyne wyth me to-morne.'
Gawen seyde he scholde.

Then thei rode syngynge away
Wyth this yonge lady on here palfray,
That was so fayre and bryghte.
580 They tolde kynge Artir wher thei had bene,
And what wondirs thei had sene
Serteynly in here syght
'Nowe thonkyd be God, cosyn Gawyn,
That thou scapist alyve unslayne,
Serteyne wyth alle my myght.'
'And I, syr kynge,' sayd syr Kay agayne,
'That ever I scapid away unslayne
My hert was nevyr so lyght.
The carle prayde you for his love that yn Bedlem was borne
590 That ye wolde dyne with hym to-morne.'
Kynge Artur sone hym hyght.   *promised*
In the dawnynge fothe they rade,
A ryalle metynge ther was imade   *royal, made*
Of many a jentylle knyght.   *gentle*

Trompettis mette hem at the gate,
Clarions of silver redy therate,   *trumpets, there*
Serteyne wythoutyn lette;   *delay*
Harpe, fedylle, and sawtry,   *psaltery*
Lute, geteron, and menstracy   *gittern, minstrelsy*
600 Into the hall hem fett.   *conducted them*

The carle knelyd downe on his kne,
And welcomyd the king wurthyly
Wyth wordis ware and wyse.   *prudent*
When the kynge to the hall was brought,
Nothynge ther ne wantyd nought
That any man kowde devyse.
The wallys glemyd as any glasse,
With dyapir colour wroughte hit was   *varied and rich*

Of golde, asure, and byse,   *blue-green colour*
610   Wyth tabernacles the halle aboute,   *ornamental niches*
With pynnacles of golde sterne and stoute;
Ther cowde no man hem preyse.   *determine their value*
Trompettys trompid up in grete hete,
The kynge lete sey grace and wente to mete
And was iservyde wythoute lette.   *served, delay*
Swannys, fesauntys, and cranys,
Partrigis, plovers, and curlewys
Before the kynge was sette.

The carle seyde to the kynge, 'Dothe gladly.   *good cheer*
620   Here get ye no nothir curtesy,   *no other*
As I undirstonde.'
Wyth that come yn bollys of golde, so grete   *bowls*
Ther was no knyght sat at the mete
Myght lyfte hem wyth his on honde.   *hand*
The kynge swore, 'By seynte Myghelle,   *Michael*
This dyner lykthe me as welle   *pleases*
As any that evyr Y fonde.'
A dubbyd hym knyght on the morne,   *Arthur dubbed the Carl*
The contre of Carelyle he gafe hym sone
630   To be lorde of that londe.

'Here I make the yn this stownde   *time/place*
A knyght of the Table Rownde,
Karlyle thi name schalle be.'
On the morne when hit was daylyght
Syr Gawen weddyid that lady bryght,
That semely was to se.

Then the carle was glade and blythe,
And thonkyd the kynge fele sythe,   *many times*
For sothe, as I you say.
640   A ryche feste had he idyght   *prepared*
That lastyd holy a fortenyght   *a whole*
Wyth game, myrthe, and playe.
The mynstrellis had yeftys fre   *generous gifts*
That they myght the better be
To spende many a day.
And when the feste was broughte to ende,
Lordis toke here leve to wende   *their, depart*
Homwarde on here way.

A ryche abbey the carle gan make
650 To synge and rede for Goddis sake
In wurschip of oure Lady.
In the towne of mery Carelyle
He lete hit bylde stronge and wele,   *had it built*
Hit is a byschoppis see,
And theryn monkys gray
To rede and synge tille domysday,
As men tolde hit me,
For the men that he had slayne, iwis.   *certainly*
Iesu Cryste, brynge us to thy blis
Above in hevyn, yn thy see. Amen.

THOMAS OF CHESTRE, Syr Launfal (c. *1400*)

This is not the first Middle English translation of Marie de France's twelfth-century poem Lanval, *since there exists another version called* Landevale, *with which Thomas of Chestre was probably familiar.*[130] *While Chestre follows Marie's basic story, he makes a number of alterations and additions, such as the hero's fight against Sir Valentyne and the punishment inflicted on Guenevere at the end of the poem.*

The poem opens at Arthur's court, which is here situated at Kardevyle (Cardiff). Sir Launfal is one of Arthur's Round Table knights and is made steward on account of his widespread generosity. In this version of the story, Merlin advises Arthur to marry Guenevere, daughter of King Rion of Ireland,[131] *although she has had many lovers. Guenevere is a much worse figure in Chestre's version than in his French source.*

1   Be doughty Artours dawes,   *In the days of mighty Arthur*
That held Engelond yn good lawes,   *Who, maintained*
Ther fell a wondyr cas.   *befell, marvel*
Of a ley that was ysette,   *lay, composed*
That hyght 'Launval', and hatte yette,
Now herkeneth how hyt was!
Doughty Artour somwhyle   *once*
Sojournede yn Kardevyle,   *Was staying*

⁵ Which was called 'Launval', and is still so called.

Wyth joye and greet solas;   *delight*
10   And knyghtes that wer profitable,   *worthy*
Wyth Artour of the Rounde Table –   *(Were there) with*
Never noon better ther nas:

Sere Persevall and Syr Gawayn,
Syr Gyheryes and Syr Agrafrayn,
And Launcelet du Lake;
Syr Kay and Syr Ewayn,
That well couthe fyghte yn playn,   *in full battle*
Bateles for to take;   *engage in*
Kyng Ban, Booght and Kyng Bos,
20   Of ham ther was a greet los –   *renown*
Men sawe tho nowher her make;
Syr Galafre and Syr Launfale,
Wherof a noble tale   *Of whom*
Among us schall awake.   *i.e. be told*

Wyth Artour ther was a bacheler,   *young knight*
And hadde ybe well many a yer: *been*
Launfal, forsoth, he hyght.   *truly, he was called*
He gaf gyftys largelyche –   *generously*
Gold and sylver and clodes ryche –   *clothes*
30   To squyer and to knyght.
For hys largesse and hys bounte   *generosity, bounty*
The kynges stuward made was he   *steward*
Ten yer, y you plyght.   *assure*
Of alle the knyghtes of the Table Rounde
So large ther nas noon yfounde,   *generous*
Be dayes ne be nyght.   *i.e. At any time*

So hyt befyll, yn the tenthe yer,
Marlyn was Artours counsalere: *counsellor*
He radde hym for to wende   *advised, go*
40   To Kyng Ryon of Irlond ryght,   *indeed*
And fette hym ther a lady bryght,
Gwennere, hys doughtyr hende.   *i.e. Ryon's, noble*
So he dede, and hom her brought;   *did, home*
But Syr Launfal lykede her noght,
Ne other knyghtes that wer hende:

12 There were never any better.
21 At that time their equal was nowhere to be found.
41 And fetch for himself there a beautiful lady/wife.

For the lady bar los of swych word
That sche hadde lemmannys unther her lord,
So fele ther nas noon ende.   *many*

They wer ywedded, as y you say,
50   Upon a Wytsonday,
Before princes of moch pryde.   *magnificence*
No man ne may telle yn tale
What folk ther was at that bredale,
Of countreys fer and wyde.   *From, far and wide*
No nother man was yn halle ysette
But he wer prelat other baronette –
In herte ys naght to hyde.
Yf they satte noght alle ylyke,   *Even if, alike*
Har servyse was good and ryche,
60   Certeyn, yn ech a syde.   *on every side (i.e. for them all)*

And whan the lordes hadde ete yn the halle
And the clothes wer drawen alle,   *removed*
As ye mowe her and lythe,   *may hear and listen*
The botelers sentyn wyn   *cup-bearers, served*
To alle the lordes that wer theryn,
Wyth chere bothe glad and blythe.   *countenance*
The quene yaf [g]yftes for the nones –   *indeed*
Gold and selver and precyous stonys –
Her curtasye to kythe.   *show*
70   Everych knyght sche yaf broche other ryng,   *gave, or*
But Syr Launfal sche yaf nothyng:
That grevede hym many a syde.   *time*

And whan the bredale was at ende,
Launfal tok hys leve to wende
At Artour, the kyng;
And seyde a lettere was to hym come
That deth hadde hys fadyr ynome –   *taken*
He most to hys beryynge.   *must (go) to his burial*
Tho seyde Kyng Artour, that was hende,   *gracious*
80   'Launfal, yf thou wylt fro me wende,

46-7 For the lady had the reputation of taking lovers in addition to her husband.
52-3 No one can reckon how many people there were at that bridal feast.
55-6 There was no one seated in the hall who was not (at least) a bishop or a baronet.
57 i.e. there is no secret about it.
59 The manner in which they were served was good and sumptuous.
67 gyftes] yftes MS.
74-5 Took leave of ... Arthur.

Tak wyth the greet spendyng,   *money for expenses*
And my suster sones two –   *sister's*
Bothe they schull wyth the go,
At hom the for to bryng.'   *To accompany you home*

Launfal tok leve, wythoute fable,
Wyth knyghtes of the Rounde Table,

Because Sir Launfal dislikes Guenevere's lewd conduct, he asks Arthur's permission to leave court. Launfal travels to Caerleon, where he falls into debt through his extravagant expenditure. When Arthur holds a great feast at Caerleon, Launfal is not invited to attend because of his poverty. Launfal goes riding in a forest and encounters a fairy called Dame Tryamour, who becomes his mistress and makes him fabulously wealthy. The only restraint she places on Launfal is to keep their relationship secret.

Launfal now holds rich feasts and gives generously to the poor and the Church. When a tournament is proclaimed at Caerleon, Launfal takes part with honour and wins the prize. After this, Launfal fights Sir Valentine of Lombardy, whom he slays. In this combat, the hero receives the assistance of his invisible squire, Gyfre.

Arthur summons Launfal back to court, where Queen Guenevere attempts to seduce him. Launfal refuses her advances and breaks faith with his fairy mistress, Tryamour, by informing Guenevere of her existence. The queen revenges the slight by accusing Launfal of attempted seduction. Arthur is furious and condemns Launfal to death.

613   The tydyng com to Artour, the kyng,
      Anoon, wythout lesyng,
      Of Syr Launfales noblesse.
      Anoon a let to hym [s]ende,   *he sent to him*
      That Launfall schuld to hym wende
      At Seynt Jonnys masse:
      For Kyng Artour wold a feste holde
620   Of erles and of barouns bolde,
      Of lordynges more and lesse.

[85-6] Took leave ... of the knights. The phrase *wythoute fable* could mean either 'without deceit' or, more probably, 'to cut a long story short'.
[616] sende] wende MS.

Syr Launfal schuld be stward of halle, *steward*
For to agye hys gestes alle, *direct*
For [he] cowthe of largesse. *knew about generosity*

Launfal toke leve at Triamour,
For to wende to Kyng Artour,
Hys feste for to agye.
Ther he fond merthe and moch honour,
Ladyes that wer well bryght yn bour,
630 Of knyghtes greet companye.
Fourty dayes leste the feste, *lasted*
Ryche, ryall and honeste – *royal, seemly*
What help hyt for to lye?
And at the fourty dayes ende
The lordes toke har leve to wende,
Everych yn hys partye. *direction*

And aftyr mete Syr Gaweyn,
Syr Gyeryes and Agrafayn,
And Syr Launfal also,
640 Wente to daunce upon the grene *grass*
Unther the tour ther lay the quene, *where*
Wyth syxty ladyes and mo.
To lede the daunce Launfal was set: *assigned*
For hys largesse he was lovede the bet, *better*
Sertayn, of alle tho. *by all those*
The quene lay out and beheld hem alle; *leaned*
'I se,' sche seyde, 'daunce large Launfalle. *generous*
To hym than wyll y go.

'Of alle the knyghtes that y se there,
650 He ys the fayreste bachelere:
He ne hadde never n[o] wyf.
Tyde me good other ylle, *Whether good or ill comes of it*
I wyll go and wyte hys wylle – *discover, inclination*
Y love hym as my lyf!' *life*
Sche tok wyth her a companye –
The fayrest that sch[e] myghte aspye, *see*
Syxty ladyes and fyf – *five*
And wente hem doun anoonryghtes, *(they) went down*

---

⁶²⁴ he] *om.* MS.
⁶³³ What is the point of lying?
⁶⁵¹ no] ne MS.
⁶⁵⁶ sche] sch MS.

| | Ham to pley among the knyghtes, | *To disport themselves* |
| 660 | Wel stylle, wythouten stryf. | *quietly, dispute* |

	The quene yede to the formeste ende,	
	Betwene Launfal and Gauweyn the hende,	
	And after her ladyes bryght.	
	To daunce they wente, alle yn same;	*together*
	To se hem play, hyt was fayr game,	*good sport*
	A lady and a knyght.	*Ladies and knights alternately*
	They hadde menstrales of moch honours,	*minstrels*
	Fydelers, sytolyrs and trompours –	*citole-players*
	And elles hyt were unryght.	*wrong*
670	Ther they playde, forsothe to say,	
	After mete the somerys day,	
	All what hyt was neygh nyght.	*Until it was nearly night*

	And whanne the daunce began to slake,	*slacken*
	The quene gan Launfal to counsell take,	
	And seyde yn thys manere:	
	'Sertaynlyche, syr knyght,	
	I have the lovyd wyth all my myght	
	More than thys seven yere.	
	But that thou lovye me,	*Unless*
680	Sertes, y dye for love of the,	
	Launfal, my lemman dere!'	
	Thanne answerede the gentyll knyght,	
	'I nell be traytour, thay ne nyght,	*will not, day nor night*
	Be God, that all may stere!'	*guide*

	Sche seyde, 'Fy on the, thou coward!	*villain*
	Anhongeth worth thou hye and hard.	
	That thou ever were ybore,	*born*
	That thou lyvest hyt ys pyte.	*shame*
	Thou lovyst no woman, ne no woman the.	
690	Thow wer worthy forlore!'	*You deserve (to be) destroyed*
	The knyght was sore aschamed tho:	*embarrassed*
	To speke ne myghte he forgo,	*refrain*
	And seyde the quene before,	*to the queen*

661 The front end (i.e. the head of the dance).
663 And beautiful ladies after her.
674 i.e. she spoke to him privately.
675 manere] marnere MS.
686 You deserve to be hanged high and hard.
689 You love no woman, nor any woman you.

'I have loved a fayr[er] woman
Than thou ever leydest thyn ey upon,
Thys seven yer and more.

'Hyr lothlokste mayde, wythoute wene,   *ugliest, doubt*
Myghte bet be a quene   *better*
Than thou yn all thy lyve!'   *life*
700   Therfore the quene was swythe wroght[h];   *very angry*
Sche taketh hyr maydenes and forth hy go<th>
Into her tour, also blyve.   *at once*
And anon sche ley doun yn her bedde;
For wrethe syk sche hyr bredde,
And swore, so moste sche thryve,   *as she hoped to prosper*
Sche wold of Launfal be so awreke   *avenged*
That all the lond schuld of hym speke,
Wythinne the dayes fyfe.

Kyng Artour com fro huntynge,
710   Blythe and glad yn all thyng;
To hys chamber than wente he.
Anoon the quene on hym gan crye: *sought his help*
'But y be awreke, y schall dye!   *Unless I am avenged*
Myn herte wyll breke a thre!
I spak to Launfal yn my game,   *jokingly*
And he besofte me of schame,
My lemman for to be.
And of a lemman hys yelp he made,   *boast*
That the lodlokest mayde that sche hadde   *ugliest*
720   Myght be a quene above me.'

King Artour was well w[ro]th,
And be God he swor hys oth
That Launfal schuld be sclawe.   *put to death*
He [s]ente aftyr doghty knyghtes,   *valiant*
To brynge Launfal anoonryghtes
To be hongeth and to-drawe.

---

694 fayrer] fayrye MS.
700 wroghth] wroght MS.
704 She made herself ill with anger.
716–17 And he begged me to do something shameful, that he might be my lover.
721 wroth] worþ MS.
724 sente] wente MS.

When twelve knights swear on the Bible that the queen has had
lovers, Sir Launfal is given the chance to preserve his life by
producing his mistress. On the appointed day, Tryamour arrives to
save him and punish Guenevere by blinding her.

The Avowing of King Arthur *(c. 1425)*

Arthur is informed about the devastations of an enormous boar
and sets off with three of his knights to kill it. Arthur vows to slay
the boar, and his companions echo him. The first extract goes as
far as the completion of Arthur's part in the adventure.

17	This is no fantum ne no fabull.	
	Ye wote wele of the Rowun Tabull,	*know well*
	Of prest men and priveabull	*prompt, worthy*
20	Was holdun in prise;	
	Chevetan of chivalry,	*paragon*
	Kyndenesse of curtesy,	
	Hunting full warly	
	As waythmen wise.	*hunters*
	To the forest tha fare	
	To hunte atte buk and atte bare,	*boar*
	To the herte and to the hare	
	That bredus in the rise.	*dwells, bushes*
	The king atte Carlele he lay.	
30	The hunter cummys on a day,	*comes*
	Sayd, 'Sir, ther walkes in my way	
	A well grim gryse.	*boar*
	'He is a balefull bare –	*boar*
	Seche on segh I nevyr are.	*before*
	He has wroghte me mycull care	*much, anxiety*
	And hurte of my howundes;	
	Slayn hom downe slely	
	Wyth feghting full furcely.	
	Wasse ther none so hardi	
40	Durste bide in his boundus.	*territory*
	On him spild I my spere	*broke*
	And mycull of my nothir gere;	*other, equipment*
	There moue no dintus him dere	*may, blows*

Ne wurche him no wowundes. *inflict*
He is masly made *massively*
All offellus that he bade; *kills all who wait for him*
Ther is no bulle so brade *stout*
That in frith foundes. *woodland*

'He is hegher thenne a horse,
50 That uncumly corse; *body*
In fayth, him faylis no force
Quen that he schalle feghte; *when*
And therto blake as a bere. *black, bear*
Feye folke wil he fere. *unlucky, frighten*
Ther may no dyntus him dere, *hurt*
Ne him to dethe dighte. *kill*
Quen he quettus his tusshes, *whets, tusks*
Thenne he betus on the busshes;
All he rives and he russhes *tears up*
60 That the rote is unryghte. *root, pulled up*
He hase a laythelych lusse *repulsive, blow*
Quen he castus uppe his tusse; *tusk*
Quo durst abide him a busse,
Iwisse he were wighte.'[132]

He sais, 'In Ingulwode is hee.' *Englewood*
The tother biddus, 'Lette him bee. *commands*
We schall that Satnace see, *Satan*
Giffe that he be thare.' *if*
The king callut on knyghtis thre;
70 Himselvun wold the fuyrthe be.
He sayd, 'There schalle no mo mene *company*
Wynde to the bore.' *go*
Bothe Kay and Sir Gavan
And Bowdewynne of Bretan,
The hunter and the howundus-squayn *keeper of the hounds*
Hase yarket hom yare. *have made them ready*
The kinge hase armut him in hie, *armed himself, haste*
And tho thre buirnes hym bie; *warriors beside him*
Now ar thay fawre all redie,
80 And furthe conne thay fare. *they rode forth*

Vnto the forest thay weynde, *travelled*
That was hardy and heynde. *those who were, valiant*
The hunter atte the northe ende
His bugull con he blaw,

     Uncoupult kenettis as he couthe;   *small hunting dogs, knew how*
     Witturly thay soghte the southe,   *certainly, South*
     Raches wyth opon mouthe,   *hunting dogs*
     Rennying on a raw;   *running, row*
     Funde fute of the bore;   *track*
90   Faste folutte to him thore.   *followed, there*
     Quen that he herd he hade care;
     To the denne conne he draw.   *withdrew to his den*
     He sloghe hom downe slely   *slew*
     Wyth feghting full fuyrsly;
     But witte ye, sirs, witturly,   *know, certainly*
     He stode butte litull awe.

     Thay held him fast in his hold,
     He brittunt bercelettus bold,   *cut in pieces, dogs*
     Bothe the yunge and the old,
100 And rafte hom the rest.   *deprived them of comfort*
     The raches comun rennying him by   *dogs came running by him*
     And bayet him full boldely,   *held him at bay*
     Butte ther was no so hardy
     Durste on the fynde fast.   *dared attack the fiend*
     Thenne the hunter sayd, 'Lo him thare.
     Yaw thar such him no mare.   *seek*
     Now may ye sone to him fare;
     Lette see quo dose beste.   *who, does*
     Yaw thar such him nevyr more,
110 Butte sette my hed open a store
     Butte giffe he flaey yo all fawre,[133]
     That griselich geste.'   *horrible, evil one*

     Thenne the hunter turnes home agayn.
     The king callut on Sir Gavan,
     On Bawdewin of Bretan
     And on kene Kay.   *sharp-tongued*
     He sayd, 'Sirs, in your cumpany
     Myne avow make I,
     Were he nevyr so hardy,
120 Yone Satenas to say;   *yonder Satan, put to the test*
     To brittun him and downe bringe,   *rip him in pieces*
     Wythoute any helpinge,
     And I may have my levynge,   *if I can survive*
     Hen till tomorne atte day.   *hence*
     And now, sirs, I cummaunde yo

To do as I have done nowe;
Ichone make your avowe.'   *each one*
Gladdely grawuntutte thay.   *they agreed*

Then unsquarut Gavan,   *answered*
130 And sayd godely agayn,
'I avowe to Tarne Wathelan,[134]
To wake hit all nyghte.'   *guard it*
'And I avow,' sayd Kaye,
'To ride this forest or daye;   *before*
Quose wernes me the waye,   *whoever, denies*
Him to dethe dighte.'   *to kill him*
Quod Baudewyn, 'To stynte owre strife,   *said*
I avow, bi my life,
Nevyr to be jelus of my wife
140 Ne of no birde bryghte;   *woman*
Nere werne no mon my mete,   *never, refuse*
Quen I gode may gete;   *while I may obtain money*
Ore drede my dethe for no threte,
Nauthir of king ner knyghte.'

Butte now thay have thayre vowes made,
Thay buskutte hom and furth rade   *got ready, rode forth*
To hold that thay heghte hade,   *to keep what they had vowed*
Ichone sere way.   *separate*
The king turnus to the bore;
150 Gavan, wythoutun any more,
To the tarne con he fare   *went to the mountain lake*
To wake hit to day.
Thenne Kay, as I conne roune,   *I can relate*
He rode the forest uppe and downe;
Boudewynne turnes to toune,   *returns*
Sum that his gate lay,   *since this was his route*
And sethun to bed bownus he.   *then, goes*
Butte carpe we now of ther othir thre,
How thay prevyd hor wedde-fee,   *proved their pledge*
160 The sothe for to say.   *to tell the truth*

Furst to carpe of oure kinge,   *speak*
Hit is a kyndelich thinge,   *it is a suitable topic*
Atte his begynnyng,
Howe he dedde his dede.
Till his houndus con he held.

The bore wyth his brode schilde
Folut hom fast in the filde,   *followed*
And spillutte on hom gode spede.   *killed them quickly*
Then the kinge con crye,
170   And carputte of venerie   *spoke of hunting*
To make his howundus hardi;
Houute on a stede.   *waited on a horse*
Als sone as he come thare,
Agaynus him rebowndet the bare.   *the boar leapt against him*
He se nevyr no syghte are   *before*
So sore gerutte him to drede.   *caused*

He hade drede and doute
Of him that was stirrun and stowte;   *stern*
He began to romy and rowte   *roar, rush*
180   And gapes and gones.   *gapes*
Men myghte noghte his cowch kenne   *lair, discover*
For howundes and for slayn men
That he hade draun to his denne
And brittunt all to bonus.   *devours, bones*
Thenne his tusshes con he quette
Opon the kinge for to sette;
He liftis uppe wythoutun lette   *hindrance*
Stokkes and stonis.   *tree stumps*
Wyth wrathe he begynnus to wrote;   *overturn*
190   He ruskes uppe mony a rote   *tears up, root*
Wyth tusshes of iii fote,
So grisly he gronus.

Thenne the kinge spanes his spere   *grasps*
Opon that bor for to bere;
Ther may no dyntus him dere,   *harm*
So sekir was his schilde.   *dependable*
The grete schafte that was longe
All to splidurs hit spronge;   *splinters*
The gode stede that was stronge
200   Was fallun in the filde.
As the bore had mente,   *intended*
He gave the king such a dinte,   *blow*
Or he myghte his bridull hente,   *before, seize*
That he evyr hit feld.   *felt*
His stede was stonet starke ded;   *struck*
He sturd nevyr owte of that sted.   *place*

To Jesu a bone he bede,	*prayer, made*
Fro wothes hym weylde.	*protect him from harm*
Thenne the king in his sadul sete,	
210 And wightely wan on his fete;	*boldly, got up*
He prays to Sayn Margarete	
Fro wathes him were;	*to guard him from danger*
Did as a dughty knyghte,	
Brayd oute a brand bryghte,	*drew forth his bright sword*
And heue his schild opon highte,	*lifted, high*
For spild was his spere.	*broken*
Sethun he buskette him yare,	*then he gets himself ready*
Squith wythoutun any mare,	*quickly, more delay*
Agaynus the fynde for to fare,	*fiend, go*
220 That hedoes was of hiere.	*terrifying, bristles*
So thay cowunturt in the fild.	*engaged in combat*
For all the weppuns that he myghte weld,	
The bore brittunt his schild,	*destroyed*
On brest he conne bere.	*carried*
There downe knelus he	
And prayus till Him that was so fre,	*gracious*
'Send me the victore,	
This Satanas me sekes.'	
All wroth wex that sqwyne,	*swine*
230 Blu and brayd uppe his bryne;	*snorted, foamed, eyebrows*
As kylne other kechine,	*furnace, kitchen*
Thus rudely he rekes.	*wildly, fumes*
The kynge myghte him noghte see,	
Butte lenyt him doune bi a tree,	*lay*
So nyghe discumford was hee	
For smelle other smekis.	*because of the foul stench*
And as he neghet bi a noke,	*drew near, oak tree*
The king sturenly him stroke,	
That both his brees con blake;	*eyebrows grew pale*
240 His maistry he mekes.	*he humbles his superiority*
Thus his maistry mekes he	
Wyth dyntus that werun dughte;	*blows*
Were he nevyr so harde,	
Thus bidus that brothe.	*fierce animal*
The kinge wyth a nobull brande,	*sword*
He mette the bore comande.	*struck, coming*
On his squrd till his hande	*sword, up to*

He rennes full rathe.	*rushes, quickly*
He bare him inne atte the throte;	*stabbed*
250 He had no myrth of that mote.	*encounter*
He began to dotur and dote	*totter, grow weak*
Os he hade keghet scathe.	*since, received injury*
Wyth sit siles he adowne.	*trouble, sinks*
To brittun him the king was bowne,	*destroy, ready*
And sundurt in that sesun	*split, time*
His brode schildus bothe.	*shoulders*

The king couthe of verery,	*knew about hunting skills*
Colurt him full kyndely;	*Chopped up the boar very suitably*
The hed of that hardy	
260 He sette on a stake.	
Sethun brittuns he the best	*afterwards, cuts in pieces*
As venesun in forest;	
Bothe the yonge and lees	*entrails and lights*
He hongus on a noke.	*hook*
There downe knelys hee,	
That loves Hur that is free;	*i.e. the Virgin Mary, gracious*
Sayd, 'This socur thou hase send me	
For thi sune sake.'	
If he were in a dale depe,	
270 He had no knyghte him to kepe.	*guard*
Forwerre slidus he on slepe;	*exhausted, he falls asleep*
No lengur myghte he wake.	

The king hase fillut his avowe.

After Arthur has fulfilled his vow, the story deals with the adventures of Kay and Gawain, before turning to Baldwin's pledge. Arthur takes an active part in testing Baldwin's vow that he will not be jealous of his wife.

781 'Now I cummawunde the,' quod the king,	
'Tomorne in the mornying,	
That thou weynde on huntyng	*go*
To wynne us the dere.	
Fare furthe to the fenne;	*go, marsh*
Take wyth the howundus and men,	
For thou conne hom beste kenne;	*can choose them best*
Thou knoes best here.	
For all day tomorne will I bide,	

790   And no forthir will I ride,
      Butte wyth the lades of pride
      To make me gud chere.'
      To bed bownut thay that nyghte,   *went*
      And atte the morun, atte days lighte,
      Thay blew hornys opon highte,
      And ferd furthe in fere.   *went, together*

      Thenne the kynge cald his huntere
      And sayd, 'Felaw, come here.'
      The tother, wyth a blithe chere,
800   Knelet on his kne;
      Dowun to the kinge con he lowte.   *bowed*
      'I commawunde the to be all nyghte oute.
      Bawdewyn, that is sturun and stowte,
      Wyth the schall he be.
      Erly in the dawyng   *dawn*
      Loke that ye come fro huntying.   *make sure*
      If ye no venesun bring,
      Full litill rechs me.'   *bothers*
      The tother unsquarut him thertille;   *answered, on this subject*
810   Sayd, 'Sir, that is atte your aune wille;
      That hald I resun and skille,
      As evyr myghte I the.'

      And atte evyn the king con him dyghte,   *evening, got ready*
      And callut to him a knyghte,
      And to the chambur full righte
      He hiees gode waye,   *hurries, quickly*
      Qwere the lady of the howse   *where*
      And maydyns ful beuteowse,
      Were curtase and curiowse,   *concerned*
820   Forsothe in bed lay.
      The kyne bede, 'Undo.'   *commanded*
      The lady asshes, 'Querto?'   *asks, for what reason*
      He sayd, 'I am comun here, loe,
      In derne for to play.'   *secret*
      Ho sayd, 'Have ye notte your aune quene here   *she*
      And I my lord to my fere?   *spouse*
      Tonyghte more neghe ye me nere,   *you may not come nearer me*
      In fayth, gif I may!'   *if*

      'Undo the dur,' quod the kinge,   *said*
830   'For bi him that made all thinge,

Thou schall have no harmynge,
Butte in thi none wille.'
Uppe rose a damesell squete,   *sweet/lovely*
In the kinge that ho lete.   *that she might let in the king*
He sette him downe on hur beddus fete
And talkes so hur tille: *to her in this way*
Sayde, 'Medame, my knyghte
Mun lye wyth the all nyghte   *must*
Til tomorne atte days lighte.

840   Take hit on non ille.   *do not be offended by it*
For, als evyr myghte I the,
Thou schall harmeles be.
We do hit for a wedde-fee,   *wager*
The stryve for to stylle.'   *to resolve the dispute*

Thenne the kyng sayd to his knyghte,
'Sone that thou were undyghte,   *get undressed at once*
And in yondur bedde ryghte
Hie the gud spede.'   *quickly hurry yourself*
The knyghte did as he him bade,

850   And qwenne ho se him unclad,   *when she saw*
Then the lady wex drede,   *grew fearful*
Worlyke in wede.   *worthy in attire*
He sayd, 'Lye downe prevely hur by,   *i.e. Arthur*
Butte neghe noghte thou that lady,   *do not draw near to*
For, and thou do, thou schall dey   *if, die*
For thi derfe dede.   *audacious*
Ne noghte so hardy thou stur,
Ne onus turne the to hur.'   *once*
The tother sayd, 'Nay, Sur.'

860   For him hade he drede.

Thenne the kyng asshet a chekkere,   *asked for a chess set*
And cald a damesel dere;
Downe thay sette hom in fere   *together*
Opon the bed syde.
Torches was ther mony light,
And laumpus brennyng full bryghte,
Butte notte so hardy was that knyghte
His hede onus to hide.
Butte fro thay began to play,

870   Quyle on the morun that hit was day,   *while, dawn*

Evyr he lokette as he lay — *stared*
Baudewynne to byde. — *to wait for Baldwin's return*
And erly in the dawyng — *dawn*
Come thay home from huntyng,
And hertis conne thay home bring, — *male deer*
And buckes of pride.

Thay toke this venesun fyne
And hade hit to kechine. — *brought it*
The kinge sende aftur Bawdewine,
880 And bede him cum see.
To the chaumbur he takes the way;
He fyndus the king atte his play;
A knyghte in his bedde lay
Wyth his lady.
Thenne sayd the king opon highte, — *out loud*
'Tonyghte myssutte I my knyghte, — *missed*
And hither folut I him ryghte; — *followed*
Here funden is hee.
And here I held hom bothe stille
890 For to do hom in thi wille, — *to punish them as you like*
And gif thou take hit now till ille, — *are offended*
No selcouthe thinge me.' — *I am not surprised*

Then the king asshed, 'Art thou wroth?' — *asked*
'Nay, Sir,' he sayd, wythouten othe,
'Ne wille the lady no lothe. — *harm*
I telle yo as quy: — *why*
For hitte was atte hur awen wille;
Els thurt no mon comun hur tille;[135]
And gif I take hitte thenne to ille,
900 Muche maugreue have Y. — *I would be greatly to blame*

HENRY LOVELICH, The Romance of Merlin (c. 1450)

*This is one of several extant Middle English versions of the French
The Story of Merlin (Lestoire de Merlin); Lovelich's Merlin covers
more of the story than the earlier Of Arthour and of Merlin, and
is more original than the prose version written about the same
time. The following extract discusses the origin of the Round Table,*

the Holy Grail, and the Siege Perilous, which is the empty place in which Judas sat.

4339 'Sire, at this Table evere there was	
4340 In memorie of Crist kept a voide plas,	
Whiche specyal place doth signefye	
The place that Judas in sat, trewelye,	*truly*
Which he forsook, whanne God hadde sayd:	
'On of yow hath me betrayed	
That with me here doth drynke and ete.'	
(It hadde ben bettere he dyde it lete.)	*prevent*
So was this place there voyde stylle,	
Tyle that aftyr-ward be Goddis wylle	
Anothir, hyht Mathy, was there-ine i-set,	*called, Matthew*
4350 As to hym there it cam be lot,	*by*
And to fulfille the nombre of the postelis twelve,	*apostles*
For thus wold God it scholde ben him-selve.	
And, Sire, this voyde place that at the table is,	
Signefieth be Josepe, Sire, i-wis;	*indeed*
And lik as Maththy was chosen therto,	
Riht so was Josepe, wit-owten mo,	*more*
So that these tweyne tables covenable were,	*two*
And thus pleside Crist mennes hertes there.	
Sire, this peple clepede this vessel	*called*
4360 'The Sank Ryal,' other ellys 'Seint Graal.'	*otherwise*
And, Sire, if ye welen don aftyr me,	*will take my advice*
The thrydde table, in worschepe of the Trenite,	
Ye scholen be-gynne, as I yow schal say,	*should*
And yow to gret worschepe it schal torne eche day,	
And to youre sowle gret mede also,	*reward*
And manye benfettes yow schal comen to,	
And thorwgh this world this word schal springe,	
As I yow seye with-owten lesenge.'	*lying*
Lo, thus spak Merlyne to the kyng,	
4370 Whiche wordis to hym were gret lykyng.	
Thanne seide the kyng to Merlyne ageyn:	
'I nolde for non thing, in certein,	*would not*
That God non thing ne loste be me[136]	
Whiche that to his pleasaunce myhte be.	
Wherfore, Merlyne, ordeyne as thow wylt,	
For uppon me ne schal not lyn the gylt.'	
'Now,' thanne quod Merlyne to the kyng,	*said*
'Where liketh yow best to ben abydying?'	*have your residence*

'Now certes,' quod the kyng ageyn,
4380 'Where thou wilt it ordeynen, in certeyn,
And where that most plesyng it myhte be
To God, that syt anhyghe in majeste.'   *on high*
Thanne answerede Merlyne, that was ful lel: *very loyal*
'In Wales, atte the town of Cardweille,
And there schalt thou holden thy feste
Atte Pentecost bothe to mest and leste.[137]
And forth to-foren, Sire, wyl I gon   *before*
That Table to ordeynen for yow echon;   *all/each one*
And also hem that there schal sytte,
4390 I wile hem ordeynen, that thow it wyte.   *understand*

Chapter 4

Ryht as Merlyne devisede in alle thing,
Riht so aftyr hym evene wrowht the kyng,   *carried out*
And there anon sente proclamaciown
Be messengeris thorwgh-owt his regyown,   *by, kingdom*
His ryals hym to meten, bothe lest and meste,   *nobles*
In Cardwel atte Pentecost feste;
Thus was the kynges proclamaciown.
And thanne from the kyng departyd Merlyne anon,
And wente to ordeyne that behoven scholde
4400 To that Table bothe for yong and olde.
And the woke to-foren Pentecost   *week before*
Thedyr cam the kyng, as he nedis most,   *thither, was obliged*
And axede of Merlyne how he hadde-i-do.   *asked*
He seide: 'Sire, riht wel it hyderto!'
'Hast thow owht ordeyned whiche scholen sitten here?'
'Ye, sire, to morwen scholen ye sen the manere   *tomorrow, see*
And that ye wenden nevere forto han seye: *believed, have seen*
Fyfty worthy knyhtes, Sire, in feye,   *together*
Of the beste that ben with-inne thi lond,   *are*
4410 Certein I do yow to undyrstond.
And therby myht thou knowen thy worthy men,
That I have chosen be fyve sithes ten.   *times*
Also the voide place there schalt thou se,
That yit fulfyld it may not be.'   *yet*
Thus Merlyne at that ryal feste
Ches there fyfty knyhtes of the beste,   *chose*
And preide hem to sitten al in fere   *together*
And there to eten with ryht good chere.

Ryht so they deden be on an on,   *did*
4420   And glad they weren everychon.   *each one*
Thanne Merlyne, that was so ful of craft,
Abowtes he wente, and not ne laft,   *omitted nothing*
And clepid the kyng there forto se   *called*
How that they seten in here degre,   *their*
And schewed him also the voide place
And thike tyme atte the table wase.   *that*
But what that place dide signifie,
Niste the kyng ne non of his compenye.   *did not know*

And whanne Merlyne thus hadde i-don,
4430   He preyde the kyng to sitten anon.
And thus viii dayes contenued the feste ryal
To lordes and ladyes and damyselis with-al;
And there ful grete giftes gaf the kyng
Bothe to lordis and to ladyes and to damyselis so yyng.   *young*
And whanne this feste gan up to breke,
Thanne to the fyfty knyhtes the kyng gan to reke,   *consider*
And axede how hem likede there,
And of here syttyng in alle manere.
Thanne they the kyng answerid ful sone:
4440   'It is owre wylle nevere hens to gone
Nether nevere to parten oure compeny onsondyr,
For so as we loven to-gederis, it is gret wondir,
For as brethren we loven to-gederis in fere,
And, tyl deth us sondre, nevere to departen ere.'
And whanne the kyng herde this,
Gret merveille he hadde ther-offen, i-wys.   *indeed*
Thanne charged the kyng to hem anon
To hym ben loveng and trewe everychon.
Thanne departyd al this compenye,
4450   Eche man to his own contre, trewelye.
Thanne cam the kyng to Merlyne there,
And axede him thanne in this manere:
'Telle me if that Goddis wylle it be
This Table fulfylled that I schal se?'
'Wyte thow wel certeyn, Sire kyng,   *know*
That in thy tyme it schal nevere haven endyng,
Nethyr he that it schal fulfylle,
Is not yit be-geten, I sey the tylle.   *I tell you*
But in the kynges tyme it schal be-falle
4460   And aftyr the schal regnen in pured and palle;   *fur, rich cloth*

And he that hym begeten schal,
Knoweth not what aventure him schal befal.
And that same that is to be bore,   *born*
Schal fulfillen the place thore,   *there*
Lyk as Josepe dide in his manere
The signefiaunce aftyr Maththy there.
And therfore, Sire, I preye to the
Thy festes here to holden, certeinle.'
'Now certes, Merlyne,' quod the kyng tho,   *said*
4470 'And at thy wille it schal be do.'
Thanne seide Merlyne to the kyng:
'Sire, it is tyme to maken a partyng;
And knowe ye wel now, Syre kyng,
That aftyr myn hens departyng   *hence*
Of a long tyme ye schole not me se,   *shall*
I seye you, Sire Kyng, ful certeinle.'
Thanne axede the kyng of hym aye
Whethir at his festes he wolde not be.[138]
Thanne answerede Merlyne in this manere:
4480 'Atte all tyme I may not ben here.'
Thanne wente Merlyne to Blasye anon,
And the establementes of the table told hym echon   *rules, all*
And of other thynges manye also
That at thylke tyme were to comen tho.[139]
And there dwelde Merlyne two yer stylle,   *dwelt*
That the kynges cowrt he nolde comen tylle.   *did not wish*
So happede it at Cardweille uppon a day
That they whiche lovede not Merlyne, gonne to say,
And axeden a qwestiown of the kyng:
4490 Why that place was voyde of syttyng,
And why that som good man mihte not sytten there,
And thanne the table fulfilled were.
Thanne answeryd the kyng: 'Certeynle,
For a gret merveyl that Merlyne told me,
That it scholde nevere ben be my day,
And thus Merlyne to me gan say.
And yit he that him engendren schal,   *shall be born*
Nys not yit born, more with-al,   *is*
That this table schal fulfylle.'
4500 They lawhen wel faste, as men that weren ille.   *laughed*
'Sire, beleve ye thanne that in tyme comenge
That better men scholen ben thanne be now reignenge,
And that in yowre lond not as goode there be

As evere here-aftyr scholen comen, sikerle?'   *truly*
'Now certes, I wot nevere,' quod the kyng.   *never knew*
'Now we reden yow to putten it in asayeng.'   *advise, to the test*

'Certes,' quod the kyng, 'I drede me thanne sore
That Merlyne wolde ben angry there-fore.'
'Sire, thanne, and ye wylen gyven us leve,
4510 His falsnesse forsothe we scholen preve.'
'And I wiste Merlyne wroth wolde not be,   *if I believed*
Wel fayn wolde I asayen it, ful sykerle.'
'Ye, Sire, if that Merlyne know of this,
Siker, there wile he ben, i-wys;   *certain*
And therfore suffreth us forto asaye,   *try*
Now, goode Sire Kyng, alle we yow praye.'
So that the kyng hem graunted it forto do,   *them*
Whanne that the feste cam therto.
Thanne weren they glad everichon
4520 That the kyng had graunted this thing be don.
And thus it taryede in-to Pentecost feste,   *was delayed*
That eche ryal there to be atte the kynges heste.   *noble, order*
And Merlyne, that knew here thowhtes echon,   *their*
Ryht there to Blase told it anon,
And of alle here ille thenkenge,   *wicked*
And of hem that weren ther-offen the begynnenge.
And he wiste wel that provyd it scholde be,
That ilke place, ful certeynle;   *same*
And sethen algates it scholde ben so,   *since always*
4530 Bettere on a schrewe thanne on a god man to proven it
          tho.   *knave*
And thus Merlyne dwelled there stylle
Into qwynyyme of Pentecost,¹⁴⁰ here wil to fulfille.

Thanne the kyng to Cardweille wente,
And with hym many lordis, veramente.   *in truth*
And they that comen to asayen this place,   *attempt*
Seiden there was fallen a wondyr case: *said*
That a fals wood cherl, in certayn,   *churl*
In a wode goode Merlyne hadde slayn.
And thus so styfly they gonnen it say,
4540 That the kyng belevyd it that day,
And more principaly the more for on thing:
Be encheson of Merlynes longe abydyng;   *reason*
And also more thanne supposed the kynge

That he wolde it not were asayed, Merlyne levynge.
Thanne uppon the even of Pentecost
There was the semblance, as nedes most.   *appearance, necessary*
Thanne axede the kyng of hem anon
Ho that place asayen scolde don.   *who, do*
Thanne he that the place assaien wolde,   *attempt*
4550 Seide there to the kyng with wordis bolde:
'Sire, I have begonnen this ilke thing,   *same*
And non but I ne schal have the asayeng.'
Thanne cam he to the table anon
There the fyfty knyhtes seten echon.
'I am comen forto sitten here
Forto beren yow compenye al in fere.'   *bear, together*
And they to hym seiden never a word,
But humblely stille seten at that bord,   *table*
And behelden what that he wolde do,
4560 And so dyde the kyng and manyon mo.   *many more*

Thanne thussone he hym sette adown   *as soon as*
Amonges al that peple there in virown.   *around*
And as sone as he was set in that sted,   *place*
He sank a-down lik a plom of led.   *lead weight*
Ne non man wyste how it cam to,   *knew*
Nether why he suffrede that deth ful wo,
Ne where his body becomen was,
There wiste no man in that plas.

The Weddynge of Sir Gawen and Dame Ragnell
(c. *1450*)

This is one of three extant versions of the 'loathly lady' story, the best known of which is Chaucer's Wife of Bath's Tale. *It involves an unnamed Arthurian knight who rapes a damsel; he is instructed to find out what women most desire, in order to preserve his life. In* Dame Ragnell, *Arthur takes a more active role than in Chaucer's version of the story.*

1   Lythe and listenythe the lif of a lord riche,
The while that he lyvid was none hym liche,
Nether in bowre ne in halle;

In the tyme of Arthoure thys adventure betyd,
And of the greatt adventure that he hym-self dyd,
That kyng curteys and royalle.
Of alle kynges Arture berythe the flowyr,
And of alle knyghtod he bare away the honour,
Where-so-euere he wentt.
In his contrey was nothyng butt chyvalry,
And knyghtes were belovid [by] that doughty,
For cowardes were eueremore shent.
Nowe wylle ye lyst a whyle to my talkyng,
I shalle you telle of Arthowre the kyng,
Howe ones hym befelle.

King Arthur, hunting in Ingleswood with his knights

On huntyng he was in Ingleswod,
Withe alle his bold knyghtes good,
Nowe herken to my spelle.
The kyng was sett att his trestylle-tree,
Withe hys bowe to sle the wylde venere,
And hys lordes were sett hym besyde;
As the kyng stode, then was he ware,

noted a great hart

Where a greatt hartt was and a fayre,
And forthe fast dyd he glyde.
The hartt was in a braken ferne,
And hard the g[r]oundes, and stode fulle derne,
Alle that sawe the kyng.
'Hold you stylle, euery man,
And I wolle goo my-self, yf I can
Withe crafte of stalkyng.'
The kyng in hys hand toke a bowe,

Alone, he stalked the hart for some distance

And wodmanly he stowpyd lowe,
To stalk vnto that dere;
When that he cam the dere fulle nere,
The dere lept forthe into a brere,
And euere the kyng went nere and nere,
So kyng Arthure went a whyle,
After the dere, I trowe, half a myle,
And no man withe hym went;
And att the last to the dere he lett flye,

and finally slew it

And smote hym sore and sewerly, –
Suche grace God hym sent.
Doun the dere tumblyd so deron,
And felle into a greatt brake of fferon;

The kyng folowyd fulle fast.
Anon the kyng bothe ferce and felle,
Was withe the dere and dyd hym serve welle.
And after the grasse he taste.
As the kyng was withe the dere
    alone,   *A knight, strong and well armed, appears*
50   Streyghte ther cam to hym a quaynt grome,
Armyd welle and sure;
A knyghte fulle strong and of greatt myghte,
And grymly wordes to the kyng he sayd:
'Welle i-mett, kyng Arthour!   *determined to kill Arthur*
Thou hast me done wrong many a yere,
And wofully I shalle quytte the here;
I hold thy lyfe days nyghe done;
Thou hast gevyn my landes in
    certayn,   *who had deprived him of his land*
Withe greatt wrong vnto Sir Gawen.
60   Whate sayest thou, kyng alone?'
'Syr knyghte, whate is thy name withe honour?'
'Syr kyng,' he sayd, 'Gromer Somer Joure,
I telle the nowe withe ryghte.'
'A, Sir Gromer Somer, bethynk the
    welle,   *'Killing me would only bring shame on you*
To sle me here honour getyst thou no delle,
Be-thynk the thou artt a knyghte,
Yf thou sle me nowe in thys case,
Alle knyghtes wolle refuse the in euery place,
That shame shalle neuere the froo;
70   Lett be thy wylle and folowe wytt,
And that is amys I shalle amend itt,   *I shall amend what is amiss.'*
And thou wolt, or that I goo.'
'Nay,' sayd Sir Gromer Somer, 'by hevyn
    kyng! *The knight (Sir Gromer Somer) swears that he shall take Arthur's life*
So shalt thou nott skape withoute lesyng,
I haue the nowe att avaylle;
Yf I shold lett the thus goo withe mokery,
Anoder tyme thou wolt me defye;
Of that I shalle nott faylle.'
Now sayd the kyng, 'So God me
    saue,   *'Ask for anything else, and I shall grant it. You are armed and I*
                         am not'
80   Save my lyfe, and whate thou wolt crave,
I shalle now graunt itt the;

Shame thou shalt haue to sle me in venere,
Thou armyd and I clothyd butt in grene, perde.'
'Alle thys shalle nott help the, sekyrly,
Ffor I wolle nother lond ne gold truly;
Butt yf thou graunt me att a certayn day,
Suche as I shalle sett, and in thys same araye.'
'Yes,' sayd the kyng, 'lo, here my hand.'
'Ye, butt abyde, kyng, and here me a stound;

90   Ffyrst thow shalt swere vpon my sword
       broun,   *Swear that in exactly one year you shall come back alone,
                              in the same array, and tell me what women love best*
To shewe me att thy comyng whate wemen love
       best in feld and town;
And thou shalt mete me here witheouten send,
Evyn att this day xij. monethes end;
And thou shalt swere vpon my swerd good,
That of thy knyghtes shalle none com with the,
       by the rood,
Nowther frende ne freynd.
And yf thou bryng nott answere withe-oute
       faylle;   *If you cannot answer that question, you must die*
Thyne hed thou shalt lose for thy travaylle, –
Thys shalle nowe be thyne othe.

100   Whate sayst thou, kyng, lett se, haue done.'
'Syr, I graunt to thys, now lett me gone;   *They agree*
Thoughe itt be to me fulle lothe,
I ensure the, as I am true kyng,
To com agayn att thys xij. monethes end,
And bryng the thyne answere.'
'Now go thy way, kyng Arthure,
Thy lyfe is in my hand, I am fulle sure,
Of thy sorowe thow artt nott ware.
Abyde, kyng Arthure, a lytelle whyle,

110   Loke nott to-day thou me begyle,
And kepe alle thyng in close;
Ffor and I wyst, by Mary mylde,
Thou woldyst betray me in the feld,
Thy lyf fyrst sholdyst thou lose.'
'Nay,' sayd kyng Arthure, 'that may nott
       be,   *Arthur pledges his faith*
Vntrewe knyghte shalt thou neuere fynde me;
To dye yett were me lever.
Ffarwelle, Sir knyghte and evylle mett,

I wolle com, and I be on lyve att the day sett,
120 Thoughe I shold scape neuere.'
The kyng his bugle gan blowe, *He gathers his companions*
That hard euery knyghte and itt gan knowe,
Vnto hym can they rake;
Ther they fond the kyng and the dere,
Withe sembland sad and hevy chere,
That had no lust to layk.
'Go we home nowe to Carlylle, *to ride home*
Thys hyntyng lykys me nott welle,' –
So sayd kyng Arthure.
130 Alle the lordes knewe by his
countenaunce *The knights note his distress*
That the kyng had mett withe sume dysturbaunce.
Vnto Carlylle then the kyng cam,
Butt of his hevynesse knewe no man,
Hys hartt was wonder hevy;
In this hevynesse he dyd a-byde,
That many of his knyghtes mervelyd that tyde,
Tylle att the last Sir Gawen *Gawain questions him*
To the kyng he sayd than,
'Syr, me marvaylythe ryghte sore,
140 Whate thyng that thou sorowyst fore.'

*King Arthur informs Gawain about his predicament, and they both
set off in search of the answer. Then Arthur meets an ugly old hag,
Dame Ragnell, who demands marriage with Gawain as a reward
for telling him the correct answer.*

225 Kyng Arthoure rode forthe on the other day,
In-to Yngleswod as hys gate laye,
And ther he mett withe a lady; *There he meets a very ugly lady*
She was as vngoodly a creature,
As euere man sawe witheoute mesure.
230 Kyng Arthure mervaylyd securly.
Her face was red, her nose snotyd withalle,
Her mowithe wyde, her tethe yalowe ouere alle,
Withe bleryd eyen gretter then a balle,
Her mowithe was nott to lak;
Her tethe hyng ouere her lyppes;
Her chekys syde as wemens hyppes;
A lute she bare vpon her bak.

Her nek long and therto greatt,
Her here cloteryd on an hepe,
240   In the sholders she was a yard brode,
Hangyng pappys to be an hors lode;
And lyke a barelle she was made;
And to reherse the fowlnesse of that lady,
Ther is no tung may telle, securly,
Of lothynesse inowghe she had.
She satt on a palfray was gay begon,   *seated on a gay palfrey*
Withe gold besett and many a precious stone,
Ther was an vnsemely syghte;
So fowlle a creature withe-oute mesure,
250   To ryde so gayly, I you ensure,
Ytt was no reason ne ryghte.
She rode to Arthoure, and thus she sayd:
'God spede, Sir kyng, I am welle
    payd,   *She tells him that his life is in her hands*
That I haue withe the mett;
Speke withe me, I rede, or thou goo,
Ffor thy lyfe is in my hand, I warn the soo,
That shalt thou fynde, and I itt nott lett.'
'Why, whatt wold ye, lady, nowe withe me?'
'Syr, I wold fayn nowe speke withe the,
260   And telle the tydynges good;
Ffor alle the answerys that thou canst
    yelpe,   *None of his answers will help*
None of theym alle shalle the helpe,
That shalt thou knowe, by the rood,
Thou wenyst I knowe nott thy
    councelle,   *she knows all about his plight*
Butt I warn the I knowe itt euery dealle;
Yf I help the nott, thou art butt dead.
Graunt me, Sir kyng, butt one
    thyng,   *let him grant her one thing, and he will be safe*
And for thy lyfe, I make warrauntyng,
Or elles thou shalt lose thy hed.'
270   'Whate mean you, lady, telle me tyghte,   *'What do you mean?*
For of thy wordes I haue great dispyte,
To you I haue no nede.
Whate is your desyre, fayre lady,
Lett me wete shortly;
Whate is your meanyng,
And why my lyfe is in your hand,

Telle me, and I shalle you warraunt,
Alle your oun askyng.'
'Ffor-sothe,' sayd the lady, 'I am no
    qued,   *'Grant that I shall marry Gawain*
280   Thou must graunt me a knyghte to wed,
His name is Sir Gawen;
And suche covenaunt I wolle make the,
Butt thorowe myne answere thy lyf sauyd
    be,   *and my answer will save your life*
Elles lett my desyre be in vayne.
And yf myne answere saue thy lyf,
Graunt me to be Gawens wyf,
Advyse the nowe, Sir kyng;
Ffor itt must be so, or thou artt butt dead,   *no other hope for you*
Chose nowe, for thou mayste sone lose thyne hed.
290   Telle me nowe in hying.'
'Mary,' sayd the kyng, 'I maye nott graunt
    the,   *'I cannot bind Gawain to this*
To make warraunt Sir Gawen to wed the;
Alle lyethe in hym alon.
Butt and itt be so, I wolle do my labour,
In savyng of my lyfe to make itt secour,
To Gawen wolle I make my mone.'

At midday on the morning following the wedding-night, Arthur
goes with his knights to see if Gawain has survived the night.

722   'Syrs,' quod the kyng, 'lett vs go and
    asaye,   *Wondering how Gawain is faring*
Yf Sir Gawen be on lyve;
I am fulle ferd of Sir Gawen,
Nowe lest the fende haue hym slayn,
Nowe wold I fayn preve.
Go we nowe,' sayd Arthoure the
    kyng.   *Arthur and his companions come to the chamber*
'We wolle go se theyr vprysyng,
Howe welle that he hathe sped.'
730   They cam to the chambre, alle in certeyn.
'Aryse,' sayd the kyng to Sir Gawen,
'Why slepyst thou so long in bed?'   *'Why sleep so late?'*
'Mary,' quod Gawen, 'Sir kyng, sicurly,
I wold be glad, and ye wold lett me be,

Ffor I am fulle welle att eas;
Abyde, ye shalle se the dore vndone,
I trowe that ye wolle say I am welle goon,   *You will see.*
I am fulle lothe to ryse.'
Syr Gawen rose, and in his hand he toke
His fayr lady, and to the dore he shoke,   *He opens the door*
And opynyd the dore fulle fayre;
She stod in her smok alle by that fyre,
Her her was to her knees as red as gold wyre,
'Lo! this is my repayre,
Lo!' sayd Gawen Arthoure vntille,
'Syr, this is my wyfe, Dame Ragnelle,   *'This is Ragnell my wife.'*
That sauyd onys your lyfe.'
He told the kyng and the queen
    hem beforn,   *He tells them how she had been transformed*
Howe sodenly from her shap she dyd torne,
'My lord, nowe be your leve.'
And whate was the cause she forshapen was,
Syr Gawen told the kyng both more and lesse.
'I thank God,' sayd the queen,
'I wenyd, Sir Gawen, she wold the haue myscaryed;
Therfore in my hartt I was sore agrevyd;
Butt the contrary is here seen.'
Ther was game, revelle, and playe,   *All rejoice*
And euery man to other gan saye:
'She is a fayre wyghte.'
Than the kyng them alle gan
    telle,   *Arthur tells them how she saved his life*
How did held hym att nede Dame Ragnelle,
'Or my dethe had bene dyghte.'
Ther the kyng told the queen, by the rood,
Howe he was bestad in Ingleswod,
Withe Sir Gromer Somer Joure;
And whate othe the knyghte made hym swere,
'Or elles he had slayn me ryghte there,
Withoute mercy or mesure.
This same lady, Dame Ragnelle,
Ffrom my dethe she dyd help me ryghte welle,
Alle for the love of Gawen.'
Then Gawen told the kyng alle togeder,   *Gawain explains more*
Howe forshapen she was withe her stepmoder,
Tylle a knyghte had holpen her agayn;
Ther she told the kyng fayre and welle,

740

750

760

770

Howe Gawen gave her the souereynte euery delle,
And whate choyse she gave to hym;
'God thank hym of his curtesye,   *Ragnell thanks him for his courtesy*
He savid me from chaunce and vilony,
780   That was fulle foulle and grym.
Therfore, curteys knyghte and hend Gawen,
Shalle I neuere wrathe the serteyn,
That promyse nowe here I make, –
Whilles that I lyve I shal be obaysaunt,   *she will always obey him*
To God aboue I shalle itt warraunt,
And neuere withe you to debate.'
'Garamercy, lady,' then sayd Gawen,   *Gawain is very happy*
'With you I hold me fulle welle content,
And that I trust to fynde.'
790   He sayd, 'My loue shalle she haue,   *he loves Ragnell*
Therafter nede she neuere more craue,
For she hathe bene to me so kynde.'
The queen sayd, and the ladyes alle,
'She is the fayrest nowe in this halle,
I swere by Seynt John!
My loue, lady, ye shalle haue euere,
For that ye savid my lord Arthoure,
As I am a gentilwoman.'
Syr Gawen gatt on her Gyngolyn,   *They have a son, Gyngolyn*
800   That was a good knyghte of strengthe and kynn,
And of the Table Round.
Att euery greatt fest that lady shold be,
Of fayrnesse she bare away the
      bewtye,   *She is the fairest one wherever she goes*
Wher she yed on the ground.
Gawen louyd that lady Dame Ragnelle,
In alle his lyfe he louyd none so welle,
I telle you withoute lesyng;
As a coward he lay by her bothe day and nyghte,
Neuere wold he haunt justyng aryghte,
810   Ther-att mervayled Arthoure the kyng.
She prayd the kyng for his
      gentilnes,   *For her sake Arthur forgives Sir Gromer*
'To be good lord to Sir Gromer, i-wysse,
Of that to you he hathe offendyd;'
'Yes, lady, that shalle I nowe for your sake,
Ffor I wott welle he may nott amendes make,
He dyd to me fulle vnhend.'

Nowe for to make you a short conclusyon,
I cast me for to make an end fulle sone,
Of this gentylle lady.

820   She lyvyd with Sir Gawen butt
      yerys v.,   *She and Gawain live five years together*
That grevyd Gawen alle his lyfe,
I telle you, securly.
In her lyfe she grevyd hym neuere,
Therfor was neuere woman to hym lever,
Thus leves my talkyng;
She was the ffayrest lady of al[l]e Englond,
When she was on lyve, I vnderstand,
So sayd Arthoure the kyng.
Thus endythe the aduenture of kyng Arthoure,

830   That oft in his days was grevyd sore,
And of the weddyng of Gawen.
Gawen was weddyd oft in his days,
Butt so welle he neuere lovyd woman
    always,   *Gawain never loved any other woman so much*
As I haue hard men sayn.
This aduenture befelle in Ingleswod,
As good kyng Arthoure on huntyng yod,
Thus haue I hard men telle.
Nowe God as thou were in Bethleme born,
Suffer neuere her soules be forlorne,

840   In the brynnyng fyre of helle!
And, Ihesu, as thou were born of a virgyn,
Help hym oute of sorowe that this tale dyd devyne,
And that nowe in alle hast,
Ffor he is be-sett withe gaylours many,
That kepen hym fulle sewerly,
Withe wyles wrong and wraste.
Nowe God as thou art veray kyng royalle,
Help hym oute of daunger that made this tale,
Ffor therin he hathe bene long;

850   And of greatt pety help thy seruaunt,
Ffor body and soulle I yeld into thyne hand,
Ffor paynes he hathe strong.

Here endythe the weddyng of
Syr Gawen and Dame Ragnelle
Ffor helpyng of kyng Arthoure.

SIR THOMAS MALORY, The Works (Le Morte d'Arthur) (c. 1460–70)

Thomas Malory's Works, *collectively known by the title* Le Morte d'Arthur *(Death of Arthur), in fact covers the whole of Arthur's life from his conception to his death. Malory's version of the story is one of the best known, and is the only Arthurian work familiar to many people.*

Eugène Vinaver, the French editor of Malory's Works, *brought into dispute the integrity of Malory's work and revealed the extent of Malory's debt to the various French Arthurian romances which he compressed into his own version of the story.*[141] *Despite this, recent British and American critics still tend to write favourably of Malory, emphasizing elements of originality in his treatment of the story of Arthur.*

Unlike many of his French sources, Malory prefers to eulogize Arthur, although he makes Lancelot and Tristan the main heroes of substantial sections of his romance. Owing to his failure to synthesize a variety of different source-material, Malory is sometimes inconsistent in his treatment of his subject matter and of the various characters – notably Gawain, who is usually the main hero in English works, but is represented as a villain in one of Malory's sources, the Prose Tristan.

The first extract taken from Malory is the famous opening section, relating how Uther begets Arthur on Igrayne (Ygerne), and how the young Arthur gains his throne after proving his worthiness by withdrawing the sword from the stone. With Merlin's advice, and the assistance of Ban and Bors, Arthur must then fight for survival against the five kings, who include Gawain's father Lot. Malory's main source for this material is the prose version of Robert de Boron's Merlin.[142]

Book 1, Chapter 1: How Uther Pendragon sent for the Duke of Cornwall and Igraine his wife, and of their departing suddenly again

It befell in the days of Uther Pendragon, when he was king of all England, and so reigned, that there was a mighty duke in Cornwall that held war against him long time. And the duke was called the duke of Tintagil. And so by means King Uther sent for this duke, charging him to bring his wife with him, for she was called a fair lady, and a passing wise, and her name was called Igraine. So when the duke and his wife were come unto the king, by the means of great lords they were accorded both: the king liked and loved this lady well, and he made them great cheer out of measure, and desired to have lain by her. But she was a passing good woman, and would not assent unto the king. And then she told the duke her husband, and said, I suppose that we were sent for that I should be dishonoured, wherefore, husband, I counsel you, that we depart from hence suddenly, that we may ride all night unto our own castle. And in like wise as she said so they departed, that neither the king nor none of his council were ware of their departing. All so soon as King Uther knew of their departing so suddenly, he was wonderly wroth. Then he called to him his privy council, and told them of the sudden departing of the duke and his wife. Then they advised the king to send for the duke and his wife by a great charge; And if he will not come at your summons, then may ye do your best, then have ye cause to make mighty war upon him. So that was done, and the messengers had their answers, and that was this shortly, that neither he nor his wife would not come at him. Then was the king wonderly wroth. And then the king sent him plain word again, and bade him be ready and stuff him and garnish him, for within forty days he would fetch him out of the biggest castle that he hath. When the duke had this warning, anon he went and furnished and garnished two strong castles of his, of the which the one hight Tintagil,[143] and the other castle hight Terrabil.[144] So his wife Dame Igraine he put in the castle of Tintagil, and himself he put in the castle of Terrabil, the which had many issues and posterns out. Then in all haste came Uther with a great host, and laid a siege about the castle of Terrabil. And there he pyght many pavilions, and there was great war made on both parties, and much people slain. Then for pure anger and for great love of fair Igraine the King Uther fell sick. So came to the King Uther, Sir Ulfius a noble knight, and asked the king why he was sick. I shall tell thee, said the king, I am sick for anger and for love of fair Igraine that I may not be hool. Well, my lord, said Sir Ulfius, I shall seek Merlin,[145] and he shall do you remedy, that your heart shall be pleased. So Ulfius departed, and by adventure he met Merlin in a beggar's array, and then Merlin asked Ulfius whom he sought. And he said he had little ado to tell him. Well, said Merlin, I know whom thou seekest, for thou seekest Merlin; therefore seek no farther, for I am he, and if King Uther will well reward me, and be sworn unto me to fulfil my desire, that shall be his honour and profit more than mine, for I shall cause him to have all his desire. All this will I undertake, said Ulfius, that there shall be nothing reasonable but thou shalt have thy desire. Well, said Merlin, he shall have his entente and desire. And therefore, said Merlin, ride on your way, for I will not be long behind.

Chapter 2: How Uther Pendragon made war on the Duke of Cornwall, and how by the means of Merlin he lay by the Duchess and gat Arthur

Then Ulfius was glad, and rode on more than a pace till that he came to King Uther Pendragon, and told him he had met with Merlin. Where is he? said the king. Sir, said Ulfius, he will not dwell long; therewithal Ulfius was ware where Merlin stood at the porch of the pavilion's door. And then Merlin was bound to come to the king. When King Uther saw him, he said he was welcome. Sir, said Merlin, I know all your heart every deal; so ye will be sworn unto me as ye be a true king anointed, to fulfil my desire, ye shall have your desire. Then the king was sworn upon the four Evangelists. Sir, said Merlin, this is my desire: the first night that ye shall lie by Igraine ye shall get a child on her, and when that is born, that it shall be delivered to me for to nourish there as I will have it; for it shall be your worship, and the child's avail as mickle as the child is worth. I will well, said the king, as thou wilt have it. Now make you ready, said Merlin, this night ye shall lie with Igraine in the castle of Tintagil, and ye shall be like the duke her husband, Ulfius shall be like Sir Brastias, a knight of the duke's, and I will be like a knight that hight Sir Jordanus, a knight of the duke's. But wayte ye make not many questions with her nor her men, but say ye are diseased, and so hie you to bed, and rise not on the morn till I come to you, for the castle of Tintagil is but ten mile hence; so this was done as they devised. But the duke of Tintagil espied how the king rode from the siege of Terrabil, and therefore that night he issued out of the castle at a postern for to have distressed the king's host. And so, through his own issue, the duke himself was slain or-ever the king came at the castle of Tintagil. So after the death of the duke, King Uther lay with Igraine more than three hours after his death, and begat on her that night Arthur, and or day came Merlin came to the king, and bade him make him ready, and so he kissed the lady Igraine and departed in all haste. But when the lady heard tell of the duke her husband, and by all record he was dead or-ever King Uther came to her, then she marvelled who that might be that lay with her in likeness of her lord; so she mourned privily and held her peace. Then all the barons by one assent prayed the king of accord betwixt the lady Igraine and him; the king gave them leave, for fain would he have been accorded with her. So the king put all the trust in Ulfius to entreat between them, so by the entreaty at the last the king and she met together. Now will we do well, said Ulfius, our king is a lusty knight and wifeless, and my lady Igraine is a passing fair lady; it were great joy unto us all, an it might please the king to make her his queen. Unto that they all well accorded and moved it to the king. And anon, like a lusty knight, he assented thereto with good will, and so in all haste they were married in a morning with great mirth and joy. And King[146] Lot of Lothian and of Orkney then wedded Margawse that was Gawaine's mother, and King Nentres of the land of Garlot wedded Elaine. All this was done at the request of King Uther. And the third sister Morgan le Fay[147] was put to school in a nunnery, and there she learned so much that she was a great clerk of necromancy, and after she was wedded to King Uriens of the land of Gore, that was Sir Ewain le Blanchemain's father.

Chapter 3: Of the birth of King Arthur and of his nurture

Then Queen Igraine waxed daily greater and greater. So it befell after within half a year, as King Uther lay by his queen, he asked her, by the faith she owed to him, whose was the child within her body; then was she sore abashed to give answer. Dismay you not, said the king, but tell me the truth, and I shall love you the better, by the faith of my body. Sir, said she, I shall tell you the truth. The same night that my lord was dead, the hour of his death, as his knights record, there came into my castle of Tintagil a man like my lord in speech and in countenance, and two knights with him in likeness of his two knights Brastias and Jordanus, and so I went unto bed with him as I ought to do with my lord, and the same night, as I shall answer unto God, this child was begotten upon me. That is truth, said the king, as ye say; for it was I myself that came in the likeness, and therefore dismay you not, for I am father to the child; and there he told her all the cause, how it was by Merlin's counsel. Then the queen made great joy when she knew who was the father of her child. Soon came Merlin unto the king, and said, Sir, ye must purvey you for the nourishing of your child. As thou wilt, said the king, be it. Well, said Merlin, I know a lord of yours in this land, that.is a passing true man and a faithful, and he shall have the nourishing of your child, and his name is Sir Ector,[148] and he is a lord of fair livelihood in many parts in England and Wales; and this lord, Sir Ector, let him be sent for, for to come and speak with you, and desire him yourself, as he loveth you, that he will put his own child to nourishing to another woman, and that his wife nourish yours. And when the child is born let it be delivered to me at yonder privy postern unchristened. So like as

Merlin devised it was done. And when Sir Ector was come he made fyaunce to the king for to nourish the child like as the king desired; and there the king granted Sir Ector great rewards. Then when the lady was delivered, the king commanded two knights and two ladies to take the child, bound in a cloth of gold, and that ye deliver him to what poor man ye meet at the postern gate of the castle. So the child was delivered unto Merlin, and so he bare it forth unto Sir Ector, and made an holy man to christen him, and named him Arthur; and so Sir Ector's wife nourished him with her own pap.

Chapter 4: Of the death of King Uther Pendragon

Then within two years King Uther fell sick of a great malady. And in the meanwhile his enemies usurped upon him, and did a great battle upon his men, and slew many of his people. Sir, said Merlin, ye may not lie so as ye do, for ye must to the field though ye ride on an horse-litter: for ye shall never have the better of your enemies but if your person be there, and then shall ye have the victory. So it was done as Merlin had devised, and they carried the king forth in an horse-litter with a great host towards his enemies. And at St Albans there met with the king a great host of the North. And that day Sir Ulfius and Sir Brastias did great deeds of arms, and King Uther's men overcame the Northern battle and slew many people, and put the remnant to flight. And then the king returned unto London, and made great joy of his victory. And then he fell passing sore sick, so that three days and three nights he was speechless: wherefore all the barons made great sorrow, and asked Merlin what counsel were best. There nis none other remedy, said Merlin, but God will have his will. But look ye, all barons, be before King Uther to-morn, and God and I shall make him to speak. So on the morn all the barons with Merlin came tofore the king; then Merlin said aloud unto King Uther, Sir, shall your son Arthur be king after your days, of this realm with all the appurtenance? Then Uther Pendragon turned him, and said in hearing of them all, I give him God's blessing and mine, and bid him pray for my soul, and righteously and worshipfully that he claim the crown upon forfeiture of my blessing; and therewith he yielded up the ghost, and then was he interred as longed to a king. Wherefore the queen, fair Igraine, made great sorrow, and all the barons.

Chapter 5: How Arthur was chosen king, and of wonders and marvels of a sword taken out of a stone by the said Arthur

Then stood the realm in great jeopardy long while, for every lord that was mighty of men made him strong, and many weened to have been king. Then Merlin went to the Archbishop of Canterbury, and counselled him for to send for all the lords of the realm, and all the gentlemen of arms, that they should to London come by Christmas, upon pain of cursing; and for this cause, that Jesus, that was born on that night, that he would of his great mercy show some miracle, as he was come to be king of mankind, for to show some miracle who should be rightwise king of this realm. So the Archbishop, by the advice of Merlin, sent for all the lords and gentlemen of arms that they should come by Christmas even unto London. And many of them made them clean of their life, that their prayer might be the more acceptable unto God. So in the greatest church of London, whether it were Paul's or not the French book maketh no mention, all the estates were long or day in the church for to pray. And when matins and the first mass was done, there was seen in the churchyard, against the high altar, a great stone four square, like unto a marble stone, and in midst thereof was like an anvil of steel a foot on high, and therein stuck a fair sword naked by the point, and letters there were written in gold about the sword that said thus: – Whoso pulleth out this sword of this stone and anvil, is rightwise king born of all England. Then the people marvelled, and told it to the Archbishop. I command, said the Archbishop, that ye keep you within your church, and pray unto God still; that no man touch the sword till the high mass be all done. So when all masses were done all the lords went to behold the stone and the sword. And when they saw the scripture, some assayed; such as would have been king. But none might stir the sword nor move it. He is not here, said the Archbishop, that shall achieve the sword, but doubt not God will make him known. But this is my counsel, said the Archbishop, that we let purvey ten knights, men of good fame, and they to keep this sword. So it was ordained, and then there was made a cry, that every man should essay that would, for to win the sword. And upon New Year's Day the barons let make a jousts and a tournament, that all knights that would joust or tourney there might play, and all this was ordained for to keep the lords and the commons together, for the Archbishop trusted that God would make him known that should win the sword. So upon New Year's Day, when the service was done, the barons rode unto the field, some to joust and some to tourney, and so it happed that Sir Ector, that had great livelihood about London, rode unto the jousts, and with him rode Sir Kay his son, and young Arthur that was his nourished brother; and Sir Kay was made knight at All Hallowmass afore. So as they rode to the joustsward, Sir Kay lost his sword, for he had left it at his father's lodging, and so he prayed young Arthur for to ride for his sword. I will well, said Arthur, and rode fast after the sword, and when he came home, the lady and all were out to see the jousting. Then was Arthur wroth, and said to himself, I will ride to the churchyard, and take the sword with me that sticketh in the stone, for my brother Sir Kay shall not be without a sword this day. So when he came to the churchyard, Sir Arthur alit and tied his horse to the stile, and so he went to the tent, and found no knights there, for they were at jousting; and so he handled the sword by the handles, and lightly and fiercely pulled it out of the stone, and took his horse and rode his way until he came to his brother Sir Kay, and delivered him the sword. And as soon as Sir Kay saw the sword, he wist well it was the sword of the stone, and so he rode to his father Sir Ector, and said: Sir, lo here is the sword of the stone, wherefore I must be king of this land. When Sir Ector beheld the sword, he returned again and came to the church, and there they alit all three, and went into the church. And anon he made Sir Kay to swear upon a book how he came to that sword. Sir, said Sir Kay, by my brother Arthur, for he brought it to me. How gat ye this sword? said Sir Ector to Arthur. Sir, I will tell you. When I came home for my brother's sword, I found nobody at home to deliver me his sword, and so I thought my brother Sir Kay should not be swordless, and so I came hither eagerly and pulled it out of the stone without any pain. Found ye any knights about this sword? said Sir Ector. Nay, said Arthur. Now, said Sir Ector to Arthur, I understand ye must be king of this land. Wherefore I, said Arthur, and for what cause? Sir, said Ector, for God will have it so, for there should never man have drawn out this sword, but he that shall be rightwise king of this land. Now let me see whether ye can put the sword there as it was, and pull it out again. That is no mastery, said Arthur, and so he put it in the stone, wherewithal Sir Ector essayed to pull out the sword and failed.

Chapter 6: How King Arthur pulled out the sword divers times

Now assay, said Sir Ector unto Sir Kay. And anon he pulled at the sword with all his might, but it would not be. Now shall ye essay, said Sir Ector to Arthur. I will well, said Arthur, and pulled it out easily. And therewithal Sir Ector knelt down to the earth, and Sir Kay. Alas, said Arthur, my own dear father and brother, why kneel ye to me? Nay, nay, my lord Arthur, it is not so, I was never your father nor of your blood, but I wot well ye are of an higher blood than I weened ye were. And then Sir Ector told him all, how he was betaken him for to nourish him, and by whose commandment, and by Merlin's deliverance. Then Arthur made great dole when he understood that Sir Ector was not his father. Sir, said Ector unto Arthur, will ye be my good and gracious lord when ye are king? Else were I to blame, said Arthur, for ye are the man in the world that I am most beholden to, and my good lady and mother your wife, that as well as her own hath fostered me and kept. And if ever it be God's will that I be king as ye say, ye shall desire of me what I may do, and I shall not fail you, God forbid I should fail you. Sir, said Sir Ector, I will ask no more of you but that ye will make my son, your foster brother Sir Kay, seneschal of all your lands.[149] That shall be done, said Arthur, and more, by the faith of my body, that never man shall have that office but he, while he and I live. Therewithal they went unto the Archbishop, and told him how the sword was achieved, and by whom; and on Twelfth-day all the barons came thither, and to essay to take the sword, who that would essay. But there afore them all, there might none take it out but Arthur; wherefore there were many lords wroth, and said it was great shame unto them all and the realm, to be over-governed with a boy of no high blood born, and so they fell out at that time that it was put off till Candlemas,[150] and then all the barons should meet there again; but always the ten knights were ordained to watch the sword day and night, and so they set a pavilion over the stone and the sword, and five always watched. So at Candlemas many more great lords came thither for to have won the sword, but there might none prevail. And right as Arthur did at Christmas, he did at Candlemas, and pulled out the sword easily, whereof the barons were sore aggrieved and put it off in delay till the high feast of Easter. And as Arthur sped afore, so did he at Easter, yet there were some of the great lords had indignation that Arthur should be king, and put it off in a delay till the feast of Pentecost. Then the Archbishop of Canterbury by Merlyn's providence let purvey then of the best knights that they might get, and such knights as Uther Pendragon loved best and most trusted in his days. And such knights were put about Arthur as Sir Baudwin of Britain, Sir Kay, Sir Ulfius, Sir Brastias. All these with many other, were always about Arthur, day and night, till the feast of Pentecost.

Chapter 7: How King Arthur was crowned, and how he made officers

And at the feast of Pentecost all manner of men essayed to pull at the sword that would essay, but none might prevail but Arthur, and pulled it out afore all the lords and commons that were there, wherefore all the commons cried at once, We will have Arthur unto our king, we will put him no more in delay, for we all see that it is God's will that he shall be our king, and who that holdeth against it, we will slay him. And therewith they all kneeled at once, both rich and poor, and cried Arthur mercy because they had delayed him so long, and Arthur forgave them, and took the sword between both his hands, and offered it upon the altar where the Archbishop was, and so was he made knight of the best man that was there. And so anon was the coronation made. And there was he sworn unto his lords and the commons for to be a true king, to stand with true justice from thenceforth the days of this life. Also then he made all lords that held of the crown to come in, and to do service as they ought to do. And many complaints were made unto Sir Arthur of great wrongs that were done since the death of King Uther, of many lands that were bereaved lords, knights, ladies, and gentlemen. Wherefore King Arthur made the lands to be given again unto them that ought them. When this was done, that the king had stablished all the countries about London, then he let make Sir Kay seneschal of England; and Sir Baudwin of Britain was made constable; and Sir Ulfius was made chamberlain; and Sir Brastias was made warden to wait upon the north from Trent forwards, for it was that time the most part the king's enemies. But within few years after, Arthur won all the north, Scotland, and all that were under their obeissance. Also Wales, a part of it, held against Arthur, but he overcame them all, as he did the remnant, through the noble prowess of himself and his knights of the Round Table.

Chapter 8: How King Arthur held in Wales, at a Pentecost, a great feast, and what kings and lords came to his feast

Then the king removed into Wales, and let cry a great feast, that it should be holden at Pentecost after the incoronation of him at the city of Caerleon. Unto the feast came King Lot of Lothian and of Orkney, with five hundred knights with him. Also there came to the feast King Uriens of Gore with four hundred knights with him. Also there came to that feast King Nentres of Garlot, with seven hundred knights with him. Also there came to the feast the king of Scotland with six hundred knights with him, and he was but a young man. Also there came to the feast a king that was called the King with the Hundred Knights, but he and his men were passing well beseen at all points. Also there came the king of Carados with five hundred knights. And King Arthur was glad of their coming, for he weened that all the kings and knights had come for great love, and to have done him worship at his feast, wherefore the king made great joy, and sent the kings and knights great presents. But the kings would none receive, but rebuked the messengers shamefully, and said they had no joy to receive no gifts of a beardless boy that was come of low blood, and sent him word they would none of his gifts, but that they were come to give him gifts with hard swords betwixt the neck and the shoulders. And therefore they came thither, so they told to the messengers plainly, for it was great shame to all them to see such a boy to have a rule of so noble a realm as this land was. With this answer the messengers departed and told to King Arthur this answer. Wherefore, by the advice of his barons, he took him to a strong tower with five hundred good men with him; and all the kings aforesaid in a manner laid a siege tofore him, but King Arthur was well victualled. And within fifteen days there came Merlin among them into the city of Caerleon. Then all the kings were passing glad of Merlin, and asked him, For what cause is that boy Arthur made your king? Sirs, said Merlin, I shall tell you the cause, for he is King Uther Pendragon's son, born in wedlock, gotten on Igraine, the duke's wife of Tintagil. Then is he a bastard, they said all. Nay, said Merlin, after the death of the duke, more than three hours, was Arthur begotten, and thirteen days after, King Uther wedded Igraine; and therefore I prove him he is no bastard, and who saith nay, he shall be king and overcome all his enemies; and, or he die, he shall be long king of all England, and have under his obeissance Wales, Ireland, and Scotland, and more realms than I will now rehearse. Some of the kings had marvel of Merlin's words, and deemed well that it should be as he said; and some of them laughed him to scorn, as King Lot; and more other called him a witch. But then were they accorded with Merlin, that King Arthur should come out and speak with the kings, and to come safe and to go safe, such assurance there was made. So Merlin went unto King Arthur, and told him how he had done, and bade him fear not, but come out boldly and speak with them, and spare them not, but answer them as their king and chieftain, for ye shall overcome them all, whether they will or nill.

Chapter 9: Of the first war that King Arthur had, and how he won the field

Then King Arthur came out of his tower, and had under his gown a jesseraunte of double mail, and there went with him the Archbishop of Canterbury, and Sir Baudwin of Britain, and Sir Kay, and Sir Brastias: these were the men of most worship that were with him. And when they were met there was no meekness, but stout words on both sides; but always King Arthur answered them, and said he would make them to bow an he lived. Wherefore they departed with wrath, and King Arthur bade keep them well, and they bade the king keep him well. So the king returned him to the tower again and armed him and all his knights. What will ye do? said Merlin to the kings; ye were better for to stint, for ye shall not here prevail though ye were ten times so many. Be we well advised to be afeard of a dream-reader? said King Lot. With that Merlin vanished away and came to King Arthur, and bade him set on them fiercely; and in the meanwhile there were three hundred good men of the best that were with the kings, that went straight unto King Arthur and that comforted him greatly. Sir, said Merlin to Arthur, fight not with the sword that ye had by miracle, till that ye see ye go unto the worse, then draw it out and do your best. So forthwithal King Arthur set upon them in their lodging. And Sir Baudwin, Sir Kay, and Sir Brastias slew on the right hand and on the left hand that it was marvel; and always King Arthur on horseback laid on with a sword, and did marvellous deeds of arms that many of the kings had great joy of his deeds and hardiness. Then King Lot brake out on the back side, and the King with the Hundred Knights, and King Carados, and set on Arthur fiercely behind him. With that Sir Arthur turned with his knights, and smote behind and before, and ever Sir Arthur was in the foremost press till his horse was slain underneath him. And therewith King Lot smote down King Arthur. With that his four knights received him and set him on horseback. Then he drew his sword Excalibur,[151] but it was so bright in his enemies' eyes, that it gave light like thirty torches. And therewith he put them on back, and slew much people. And then the commons of Caerleon arose with clubs and staves and slew many knights; but all the kings held them together with their knights that were left alive, and so fled and departed. And Merlin came unto Arthur, and counselled him to follow them no further.

While much of Malory's work (like those of his sources) relates the adventures of various Arthurian knights rather than the king himself, the Accolon episode is an exception: Arthur is the main hero, who succeeds in overcoming a serious threat to his life.

The Accalon episode begins when Arthur and many of his knights pursue a great hart, and the king, Accolon and King Urien become separated from the others and arrive at a magical ship which Morgan has contrived with the intention of murdering her half-brother. While hunting does not have an important role in itself in Malory's lengthy Works, *there are a number of other instances when hunting plays an important function in initiating an individual adventure.*[152]

Book 4, Chapter 6: How King Arthur, King Uriens, and Sir Accolon of Gaul, chased an hart, and of their marvellous adventures

Then it befell that Arthur and many of his knights rode a-hunting into a great forest, and it happed King Arthur, King Uriens, and Sir Accolon of Gaul followed a great hart, for they three were well horsed, and so they chased so fast that within a while they three were then ten mile from their fellowship. And at the last they chased so sore that they slew their horses underneath them. Then were they all three on foot, and ever they saw the hart afore them passing weary and enbushed. What will we do? said King Arthur, we are hard bestad. Let us go on foot, said King Uriens, till we may meet with some lodging. Then were they ware of the hart that lay on a great water bank, and a brachet biting on his throat, and more other hounds came after. Then King Arthur blew the prise and dight the hart. Then the king looked about the world, and saw afore him in a great water a little ship, all apparelled with silk down to the water, and the ship came right unto them and landed on the sands. Then Arthur went to the bank and looked in, and saw none earthly creature therein. Sirs, said the king, come thence, and let us see what is in this ship. So they went in all three, and found it richly behanged with cloth of silk. By then it was dark night, and there suddenly were about them an hundred torches set upon all the sides of the ship boards, and it gave great light; and therewithal there came out twelve fair damosels and saluted King Arthur on their knees, and called him by his name, and said he was right welcome, and such cheer as they had he should have of the best. The king thanked them fair. Therewithal they led the king and his two fellows into a fair chamber, and there was a cloth laid richly beseen of all that longed unto a table, and there were they served of all wines and meats that they could think; of that the king had great marvel, for he fared never better in his life as for one supper. And so when they had supped at their leisure, King Arthur was led into a chamber, a richer beseen chamber saw he never none; and so was King Uriens served, and led into such another chamber; and Sir Accolon was led into the third chamber passing richly and well beseen. And so they were laid in their beds easily. And anon they fell asleep, and slept marvellously sore all the night. And on the morrow King Uriens was in Camelot abed in his wife's arms, Morgan le Fay. And when he awoke he had great marvel, how he came there, for on the even afore he was two days' journey from Camelot. And when King Arthur awoke he found himself in a dark prison, hearing about him many complaints of woful knights.

Chapter 7: How Arthur took upon him to fight to be delivered out of prison, and also for to deliver twenty knights that were in prison

What are ye that so complain? said King Arthur. We be here twenty knights, prisoners, said they, and some of us have lain here seven year, and some more and some less. For what cause? said Arthur. We shall tell you, said the knights. This lord of this castle, his name is Sir Damas, and he is the falsest knight that liveth, and full of treason, and a very coward as any liveth, and he hath a younger brother, a good knight of prowess, his name is Sir Ontzlake; and this traitor Damas, the elder brother, will give him no part of his livelihood, but as Sir Ontzlake keepeth through prowess of his hands, and so he keepeth from him a full fair manor and a rich, and therein Sir Ontzlake dwelleth worshipfully, and is well beloved of all people. And this Sir Damas, our master, is as evil beloved, for he is without mercy, and he is a coward, and great war hath been betwixt them both. But Ontzlake hath ever the better, and ever he proffereth Sir Damas to fight for the livelihood, body for body, but he will not do; other else to find a knight to fight for him. Unto that Sir Damas hath granted to find a knight, but he is so evil beloved and hated that there is never a knight will fight for him. And when Damas saw this, that there was never a knight would fight for him, he hath daily lain await with many knights with him, and taken all the knights in this country to see and espy their adventures, he hath taken them by force and brought them to his prison. And so he took us severally as we rode on our adventures, and many good knights have died in this prison for hunger, to the number of eighteen knights; and if any of us all that here is, or hath been, would have foughten with his brother Ontzlake, he would have delivered us, but for because this Damas is so false and so full of treason we would never fight for him to die for it. And we be so lean for hunger that unnethe we may stand on our feet. God deliver you, for his mercy, said Arthur. Anon, therewithal there came a damosel unto Arthur, and asked him, What cheer? I cannot say, said he. Sir, said she, an ye will fight for my lord, ye shall be delivered out of prison, and else ye escape never the life. Now, said Arthur, that is hard, yet had I lever to fight with a knight than to die in prison; with this, said Arthur, I may be delivered and all these prisoners, I will do the battle. Yes, said the damosel. I am ready, said Arthur, an I had horse and armour. Ye shall lack none, said the damosel. Meseemeth, damosel, I should have seen you in the court of Arthur. Nay, said the damosel, I came never there, I am the lord's daughter of this castle. Yet was she false, for she was one of the damosels of Morgan le Fay. Anon she went unto Sir Damas, and told him how he would do battle for him, and so he sent for Arthur. And when he came he was well coloured, and well made of his limbs, that all knights that saw him said it were pity that such a knight should die in prison. So Sir Damas and he were agreed that he should fight for him upon this covenant, that all other knights should be delivered; and unto that was Sir Damas sworn unto Arthur, and also to do the battle to the uttermost. And with that all the twenty knights were brought out of the dark prison into the hall, and delivered, and so they all abode to see the battle.

Chapter 8: How Accolon found himself by a well, and he took upon him to do battle against Arthur

Now turn we unto Accolon of Gaul, that when he awoke he found himself by a deep well-side, within half a foot, in great peril of death. And there came out of that fountain a pipe of silver, and out of that pipe ran water all on high in a stone of marble. When Sir Accolon saw this, he blessed him and said, Jesu save my lord King Arthur and King Uriens, for these damosels in this ship have betrayed us, they were devils and no women; and if I may escape this misadventure, I shall destroy all where I may find these false damosels that use enchantments. Right with that there came a dwarf with a great mouth and a flat nose, and saluted Sir Accolon, and said how he came from Queen Morgan le Fay, and she greeteth you well, and biddeth you be of strong heart, for ye shall fight to-morn with a knight at the hour of prime, and therefore she hath sent you here Excalibur, Arthur's sword, and the scabbard, and she biddeth you as ye love her, that ye do battle to the uttermost, without any mercy, like as ye had promised her when ye spake together in private; and what damosel that bringeth her the knight's head, which ye shall fight withal, she will make her a queen. Now I understand you well, said Accolon, I shall hold that I have promised her now I have the sword: when saw ye my lady Queen Morgan le Fay? Right late, said the dwarf. Then Accolon took him in his arms and said, Recommend me unto my lady queen, and tell her all shall be done that I have promised her, and else I will die for it. Now I suppose, said Accolon, she hath made all these crafts and enchantments for this battle. Ye may well believe it, said the dwarf. Right so there came a knight and a lady with six squires, and saluted Accolon, and prayed him for to arise, and come and rest him at his manor. And so Accolon mounted upon a void horse, and went with the knight unto a fair manor by a priory, and there he had passing good cheer. Then Sir Damas sent unto his brother Sir Ontzlake, and bade make him ready by to-morn at the hour of prime, and to be in the field to fight with a good knight, for he had found a good knight that was ready to do battle at all points. When this word came unto Sir Ontzlake he was passing heavy, for he was wounded a little tofore through both his thighs with a spear, and made great dole; but as he was wounded he would have taken the battle on hand. So it happed at that time, by the means of Morgan le Fay, Accolon was with Sir Ontzlake lodged; and when he heard of that battle, and how Ontzlake was wounded, he said that he would fight for him, because Morgan le Fay had sent him Excalibur and the sheath for to fight with the knight on the morn: this was the cause Sir Accolon took the battle on hand. Then Sir Ontzlake was passing glad, and thanked Sir Accolon with all his heart that he would do so much for him. And therewithal Sir Ontzlake sent word unto his brother Sir Damas, that he had a knight that for him should be ready in the field by the hour of prime. So on the morn Sir Arthur was armed and well horsed, and asked Sir Damas, When shall we to the field? Sir, said Sir Damas, ye shall hear Mass. And so Arthur heard a Mass, and when Mass was done there came a squire on a great horse, and asked Sir Damas if his knight were ready, for our knight is ready in the field. Then Sir Arthur mounted upon horseback, and there were all the knights and commons of that country; and so by all advices there were chosen twelve good men of the country for to wait upon the two knights. And right as Arthur was on horseback there came a damosel from Morgan le Fay, and brought unto Sir Arthur a sword like unto Excalibur, and the scabbard, and said unto Arthur, Morgan le Fay sendeth here your sword for great love. And he thanked her, and weened it had been so, but she was false, for the sword and the scabbard were counterfeit, and brittle, and false.

Chapter 9: Of the battle between King Arthur and Accolon

And then they dressed them on both parts of the field, and let their horses run so fast that either smote other in the midst of the shield with their spear-heads, that both horse and man went to the earth; and then they start up both, and pulled out their swords. The meanwhile that they were thus at the battle, came the damosel of the lake into the field, that put Merlin under the stone; and she came thither for love of King Arthur, for she knew how Morgan le Fay had so ordained that King Arthur should have been slain that day, and therefore she came to save his life. And so they went eagerly to the battle, and gave many great strokes, but always Arthur's sword bit not like Accolon's sword; but for the most part, every stroke that Accolon gave he wounded sore Arthur, that it was marvel he stood, and always his blood fell from him fast. When Arthur beheld the ground so sore be-bled he was dismayed, and then he deemed treason that his sword was changed; for his sword bit not steel as it was wont to do, therefore he dread him sore to be dead, for ever him seemed that the sword in Accolon's hand was Excalibur, for at every stroke that Accolon struck he drew blood on Arthur. Now, knight, said Accolon unto Arthur, keep thee well from me; but Arthur answered not again, and gave him such a buffet on the helm that it made him to stoop, nigh falling down to the earth. Then Sir Accolon withdrew him a little, and came on with Excalibur on high, and smote Sir Arthur such a buffet that he fell nigh to the earth. Then were they wroth both, and gave each other many sore strokes, but always Sir Arthur lost so much blood that it was marvel he stood on his feet, but he was so full of knighthood that knightly he endured the pain. And Sir Accolon lost not a deal of blood, therefore he waxed passing light, and Sir Arthur was passing feeble and weened verily to have died; but for all that he made countenance as though he might endure, and held Accolon as short as he might. But Accolon was so bold because of Excalibur that he waxed passing hardy. But all men that beheld him said they saw never knight fight so well as Arthur did considering the blood that he bled. So was all the people sorry for him, but the two brethren would not accord; then always they fought together as fierce knights, and Sir Arthur withdrew him a little for to rest him, and Sir Accolon called him to battle and said, It is no time for me to suffer thee to rest. And therewith he came fiercely upon Arthur, and Sir Arthur was wroth for the blood that he had lost, and smote Accolon on high upon the helm, so mightily, that he made him nigh to fall to the earth; and therewith Arthur's sword brast at the cross, and fell in the grass among the blood, and the pommel and the sure handles he held in his hands. When Sir Arthur saw that, he was in great fear to die, but always he held up his shield and lost no ground, nor bated no cheer.

Chapter 10: How King Arthur's sword that he fought with brake, and how he recovered of Accolon his own sword Excalibur, and overcame his enemy

Then Sir Accolon began with words of treason and said, Knight, thou art overcome, and mayst not endure, and also thou art weaponless and thou hast lost much of thy blood, and I am full loath to slay thee, therefore yield thee to me as recreant. Nay, said Sir Arthur, I may not so, for I have promised to do the battle to the uttermost, by the faith of my body, while me lasteth the life, and therefore I had lever to die with honour than to live with shame; and if it were possible for me to die an hundred times, I had lever to die so oft than yield me to thee; for though I lack weapon, I shall lack no worship, and if thou slay me weaponless that shall be thy shame. Well, said Accolon, as for the shame I will not spare, now keep thee from me, for thou art but a dead man. And therewith Accolon gave him such a stroke that he fell nigh to the earth, and would have had Arthur to have cried him mercy. But Sir Arthur pressed unto Accolon with his shield, and gave him with the pommel in his hand such a buffet that he went three strides aback. When the Damosel of the Lake beheld Arthur, how full of prowess his body was, and the false treason that was wrought for him to have had him slain, she had great pity that so good a knight and such a man of worship should so be destroyed. And at the next stroke Sir Accolon struck him such a stroke that by the damosel's enchantment the sword Excalibur fell out of Accolon's hand to the earth. And therewithal Sir Arthur lightly leapt to it, and gat it in his hand, and forthwithal he knew that it was his sword Excalibur, and said, Thou hast been from me all too long, and much damage hast thou done me; and therewith he espied the scabbard hanging by his side, and suddenly he start to him and pulled the scabbard from him, and threw it from him as far as he might throw it. O knight, said Arthur, this day hast thou done me great damage with this sword; now are ye come unto your death, for I shall not warrant you but ye shall as well be rewarded with this sword or ever we depart as thou hast rewarded me, for much pain have ye made me to endure, and much blood have I lost. And therewith Sir Arthur rushed on him with all his might and pulled him to the earth, and then rushed off his helm, and gave him such a buffet on the head that the blood came out at his ears, his nose, and his mouth. Now will I slay thee, said Arthur. Slay me ye may well, said Accolon, an it please you, for ye are the best knight that ever I found, and I see well that God is with you. But for I promised to do this battle, said Accolon, to the uttermost, and never to be recreant while I lived, therefore shall I never yield me with my mouth, but God do with my body what he will. Then Sir Arthur remembered him, and thought he should have seen this knight. Now tell me, said Arthur, or I will slay thee, of what country art thou, and of what court? Sir knight, said Sir Accolon, I am of the court of King Arthur, and my name is Accolon of Gaul. Then was Arthur more dismayed than he was beforehand; for then he remembered him of his sister Morgan le Fay, and of the enchantment of the ship. O sir knight, said he, I pray you tell me who gave you this sword, and by whom ye had it.

Chapter 11: How Accolon confessed the treason of Morgan le Fay, King Arthur's sister, and how she would have done slay him

Then Sir Accolon bethought him, and said, Woe worth this sword, for by it have I gotten my death. It may well be, said the king. Now, sir, said Accolon, I will tell you: this sword hath been in my keeping the most part of this twelvemonth; and Morgan le Fay, King Uriens' wife, sent it me yesterday by a dwarf, to this intent, that I should slay King Arthur, her brother. For ye shall understand King Arthur is the man in the world that she most hateth, because he is most of worship and of prowess of any of her blood. Also she loveth me out of measure as paramour, and I her again; and if she might bring about to slay Arthur by her crafts, she would slay her husband King Uriens lightly, and then had she me devised to be king in this land, and so to reign, and she to be my queen; but that is now done, said Accolon, for I am sure of my death. Well, said Sir Arthur, I feel by you ye would have been king in this land. It had been great damage to have destroyed your lord, said Arthur. It is truth, said Accolon, but now I have told you truth, wherefore I pray you tell me of whence ye are, and of what court. O Accolon, said King Arthur, now I let thee wit that I am King Arthur, to whom thou hast done great damage. When Accolon heard that he cried aloud, Fair, sweet lord, have mercy on me, for I knew not you. O Sir Accolon, said King Arthur, mercy shalt thou have, because I feel by thy words at this time thou knewest not my person; but I understand well by thy words that thou hast agreed to the death of my person, and therefore thou art a traitor; but I wyte thee the less, for my sister Morgan le Fay by her false crafts made thee to agree and consent to her false lusts, but I shall be sore avenged upon her an I live, that all Christendom shall speak of it. God knoweth I have honoured her and worshipped her more than all my kin, and more have I trusted her than mine own wife and all my kin after. Then Sir Arthur called the keepers of the field, and said, Sirs, come hither, for here are we two knights that have fought unto a great damage unto us both, and like each one of us to have slain other, if it had happed so; and had any of us known other, here had been no battle, nor stroke stricken. Then all aloud cried Accolon unto all the knights and men that were then there gathered together, and said to them in this manner: O lords, this noble knight that I have fought withal, the which me sore repenteth, is the most man of prowess, of manhood, and of worship in the world, for it is himself King Arthur, our alther liege lord, and with mishap and with misadventure have I done this battle with the king and lord that I am holden withall.

Chapter 12: How Arthur accorded the two brethren, and delivered the twenty knights, and how Sir Accolon died

Then all the people fell down on their knees and cried King Arthur mercy. Mercy shall ye have, said Arthur: here may ye see what adventures befall ofttime of errant knights, how that I have fought with a knight of mine own unto my great damage and his both. But, sirs, because I am sore hurt, and he both, and I had great need of a little rest, ye shall understand the opinion betwixt you two brethren: As to thee, Sir Damas, for whom I have been champion and won the field of this knight, yet will I judge because ye, Sir Damas, are called an orgulous knight, and full of villainy, and not worth of prowess your deeds, therefore I will that ye give unto your brother all the whole manor with the appurtenance, under this form, that Sir Ontzlake hold the manor of you, and yearly to give you a palfrey to ride upon, for that will become you better to ride on than upon a courser. Also I charge thee, Sir Damas, upon pain of death, that thou never distress no knights errant that ride on their adventure. And also that thou restore these twenty knights that thou hast long kept prisoners, of all their harness, that they be content for; and if any of them come to my court and complain of thee, by my head thou shalt die therefor. Also, Sir Ontzlake, as to you, because ye are named a good knight, and full of prowess, and true and gentle in all your deeds, this shall be your charge. I will give you that in all goodly haste ye come unto me and my court, and ye shall be a knight of mine, and if your deeds be thereafter I shall so prefer you, by the grace of God, that ye shall in short time be in ease for to live as worshipfully as your brother Sir Damas. God thank your largeness of your goodness and of your bounty, I shall be from henceforward at all times at your commandment; for, sir, said Sir Ontzlake, as God would, as I was hurt but late with an adventurous knight through both my thighs, that grieved me sore, and else had I done this battle with you. God would, said Arthur, it had been so, for then had not I been hurt as I am. I shall tell you the cause why: for I had not been hurt as I am, had it not been mine own sword, that was stolen from me by treason; and this battle was ordained aforehand to have slain me, and so it was brought to the purpose by false treason, and by false enchantment. Alas, said Sir Ontzlake, that is great pity that ever so noble a man as ye are of your deeds and prowess, that any man or woman might find in their hearts to work any treason against you. I shall reward them, said Arthur, in short time, by the grace of God. Now, tell me, said Arthur, how far am I from Camelot? Sir, ye are two days' journey therefrom. I would fain be at some place of worship, said Sir Arthur, that I might rest me. Sir, said Sir Ontzlake, hereby is a rich abbey of your elders' foundation, of nuns, but three miles hence. So the king took his leave of all the people and mounted upon horseback, and Sir Accolon with him. And when they were come to the abbey, he let fetch leeches and search his wounds and Accolon's both; but Sir Accolon died within four days, for he had bled so much blood that he might not live, but King Arthur was well recovered. So when Accolon was dead he let send him on a horse-bier with six knights unto Camelot, and said: Bear him to my sister Morgan le Fay, and say that I send her him to a present, and tell her I have my sword Excalibur and the scabbard. So they departed with the body.

Chapter 13: How Morgan would have slain Sir Uriens her husband, and how Sir Uwaine her son saved him

The meanwhile Morgan le Fay had weened King Arthur had been dead. So on a day she espied King Uriens lay in his bed sleeping. Then she called unto her a maiden of her counsel, and said, Go fetch me my lord's sword, for I saw never better time to slay him than now. O madam, said the damosel, an ye slay my lord ye can never escape. Care not you, said Morgan le Fay, for now I see my time in the which it is best to do it, and therefore hie thee fast and fetch me the sword. Then the damosel departed, and found Sir Uwaine sleeping upon a bed in another chamber. So she went unto Sir Uwaine, and awaked him, and bade him, Arise, and wait on my lady your mother, for she will slay the king your father sleeping in his bed, for I go to fetch his sword. Well, said Sir Uwaine, go on your way, and let me deal. Anon the damosel brought Morgan the sword with quaking hands, and

[she] lightly took the sword, and pulled it out, and went boldly unto the bed's side, and awaited how and where she might slay him best. And as she lifted up the sword to smite, Sir Uwaine leapt unto his mother, and caught her by the hand, and said, Ah, fiend, what wilt thou do? An thou wert not my mother, with this sword I should smite off thy head. Ah, said Sir Uwaine, men saith that Merlin was begotten of a devil, but I may say an earthly devil bare me. O fair son, Uwaine, have mercy upon me, I was tempted with a devil, wherefore I cry thee mercy; I will never more do so; and save my worship and discover me not. On this covenant, said Sir Uwaine, I will forgive it you, so ye will never be about to do such deeds. Nay, son, said she, and that I make you assurance.

Chapter 14: How Queen Morgan le Fay made great sorrow for the death of Accolon, and how she stole away the scabbard from Arthur

Then came tidings unto Morgan le Fay that Accolon was dead, and his body brought unto the church, and how King Arthur had his sword again. But when Queen Morgan wist that Accolon was dead, she was so sorrowful that near her heart to-brast. But because she would not it were known, outward she kept her countenance, and made no semblant of sorrow. But well she wist, an she abode till her brother Arthur came thither, there should no gold go for her life. Then she went unto Queen Guenever, and asked her leave to ride into the country. Ye may abide, said Queen Guenever, till your brother the king come home. I may not, said Morgan le Fay, for I have such hasty tidings, that I may not tarry. Well, said Guenever, ye may depart when ye will. So early on the morn, or it was day, she took her horse and rode all that day and most part of the night, and on the morn by noon she came to the same abbey of nuns whereat lay King Arthur; and she knowing he was there, she asked where he was. And they answered how he had laid him in his bed to sleep, for he had had but little rest these three nights. Well, said she, I charge you that none of you awake him till I do, and then she alit off her horse, and thought for to steal away Excalibur his sword. And so she went straight unto his chamber, and no man durst disobey her commandment, and there she found Arthur asleep in his bed, and Excalibur in his right hand naked. When she saw that, she was passing heavy that she might not come by the sword without she had awaked him, and then she wist well she had been dead. Then she took the scabbard and went her way on horseback. When the king awoke and missed his scabbard, he was wroth, and he asked who had been there, and they said his sister Queen Morgan had been there, and had put the scabbard under her mantle and was gone. Alas, said Arthur, falsely ye have watched me. Sir, said they all, we durst not disobey your sister's commandment. Ah, said the king, let fetch the best horse may be found, and bid Sir Ontzlake arm him in all haste, and take another good horse and ride with me. So anon the king and Ontzlake were well armed, and rode after this lady, and so they came by a cross and found a cowherd, and they asked the poor man if there came any lady late riding that way. Sir, said this poor man, right late came a lady riding with a forty horses, and to yonder forest she rode. Then they spurred their horses, and followed fast, and within a while Arthur had a sight of Morgan le Fay, then he chased as fast as he might. When she espied him following her, she rode a greater pace through the forest till she came to a plain, and when she saw she might not escape, she rode unto a lake thereby, and said, Whatsoever come of me, my brother shall not have this scabbard. And then she let throw the scabbard in the deepest of the water so it sank, for it was heavy of gold and precious stones. Then she rode into a valley where many great stones were, and when she saw she must be overtaken, she shaped herself, horse and man, by enchantment unto a great marble stone. Anon withal came Sir Arthur and Sir Ontzlake whereas the king might know his sister and her men, and one knight from another. Ah, said the king, here may ye see the vengeance of God, and now am I sorry that this misadventure is befallen. And then he looked for the scabbard, but it would not be found, so he returned to the abbey there he came from. So when Arthur was gone she turned all into the likeliness as she and they were before, and said, Sirs, now may we go where we will.

Chapter 15: How Morgan le Fay saved a knight that should have been drowned, and how King Arthur returned home again

Then said Morgan, Saw ye Arthur, my brother? Yea, said her knights, right well, and that ye should have found an we might have stirred from one stead, for by his army-vestal countenance he would have caused us to have fled. I believe you, said Morgan. Anon after as she rode she met a knight leading another knight on his horse before him, bound hand and foot, blindfold, to have drowned him in a fountain. When she saw this knight so bound, she asked him, What will ye do with that knight? Lady, said he, I will drown him. For what cause? she asked. For I found him with my wife, and she shall have the same death anon. That were pity, said Morgan le Fay. Now, what say ye, knight, is it truth that he saith of you? she said to the knight that should be drowned. Nay truly, madam, he saith not right on me. Of whence be ye, said Morgan le Fay, and of what country? I am of the court of King Arthur, and my name is Manassen, cousin unto Accolon of Gaul. Ye say well, said she, and for the love of him ye shall be delivered, and ye shall have your adversary in the same case ye be in. So Manassen was loosed and the other knight bound. And anon Manassen unarmed him, and armed himself in his harness, and so mounted on horseback, and the knight afore him, and so threw him into the fountain and drowned him. And then he rode unto Morgan again, and asked if she would anything unto King Arthur. Tell him that I rescued thee, not for the love of him but for the love of Accolon, and tell him I fear him not while I can make me and them that be with me in likeness of stones; and let him wit I can do more when I see my time. And so she departed into the country of Gore, and there was she richly received, and made her castles and towns passing strong, for always she dread much King Arthur. When the king had well rested him at the abbey, he rode unto Camelot, and found his queen and his barons right glad of his coming. And when they heard of his strange adventures as is afore rehearsed, then all had marvel of the falsehood of Morgan le Fay; many knights wished her burnt. Then came Manassen to court and told the king of his adventure. Well, said the king, she is a kind sister; I shall so be avenged on her an I live, that all Christendom shall speak of it. So on the morn there came a damosel from Morgan to the king, and she brought with her the richest mantle that ever was seen in that court, for it was set as full of precious stones as one might stand by another, and there were the richest stones that ever the king saw. And the damosel said, Your sister sendeth you this mantle, and desireth that ye should take this gift of her; and in what thing she hath offended you, she will amend it at your own pleasure. When the king beheld this mantle it pleased him much, but he said but little.

Chapter 16: How the Damosel of the Lake saved King Arthur from a mantle that should have burnt him

With that came the Damosel of the Lake unto the king, and said, Sir, I must speak with you in private. Say on, said the king, what ye will. Sir, said the damosel, put not on you this mantle till ye have seen more, and in no wise let it not come on you nor on no knight of yours till ye command the bringer thereof to put it upon her. Well, said King Arthur, it shall be done as ye counsel me. And then he said unto the damosel that came from his sister, Damosel, this mantle that ye have brought me, I will see it upon you. Sir, she said, it will not beseem me to wear a king's garment. By my head, said Arthur, ye shall wear it or it come on my back, or any man's that here is. And so the king made it to be put upon her, and forthwithal she fell down dead, and never more spake word after and burnt to coals. Then was the king wonderly wroth, more than he was toforehand, and said unto King Uriens, My sister, your wife, is alway about to betray me, and well I wot either ye or my nephew, your son, is of counsel with her to have me destroyed; but as for you, said the king to King Uriens, I deem not greatly that ye be of her counsel, for Accolon confessed to me by his own mouth that he would have destroyed you as well as me, therefore I hold you excused; but as for your son, Sir Uwaine, I hold him suspect, therefore I charge you put him out of my court. So Sir Uwaine was discharged. And when Sir Gawaine wist that, he made him ready to go with him, and said, Whoso banisheth my cousin-germain shall banish me. So they two departed, and rode into a great forest, and so they came to an abbey of monks, and there were well lodged. But when the king wist that Sir Gawaine was departed from the court, there was made great sorrow among all the estates. Now, said Gaheris, Gawaine's brother, we have lost two good knights for the love of one. So on the morn they heard their masses in the abbey, and so they rode forth till that they came to a great forest.

HERMANN OF TOURNAI, Concerning the Miracles of St Mary of Laudun (De Miraculis S. Mariae Laudunensis) (1146)

In his account of a journey to Devon and Cornwall, Hermann of Tournai mentions a number of places and things associated with Arthur by the local people. He then recounts an interesting experience concerning the strong local belief (also held by the Bretons) that Arthur was still alive.

Then we came from Exeter into the area which is called Dumnonium [Devon and Cornwall], where people showed us the chair and oven of King Arthur, famous in the stories of the Britons, and they said that this had been Arthur's land ... In the town which is called Bodmin...

There was a certain man with a withered hand, who was keeping watch beside the shrine, hoping to recover his health. However, just as the Bretons are accustomed to quarrel with the French about King Arthur, so this man began to dispute with one of our household, called little Hagan, who was from the household of Guy, archdeacon of Laon, saying that Arthur was still alive. From this argument arose a great uproar; many people rushed into the church with weapons and, if Algard the cleric had not intervened, it would probably have resulted in bloodshed. We believe that God was displeased with the riot beside his shrine, for the man with the withered hand, who caused the disturbance over Arthur, did not recover his health.

ALAIN DE LILLE, English Prophecies of Merlin Ambrosius (Prophetia Anglicana Merlini Ambrosii Britanni) (c. 1167–83)

Alain de Lille provides further evidence for the Breton belief in the legend of Arthur's survival, perhaps derived from Merlin's prophecy about Arthur's fate remaining in doubt.

Arthur's fate will be uncertain. It is indeed true that today there are various opinions among men about his life and death. If, however, you should doubt me, visit the kingdom of Armorica (that is, Lesser Britain [Brittany]) and proclaim through the streets and villages that Arthur the Briton died just as other men die. Then, certainly, you will discover the truth of that prophecy of Merlin which says that Arthur's fate will be in doubt since, even should you manage to escape unharmed from that place, you will be either overwhelmed by the curses of those who hear you, or pelted with stones.

PETER OF BLOIS, Confessions (De Confessione) (c. 1190)

Peter of Blois attests to the popularity of Arthurian stories, which contemporary audiences prefer to more serious works.

Often a certain prudent, honourable, strong, likeable and in every way worthy man is described in tragedies, in other poetic works and in the songs of entertainers. They even cruelly recite tales of violence or injustice, such as certain fables about Arthur, Gawain and Tristan which, when heard, move the audience to compassion, and even to tears.

RALPH OF COGGESHALL, English Chronicle (Chronicon Anglicanum) (1187–1224)

Ralph was abbot of Coggeshall, near Colchester in Essex, from 1207 to 1210, and is considered an invaluable source for the period 1187–1224. This brief extract describes the reputed discovery of Arthur's tomb at Glastonbury in 1191, with the inscription that he was buried in the Isle of Avalon. Support for this statement that the resting-place of Arthur was found when preparing a monk's grave is given by Robert of Gloucester (see p. 81, above).

AD 1191 In this year were found at Glastonbury the bones of the most famous Arthur, formerly king of Britain, in an extremely old sarcophagus, in the vicinity of which were placed two ancient pyramids on which there were engraved certain letters, but, because of their barbarous character and worn state, they could not be read. These things were found for the following reason: for when people were digging the earth to bury a certain monk who had had a strong desire to be buried in this place during his lifetime, they found this coffin, over which was placed a lead cross, upon which were engraved the following words: 'Here lies the famous King Arthur, buried in the Isle of Avalon.' This place had formerly been surrounded by marshes, and was called the Island of Avalon, that is 'Island of Apples'.

GERALD OF WALES (Giraldus Cambrensis)

Instruction of a Prince (De Principis Instructione) (c. 1193–9)

Gerald of Wales must have been particularly interested in the discovery of Arthur's tomb, for he writes two descriptions; one (the first extract) soon after the discovery and another (the second extract) years later in his work, Mirror of the Church (Speculum Ecclesiae). While Ralph of Coggeshall's description of the discovery is possibly earlier, Gerald's is considerably more detailed. He provides a number of personal details, relating how the abbot showed him one of the shin-bones for its remarkable length, and that he also saw the skull, which had been damaged by various wounds.

The memory of Arthur, that most renowned King of the Britons, will endure for ever. In his own day he was a munificent patron of the famous Abbey at Glastonbury, giving many donations to the monks and always supporting them strongly, and he is highly praised in their records. More than any other place of worship in his kingdom he loved the Church of the Blessed Mary, Mother of God, in Glastonbury, and he fostered its interests with much greater loving care than that of any of the others. When he went out to fight, he had a full-length portrait of the Blessed Virgin painted on the front of his shield, so that in the heat of battle he could always gaze upon Her; and whenever he was about to make contact with the enemy he would kiss Her feet with great devoutness.

In our own lifetime Arthur's body was discovered at Glastonbury, although the legends had always encouraged us to believe that there was something otherworldly about his ending, that he had resisted death and had been spirited away to some far-distant spot. The body was hidden deep in the earth in a hollowed-out oak-bole and between two stone pyramids which had been set up long ago in the churchyard there. They carried it into the church with every mark of honour and buried it decently there in a marble tomb. It had been provided with most unusual indications which were, indeed, little short of miraculous, for beneath it – and not on top, as would be the custom nowadays – there was a stone slab, with a leaden cross attached to its under side. I have seen this cross myself and I have traced the lettering which was cut into it on the side turned towards the stone, instead of being on the outer side and immediately visible. The inscription read as follows: HERE IN THE ISLE OF AVALON LIES BURIED THE RENOWNED KING ARTHUR, WITH GUINEVERE, HIS SECOND WIFE.

There are many remarkable deductions to be made from this discovery. Arthur obviously had two wives, and the second one was buried with him. Her bones were found with those of her husband, but they were separate from his. Two thirds of the coffin, the part towards the top end, held the husband's bones, and the other section, at his feet, contained those of his wife. A tress of woman's hair, blond, and still fresh and bright in colour, was found in the coffin. One of the monks snatched it up and it immediately disintegrated into dust. There had been some indications in the Abbey records that the body would be discovered on this spot, and another clue was provided by lettering carved on the pyramids, but this had been almost completely erased by the passage of the years. The holy monks and other religious had seen visions and revelations. However, it was Henry II, King of England, who had told the monks that, according to a story which he had heard from some old British soothsayer, they would find Arthur's body buried at least sixteen feet in the ground, not in a stone coffin but in a hollowed-out oak-bole. It had been sunk as deep as that, and carefully concealed, so that it could never be discovered by the Saxons, whom Arthur had attacked relentlessly as long as he lived and whom, indeed, he had almost wiped out, but who occupied the island [of Britain] after his death. That was why the inscription, which was eventually to reveal the truth, had been cut into the inside of the cross and turned inwards towards the stone. For many a long year this inscription was to keep the secret of what the coffin contained, but eventually, when time and circumstance were both opportune the lettering revealed what it had so long concealed.

What is now known as Glastonbury used in ancient times to be called the Isle of Avalon. It is virtually an island, for it is completely surrounded by marshlands. In Welsh it is called 'Ynys Avallon', which means the Island of Apples. 'Aval' is the Welsh word for apple, and this fruit used to grow there in great abundance. After the Battle of Camlann, a noblewoman called Morgan, who was the ruler and patroness of these parts as well as being a close blood-relation of King Arthur, carried him off to the island now known as Glastonbury, so that his wounds could be cared for. Years ago the district had also been called 'Ynys Gutrin' in Welsh, that is the Island of Glass, and from these words the invading Saxons later coined the place-name 'Glastingebury'. The word 'glass' in their language means 'vitrum' in Latin, and 'bury' means 'castrum' or 'civitas'.

You must know that the bones of Arthur's body which were discovered there were so big that in them the poet's words seem to be fulfilled:

All men will exclaim at the size of the bones they've exhumed.[153]

The Abbot showed me one of the shin-bones. He held it upright on the ground against the foot of the tallest man he could find, and it stretched a good three inches above the man's knee. The skull was so large and capacious that it seemed a veritable prodigy of nature, for the space between the eyebrows and the eye-sockets was as broad as the palm of a man's hand. Ten or more wounds could clearly be seen, but they had all mended except one. This was larger than the others and it had made an immense gash. Apparently it was this wound which had caused Arthur's death.

Mirror of the Church (Speculum Ecclesiae) (1216)

The following extract, written twenty-five years after the discovery of Arthur's body, is Gerald's second account. While it contains basically the same material as his earlier version, it provides some additional information, such as on the woman's hair. Unfortunately, this text survives only in a single, fragmentary manuscript (London, British Library, MS Cotton Tiberius B. xiii).

In our own lifetime,[154] when Henry II was reigning in England, strenuous efforts were made in Glastonbury Abbey to locate what must have once been the splendid tomb of Arthur. It was the King himself who put them on to this, and Abbot Henry, who was later elected Bishop of Worcester, gave them every encouragement. With immense difficulty Arthur's body was eventually dug up in the church-yard dedicated by St Dunstan.[155] It lay between two tall pyramids with inscriptions on them, which pyramids had been erected many years before in memory of Arthur. The body was reduced to dust, but it was lifted up into the fresh air from the depths of the grave and carried with the bones to a more seemly place of burial. In the same grave there was found a tress of woman's hair, blond and lovely to look at, plaited and coiled with consummate skill, and belonging no doubt to Arthur's wife, who was buried there with her husband. The moment that [he saw] this lock of hair, [one of the monks], who was standing there in the crowd, jumped down into the deep grave in an attempt to snatch hold of it before any of the others. It was a pretty shameless thing to do and it showed little reverence for the dead. This monk, then, of whom I have told you, a silly, rash and impudent fellow, who had come to gawp at what was going on, dropped down into the hole, which was a sort of symbol of the Abyss from which none of us can escape. He was determined to seize hold of this tress of woman's hair before anyone else could do so and to touch it with his hand. This was a fair indication of his wanton thoughts, for female hair is a snare for the feeble-minded, although those with any strength of purpose can resist it.[156] Hair is considered to be imperishable, in that it has no fleshy content and no humidity of its own, but as he held it in his hand after picking it up and stood gazing at it in rapture, it immediately disintegrated into fine powder. All those who were watching were astounded by what had happened. By some sort of miracle, not to say . . ., it just disappeared, as if suddenly changed back into atoms, for it could never have been uncoiled and examined closely . . .: this showed that it was even more perishable than most things, proving that all physical beauty is a transitory thing for us to stare at with our vacant eyes or to grope for in our lustful moments, empty and availing nothing. As the philosopher says: 'Physical beauty is short-lived, it disappears so soon, it fades more quickly than the flowers in springtime.'[157]

Many tales are told and many legends have been invented about King Arthur and his mysterious ending. In their stupidity the British people maintain that he is still alive. Now that the truth is known, I have taken the trouble to add a few more details in this present chapter. The fairy-tales have been snuffed out, and the true and indubitable facts are made known, so that what really happened must be made crystal clear to all and separated from the myths which have accumulated on the subject.

After the Battle of Camlann ... killed his uncle ... Arthur: the sequel was that the body of Arthur, who had been mortally wounded, was carried off by a certain noble matron, called Morgan, who was his cousin, to the Isle of Avalon, which is now known as Glastonbury. Under Morgan's supervision the corpse was buried in the churchyard there. As a result the credulous Britons and their bards invented the legend that a fantastic sorceress called Morgan had removed Arthur's body to the Isle of Avalon so that she might cure his wounds there. According to them, once he has recovered from his wounds this strong and all-powerful King will return to rule over the Britons in the normal way. The result of all this is that they really expect him to come back, just as the Jews, led astray by even greater stupidity, misfortune and misplaced faith, really expect their Messiah to return.

It is worth noting ... just as, indeed ... placed by all, as ... are called islands and are known to be situated in salt water, that is to say in the sea. It is called Avalon, either from the Welsh word 'aval', which means apple, because apple-trees and apples are very common there, or from the name of a certain Vallo who used to rule over the area long ago.[158] In remote times the place used to be called 'Ynys Gutrin' in the Welsh language, that is the Island of Glass, no doubt from the glassy colour of the river which flows round it in the marshland. As a result the Saxons who occupied the area later on called it 'Glastonia' in their language, for in Saxon or English 'glass' corresponds to the Latin word 'vitrum'. From what I have said you can see why it was called first 'the Isle of Avalon' and then 'Glastonia'. It is also clear how this fantastic sorceress came to be adopted by the story-tellers.

It is worthy of note that the Abbot called ... also from the letters inscribed on it, although they had been almost obliterated long ago by the passing of the years, and he had the aforesaid King Henry to provide the main evidence.

The King had told the Abbot on a number of occasions[159] that he had learnt from the historical accounts of the Britons and from their bards that Arthur had been buried in the churchyard there between two pyramids which had been erected subsequently, very deep in the ground for fear lest the Saxons, who had striven to occupy the whole island after his death, might ravage the dead body in their evil lust for vengeance. Arthur had attacked them on a great number of occasions and had expelled them from the Island of Britain, but his dastardly nephew Mordred had called them back again to fight against him.[160] To avoid such a frightful contingency, to a large stone slab, found in the tomb by those who were digging it up, some seven feet[161] ... a leaden cross had been fixed, not on top of the stone, but underneath it, bearing this inscription: HERE IN THE ISLE OF AVALON LIES BURIED THE RENOWNED KING ARTHUR, WITH GUI-NEVERE, HIS SECOND WIFE. They prised this cross away from the stone, and Abbot Henry, about whom I have told you, showed it to me. I examined it closely and I read the inscription. The cross had been attached to the under side of the stone and, to make it even less easy to find, the surface with the lettering had been turned towards the stone. One can only wonder at the industry and the extraordinary prudence of the men of that period, who were determined to protect at all costs and for all time the body of this great man, their leader and the ruler of this area, from the possibility of sudden desecration. At the same time they ensured that at some moment in the future, when the troubles were over, the evidence of the lettering cut into the cross might be discovered as an indication of what they had done.

... it had indicated, so Arthur's body was discovered, not in a stone sarcophagus, carved out of rock or of Parian marble, as would have been seemly for so famous a King, but in wood, in an oak-bole hollowed out for this purpose and buried deep in the earth, sixteen feet or more down, for the burial of so great a Prince, hurried no doubt rather than performed with due pomp and ceremony, as this period of pressing disturbance made only too necessary.

When the body was discovered from the indications provided by King Henry, the Abbot whom I have named had a splendid marble tomb built for it, as was only proper for so distinguished a ruler of the area, who, moreover, had shown more favour to this church than to any other in his kingdom, and had endowed it with wide and extensive lands. By the judgement of God, which is always just and which in this case was certainly not unjustified, who rewards all good deeds not only in Heaven above but on this earth and in our terrestrial life ..., church ... others of his kingdom ... the genuine [remains] and the body ... of Arthur to be buried in a seemly fashion ... and gloriously ... and ... inhumed.

The Journey Through Wales (Itinerarium Kambriae) *and* The Description of Wales (Descriptio Kambriae) (c. 1191)

Gerald reports a local Welsh legend which associates a pair of mountain peaks resembling a throne as being King Arthur's 'Chair'. In fact, there are numerous places in Wales and throughout Britain connected with Arthur.

The Description of Wales

Except to the north, the region is sheltered on all sides by lofty mountains: to the west by Cantref Bychan; to the south by a range of hills the chief of which is Cadair Arthur, or Arthur's Chair, so called from two peaks which rise up in the form of a throne.[162] This summit is a very lofty spot and most difficult of access, so that in the minds of simple folk it is thought to have belonged to Arthur, the greatest and most distinguished King of the Britons.

GERVASE OF TILBURY, Imperial Leisure (Otia Imperialia) (c. 1211)

Of English birth, Gervase of Tilbury is believed to have lived from about 1150 to 1220. He lectured in canon law at Bologna, composing Imperial Leisure *for the entertainment of the German emperor, Otto IV. In the first extract, Gervase refers briefly to the tradition of Avalon and Arthur's return. The second deals with a reported sighting of Arthur still being alive, but for some inexplicable reason living on Mount Etna in Sicily rather than in Britain![163] It also records the existence of local legends in Britain and Brittany that Arthur goes hunting by moonlight with his followers.*

Arthur was mortally wounded, although he had destroyed all his enemies. After this, according to a popular British tradition, he was carried off to the Isle of Avalon to be healed of his wounds, which break open again every year, by Morgan the fairy's restorative cure. The British foolishly believe that he will return to his kingdom after a period of time.

Mount Etna is in Sicily ... The common people call this mountain Mongibel. The locals report that in our time the great Arthur has appeared in this deserted place. For, one day, one of the bishop of Catania's grooms had gone there in search of a horse which had thrown him and galloped off. Pursuing the animal through difficult and dangerous parts of the mountain without success, the groom became increasingly fearful as darkness fell. What more? The boy found a very narrow path through a cleft in the rock; entering, he came upon a spacious plain full of all kinds of delights, where in a palace constructed with marvellous workmanship he found Arthur reclining on a royal couch.

When he had recounted how he had found the place, and the reason for his journey was known, the bishop's horse was returned to him immediately. Arthur asked him to commend him to his master, adding that since ancient times he had resided there; he had been ill for a long time, since every year the wounds reopened which he had received in the war against his nephew Mordred and Childric, the leader of the Saxons.

Indeed, as I have heard from local accounts which provide evidence that he is still alive, there are many records of sightings and fabulous stories reported. Similar stories are told also of the woods of both Greater and Lesser Britain, according to the accounts of guards, called 'foresters' by the common people, who protect the royal animals. On certain days at about noon, and in the first silence of night, at the time of full moon, frequently a large group of knights is seen hunting with dogs, and hunting horns are heard; the foresters swear that these are the followers and household of Arthur.

CAESARIUS OF HEISTERBACH, Dialogue of Miracles (Dialogus Miraculorum) (c. 1240)

This brief story, like the earlier one by Gervase of Tilbury, is also set in Sicily and involves a lost horse. According to the old man in the story, Arthur lives on a Mount Gyber.

At the time when the Emperor Henry was subduing Sicily, there was a certain Decanus, a German as I believe, in the church of Palermo. One day, when Decanus had lost his best palfrey, he sent his servant to many places in search of it. An old man whom the servant met asked him, 'Where are you going, and what are you looking for?' He replied, 'I'm looking for my master's horse.' The man told him, 'I know where it is.' He asked, 'And where is it?' The man replied, 'On Mount Gyber: my lord King Arthur has the horse there. This same mountain emits flames, like Vulcan.' He continued, instructing the servant, who was dumbfounded by his words, 'Tell your master that he should go there to Arthur's solemn court in a fortnight. However, if you omit to inform him, you will be punished severely.' The servant returned, and related what he had heard to his master, but in some trepidation. Decanus, hearing that he had been invited to Arthur's court, and ridiculing it, fell ill and died on the day appointed. This account was told to us by Godescalcus, canon of Bonn, who said that he was there at that same time.

ÉTIENNE DE BOURBON, Treatise on Various Prophetic Matters (Tractatus de diversis materiis praedicabilibus) (1251–60)

This story about a peasant and a succubus uses the familiar themes of Arthur's nocturnal hunting-party and splendid palace as background to a short moral tale.

On occasions, demons enjoy changing their appearance into the likeness of knights hunting or amusing themselves, who commonly claim to belong to the household of Alcuin[164] or Arthur. I have heard that, when a certain peasant was carrying a bundle of sticks around Mount Catum by moonlight, he saw an immense number of hunting dogs as if they were barking after their prey, followed by a considerable body of men on foot and horseback. When the peasant asked one of them who they were, he replied that they were members of King Arthur's household, to whose nearby court they were going, and he would be welcome there.

Then it seemed to this peasant that he followed them, and that he entered into a large and most noble palace and saw knights and ladies playing and dancing, eating and drinking from splendid vessels;

finally, he was told to go to bed, and he was led into a chamber to a most elaborately ornamented bed, in which a certain lady of extremely beautiful appearance was lying. After he had got into the bed and fallen asleep, he found himself, when woken up in the morning, lying shamefully playing with himself on a pile of sticks.

MATTHEW PARIS, History of the English (Historia Anglorum) (c. 1253)

The 'Round Table' described here by Matthew Paris denotes a kind of violent tournament. Although the precise details are unclear, there is an intentional imitation of Arthurian custom.

In 1252 the knights of England, in order to test their strength and skill in military exercise, decided to try their manhood, not in the usual spear contest called a tournament, but rather in that military sport called a Round Table. When two of the finest knights, namely Arnald de Muntein and Roger de Lemburne, charged each other with lances, Arnald was mortally wounded, falling headlong to his death. It was believed that he was second to none in military prowess in England.

The Song of the Welsh (thirteenth century)

This Latin poem probably dates from the reign of Henry III (1216–72). The reference to mutual slaughter among the 'Saxons' (or English) suggests that it might have been written during or shortly after the Baronial War of 1263–5, when Simon de Montfort led a rebellion against the king. De Montfort won the battle of Lewis (14 May 1264), but was defeated in a bloody encounter at Evesham (4 August 1265).[165] At a meeting in Shrewsbury, in 1267, Llywelyn the Great desired recognition of his title as prince of all Wales, and the retention of the lands he had conquered during the Baronial War. This was confirmed in the treaty of Montgomery, 29 September 1267. Perhaps for 'Britons' one should understand the 'Bretons' of Brittany.

The Cambrians (i.e. Welsh), who are used to slaying the Saxons, salute their relations the Britons and Cornishmen; they require them to come with their sharp swords to conquer their Saxon enemies. Come now, vigorously, armed with coats of mail; a great part of the Saxons are fallen in mutual slaughter, the remainder shall be slain by us: now is the time to show of what blood you are sprung. The soothsayer Merlin never said a thing that was vain; he foretold that the mad people should be expelled. However, you do not keep this wise counsel; observe deceitful people of whom the whole race is accursed. If our valiant predecessor, King Arthur, had been now alive, I am sure not one of the Saxon walls would have resisted him; he would have been hard to them, in spite of their prayers, as they have deserved. May the Omnipotent procure him a successor only similar to him, I would not desire a better, who may deliver the Britons from their old grievances, and restore to them their country and their country's glory. May it please the uncle of Arthur to obtain this for us, a certain very great saint, to send the Englishman over the sea; we know that his festival is approaching on the kalends of March (St David's Day), may he make it his study to recall the Britons to their native land. Sons imitate their virtuous fathers, so let the Britons take Arthur as their example in valour; they show from what a good and brave man they are descended; as Arthur was, so let them be, conquerors! The Roman power reigned at Paris, the bold giant Frollo, with the bearish mind; him Arthur slew; every person of good faith believes it: witness the tent and the Parisian island. He is a madman who kills the noble Britons: it seems that he holds them thus hated; for he invidiously proclaims that hateful always and incessantly, who he hears are victorious. Of this nation there have been four great commanders, Arthur and Broinsius, powerful warriors; Constantine and Brennius, more powerful, if it were possible; these held the monarchy by reason of their being the best.

The Waverly Annals (Annales de Waverleia) (c. 1278–84)

This work provides a brief account of Edward I's exhumation of Arthur's bones at Glastonbury and the surrender, by the defeated Welsh, of a crown and other regalia which they believed had belonged to Arthur. The Annals *also describe a Round Table held by Edward I in imitation of Arthur.*

In 1278, at Easter, King Edward I and the queen went to Glastonbury, where the king had the tomb of Arthur opened and the bones taken out and examined, and honourably deposited in the treasury of the monastery; and it can be said with certainty that the bones were placed there.

In 1283 the crown of the famous King Arthur, which had been kept by the Welsh for a long time in great honour, together with other precious jewels, was presented to our lord the king; and thus the spoils of the Welsh were transferred, albeit unwillingly, to the English.

In 1284, about the feast of the Blessed Peter ad Vincula (1 August), the earls, barons and knights of the kingdom of England, and even a large number of notable people from overseas, assembled to hold a Round Table at Nevin near Snowdon: celebrated with dances and jousts enjoyed in turn, as a symbol of triumph over the insolence of the lightly armed Welsh.

ADAM OF DOMERHAM, History of the Affairs of Glastonbury (Historia de Rebis Gestis Glastoniensibus) (c. 1278–91)

Although writing about a hundred years after the initial exhumation of the bodies of Arthur and Guenevere, during the reign of Edward I (1272–1307), Adam of Domerham provides some details absent from contemporary accounts by Ralph de Coggeshall and Gerald of Wales, notably the fact that curtains were placed around the area being dug. Being a monk of the abbey, perhaps Domerham had access to an earlier account of the 'discovery' which is now lost. He also provides another account of Edward's visit to Glastonbury and the (recent) second exhumation.

King Richard I . . . confirmed Henry de Soliac, prior of Bermundsey, as abbot [of Glastonbury], a man of royal descent . . . Henry, frequently warned to speak decently of the famous King Arthur (for Arthur's body had rested, beside the old church, between two stone pyramids which were nobly inscribed, for six hundred and forty-eight years), ordered on a certain day for the place to be surrounded by curtains and to be dug ... Therefore the abbot and those assembled, lifting up their remains [i.e. those of Arthur and Guenevere], carried them into the larger church with rejoicing, placing them in a mausoleum with a noble inscription divided into two parts: for the king's body was placed by itself at the head of the tomb, and the queen at his feet, on the east part, where they have rested magnificently up to the present day. This is the epitaph inscribed on the tomb:

> Here lies Arthur, flower of kings, of glorious reign,
> Whose manners and integrity deserve eternal praise.
> Here lies the second wife of Arthur,
> Whose virtue deserves a rich heavenly reward.

AD 1277–8

Lord Edward I, famous king of England, together with his wife, Lady Eleanor, came to Glastonbury to celebrate Easter ... On the following Tuesday ... at twilight, the lord king had the tomb of the famous King Arthur opened. There, in two caskets with their images and arms depicted on them, were found, separately, the bones of the said king, of wondrous size, and those of Queen Guenevere of marvellous beauty. The image of the queen was clearly crowned, while the crown had fallen from the image of the king, which displayed the loss of his left ear, and the traces of the wounds from which he had died.

Also writing was found over both of them. On the following morning, that is the Wednesday, the lord king wrapped King Arthur's bones in precious silk, while the queen wrapped those of Queen Guenevere, and, replacing them in their coffins, they affixed their seals and ordered that the coffins should be swiftly relocated before the high altar, leaving the skulls of both of them outside on account of popular devotion.

WALTER OF COVENTRY, The Historical Collections of Walter of Coventry (Memoriale Fratris Walteri de Coventria) (c. 1293–1307)

The Historical Collections is a compilation of history, extending from the arrival of Brutus to the year 1225, and considered to be most valuable for the early thirteenth century. Although Walter of

Coventry's account of Arthur's life is derived from Geoffrey of Monmouth, he transfers the site of the famous Pentecostal feast to Karnarvan (Caernarfon), presumably in honour of Edward I (1272–1307), who started to build the castle there in 1283 after his victory over the Welsh. The town grew from that date. Previously there had been a Roman settlement at nearby Segontium. In the following extract Richard I gives Arthur's sword, Caliburn, to Tancred of Sicily in March 1191 in exchange for military equipment.

On the fourth day, the king of Sicily sent many great gifts in both gold and silver, as well as horses and silk garments, to the English king; but he received nothing in return except a little ring, which he accepted as a token of mutual friendship. Moreover, the king of England gave to King Tancred an excellent sword called Caliburn, formerly belonging to King Arthur of England. Then Tancred gave to the King of England four great ships, called 'Ursers', and fifteen galleys.

PIERRE DE LANGTOFT, Chronicle
(early fourteenth century)

Pierre de Langtoft, a canon of Bridlington in Yorkshire writing in the early fourteenth century, devotes the first volume of his Chronicle to the Brut story, emphasizing the role of Arthur.[166] Langtoft also describes, in his second volume, how Edward I utilized Geoffrey of Monmouth's account of Merlin's prophecies and Arthur's legendary conquest of numerous kingdoms to claim a right to the crown of Scotland, where he set up John Baliol as a figurehead king. This is also reported in other contemporary chronicles, where Edward's letter to the Pope is sometimes quoted.[167]

Of the Union of England and Scotland

Ah, God! how often Merlin said truth
In his prophecies, if you read them!
Now are the two waters united in one,
Which have been separated by great mountains;
And one realm made of two different kingdoms

Which used to be governed by two kings.
Now are the islanders all joined together,
And Albany reunited to the royalties
Of which King Edward is proclaimed lord.
Cornwall and Wales are in his power,
And Ireland the great at his will.
There is neither king nor prince of all the countries
Except King Edward, who has thus united them;
Arthur had never the fiefs so fully.
Henceforward there is nothing to do but provide his expedition
Against the King of France, to conquer his inheritances,
And then bear the cross where Jesus Christ was born.

With the subjugation of Scotland achieved, Edward set his sights on continental territory, and again Arthur provided a noble precedent. Arthur's supposed continental possessions were used by Edward I as a justification for present-day English ownership.

While the king and his counsellors
Were in debate with the clergy,
Count William of Flanders has sent messengers,
The lord of Blancmount, a prudent and bold knight,
And the lord of Kew, and the treasurer,
Receiver of Flanders, who will willingly
Make entire friends of the English and Flemings,
That in one land and the other, on all coasts,
The merchants may in good love and peace
Arrive with their wares, and sell for money.
And when King Edward shall raise his banners,
The count and his Flemings shall be his allies
Against King Philip and against the twelve peers,
Who wrongfully hold from him the land with the manors
Which King Arthur to the duke Sir Beduer
Gave in Aquitaine, as to his butler;
Which King Edward and King Henry his father,
And all their ancestors, held hitherto.
The gentle count of Henault, with all the Henaulters,
The duke John of Brabant, and his Hollanders,
Have by the count of Flanders and his knights
Confirmed the alliance as his dear friends.

Edward I's failure in France is attributed by Langtoft to his frugality, which is then compared unfavourably with Arthur's largesse.

King Edward, I tell you, would have gained a great advantage,
If he had had his earls then and there.
Listen to the fault in which all the sin lay.

An Example of the Noble King Sir Arthur

In ancient histories we find written
What kings and what kingdoms king Arthur conquered,
And how he shared largely his gain.
There was not a king under him who contradicted him,
Earl, duke, or baron, who ever failed him
In war or in battle, but each followed him.
The king sir Edward has given too little;
Whereby at his departure, when he put to sea
Against the king of France, the affront was shown him
That not one of his earls undertook the expedition.
The commonalty of Scotland hears the news,
Each on his own part rejoices over it.
The rabble of the lower people resumed war anew;
The earl and the baron suffered by dissimulation
That William Wallace made himself their chieftain
By false pretence, which none understood.
That he sought to raise himself up a great man of Scotland.
The Wallace immediately assaulted the castles
Through the land of Scotland, and took them from the English.

Like his ancestors, Edward I fails to live up to the example of Arthur.

Idleness and feigned delay, and long morning's sleep,
Delight in luxury, and surfeit in the evenings,
Trust in felons, compassion for enemies,
Self-will in act and counsel,
To retain conquest without giving distributions of gain,
Overthrew the Britons in old times.
We may take example of Arthur the wise;
He was always the first in all his expeditions

In morning and in evening, with great magnanimity;
Felons in company, and hostile people,
According to their desert, he condemned them all.
He was temperate in deed and in counsel;
A prince more courteous in conquering lands
Was never born among Christians.
Wherefore I tell you, listen to the reason,
If our king had performed the perambulations
Through England, as he had granted
And strengthened by writing, as is well witnessed,
And of the land of Scotland had shared and given
To his English barons, by just quantities,
The land over there would have been in his power,
And his men heritors of it for ever.

*Edward I's 1306 feast was considered to be the most splendid since
the time of King Arthur.*

Anno Domini 1306

After the festival of Easter in the year here named,
King Edward has proclaimed his feast of Whitsuntide
To be held at Westminster with clergy and with barons,
Where, with great nobleness, to his eldest son,
Edward prince of Wales, he has given arms.
Three hundred knights of account in truth
Were dubbed at the cost of King Edward.
Several of the most noble were married on that occasion.
The earl of Warenne, with his newly received title,
Espoused the daughter of the count de Barre.
The earl of Arundel, in possession of his fees,
Took there the damsel whose father was named
William de Warenne, who had departed to God.
Sir Hugh son of Hugh, called Despenser,
Took there the maiden of noble kindred,
Whom Gilbert de Clare had begotten
On Joan the countess surnamed of Acres.
No soul wonders there was game and joy enough,
Where a feast was held with such ceremonies.
Never in Britain, since God was born,
Was there such nobleness in towns nor in cities,

Except Caerleon in ancient times,
When sir Arthur the king was crowned there.
The prince, whom God preserve! of whom we have spoken,
After the said feast has taken his leave
With joyous company, and gone towards the north.

On his death, Edward I is once more compared with Arthur.

Of the Death of the Illustrious King Edward

Belinus and Brennius, Britons in their pride,
Took Rome by force, and put a truce upon it;
King Arthur afterwards, without wound and without blemish,
Conquered all France, and took possession as his own.
Gawain and Angusele, of his nourishing,
In wars and battles used to follow Arthur.
One must well, among kings who have reigned since that time,
Speak of King Edward and of his memory
As of the most renowned combatant on steed.
Since the time of Adam never was any time
That prince for nobility, or baron for splendour,
Or merchant for wealth, or clerk for learning,
By art or by genius could escape death.
Of chivalry, after King Arthur,
Was King Edward the flower of Christendom.
He was so handsome and great, so powerful in arms,
That of him may one speak as long as the world lasts.
For he had no equal as a knight in armour
For vigour and valour, neither present nor future.

WILLIAM RISHANGER, Chronicles *(Chronica)* (c. 1300–27)

Roger Mortimer holds a splendid 'Round Table' tournament at his castle of Kenilworth in imitation of King Arthur.

AD 1279 The famous knight, Roger de Mortimer held a military game at Kenilworth, which was called a 'Round Table'; it involved a hundred knights and as many ladies, and to which numerous knights flocked from various kingdoms for the exercise of arms.

MONK OF MALMESBURY, The Life of Edward II (Vita Edwardi Secundi) (c. 1325)

Despite the 'discovery' of Arthur's body at Glastonbury more than a hundred years before, the Welsh continue to believe in Merlin's prophecy of Arthur's return.

AD 1315 Furthermore, on account of Merlin's prophecy, the Welsh believe that they will recover England. This is a frequent cause of their rebellion, since they wish to fulfil the prophecy; however, since they are ignorant of the right time, they are often deceived, and labour in vain.

RANULPH HIGDEN, Polychronicon (1327–42)

Because continental writers are silent about the famous exploits attributed to Arthur by Geoffrey of Monmouth, Higden, despite devoting a reasonable amount of attention to Arthur's reign in his work, is rather dubious about the accuracy of this information. His translator, Trevisa, believes this viewpoint, first expounded by William of Newburgh,[168] is unproven and maintains that, just as St John's gospel contains material absent from those of the other apostles, so Geoffrey of Monmouth records information disregarded by other historians.

Since Geoffrey [of Monmouth] is the only writer to extol Arthur, many have wondered how it is possible to learn the truth about what is said about him, because if Arthur (as Geoffrey writes) had acquired thirty kingdoms, if he had conquered the kingdom of the Franks, and killed Lucius procurator of the republic in Italy, why do all Roman, French and German historians utterly fail to mention such a man, while recording the minor deeds of lesser men?

Geoffrey relates how his Arthur overcame Frollo, king of France, and yet no mention of Frollo is found in French records. Also he says that Arthur killed Lucius Hiberius, procurator of the [Roman] republic in the time of the Emperor Leo, although among all the Roman histories there is no mention of any Procurator Lucius at that time, while this Arthur neither ruled, nor was even born in the time of Leo, but during Justinian's reign, who was the fifth emperor after Leo.[169] Moreover, Geoffrey asserts that he finds it astonishing that Gildas and Bede make no mention of Arthur in their accounts; but I find it quite incredible that Geoffrey himself should glorify such a man, whom all ancient, true and famous histories leave almost untouched; but it is the custom of every nation to extol someone of their own country with excessive praise: thus the Greeks celebrate their Alexander, the Romans their Octavian, the English their Richard, the French their Charlemagne, and the British their Arthur.

ADAM OF MURIMUTH, Continuation of the Chronicles (Continuatio Chronicarum) (1338–47)

Adam of Murimuth describes Edward III's foundation of a Round Table fellowship at Windsor Castle in January 1344, and the king's decision to build a Round Table in imitation of King Arthur. He relates how the enterprise was later abandoned for 'certain reasons', but does not specify what they were. Instead, Edward established the Order of the Garter.

On the Thursday following this tourney (in which King Edward III had led nineteen of his household knights against all comers), the lord king gave a great feast at which he founded his Round Table, and several earls, barons and knights swore oaths that they wished to be received into this Round Table fellowship, under the rules which pertained to the said Round Table. Then the king ordained a day to celebrate the Round Table at the forthcoming Pentecost feast, and he gave permission for everyone present to return home, thanking them for their services.

The king later ordered that a noble edifice should be built to house the aforesaid Round Table and form the fellowship's meeting-place; to achieve this, he ordered the organization of stonemasons, carpenters and other workmen, and the provision of sufficient wood and stone, sparing no labour or expense. The work was later abandoned for certain reasons.

This slightly different account of the same event occurs in Cotton MS Nero D.x.

At Windsor Castle ... the lord king made a solemn vow on sacred relics that he would within a certain time, if his health lasted, establish a Round Table on the model and according to the custom and rule which the Lord Arthur, once King of England, had set down – that is to the number of three hundred knights – and he (Edward) would foster and maintain the Table-fellowship with the same number.

JEAN LE BEL, Chronicle *(Chronique)* *(mid-fourteenth century)*

The French chronicler Jean le Bel indicates that the English King Edward III wished to associate himself with Arthur. Describing Edward on his return to England after a successful Scottish campaign, le Bel relates that 'everyone said that he was a second King Arthur' (Chronicle I, p. 119). He describes the 1344 Windsor Feast as 'made in the style of the Round Table' (Chronicle II, pp. 34–5), and he reports Edward III's wish to restore Windsor Castle in 1344 (Chronicle II, p. 26).

When he had returned to England, he decided out of the nobleness of his heart to restore the castle of Windsor, which King Arthur had built, and where he had originally established the Round Table.

JEAN FROISSART, Chronicles *(Chroniques)* *(after 1377)*

Another French chronicler to make Arthurian comparisons with the contemporary English monarchy is Jean Froissart, who compares Edward III's queen, his compatriot Philippa of Hainault, to

Guenevere on her arrival in England in 1327 (Chronicles II, p. 196). Later, in his discussion of Edward III's reign after the king's death, Froissart recalls the following:

There was never anyone his equal since the time of King Arthur, who was formerly King of England, which was called Great Britain in his time.

APPENDIX: ARTHURIAN COURTS

In Arthurian literature, feasts frequently play a crucial role in the structure of a work and are sometimes described in elaborate detail. The main reason for this emphasis on feasting is to stress the importance of feudal relationships and loyalties in the Arthurian world; this explains the concentration on the details of those attending and the protocol observed at them.

Medieval kings, eager to expand the image of their power and maintain control over unruly magnates, held regular courts at Christmas, Easter and Pentecost. Arthur's great feasts, like those of later rulers contemporary with the writers in this anthology, are held at regular intervals and are attended by his important vassals. They are intended to enhance Arthur's prestige and renown, providing both potential allies and enemies with lavish displays of regal power and wealth. Arthur's large-scale banquets are generally connected with the major religious festivals of Christmas, Easter, Ascension, Pentecost and All Saints, but are also held to celebrate other important occasions, such as coronations and important marriages. The writers of Arthurian literature have credited Arthur with the historical practice of Crown-Wearing at official banquets, a custom which was already well established before the Norman Conquest. The king wears his crown at these high feasts, in the presence of all his barons, bishops and knights who have been summoned to witness the monarch's majesty, munificence and authority.

While Geoffrey of Monmouth depicts the Pentecostal feast at Caerleon and that of Christmas at York, later writers frequently visualize celebrations at many other sites, depicting the peripatetic nature of the Arthurian court. The interesting choice of settings for Arthur's courts made by different authors may perhaps be utilized to indicate relationships existing between different texts.

Since the Roman city of Caerleon quickly fell into disuse after the departure of the legions in the fifth century, Geoffrey of Monmouth's employment of this place as Arthur's principal seat was presumably intended to recall this earlier period. Its retention by later writers probably suggests their indebtedness to Geoffrey's *History of the*

Kings of Britain for this traditional association of Caerleon with Arthurian festivity.

References to 'Carduel' are generally considered to represent Carlisle, formerly a major Roman town called Luguvallium. The city regained prominence at the end of the thirteenth century when Edward I used it as a base for his invasion of Scotland. Carlisle is first specifically named as the location of Arthur's court in *Landavall*,[170] an English version of Marie de France's *Lanval*, which probably predates 1337. Later fourteenth-century English poets frequently refer to Carlisle in association with Arthur. *Sir Gawain and the Green Knight* depicts the Christmas feast at the legendary Camelot, suggesting the poet's knowledge of French texts such as *The Prose Lancelot*. However, the location of Arthur's court in the *Green Knight* (a later version of this poem) is transferred to Carlisle, which also serves as the base for Arthur's hunting interludes in *The Anturs of Arther, The Avowing of King Arthur* and *Syre Gawene and the Carle of Carelyle*.

Advent

CARDUEL   *The Prose Lancelot* (p. 275)

Christmas

CAERLEON   Pseudo William of Malmesbury, *Concerning the Ancient Church of Glastonbury* (p. 240)
CAMELOT   *Sir Gawain and the Green Knight*, l. 37 (p. 439);
CARDUEL   *Meraugis de Portlesguez*, ll. 843–4 (p. 234)
CARLISLE   The Alliterative *Morte Arthure*, l. 64 (p. 99)
LONDON   Lawman, *Brut*, ll. 11345–52 (p. 73)
TINTAGEL   Heinrich von dem Türlin, *The Crown* (p. 385)
YORK   Geoffrey of Monmouth, *History of the Kings of Britain* (p. 36)

Easter

CAERLEON   *My Lord Gawain, or the Avenging of Raguidel* (p. 221)
CARDIGAN   *Erec and Enide* (p. 141)

Ascension

CAMELOT   Chrétien de Troyes, *Lancelot* (p. 157)

Pentecost

CAERLEON   Wace, *Brut*, ll. 1663–97 (p. 53); Robert Biket, *The Lay of the Horn* (p. 211); Robert Mannyng of Brunne, *Chronicle* (p. 85); Jehan, *The Marvels of Rigomer*, l. 1ff. (p. 366); Robert of Gloucester, l. 3882 (p. 79); Malory, *The Works* (p. 499)

CAMELOT	*The Knight of the Parrot* (p. 369); *The Grail Quest* (p. 286)
CANTERBURY	*Meraugis de Portlesguez* (p. 238)
CARDIGAN	*Claris and Laris*, ll. 6041–341 (p. 353)
CARDUEL	*The Knight With Two Swords*, ll. 1–65 (p. 317); Manessier (p. 187); *Didot Perceval*, Ms.D. l. 1697 (p. 189); *Yvain, or the Knight of the Lion*, ll. 5–13 (p. 160)
KARNARVAN (CAERNAVAN)	Walter of Coventry, *The Historical Collections*
KYNKE KENADONNE	Malory, *The Works* (p. 490)
LONDON	*Huth Merlin* (p. 268)
ORGUENIE (ORKNEY)	*The First Perceval Continuation* (p. 171)
PONTEFRACT	*Yder*, l. 57 (p. 242)

St John

CAERLEON	Gerbert de Montreuil, *Perceval Continuation*, ll. 1333–62 (p. 183)
CAMELOT	*The Prose Lancelot* (p. 283)
CARDIGAN	*The Second Perceval Continuation*, ll. 28520–78 (p. 177); *Escanor* (p. 360)
LONDON	Robert de Blois, *Biausdous*, l. 4595 (p. 351)

Assumption

LONDON	*The Story of Merlin* (p. 272)

Unspecified Dates

CAMELOT	*Huth Merlin* (p. 268); *The Romance of Laurin*, l. 13034 (p. 334); *Huth Merlin* (Arthur's Wedding, p. 265)
CARDIGAN	*Claris and Laris*, ll. 6094, 14090 (pp. 353, 358)
CARDUEL	*Fergus of Galloway*, l. 715 (p. 248)
CAERLEON	*Perceval*, ll. 4003, 4606 (pp. 162, 169); *The Romance of Hunbaut*, ll. 46–201 (p. 332); Pierre de Langtoft, *Chronicle* (p. 533)
CARLISLE	*The Parlement of the Thre Ages*, l. 467 (p. 126); *The Anturs of Arther*, ll. 689–90 (p. 437); *The Avowing of King Arthur*, l. 29 (p. 466)
GLASTONBURY	*Lybeaus Desconus*, ll. 41–2 (p. 397)
LOGRES (LONDON)	*The Book of Arthur* (p. 298); Robert de Blois, *Biausdous* (p. 351)
MONTAGU	Robert de Blois, *Biausdous*, l. 3370 (p. 347)
MOUNT GYBER	Caesarius of Heisterbach, *Dialogue of Miracles* (p. 525)

WINCHESTER   Chrétien de Troyes, *Cligés* (p. 147); *The Romance of Laurin*, ll. 10868ff. (p. 334)
CIRENCESTER   Robert of Gloucester, *Chronicle*, l. 9740 (p. 82)
KELLIWIG   'Culhwch and Olwen' (p. 7)

NOTES

1. **(p. 6):** In the mid-twelfth-century manuscript edited by J. Williams, Rolls Society (London, 1860), p. 4, the battle of Badon takes place in AD 518, and the battle of Camlann in AD 539. These dates are only conjectural, and other dates have been proposed: for example, 490 and 511 respectively by L. D. Alcock, *Arthur's Britain: History and Archaeology* (London and New York: 1971), p. 55.

2. **(p. 6):** In fact, Arthur may have had the cross on his shield rather than on his shoulder, since the Old Welsh words for shoulder (*scuid*) and shield (*scuit*) are very similar, and the word *scuit* may have been mistaken for *scuid* when being translated into Latin. Alternatively, the 'cross' may have been a small relic, perhaps only a chip of wood (see Alcock, *Arthur's Britain*, p. 52).

3. **(p. 6):** The battle of Camlann is mentioned also in a Welsh bardic elegy on Llewelyn ap Gruffudd, *Gruffudd ab yr Ynad Coch*, written in 1282.

4. **(p. 7):** See the 1993 Everyman edition, trans. Jones and Jones for a discussion of the date.

5. **(p. 7):** See D. D. R. Owen's introduction to the 1993 Everyman edition of Chrétien de Troyes's *Arthurian Romances*, p. xvi, for a brief discussion of this problem.

6. **(p. 15):** It was customary in the early Middle Ages to receive such compensation for slain men.

7. **(p. 16):** A short passage on what later happened to St Cadoc is omitted.

8. **(p. 16):** Although the Latin word *serpens* is used in the text, rather than *draco* (which can mean either 'serpent' or 'dragon'), since the monster has wings and claws it is obviously a dragon.

9. **(p. 19):** For further information on Gildas and *The Life of Gildas*, the reader might like to refer to H. Marsh, *Dark Age Britain* (Newton Abbot: David and Charles, 1970), pp. 36ff.

10. **(p. 19):** This island is probably either Anglesey or the Isle of Man, both known as *Mona* in Latin, although *Minau* is the word found in the text.

11. **(p. 20):** The Latin word *vitro* (*vitrum, -i*) can mean 'woad' as well as 'glass'.

12. (p. 20): The marshy land around Glastonbury is still prone to flooding; in Arthur's time, Glastonbury may have been an island.

13. (p. 21): See the extract on Caradoc of Llancarfan's *Life of St Gildas*, where Gildas appears to forgive Arthur, pp. 19–20.

14. (p. 25): See pp. 14–19 of the introduction to the Penguin edition of Geoffrey of Monmouth's *History of the Kings of Britain*, trans. Thorpe, for a discussion of the problem of his sources.

15. (p. 26): See also Malory's later version.

16. (p. 26): See also Lawman's *Brut* for another account of the Saxon war, Mannyng's *Chronicle* and Malory's *Le Morte d'Arthur* for Arthur's coronation, and *Of Arthour and of Merlin* for a further description of Arthur's marriage.

17. (p. 26): It is during this period of peace that many of the Arthurian stories of romance and chivalry are set. In some manuscripts, Chrétien de Troyes's romances are inserted at this point in Wace's *Brut*.

18. (p. 26): See Geoffrey of Monmouth, *History of the Kings of Britain*, Book IX, Chapter 13; Wace retains Geoffrey's separate dining-custom but hints disapproval (ll. 1909–12). There is some historical evidence that such a custom was practised in Anglo-Saxon England. At Edgar's coronation at Bath Abbey in 973, his queen feasted separately, acting as hostess to abbots, abbesses and bishops. A similar feast is recorded at the marriage and coronation of Edith to Edward the Confessor in 1045 (*Vita St Oswaldi*, I, 438).

19. (p. 26): See the alliterative *Morte Arthure* (pp. 96–114).

20. (p. 26): See Mannyng (pp. 85–96).

21. (p. 27): See the French *Mort Artu* (*The Death of Arthur*) for a brief account of the war against the Romans. The 'Wheel of Fortune' episode in the alliterative *Morte Arthure* occurs shortly after Arthur's victory, while he is invading Italy.

22. (p. 27): See also Jehan de Waurin, and versions in *The True History of Arthur's Death*, *The Parlement of the Three Ages* and the stanzaic *Morte Arthur*.

23. (p. 40): In his *Ecclesiastical History*, Book I, Chapter 15 (AD 731), Bede gives a brief mention of the battles of Mount Badon but makes no reference to Arthur.

24. (p. 60): See the introduction to R. Allen's Everyman translation (London: 1992), especially pp. xx–xxvi, xxxii–xxxiv.

25. (p. 73): This is the only mention of Argante. In other versions of this legend it is the sorceress Morgan le Fay, Arthur's half-sister, who heals him of his wounds.

26. (p. 78): Paneter (pantler) is not quite as important a figure as a

'steward', Kay's usual office. For details of the office of pantler see John Russell's *Boke of Nurture* (Harl. Ms. 4011) in *The Babees Boke*, ed. F. J. Furnivall, Early English Texts Society 32 (1868), pp. 66–9, 120.

27. (p. 79): The twelve companions: originally referring to Roland, Oliver and their companions in *Chanson de Roland* and the French Charlemagne romances, this term was sometimes adopted into Arthurian literature to describe the Round Table companions. (See also Andrew of Wynton, *Chronicle*, l. 4336.)

28. (p. 82): A performer of deeds of prowess.

29. (p. 85): See above, p. 37; Mannyng's version is, in fact, a translation of Wace.

30. (p. 85): i.e. tying ropes to the banks.

31. (p. 85): i.e. setting bowlines on bowsprits.

32. (p. 85): *wale*: horizontal timber round the top of the sides of a boat.

33. (p. 86): i.e. to get the men and horses on board.

34. (p. 90): *what wiltow her?* = what do you want here?

35. (p. 91): Alas that she was ever entrusted to me.

36. (p. 91): ... it is completely against my will.

37. (p. 91): I wish I were sunk in the earth.

38. (p. 93): If he hadn't been crafty and cunning.

39. (p. 95): He made them into a trimming for his cloak.

40. (p. 96): See L. D. Benson, 'The Date of the Alliterative *Morte Arthure*', *Mediaeval Studies Presented to L. H. Hornstein*, ed. J. B. Bessinger and R. K. Raymo (New York: New York University Press, 1976), pp. 19–40; *Morte Arthure*, ed. Mary Hamel (New York: 1984), p. 54; Juliet Vale, 'Law and Diplomacy in the Alliterative *Morte Arthure*', Nottingham Medieval Studies 23 (1979), p. 44.

41. (p. 96): W. Matthews, *The Tragedy of Arthur: A Study of the Alliterative Morte Arthure* (Berkeley: University of California Press, 1960); K. Göller, 'Reality versus Romance: A Reassessment of the Alliterative *Morte Arthure*', *Arthurian Studies II: The Alliterative Morte Arthure*, ed. K. Göller (Cambridge: D. S. Brewer, 1981).

42. (p. 96): John Finlayson, '*Morte Arthure*: the date and a source for contemporary references', *Speculum* 42 (1967), p. 638; G. R. Keiser, 'Edward III and the Alliterative *Morte Arthure*', *Speculum* 48 (1973), p. 45.

43. (p. 97): *Morte Arthure*, ed. Hamel, pp. 35–6.

44. (p. 97): See *Morte Arthure*, ed. J. Finlayson (London: 1967), pp. 18–19; Hamel (p. 332) suggests that Arthur's speech in ll. 2399–405 indicates deterioration in character.

45. (p. 97): See, for instance, l. 43, or l. 100, where Lucius's ambassador demands the reason for Arthur's aggression.

46. (p. 98): This poem is printed in *Political Poems and Songs Relating to English History, from the Accession of Edward III to the Reign of Henry VIII*, ed. T. Wright (London: Rolls Series, 1859–61), pp. 1–25.

47. (p. 126): From the Old French word *bliaut*, meaning a woman's long-sleeved garment. For other accounts of King Rion and his beard mantle, first mentioned by Geoffrey of Monmouth, see also the *Huth Merlin*, *Lestoire de Merlin* and *Le Chevalier as Deus Espees*, in which the young hero, later revealed as Meriadeuc, defeats Rion on Arthur's behalf.

48. (p. 126): Here the poet mistakes the Cornish island for that in France of the same name, and apparently believes that Arthur confronted a real dragon, not a dream one.

49. (p. 126): While all the men of Brittany bowed at his feet.

50. (p. 129): Usually considered to be Caerleon in South Wales, it could also be identified with Chester.

51. (p. 130): The whole of this opening section of Fordun's Chapter 25 is taken directly from Geoffrey of Monmouth's opening section on Arthur.

52. (p. 130): The principle of primogeniture was not established until the thirteenth century (see A. L. Poole, *From Domesday Book to Magna Carta 1087–1216* [Oxford: Clarendon Press, 1954], p. 2). For example, when Richard I died in 1199, he was succeeded by his brother, John, rather than his adolescent nephew, Arthur.

53. (p. 130): See Geoffrey of Monmouth, *History*, Bk IX, Ch. 11.

54. (p. 131): See G. Neilson, *Huchown of the Awle Ryale* (Glasgow: James Maclehose and Sons, 1902); more recent critics tend to doubt the existence of Huchon.

55. (p. 135): Would not give away a hair's breadth.

56. (p. 139): The praiseworthy few.

57. (p. 140): As he had deserved by his deeds.

58. (p. 156): In fact, medieval writers state that Arthur held his court in many different places: Caerleon, Carduel and Carlisle are all at least as common as Camelot. See the Appendix on Arthurian courts, pp. 539–42.

59. (p. 156): Guenevere rebukes Kay for his churlish reputation in Chrétien de Troyes's *Yvain*, although in *Lancelot* she treats him with more respect, probably due to Arthur's presence.

60. (p. 162): in the German *Diu Krône* (*The Crown*) by Heinrich von dem Türlin.

61. (p. 177): Giglain is the hero of a contemporary French poem,

The Fair Unknown; an extract from the Middle English version of this poem can be found pp. 396–403.

62. (p. 183): Perceval had broken Kay's arm when he had rudely interrupted his meditation on the drops of blood in the snow in Chrétien de Troyes's *Perceval*.

63. (p. 186): A reference to an episode in Chrétien de Troyes's *Erec and Enide*.

64. (p. 186): Gerbert's castigation of homosexuality at this point would probably be more appropriate to a sermon than a romance. This is a particularly rare topic in Arthurian literature, although there are numerous instances of close friendship between Arthurian knights, notably Gawain and his cousin Ywain, and physical contact between men appears to have been more socially acceptable than it is today.

65. (p. 188): The word *Didot* is the name of a fairly recent owner of MS D and has no connection with the romance itself. It is retained merely to distinguish the work from the various other Perceval texts.

66. (p. 191): This phrase reveals Elaine's desire that Perceval should become her knight and pay her love-service; the word 'might' indicates her uncertainty of his response.

67. (p. 191): It is customary in Arthurian literature for a knight to hang his shield outside his tent so that potential challengers could announce their desire to joust with him by striking it.

68. (p. 195): In this work Kay murders Loholt, the son of Arthur and Guenevere.

69. (p. 209): See *Two Old French Gauvain Romances*, ed. R. C. Johnston and D. D. R. Owen (Edinburgh: Scottish Academic Press, 1972).

70. (p. 211): *Le Mantel* can be found in *Romania*, ed. F. A. Wulff (1885), pp. 358–80. *The Boy and the Mantle* can be found in Thomas Percy, *Reliques of Ancient English Poetry* II (London: Everyman, 1906), p. 188.

71. (p. 211): Scribal Prologue, probably borrowed from the prologue of *Le Mantel Mautaillie* (see *Le Lai du Cor*, ed. C. T. Erickson [Oxford: 1973], p. 49n).

72. (p. 211): It is uncertain whether Biket intends Brittany or Britain here (see ibid., pp. 50–51nn.).

73. (p. 211): Perhaps Maundy Thursday, but here probably a day of general absolution immediately before Whit Sunday (see ibid., p. 51nn.).

74. (p. 212): *serreine*: Erickson (p. 53nn.) attests to the medieval French knowledge of these mythical enchantresses, first mentioned

in Homer's *Odyssey*, who lured sailors to their deaths with their beautiful singing.

75. (p. 212): Erickson (p. 53nn.) contrasts the messenger's simple attire with the rich robes of Arthur and the other kings.

76. (p. 213): Erickson (p. 55nn.) observes that Mangoun can be identified with Mangon, brother of the Fisher King in *Perlesvaus*, who also appears in other Arthurian stories, usually as an abductor of ladies. (See also R. S. Loomis, *Arthurian Tradition and Chrétien de Troyes* [New York: 1949], pp. 244–50.) Erickson (p. 5) associates the figure of Moraine with Morgan la Fay.

77. (p. 217): The use of this toast was, according to Geoffrey of Monmouth, Bk. VI, Ch. 12, already an established tradition in Britain when Vortigern was served a drink by Hengist's daughter, Rowena. 'Wassail' (from Old Norse *waes heill*), meaning 'be in good health', to which the reply was 'Drink heill', meaning 'I drink to your health'.

78. (p. 227): Usually a small landowner, a vavassor was a feudal tenant of slightly lower status than a knight. However, a vavassor could be quite a wealthy man and influential member of the community. Chaucer's Franklin, who is described as a vavassor, is a justice of the peace, a sheriff and a Member of Parliament.

79. (p. 232): Here the poet is making a pun, for the dwarf's name is derived merely from his love for the lady: the love (*drue*) of Ydain.

80. (p. 237): Gawain is often known as the *chevalier as damoiseles* (the ladies' knight) because of his special concern to protect their interests and fulfil their desires.

81. (p. 240): Ider (or Yder) appears in a number of Arthurian works, including the French romance *Yder*, of which he is the hero, where he undertakes a similar adventure against three giants.

82. (p. 241): See *Yder*, ed. and trans. A. Adams (Cambridge: 1983), p. 13.

83. (p. 248): The hunt for the white stag first occurs in Chrétien de Troyes's *Erec and Enide*, but reappears in a number of other works; the hunt in *Fergus of Galloway* is probably derived from an episode in *The Second Perceval Continuation*, where it is Perceval's hound who kills the stag. Guillaume le Clerc took material from a number of episodes in the *Perceval Continuations* for his *Fergus of Galloway* (see D. D. R. Owen's notes [Everyman, 1991], p. 115 and his Appendix, pp. 130–31).

84. (p. 248): The word 'Wales' here means the Dark Age British kingdom of Strathclyde (see *Fergus of Galloway*, trans. Owen, p. 117).

85. (p. 259): an official set over others.

86. (p. 263): For a full account of this story, see the Accalon episode, which is included in Malory's account, pp. 501–9.

87. (p. 266): This is related in detail in the *Prose Lancelot*.

88. (p. 268): Here the text is defective.

89. (p. 272): The Assumption of the Virgin Mary on 15 August.

90. (p. 275): Dante, *Inferno*, Canto V. Francesca da Rimini, d. 1285, slain by her husband Giovanni when discovered with his brother Paolo. According to Dante, when the lovers are reading the *Prose Lancelot* together, the description of the first kiss so inflamed them that they committed the sin which caused their discovery.

91. (p. 303): The French term 'a fine force' indicates that the duke held his followers back by the force of his personality.

92. (p. 307): The damsel is pleased that Arthur's complaint is nothing more serious. She may, perhaps, have been concerned that he might have received a wound in the fight against the brigands. Her later behaviour indicates that she finds him physically attractive.

93. (p. 310): This theme occurs elsewhere, in stories about Tristan and Lancelot.

94. (p. 313): This is an obscure reference which I have been unable to trace. In his edition of *Livre d'Artus* (*The Book of Arthur*) Sommers notes two references to a 'Land of Shepherds' (Terre des Pastures) p. 150, n. 3, where King Rion of Ireland claims to own it, and p. 246, l. 10.

95. (p. 314): The giant, like most of Arthur's enemies in this work, is identified as a Saxon.

96. (p. 317): In this poem he is called King Ris.

97. (p. 318): Baudemagus's kingdom of Gorre is the land to which Guenevere is abdicated in Chrétien de Troyes's *Lancelot*. The name 'Gorre' may be a corruption of Old French *Voirre* ('glass'), since Glastonbury, the place to which she is carried off in the *Life of St Gildas* (see above, pp. 19–21) was associated in that work with the City or Isle of Glass, and also in Chrétien de Troyes's *Erec and Enide*, ll. 1946–7. (See D. D. R. Owen's notes to *Lancelot*, Everyman edn, p. 513.)

98. (p. 333): Here the text is defective. There may be a parallel with Chrétien de Troyes's *Erec and Enide* at this point, with Gawain telling his sister to take no garment with her except a surcoat.

99. (p. 335): The original French wording is quite concise: *Keux a fait l'iaue corner.* This reference to the etiquette of dining, which was the subject of contemporary courtesy books in both French and English, is a common occurrence in Arthurian literature (see J. W. Nicholls, *The Matter of Courtesy: Medieval Courtesy Books and the Gawain-poet* [Cambridge: D. S. Brewer, 1985]).

100. **(p. 335)**: Here, as in the original text, the masculine gender is used for the knight until Arthur and his courtiers are informed that she is female.

101. **(p. 337)**: Here Kay deliberately misinterprets the damsel's words 'hard-pressed' (*tenus si cours*).

102. **(p. 337)**: See Geoffrey of Monmouth's *History*, Bk IX, Ch. 11.

103. **(p. 353)**: This episode is reminiscent of the famous scene in Chrétien de Troyes's *Yvain* (518ff.), from which it probably derives.

104. **(p. 357)**: Mail and armour were cleaned by being rolled in barrels of sand. See *Sir Gawain and the Green Knight* (Everyman, 1996), l. 2018; and second edn J. R. R. Tolkein and E. V. Gordon, rev. N. Davis (Oxford: Clarendon Press, 1967) notes to p. 124; and Lawman, *Brut* (Everyman, 1992), l. 22287.

105. **(p. 360)**: See pp. 530–34 for Pierre de Langtoft's comparison of Edward I and Arthur.

106. **(p. 364)**: There was a real Brien of the Isles during the reigns of King John and Henry III, who played an active part in political affairs, and seems to have been one of John's closest henchmen. It is possible that this episode in *Escanor* may have been inspired by King John's reaction to Welsh incursions in 1211–12. At first John contemplated sending a punitive expedition under Brien Delisle, but then changed his mind and decided to lead a large-scale expedition into North Wales in person (see W. 'L. Warren, *King John* [London: Methuen, 1990] pp. 4, 140, 199). Brien appears in various Arthurian works, including *Perlesvaus*, where he joins Kay in devastating Arthur's lands, but it is never clear which islands he controls.

107. **(p. 372)**: The Sparrowhawk contest in Chrétien de Troyes's *Erec and Enide* is an obvious model for this episode; there is also a parallel in *The Marvels of Rigomer*, where there is a speaking bird called Willeris.

108. **(p. 372)**: The damsel seats herself on Arthur's horse in front of him so that the other knight can perceive her beauty and, hopefully, admit defeat in the contest.

109. **(p. 377)**: Derived from the Roman measure of 1,000 paces, the 'mile' was used throughout Europe in the Middle Ages, but varied in length from country to country. Since the story is set in Britain, distances are given in English miles rather than French.

110. **(p. 378)**: The Old French *aulne* in the original text, translated here by the English equivalent term 'ell', is approximately forty-five inches.

111. **(p. 379)**: Here 'Love' is personified as being feminine, so the figure is that of Venus rather than her archer son, Cupid.

112. (p. 391): Unless night separated the two armies.

113. (p. 391): Where there was greatest need.

114. (p. 392): See the *Prose Lancelot*, pp. 274–86.

115. (p. 392): Blaise was a hermit, who assisted Merlin's pregnant mother and befriended the young magician. Merlin dedicated to him the story of the Grail. Blaise also wrote an account of Arthur's battles.

116. (p. 396): See Chaucer's *Sir Thopas*, l. 900.

117. (p. 399): He knew a lot about entertainments.

118. (p. 402): *falchion*: a heavy, curved sword best suited for chopping, similar to the later cutlass.

119. (p. 403): See Mills's introduction to the Everyman edition (London: 1992), p. xix.

120. (p. 407): Although the text is continuous in T, it seems certain that twelve lines have been omitted by the scribe. (Mills)

121. (p. 422): Where he most liked to reside.

122. (p. 422): The old head wound which he had received in the duel against Lancelot.

123. (p. 423): And stirred the blood and bones of knights.

124. (p. 424): They made a mound over each body.

125. (p. 426): Lancelot du Lake comes to help you.

126. (p. 426): The Tarne Wathelan appears in other English Arthurian poems of this period, including *The Weddynge of Sir Gawen and Dame Ragnell* and *The Avowing of Arthur*. The famous tarn, since drained, lay on the main road south of Carlisle (see Mills, p. 199n.).

127. (p. 426): See, for instance, *The Weddynge of Sir Gawen and Dame Ragnell* (p. 481), *The Carle of Carelyle* (p. 456) and *The Avowing of King Arthur* (p. 466).

128. (p. 427): There is a parallel in the opening scene of Chrétien de Troyes's *Erec and Enide*, where Arthur hunts the white stag and Erec encounters an adventure with the queen and one of her damsels.

129. (p. 439): See H. Schnyder, 'Aspects of Kingship in *Sir Gawain and the Green Knight*', *ES* XL (1959), pp. 289–94.

130. (p. 459): Fellows (*Love and Chivalry* [Everyman, 1993], p. xviii) observes that there are 'many close verbal parallels between *Syr Launfal* and *Landevale*'.

131. (p. 459): In most works Guenevere is the daughter of King Leodigan of Camelide. See, for example, the extract from *Of Arthour and of Merlin*, pp. 392–5.

132. (p. 467): Whoever dares wait to receive a blow from him / Is valiant indeed.

133. (p. 468): But set my head on a stake if he doesn't rip the skin off all four of you.

134. (p. 468): A tarne is a small mountain lake. The Tarn Wathelan occurs in several Arthurian poems from the North of England, including *The Anturs of Arther*, pp. 426–36.

135. (p. 475): Otherwise no man would approach her.

136. (p. 476): ... should lose anything through me.

137. (p. 476): ... for important and minor vassals.

138. (p. 478): Whether he [Merlin] would always be at his feasts.

139. (p. 479): That were still in the future at that time.

140. (p. 480): The fiftieth day after Easter.

141. (p. 490): See *The Works of Sir Thomas Malory*, ed. E. Vinaver, third rev. edn P. J. C. Field, 3 vols (Oxford: Clarendon Press, 1990).

142. (p. 491): See Robert de Boron, *Merlin*, ed. A. Micha, Textes littéraires français (Paris and Geneva: Droz, 1980), pp. 197–290.

143. (p. 491): Already the location of Uther's seduction of Ygerna in Geoffrey's *History*, the small town of Tintagel (on the north coast of Cornwall, facing the Bristol Channel) is only about four miles from Camelford, a conjectured site for Arthur's last battle against Mordred. Unfortunately the extant ruins of Tintagel Castle date only from the thirteenth century, being the remains of the castle built by Henry III's brother, Richard Duke of Cornwall.

144. (p. 492): Whereas Tintagel can still be identified, the location of castle Terabyl (or the *castellum Dimilioc* in Geoffrey of Monmouth's *History*) is unknown.

145. (p. 492): The abrupt introduction of Merlin suggests that Malory would have assumed that his readers would already be familiar with this figure. Different versions of the story of Merlin's birth and early years (omitted by Malory) are related by Geoffrey of Monmouth and in various French works, such as Robert de Boron's *Merlin* and the *Huth Merlin*.

146. (p. 493): Malory gives the title of 'king' to many characters who are of less exalted station in his sources; Geoffrey calls him Lot of Lodonesia (Lot of Lothian).

147. (p. 493): According to the prose version of Robert de Boron's *Merlin*, Morgan was Ygerne's bastard daughter. On Ygerne's marriage to Uther, Morgan was placed in a convent, where she learned a great deal about astronomy and physics, earning herself the name *Morgain la fee* (*Merlin*, ed. Micha, pp. 244–5).

148. (p. 494): In the original French, he is called *Antor*, as in Lovelich's English metrical life of Merlin, *The Romance of Merlin*.

149. (p. 497): There are more details in Malory's French source, where Antor tells Arthur that he should forgive Kay if he is foolish

or wicked because he acquired those bad habits for Arthur's sake since, while Arthur received milk from Kay's mother, Kay himself was nurtured by a whore (*garce*). (See *Merlin*, ed. Micha, p. 278).

150. (p. 497): 2 February: the celebration of Christ's circumcision, so called from the practice of lighting numerous candles.

151. (p. 500): While Malory's *Excalibur* appears to be the sword which Arthur drew from the stone, in the *Huth Merlin* it is the sword presented to Arthur by the Lady of the Lake (see first extract from the *Huth Merlin*, pp. 261–3). In a number of Arthurian texts, including *The Story of Merlin* and *The Book of Arthur*, Arthur gives (or perhaps lends) *Excalibur* to his favourite nephew, Gawain.

152. (p. 501): For example, the adventure of the white hart, which takes place at Arthur's wedding feast.

153. (p. 519): Virgil, *Georgics*, l. 497.

154. (p. 520): The *Speculum Ecclesiae* is dated *c.* 1216, so that Gerald wrote this second account a quarter of a century after the discovery. (Thorpe)

155. (p. 520): According to William of Malmesbury there was a church in Glastonbury as early as AD 166. There was certainly a Celtic monastery there before the Saxon conquest. St Dunstan became Abbot *c.* 943. (Thorpe)

156. (p. 520): This is an interesting example of hair fetish: there were not many things which Gerald did not know. (Thorpe)

157. (p. 521): Untraced.

158. (p. 521): Nothing is known of this Vallo, although folklorists have taken him up. (Thorpe)

159. (p. 522): Henry de Soilli became Abbot two months after the death of Henry II. (Thorpe)

160. (p. 522): Cf. Geoffrey of Monmouth, *History of the Kings of Britain*, Bk XI, Ch. 1. (Thorpe)

161. (p. 522): The figure VII comes just where the manuscript is damaged and it may have been misread by the editor. (Thorpe)

162. (p. 523): Cadair Arthur is now called Brecon Beacons or Bannau Brycheiniog. (Thorpe)

163. (p. 523): The Normans took various legends about Arthur with them when they conquered Sicily, but it is a little farfetched to transfer Arthur's place of retirement there!

164. (p. 525): Born in York *c.* 737, Alcuin became the emperor Charlemagne's chief adviser in 781, educating the royal family. It was largely through his influence that the court of Aachen became an important cultural centre, resulting in the Carolingian renaissance. Alcuin became abbot of Tours in 796 and died in 804.

165. (p. 526): Robert of Gloucester, in his *Metrical Chronicle* (in a

passage not included in this anthology) states that Evesham was more of a slaughter than a battle.

166. (p. 530): Langtoft's version of the story of Arthur is found in Pierre de Langtoft, *Chronicle*, ed. and trans. T. Wright, Roll Series (London: 1866), Vol. 1, pp. 134–225.

167. (p. 530): See, for instance, *Annales Londonienses* in *Chronicles of the Reigns of Edward I and Edward II*, ed. W. Stubbs, Rolls Series (London: 1882), Vol. 1.

168. (p. 535): See above, pp. 40–45, for Newburgh's criticism of Geoffrey of Monmouth.

169. (p. 536): Justinian was emperor of the Eastern Roman, or Byzantine, Empire (527–65); Leo I was emperor 457–74.

170. (p. 540): *Landavall*, ed. A. J. Bliss (London: 1960), p. 4.

LIST OF SOURCES

Part 1: Early Works

Gildas, *The Ruin of Britain and Other Works*, ed. and trans. M. Winterbottom (London and Chichester: Phillimore, 1978), pp. 28–9.

Nennius, *History of the Britons* in *Arthur of Britain*, ed. Sir E. K. Chambers (London: Sidgwick & Jackson, 1927), pp. 238–40, trans. R. D. White.

The Annals of Wales in *Arthur of Britain*, ed. Sir E. K. Chambers (London: Sidgwick & Jackson, 1927), pp. 240–41, trans. R. D. White.

The Mabinogion, ed. and trans. G. Jones and T. Jones (London: Everyman, 1949; rev. edn 1993), pp. 90–95.

The Life of St Goeznovius in *Arthur of Britain*, ed. Sir E. K. Chambers (London: Sidgwick & Jackson, 1927), pp. 241–3, trans. R. D. White.

Lifric of Llancarfan, *The Life of St Cadoc* in *Arthur of Britain*, ed. Sir E. K. Chambers (London: Sidgwick & Jackson, 1927), pp. 243–6, trans. R. D. White.

The Life of St Carannog in *Arthur of Britain*, ed. Sir E. K. Chambers (London: Sidgwick & Jackson, 1927), pp. 246–7, trans. R. D. White.

The Life of St Iltud in *Arthur of Britain*, ed. Sir E. K. Chambers (London: Sidgwick & Jackson, 1927), p. 248, trans. R. D. White.

The Life of St Padarn in *Arthur of Britain*, ed. Sir E. K. Chambers (London: Sidgwick & Jackson, 1927), pp. 248–9, trans. R. D. White.

Caradoc of Llancarfan, *The Life of St Gildas* in *Arthur of Britain*, ed. Sir E. K. Chambers (London: Sidgwick & Jackson, 1927), pp. 262–4, trans. R. D. White.

William of Malmesbury, *The Deeds of the English Kings*, ed. W. Stubbs, Rolls Series (London: Longman, 1887–9), Vol. I, p. 11; Vol. 2, p. 342, trans. R. D. White.

Part 2: Geoffrey of Monmouth and the 'Brut' Chronicle Tradition

Geoffrey of Monmouth, *History of the Kings of Britain*, trans. L. Thorpe (Harmondsworth: Penguin, 1966), pp. 204–8, 212–21, 257–61.

William of Newburgh, *History of English Affairs*, ed. and trans. P. G. Walsh and M. J. Kennedy (Warminster: Aris and Philips Ltd, 1986), pp. 29–37.

Wace, *Brut*, ed. G. Jones, trans. E. Mason (London: Everyman, 1962), pp. 55–71.

Lawman, *Brut*, ed. and trans. R. Allen (London: Everyman, 1992), pp. 290–95, 264–76.

Robert of Gloucester, *Metrical Chronicle*, ed. W. A. Wright, Rolls Series (London: 1887), ll. 3861–974, 9847–53.

Robert Mannyng of Brunne, *Chronicle*, ed. F. J. Furnivall, Rolls Series, 2 vols (London: 1887), ll. 9735–68, 10543–614, 12033–492.

The Alliterative Morte Arthure, ed. Larry D. Benson (Exeter: University of Exeter Press, 1986), ll. 26–488, 3218–560.

The Parlement of the Thre Ages, ed. M. Y. Offord, Early English Texts Society, Old Series 246 (London: 1959), ll. 462–512.

Jehan de Waurin, *Chronicles and Ancient Histories of Great Britain*, ed. W. Hardy, Rolls Series, 3 vols (London: 1864), pp. 446–8, trans. R. D. White.

John de Fordun, *Chronicle of the Scottish People* in *The Historians of Scotland*, ed. W. F. Skene (Edinburgh: Scottish Text Society, 1871), Vol. 1, pp. 109–11, trans. R. D. White.

Andrew of Wyntoun, *Chronicle* in *The Original Chronicle of Andrew of Wyntoun*, ed. F. J. Amours, 6 vols (Edinburgh: Blackwood, 1903–14), ll. 1903–14, 4257–360.

William Stewart, *The Buik of the Chronicles of Scotland*, ed. W. Turnball, Rolls Series, 3 vols (London: 1858), ll. 26225–76, 26947–27020, 27682–906, 27906–42.

Part 3: Arthur in Early French Romance

Chrétien de Troyes, *Eric and Enide* in *Arthurian Romances*, trans. D. D. R. Owen (London: Everyman, 1987), pp. 1–2, 20–25.

Chrétien de Troyes, *Cligés* in *Arthurian Romances*, trans. D. D. R. Owen (London: Everyman, 1987), pp. 96–8, 107–13.

Chrétien de Troyes, *Lancelot, or the Knight of the Cart* in *Arthurian Romances*, trans. D. D. R. Owen (London: Everyman, 1987), pp. 185–8.

Chrétien de Troyes, *Yvain, or the Knight of the Lion* in *Arthurian Romances*, trans. D. D. R. Owen (London: Everyman, 1987), pp. 281–3.

Chrétien de Troyes, *Perceval, or the Story of the Grail* in *Arthurian Romances*, trans. D. D. R. Owen (London: Everyman, 1987), pp. 427–37.

The First Perceval Continuation in *Perceval: The Story of the Grail*, trans. N. Bryant in *Arthurian Studies 5*, ed. D. S. Brewer (Woodbridge: D. S. Brewer, Rowman and Littlefield, 1982), pp. 98–102.

The Second Perceval Continuation in *Perceval: The Story of the Grail*, trans. N. Bryant in *Arthurian Studies 5*, ed. D. S. Brewer (Woodbridge: D. S. Brewer, Rowman and Littlefield, 1982), pp. 179–82.

Gerbert de Montreuil, *Perceval Continuation* in *Perceval: The Story of the Grail*, trans. N. Bryant, *Arthurian Studies 5*, ed. D. S. Brewer (Woodbridge: D. S. Brewer, Rowman and Littlefield, 1982), pp. 205–9.

Manessier, *Perceval Continuation* in *Perceval: The Story of the Grail*, trans. N. Bryant, *Arthurian Studies 5*, ed. D. S. Brewer (Woodbridge: Rowman and Littlefield, 1982), pp. 300–301.

The *Didot Perceval*, ed. W. Roach (Philadelphia: University of Pennsylvania Press, 1971), pp. 140–53, trans. R. D. White.

Perlesvaus, or *The High Book of the Grail*, trans. N. Bryant (Cambridge: D. S. Brewer, Rowman and Littlefield, 1978), pp. 184–96.

The Bridleless Mule in *Two Old French Gauvain Romances*, ed. R. C. Johnston and D. D. R. Owen (Edinburgh: Scottish Academic Press, 1972), ll. 1–58–133, trans. R. D. White.

Robert Biket, *The Lay of the Horn* in *Le Lai du Cor*, ed. C. T. Erickson (Oxford: Anglo-Norman Text Society, 1973), trans. R. D. White.

Béroul, *The Romance of Tristan*, trans. A. S. Frederick (Harmondsworth: Penguin, 1970), pp. 139–43.

Raoul de Houdenc, *My Lord Gawain, or the Avenging of Raguidel*, ed. C. Hippeau (Paris: 1862; repr. Geneva: Slatkine, 1969), ll. 1–383, 3900–4474, trans. R. D. White.

Raoul de Houdenc, *Meraugis de Portlesguez*, ed. M. Friedwagner (Halle: Niemeyer, 1897; repr. Geneva: Slatkine, 1975), ll. 855–907, 1060–110, 1256–411, 5834–932, trans. R. D. White.

Pseudo William of Malmesbury, *Concerning the Ancient Church of Glastonbury* in *Arthur of Britain*, ed. Sir E. K. Chambers, trans. R. D. White.

Yder, ed. and trans. Alison Adams, *Arthurian Studies 8* (Cambridge: D. S. Brewer, 1983), pp. 29–33, 201–11.

Guillaume le Clerc, *Fergus of Galloway*, trans. D. D. R. Owen (London: Everyman, 1991), pp. 12–25.

Gliglois, ed. C. H. Livingstone, *Harvard Studies in Romance Studies 8* (Cambridge: Mass.: Harvard University Press, 1932), ll. 2671–887, trans. R. D. White.

Huth Merlin, ed. G. Paris and J. Ulrich, Société des Anciens Textes Français, 2 vols (Paris: Firmin-Didot, 1886), ll. 195–200, 218–20, 60–66, trans. R. D. White.

Part 4: The Vulgate Cycle

The Story of Merlin in *The Vulgate Version of the Arthurian Romances*, ed.
  H. Oscar Sommer, 8 vols (Washington D.C.: Carnegie Institution, 1909–
  16; repr. New York: 1979), Vol. 2, pp. 319–22, trans. R. D. White.
The Prose Lancelot, trans. R. D. White from *Lancelot du Lac: The Non
  Cyclic Old French Prose Romance*, ed. E. Kennedy (Oxford: 1980), pp.
  584–96.
The Grail Quest, ed. and trans. P. M. Matarasso (Harmondsworth: Penguin,
  1969), pp. 34–8.
The Death of Arthur, trans. J. Cable (Harmondsworth: Penguin, 1971), pp.
  69–74, 221–5.
The Book of Arthur in *The Vulgate Version of the Arthurian Romances*, ed.
  H. Oscar Sommer (Washington D.C.: Carnegie Institution, 1909–16; repr.
  New York: 1979), Vol. 7, pp. 213–25, trans. R. D. White.

Part 5: Later French Romance

The Knight With Two Swords, ed. W. Foerster (Amsterdam: Rodopi, 1966),
  ll. 1–312, 3161–446, 6892–979, trans. R. D. White.
The Perilous Cemetery, ed. B. Woledge, Classiques Français du moyen age
  (Paris: Champion, 1936), ll. 17–374, trans. R. D. White.
The Romance of Hunbaut, ed. M. Winters (Leiden: Brill, 1984), ll. 46–201,
  trans. R. D. White.
The Romance of Laurin, ed. L. Thorpe, Nottingham Medieval Studies
  (Nottingham: University of Nottingham Press), pp. 263–4, 300–302,
  trans. R. D. White.
The Rise of Gawain, ed. and trans. M. L. Day, Garland Library of Medieval
  Literature, A (New York: Garland, 1984), Vol. 15, pp. 97–123.
Robert de Blois, *Biausdous*, ed. J. Ulrich, 3 vols (Berlin: Mayer and Müller,
  1889), Vol. 1, ll. 3364–636, 4483–610, trans. R. D. White.
The Romance of Claris and Laris, ed. J. Alton (Tübingen: 1884; repr.
  Amsterdam: Rodopi, 1966), ll. 4575–685, 6041–341, 6848–979, trans.
  R. D. White.
Girart d'Amiens, *Escanor*, ed. R. Trachsler, Textes littéraires français
  (Geneva: Droz, 1994), ll. 10364–603, 16784–877, 17473–538, trans. R.
  D. White.
Jehan, *The Marvels of Rigomer*, trans. T. E. Vesce, Garland Library of
  Medieval Literature (New York: Garland, 1991), pp. 3–5.

The Knight of the Parrot, ed. F. Heuckenkamp (Halle: Niemeyer, 1896), pp. 1–12, 26, 30, 40–43, trans. R. D. White.

Part 6: German and English Romances

Heinrich von dem Türlin, *The Crown*, trans. J. W. Thomas (Lincoln and London: University of Nebraska Press, 1989), pp. 54–8, 121–3.

Of Arthour and of Merlin, ed. O. D. Macrae-Gibson, Early English Texts Society 268 (London: Oxford University Press, 1973), Vol. 1, ll. 2196–222, 6375–594.

The Fair Unknown, ed. M. Mills, Early English Texts Society 261 (London: 1969), ll. 1–275.

Sir Percyvell of Gales in *Ywain and Gawain, Sir Percyvell of Gales, The Anturs of Arther*, ed. M. Mills (London: Everyman, 1992), ll. 485–696.

Yvain and Gawain in *Yvain and Gawain, Sir Percyvell of Gales, The Anturs of Arther*, ed. M. Mills (London: Everyman, 1992), ll. 3385–3772.

'The Stanzaic *Morte Arthur*', ed. L. D. Benson (Exeter: Exeter University Press, 1986), ll. 2946–3223.

The Anturs of Arther in *Yvain and Gawain, Sir Percyvell of Gales, The Anturs of Arther*, ed. M. Mills (London: Everyman, 1992), ll. 260–493, 617–714.

Sir Gawain and the Green Knight, ed. J. J. Anderson (London: Everyman, 1996), ll. 25–490.

Syre Gawene and the Carle of Carelyle, ed. A. Kurvinen (Helsinki: Suomalaisen Tiedeakatemian Toimituksia Annales Academiae Scientianum Fennicae, 1951), ll. 565–660.

Thomas of Chestre, *Syr Launfal* in *Of Love and Chivalry*, ed. Jenny Fellows (London: Everyman, 1993), ll. 1–86, 613–726.

The Avowing of King Arthur, ed. R. H. Dahood, Garland Library of Medieval Literature (New York and London: Garland, 1984), ll. 17–283, 781–900.

Henry Lovelich, *The Romance of Merlin*, ed. J. Kock, Early English Texts Society, 3 vols (London: 1904–13), ll. 4339–568.

The Weddynge of Sir Gawen and Dame Ragnell, ed. W. F. Bryan and G. D. Dempster in 'Sources and Analogues of Chaucer's *Canterbury Tales*' (Atlantic Highlands, N.J.: Humanities Press, 1941; repr. 1958), ll. 1–140, 225–96, 722–855.

Sir Thomas Malory, *Le Morte d'Arthur*, ed. Sir John Rhys, 2 vols (London: Everyman, 1906), pp. 5–17, 97–112.

Part 7: Historical Texts

Hermann of Tournai, *Concerning the Miracles of St Mary of Laudun* in *Arthur of Britain*, ed. Sir E. K. Chambers (London: Sidgwick & Jackson, 1927), p. 249, trans. R. D. White.

Alain de Lille, *English Prophecies of Merlin Ambrosius* in *Arthur of Britain*, ed. Sir E. K. Chambers (London: Sidgwick & Jackson, 1927), p. 265, trans. R. D. White.

Peter of Blois, *Confessions* in *Arthur of Britain*, ed. Sir E. K. Chambers (London: Sidgwick & Jackson, 1927), p. 267, trans. R. D. White.

Ralph of Coggeshall, *English Chronicle*, ed. J. Stevenson, Rolls Series (London: Longman, 1875), trans. R. D. White.

Gerald of Wales, *Instruction of a Prince, Mirror of the Church, The Journey Through Wales* and *The Description of Wales* in *The Journey Through Wales and the Description of Wales*, trans. L. Thorpe (Harmondsworth: Penguin, 1978), pp. 96, 281–8.

Gervase of Tilbury, *Imperial Leisure* in *Arthur of Britain*, ed. Sir E. K. Chambers (London: Sidgwick & Jackson, 1927), pp. 276–7, trans. R. D. White.

Caesarius of Heisterbach, *Dialogue of Miracles* in *Arthur of Britain*, ed. Sir E. K. Chambers (London: Sidgwick & Jackson, 1927), pp. 277–8, trans. R. D. White.

Étienne de Bourbon, *Treatise on Various Prophetic Matters* in *Arthur of Britain*, ed. Sir E. K. Chambers (London: Sidgwick & Jackson, 1927), p. 278, trans. R. D. White.

Matthew Paris, *History of the English* in *Arthur of Britain*, ed. Sir E. K. Chambers (London: Sidgwick & Jackson, 1927), p. 279, trans. R. D. White.

The Song of the Welsh in *The Political Songs of England, from King John to King Edward II*, ed. and trans. T. Wright (London: Camden Society, 1839), pp. 56–8.

The Waverly Annals in *Annales Monastici*, ed. H. R. Louard, Rolls Series (London: Longman, 1865), Vol. 2, pp. 389, 401, trans. R. D. White.

Adam of Domerham, *History of the Affairs of Glastonbury* in *Arthur of Britain*, ed. Sir E. K. Chambers (London: Sidgwick & Jackson, 1927), pp. 280–81, trans. R. D. White.

Walter of Coventry, *The Historical Collections of Walter of Coventry*, ed. W. Stubbs, Rolls Series (London: Longman, 1872), Vol. 1, pp. 432–3, trans. R. D. White.

Pierre de Langtoft, *Chronicle*, ed. and trans. T. Wright, Rolls Series, 2 vols (London: Longman, 1866), Vol. 2, pp. 265–7, 279–81, 297–9, 327–9, 369, 379–81.

William Rishanger, *Chronicles* in *Arthur of Britain*, ed. Sir E. K. Chambers

(London: Sidgwick & Jackson, 1927), trans. R. D. White.

Monk of Malmesbury, *The Life of Edward II* in *Chronicles of Edward I and Edward II*, ed. W. Stubbs, Rolls Series (London: 1882–3), p. 281, trans. R. D. White.

Ranulph Higden, *Polychronicon Ranulphi Higden, Monarchi Cestrensis (With English Translations of John Trevisa and an Unknown Writer of the Fifteenth Century)*, ed. Churchill Babington and J. R. Lumby, Rolls Series, 9 vols (London: 1865–86), Vol. 5, pp. 334–6, trans. R. D. White.

Adam of Murimuth, *Continuation of the Chronicles*, ed. E. M. Thompson, Rolls Series (London: 1889), Vol. 1, pp. 155–6, 232, trans. R. D. White.

Jean le Bel, *Chronicle*, eds J. Viard and E. Déprez (Paris: 1904–5), Vol. 2, p. 26, trans. R. D. White.

Jean Froissart, *Chronicles*, eds. S. Luce, G. Raynaud, C. Mirot and A. Mirot (Paris: Renouard, 1969–), Vol. 8, p. 389, trans. R. D. White.

SUGGESTIONS FOR FURTHER READING

Alcock, L., *Arthur's Britain* (London and New York: 1971).

Ashe, G., *King Arthur's Avalon* (London: Collins, 1955, 1957; new edn 1966; Fontana, 1979).

Barber, R., *King Arthur, Hero and Legend* (Boydell Press, 1986, 1990).

Bromwich, R., ed. and trans., *Trioedd Ynys Prydein: The Welsh Triads* (Cardiff: 1961).

Bromwich, R., Jarman, A. O. H. and Roberts, B. F., eds, *The Arthur of the Welsh: The Arthurian Legend in Medieval Welsh Literature* (Cardiff: University of Wales Press, 1991).

Bruce, J. D., *The Evolution of the Arthurian Romance*, 2 vols (Gloucester Ma.: 1958).

Burrow, J. A., *A Reading of Sir Gawain and the Green Knight* (London: Routledge & Kegan Paul, 1965).

Chambers, Sir E. K., *Arthur of Britain* (London: Sidgwick & Jackson, 1927).

Davenport, W. A., *The Art of the* Gawain-*Poet* (London: 1978).

Göller, K. H., ed., *The Alliterative Morte Arthure*, Arthurian Studies II (Cambridge: 1981).

Hibbert, C., *The Search for King Arthur* (London: Cassell Caravel Books, 1970).

Keen, M., *Chivalry* (New Haven and London: Yale University Press, 1984).

Kennedy, E., *Lancelot and the Grail* (Oxford: Clarendon Press, 1986).

Knight, S., *Arthurian Literature and Society* (London: 1983).

Lacy, N. J. [et al.], eds, *The Legacy of Chrétien de Troyes*, 2 vols (Amsterdam: Rodopi, 1986, 1988).

Lawton, D. A., ed., *Middle English Alliterative Poetry and its Literary Background* (1982).

Loomis, R. S., ed., *Arthurian Literature in the Middle Ages: A Collaborative History* (Oxford: 1959).

——, *Celtic Myth and Arthurian Romance* (New York: Columbia University Press, 1927).

——, *Wales and the Arthurian Legend* (Cardiff: 1956).

Luttrell, C., *The Creation of the First Arthurian Romance. A Quest* (London: Arnold, 1974).

Maddox, D., *The Arthurian Romances of Chrétien de Troyes* (Cambridge: Cambridge University Press, 1991).

Morris, R., *The Character of King Arthur in Mediaeval Literature*, Arthurian Studies 4 (1982).

Nicholls, J. W., *The Matter of Courtesy: Medieval Courtesy Books and the Gawain-Poet* (1985).

Thomas, C., *Tintagel: Arthur and Archaeology* (London: B. T. Batsford/English Heritage, 1993).

Vale, J., *Edward III and Chivalry* (Boydell Press, 1982).

Vinaver, E., *The Rise of Romance* (Oxford: Clarendon Press, 1971).

Whitaker, M. A., *Arthur's Kingdom of Adventure* (Cambridge: 1984).

Whitaker, M., *The Legends of King Arthur in Art* (Cambridge: 1990).

BIBLIOGRAPHY

The Alliterative Morte Arthure, ed. L. D. Benson (Exeter: University of Exeter Press, 1986). (Suitable for the general reader.)

'The Alliterative *Morte Arthure*', ed. M. Hamel, Garland Library of Mediaeval Literature, 9 (New York and London: Garland, 1984). (Suitable for students.)

Annales Cambriae [*The Annals of Wales*], ed. J. Williams ab Ithel, Rolls Series (London: 1860).

Annales de Waverleia [*The Waverly Annals*] in *Annales Monastici*, ed. H. R. Luard, Rolls Series, Vol. II (London: Longman, 1865).

L'Atre Périlleux [*The Perilous Cemetery*], ed. B. Woledge, Classiques Français du Moyen Age (Paris: Champion, 1936).

The Avowing of King Arthur, ed. R. H. Dahood, Garland Library of Medieval Literature (New York and London: Garland, 1984).

Bel, Jean le, *Chronique*, eds J. Viard and E. Déprez, Société de l'Histoire de France, 2 vols (Paris: 1904–5).

Béroul, *Le Roman de Tristan* [*The Romance of Tristan*], trans. A. S. Frederick (Harmondsworth: Penguin, 1970).

Biket, Robert, *Le Lai du Cor* [*The Lay of the Horn*], ed. C. T. Erikson, Anglo-Norman Texts Society (Oxford: 1973).

Blois, Robert de, *Biausdous*, ed. J. Ulrich, 3 vols (Berlin: Mayer and Müller, 1889).

Boece, Hector, *The Chronicles of Scotland*, ed. R. W. Chambers and E. C. Batho, Scottish Texts Society, Vol. I (Edinburgh: 1938).

Burton, Thomas of, *Chronica Monasterii de Melsa* [*Chronicle of the Monastery of Meaux*], ed. E. A. Bond, Rolls Series, Vol. I (London: 1866).

Cambrensis, Giraldus, *Opera* [*Complete Works*], eds J. S. Brewer, J. F. Dimock and G. F. Warner, Rolls Series (London: 1861–91).

——, *The Journey Through Wales and the Description of Wales*, trans. L. Thorpe (Harmondsworth: Penguin, 1978).

Chambers, Sir E. K., *Arthur of Britain* (London: Everyman, 1927; reissued Cambridge, 1964).

Chestre, Thomas of, *Syr Launfal* in *Of Love and Chivalry*, ed. J. Fellows (London: Everyman, 1960).

Li Chevalier as Deus Espees [*The Knight With Two Swords*], ed. W. Foerster (Amsterdam: Rodopi, 1966).

Coggeshall, Ralph of, *Chronicon Anglicanum* [*English Chronicle*], ed. J. Stevenson, Rolls Series (London: Longman, 1875).

Coventry, Walter of, *Memoriale Fratris Walteri de Coventria* [*The Historical Collections*], ed. W. Stubbs, Rolls Series (London: Longman, 1872).

Didot Perceval, ed. W. Roach (Philadelphia: University of Pennsylvania Press, 1971).

Fordun, John de, *Chronica Gentis Scotorum* [*Chronicle of the Scottish People*], ed. W. F. Skene, Vol. I (Edinburgh: 1871).

Froissart, Jean, *Chroniques*, ed. G. T. Diller (Geneva: Droz, 1972).

Gildas, *The Ruin of Britain and Other Works*, ed. and trans. M. Winterbottom (London and Chichester: Phillimore, 1978).

Girart d'Amiens, *Escanor*, ed. R. Trachler, Textes Litteraires français (Geneva: Droz, 1994).

Gliglois, ed. C. H. Livinston, *Harvard Studies in Romance Language 8* (Cambridge, Mass.: Harvard University Press, 1932; repr. New York, 1966).

Gloucester, Robert of, *Metrical Chronicle*, ed. W. A. Wright, Rolls Series (London: 1887).

Guillaume le Clerc, *Fergus of Galloway*, ed. W. Frescoln (Philadelphia and Pennsylvania: W. E. Allen, 1983).

——, trans. D. D. R. Owen (London: Everyman, 1991).

Higden, Ranulph, *Polychronicon Ranulphi Higden, Monarchi Cestrensis*, ed. Churchill Babington and J. R. Lumby, Rolls Series, 9 vols (London: 1865–86).

Hunbaut, *The Romance of Hunbaut*, ed. M. Winters (Leiden: Brill, 1984).

Huth Merlin, ed. G. Paris and J. Ulrich, Société des Anciens Textes Français, 2 vols (Paris: Firmin-Didot, 1886).

Jehan, *Les Merveilles de Rigomer* [*The Marvels of Rigomer*], trans. T. E. Vesce, Garland Library of Mediaeval Literature (New York: Garland, 1991).

Langtoft, Pierre de, *Chronicle*, ed. and trans. T. Wright, Rolls Series, 2 vols (London: 1866).

Laurin, *Le Roman de Laurin*, ed. L. Thorpe, Nottingham Medieval Studies (Nottingham: University of Nottingham Press: 1958).

Lawman, *Brut*, ed. and trans. R. Allen (London: Everyman, 1992).

Lovelich, Henry, *The Romance of Merlin*, ed. E. A. Kock, Early English Texts Society, 3 vols (London: 1904–13).

Lybeaus Desconus [*The Fair Unknown*], ed. M. Mills, Early English Texts Society 261 (London: 1969).

The Mabinogion, trans. G. Jones and T. Jones (London: Everyman, 1993).

Malmesbury, Monk of, *Vita Edwardi Secundi Auctore Malmesberiensis* [*The Life of Edward II*] in *Chronicles of Edward I and Edward II*, ed. W. Stubbs, Rolls Series (London: 1882–3).

Malmesbury, William of, *De Rebus Gestis Regum Anglorum* [*The Deeds of the English Kings*], ed. W. Stubbs, Rolls Series, 2 vols (London: 1887–9).

Malory, Sir Thomas, *Le Morte d'Arthur*, ed. Sir John Rhys, 2 vols (London: Everyman, 1906).

——, *The Works of Sir Thomas Malory*, ed. E. Vinaver, rev. P. S. C. Field, 3 vols, 3rd edn (Oxford: Clarendon Press, 1990).

Mannyng, Robert, of Brunne: *Chronicle*, ed. F. J. Furnivall, Rolls Series, 2 vols (London: 1887).

Monmouth, Geoffrey of, *Historia Regum Britanniae* [*History of the Kings of Britain*], ed. A. Griscom (London: 1929).

——, *Geoffrey of Monmouth: History of the Kings of Britain*, trans. L. Thorpe (Harmondsworth: Penguin, 1966).

La Mort le Roi Artu [*The Death of Arthur*], ed. J. Frappier, Textes Littéraires Français (Paris: M. J. Minard, 1964).

——, trans. J. Cable (Harmondsworth, Penguin Classics, 1971).

Murimuth, Adam of, *Continuatio Chronicarum* [*Continuation of the Chronicles*], ed. E. M. Thompson, Rolls Series (London: 1889).

Newburgh, William of, *Historia Rerum Anglicarum* [*History of English Affairs*], ed. and trans. P. G. Walsh and M. J. Kennedy (Warminster: Aris & Philips Ltd, 1986).

Of Arthour and of Merlin, ed. O. D. Macrae-Gibson, Early English Texts Society 268 (London: Oxford University Press, 1973).

De Ortu Walwanii [*The Rise of Gawain*], ed. and trans. M. L. Day, Garland Library of Mediaeval Literature, A, Vol. 15 (New York: Garland, 1984).

Papegau, *Le Chevalier du Papegau* [*The Knight of the Parrot*], ed. F. Heuckenkamp (Halle: Niemeyer, 1896).

Paris, Matthew, *Historia Anglorum* [*History of the English*], ed. R. Madden, Rolls Series (London: 1866–9).

The Parlement of the Thre Ages, ed. M. Y. Offord, Early English Texts Society, Old Series 246 (London, 1959).

Perceval: The Story of the Grail, ed. N. Bryant, *Arthurian Studies 5* (Woodbridge: D. S. Brewer, Rowman and Littlefield, 1982).

Perlesvaus: Le Haut Livre du Graal [*Perlesvaus: The High Book of the Grail*], ed. W. A. Nitze and T. Atkinson Jenkins (Chicago: University of Chicago Press, 1932).

——, trans. N. Bryant (Cambridge: D. S. Brewer, Rowman and Littlefield, 1978).

Pieces from the Mackulloch and the Gray MSS., together with the Chepman and Myllar Prints, ed. G. Stevenson, Scottish Texts Society (Edinburgh: 1917).

Prose Lancelot: Lancelot du Lac (The Non-Cyclic Old French Prose Romance), ed. E. Kennedy (Oxford: 1980), trans. C. Corley, *Lancelot of the Lake* (Oxford and New York: Oxford University Press, 1989).

La Queste del Saint Graal [*The Grail Quest*], ed. A. Pauphilet (Paris: *Classiques Français du Moyen Age* 33, Champion, 1978).

——, trans. P. M. Matarasso (Harmondsworth: Penguin, 1969).

Raoul de Houdenc, *Meraugis de Portlesguez*, ed. M. Friedwagner, Sämtlich

Werke I (Halle: Niemeyer, 1897; repr. Geneva: Slatkine, 1975).

——, *Messire Gauvain, ou La Vengeance Raguidel* [*My Lord Gawain, or the Avenging of Raguidel*], ed. C. Hippeau (Paris: 1862; repr. Geneva: Slatkine, 1969).

Rishanger, William, *Chronica et Annales Regnantibus Henrici III et Edwardi I* [*Chronicles and Annals of the Reigns of Henry III and Edward I*], ed. H. T. Riley, Rolls Series (London: 1865).

Li Romans de Claris et Laris [*The Romance of Claris and Laris*], ed. J. Alton, *Bibliothek des Literarischen Vereins in Stuttgart* CXVI (Tübingen: 1884; repr. Amsterdam: Rodopi, 1966).

Sir Gawain and the Green Knight, ed. J. J. Anderson (London: Everyman, 1996).

The Song of the Welsh in *The Political Songs of England, from King John to King Edward II*, ed. and trans. T. Wright, (London: Camden Society, 1839).

'The Stanzaic *Morte Arthure*', ed. L. D. Benson (Exeter: University of Exeter Press, 1986).

Stewart, William, *The Buik of the Chronicles of Scotland*, ed. W. Turnbull, Rolls Series, 3 vols (London: 1858).

Syre Gawene and the Carle of Carelyle, ed. A. Kurvinen (Helsinki: Suomalaisen Tiedeakatemian Toimituksia Annales Academiae Scientianum Fennicae, 1951).

Tilbury, Gervase of, *Ex Otiis Imperialiabus* [*Imperial Leisure*], ed. J. Stevenson, Rolls Series (London: 1875).

Troyes, Chrétien de, *Arthurian Romances*, trans. D. D. R. Owen (London: Everyman, 1987).

——, *Le Chevalier de la Charrete* [*The Knight of the Cart*] ed. M. Roques, Classiques Français du Moyen Age 86 (Paris: Champion, 1983).

——, *Cligés*, ed. A. Micha, Classiques Français du Moyen Age 84 (Paris: Champion, 1982).

——, *Le Conte du Graal* [*The Story of the Grail*], ed. W. Roach, Textes Littéraires Français 71 (Geneva: Librairie Droz, 1959).

——, *Erec et Enide*, ed. M. Roques, Classiques Français du Moyen Age 80 (Paris: Champion, 1981).

——, *Yvain, ou Le Chevalier au Lion* [*Yvain, or the Knight of the Lion*], ed. T. B. W. Reid (Manchester: Manchester University Press, 1942).

Türlin, Heinrich von dem, *Diu Kröne* [*The Crown*], trans. J. W. Thomas (Lincoln and London: University of Nebraska Press, 1989).

Two Old French Gauvain Romances, ed. R. C. Johnson and D. D. R. Owen (Edinburgh: Scottish Academic Press, 1972).

Vera Historia [*The True Account of Arthur's Death*], ed. and trans. M. Lapidge, *Arthurian Literature I*, ed. R. Barber (Woodbridge: D. S. Brewer, 1981).

The Vulgate Version of the Arthurian Romances, ed. H. O. Sommer, 8 vols

(Washington D.C.: The Carnegie Institution, 1909–16; repr. New York, 1979).

Wace, *La Partie Arthurienne du Roman de Brut*, ed. I. Arnold and M. M. Pelan, *BFR* (Paris: Klinksieck, 1962).

Waurin, Jehan de, *Recueil des Croniques et Anchiennes Istories de la Grant Bretaigneà Present Nomme Engleterre* [*Chronicles and Ancient Histories of Great Britain*], ed. W. Hardy, Rolls Series, 3 vols (London: 1864).

The Weddynge of Sir Gawen and Dame Ragnell in '*Sources and Analogues of Chaucer's* Canterbury Tales', eds W. F. Bryan and G. D. Dempster (Atlantic Highlands, N.J.: Humanities Press, 1941; repr. 1958).

Wolfram von Eschenbach, *Parzival*, ed. K. Lachmann (Berlin: 1965).

——, trans. A. T. Hatto (Harmondsworth: Penguin, 1980).

Wyntoun, Andrew of, *The Original Chronicle of Andrew of Wyntoun*, ed. F. J. Amours, Vol. 5, (Edinburgh: 1903–14).

Yder, ed. and trans. A. Adams, *Arthurian Studies 8* (Cambridge: D. S. Brewer, 1983).

Ywain and Gawain, Sir Percyvell of Gales, The Anturs of Arther, ed. M. Mills (London: Everyman, 1992).

ACKNOWLEDGEMENTS

The editor and publishers wish to thank the following for permission to use copyright material for the photographic section:

Aerofilms for Plate 8;

Janet and Colin Bord/Fortean Picture Library for Plates 1, 2, 3 and 4;

Bridgeman Art Library, London for Plate 12, from Bibliothéque Nationale, Paris, Gaultier Map, 1470, Italy MS.Fr. 112, f.5; Plate 14, from a manuscript of Histories by the Boucicaut Master, Bibliothéque Nationale, Paris, MS Arsenal 5077, f.298;

Bridgeman Art Library, London/Giraudon, Paris for Plate 11, from Musée Conde, Chantilly, Tristram Book III, fol. I;

The British Library for Plate 5, from MS Additional 12228, f.221v; Plate 6, from MS Cotton Nero A.x, f.94v; Plate 7, from MS Royal 14, fol. III, f.89); Plate 15, from MS Additional 10294, f.89;

The Conway Library for Plates 9 and 10;

Lambeth Palace Library for Plate 13, from St Albans's Chronicle, late 15th century, Lambeth Palace Library, MS 6, f.62v; Plate 16, from St Alban's Chronicle illustrated by a Flemish artist c. 1470, Lambeth Palace Library, MS 6, f.66v. Courtesy of the Archbishop of Canterbury and the Trustees of Lambeth Palace Library;

Scala for Plate 18;

Michael White for Plate 17.

The editor and publishers wish to thank the following for permission to use copyright material for the texts:

Aris & Phillips Ltd for material from William of Newburgh, *History of English Affairs*, ed. and trans. P. G. Walsh and M. J. Kennedy (1986), pp. 29–37;

Boydell & Brewer Ltd for material from *Perceval: The Story of the Grail*, trans. N. Bryant in *Arthurian Studies 5*, ed D. S. Brewer (D. S. Brewer, Rowman and Littlefield, 1982), pp. 98–102, 179–82, 205–9, 300–301; *Perlesvaus, or The High Book of the Grail*, trans. N. Bryant (D. S. Brewer, Rowman and Littlefield, 1978), pp. 184–96; *Yder*, ed. and trans. Alison Adams in *Arthurian Studies 8* (1983), pp. 29–33, 201–11;

The Council of the Early English Text Society for material from *The Parlement of the Thre Ages*, ed M. Y. Offord, *EETS*, OS 246 (London, 1959) from Thornton BM Additional MS 31042, ll. 462–512 (text T); Henry Lovelich, *The Romance of Merlin*, ed. J. Kock (1904). ii. 4339–568, ES 93, 112 OS 485; *of Arthour and of Merlin*, O. D. Macrea-Gibson, *EETS*, 268, Vol. I (1973), ii. 2196–222, 6375–594; and *The Fair Unknown* (*Lybeaus Disconus*), ed. M. Mills, *EETS*, 261 (1969), ll. 2946–3223, Lambeth Palace 306;

Garland Publishing Company for material from *The Rise of Gawain*, ed. and trans. M. L. Day, *Garland Library of Mediaeval Literature*, Vol. 15 (1984), pp. 97–123; Jehan, *The Marvels of Rigomer*, trans. T. E. Vesce, *Garland Library of Mediaeval Literature* (1991), pp. 3–5; and *The Avowing of King Arthur*, ed. R. H. Dadood, *Garland Library of Mediaeval Literature* (1984), ll. 17–283, 781–900;

Oxford University Press for material from *Lancelot of the Lake*, trans. Corin Corley (1989). Copyright © Corin Corley, 1989;

Penguin UK for material from Geoffrey of Monmouth, *History of the Kings of Britain*, trans. Lewis Thorpe (Penguin Classics, 1966), pp. 204–8, 212–21, 257–61. Translation copyright © Lewis Thorpe, 1966; Bérol, *The Romance Tristan*, trans. Alan S. Fedrick (Penguin Classics, 1970), pp. 139–43. Translation copyright © Alan S. Fedrick, 1970; *The Quest for the Holy Grail*, trans. Pauline M. Matarasso (Penguin Classics, 1969), pp. 34–8. Translation copyright © Pauline M. Matarasso, 1969; *The Death of King Arthur*, trans. James Cable (Penguin Classics, 1971), pp. 69–74, 187–90, 221–5. Translation copyright © James Cable, 1971; and Gerald of Wales, *The Journey Through Wales/The Description of Wales*, trans. Lewis Thorpe (Penguin Classics, 1978), pp. 96, 281–8. Translation copyright © The Estate of Lewis Thorpe, 1978;

Phillimore & Co Ltd for material from *Gildas: The Ruin of Britain*, ed. and trans. Michael Winterbottom (1978), pp. 28–9, sections 25–7;

The University of Nebraska Press for material from Heinrich von dem Türlin, *The Crown: A Tale of Sir Gawein and King Arthur's Court*, trans. J. W. Thomas (1989), pp. 54–8, 121–3. Copyright © 1989 by the University of Nebraska Press.

Every effort has been made to trace the copyright holders but if any have been inadvertently overlooked the publishers will be pleased to make the necessary arrangements at the first opportunity.